"We should not be together." There was an edge to his voice. "It was wrong of me to bring you here."

"But why? It is so beautiful, and I want to be alone with you."

"That is the reason, don't you see?"

"I don't understand."

His tone was distant. "You are another man's wife, Eve, and you always will be."

They were standing no more than two feet apart, their eyes locked. The seconds passed in silence, the only noises the sounds of the bush and the running water. He was contemplating her in the way that made her feel he could see inside of her. She felt wonderfully uncomfortable.

Then she lifted her hand to his face, and when he did not draw away, she said, "I cannot help what has happened in the past. While I am responsible for many mistakes, and I acknowledge them, all I know is that I love you now . . . and have loved you since the moment I first saw you."

OUTBACK

Joy Chambers

BALLANTINE BOOKS • NEW YORK

Copyright © 1993 by Joy Chambers

All rights reserved under International and Pan-American Copyright Conventions. Published in the United States of America by Ballantine Books, a division of Random House, Inc., New York, and simultaneously in Canada by Random House of Canada Limited, Toronto.

Library of Congress Catalog Card Number: 93-90509

ISBN: 0-345-37656-0

Manufactured in the United States of America

First Edition: November 1993

ONE

Alan

January 1849

It was just after three in the afternoon on a bone-aching winter's day on the Southampton Docks in the south of England, and already it was almost dark. A fog, interspersed with sleet and a fine rain, drifted indifferently over the harbor. A young naval lieutenant stood on the Baltic wharf looking up at the vessel, a sloop, berthed beside him. She was the HMS *Coral Regis*, a small fleet ship of war that carried guns only on her upper decks. He had remained there a long time, his eyes roving back and forth from stem to stern, when suddenly there was a movement at the bulwark above and he looked up into the face of his boatswain.

"Good-bye, Lieutenant Fletcher," the sailor called down to him.

Fletcher lifted his hand in a farewell salute, then reversing the collar of his overcoat up around his chin, he positioned his seaman's bag more comfortably over his square shoulders and walked swiftly away through the drizzling rain.

The wharf laborers, moving lethargically in the icy air, glanced at him a second time as he strode toward American wharf. There was an energy about him, not just the vitality that comes with youth, but a virile quality that somehow made him unforgettable. He wore no beard or mustache, as was characteristic of men of the sea, and his skin was smooth and sunbrowned, exuding health and strength. His gait showed barely any of the mariner's roll, which was surprising for a man who had spent over ten years at sea. His walk was easy and flowing, as if he were more used to traveling over hills and valleys. His blue-gray eyes were the brightest thing on this dismal seafront, and they flickered now across the hawkers calling for his attention in the dark, cold alleys leading from the docks.

He crossed the Chantrey meadows and halted under the gloomy shapes of naked trees, rigid like twisted wire, on the edge of the public football oval. He stood reflectively before he turned into the deserted stand and, dropping his bag to his feet, sat down out of the wind.

Today he had resigned his commission in the Royal Navy!

He would miss it, for the ocean had become his love. Yet he supposed in time he could come to tolerate a life upon land. He must. Tomorrow Alan Fletcher would assume his new responsibilities in Somerset, beneath the Mendip Hills, as squire of Long Moss House.

When eventually he rose to his feet, it was totally dark, and hoisting his bag to his right shoulder and adjusting his hat more firmly over his eyes, he proceeded on his way.

The news of his father's death had arrived when he had been in Nelson's Dockyard in Antigua. It was sad for him to realize he would never see his parent again, but they had never been close. His father had been opposed to his joining the navy from the start. It had been different with his mother. A soft expression passed across his face at the thought of her. He closed his eyes and he was a child again. He saw her coming across the lawn of Long Moss House, wide lemon silk skirts enveloping him as she bent down to hug him. She had shone in his life like the morning star!

On the morning of her funeral, the wives of all the tenant farmers had come and gathered together at the front of the wide stone steps. Beyond them had been a dray, and on the back of it, a blanket made entirely of flowers. Each had toiled through the night to weave it. They had interlaced lily of the valley with bluebells and marigolds, wild rose and daffodils, juniper and scarlet rhododendron. Woven into it were the words "Lady Fletcher of Long Moss House loved and missed." His father had draped her coffin with it, and when they had laid her to repose in the family crypt, he had left it there, so bright and pretty against the insipid, gray coldness of her resting place.

Tomorrow Alan would meet again his cousin, Abel Crenshaw, his only male blood relative, his mother's sister's son, who had been handling the estate's affairs since his father's death. Abel would help him to understand the complexities of the place.

He did not know his cousin well, for Abel was ten years older than he, but he recalled him as a quiet, sober man, clever and conscientious.

Tiny snowflakes were falling and the January chill bit through his thick greatcoat. He would spend the night at the Dolphin Hotel and travel on the morrow to Somerset. The byways were more deserted, now that the day's work was over, and on the corner of Orchard Place, he stopped beneath the gas lamp to let a solitary cabriolet pass. He turned toward a long alleyway connecting Orchard Place to Canal Terrace and onto High Street. He did not notice the two shadowy forms that had been trailing him from the moment he had stepped ashore. They slithered from the doorway where they had been concealed and followed him.

He strode vigorously to the center of the alley where an old Tudor coach house projected out over the passage. Suddenly he was aware of running footsteps behind him. He spun around and blinked in the darkness, dropping his bag to the ground just as a figure leaped at him.

With perfect reflexes, he sidestepped the hurtling body. The man fell to the ground, having only cuffed Alan with his arm and having totally missed him with the long, razor-sharp dirk he had aimed at his throat.

As Alan wavered to keep his balance, a second form sprang from the side, stabbing at him with a thick dagger. He threw up his left arm to ward off the blade. There was searing pain as it entered his flesh. He swung around and kicked into the ribs of his attacker. There was a loud howl and the man fell moaning to the alley floor.

The first assailant lunged up and forward, crying obscenities, just as another person entered the lane. He was a baker making his way home from his shop in Canal Walk, a stout, lumbering man, and was well into the passage before he realized what was before him. "Hey, what happens here?" he shouted.

"Some bastard is coming," warned the figure on the ground, but Alan had the other attacker by the throat and had seized his knife.

As the corpulent baker came up to them, the man with the injured ribs stood. He lifted his dagger and sank it deep into the newcomer's chest. There was a gurgling sound of death as the baker dropped to the floor.

Alan was peripherally aware of what had happened but could not turn his attention from the man he fought until he managed to push him to arm's length and hit him a blow that knocked him senseless to the ground. He turned sharply to face the killer, but his foot caught under the body at his feet, and he twisted sideways into a fall. As he went down, the killer smashed the side of Alan's head with all the force he could muster. There was a sickening crunch as his head hit the cobblestones.

Alan was motionless, the wound in his forearm bleeding into the snow. The baker lay crumpled with a dagger in his heart. The first attacker lay unconscious, and the murderer leaned against the wall, breathing heavily and holding his ribs.

For some moments, all was still. Then, the killer collected himself, and peering hurriedly up and down the dark passageway, he picked up his cohort's fallen dagger and moved quickly to his side. "Come on, you, ged up! We can't 'ang around 'ere. Ged up, I say!" He began to slap the man to bring him back to consciousness, then lifted him to his feet. Together they hobbled out of the alley.

Alan was vaguely aware of the cold at his back and then of hands roughly shaking him. The light from a firebrand shone in his eyes and he began to discern people above and around him.

"Coom on, it's off to prison with ye! Murder's a hangin' offense!"

Murder! What were they talking about? Then he remembered the man who had come into the alley when he was being attacked. They had killed him!

He was pulled into a standing position, and then through the haze and pain, he focused on a policeman. "Coom on, young fella!" He was prodded gently in the ribs. "It's off to jail with ye!"

Alan looked in amazement at the plump face under the policeman's helmet. "I committed no murder. It was the other two. Did no one see them?" He looked to the faces encircling him. They looked back at him in silence.

"I was attacked. This poor man was an innocent witness."

He kept down the nausea that rose in his throat as the policeman pushed him steadily along through the collection of people and the now heavily falling snow.

That night he lay awake, his senses invaded by the smell of bodies and straw. At least they had dressed the wound on his forearm and cleaned the blood from his forehead, which had hit the pavement, but still his arm and his brow ached.

Over and over, he analyzed the attack. It had obviously been a mistake. They must have thought he was someone else. He fell into a fitful sleep thinking that tomorrow his name would be cleared.

Alan Fletcher was formally charged before the city magistrate with the murder of "Byard Tennyson, baker of the City of Southampton."

Two witnesses had appeared to say they had seen Alan kill the baker in cold blood. They stated that the baker had hit out with his dying breath and had knocked the attacker, Fletcher, down. Fletcher's head had struck the ground, and he had lost consciousness. One of the witnesses had a broken rib, the other a sore head!

For three weeks he was detained in Southampton jail, where daily he asked to see Vice Admiral St. Nevis, his commanding officer, and to have his family solicitor and his cousin, Abel, notified. In due course, official and unhurried, contact was made. During this same time, he was informed that he was to be tried at the coming February assizes, the periodic sessions held in each county to administer civil and criminal justice. He saw his family solicitor, old Mr. Bader, who proved entirely inadequate to the calamitous situation but told Alan that Abel had retained a barrister to defend him.

At nine o'clock in the morning of the following day, he was taken from the cell he shared with eight others to meet his defense lawyer. He urged himself to optimism. Surely this must all right itself. A warden led him along a dusty passageway, up a flight of steps to a door with a small metal grille in its center and a jailer lounging before it.

The room he entered was about ten feet square. A tired brocade curtain hung across a window to the left, and a corpulent, middle-aged man sat in front of it, leafing through some papers. There was a small table to his side and an empty chair to which he motioned Alan with a courteous wave of his hand and a wide, friendly smile.

His eyes were large and he blinked continually as he spoke. "Lieutenant Fletcher?"

"Yes," said Alan as he sat.

"I'm Eams, Colin Eams, your barrister-at-law."

"How do you do."

"Now then," Eams went on, "I have the facts here, and I should like to hear what you have to say about them." He placed his fat hands palm upward on the table in a polite gesture to elicit information.

Alan met his eyes. "What facts are they?"

"Why, what I got from the prison records, indeed. About events on the night of January tenth. I've read it all, Lieutenant Fletcher. Now then, what have *you* to say?"

Alan told him what had occurred, and all the while Eams blinked and nodded sagely. When Alan completed his account, Eams leaned forward to pat his arm. "I understand—" he gave another of his smiles "—and I believe you, indeed. Unfortunately, you have no witnesses to give credence to your side of the story."

"No."

"Mmm, indeed, pity, pity." He clutched his hands together and leaned forward. "I have won many a case, Lieutenant, and would feel confident but for this new evidence. That's what's worrying me indeed."

Alan's face grew grave. He drew his right hand across the cut on his forehead. "What new evidence?"

Eams's eyes seemed to become even larger, and the blinking more disconcerting as he bent closer. "Haven't they told you? There's a local fellow, a Southampton man, who attests he saw you in the baker's shop the very afternoon of the murder, arguing fit to screaming with the dead man."

Alan's voice was cold and serious. "What time of day does this 'new' witness say he saw the argument?"

"About thirty minutes past the hour of three in the afternoon."

Alan nodded. "That is what I expected." Then to himself he added, "While I sat alone in the cricket ground. Of course . . ."

"What is that you say?"

Alan looked directly at the large man. "I wonder why they are doing this to me."

"Who?"

"Whoever they are."

The chair squeaked as Eams leaned back. He stretched his hand out and tapped with his fingernail on the table. Alan noticed the skin on his knuckles was cracked.

The barrister drew in his breath noisily. "Young man, I am your ally, but unfortunately your defense is very weak. You see, in fact, there is only your word. Yes, indeed." He looked sympathetically at Alan. "What time did you leave the *Coral Regis*?"

"Around the hour of three in the afternoon."

"And when were you attacked by the footpads?"

"Perhaps an hour and a half later."

"And you had never seen either of the men before?"

"No I had not."

"Why were you in the laneway?"

"It was the shortest way to the Dolphin Hotel. I intended to stay there."

Eams nodded and fell silent for a time before he lifted his bulk from the chair and, with another of his amicable smiles, said, "I have won many a difficult case. Give me a night to think about it. To reflect. I shall return tomorrow."

During the next twenty-four hours, Alan went over the meeting many times in his mind. He examined all the possibilities, and when the hour arrived to confront Eams again, he was thoughtful as he entered the interview room.

"Sit down, Lieutenant Fletcher, indeed do," Eams welcomed him with his customary friendliness, pointing to the empty chair.

They sat looking at each other for a few seconds, Eams blinking and Alan staring.

"Sooo," the big man began. "I have been pondering about what will be best for you . . . best in the long run. Indeed, we must do what is best."

"And what is that?"

"Even with all my deliberations, I am still not entirely sure." He shook his head and dropped his voice. "Murder is a hanging offense, my friend."

"I murdered no one."

"Indeed I know that. But you have . . . that is, *we* have no witnesses. The prosecution has. But we must not be despondent."

"Do you think I have a chance?"

"Lieutenant, you are an intelligent man." Eams smiled sadly. "There is a witness who says he heard you argue and threaten the dead man. There are witnesses who say they saw you stab the dead man. It is all to the prosecutor's advantage, indeed. But I am determined to do my best for you, my friend, and that will not be inconsiderable."

Alan nodded. "My cousin is very concerned for my welfare?"

"Very concerned, I would say, yes."

"And yet he has not been to see me."

"Has he not? Ah well, indeed he is very busy, no doubt . . .

a very busy man. But he expressed great anxiety in respect to your welfare when he spoke to me. Of that you can be certain.''

It was then Alan smiled back at Eams for the first time. Really smiled.

Eams blinked. He looked most uncomfortable. "Why are you amused?''

"Because now, Colin Eams, I know what I did not know before. Now I realize the two men who attacked me were hired to do so! They were not chance footpads. I was to have been found dead, the unlucky victim of a robbery, conveniently out of the way in a Southampton lane. But the ill-fated baker changed things. The attackers became 'witnesses,' and I falsely charged as the murderer. I am still to be conveniently out of the way . . . hanged on a gibbet!''

Eams said nothing, but there was no smile on his face.

Then he shook his head, as he rose awkwardly. "Now, Lieutenant.'' He came closer. "Why do you say this? I . . . I . . . am astounded.''

"Now,'' Alan cut across him, "a third 'witness' to authenticate the story has been procured. An 'impartial' local man who has 'heard' me argue with the dead baker. Undeniably a secure trap now! It must be costing him a great deal of money.''

Eams's hand went out and took Alan by the shoulder. "Perhaps life in a cell has affected your judgment, my friend, but I'm sure you are wrong.''

"Friend?'' Alan shook off the man's hand. "No, Eams, I think not. The entire Fletcher lands are to be his, are they not? And all of you will be very well paid to make sure I die on the gallows. How greatly my cousin Abel must desire my estate!''

"That is a terrible accusation to make, young man, especially against me. Indeed, I cannot believe you mean it!''

"But I do mean it. I would rather one of the thieves sharing my cell represent me, than you.''

"You are mad, quite mad,'' Eams retorted, head shaking, eyes blinking.

"Get out!'' Alan brusquely swept the sheaf of papers to the floor, and called to the guard.

The following day, he was returned to the same room, but this time Commodore James Trent of the Royal Navy awaited him there. Alan knew this man; he had served under him briefly as a midshipman some ten years before. He saluted, but the naval officer came forward and took his hand.

"Hello, Alan. The vice-admiral is at sea. I hope I can help in his stead.'' Trent was a fair-minded man, and his face was troubled. ''I've just spoken with the head jailer. This all sounds wretched for you, I'm afraid. Yet I know you wouldn't be involved in a mess like this. What happened?''

At last someone had asked Alan unequivocally for his version of the events.

Step by step, he related the incidents of January 10 from the moment of his departure from the *Coral Regis* to the assault in the alley and the baker's intervention.

When he finished, he stood looking at Commodore Trent, who had listened without interrupting and now spoke at last. ''I believe every word you say, Alan. No one with your fine record would be involved in such a rum affair.''

Relief sounded in Alan's voice. ''Thank you, sir. It is good to hear you say that.''

''I have read what you've done since I last saw you, and I am proud of you. I noted that a few months after you served with me, you were in Aden during the annexation. You were mentioned in dispatches . . . most unusual for one so young . . . and commendable.''

''Well, sir—'' Alan smiled wearily ''—I had been there long enough to know a few Arabic words, and more than a few oaths. They came in handy when dealing with the tribesmen.''

The older man nodded. ''Your record shows you have been mentioned in dispatches at other times. The war office clearly valued your achievements. They gave you your own ship. Perhaps the youngest captain in the Royal Navy.'' He touched Alan affectionately on the shoulder. ''You are a fine sailor, and a brave man. I know. Do you have someone to defend you?''

''No, I do not.''

''Then I shall find you someone.''

The commodore's choice was Barrister-at-law Finnigan McGuire, who quickly came to believe in Alan's innocence, and in the short week available to him before the assizes, did as much as he could. On the afternoon before the trial, Finnigan took Alan's hand, and his brow crinkled.

''The case against you is strong, but I shall fight for you, Alan! I really shall.''

''Yes. I know you will.''

The next morning, the day of the assizes, a jailer came for him before the hour of seven. He was given some lukewarm water to wash in, and clean clothes to wear, which Finnigan had arranged. He was then taken through the streets to the court building.

The judge presiding was the usual circuit judge, His Worship, the Right Honorable Alexander Netterville, a man with a reputation for being objective although harsh when imposing a sentence.

The courtroom was filled to capacity.

For the first time in over two years, Alan saw his cousin Abel, and all the disgust and fury he felt for the man exploded inside him. Then he calmed himself while Abel sat there impassively, much as Alan remembered him: solemn face, sandy hair, medium height and build.

The trial began. The two witnesses claiming to have seen the attack were from London. The first of them took the stand and identified Alan as the man he and his companion had seen stab the baker. Finnigan took the attitude that he was a liar, and used strong words to press his charge. The judge reprimanded him, reminding the jury that the witness was not on trial. Then Finnigan tried another defense; he suggested that the alley was dark, so dark, in fact, that the two Londoners could not be sure whom they saw, and for a time there were jurors who looked at Alan more sympathetically.

The second witness, Christopher Scales, a tall, thin man with a high forehead, said he was positive of Alan's identity whether the alley was dark or not. There was no doubt in his mind that the killer had worn the greatcoat of a naval lieutenant. "Aye," he said, "it were him, all right. 'Is eyes glinted there in the alley, they did. Fair give me the 'orrors! And who could ever forget them eyes when turned upon ye?"

There was a whisper of agreement from some of the crowd.

Finnigan asked why they had not attempted to help the baker, and Scales replied that Alan had dealt the death blow before they could reach him.

When his cousin, Abel, was called to the stand, he took the Bible in his hand and spoke so softly, the judge made him repeat the oath.

"Speak more loudly, Abel Crenshaw . . . louder!"

Finnigan tried to reveal Abel's real attitude toward his cousin, but Abel only spoke of his "love."

"I was looking forward to dear Alan coming home," he reiterated during the cross-examination.

Abel implied that Alan sometimes had a violent temper. "While I do hate to say anything against my cousin, I must admit he kicked my terrier once . . . In the stomach, it was." He dropped his eyes to his agitated hands. "Died shortly afterwards.'' He omitted the fact that Alan's kick had been an automatic reaction when the animal had attacked him.

Alan shook his head. It is you I should have kicked, Abel.

The man had been thorough, most thorough, in his planning. There were even letters to Mr. Bader saying he would be delighted to stay on and aid his returning cousin with the running of the estate. Or if his cousin did not want him, he would be happy to leave Long Moss and return to his own thriving business in the wool trade.

For Alan, the whole proceeding was like a bizarre dream. He felt as if it must all disintegrate . . . the people, the room, the court . . . and once again he would be standing on the poop deck of the *Coral Regis*, setting sail with the east wind and the evening tide.

When old Mr. Bader took the stand, he did his best for Alan. He told of Alan's sunny nature and praised his friendliness to all the tenant farmers. It was his belief that Alan would harm no creature or person. He pointedly spoke of Alan's kindness to animals, which allowed Finnigan to reveal that there had, in fact, been a reason for Alan to treat the terrier as Abel had described.

The rector from the family church came down from Sedgemoor, and he, too, gave evidence of Alan's good character.

Commodore Trent was better than his word. When he was called by Finnigan, he spoke glowingly of Alan and his service record. He told the court that in his opinion, ex-Lieutenant Fletcher was an honorable man of high moral principle, had been an exemplary officer in Her Majesty's navy, and could never have performed the base act of which he was accused. It was a peerless commendation, and for a short time Alan thought he had a chance.

Then came the testimony of the local Southampton man.

''I call Benjamin Breely to the stand.''

The man who walked through the court was in his early twenties. He had golden hair, and his face was round and smooth. His big, blue, candid eyes looked interestedly about as he took the stand. His dress was fashionable, but there was no suggestion of the dandy about him, and when he took the oath, his tones were sincere and distinct. There was an intangible quality about him, somehow synonymous with truth and honesty.

Oh, Abel! How you must have searched to find this one! He is perfect! A masterstroke! A corrupted man who looks sinless. The jury will believe whatever he says.

Alan stood listening to the testimony of the cherub.

The prosecutor was examining him.

"I was on my way to the baker, Mr. Tennyson. He made the best cakes in Southampton, don't you know!"

"And tell us what happened."

"I had just opened the door, and stepped inside. It was twilight and the lamps were lit. Mr. Tennyson was out in the back . . . out where he bakes . . . and there was another man with him. The man with him was shouting. I do remember what he said. 'You'll give me what is mine, Tennyson. I'm not going to ask you anymore. It's been long enough.' And he sort of pushed Mr. Tennyson roughly against the wall. 'Leave me alone!' Mr. Tennyson said. 'I haven't got it!' And the man answered, 'Blast your eyes! If you don't hand it over now, I swear I'll do for you!' "

The noise in the court rose.

"Quiet! Silence in the court!"

The Crown prosecutor continued. "Mr. Breely, what took place after that?"

The cherub looked serious. "Well, you see, sir, that was when they turned and saw me."

"Yes," said the prosecutor, "go on."

"I remember they both came out to the front of the shop, and Mr. Tennyson went behind the counter. The other man stood there for a few moments looking threatening-like. Then he said quietly, real cold-like, 'I'm warning you Tennyson,' and he brushed past me and went out the door."

"Is this man you speak of here, today?" asked the prosecutor.

The young man's artless eyes looked around the room. He nodded his golden head. "Yes, sir, he is, sir."

"Point to him, please."

The cherub lifted his inoffensive right hand and with a definite motion, pointed at Alan.

In cross-examination, Finnigan attempted to discredit Benjamin Breely's evidence, to say that no encounter such as he described took place in the baker's shop, but Breely merely held to his story, an attentive expression on his face. Again, in Finnigan's final speech, he argued that it hardly seemed sensible that a young man returning home to inherited wealth would kill a humble baker, but when the jury retired, there were only four men who tended to believe Alan, and finally even they succumbed to the evidence.

When they found him guilty, Alan was not surprised. The

judged coughed and moved uncomfortably in his chair. Twice more he coughed before, at last, he spoke. He had listened closely and concentrated earnestly for many days. "Alan Fletcher, you have been found guilty of murder, and with this finding goes the death sentence. But due to your impeccable record in Her Majesty's navy . . . that . . . and my own very complex feelings about this trial . . . I commute the death sentence to transportation . . . transportation for life, to the colonies."

This brought loud murmurs of opinion, and the voice that brought silence this time was the prisoner's. At the sound of Alan's voice, the room became still.

At the Southampton assizes in 1849, it was unheard of for a prisoner to speak after sentencing, and the whole congregation looked to Judge Netterville to silence him. It appeared for a moment as if he would, for he bent forward in his great oak chair and even lifted his hand palm upward to the prisoner, but then he dropped it back on his bench, and for the only time in his life, he allowed a sentenced man to speak!

Alan's eyes passed over the people.

Slowly, and in a voice almost devoid of emotion, he spoke. "That you have found me guilty does not make me so! I do not blame the jury or the judge for what has transpired. The liars did not flinch, and the evidence against me was powerful. You leave now to return to your homes. My cousin leaves now to return to mine! And I go . . . to a prison ship." Here he stopped and looked directly at Abel. His cousin stood transfixed on the far side of the court, his hands clenching and unclenching just as they had throughout the trial. For the space of a second or two, it seemed as if Alan might smile, then he said, "At least I need look on your face no more."

People moved and whispered, but fell quiet when he spoke again.

"There are good men here." And his eyes found Finnigan and Commodore Trent and Mr. Bader. "There are good men here who have been duped!" And his eyes moved across the gathered people, to the jury, to Judge Netterville. A hiatus followed as the crowd waited for his last words. "The others are not men!" Then he turned his back on them, signaled to the guard, and left the dock.

Pandemonium broke out behind him.

TWO

The Young Eve, the Young Clare

**The same day as the jury's decision. Bitterly cold.
Boston, New England**

In the failing light, two sisters in matching blue bonnets and coats hurried down the steps of Miss Scrowcroft's School for Young Ladies in Exchange Street. They were pleased to be out in the brisk air after having remained late at school to help make dolls to send with missionaries to the "starving heathens of Africa."

The first girl, her eyes merry, turned to her sister. "Eve, we have plenty of time before meeting Mummy and Daddy at the ship. Shall we go by Delaney's?"

Eve's perfect brow puckered. Delaney was a cobbler, an old man with long gray hair who mended their shoes. Clare thought him funny and had taken a liking to him; she often went visiting in his little dark shop in Bread Street, not far from the wharves. He always gave the girl cups of China tea.

Eve shook her head. "We'll be late if we do."

"No we won't. Come on." Clare took her sister's hand to hurry her along.

Eve was still reluctant. "I'm not sure. Daddy said to come straight to the brig at India wharf after leaving school. We should do what he said, Clare."

Their father, Phillip Herman, was a trader, and he was out-fitting the brig *Ipswich* for a voyage around the horn to California.

Clare laughed, a tinkle of a sound, and pulled her sister into a run. They crossed an empty allotment between State Street

14

and Doane Street where the wind whipped the skirts of their coats high in the air. They avoided the dirty water lying in a pool near the Customs House and passed into India Street, where a few youths loitered despite the biting wind.

As they passed a row of stark, leafless trees along the street, the wind grew in fury, and sleet fell across their path. Eve looked sideways to the pretty eyes so like her own. "I hope Mother is already at the ship. She shouldn't be about in this cold."

Clare nodded. "Yes, she was coughing so much again this morning, she couldn't stop. It's awful when that happens."

"Yes," murmured Eve, and then she added to herself, "and I truly think she's getting thinner."

By the time they came near the Mariners' Hotel, the light was failing and there were fewer folk about. A block ahead, the cloaked figure of a woman bent forward, talking to an old crone.

Eve and Clare both halted. "Isn't that Mummy?" said Eve.

"Yes it is. Who is the woman she's talking to?"

"Just an old Irish woman, I suppose."

There were lots of Irish in Boston now; they had covered all of the old North End with workers' housing. Many of their aged folk idled hereabout, waiting in the passages leading from the docks, usually with some trinkets to sell. It was best to ignore them, but the girls' mother seemed deep in conversation.

"Quickly," said Clare, "let's catch up to her."

Eve stayed her sister with her hand. "No. Watch."

Their mother's inexplicable behavior had interested Eve, and when, half a minute later, Ada Herman followed the old woman into a side alley and away from the direction of India wharf, the two girls looked questioningly at each other.

Eve started off at a run. "Come on," she cried.

They reached the lane entrance in time to see their mother's figure disappear through a doorway about forty yards down the dark passage and now interest flickered in Clare's bright eyes, too. "Why is she going in there?"

They hurried down the alleyway.

When they reached the unpainted, chipped and cracked oak door, Clare shrugged her shoulders. "Should we knock?"

Eve hesitated. "I . . . I don't know." Then she pointed. "Look, a window; let's look through."

The window, too, was cracked and there was a small hole in the dirty pane of glass, but they could make out their mother and the old woman inside; they stood silhouetted in front of a

glowing fireplace, and the old woman's ancient eyes looked up
into their mother's face.

"I think I can hear," Eve whispered.

They strained to catch the crackling tones of the old woman
through the hole in the window as her ancient hands took their
mother's cloak and placed it on a chair.

"Ah, my dear, must I convince, eh? Then listen carefully. I
am the seventh daughter of a seventh daughter. Do ye know
what that signifies? Some say not so much as the seventh son of
a seventh son, but I am living proof that they be wrong. I've had
the gift since childhood, I have, and what Matthis sees is always
true. Cross my palm with silver, pretty one, and I'll tell ye what
ye dearly want to know."

The two girls giggled nervously, watching as their mother
opened her small, soft purse and removed one-cent and three
half-cent coins, handed them to the Irishwoman, and turned to
leave. They heard her say, "I've changed my mind; I'm going."

The old woman put her wrinkled hand out to rest on her arm.
"Charity I will accept, dearie, but don't ye want to hear what
will become of ye? And of yeer husband, who moves ye from
one place to another, regular-like."

The young woman's amazed, beautiful face turned pale.
"How can you possibly know this?"

Eve and Clare were frozen in fascination as the crone beckoned their mother and then lit four candles from the fire in the
grate. She placed each one in a line on a tiny occasional table
covered with a many-colored cloth.

"Off to meet yeer husband, eh? Is that right? On the wharf is
it? Visiting a ship, eh?"

From the window the girls could see in the candle glow the
old woman's face. The skin under her brows fell in so many
layers, the woman's eyes were half-closed. But what Ada Herman could see up close was astonishing. The irises were almost
golden, they were so bright, and the whites were as clear as a
child's.

"Who are you truly?" Ada whispered.

"Ha, ha, ha." The laugh was a phantom sound. "Who am
I? As I told ye, Matthis. Matthis is who I am."

Ada's voice was uncertain. "What . . . do you really want?"

The old woman made the laughing sound again. "Only a few
minutes of yeer time, my dear. Not much to ask in this life."

Eve squeezed Clare's gloved hand, and Clare dug her sister
with her elbow. "Eve," she whispered, then she giggled again

uncertainly, "perhaps we should go." But Eve was too interested to leave.

Matthis lifted two of the candles and placed them on top of a decrepit oak cabinet with highly polished hinges. It seemed anomalous that the hinges should be brought to such a high shine on so feeble a piece of furniture. The two girls could just make out a painting of a tiger and a bear in a black frame above the cabinet. The animals appeared to be fighting, but as Eve concentrated, somehow they seemed to be embracing.

Ada Herman sat down uncertainly on a stool beside the small table, and Eve and Clare heard more clearly as Matthis's voice rose slightly as she, too, sat. "I likes to air my gift, in fact, cannot help it, if the truth is spoken, but I have told ye all I can without help. I can only read so much from a body, my dear."

She sniffed and shuffled a pack of worn cards. "Take one."

Ada did so.

"Take another."

Ada took another.

"Turn them up."

Eve and Clare could not see the cards, but the old crone's screechy voice rang and echoed in the small room.

"Aah . . . now I see . . . yes, yes, quite clearly." She stopped speaking and smiled a worn smile at her subject. "Before I begin, I shall need another coin. Do ye have a silver one? I can see a lot more when I'm pleased, ye understand."

The young woman gave her what was the last coin in her purse, a silver half dime. "It's all I have."

"It is more than sufficient." The old face contorted into a genuinely happy smile, showing wide gaps between long teeth. "Now, take three more cards."

Matthis took up her visitor's soft, white left hand in her gaunt and bony ones, and traced upon the lines with a long, yellow fingernail. "You will travel far. You have traveled already, I can see. Take another card."

It seemed to Eve, standing there in the dark, deserted alley with the February cold seeping through her coat and boots, that her mother was almost in a trance, her eyes never leaving Matthis's goblinlike face.

The cracked tones continued. "As was clear to me when ye came toward me in the street, yeer health is not good. It is the coughing and the pain in the chest. Ye have good days and bad days. Yeer husband has been to see yeer doctor. There has been talk of a warmer climate between them."

"Really?"

"I see two letters big and bright in yeer life . . . a *P* and, I think, an *M*. . . . No! No, wait a bit. It's an *H*."

"Yes, yes," replied her subject, "they are his initials, P.H. Phillip Herman, my husband."

"She can see Daddy," Eve whispered, captivated.

"Certainly, Phillip Herman," Matthis continued. "Now, as ye came down India Street, I was trying to concentrate on yeer own name, but it was escaping me." There was a deep frown lodged among the confusion of creases in Matthis's brow. She gave a grunt of concentration and shook her head. Then, looking up abruptly, she asked, "What the devil is yeer name?"

"Ada, Ada is my name."

She tapped with her misshapen middle finger on one of the cards and the two girls started as she asked, "Then, who is this 'Eve'?"

Clare poked her sister in her side. "How does she—"

"Shh," replied Eve, pressing her face close to the grimy window-pane.

"Eve is my daughter," came the reply.

Matthis slapped her hands together. "Of course, of course, yeer daughter, and she be the eight of diamonds, ye see, my dear. No, I don't aspose ye do, but be that as it may, there she is on the table, large as life, yeer daughter Eve." Matthis tapped again on the card. "And this Eve is a fiery young filly, with a kind heart, I see. . . . There'll come a time when she's a fine lady in silks and pearls. Diamonds, too."

Eve let out a squeak of pleasure, and Clare whispered, "What about me?" Suddenly Matthis's face turned toward the window. The sisters stiffened in alarm, but Matthis could see nothing; there was now no light at all in the lane. The multitude of grooves in her brow drew even more closely together as their mother's eyes turned and followed the old woman's gaze. "What is it?" Ada Herman asked.

"Not sure . . . not sure," the ancient answered, peering at the window as the girls stood transfixed in the cold, damp alley. Eve could feel Clare shaking with fear beside her, but Matthis just took a deep breath and turned back to face her subject as the sound of the crackling, ghostly mirth came through the hole in the window.

"Why, never since I've been using the gift have I seen so much money," they heard her say. "Quite tickles my fancy, it do."

"Really? Money? Where? For us?" The young woman was excited now.

Matthis shook her head. "No, my dear, I'm afraid not for ye . . . though don't fret, for ye will have enough, enough. After ye have left Boston and gone away."

"And when will that be?"

Matthis took up the six cards that Ada had already chosen from the pack. "Sooner than ye think."

Eve and Clare turned to look at each other.

"Take another," Matthis croaked.

Ada Herman did so.

This time Matthis took the card and added it to the six she already held, shuffled them and put them down in a line on the tablecloth. She looked at them without speaking for some seconds.

It was an effort for the girls to hear as their mother's voice dropped in awe. "What else can you see?" she asked.

"Give Matthis your right hand."

Matthis was nodding to herself. She handed all the cards she had chosen back to the young woman. "Now, return them to my well-used pack, used to tell many a heart what it desired to know, and for one last time, I shall look into the future which surrounds yeer soul."

Matthis mixed the cards once more.

Eve's heart was racing and a high color came to her neck and cheeks.

"Take another," Matthis said again.

This time the smooth, pale hand reached into the pack and took out, for the second time, a card she had taken before.

Matthis started slightly and her wrinkled mouth tightened. She shook her head and muttered, "What? Eight of diamonds again. Confusing me . . . confusing me . . ."

"Why? What does it mean?" the sisters heard their mother ask.

"Don't like to be confused," came the answer. "Show me yeer palms again."

Eve and Clare stared wide-eyed at the ancient face as it came down close to their mother's hand in scrutiny.

Now Ada's voice came urgently to them. "My little daughters, can you see them? Do they have happy lives?"

Matthis's yellow eyes lifted sharply up, her voice so high-pitched and shrill, it echoed through the window, startling Eve and Clare, who pulled sharply back from the glass. "Daughters!

So that's it. Plural. There is not one alone. . . . Matthis was seeing only one, but there be two!''

"Yes I have—"

"Quiet, quiet, let the gift work."

Their mother fell silent, and Clare's pretty forehead wrinkled in dismay as she whispered, "Eve, I don't think I like this now."

But her sister was entranced as the ancient one closed her eyes and the croaking tones revealed her vision. "Ah, finally I see. Yes, yes, there they are . . . behind ye, clear as daylight now." She shook her head and grinned with real satisfaction. Then she moved her body uncomfortably and, opening her eyes, turned to the window again. Eve felt her heartbeat quicken as Matthis seemed to look directly at her.

"Strange, for I feel they are . . ." But the ancient did not finish the sentence, and turned back to her subject.

It was at that moment Eve felt Clare leave her side. "She's scary. I'm cold and I don't like it anymore."

Eve hardly noticed as her sister ran up the lane, her footsteps crunching on the cold cobblestones; Eve's whole self was concentrated, her gaze fixed through the glass on the mysterious old fortune-teller clearing her throat before she spoke again. "Yeer daughters will travel much further than ye. Across the wide ocean, and one will travel oceans in multiple, though which girl, I cannot say." She nodded her head again, eyes closed, and raised her bony fingers to her temple. "One will be loved by many, the other will be loved by few. In the few will be noble men, and in the many will be ignoble."

"Oh dear," whispered Eve, entranced, watching the flickering light make strange shadows on the two figures through the window.

The old woman dropped her voice, and her words came slowly. Eve had to strain to hear, and she did not catch all the words this time. "Aha . . . Father . . . what does . . . marriage . . . two outstanding men, remarkable . . . clutch it . . . deaths . . . trees and hills . . ." Then Matthis stopped speaking and drew her gnarled hand across her brow in a contorted movement before Eve thought she heard her say, "and Boston again . . ." Her mother was motionless.

The old crone's voice rose again.

"There is a vital word. It is difficult to decipher in the ever-lasting mist. Can I see it? Try, Matthis, try; the word begins . . . M . . . A . . . Y . . . F? Yes, that is right. This word is of

life importance to your daughter named Eve. Can I make out
the rest? M-a-y-f . . . No, it fades.''

She shook her head and focused on her subject again. ''Listen, my dear.'' Matthis raised her long, gnarled hand again, this
time close to the lovely face opposite. ''I have seen that ye will
leave Boston, and ye will live elsewhere, long enough to see a
fine house built of yeer own, and to sleep in a bed of fashioned
mahogany when all about ye live in shacks and tents.''

Her mother answered, but Eve could not hear anything she
said.

Then Matthis continued. ''It doesn't matter. It is across the
wide continent, though ye shall travel on the sea to get there. It
be filled with hopeful men, hopeful of finding . . . gold!''

Eve's mouth made a silent ''Oh,'' her breath on the windowpane.

Suddenly Matthis's whole body came sharply round to the
window. Eve heard the sound of the ghostly, eccentric laughter
again, then Matthis seemed to look directly into Eve's eyes. The
crone jumped to her feet. ''Aha . . . now I understand. . . . I
was feeling it all the time; they are here, somewhere!''

''Who are?'' asked Ada Herman in amazement as Matthis
moved toward the window, her hand twisting like a claw as it
pointed directly at Eve.

Eve was thunderstruck. The black form on the other side of
the window headed straight for her, like a phantom from a nightmare. Then coming to life, she ran off in fright down the lane
just as snowflakes began to fall.

Back inside the small, oddly smelling room, Matthis rounded
on Eve's mother. ''Yeer daughters were here, very close. Outside the window, I think . . . perhaps listening. I did not realize
for some time, though I kept feeling another presence. They are
gone now.''

An hour before, Ada Herman would have been filled with
disbelief at such a revelation, but now she accepted it as indis-
putable fact.

The ancient moved back to her and touched Ada's hair in a
jerky, almost affectionate, movement. Ada's eyes opened and
widened, but she did not draw away. For a few moments neither
spoke, then Matthis said, '' 'Tis best I say good-bye to ye now,
my dear,'' and her bony hand propelled Ada to the door.

As the door squeaked open, Ada could not refrain from asking
the question that concerned her most. It had been in her mind
the whole reading. ''Please, one last thing. I know I am sick,

and that I worsen slowly. Do you know how long I have yet to live?''

''It is best ye do not know.''

''Why, why?'' The young woman closed her eyes. ''Is it so short a time? Please . . . Will I see my little girls grown into women?''

Matthis shook her forefinger to emphasize her words. ''It is hard to see the length of *one* life exactly, even for those as gifted as Matthis, even for the seventh daughter of a seventh daughter. And what if I could see? Should I tell ye?''

''Yes, you must,'' the young woman answered from her soul.

The ancient one considered this for a long time, then gave a strangled sigh. ''You are a strong, brave woman, Ada Herman, and your daughters are like you, though one more than the other, I suspect. And because you are so brave, your final question will have this final answer. ''You will not see your girls grown to full womanhood.''

By the time Ada found herself out in the dark street in the falling snow, Eve had already reached India wharf, where her run had slowed to a hurried walk. She assumed her sister had reached the ship well before her. She did not feel the fierce cold as she hastened by the large, well-lit central arch that graced the warehouses, and she was oblivious to the six or seven Irish immigrant laborers who stopped their work to watch her pass, a pretty girl of thirteen with long, fair curls trailing over her shoulders from underneath her bonnet.

Her mind was a blur of thoughts about the weird and occult Matthis and what she had said.

The things Matthis had told her mother were fantastic. And the word, what was the word she had begun to spell? M-a-y-f. Whatever could it be? It appeared someday she and Clare would be going to a faraway land. And what of the present? They were all going away again, to a warmer climate.

She was soon past the gaslit brick warehouse buildings and the ships berthed along India wharf and was heading toward the brig *Ipswich*, where she was to meet her father. The brig sat low in the water, for it was almost completely loaded with stores for its coming long voyage around the Horn. A figure appeared at the top of the gangplank in the wan lantern light and waved to her through the falling snow.

It was Clare.

''Why did you run off?'' she asked her sister as she joined her on deck.

But before Clare could reply, her father appeared. "There you are at last, my precious darlin'! What's this Clare's been telling me about listening through a broken window to an old Irish woman telling your mother all manner of strange things?"

Phillip Herman listened intently to what his daughters had to say, which was most of what they had heard, although Eve did not refer to the letters Matthis had spelt out after Clare had run off . . . Mayf. For some reason she wanted to keep them to herself. Their father had been quite taken aback when the girls told him they knew they were going to the gold fields. By the time his wife arrived, he was looking abashed.

When Ada took him aside in a passageway, he knew full well she would accuse him of deciding to go to California without telling her, and sure enough, she did.

Phillip put his arm around her. She shook it off. He took up her hand. She removed it.

"Oh, Adee, I am sorry. I never wish to hurt you. Never. But yes, it is true, I am thinking of taking us on her."

She looked accusingly. "Thinking of it? More like you've booked passage. Be honest, you have, haven't you?"

His mouth drew down with guilt. "Oh, Adee, there I was supplying them with stores for the voyage, and when I found out the destination, I was tempted. I began considering, and then planning, and before I knew it, I was committed. And I'd not said a word to you. Forgive me, but don't you see, my darlin', it is all for you. California is warm and the sun shines all the time. In truth, I believe your cough will disappear over there and you'll be well again, and they say it will be a state by year's end."

Tears rose to her eyes and she looked away from him.

"Adee, California is the place for us. Listen, dearest. It is not for the gold we go. A trader can make a fortune supplying the diggers with necessities. We will have our own home at last. I shall be successful."

"It's a fine speech you make, Phillip Herman, and I've heard it one way and another many times in the last fifteen years."

Just then the ship's master, Captain Bernard Yorke, came to introduce himself.

"How d'you do, marm. Pleased to make your acquaintance." The captain's strong face broke into a warm smile. "Terrible weather, it is. It will be better, I hope, in forty-eight hours when we set sail."

"Yes, I hope so," Ada replied.

There was silence for a few moments.

"Would you like to see the ship's accommodations, Mrs. Herman? She's a fine, seaworthy vessel, she is."

Ada looked to Phillip. He shrugged.

"No doubt I should, Captain, if we are to live in them for many weeks," Ada replied in a quiet voice.

Ada had resigned herself. Her husband believed in a dream, and she believed in him. She thought of what Matthis had said. She really had no option but to go to California.

When they joined their daughters and the captain had said his farewells, Ada turned to her husband. He looked so remorseful. She loved him so much. "Phillip Herman, it was a fait accompli . . . long before you ever made the arrangements. I shall come with you."

He whooped with joy and hugged her to him, while the ghostly voice of Matthis echoed in her brain, "You will not see your girls grown to full womanhood."

THREE

The Voyage

Alan awoke to the sound of timbers creaking and water lapping against the side of the ship, and for a few seconds he felt content. Then he remembered where he was, aboard the convict ship *Mount Stewart Elphinstone* at anchor in Cork Harbour, Ireland.

Suddenly, the stench of bodies, the smell of the bilge, the stink of rats, assailed his sense of smell.

He opened his eyes, then wished he had not. The rows of tiny wooden bunks that reached from floor to ceiling were filled with all manner of disreputable-looking men. Some played at pitch-and-toss a few feet away, and others sat on the decking, playing cards. The only paper they had been issued were religious books. Every eight prisoners had been given two Books of Common Prayer, two Books of Psalms, and a copy of the New Testament; a single Bible had been supplied for every sixteen men. Yet cards had appeared even before they had reached Cork.

The night they had boarded, they were given a lecture on the "evils of idleness" by the surgeon superintendent, the man responsible for the convicts, Mr. George Mocksey. He had waved his arm across the prisoners gathered in the stern of the ship below him, his large, heavy face settling in severe lines.

"Now, all of you, listen here and listen carefully. This is not my maiden voyage, so I have the advantage of all of you, in every way. There are a few things you should know and heed. You are accountable to me until I land you at our destination, and you will follow my rules. There will be no trafficking of spirits or food. I will not tolerate movement between cots after lamps out. There will be no buggery on my ship! It's fifty lashes for any transgression."

He looked sidelong at his assistant, a young, handsome man in his twenties standing at attention beside him, then his eyes came back to the prisoners, and he leaned forward, his pale hands gripping the rail of the deck above them. "We head for New South Wales, though I cannot tell you upon what part of that colony you will disembark. Reform is possible on the long journey ahead. I hope there are those who will see the voyage as an opportunity. Read your Bible, attend the classes, foster no evil thoughts, and remember that every one of you is here to pay his debt to the society he wronged."

The surgeon was an optimist! Alan thought to himself. His comrades were the scruffiest, filthiest men he had ever encountered: thieves and robbers, poachers, burglars, pickpockets, smugglers, vagrants, kidnappers, and rapists. There were 232 of them, 120 of whom were exiles, prisoners who had served part of their sentences in Great Britain, and on condition of deportation, would work as free men for a master after arrival in the colony. Yet there was not a man here, exile or not, who looked forward to the future. The great majority left family members behind, with no hope of ever seeing them again. The faces that Alan looked into were those of despair.

Thank God they were not shackled! One of the prisoners had shouted to the entire "between decks" that when his father had been shipped out twenty years before they had been ironed for the whole voyage! How did they live through it?

They had been in Cork three days, and now, once more, they were to set sail. How he wished he were above, where he belonged.

He prayed for numbness, repressing a desire to scream. He did not belong here. He was a "lifer" and it was wrong, all wrong. For the first time since the appalling events in Southampton, Alan Fletcher was feeling sorry for himself.

When the weather was fair, the prisoners were allowed fresh air for two hours, twice a day. They were brought up in three divisions. Sometimes they were put to work, scrubbing and holystoning the decks or scraping and swabbing, but much of their time was free. They were encouraged to sing and dance and to take classes, but convicts have no mind to learn and this last suggestion died a natural death. Buckets of water were thrown over them every morning, and twice weekly they carried the bottom boards of their berths on deck and washed them with saltwater. Once in two weeks, the convict contingent in its entirety was brought above and the prison fumigated. Still, it was impossible to keep between decks clean, even with the methodical efforts of the surgeon superintendent and his assistant, so that they longed for the intervals on deck, out of the stink of the hold.

It was during a respite above decks that Alan noticed a small, middle-aged, Irish convict watching him. He was easily the oldest prisoner on board, the average age being twenty-six. Daniel Dwyer did not interfere with Alan's solitude until a week after they departed Tenerife. The early company had come up from the hold at six o'clock in the morning. The ship was entering the tropics, and the sea air was glorious. It was a gleaming morning and the line of prisoners stretched in a circle around the deck. They were having a shave and a haircut. The shave was a weekly event, the haircut fortnightly.

When Alan finished his turn, he found a spot as remote from his comrades as possible, and sat alone staring to windward. He was interested in the course the ship was taking. Daily, it was becoming more evident to him that the *Mount Stewart Elphinstone* was not set for Rio, the Falklands and the Horn, but was headed south-southeast toward Cape Town. He breathed deeply, picturing himself on the *Coral Regis*. He was staring at the horizon when a shadow fell across him. He looked up to see two prisoners about to sit down. There was no restriction on talking as long as the numbers did not become too large, and many of the men congregated in small, clan-like groups. Usually Alan would turn away from conversation, and these two men he found particularly obnoxious.

One was Thadius Boucher, a London thug being transported for kidnapping, and the other was Paul Cratten, a one-eyed, illiterate thief from the streets of Manchester. Alan stood to leave.

The London ruffian, though not tall, was powerfully built, a massive man. He barred Alan's way.

"Why would ye be movin' away, Fletcher?"

Alan looked steadily in his eyes. "I don't like the air up here when it becomes infested with the stench from below."

"What does that mean, ye bastard? Are ye insultin' us?"

Boucher looked to Cratten, whose mean face was blank, then moved menacingly closer. He took Alan's wrist in his right hand, and he brought his flat, ugly face closer. "Listen, Mr. 'Igh an' Mighty, I've bin noticin' 'ow none of us are good enough for ye. Well, I'll be changin' yer uppity face for ye. Yeah, I'll do for ye I will one night when ye be asleep!" He made a sinister sound between missing teeth and began to twist Alan's arm.

Suddenly a lilting Irish voice came from behind. They turned in surprise. "Be much more likely he'll do for you, Thadius Boucher. I wouldn't be meddling with a 'lifer' now. He's probably murdered the likes of you!"

It was the middle-aged Irishman speaking.

The big villain's eyes narrowed with interest, perhaps even with admiration. He did not move out of Alan's way, but he released his wrist. "Well now, we might just be preferin' it 'ere without the likes of ye, anyway, Mr. Bloody 'Igh an' Mighty."

Alan moved around him, and the Irishman fell immediately in step with him.

"How the devil did you know that?" Alan questioned, once they were out of earshot.

"Know what?"

"That I was a lifer?"

The small man looked up at Alan. "Ah, I must confess that a few days out of Cork Harbour, I overheard the sergeant of the guard say as ye were one, and by our Lord Jesus, I didn't think you had the appearance for it at all. Still don't." Then he smiled a huge smile; his mouth was wide and generous, and the proportions of it seemed to reach his ears. "You see, I've watched you a bit. I notice how you remain aloof, and I'm thinking you have a story to tell!''

"And I'll be certain you have, too,'' countered Alan.

"Yes, well, there you are, and if you like, I'll tell you mine first.''

"All right, if you must, though I would certainly rather not hear it.''

The Irishman stopped walking suddenly, and Alan turned back to him.

There was a serious expression pulling the corners of the older man's mouth down. "Now, look, young man. There are precious few aboard as I'd want to be knowing well. But you are different. I remarked it as soon as I looked into these eyes of yours. A man's going to need friends before this voyage is over. It's time you accepted whatever it is you cannot accept.''

For some seconds, Alan stood looking down at the man. He had said what was true, of course. The eyes looking up at his were actually concerned, even friendly.

Abruptly he held out his hand. "I am Alan Fletcher,'' he said. "And yes, I will tell you my story, although I do not think you will believe me.''

The Irishman took Alan's hand in both of his. "I am Daniel Dwyer, and I will believe you, lad.''

They sat at the bottom of the main brace, on the recently holy-stoned deck and Daniel began. Instinctively he told Alan the whole truth, and instinctively Alan knew he spoke from his soul.

Daniel Sean Dwyer had been brought up the eldest son of a master builder in Killorglin, County Kerry. He had gone to Dublin College, and when he was twenty-one, had entered a firm of architects. He had learned quickly, and his main field of work had been on the restoration of churches.

He had been over thirty when he married pretty Audrey Mc-Allister, whom he worshiped, and shortly afterward, with the money left him upon his father's death, he had begun his own business in Tralee, where he employed his brothers, who had followed in his father's footsteps, and for many years he had prospered as an architect-builder.

He and Audrey had been married for twelve years before she fell with child at the advanced age of thirty-six. She died in childbirth. "She was me darlin' colleen, Audrey was . . . and life was never the same without her!''

Daniel had begun to drink, and the business suffered. There were lean years, and when the great famine saw the people of

Ireland starving and dying, his business collapsed. When his last brother left him to go back to the family in Killorglin, Daniel, in desperation, did what so many have been tempted to do. He forged some checks. They were not for enormous sums, but large enough to have him transported for seven years!

"So there you see, Alan Fletcher, I'm fifty-five years of age and not smart enough but to be doing something unlawful!"

At that moment the sergeant of the guard's voice sounded. "All right, time's up! Step lively! All muster here!"

"Shall we continue our conversation below, lad?"

Alan nodded. "I'll come to you."

On Daniel's bunk they passed the hours. It was the first of many such days on the voyage.

Alan told Daniel all that had happened to him, and at times throughout his narrative, the older man shook his head sympathetically. When Alan recounted the trial, Daniel simply closed his eyes and sighed, and when the tale was done, Daniel took Alan's hand and patted it slowly. It was a fatherly gesture, and Alan did not remove it, for he was comforted by the older man's touch.

"Well, Alan," Daniel said, "I don't doubt a single word. The minute I laid eyes on you, I could see there was something terribly awry for such as you to be on this ship. Nevertheless, here you are and here I am. And perhaps all the more reason that we be friends?"

Alan looked into Daniel's eyes. Telling their stories had been a strain, but now he felt lightened and was glad he had done so. "Yes, Daniel, and friends we will be."

The *Mount Stewart Elphinstone* arrived in Table Bay nine weeks after departing Spithead. She had made swift passage and in the ninth week had logged three, splendid, daily distances, all close to two hundred miles. As the sun set and night fell, the lights of Cape Town shimmered in the distance across the black water; and at dawn, the watch could see the glow on the rooftops nestling at the feet of the flat-topped mountain that gave the bay its name. It was August and the ship had sailed from summer into the winter of the southern hemisphere. There was a stale, chilly, damp belowdecks now, where before there had been heat and perspiration. After sojourning briefly in this outpost of the empire, they weighed anchor with the evening tide on the third day. They rounded the Cape of Good Hope and twenty miles later passed to the south of Cape Agulhas. In front of them lay

the Southern ocean and their straight course for New South
Wales. For two weeks they sailed with the wind.

Alan first noticed the change in the weather after the evening
meal. He was on Daniel's bunk talking, as was their habit until
"lights out." Two youths had the berths opposite and above,
and they also were in the conversation. These young men had
begun their days in the "Rookery" of St. Giles, one of the
labyrinthian confusions of sordidness north of the Strand in London, a home for thieves, prostitutes, and worse. They were nicknamed Swiftie and Lawless; their real names, Jonathan Lochran
and Arnold Drake, were used only at roll call. Both had been
professional pickpockets. Swiftie was eighteen, and Lawless had
recently turned twenty-three.

Both young men had taken a strong liking to Alan. They
called him "the guverner" and would linger in his company.
The way he spoke enchanted them.

Although it was always stuffy belowdecks, Alan had noticed
an intangible change in the air, and he could feel a gradual
reduction of humidity.

"I think the glass will be dropping," he said softly to Daniel.

"What does that mean, guverner?" asked Swiftie, leaning
across toward him.

Alan turned to him. The boy had a cheeky, thin, gray face.

" 'The glass' is a term for the barometer. It is an instrument, a long glass filled with mercury, which measure the
atmosphere. When the mercury drops, it indicates a change
in the weather."

"Cor," replied Swiftie. "What does 'in . . . indicet' mean?"

"Indicate," corrected Daniel from where he lay. "It means
'shows.' "

"Ah!" observed the youth.

"So ye think there's to be a change in the weather, do ye,
guverner?" asked Lawless, not to be left out.

"Yes, Lawless."

"Well, how is it ye know such things? How can ye tell?"

"If you had been to sea as many times as I have, lad, you
would be able to tell, too. And I'm afraid the change is not a
pleasant one."

"Bloody hell!" commented the youth.

For the next hour or so, nothing altered greatly. Then the
batch of prisoners who had not completed their exercise above
came below, complaining loudly at the curtailment of their recreation.

On the deck above, there was the scurry and hustle of movement that Alan recognized as preparation for a storm. He could imagine the sailors working to bring in the canvas. He could picture them reefing the main topsail and shortening sail and dropping rope to the deck, as the ship began to bow before the rising wind. Things began to slide and bump, and the ocean was swelling in the wind.

"Now, lads," Alan said to those about him, "when the storm hits, it may prove to last a long time, even days. During the worst of it, the ship will be thrown about, but do not be tempted to leave your bunks. Take a good firm hold with your hands and feet, and brace yourselves . . . and stay there."

The rain started to fall heavily, and came with the spray into the hold. The hatches were not battened down immediately, so that much water was taken in and the bedding was drenched on the bunks near the openings. Finally, because of the curses and cries of the soaked convicts, orders were given to close the hatches. The hold, though cold and damp, now became unbearably fetid from the lack of ventilation.

The night was ghastly. The wind grew stronger, and the ship began to pitch and toss. Waves ran higher than the yardarms as the vessel labored ponderously against them.

Men screamed and retched, cursed and vomited. Everything movable rushed back and forth and even leapt from the floor.

When there was a brief lull in the din, Swiftie's frightened voice sounded across the darkness. "Have ye ever been in a gale as bad as this, guverner?"

"Yes," shouted Alan, "and I am sorry to say, lad, it is far from over."

"Oh Gawd! D'ye think she'll sink, guv?"

"No, laddie. Take no notice of the others, for as you see, I am still here, just as you will be when it's over."

"Hope so, guv."

The wailing was long and intense, and still the ship fought the wind. She continued to pitch viciously, and somewhere a man was calling out that his arm was broken.

Why don't they let her run before it? Furl the fore-topsail and yield to it! The hands all must be at the pumps. The wind is so violent, it must be pushing the white tops of the waves to many feet above the ship's side. She shuddered under the impact as she continued to take the relentless blows. Soon she must lose spars and sail, if she had not already.

Up above, the helm was lashed, and all available hands worked the pumps. She was a sturdy vessel, 611 tons, making her third trip from England to New South Wales, and had indeed hit turbulent seas before, but this was a powerful wind, and now her frailties appeared. She began to lean and stay down for interminable periods.

Alan knew she was spending too much time over on her side. With this battering, her seams must be opening and closing like the mouth of a chattering monkey. Why is the master fighting it? She cannot take much more. The shuddering was running in quick succession through the ship, spreading through everything down to the bunk boards. The pressure on the beams must be so great, the risk of splitting will soon be reality. The ship took a deep dive and leaned. It seemed to stay there endlessly. Alan counted the seconds. This was too long!

Then suddenly he felt her turn, just when he thought she would stay down forever. Good man! At last! At last!

Now, finally, the ship established a rhythm in her dives. The vicious plunging up and down turned to an unsteady rising and falling. They had brought her to, and she was running before it. No doubt she would be many a league off course when the storm abated, but she would not be at the bottom of the ocean.

And so the *Mount Stewart Elphinstone* ran before the gale for six hellish days, while the prisoners, locked in foul blackness, existed as best they could. Occasionally food was brought along the gangways and dumped inside the hold. The convicts fended for themselves.

When at last the wind moderated and a modicum of comfort returned to the motion of the ship, the guard came to open the hatches. Up rose the stench from the vomit and excreta below into the faces of the soldiers, and to a man, they turned away and retched in the scuppers.

All the convicts looked haggard and ill. The surgeon and his assistant examined 232 men in the hold, and fifty proved too sick to move from their bunks. Seven had concussions, three had fractured wrists, two had broken fingers, two had broken arms, one a broken ankle, and one a dislocated hip. Seventeen had swollen joints from various sprains. Two hundred thirty-one had bruises, black eyes, cuts, and lumps. And one was dead.

Alan was the least injured of them all. With his expertise, he had braced himself properly during the worst of the storm, and though he had felt fiercely ill during most of it, he had come away with only a few bruises and cuts.

Swiftie and Lawless were much worse off. Swiftie had cut his head badly on the side of his bunk. Lawless had been thrown from his, and it was he who had dislocated his hip. Daniel was ministering to them as best he could, and in time, Lawless's hip would mend, but not successfully, and ever afterward he was to be slightly lame.

The hold was cleaned in cursory fashion by the convicts who could walk, and then they were all mustered on deck. They were deep in the Southern ocean now, and the light wind carried sleet. Wrapped in blankets, the felons crowded aft, while amidships stood the soldiers and their wives and children who were accompanying them to New South Wales. Farther forward the sailors gathered.

They all listened while prayers were held giving thanks for survival.

As prayers ended and the sailors, soldiers, and their families dispersed, the commander of the guard gestured to the sergeant, who called the convicts to order. "Now, quiet! Silence for the first mate, Mr. Connah."

He stood on the quarterdeck looking down at the motley gathering crowded in the stern. "We have all come through a bad gale. Thanks be to the Lord for our deliverance. But we are many leagues off course. The master is presently calculating the distance. Until this is rectified, provisions and water will be restricted. Beginning tomorrow, all prisoners will go onto half rations."

Groans and grumbles met the news.

"Quiet now, no complaints! Sergeant, take them below!"

Throughout the voyage, they had been divided into "messes" of six men. Each mess was apportioned weekly, receiving measures of bread, flour, beef, pork, rice, boiled peas, butter, suet, raisins, oatmeal, sugar, vinegar, and lime juice. Alan had found the rationing fair and as good as that in many a ship in Her Majesty's navy. But half rations were another matter.

When they were all once more in the hold, they were set to work cleaning it thoroughly, and for the next few hours there was too much to do for any of them to vent their anger; but when night fell, the unhappy rumblings of the day gave way to temper. As the night passed, a number of fistfights broke out.

On the next morning, though there was still grumbling and discord, all seemed calmer. It was late that afternoon when Alan sensed that something more was awry. He and Daniel had been taking turns nursing Swiftie and Lawless. The worst of the cases had been taken to the ship's hospital, but it was so full, the other injured had to remain in their bunks.

Once, while Alan was dabbing Swiftie's hot head with a wet rag, the boy had looked up, his eyes glassy in his pale exhausted face, and said, "Thanks for lookin' after us, guv. Just like a real mum, ye be." A weak grin covered his features.

Daniel, who sat leaning on one end of his bunk across from the boy, asked quietly, "Tell us Swiftie, lad, where is your mum and all? Does she know her son is a prisoner of Her Majesty?"

Swiftie shook his head. "Never had one. Not as I recall." Then his tone took on faint derision as if Daniel should know better. "Lots of us in the Rookery never had a mum, Daniel!"

"Too right," commented Lawless from where he lay, "and those of us what did, could've done without her."

At that moment, Alan lifted his eyes and noted a group of men in a huddle nearby. Although they appeared to be playing cards, it was the particular individuals that drew his attention. Thadius Boucher's arm was around a Surry poacher, Samuel Cooper. On the far side of Cooper was Paul Cratten, and next to him, another thief and troublemaker, "Gaffer" Gordon. The other two were Davey Keating from Dublin and Luke Talbot, the only other lifer, who enjoyed telling how he had bashed two policemen so badly that later they had died. These were the most feared men between decks, and it augured ill that they had their heads together. Alan had a premonition of trouble.

Over the next twenty-four hours, Alan observed the same six men together several times, even during the burial of the poor devil who had died.

Alan had guessed what they were planning, so it was no surprise when Boucher and Talbot came to his bunk that night. Boucher put his heavy hand to his mouth and in conspiratorial fashion said, "We'd like a word with ye, Fletcher, private like!"

"The hall of residence seems a trifle overcrowded for privacy!"

It was Talbot who replied, "Com' on down then, will ye, mon? It be urgent we speak! Over 'ere." He beckoned Alan.

The eternal card games were taking place in the corridors between the beds, and this did in fact leave a certain number of cots unoccupied. Boucher and Talbot led him to an empty spot against the bulwark.

Alan spoke first. "Well, what is so important?"

"We've 'ad enough. We're gonna do sommat about it!" began Boucher.

Talbot nodded. "Those bastards! Half rations!" He spat on the floor. "Didn't hear nothin' about *them* goin' on half rations, did we?" Then he lowered his voice. "We reckon we can take it . . . the ship."

Alan kept silent. "Now, there be twenty of us in it definite," Talbot continued. "We'll recruit more just 'afore we mutiny. Most o' the real cons will join wiv us. Cratten and Keating 'ave talked to a few of the exiles, and they be for it as well. But ye . . . well, we'd like ye in with us now, mon. Ye be real popular with them young uns, and they'll com' easy if ye be wiv us. Besides, ye've nothin' to lose. Ye bein' the only other lifer like mesel'!"

"How do you intend to seize her?"

"In the wee hours, when the guards be groggy and the ship asleep," answered Boucher. "The night after tomorrow. That be Friday. Them soldiers gets drunker Friday night than any other, eh?"

Talbot grinned. He put his big paw confidentially on Alan's shoulder. "We'll get rid o' the master an' Mocksey an' them officers. Then we puts the rest of 'em ashore at the first point o' land. After that, we be free!"

"Free to be pirates . . . if you get away with it," Alan answered softly. "And what do you mean by 'get rid of the officers'?"

"Get rid of 'em, see," said Boucher, drawing his finger across his throat.

"It is not a simple thing to take a ship. Not without guns and weapons."

"We'll soon 'ave those!" answered Boucher.

Alan was skeptical. "Perhaps you should think on this a little longer. So we are on half rations. But we haven't been ironed, and they've been light on the lash. But if you mutiny and fail . . ."

Talbot shook his head. "By Christ, we won't bloody fail."

Alan's expression did not change. "And the women and children?"

A lascivious grin widened across Boucher's mouth, and Talbot pursed his lips. "Well, some of us be for takin' the women along wie us."

Alan looked from one to the other. "But they are the soldiers' wives."

Talbot smiled. "So?"

Alan closed his eyes in thought for a second or two before he spoke again. "I ask you to take this into account. There have been only a handful of successful mutinies in the entire history of the navy. There has been only *one* successful mutiny on board a convict ship. That was fifty years ago, and it was carried off by the blasted *guard*, not the convicts!''

Boucher spat on the back of his hand. "Look, ye bastard, we're goin' ta do it! Ye'll not be frightenin' us wie all that stuff. Now, are ye wie us?''

Alan shook his head. "The soldiers are armed, you fools . . . armed! Whether they be drunk or not, they are military men, used to fighting. There is water surrounding us. You cannot get away. They will have you trapped and—''

"Christ sake," interrupted Boucher angrily, "are ye wie us or agin us?''

"I don't think you have a chance. Ask me again when we are on dry land.''

Talbot's face clouded. "Are ye sayin' ye'll not join wiv us?''

"I'm saying I will not join you.''

"Bloody coward!'' said Boucher loudly.

"Shaddup, Boucher!'' snapped Talbot. "Quiet, you fool.'' Then he tapped Alan on the chest. "It's wrong of ye not to throw in wiv us. Ye'll be sorry. Just keep out of the way an' don't interfere. An' don't say nothin'.''

"Certainly." Alan turned from them and went back to his bunk. He desired to be free as much as any man on board. He had been given a life sentence, from which there was no release. Convict lifers did not get their sentences reduced. They were convicts "for life" as the sentence read. But mutiny was not the way. He would wait until the voyage was over, then he would watch for his opportunity to escape.

The next day during recreation on deck the mutineers made one last approach to Alan. This time it was Cratten and Samuel Cooper. The thief stood silently watching with his single blood-shot eye, while Cooper asked if Alan would not reconsider. When Alan refused, the poacher paid him as close to a compliment as he could muster. "I'm sorry ye won't come along with us, man. I reckon ye'd be good in a scuffle.''

"Thanks Cooper," replied Alan.

The following forty-eight hours passed quietly. Then on Friday night, just before ten o'clock, one of the youths, a lad about seventeen, called Kerry Tyson came to join Alan and Daniel by Swiftie's bunk. Swiftie had been regaining his health, but Lawless had deteriorated and had been removed to the hospital.

Kerry had a strange look in his eyes and seemed unnaturally stimulated.

"We are goin' to be takin' the ship tonight, Swiftie my dear; I've been in a meetin' with Talbot," he said in an excited whisper.

Swifty looked astonished. "What do you mean, Kerry?"

"Now, listen, lad," Alan said, taking Kerry by the arm and sitting him on the bunk as Swiftie moved his legs to accommodate, "do not become involved. This is a convict transport. I should guess that already someone has turned informer. That means the guard will be in wait. It's the way of most mutinies."

Daniel nodded in agreement as Alan went on. "I do not want you involved. You or any of the other lads. Men might be killed, and if the mutiny fails, it will mean severe punishment: irons and flogging at the least. They will deal brutally with those they catch."

Kerry did not look quite so inflamed with excitement at the thought of irons and flogging. He rested his head against the upright of the bunk. "What'll I do?"

Alan took his arm. "Go back to Talbot and tell him you have decided to stay out of it. Say I talked to you, if you like. And tell the others I said to stay in their bunks."

"Yeah, Kerry," whispered Swiftie. "The guv wouldn't lead ye astray."

The youth nodded solemnly and left to find Talbot as the shout from the guard ordered them to retire.

After what seemed a long time, Alan fell asleep.

At three in the morning he was awakened by an uproar of gunshots and men screaming. There was thudding and shouting from above, and from the direction of the fore hatchway, a brief, rousing cry of "Forward boys! Attack! Attack!"

He raised himself on his elbow and strained to peer through the gloom. He could make out that the hatch was open and prisoners were climbing up to the deck. Later he was to learn that all of the stanchions on the fore hatch had been loosened by a guard who had been bribed to help the mutineers . . . or so they thought. Now they realized that the soldier had duped them.

After another volley of shots and more shouting, a man fell back grotesquely from the hatchway, screaming in agony. This was followed by screeches of terror and more gunfire from above. Men scrambled back from the opening as others tumbled from their bunks, bumping into one another and yelling in the confusion to avoid being hit.

Alan leaped down from his bunk and called out, "Daniel! Daniel! Where are you? Swiftie, where are you?"

"We be here, Alan," the Irishman's voice sounded at his elbow. "The guard were waiting for them, as you foresaw."

Swiftie's white face was peering from behind Daniel's shoulder. In the rear were Kerry and some other youths. Good! They were safe.

When the convicts returned to their cots, the hold fell into an uneasy peace, except for the four who were groaning at the bottom of the hatchway.

Within a few minutes, the prison door opened, and in the light of firebrands held by sailors, a dozen soldiers entered with rifles leveled. The sergeant and the assistant surgeon, Anthony Miller, followed.

Miller was on his first voyage in a transport. He was an earnest young man from a farm in Essex. He had been shocked at the attempted takeover of the ship, but he had rallied quickly. Now, with armed soldiers at his heels, he walked through the gangway, looking left and right. "Listen, you lot, stay exactly where you are. We have the ringleaders, all bar one."

Alan felt a presentiment at the young man's statement.

When the assistant surgeon reached the injured, he knelt down. "Now, steady. We shall soon have you mended, damn fools though you are!"

When the wounded men had been removed to the already crowded hospital, the sergeant turned to the prisoners, his features ruddy in the glow from the firebrands. "Where is Fletcher? Alan Fletcher?" he shouted.

"Here," replied Alan from the mass of dark shapes and shadows.

"Come with me, you."

Alan left his bunk, and as he passed the row where Daniel lay, the older man called, "What the devil is going on, sonny?"

Alan shrugged his shoulders. "Don't know, Dan." But he had a theory about the request for his company.

He followed the sergeant out the prison door to a part of the ship the prisoners never saw. Up a rear gangway, they went through the black night to the cabin of the surgeon superintendent George Mocksey.

Two men shared the command of convict transports. The master, who captained the ship and took care of navigation and the crew; and the surgeon superintendent, who was solely responsible for the welfare of the prisoners. On most ships, each man kept to his own designated duties. So it was on the *Mount Stewart Elphinstone*. Master Henry Loney preferred to remain indifferent, Pontius Pilate–like. He left the scurrilous riffraff belowdecks entirely to the surgeon superintendent. George Mocksey was on his fourth trip to New South Wales. The pay until recently had been poor, and the trips were exacting. There was no luxury on a transport. His responsibilities were vast. He rationed the food and handled its distribution. Every cask of provisions was opened in his presence. He inspected the convicts and visited the hospital daily. The prisoners' cleanliness and the cleaning of their quarters were his specific responsibilities. He locked the prison at night and tended all sick on board, including the crew and soldiers and their wives and children. His list of duties seemed endless. At least on this voyage, he had an assistant, thank God.

George Mocksey fulfilled his obligations adequately, but he was an embittered and disillusioned man who had drifted permanently into the convict service. His wife and daughter had accompanied him on his first voyage to New South Wales, and the child had died of cholera in Rio de Janeiro. It was exactly ten years since the tragedy, and he still had not forgiven the world. He was now in his forty-eighth year. His wife could bear no more children, and his marriage had gone sour. On his recent stay in England, he had not bothered to journey to Sheffield to see her.

As the sergeant of the guard stood in front of Alan and knocked on Mr. Mocksey's door, the surgeon superintendent was studying the crimes list. Mocksey had once been a good-looking man, but over the past ten years, his hairline had receded and his face had dropped to form jowls, giving him an unhappy appearance. And his appearance reflected himself.

He put down the book at the sound of the tapping. "Come in."

The sergeant entered, followed by Alan.

"Wait outside, Sergeant. I will call if I need you. And send for the others. I will have them all here together."

As he entered the cabin, Alan looked around him. It was small, as they all were, but how well it reminded him of his past: the lamp swinging moodily to and fro from deck beams overhead, a map or two on the walls, a cot against the bulkhead.

He gave the suggestion of a sigh as he brought his eyes around to the surgeon superintendent.

While Alan had surveyed the cabin, Mocksey had been studying him. Strange he had not noticed Fletcher. He should have read the crimes list before. It made puzzling reading. The man had once captained his own ship in the Royal Navy. Now it seemed he was keen to get another. It was odd he was not caught with the others on deck. Still, the informant had insisted that Fletcher was one of the ringleaders.

Mocksey had to admit that he had more than once heard the guards talking about Fletcher. For a convict he must be unique. He was to have become the squire of a large estate in Somerset. Instead, he had committed murder!

"Well, Fletcher, do you know why you are here?" His accent was that of the north country man.

"I can only guess that I have somehow been implicated in the mutiny."

"Somehow implicated is it? A little stronger than that, prisoner! You have been named as one of the ringleaders."

Alan's eyes met Mocksey's. "By whom?"

"Now, listen Fletcher," Mocksey said, rising to his feet. "I'll do the interrogating here."

"Of course," Alan answered, falling silent to mollify him.

The surgeon coughed, and pointed to the pages he had been reading. "I admit, to my astonishment, I see you were captain of your own ship?"

"Yes, for eighteen months, the *Coral Regis*. My cabin bore a close resemblance to this. Perhaps a mite larger."

"Really?" The surgeon superintendent was watching his aristocratic killer-convict closely. He came around his desk. "Surely as a former naval officer, you knew better than to get involved in this particular uprising."

"Yes, I did," answered Alan, glancing over his head to the map on the wall.

Mocksey felt disconcerted and his voice rose impatiently. "What the devil does that mean?"

"I was not involved in the uprising."

"My information is to the contrary."

"Then your information is incorrect."

Surgeon superintendent Mocksey turned away. "Silence!" He stood with his back to Alan as the seconds passed, then he turned and demanded, "All right, Fletcher, let me have your story. Who do you say were the ringleaders?"

"I do not say." He was looking directly at the commander. "What I do say is, I am not one of them!"

The Surgeon felt himself becoming angry, affronted. This man was a convict. A criminal should be more accommodating. It was all his easy years in affluence that made him this disagreeable.

For some time the noises of the creaking timber and the grating of the hanging lantern were intensified by the silence between the two men. Their shadows grew and diminished alternately as the lamp swung above them.

A sharp knocking on the door interrupted the stillness.

Mr. Mocksey coughed and cleared his throat as he returned to his place behind the desk. When he was seated, he called loudly, "Enter!"

Through the cabin door were pushed four men. Talbot limped badly from a deep cutlass slash in his right leg. Boucher's thick frame was stooped. There was a gash on his cheek, and he nursed a bullet wound in his right shoulder. Keating's head was covered with a bloody bandage—a shot had ripped off his ear—and Cooper's left hand was bandaged where a bullet had passed cleanly through. The two thieves, Cratten and Gordon, were not with them.

Behind the four prisoners came Mr. Miller, the first mate, the sergeant of the guard, and two soldiers with rifles at the ready. The four rebels registered Alan's presence. Obvious surprise appeared on the faces of Cooper and Keating, but Boucher and Talbot showed no emotion.

"This is what's left of the ringleaders, sir," said the sergeant.

"Thanks, Sergeant. The others are dead, I gather?"

"Yes, sir," answered Mr. Miller.

The surgeon superintendent stood again. His mouth had set in a hard, straight line, and he presented himself truly in charge. He turned briefly to face the mate. "Mr. Connah, you will note sentence. Please pass it on to Master Loney to be recorded in the log."

"Aye, aye, sir."

Alan had been standing apart from the other four, and now the surgeon superintendent signaled with his hand for him to join them. "You, too, Fletcher, along with your comrades."

He rapped his fist on the desk in emphasis. "Mutiny is the most serious crime on the sea. You are all guilty of inciting the prisoners to rise and attempt a bloody takeover of the *Mount Stewart Elphinstone*. My decision is to separate you from the others for the rest of the voyage. You will be ironed and will take but two hours' exercise a day. When your wounds are sufficiently healed, you will take your punishment. Each of you will be confined in the box for a total of six hours a day for seven consecutive days.''

As he made this statement, there was a groan from Cooper while Keating mouthed the words, "Oh God!"

This was a ghastly punishment, even more feared than flogging.

The "box" was infamous. It was described in the log as "a strictly confining wooden structure, something like a sentry box, only much smaller, somewhat over six feet high, with only enough room for a man to stand. Six auger holes enable a man to see and breathe as he stands inside. Half a dozen hours in the box are all a strong man can endure. After a week of six hours in the box each day, his spirit is broken.''

"Sergeant! Mr. Connah!" the commander called out.

"Yes, sir!"

''As Fletcher has no injury, he can begin the box this coming afternoon. And all prisoners will be ironed at night until we complete our journey." He turned his back on them, saying as he did so, "Take them away!"

As the sergeant began to hustle the sentenced men to the door, Samuel Cooper, to the surprise of all, spoke. His voice was subdued, but what he said was unmistakably plain.

''Excuse me, Mr. Mocksey, sir, but if ye include Fletcher along with us, it's a proper disgraceful act and no mistake. For he's not guilty of nothin'.''

"Shaddup, you!" said Boucher, putting out his left hand to silence him.

Alan stopped walking and faced Cooper. He looked intently at the man. There was more in the character of the Surry poacher than he had suspected.

''What is that you say?'' asked the surgeon superintendent, turning back toward them.

"You bloody fool!" growled Talbot.

"I said that Fletcher was not one of us, sir! He would have nothin' to do with the mutiny.''

The commander's face was curious. His brows drew closer as he regarded the little man. "Really now?"

''Yes, sir! We wanted him to join with us, but he would be havin' none of it. Twice we asked him and twice he refused.''

The surgeon looked across at Alan, and their eyes met once more. "Why, it seems you have a champion, Fletcher."

Cooper spoke again. " 'Taint fair for ye to suffer for somethin' ye had naught to do with, Fletcher."

"Thank you, Cooper."

"So," declared Mr. Mocksey reflectively, "we have one who is at variance with the proceedings. Well, what about you other three? Was Fletcher with you or against you?"

Boucher turned from Cooper to the commander, his eyes narrowing to slits. "I dunno what goes on 'ere, but 'e were wi us right enough, right from the start. It was 'is idea, ye might say. But once the firin' started, 'e disappeared! Where did ye run to, Mr. 'Igh and Mighty? Back to yer bunk, yer coward?" He stared at Alan with obvious hatred.

Alan simply looked away. He found the man contemptible.

The surgeon superintendent pursed his lips. "And you other two, come, what do you say? Was he with you or not?"

As Talbot and Keating's eyes met, Alan knew it was useless to defend himself. Talbot answered, "Yeah, that's right, we were all in together. I suppose it's true it were 'is idea."

"But it's not true, they—" began Cooper.

"Silence! I'll have no more of this," interrupted Mr. Mocksey, bringing his hand down heavily on his desk. He took a deep breath and looked around the five faces of the felons in front of him. Four signaled their circumstances and social inferiority in every nuance of their beings, whereas Fletcher had the bearing of the privileged. Yes, he looked like the heir to a large estate. Yes, he looked like a captain of a ship of the line.

Surgeon superintendent Mocksey was irritated, his irritation aggravated by many emotions. He felt inferiority, envy, enmity, hostility. He did not wish to examine his feelings too closely. All he knew was that he had just heard three of the mutineers agree that Fletcher had been the ringleader, and, too, there was the evidence of the informer. This salved his conscience. "I am in charge here," he said, "and while I'm not Solomon, I have heard three out of four say you were a mutineer, Fletcher, and the leader. You will begin your days in the box as sentenced. How many will remain at my discretion. Take them away, Sergeant!"

"Oh no!" whispered Cooper, his face wrinkling with dismay.

"You heard," came the sergeant's loud voice. "Com' on, you lot. Move!"

As they departed, Alan looked down at Cooper. There was a

message in his eyes as from one man to another when words are unnecessary and perhaps would not do as well. Cooper shook his head sadly at Alan and shrugged his shoulders. When they were outside in the gangway, Alan placed his hand on the little man's bony shoulder. "Thank you, Samuel Cooper," he said softly. "It took a brave man to speak the truth back there."

"Didn't do no good," came Samuel's defeated reply. "Fact is, made it ten times worse."

"Yes, but there was honor in the deed."

Anthony Miller had not spoken during all the preceedings. He returned to the hospital to inspect the wounded in a thoughtful mood.

Soon the first rays of dawn broke over the horizon.

The *Mount Stewart Elphinstone* glistened, catching the wind on the rolling ocean. Her unfurled sails were a spotless white against the blue of the sea as she continued majestically running the easting down.

As a medieval castle was magnificence and grandeur on the outside, hiding offensive dungeons within, so too did this splendid sight carry rancorous, dark holes. To one of these, beneath the forecastle, the prisoners were taken.

Some hours later, when the guards came to take Alan above, Samuel Cooper called across the dank enclosure, "Courage, my friend!" and Alan nodded appreciatively.

When he came up on deck, the convicts, in a mass, were watching him from aft. Each man was wrapped in a blanket against the biting wind. He made out Daniel, white-faced with alarm. Some of the wives and children of the soldiers had also gathered a little distance away to watch.

He stood in front of the grim wooden box that had been erected amidships that morning. One of the soldiers unlocked the door, a thick, solid plank hinged at the side. It looked like an open coffin. It was made of solid wood, with small air holes in the door. Above his head he would have only about an inch or so to spare. Six hours in here? What fiend had conjured up this? It would be like being smothered!

"Turn around, Fletcher. Ye'll have to back in, matey."

Because of his double irons, this was achieved with difficulty. He stood in the rectangle, looking out at the guards, the closeness of the thing oppressing him already. One of the soldiers shook his head in sympathy. Then the door was closed.

Blackness! Nothing but blackness!

Why could he not see? There were five or six perforations in the door. He had noticed them before. He moved his head to left and right, but there was no light. Why? What was wrong?

Then he realized. All the tiny auger holes were far below the level of his eyes. Panic rose in his chest as if to stifle him. He pushed it down by remembering what he had said to his father about going to sea. "I will accept responsibility for my decision." And so he must accept responsibility for being in this Godless black hole. If he had not joined the navy, he would have been at home all those years, and Able would not have had the opportunity to thwart him, and so lead him to this.

The feeling of panic built as he heard the wind rattle the door. He must lift his arms, but of course, he could not.

His throat was dry, and his mind was clouded with hysteria. If only he could lift his arms. God, he must not scream! They had only just closed the door on him. There would be six hours of this to endure each day until Mocksey chose to stop it. How many days would there be? No, don't think of how long. Simply think of now. Courage! As Samuel Cooper had said. He must concentrate on other things. That's it. He would pretend he was simply standing with his eyes closed, thinking. Spend the time meditating and recall days gone by when there were no prisons, no horrors in his life.

What of the days at Long Moss House when his mother had been alive? Yes, he would remember them one by one. From his first memories. He would see again the house and the stream that came down from the Mendip Hills to run by the stables, where the delicate fronds of the weeping willows brushed the water. He would picture her, his mother, coming to him through the spring flowers, her pale skirt brushing the daffodils of the meadow, her arms full of red and pink tulips. She would call and wave and hold her hat to stop it flying away in the breeze. He was four and the sun was shining brightly.

He would look up at Sophie, pretty Sophie his nurse, with her cupid's-bow mouth and happy eyes and fair curls, smiling down at him indulgently. His mother would turn to her and load her arms with the flowers, and laugh. Sophie would laugh, too, a carefree sound from behind the blooms, and then his mother would bend forward, and the rose would fall from her hatband as she leaned down to lift him in her arms. Then he, too, would laugh, and Sophie would pick up the fallen flower in her fine fingers and run, looking back and calling to them joyfully, and the sweet aroma of his mother would envelop him, clean and warm.

But it was not warm. It was bitterly cold, and his feet had gone to sleep. There was stiffness throughout him. He ached in every muscle. What was that noise? It sounded like hammering on the wood around him. What was going on? Oh, yes, that was it. Rain! Of course it was rain. Everything was disoriented. He had not recognized the sound on the wood, so close it was to his ears. It sounded like beads of lead dropping.

Pain seared through him. If only he could lift his arms. He felt as if he were suffocating.

How long had he been in here? It must be many hours.

He did not know how much later it was when the water began to drip on his shoulder.

At first the drips on his shoulder had been bearable, but after hours of heavy rain, they became a trickle, then two streams, one running over his shoulder and the other across his forehead, into his eye, and down his face. When he moved his head, it ran into his ear. He found that by leaning his head forward on the door, he could make one stream hit the back of his head, and the other, his shoulder blade. He remained in this position until his whole body screamed from tension. Then he was forced to return to his first position.

It was bitterly cold in these latitudes, and with the added torture of the rain, his shivering racked his entire frame. For what had seemed like an eternity, he had wanted desperately to stretch his arms above his head. Now he could not feel his arms. He did not know whether he could feel his legs or not.

Courage! he told himself. Nothing lasts forever! If only the mind could leave the body. But it could not, and the cold and wet forced itself into every corner of his brain.

They had forgotten him . . . . God . . . they were going to leave him here. He felt himself slipping . . . slipping into unconsciousness. His body had crumpled, as much as the restricted space allowed. There was more agony coming from somewhere. He thought it must be from his knees.

The horror continued relentlessly.

Alan thought he was hallucinating when the blackness in front of his eyes turned red. Then, slowly, he focused. The door had opened. His mind recognized the red coats of soldiers in the lantern light. What was that behind them? Something white. Yes, a white face, with concerned eyes. But whose? The numbness that was his mind finally identified the assistant surgeon.

''Com' on, lad,'' said the same corporal who had put him in

six hours before, "Mr. Miller 'ere wants you taken straight to the 'orspital."

He tried to step out of the box, but instead fell forward. They caught him before he hit the deck.

An hour later, Alan lay sleeping. His soaking clothing had been removed and replaced with dry ones. He had been put to bed in the ship's hospital and fed warm broth. Anthony Miller, the assistant surgeon, was concerned for his health and spent much of the night beside him.

At eight o'clock the next morning, two guards appeared as Miller was about to go off duty.

"We've come for Fletcher, sir. He's to be returned to the forecastle and placed in the box again this afternoon at one o'clock sharp."

"Has this order come from Mr. Mocksey?"

"Yes, sir, none other."

Anthony Miller looked across at Alan, who lay with his eyes closed. Then he shook his head. He was worried and unsure. "This . . . this is not right. It is inhuman. The temperatures are falling. I will go to Mr. Mocksey. Do nothing until I return. Leave Fletcher where he is."

When he found Mr. Mocksey, he was on deck measuring out lemon juice from a large cask. His solid back was bent forward to three crew members.

It was not raining, but there was a cold wind blowing again, and the rain clouds were still in evidence, hanging threateningly above the ship.

Fear rose in the young man and his heart raced as he came up behind the man booming instructions. He took a deep breath and spoke quietly. "Excuse me, Mr. Mocksey, but I need a word with you, now, please. Urgently."

The man stood up and turned in a slow and measured movement. He did not like to be interrupted in the middle of any of his procedures, and his voice became heavy with sarcasm. "Oh! So it's a word you need, is it? Well, well."

"Yes, sir, it's important."

"It can wait until I finish here," he snapped, turning back to the cask.

Then Anthony Miller amazed himself as he heard his voice saying, "No, sir, Mr. Mocksey, it cannot wait. I . . . I demand to speak with you now!"

The surgeon looked up quickly. This was not like Miller. He handed the nearest crew member the measuring spoon, and beckoning his assistant, walked to the starboard side of the deck, where he stood indignantly. "What the hell do you mean by 'demanding' to speak with me?"

The earnest eyes looked back at him. "It's about Alan Fletcher."

"What about him?"

"Two guards have come to the hospital not five minutes ago to return him to the forecastle. They say that at one o'clock, he is to be placed again in the confinement box. On your orders, they say."

"So?"

Anthony Miller's hands were sweating even in the chill wind. He put them behind his back and held them together tightly. "The man endured freezing temperatures in that thing for hours. And he was totally drenched. The damn thing leaks. His legs and arms were numb, and he could not walk. It is a wonder he is not delirious or dreadfully ill with pneumonia. I must formally object to his being placed in it again, at least until we are in warmer waters."

Mr. Mocksey stiffened. "Mr. *Assistant* Surgeon, is Fletcher ill?"

"He's certainly not well enough to g . . . go back into that thing."

His superior's eyes grew hard. "Is he delirious? Does he have pneumonia?"

"I . . . I don't know. I don't think so. But he is sickly."

"There's many a sick man has taken his punishment before today."

Miller summoned up all his courage. "You are supposed to keep the prisoners on board this ship well, not inflict upon them punitive measures that could jeopardize their lives!"

For a second or two, the commander looked as if he were going to lash out and strike the face in front of him. His lips twitched and the veins in his neck swelled. "Are you daring to suggest I am not carrying out my duty in a responsible manner?"

Once more Anthony Miller found himself saying words that astonished him. "No, Mr. Mocksey, I'm not. I think that in the majority of your work, you are, at the least, capable. It is only where this one man is concerned that you have lost your sense of justice. You seem to bear him a grudge."

The surgeon superintendent pulled himself up to his full height. "The punishment of convicts on board this vessel is my responsibility. Mine, do you hear? Fletcher will continue in the box for six hours each day, no matter if this blasted ship freezes or sinks! Do you understand, boy?''

The young man braced himself to contain his own rage. ''Maximum time in the box is supposed to be four hours!''

''That is in the tropics, Miller. Don't try to teach me the rules!''

''But this freezing cold and damp is just as bad as heat . . . worse! He may die, and you will be responsible!''

The older man was livid, but as Fletcher was an aristocrat, if he did die in the box, there could be an inquiry. Perhaps he should be careful.

''All right,'' he said. ''If you want to pamper the prisoner and take him to the hospital each night after his punishment, then that is your affair. I will not hinder you. But he will do his days in the box as I see fit. I am in authority here, and will not speak about this again. Return to your duties.''

He turned his back on Anthony Miller and walked away.

For longer than a minute the assistant surgeon remained rigidly at the bulwark. His hands shook nervously, and he was damp with perspiration, but he felt a strength he had never known before. He had fought as well as he knew how. He had not stopped the vile torture, but he had gained the chance to keep Alan Fletcher alive. To that end he would do his utmost.

For twelve days the horror continued for Alan. On some days, there was only the freezing wind; on others, there was sleet and rain. And always, relentlessly, there was the wood bearing down on him, confining him in the horrible, phobia-making darkness where the searing pain continued.

Yet after this hell, always came a respite: when Anthony Miller would tend him caringly, like a brother. Night after night Miller would dry him, put him to bed, comb his hair, speak softly to him, and feed him. The young man even made him a leather cape which he wore in the box as a defense against the icy, wet, interminable days.

On the eleventh and twelfth days, Alan was delirious. He remembered nothing of the box or of the interval in the assistant surgeon's care. It was not until he opened his eyes in the hospital cot on the fifteenth day after the ordeal had begun that he understood how many times he had gone into the box.

On the twenty-third day, he was returned from the hospital to the forecastle where he remained ironed for the rest of the journey.

Anthony Miller put out his hand to Alan as he left. "You have a magnificent constitution. I don't know how you survived, but thank God you did."

Alan took the younger man's hand. "Yes, I did survive, because of you. You are an honorable and benevolent man, Mr. Miller, and I thank you."

The ship was already in warmer waters, and the weather more equable. Soon the temperatures climbed from the forties to the sixties.

The ship's carpenter erected three more boxes, and Samuel Cooper, Boucher, Talbot, and Keating did their time. They spent seven days in the boxes, six hours a day.

On the fifth day, Boucher screamed so loudly, the whole ship could hear, and Keating took up his call. On the sixth day Boucher raged again, having taken leave of his senses. After his confinement, Anthony Miller took him to the hospital, where he had convulsions. On the seventh day as the guards went to back him into the box, he became quite deranged. He smashed one guard in the face and pushed the other to the deck. Then, before the stunned onlookers, he pulled himself up over the bulwalk and leapt overboard. The soldiers rushed to the side, only to see his white face upturned in supplication as he sank beneath the waves.

When the ship reached Sydney, the capital of New South Wales, one hundred and fifty-four days after departing Spithead, it was late in October, 1849 and the *Mount Stewart Elphinstone* was not allowed to land its prisoners. For the previous decade, there had been open discontent in the colony over the sending of any more felons out from Great Britain.

Hence, no one was allowed ashore from the *Mount Stewart Elphinstone* except for two prisoners bound for Hobart. The ship rode at anchor for one week while the politicians argued. Finally, it was decided to send it on to the settlement at Moreton Bay, five hundred miles to the north, where labor was in short supply.

Of the two hundred and thirty-two men embarked in the United Kingdom only four had died on the voyage. Mr. Loney and Mr. Mocksey were commended for bringing so many prisoners through alive.

FOUR

Sydney Town

February 1853

Sydney Harbor's 260 miles of shoreline, with its headlands, reaches, coves, bays, and creeks, basked in the stark bright iridescence found only in the great southlands. The combined fleets of the world, naval and mercantile, could anchor here. Across spits of sandstone and scrubby trees was Sydney town, nestled along a cove and surrounded by windmills.

From halfway up the waters of Port Jackson, the town gave the illusion of elegance, but as ships drew near to Circular wharf, the encrustation of swiftly built dwellings along the seafront, the narrow, unpaved streets, and the blight of the rookeries of "the Rocks" became all too apparent.

Indeed the settlement was a haphazard affair, but it was not without grand edifices of durable red and gray sandstone. Government House was a substantial monument for Her Majesty's representative, and there were others, all imposing enough: the Customs House, the Supreme Court, the Legislative Council building, and the Australian Library in Macquarie Street. Farther west, the best hotel, the Royal, with its portico supported by wide Doric columns, invited the affluent traveler. Yet the most impressive buildings were the churches: St. Andrew's and St. Mary's cathedrals and the churches of St. James and St. Phillip. The colonists held their God in conscientious and pious esteem.

Neither were the outer districts without occasional grandeur. The colony's wealthy had resided there for decades. But Sydney town itself was vastly overcrowded. The gold that had been

51

discovered at Summerfield Creek exactly two years before had been responsible for the now extending conglomerate of men of all races and creeds who had descended from ships, sanguine in the belief that they were the chosen of the goldrush.

Phillip had left San Francisco for Sydney the previous June. He had done well in California, but after his darlin' wife, Ada, had died in April, he had been inconsolable. They had been in California for just three years.

Forty-nine days after Ada's death, Phillip and his daughters, Eve and Clare, had caught the clipper *Fair Wind* and sailed out of San Francisco harbor on their way to the southern gold fields of New South Wales, where Phillip wanted to try his luck again.

Two days out of Honolulu, he had fallen ill. With the aid of the ship's doctor, his daughters nursed him, but he steadily worsened, and in the gray light of a cold, wet morning, at latitude 15 degrees and longitude 163, he joined his darlin' Ada. His illness had never been diagnosed.

The *Fair Wind* sailed on and carried the two sisters across the wide Pacific Ocean to deposit them upon the dock at Sydney Cove on the bleak, inhospitable southern winter day of July 31.

The few friends they had made on the voyage soon dispersed, and the woebegone sisters found that the cold weather echoed their reception in the unfamiliar colony. Within a week, they had been duped out of their father's savings by a local swindler and were alone and friendless. But they had each other, and they had the will to survive.

The miserable and destitute of Sydney town gravitated to the Rocks, the oldest area, not only of the colony, but of the country. Here, many houses and cottages from early in the century still stood in partially formed lines along the terraces of stone. It was a jumble of lanes, byways, and steep passages, home to vagrants, maritime deserters, the disillusioned of the goldrush, and all types of criminals.

The despairing sisters soon found their way to this part of the town, and were at once noticed by Mrs. Maggs, who ran the Ship Inn, a tavern of more than dubious reputation, which backed onto the harbor near Dawes Point around from the battery. The old woman had been quick to see that two pretty teenage girls would enhance business for very little outlay. In return for lodgings and sixpence a week to divide between them, they had been taken in by Mrs. Maggs and her husband.

The girls lived in a room at the back of the tavern, their single window opening out onto the waters of the harbor. They were called "serving girls," although a better description would have been "cleaners-cooks-barmaids-servants." Each day, they worked from the hour of ten in the morning until the inn closed, which was often two o'clock the next morning.

They had been half a year under the subjection of the Maggses when February 1853 discharged its heat and humidity upon the population. In that time, they had experienced enough to change them from the simple and artless teenagers who had disembarked from the *Fair Wind* into rather shrewd young women.

Every Monday Eve was sent by Mrs. Maggs to pick up her weekly parcel of tobacco, while Clare took a delivery of rum in another direction.

"And don't dawdle all day in gettin' there and back. It ain't no flamin', bloody holiday."

"I don't dawdle," Eve answered, dodging a badly aimed cuff at her head as she scurried past the old woman.

"Don't back-answer me," the woman shouted after her as she left the tavern. "Flamin', bloody cheek!"

The girl smiled as she gained the street. It was such a pleasure to be out in the open air. She had removed her apron and donned a calico bonnet to protect her face from the enervating sun. How she looked forward to this respite away from the chores of the tavern and the demands of the "Maggots," as she and Clare had soon dubbed the tavern owners.

She needed to traverse the entire length of George Street, for Mrs. Maggs was not one to forgo a bargain, and the cheapest tobacco in the town was to be had from a Chinese store in a lane at the side of the Hay Market, about a mile and a half from the Ship Inn.

Eve, now seventeen, had a swift step and stately bearing. She held her head high, her blond curls peeping from under her bonnet, and even though her dress was worn in places, her natural vivacity and youthful charm gave her a dignity that overcame her poor appearance. She drew second glances from many of the habitués of the Sydney streets.

As she turned into George Street, she found her way barred by a tall ex-sailor called Grayson, a deserter from an American clipper ship and a frequent customer at the Ship Inn. He often joked about how he was cousin to Eve and Clare because of his Boston origins. He was the barmaid's lover, a girl named Lucy, but had recently turned his attentions to the sisters. Eve had deflected his advances, having become quite adept at this skill, but Clare was obviously attracted to him and had responded.

Grayson and Clare had often left the tavern together, and on more than one occasion Clare had not returned until the following morning. It had caused more than one row between the two sisters.

Now Grayson bent into her face, smiling broadly. "Hey, is that you, Eve, under there?"

"Yes. Hello, Grayson."

"Wasn't sure for a moment. How are you?"

"Well, thank you," she responded as she went to pass by.

"What's the hurry?"

"I'm going for Mrs. Maggs's tobacco. You know what she's like. I can't stand here talking."

"Now, wait a bit," he answered, taking her arm. "Come in to Stanley's and have a quick drink." His hand went skillfully from her arm to her waist, and he moved her sideways into the darkened entry of Stanley's Pub.

"Grayson, I can't."

"Now, a few minutes won't hurt." He pushed her gently up against the stone wall of the passage and, putting his arms to either side of her body, pinioned her against the wall. He bent down to her. He was a handsome man, in his mid-twenties. His face was smooth, a healthy brown from the sun, his eyes were the color of sky, and his mouth could have been chiseled by Michelangelo. He was looking into her eyes and smiling.

For a moment, she returned his look. Then she startled him. "Where the devil did you take my sister Saturday night?" Her alert brown eyes animated in points of light as she pushed him sharply so that his head jerked back abruptly. "I know what you're up to, Grayson. You stay away from her, damn it! And poor Lucy knows nothing of it for a start! Men like you think you can treat girls like playthings, then discard them like rubbish. Well, the likes of you won't get away with it with my sister. So leave Clare alone. And leave me alone!" She threw off his arms, and moved out of the stone entry, soon disappearing into the distance.

Eve's walk became quite spirited as she crossed the street and continued past the three-foot-high stone wall surrounding the cove and the ships berthed on her left. She was unaware of the urchins playing around the piles of cannonballs stacked at intervals along the seafront, and totally ignored the fish seller who lifted a whiting from his cart to dangle for her inspection.

She was thinking about Grayson, handsome dog that he was. Lord above, did he want all the girls in Sydney town? That was the trouble, poor girls were at the mercy of men like Grayson. How angry she had been when Clare had finally returned home on Sunday morning. Why couldn't she see the sort of man he was? And it wasn't the first time. Her sister had done it before with other men. No proper man would ever look at her if she continued this way. How could Clare, who was so like Eve in so many ways, be so different in this one?

And poor Lucy, she was totally in love with Grayson. She already had a child by some cove who had run out on her. What sort of life was that?

Eve knew Clare had no intention of hurting Lucy. Clare never really wanted to hurt anyone; she just didn't think at times. These days her way of enjoying life was to love and be loved by handsome men. Grayson certainly fell into that category.

Eve's perfect brow puckered. That was one thing that was not going to happen to Evelyn May Herman. She did not know how she was going to achieve it, but she would lift herself up out of this mess, no matter what! She felt sure she was capable of getting somewhere in this life. If only she could get some money. If only.

She had heard this very morning that Sully Tomkins, around in Hunter Street, was looking for someone to lease his shed. It had small living quarters at the back, and he wanted four shillings a week for it. The news had sent a thrill down Eve's spine, for she knew something that no one else did. Oh, how much she would like to rent that shed.

She had something that she doubted anyone else in the whole of New South Wales had, something that could earn her a lot of money and enable her and Clare to live properly, respectably. It had been left at the Ship Inn by an American man off to the gold fields. "You keep this," he had said to Eve, "it's too damn cumbersome. Don't know why I brought it with me." When Mrs. Maggs had taken no interest, simply calling it a "newfangled thing," Eve had removed the object and put it by her bed. She had been studying it in the privacy of their little room, studying and using it and learning all about it.

The newfangled thing was a machine. There was a needle with an eye near the point, which contained a thread. You placed a piece of cloth in it, and there was a sort of shuttle that carried another thread below the cloth on a small reel. The needle was fastened to an arm that vibrated on a pivot. Movement of the arm by a wheel forced the needle through the cloth. The shuttle carried the under thread through the loop of the upper thread, thus making a locked stitch. The machine had come with a tin full of various fitting parts and numerous special needles. On the tin was the name Elias Howe and a New York address. With it she could sew things so very much faster than the most skillfull seamstress ever could.

Eve had enterprising ideas. There were so many folk in Sydney who needed things mended and sewn. If only she could earn enough money to rent Sully Tomkins's shed.

The dream was running through her mind as she hurried on between the lofty houses decorating either side of this part of George Street. Eve had become accustomed to Sydney; it wasn't such a bad place. She had seen many worse, such as the ramshackle villages in the West Indies and South America where the *Ipswich* had anchored on its way to California. Yet in her heart, she longed to be away from Sydney, out in the country somewhere.

She was still deep in meditation when she came to the Post Office with its line of billboards across the footpath announcing the WANTED of the colony.

Then her path took her on by the formidable Royal Hotel with its solid Doric columns, and the large covered-in marketplace a few paces on, abounding with salesmen and their wares.

It was not until she passed the police office that she came out of her reverie. There was always at least one poor devil manacled in the stocks outside. Today there were two. A shiver ran through her, for while she tried not to look at them, she could not help it. They were covered in flies and looked half-dead. She ran by.

By the time she reached St. Andrew's Cathedral, which sat sedately in its sward of green, her pace had slowed in the debilitating heat. From there it was downhill for a quarter of a mile, past rows of two- and three-story houses, until she came at last to the Hay Market at the foot of Brickfield Hill.

She made her way through the center of the business area past the turret clock and then into the back lane at the side of the market.

"Hello, Mr. Ling."

"Hello, Eve."

"I am come for the tobacco."

He took the pouch Eve had brought and moved to the back of his shop in the short, trotting steps of the Oriental.

Eve waited, passing among the large, cubical chests lined with sheet lead and full of tea leaves. Some of them had quaint

Chinese characters written on them. Here she lingered, dipping in her hands and lifting fistfuls of the aromatic tea leaves to smell.

On her return journey, she walked swiftly until she came to Hastey's Auction Room, one of the many on George Street. Old Hastey was shouting from behind a high, horseshoe-shaped desk, his gavel in his hand. His beard was so long, it almost reached his waist. Eve often wondered why he bothered to wear the neat bow tied at his throat, for it could only be seen from the side.

The crowd spilled out onto the street, for the room was quite full. Eve edged her way through to get a better view. At the front were four rows of wooden forms filled with buyers. Today, Hastey's wife was here. She helped only during large auctions with numerous lots. Everyone knew her name was Doreen, because he would always turn to her and ask, "What is next for these lucky folk, Doreen, my sweet?" She was a fine-looking woman, long and slender, with straight golden hair pulled into a topknot. She was presently holding a gilded cage inside of which were two yellow canaries.

"I have heard one and tuppence for this fine cage and grand specimens of bird life. Do I hear more?" Hastey cried out. "My fellow travelers, these birds are direct descendants of a pair owned by the Queen of Tonga herself! Why, the cage alone is worth one and tuppence!"

There were no more bids. Hastey looked disappointed as he knocked down the canaries to a lady in the front row.

The next lot was 150 dozen kangaroo skins.

"Now, my friends, my fellow travelers, here I have a sample of the superb hides that I offer today. Hold it up, Doreen, my sweet."

Eve had come to the front of the standing crowd, and right next to the table where Hastey's assistant stood with items yet to come up for bid. This was what fascinated her most, the divers things for sale. She took delight in wondering from what faraway place they had come, how they had arrived here, and who had owned or made them. She conjured up stories about them, and her fantasies lifted her up out of the grime and poverty of Sydney town.

Among the remaining lots was a large, ornate harpsichord, set near two bales of calico. There were also four ivory-handled hammers, a box of cutlery, an anchor and a chain, six down pillows, a leather-bound dictionary, some baby linen, a watercolor drawing of a horse, a sign that said, LANSDOWN STATION, IN THE DISTRICT OF MORETON BAY, 8,000 SHEEP, and closest to her, the thing that brought a wishful smile to her face, a string of pearls, with a diamond clasp and a matching brooch. They lay in a red velvet box. Her mother used to have a set of pearls. They were so lovely. Whatever had become of them? How she missed her mother and father, and often felt lonely, especially now that Clare spent so much time with men.

Hastey was calling loudly to his audience about the next item, and Eve heard him say, "I start the bidding at ten sovereigns! Do I hear ten?"

Someone began the bidding.

Ten sovereigns, Eve thought. Fancy having ten whole sovereigns. A fortune. If only she had ten sovereigns, she could rent Sully Tomkins's shed, begin her sewing business, and transform her and her sister's life. Well, really eight sovereigns . . . Why, even five would do.

The bidding continued.

She looked down at the jewels, so clean, pure, lustrous.

The bidding ended. The item was sold.

These pearls were so beautiful. She put out her hand and, with the tip of a finger, touched them.

Suddenly her wrist was in a vice-like grip, and Hastey's assistant was shouting, "So we have a would-be thief in our midst, do we?"

Eve looked up to him in surprise. "But I wasn't—"

"Wasn't, my eye! You thought no one was looking."

Doreen and Hastey turned to the noise, as did everyone in the room.

Indignation sprang to Eve's face. She threw off the man's hand and began to defend herself. "I was only touching them. My mother used to have some."

This brought gales of laughter. A thin girl in a cheap calico bonnet and threadbare dress, wearing shoes that had seen better times and carrying a tobacco pouch, had a mother who wore pearls and diamonds!

Hastey's assistant grabbed her again and dragged her roughly forward. "Tell it to the police. Come on."

"No, damn it, leave me alone! I was only looking at them." Eve was pulling away, but the man held her fast.

"You thieves are all alike. You can explain it to the police, anyway."

Just then, someone spoke. He was a clergyman, in black frock coat with reversed collar. He held his hat in his hand, and his thick, dark hair was only faintly streaked with gray at his temples, although he was a man in his sixtieth year. He had been standing beside Eve.

"Stop it! This child is with me."

Hastey's assistant raised his eyebrows. "Oh, I see, Reverend. Really? With you, is she? Then all I can say is, you should spend a touch more money on outfitting your daughter."

More tittering and laughter sounded.

The cleric had the intense eyes of a zealot, yet he was, in fact, a moderate and temperate priest. Those eyes rested now with all their force on Hastey's assistant. "You merely show your stupidity. I did not say she was my daughter. What I did say is that she is with me. She wished only to touch the pearls. I saw many women handling them before the auction began. If you do not want your goods touched during the auction, there should be a sign to say so." He took Eve's arm. "Come away from here."

The man reluctantly released her, and they made their way through the crowd to the street.

Eve could not believe what had happened. Thank heavens this minister had saved her from being taken to that awful police office. The touch of his hand made her feel suddenly quite happy, somehow warmed, with a sense of well-being.

He smiled down at her, and to Eve's surprise, his eyes seemed to soften. She responded with a smile of her own. "I don't know how to thank you, sir. They would not have believed me."

"Perhaps not, young lady, but for my part, I think your honesty shows in your face."

Eve was very moved by his words. "Oh, sir, thank you. I was brought up to be truthful and never to covet things."

The reverend could not help smiling to himself. She was certainly forthright. He felt quite drawn to her. "I should stay away from this auction room for a time," he suggested.

She nodded.

"Do you live near here?"

This reminded her. She must leave. She had been long enough now. Mrs. Maggot would be waiting.

"Yes, I do. Not far away. But I must go. I am very late, sir. I have been on an errand and am very late. Thank you again, and good-bye, sir."

The minister's eyes were still upon her as she turned and moved quickly away through the people to the street. He shook his head. There were dozens of waifs like her in Sydney town, but this child had appealed to him, and now he realized why. She reminded him of his darling Josephine. The shape of her brow and the earnest round, brown eyes beneath, even her smile of gratitude, brought to mind his sweet sister. Josephine had been about the age of this girl when she died. He took a deep breath and shook his head sadly before he walked away.

Eve was so concerned with the hour, she really hurried now, breaking into a run by the time she reached the deserted barrack-square.

It was well after four o'clock when she passed the battery of cannon facing out across the water at Dawes Point. There was Mrs. Maggs sitting on her stool beside the swing-arm doors of the tavern, holding her empty pipe in her hand and tapping impatiently with her wooden clogs on the worn stone doorstep.

"Where the bloody hell have ye been, gel? Me tongue's hangin' out for me pipe, and ye dawdlin' along as if it were a month of Sundays."

"You saw me running," the girl replied.

"Aha! I wasn't born yesterday. Sure, ye run, the last few bloody yards when I can see ye."

Eve handed her the pouch of tobacco, and the woman called, "Sly wench!" to the girl's retreating back, then abruptly forgot her annoyance in the prospect of a puff on her pipe.

That night, Grayson came to the tavern around eleven o'clock. Eve watched him, and when he was not making eyes at Lucy, he was making eyes at Clare, and for fifteen minutes around midnight, he and Clare were both missing. Lucy did not notice, and Eve did not mention it. When the tavern closed just before the hour of two, he left in company with Lucy.

"Why are you friendly with Grayson?" Eve asked her sister when they were at last in bed.

"Why not?" answered Clare.

"You know why not. It's not proper."

"Don't be such a prig, Eve. He's so handsome, and quite a gentleman, really, when you get to know him."

"But what about Lucy? She's in love with him."

Clare's voice dropped with guilt. "Yes, I suppose she is, but I think I am, too."

Eve half rose and leaned on her elbow to face Clare. She could make out her sister's dark form in the cot opposite, below the barrels of rum that were stacked against the wall. Eve was not at all sure Clare was in love. She *seemed* to be in love every few months. It disconcerted her that her sister was so changed since they had arrived in Sydney. "I know he's handsome, but I think you are a damn fool to be involved with him at all. I don't think he loves anyone but himself."

She could see Clare's dark figure in the meager light. Her sister's voice took on an exasperated note. "Oh, for heaven's sake, Eve, I can't explain it to you. If you haven't experienced what it's like being with a man, then it's like talking to a child."

Eve knew she was not worldly like Clare, but she did not want to be. When she spoke now, her voice held an edge of exasperation. "Why do you do that thing with him? He's only taking advantage of you; can't you see that?"

Her sister sprang to his defense. "No, he's not. You just don't understand." Her voice dropped to a confidential tone. "Evelyn, he makes me feel wonderful all over. I've never felt as good as I do with him. And do you know what?"

"What?"

"He's going to buy me that dress in Penny's Store up by the quay." Her voice lifted with excitement. "You know that lovely one, all red satin with lace and pearl buttons. How I do yearn for that. I haven't had a new dress for so long, and it's so beautiful, isn't it?"

"Yes, it is. But I still think it's wrong."

"Why?"

"Oh hell, Clare, Lucy thinks Grayson is serious about her. She'll be heartbroken."

Her sister was silent for such an extended time that Eve spoke again. "Well?"

Clare signed sadly. "I do feel awful about Lucy. I don't want to hurt her, honestly, but Grayson swears it's never been serious with her, that Lucy's known all along he didn't intend to stay with her; so it's not my fault." Then her voice became intimate. "Eve, he says he's never been with a girl who has a figure as beautiful as mine."

"Do you really believe that?"

"Yes, of course. I know he wouldn't lie to me."

Eve could feel her eyes filling with tears of frustration. She was angry with Clare, angry with Grayson, angry with the way their lives were. "What would Mummy and Daddy think?" she demanded. "They would be ashamed of you."

Her sister fell quiet again. The only sound was the constant lapping of the water below their window. "Don't be angry, darling,'' Clare whispered. "It's pointless to wonder what they would think."

"Well, it's not to me." Eve turned away to face the wall. She was at a loss to continue this conversation. More and more she did not understand Clare. She was trying not to feel lonely and frightened. "How I wish we could get away from this place, build for ourselves a proper, respectable life. Be as we used to be, happy and free of worry. Oh, how I do wish that."

The next morning, as Eve and Clare were sweeping the stone corridor that led to a grassy yard at the side of the inn where horses were tethered, Mr. Maggs came out of the taproom. He was a big man and almost filled the corridor as he came by. He squeezed Clare's bottom in an intimate manner as he moved past.

"Men," she laughed, stopping work to lean on her broom. "They all think about one thing."

"Because you let them, for heaven's sake," her sister answered.

"Well, in this 'very mess' of a world, we might as well have fun with them."

Eve shook her head. "Oh, Clare, don't say that. What about Daddy? He wasn't like these men. And Grandpa. Can't you remember?"

Clare shook her head sadly. "They're dead. Dead men don't count."

Now Eve stopped sweeping and placed her broom against the wall. She sighed. "Clare, I hate the way you are so changed."

Clare moved to her and took up her hands. "No, darling, I've grown up, that's all." Then she hugged Eve tightly. "And you will, too, one day."

Eve sighed. She did love her sister, even though she could not accept what she was doing. She tilted her chin. "No, Clare, I don't want to be like you. You place no value on yourself, and that's an awful mistake."

Clare turned sharply away, and Eve realized she had hurt her. Eve moved to her and smoothed her hair affectionately. "I'm sorry, but I wish you would listen to me."

Suddenly shouts sounded from the street and were answered in the taproom. "Hey, come and look, ye all!"

"Old Sam Wright's boat has been hit by a ferry, and there's someone swimming for his life in the harbor!"

Sam Wright was an ex-convict who had died a few months

before, and the rumor was that he had been worth a million guineas sterling, but he had left only the house he lived in to his wife, and his old fishing boat to his son. The speculation as to where the rest of his money had gone was still rife in Sydney town.

The sounds of shouting intensified and people were running into the street. The two sisters, as eager as anyone else to see the sight, followed the crowd heading west to Walsh Bay at the entrance to Darling Harbor, a short distance away. Even Mrs. Maggot had left the tavern and was clopping along around the hill, pipe in hand.

When the sisters reached the bay, men and women were pressing forward over the piles of the seawall to catch a glimpse of what was happening. It was not long before it was over and a bedraggled man was helped ashore.

Those gathered began to disperse, and Eve looked around for Clare, who had been beside her only a few moments earlier. There she was, leaning on a hitching rail, tête-à-tête with Grayson. Eve went over. Grayson smiled roguishly at her. She nodded stiffly.

"We had better get back, Clare. The rotten Maggots will be on us otherwise."

"You go ahead, Eve, love. I'll be by in just a minute."

Eve started back toward Dawes Point, and Grayson took a swift glance after her. Some of the crowd were still milling about in the narrow street, where a hot breeze was blowing, lifting a little dust on the unpaved thoroughfare. They had been joined by a few well-dressed folk, for this part of Sydney was over the hill from the Rocks and had an occasional better house and a sprinkling of enticing shops.

Eve did not get around to this section of town very often, even though it was close by. Her errands and her work took her the other way into Sydney proper. She stopped, intrigued by a brightly colored sign that hung on two chains from an ornamental metal arm. It had an open book painted on it and the words:

Welcome, All Lovers of the Written Word,
William Pell, the Wandering Poet,
Seller of Fine Poetry and Books

How she missed her own books. How she missed her piano. How she missed the afternoons with her mother when they would read and play piano and sing. She and Clare had begun to learn to play when they were only four. She remembered entering a city contest in Boston when she was only ten years old. She had won the pianoforte for all the children under fourteen, and Clare had won the singing. She made a soft, wistful sound and began to peruse the titles of the books stacked in the wooden stands along the front of the shop. Her hand was reaching for a leather-covered volume of Wordsworth when she stopped and looked more closely at the back of the man who exited from the shop door, a few yards away.

It was the clergyman from the auction. He was taking leave of a gentleman who appeared to be the shop owner. They said their good-byes, and the clergyman tipped his hat and walked toward a cabriolet waiting in the narrow roadway.

As he stepped up into the cab, his hand went into the pocket of his frock coat, and he took out his handkerchief. With it came out a gold watch, which fell to the ground while he continued into the cab, oblivious.

The vehicle moved.

"Sir! Sir!" Eve called. "You have dropped your watch." She ran forward, picked up the timepiece, and shouted again as the cab driver realized what had happened and halted.

The reverend looked down, and a joyful smile spread across his face as he recognized Eve. "My goodness, it is the young lady of yesterday!" He opened the door and stepped back down to Eve, who handed him his property.

"You dropped it from your pocket, sir."

"Really? God bless you; thank you, child."

Eve smiled.

"We didn't actually introduce ourselves yesterday, did we?" He bowed ever so slightly from the shoulders. "I am Leslie Billings, of All Saints' Church in Bathurst town, across the Blue Mountains." He held out his hand, and she placed hers in his. She was experiencing the same happy glow that she had in his company the day before. "How do you do. I am Eve Herman, of the Ship Inn, lately of America, sir."

"I am truly happy to meet you, child."

"And I, you, though I fear I must go again. I really shouldn't be here. There'll be the devil to pay when I get back. We all came to see poor Charlie Wright swimming from his sunken boat."

"Yes, I, too, saw the fellow," the reverend said. "Lucky to be alive." Then he took up her right hand and placed his watch in her palm.

"What?"

"You must have it." He had almost said, "You must have it, Josephine." The style of the girl was so like his dead sister, it was disconcerting. "I insist. Do just as you please with it. It's yours."

"Oh, I couldn't, sir. It's gold, sir."

She had never held anything more beautiful. It was intricately worked with filigree and was very heavy. She went to return it to him, but he shook his head.

"Yes, it is, solid gold, and, child, you must allow me the pleasure of giving it to you. I repeat: Do just as you like with it. That is why I want you to have it."

She didn't know what to say. It was like a miracle. "Oh . . . I . . . it is so beautiful. And after what you did for me yesterday. You are too generous. Thank you so much, sir."

He simply smiled. It was such a poignant feeling he had about this thin girl with fair curls and brown eyes and a smudge of dirt on her cheek.

"This Ship Inn you mentioned, is it near here?"

"Yes, sir, at Dawes Point. I live there."

"Do your parents own it?"

She shook her head. "My parents are dead, sir."

"I see."

The Reverend Leslie Billings was studying her. He suspected she was unhappy at this Ship Inn, for she had seemed alarmed the twice she had mentioned it. He wanted to help her, if he could.

If only he had known her thoughts. How she was longing that this moment could last, that somehow she could stay in his company.

"Well, thank you, again, sir. Good-bye."

"Good-bye, Miss Herman."

She was reluctant to leave, and backed away from him.

He lifted his hand. "I leave Sydney tomorrow. If ever you find yourself in Bathurst, do please come and see me and my wife."

She nodded and turned quickly from him now, for her eyes had filled with tears. She started off at a run along the street. He watched her until she disappeared out of sight, before he turned and entered the cabriolet.

The tears ran from Eve's eyes as she hurried along. What a kind, lovely old man.

She was put immediately to work on her return, for the tavern was full of seamen, four ships having berthed on the morning tide. She had to wait some hours before she found a minute to take Clare aside into their little room.

"Clare, darling, a miracle has happened."

Her sister's eyes widened. "What?"

Eve took the gold watch from her pocket.

"Oh, Evelyn, where did you get it?"

Eve turned it in her hands and opened it. The face had a diamond where the XII, the IX, the VI, and the III would normally be.

"A kind man gave it to me. A minister, from Bathurst, across the Blue Mountains."

"Oh, Lord, Eve, it must be worth ten or fifteen sovereigns at least."

"Yes."

Clare's smile widened as a thought formed in her mind. "Oh, Eve, we must sell it. We'll be able to buy all sorts of lovely things."

"Sell it? But I don't think I could do that."

"Of course you could. He gave it to you, didn't he? You can do as you like with it. Don't be so silly."

Eve frowned. Her sister's remark had stirred the notion of her dream again. She recalled the minister and what he had said to her. She looked at Clare, who was smiling with delight at the splendid object, and suddenly her own eyes began to shine with the possibility of her dream. Everything could be achievable. Slowly she closed both her hands over the timepiece and held it up to her heart. "Well, he did say for me to do anything I like with it. And even though I'd like to keep it, I suppose he would approve if I sold it."

"Of course he would. He *gave* it to you," Clare argued, imagining herself in the red satin dress with bright new shoes and a feathered hat. Perhaps now she could have gloves like the gentry wore.

A flush of pink had risen to Eve's cheeks, and her skin glowed with the light of her dream. "All right, the first chance I have, I am slipping round to Hunter street to Sully Tomkins."

"Why?"

"Because we are going to rent his premises . . . and start a business with this." She turned to pat the sewing machine affectionately. "We are getting out of this blasted hole. The Maggots can go to flamin' blazes. We are going to have a good, respectable life of our own."

"Oh," was all Clare could manage to say.

Within forty-eight hours the sisters were instated in Hunter Street. The following Tuesday a letter came addressed to: "Miss E. Herman, c/o the Ship Inn, Dawes Point, Sydney."
Mrs. Maggs took it and opened it.
It read:

> *All Saints' Parsonage*
> *Bathurst*
> *Fri., 4th February, 1853*

Dear Miss Herman,

Since our two chance meetings in the streets of Sydney this week, I have thought often about you. And in retrospect I am come to the conclusion you are not happy in your present circumstances at the Ship Inn.

Please ignore the rest of this letter if I have misjudged your sentiments.

I do not wish to appear presumptuous, but my wife has encouraged me to write and tell you of a house the church owns here in Bathurst. It is a rambling old building with a number of bedrooms. We have a gentle, motherly, elderly lady, Miss Hopkins, who is in residence here, with five orphan girls, three of whom I would calculate are similar in age to your own.

I have spoken to the church fathers and we would like to offer you and your sister lodgings here with Miss Hopkins. The older girls all have work in the town and do odd jobs for the church and generally take care of the house itself. The younger ones attend our church school. It is a happy and healthy outdoor life they lead.

Once again, I do hope I have not misread your feelings in our two brief meetings.

My wife and I have enclosed a bank note for two pounds, which should well cover the cost of transferring yourselves by coach to our small town here on the plain across the mountains.

> *Yours faithfully,*
> *Leslie Billings*
> *Rector, All Saints' C of E*

Mrs. Maggs's face contorted into a delighted, toothless grin. She shook her pipe gleefully in the air.

"Ah, Lordy me! Easiest two bloody quid I've ever made."

She tucked the bank note into her voluminous pocket, turned, and walked out into the yard, crossed to the water's edge, crumpled the letter into a ball, and threw it as far as she could into the water of the harbor.

"That'll bloody teach ye to walk out on me, gel!"

FIVE

From Bondage

Wednesday, February 2, 1853
The same day that Eve met Reverend Billings at Hastey's Auction Rooms.

"All right, you lags! Ten minutes' rest. Bring in the water. Move!"

Alan and Daniel, who had been working side by side, put down their shovels and moved toward the water cart. Dan's face was red from the intense heat, and although he was now fifty-eight, he worked side by side with the youngest of the convicts. Still, the worst of the summer heat took its toll upon him, and often after a water break, he was the last to rise to his feet.

. This year the entire Moreton Bay district was stifling, made worse by the bush fires that ringed the settlement. The horizon was lost in smoke clouds, and the temperatures rose daily to over one hundred degrees. So many of the laborers had fainted that the sergeant in charge begrudgingly agreed to more water breaks and to halt work entirely between noon and two o'clock each day.

The convicts jostled one another in their eagerness for the

water. Alan's hand went around Daniel's shoulder as they joined the line. "Are you all right, Danny?"

"Yes, son. The summers never seem to improve, do they?"

It had been the same since they had arrived here exactly three years and three months ago. Had they undergone this hell for years? Alan remembered the day they had landed at Moreton Bay. November 1, 1849.

They had been greeted in true Australian fashion that day, too: searing ninety-four-degree heat, sticky humidity, and flies.

They were led single file down the gangplank to the wooden wharf on the shore of the Brisbane River, named after Sir Thomas Brisbane, the governor of New South Wales from 1821 to 1826. There they waited for over two hours, each man carrying his worldly possessions in a cloth bag: two blankets; and his regulation dress, comprising two jackets and waistcoats of kersey cloth, two pairs of duck trousers, two coarse linen shirts, yarn stockings, and one woolen cap. During the worst of the voyage's cold, most convicts had worn their entire wardrobe day and night, but now as the sun beat down on them from a cloudless sky, many wore nothing on their upper bodies, and some tucked their waistcoats up under their caps, Arab style, to get relief.

The last prison transport ever to land its human cargo in the colony of New South Wales, the *Bangalore*, came exactly six months later. It and the *Mount Stewart Elphinstone* were the only ones to come directly to Moreton Bay at any time, though since the first fleet landed in 1788, over seventy thousand men and women convicts had been brought to New South Wales, as well as many tens of thousands to the other colonies and Norfolk Island, the "horror island," which earned its ghastly reputation by the constant ill treatment of prisoners there, isolated in the Pacific a thousand miles to the east of Moreton Bay.

In the enervating heat, the prisoners soon broke ranks, and the guards, tired and lethargic themselves, allowed them to find shade. Daniel picked up a dirty piece of newspaper as it drifted by in the hot breeze. It was the first newspaper he had seen since before he had been sentenced, and it cheered him just to hold one.

"Lads, listen to this! They don't want the likes of us here in their precious little colony!"

"What's that you say, Dan?" asked Samuel, who was now an accepted member of the little band.

"This." He held up the paper and shook it. "An article concerning all you dear, delightful companions of our happy voyage!''

Soon thirty or forty of the men gathered around him.

"This is the *Moreton Bay Courier* of October twenty-fifth, 1849, which was last Thursday." His musical Irish voice emphasized the more expressive words. "This continued influx of convicts to our *beautiful* colony may, in some cases, give impetus to the progress of certain districts; but there will be consequences, which generations to come may have *grave* cause to regret. It is our *children* we must remember. There are numerous objections to the presence of these *unseemly* arrivals, not the least of which are the apprehension of *danger* and the strong sense of *indignity*."

"Bleedin' cheek!" commented Swifty.

Daniel nodded and went on. "This is the choice part. These criminals are from the *dregs of society*. We must refuse to accept *vice* for the economic advantage of cheap labor. There is at last a growing interest in societies organized against this insult, the *antitransportation leagues*. These ships arrive, not with luxuries for our women or commodities for a *civilized* community, but with the *lowest, most immoral insult* to any settlement, criminals from Great Britain!''

"Gawd, who do they think they are?" remarked Kerry. "They waz all bloody convicts theirselves. And now they be manifestin' all holy!''

"Yes," agreed Peter Biggs, an embezzler from Birmingham, "the worst bastards are the reformed bastards!''

At this, there was much laughter and loud agreement.

"Well, I've been pardoned," called one of the exiles. "I'm as good as the pompous berk who wrote that.''

Daniel handed the paper to Alan. "Some of it seems to have been quoted by a cove called Henry Parkes.''

Alan's eyes ran over the article. "No doubt he believes he has a cause." Then he smiled to himself thinking how five months ago he had thought precisely the same of his companions as this journalist.

"He sounds just like a flamin' politician to me," decided Evan Evans, a burglar from Wales.

Swiftie, although he could not read, was looking over Alan's shoulder. "They certainly do not seem to want us.''

Alan ruffled Swiftie's hair affectionately with his long fingers. "They would not even allow us to set foot in Sydney, and it's clear they take us under sufferance here, albeit they need the labor force.''

Lawless waved his hand in disgust. "This all looks like a bleedin' dung heap anyway. What sane man would possibly *choose* to come 'ere?''

This gave rise to immediate agreement, loud derision of the locality, and an offering of scathing opinions.

"Yeah, 'beautiful,' that arse called it! Why, the river looks like shit!''

"The bleeders can 'ave their stinkin' hot Moreton Bay.''

"Friggin' hole should be called 'Mangrove Bay,' I reckon.''

In the distance, a group of adults and their children milled around. A number of the convicts turned toward them, and hailing them, gestured with rude and obscene signs.

Abruptly across the babble, the sergeant's voice broke, sonorous, in parade fashion. "All right! Attention! Jump to it! We be movin' out!''

They spent the night in rough wooden barracks on the outskirts of Brisbane town. The buildings had been unused for years. Dust was inches thick under the bunks and along the skirting boards. Big black cockroaches ran up the wooden walls and across the floor in the candlelight, and small brown spiders with long, thin legs shook in their webs in the corners of the unused bunks.

It was still eighty degrees at ten o'clock, over three hours after sunset.

It took the authorities in Brisbane a week to decide what to do with them. On the seventh morning after their arrival, they were divided. The exiles went to be assigned to settler masters, and the convicts were separated into two chain gangs to clear the bush and build roads. There were forty-eight men in Alan's gang, all those having names beginning with the letters A to L; those beginning with M to Z made up the other.

They were herded into carts to be taken away, Daniel declared. "It's a miracle. God saw fit to give the five of us names that come early in the alphabet, so we all stay together. I tell you, it's the divine working.''

Lawless lifted his eyes skyward as he patted Daniel on the back. "And I tell ye, Daniel, my dear, it were yer ma and pa workin'. That's where ye got 'Dwyer' from. There was naught divine in it!''

"Lawless, it's a poor, ignorant heathen you are,'' Daniel replied.

They traveled much of the day in a southwesterly direction, and in the late afternoon, made camp in tents on the banks of the Bremer, a tributary of the Brisbane River.

They cooked over open fires in the short summer evening. It was dark by seven o'clock, so different from the long twilights of the old country.

Many of the chain gangs in the past had been left in the care of exile and convict overseers, and abuses had been rife. This was not the case with Alan's gang, where soldiers had been made available to keep order, though the Crown surveyor who accompanied them was in charge.

After the evening meal, the convicts were allowed to sit in recreation on the riverbank, in view of their guards. The inevitable card games began in the dusk, and it was apparent that those who had gambled away their rations at sea would be the same to lose them on the land.

It was a cooler evening than the previous ones, made so by an appeasing breeze coming from downriver. Alan sat in thought. Now and then his hand would wave in front of his eyes to chase an insistent fly. The intense heat in this land fostered flies and snakes and other vermin. For a moment he was sick at heart for England. He looked across the narrow river to where some olive green weeping willows, planted by a settler, drooped to the dark water.

Sharply, a picture of the dignified willows at Long Moss House came to him: vivid, bright green fronds trailing to the clear stream that ran to graceful hills. He wondered for a moment if he would ever see Long Moss House again, then, quite surely, he knew he would not. He had crossed the Rubicon and inherited this sun-smothered land, the antipodes of England. His heart was heavy with yearning for the past; then, philosophically, he took stock of the present.

Unlike many of the convicts and even the free settlers, Alan realized that unfavorably comparing this land with the one he had left would serve no purpose but to promote more discontent, and there was enough of that emotion already in his life. So with a deep breath, he assessed the view before him with an unjaundiced eye.

It was simple terrain. It reminded him of the country near Port Nolloth in South Africa, where he had been with the navy. The hills were a blue-purple in the twilight, and nearby, stately slate gray gums threw long shadows across the tethered horses below. In the distance, large, severe granite rocks reflected a metal glossiness in the last rays of the sun. Yes, one could find a type of beauty here: different, stark, un-European, but beautiful nevertheless. He breathed a sigh. Perhaps a man could grow to love this country in time, if all his days were not spent in chains.

For the next three years, they lived nomadic lives, working southwest of the little district of Ipswich, which lay twenty-three miles from the settlement of Brisbane and had been opened to free settlers in 1843.

Because of close daily contact, some guards always became friendly with the prisoners. To discourage such association, the soldiers and the surveyor were recalled and replaced every six months. But there was mateship born of shared experience, and the new arrivals always followed the same pattern as their predecessors.

There were few attempts at escape; even though the guards were often sociable, they were still soldiers. The prisoners were well watched and, every sundown, ironed for the night. Alan was constantly alert, for he had always known that the only hope for him was to escape. "No one's soul could withstand a lifetime of this, Daniel," he confided, and the older man nodded. "Simply tell me the moment, son, and I'll be ready."

Samuel, Lawless, and Swiftie had long since agreed that if ever the opportunity arose, they were all of the same mind.

There were a number of occasions when Alan had come close to attempting escape, but each time he was thwarted before he could try. In 1852 his schemes had come nearest to fruition. The first time, several soldiers had fallen ill with fever, and because of their diminished numbers, escape appeared possible. Unfortunately, Swiftie and Lawless came down with the same fever. Alan had seen malaria in the ports of South America, and this was similar. He would not go without the two young men, and by the time they were better, so, too, were the soldiers. The other occasion, after months of bribery with their rum rations, Alan had convinced the exile overseer to forget to lock their shackles and to escape with them. The lives of the exile overseers on the chain gangs were almost as bad as those of the convicts. The escape was to take place on a Friday night, when the soldiers received their rum ration and the overseer locked the shackles of the prisoners by himself. Two days before the plan was to go into action, the man fell and broke his leg; he was taken to the nearest settlement, and they never saw him again.

It was virtually impossible to escape during the day, for while they worked, mounted soldiers patrolled around them. Three times in the first eighteen months, men had been tempted to make a break for it into the scrub, only to be shot dead.

Theirs was hard, monotonous, heavy, backbreaking labor. They built roads and cleared bushland. In the summer, the mind-deadening heat from the fierce Australian sun hammered into them. The only variations from this perpetual condition were rainstorms exploding lightning and thunder; or short dust storms, forcing them to retreat inside the tents. In the winter they shivered from the overnight frosts and the westerly winds, but the winters were brief. The summers were long and almost unbearable.

Occasionally a kindly farmer would augment their rations with fresh milk or fruit, and there was the bright spot, the weekly tots of rum. Their muscles hardened and their hands grew callused. The puny youths of the *Mount Stewart Elphinstone* developed into strong, powerful men.

And so the days turned into weeks . . . into months . . . into years . . . and through it all . . . the felon endured.

The pattern of the six-month change in their guard and surveyor altered just before Christmas 1852. The guards had been waiting for their replacements for over three weeks. On the sultry, hot Sunday evening of December 12 a stranger rode into camp just at sunset. Behind him came the ration cart and five other horse-drawn carriers, all empty. His loud voice called across the encampment, "Where the devil are Surveyor Clarke and Corporal Raleigh?"

He was a thin man in sergeant's uniform, and he looked weary from his long ride. There was two days' growth of whiskers on his ruddy face, and his hair hung lankly across a furrowed brow. His uniform was open at the neck, and his lean fingers pulled at the opening in habitual movement. "Hey! Who's in charge of this rum lot? You, man!" he shouted to a soldier who passed nearby. "Where's the corporal?"

"Why, he be with the lags, sir; it's washup time over yonder." The redcoat gestured with his hand toward the southern end of the camp.

Corporal Raleigh's face broke into a smile when he saw the newcomer, then seeing no accompanying soldiers, he frowned. "Where's the replacement troop? Ye have come to replace us, haven't ye?"

"Aye, in a way, that is so. But my orders are for you all to accompany me, along with this lot—" he waved his hand over the convicts "—across south of the Beau Desert property. Seems someone important wants the land cleared and a road and bridges built, and your beauties are to do the job, eh? Special orders. When you have delivered the prisoners, you return to Moreton Bay. I stay on in command with a new troop until the job's done. There will be two years' work in it." He wiped the back of his hand across his perspiring brow. "We leave at sunrise."

When, many days later, they reached their destination, they found a disused shed which they adapted to house eighteen men while the others lived as before, in tents. Each tent held seven men and was made semipermanent by being fortified on the inside with wooden planking and floorboards, leaving only the front flap free for entry and exit.

Surveyor Clarke and Corporal Raleigh and his men left a few days before Christmas, and Sergeant Eric Dobbs with twelve recently arrived horse soldiers took charge. The new surveyor did not join them until January, and the convicts meanwhile cleared the bush, chopping down trees and removing the scraggy shrubs and plants of the scrub.

Christmas day was a Saturday, and in honor of the birth of Christ, the convicts rested. They spent the day lying in the shade of the eucalyptus trees on the banks of a stony creek running west from the feeble Albert River. It passed, as the others before it had, heat, flies, cockroaches and sweat being the yuletide gifts to the convicts.

Within a week of his arrival, it was obvious that Dobbs was not simply strict. He resorted to the lash for even petty offenses. Standing trancelike, he would watch the punishment, while his hand pulled mechanically at his shirt collar.

Eric Dobbs had joined the army as a ten-year-old drummer boy. His character had been fashioned by hardship, discipline, and orders. He had risen to the rank of sergeant by being a sycophant and a bully. He saw weakness as a thing to be exploited, yet in the army's normal chain of command, his cruelty was not apparent. It was only now, when he was in sole charge, that it emerged. He made sport of all in his care, especially the weak and the sick. He occasionally vented his spleen on his own soldiers as well. While the magistrate rode from the Brisbane settlement regularly and the prisoners were encouraged to bring grievances to him, there was rarely a complaint, for fear of retaliation when he left.

When Mr. Stonebridge, the engineer-surveyor, arrived, nothing actually changed. He was a kindly man, whose name was not lost on the prisoners. It was a source of constant amusement to them that Mr. Stonebridge built stone bridges, and they called him "Stoney" affectionately behind his back. He was a big man, but his size did not mirror his courage. His was a genteel nature, opposed to violence and conflict, preferring appeasement and conciliation. He simply did his job. He built his roads and his bridges with care, but each evening he left to billet in relative comfort at a nearby farm, leaving Dobbs in charge.

The sergeant had a simple opinion of the forty-six men in his chain gang: bloody lags, all of them. But they would not get the better of him. Of course, the prisoner called Fletcher stood out from his ill-educated comrades. His incongruity among them was apparent whether he bent double in a field or waited, half-naked, to be doused with a bucket of water at washup time. Some obviously idolized him, and it was plain that all respected him. But Eric Dobbs was not impressed. He would spare no one. He would break Fletcher just as he would break them all, though it was difficult to find a reason to discipline Fletcher. Even when Dobbs goaded him, he had never received anything more for his efforts than a brief penetrating look.

With Dobbs in charge, Alan knew he had to escape. He had been shaping a plan, and by now, the first week in February, he had the details clear. He had chosen the following Friday night as the time. Each Friday fortnight, the sergeant allowed his soldiers double rum rations, and though they did not get hopelessly drunk, they were not as clearheaded as usual.

Alan reviewed his plan for the others as they rested during the water break until the peace was broken by an overseer calling them all back to work.

They stood from under the tree where they had been sitting, and suddenly Daniel's face turned dark red. He leaned back against the tree trunk and his breath came in short gasps.

"Daniel, what's wrong?"

"Don't know, sonny. Feel a bit tight in the chest, bit dizzy."

Alan looked to Swiftie. "Get some more water, lad." The young man quickly complied and held a cup to Daniel's lips. He sipped a little.

At that moment the overseer shouted again. Alan motioned Swiftie and the others who had gathered around to leave, while he remained on the ground beside Daniel, lifting his arm to feel his pulse.

Sergeant Dobbs, sitting in the shade of a gum thirty yards away, noticed the two men still on the ground. "Hey!" he shouted. "You two get up, move off. Rest time's finished. I'm tired of all this bloody fainting and malingering. Flamin' tired of it, I say!"

Daniel's eyes were glazed. He tried to rise but he fell back, an expression of pain crossing his face. "Go, son, go. I'll not have Dobbs screaming at you, too."

"Where does it hurt, Dan?"

"It'll pass, Alan. Don't be worrying. I'll be all right. Go. Please go . . ."

By now, Dobbs had realized who the two men were. Fletcher and Dwyer! Now, they were too brotherly by half. Pulling at his shirt collar, he rose and hastened across. "What the devil goes on here? You two have been called back to work, don't you know?"

Alan did not look up as he said, "Can't you see he cannot rise? He must rest. He needs a doctor."

"A doctor!" Dobbs's voice rose. "More like he's feignin'. Doesn't want to work in the heat. I've got a bridge to build, Fletcher, and you and Dwyer sitting here in the shade won't get it done. Come on, Dwyer, move!"

Alan's voice held steady as he looked up into the face above him. "Leave him alone. The others are half his age. He's sick, I tell you!"

Dobbs was all agitation. There was an excited sound now in his voice. "Shut up, Fletcher! I'm tired of this, I am. Sick nothin'! Get up this instant, Dwyer, if you know what's good for you." He moved his foot to Daniel's side and dug at him, but Daniel did not move. Then he grabbed Alan's shirt collar, pulling him away so that he overbalanced. "I told you to get back to work, Fletcher! I'll deal with you for insubordination later."

He turned his back on Alan and stood towering above the older man.

Alan regained his feet but did not move away.

Then Dobbs bent down and grabbed Daniel under the armpits to lift him bodily to his feet. Daniel was shaking; he could not rise. Dobbs let go, and Daniel fell heavily back to the ground.

"Look, you bastard, you're not the only one who's hot. We're all bloody hot."

Daniel's hand went to his forehead. His eyes blinked. He tried once more to rise, but he could not.

Dobbs's shouting could be heard a hundred yards away. "Blast your eyes! You're nothin' but useless, bloody well useless! I give you lags hours off work in the best part of the day, and still you play these games on me!" He shook his fist at the convicts who stood watching. Again he tugged habitually at his shirt collar. He seemed to lose all rationality as he looked down at Daniel, lifted his foot, and kicked him in the side.

It was too much for Alan. With a movement so swift that the onlookers hardly grasped what they saw, Alan's left hand went out and pulled Dobbs around to him. Amazement covered the vicious man's features as he saw the fist bursting into his face.

With all the force of Alan's might, it exploded into Dobbs's mouth! Up through his whole body from the soles of his feet rose the blow. Up out of his life came the outrage, the injury, the fury, the affront, that he had carried for years. He hit his cousin, Abel, he hit the liars at his trial, he hit Mocksey, he hit all the injustice he had seen and suffered, and, too, he hit Dobbs. The violence of the blow actually lifted the sergeant from the ground before he fell heavily backward with a loud cry.

Two soldiers came running over; they brought Dobbs groaning to his feet. A large swelling appeared rapidly at the side of his face. Blood covered his broken teeth.

" 'Strewth, Sergeant, I think 'e's gone and broke your friggin' jaw!"

There was seething hatred in the sergeant's face now as he held his chin and moaned. He was livid and in agony! "Lock him up! Iron him! Get me to a doctor, quickly!" he screamed through broken teeth.

Two more soldiers hurried over and took Alan roughly by the shoulders.

Horses were hastily brought.

Before he mounted, Dobbs turned back. His hand shook as he lifted it toward Alan. It was difficult for him to speak, but the evil menace in his words was not lost on those who heard him. "I'll do for you, Fletcher. You wait. You'll suffer. You'll wish you were a bloody dead man."

From the second Alan had hit him, he did not look in Dobbs's direction again. He had disassociated himself from the man. His eyes and thoughts were only for Daniel.

As Dobbs departed and the soldiers took Alan away, he shouted, "For God's sake, do something for Daniel Dwyer. It's he who should see a doctor!"

At last Daniel was carried to his tent, and Swiftie sent to tend him. Mr. Stonebridge was over a mile away from the camp at the quarry where they dug out the stone. By the time a soldier had been dispatched to him and he had returned, Alan had been chained to a tree trunk and left waiting outside the barracks.

The engineer rode up to where Alan stood, and dismounted. He shook his head ruefully a number of times. "Ah, Fletcher . . ." he began and then stopped and shook his head again. It was clear he was baffled by the situation and unsure of what action he should take. He liked Fletcher. The man was a fine worker and an intelligent help to him often. There were even times he sought his opinion. Why had he caused this trouble and hit Dobbs? Dobbs would retaliate in an ugly fashion, there was no doubt about that. It discouraged him to think about it. Once more he shook his head. "Fletcher, you have brought this on yourself. It behooves me to ask you why you hit the sergeant."

"Because the man is an animal. He kicked Dan Dwyer. I have done no more than he deserved, Mr. Stonebridge; you know that."

Mr. Stonebridge agreed with Fletcher, but he could not say so. Instead he stood awkwardly tapping his large chin with his fingers. "I will send for the magistrate. It is more his affair, but as it is five o'clock in the afternoon, I fear he'll not be here until tomorrow or even the next day. I am sorry, Fletcher, but there is little I can do. Sergeant Dobbs will no doubt stay with Dr. Chester on the Beau Desert property tonight if his jaw is broken as they say, but I'm afraid you'll have to take whatever he metes out to you in the morning. After all, man, I mean to say, you are a convict."

Alan made no reply, and the engineer coughed, an embarrassed sound, before he turned and walked away.

Alan was taken to his tent, where he was chained to the center pole. A yard away, Daniel lay on his bunk; a damp towel rested on his forehead, and Swiftie was beside him.

When the soldiers left, Alan turned as best he could to his friends. "How is he, Swiftie?"

For answer Daniel opened his eyes. He raised himself on his elbow, drank some water, and replied, "I'm feeling much better now, laddie, have done so ever since you smashed Dobbs."

Alan smiled.

"It were beautiful, guverner," Swiftie approved, "the best thing I've ever seen. Broke his bloody jaw straight off." Then he frowned and looked unhappy. "Though Gawd knows what will happen now."

Daniel sat up. He clearly was not yet back to normal, but he certainly had improved. "Well, I know what has to happen now. I don't think we have any alternative."

Alan and Swiftie both looked questioningly.

The older man took a deep breath and shook his head decisively. He wagged his finger in the air for emphasis as he spoke. "Now is the time to be putting your plan of escape into action, Alan. Tonight must be the night. We cannot wait until next Friday."

Alan opened his mouth to reply, but Daniel went on before he could speak. "Dobbs will stay the night with the doctor for certain. Stoney will go to the farm as usual. It will be the first night ever the soldiers won't have a commander here, and we know what they'll be doing."

"They'll drink their heads off with Dobbs out of the way, and no mistake," interjected Swiftie.

"Yes," agreed Alan, "but, Danny, my friend, you cannot run for it. And I'll not leave you here."

Daniel looked across at Alan and, putting his hand on his chest, patted over his heart. He looked determined as he spoke. "Now, you listen, Alan Fletcher. This old heart's still abeating, and I'm feeling pounds better, that's the truth. It was more the blasted heat than anything. This is the finest opportunity we've ever had. The soldiers will begin drinking early as Swiftie suggests, and I'll be a darn sight better away from here. I want no more talk of me, for there's too much at stake. Far too much. So be it."

For some seconds Alan looked skeptically at his friend who sat on the bunk smiling benignly at him. Then he nodded gently.

When at last he spoke, it was decisively. He outlined the plan again.

It was six o'clock when the men returned from the fields to the camp, and Mr. Stonebridge left as usual for the nearby farm.

As Swiftie had predicted, the soldiers began drinking immediately, positive they would not see Dobbs that night.

Within an hour, the convicts had eaten their evening meal, and the soldiers, eager for the night ahead, decided to put the men in their leg irons. This normally did not happen until "lights out" at ten o'clock, and the prisoners spent the hours after sunset in a recreation compound near the guardhouse. Tonight, as they were sent to their tents and ironed, there were loud and angry complaints. To keep them quiet, the soldiers brought rum in a bucket to distribute to each man.

The guards slept in a large wooden hut next to the main barracks in the center of the camp. As the sun went down, five of them congregated there with the rum barrel. Two had gone with Dobbs, two patrolled the camp, one minded the horses, and the other two were putting the prisoners in irons.

In Alan's tent, the last in a line of four from the barracks, Lawless, Swiftie, Daniel, Sam, and the two others, Peter Biggs and Evan Evans, were tense with excitement.

"Goodo!" Lawless had said when told. "At last. We shall be free men, Swiftie my dear."

Swiftie grinned. "I'm game, matey."

They tried the board they had been loosening for weeks at the tent side, and it lifted up and out of its position easily. It exposed the canvas, which later they would rip open and use as an exit.

For an hour, Alan had timed the two patrolling soldiers. With relaxed discipline, they walked side by side and passed the back of the tent approximately every four minutes. The drinking soldiers were doubtless set for a night of gaiety, and a general echo of noisiness reverberated through the camp from the convicts who had already received their rum.

When the overseer and two guards arrived outside Alan's tent, it was perhaps twenty minutes after sunset. An early moon had risen, spreading a weak radiance across the camp.

"Outside 'ere, you lot!" called the overseer, the chains clinking in his hands.

"But what will we do with Dan Dwyer? He can't get off his bunk," came Swiftie's worried voice, "and Alan Fletcher still be chained to the tent post."

The overseer put down his lantern and poked his head in through the tent flap. Light was given inside by one hurricane lamp, but no shadows were thrown on the canvas because of the planking. "The rest o' you then, ged out here. I'll handle them later."

Alan had hoped that the overseer and the soldiers would enter the tent without encouragement. He needed them inside to disarm them. Any attack outside risked discovery.

Sam, Lawless, Evans, and Biggs issued from the tent.

"Where's Lochran?" asked the overseer. "You, Lochran, get out here with the rest like I told you!"

Once more, Swiftie's plaintive voice came from inside the tent. "I really don't like the looks of Dwyer. Someone should do somethin' quick. Methinks he's dyin'!"

At that point, the overseer just wanted the prisoners chained so he, too, could join the festivities. "Oh damn, that's all we need, is Dwyer dyin'," he grumbled impatiently as he came inside. He walked forward to where Daniel lay moaning on his bunk.

At that moment the heavy tread of the two patrolling soldiers passed by the back of the tent. Alan's and Swiftie's eyes met across the head of the overseer as he bent down to Daniel. They had four minutes!

Daniel rolled his eyes back and at the same time groaned loudly.

That was the signal for Biggs outside. He was a large man and he moved himself across the tent opening, blocking the view inside from the soldiers. At precisely that moment, Swiftie acted. He was now a powerful young man with wide shoulders and muscular arms. He brought a rabbit-killer punch to the back of the overseer's neck as he bent over Daniel. The man crumpled.

Swiftie moved rapidly to the right of the tent opening. Then Alan's voice sounded in alarm, "Quick, guards, the overseer's collapsed!"

The two soldiers outside acted on impulse. One pushed past Biggs to enter the tent, and the other automatically followed. With an anxious look toward the guards' quarters, Biggs thrust as hard as he could on the back of the second man, called Parker, who still held the bucket of rum in one hand and his weapon in the other. He fell forward into the tent, followed immediately by Biggs, Lawless, Evans, and Sam.

In one movement as the first soldier came through the tent flap, Swiftie ripped the gun from his hands and pushed it hard in the shocked man's stomach, while Evans grabbed him from behind and took his bayonet.

The other soldier, Parker, who had lost his balance from the smash in his back, was leaped upon by Biggs. There was a half-smothered cry from him as Sam grabbed his rifle. Biggs pinioned the soldier beneath his body, saying, "If you call out, you be a dead man!"

Now Swiftie handed the rifle he held to Alan.

The overseer had risen with the idea of dashing out, but when he saw the guns had changed hands, he held still while Lawless relieved him of his keys and unlocked Alan's manacles.

The noise of the roisterers floated to them across the camp.

"Nice of your mates to be busy enough to ignore us," Alan said as he bent to relieve Parker of his belt and bayonet.

The man looked up defiantly from beneath Biggs. "You're mad, Fletcher. Where can you go? You'll hang for this!"

Then Alan's voice grew menacing. "Silence now, or you won't live to know what happens next. Bind them, fast!"

The overseer and the other soldier, Gatling, were pushed to the floor beside Parker. With the bonds made earlier from their blankets, they began to tie the three men.

"Quickly, lads," urged Alan. Then getting down on one knee, he asked the captives, "How many guards are down with the horses?"

"Damn you," answered Parker, "I'll not tell."

Evans brought the bayonet close to Parker's face. "Then ye shall just have to die with this bayonet in yer gizzard."

Alan leaned forward. "We are desperate, and though I admire your courage, I don't see why you would both want to die here on this tent floor tonight."

Gatling, in fear, answered for his comrade, "One guard. There's only Bates down with the horses."

"Thank you. You are a sensible man. Now, gag them."

Parker, still hostile, spoke quickly before Evans stuffed a gag in his mouth. "You'll hang, Fletcher. They'll hang you for sure in the end."

Alan, in the act of rising and buckling the soldier's belt around his waist, knelt back on his knee and looked down into Parker's eyes. The expression the soldier read there was sinister, whether it was or not, only Alan knew. Then, to Parker's surprise, Alan smiled broadly. "I have avoided that consequence once already, soldier. And you should avoid dabbling in prophecy, for I will continue. I will *never* hang!" He lifted his eyes from Parker's and stood, just as they heard the approach of the two patrolling soldiers.

Four minutes exactly!

As the sound of their boots drew close, the odor of the rum bucket, which had spilled, rose to Alan's nostrils. Forever afterward, the smell of rum would bring back the memory of this: the inside of the boarded tent, the heavy breathing of those about him and the red coats on the floor below, their buttons glinting in the mellow lamplight.

The footsteps halted. The soldiers were talking. "Now, where the devil are Parker and Gatling? Said they'd bring us a measure after chaining the lags."

"Yeah, well they were doing Fletcher's tent before. They'll not be far. Somewhere 'ereabouts no doubt."

Alan looked down to where Gatling and Parker lay at his feet. Yes, they were hereabout, all right!

Swiftie stifled a nervous laugh.

The voice outside continued, "We'll find them if they don't find us. Hey, I wonder how bloody old Dobbs is?"

The ground crunched beneath their feet as the soldiers walked away, and the other's answer drifted back. "Who cares? I reckon the bastard deserved it."

As soon as their voices faded, Lawless moved to the front of the tent and looked cautiously through. "Two guards on the verandah. Can see no others, guv."

"Good," answered Alan, turning to where Swiftie and Biggs were already prying the plank from the side of the tent, "then it's out we go."

With the planking lifted away, Evans began to cut through the canvas of the tent with the bayonet he had taken from Gatling. As soon as the hole was cut, they crawled through. Lawless, Daniel, Evans, Swiftie, and Biggs, followed by Sam and Alan, carrying the rifles.

Just before Sam stepped through, he turned back. The spilled bucket of rum was on the floor, but the dispensing cup sat beside it, with rum still left in the bottom. He picked it up, gulped it down, winked at Alan, and disappeared through the opening.

Twelve yards out, the tall grass and scrub began. There were no trees, so the escapees could not walk upright. They doubled over, moving as swiftly as possible under cover of the grass.

They would get as close as possible to Bates, the guard with the horses, and then Alan and Sam would take him by surprise, while the others freed the animals. As they edged through the bush, the laughter of the merry soldiers sounded in the distance.

It was a hot, humid, still night, though the escapees perspired as much from the tension as from the temperature. Daniel, breathing in a labored fashion, was the slowest of the seven, and now, half supported by Alan, brought up the rear. By the time they all came together about ten yards from the man with the horses, minutes had passed. Alan looked around the ring of strained faces in the moonlight.

Suddenly the alarm was raised! Shouting and yelling broke out behind them.

What Alan had feared had occurred. The two patrolling guards had gone in search of Gatling, Parker, and the promised rum, leaving their beat to walk between the tents. The rent in the canvas, though not obvious at a distance, was clearly visible up close. They had realized something was amiss and had found their mates and the overseer inside.

Bates, at the horse yard, leapt to his feet and grabbed his rifle. He turned, uneasy and alert, in the direction of the yelling.

There were only seconds to make a decision.

With a violent leap, Alan came up and over the intervening space. At the sound from the brush, the soldier, who was young and had drunk no rum, turned and fired.

Alan charged arms extended. The cartridge hit him in the left forearm, but the momentum of his spring carried him forward onto the man. They both fell heavily to the ground, Alan on top. Bates began to struggle, but Sam was now beside them, pushing his rifle in the soldier's face. "Lie still, matey, or I'll blow your head off!"

The man stiffened, and lay still. Alan stood.

"Are you all right, guverner?" Sam asked, grabbing the soldier's fallen rifle and throwing it to Lawless.

"Yes," replied Alan, who was so stimulated that he felt nothing, although the blood ran freely from the wound.

Swiftie and Lawless were already at the horse railings and removing the bar that held the gate.

The rifle shot had signaled to the camp the direction of the escapees, and soldiers were already tumbling out of their quarters, guns in hand, looking dazedly around. Speed, they needed speed. The bar was thrown aside and the gate opened.

Some of the horses had reared at the sound of the gunshot and now jostled one another as the convicts tried to put makeshift bridles over their heads. All but four of the animals escaped from the yard.

Even in their disarray the soldiers were well trained enough to assess the situation. Five ran toward the horse yard and fired at the convict uniforms. The bullets whistled past and thudded into the open gate beside Alan and Sam.

"Hey, stop! I'm down here!" shouted Bates as he crawled quickly away.

While the soldiers reloaded, Alan turned to those with him. There was an excited light in his eyes, giving him a wild, ferocious look. The bayonet was lodged in the scabbard at his waist. Blood ran down over the back of his hand and dripped from his fingers. There, like an untamed Delacroix mountain brigand, he stood in the moonlight with the rifle raised high in his good hand.

"All right, boys, mount quickly! Sam and I shall hold them."

Onto the rails of the fence yard they climbed, and from there to the bare backs of the animals. Daniel, Evans, and Biggs could ride, but Swiftie and Lawless had spent their days in the byways of London and had never been on a horse. They were willing but awkward. They mounted behind the more skillful.

Alan had already turned back to the soldiers. They would soon be upon them. "Aim low," he said to Sam.

He fired. Sam, too, fired beside him. One soldier fell with a wound in his leg, and the others pulled up sharply and dropped to their knees in battle fashion. Most had not realized that the escapees had the rifles of their bound comrades. They had believed they were firing on unarmed men.

While the guards on their knees rallied and took aim, Alan and Sam turned in the darkness and ran back to the others. They mounted the free horse and charged away at the same time that the soldiers fired. The escapees, riding spiritedly off, heard the gun blasts. It was Swiftie who uttered a cry and fell forward heavily onto Daniel's back.

"Oh no!" said Daniel, still pressing the horse onward, "are you hit, laddie? Are you hit?" He threw his left arm backward around his young friend to steady him as more gunshots echoed after them.

Onward they sped, taking the horses down a steep incline.

They were making for the Albert River to ford it. It was not a wide or deep river, and once over, they would head south and up through the rain forest and the mountains. They knew the countryside around the camp for miles and were not disoriented in the darkness.

"Are you all right, Swiftie? Laddie, answer me, please!" Daniel cried.

The young man only groaned.

Daniel felt his throat constrict with fear for the boy. They rode on another minute or so, then he sensed the young man beginning to slide. In an anguished voice he called, "Alan! Alan! They hit Swiftie!"

"Halt!" Alan shouted as he brought his horse, a large pale gray stallion, to a standstill.

It was then Swiftie made a strange strangled sound and slipped sideways.

Alan dismounted and ran back in time to catch him as he slid off the horse. Swiftie buckled at the knees, and Alan eased him to the bush floor. "Easy, lad, easy."

Lawless, his face blanched, jumped down and came to his friend. The others, too, dismounted and gathered around.

Swiftie's face was contorted with pain. Blood gushed from the middle of his back down over Alan's good arm, staining the earth in the darkness.

Biggs looked back toward the camp. "We'll not have long before they catch some of the horses and mount a chase."

Daniel dug him in the ribs to silence him.

Lawless's eyes filled with tears. "Oh Gawd, matey! Oh Gawd!" He touched Swiftie's face tenderly and took his hand.

In the moonglow Swiftie looked at Lawless and then up to Alan, who held him. He sighed deeply, and they saw his face change as the pain left him. There was almost a saintly peace in his drawn young face.

"Lawless . . . guverner . . . I . . . There be no more hurt. . . ." He closed his eyes, then opened them again. They were glassy as he tried to concentrate on Alan's face above. "I'm dyin' . . . aren't I, guverner?"

Alan looked at the young face upturned to his. He would have been twenty-one in a few weeks' time. Spasms of pain ran through him. Swiftie had become like a cherished young brother. He fought back the anguish that rose in his throat as he searched for an answer. "Ah, lad, you've been so brave . . . courageous . . . dear Swiftie. . . ."

The tears were now streaming down Lawless's face; he was distraught. He repeated, "No, matey, no," as Daniel gripped his shoulders, murmuring a prayer.

With effort Swiftie spoke again. "But . . . I'm dyin' a free man . . . aren't I, guverner?"

"Yes, Swiftie, my dear dear lad, you are. . . ."

The death rattle was a gentle thing.

The others rose while Lawless remained kneeling, sobbing quietly and holding his friend's hand.

"What'll we do, Alan?" Daniel asked. "We can't leave the boy here."

"No, no, we won't leave him here. We shall take him on with us."

"But how can we ride with a dead man?" demanded Biggs.

Sam turned savagely. "If the guverner says we do, we damn well do!"

Alan motioned to his horse. "I will ride with him."

At that moment there was the noise of men and animals not far behind, and a loud shout sounded clearly through the bush. They lifted and lay Swiftie's body across the horse in front of Alan, and remounted speedily.

Even bareback, Alan was a masterful rider, and though it was nigh on five years since he had sat a horse, he was as comfortable as if it had been five hours. While his arm was painful now and continued to seep blood, it was not flowing freely as it had been minutes before. Luck had indeed been with him, for the cartridge had hit no nerves, and lodged between the radius and the ulna, leaving him use of his hand and fingers.

After a five-minute ride over rough ground and through trees and scrub, they came to the river. They had made good time, and the camp was nearly a mile behind. They reined in at the river's edge and listened. Their mounts snorted, and their own heavy breathing was loud in their ears. The sounds of horses and men were not far behind.

Alan looked around the anxious eyes in the darkness. "They are coming this way, and are aware of the general direction we rode. We must cross the river. So, too, will they, but they will be unsure after that. There cannot be many of them. How much of the country can they search?"

"Nevertheless," spoke up Biggs, "maybe we should be separatin', Alan. Might 'ave more of a chance in two groups."

"If you wish, Peter," Alan replied, pressing his horse on into the river.

As they reached the other bank, the noise of pursuit was closer. Another gunshot sounded.

"Listen, Alan," Peter Biggs shouted, "Evans and I are of a mind to go our own way."

"All right," replied Alan, "you already have one of the bayonets. Give them a rifle, Sam."

Sam reluctantly handed over one of the guns.

"Good luck," Alan added as he turned his horse away. "Come on then, lads! Let's go."

Without saddles, it was the hardest ride they would ever make. Alan's sense of direction was the single distinction that ensured them their freedom. As a navigator at sea, he had studied the stars of both the northern and southern hemispheres, and now he took the men unerringly south.

Those who gave chase had guessed accurately at first and followed across the river. There they divided into two parties, and after an hour, were hopelessly lost in the bush. When the following morning dawned, only one of the groups of searchers was back in camp. They had arrived tired and defeated shortly before midnight. The others rode in three hours after the sun was up. They had been lost in the hills all night.

In contrast, when morning dawned over the escapees, they were on a rise close to nineteen miles due south of the camp. They had made slow but steady progress, resting briefly every half hour or so. At one point, they had been forced to retrace their steps when the bush was too dense for penetration; nevertheless, they had ridden for eight hours, averaging almost two and a half miles per hour.

As the sun came up, Sam dug the cartridge from Alan's arm with a bayonet. Amazingly, it had entered in the same spot where he carried a scar from the stabbing years before, in Southampton.

"Don't worry, guv," the little man kept saying as Alan grimaced throughout the operation, "I've removed a thousand cartridges from pheasant and the like. There'll hardly be a mark when I finish."

This was more appeasement than truth. Alan carried an L-shaped scar on his left arm ever afterward.

There, on the hilltop, they buried Swiftie beneath a grove of tall eucalyptus, looking down to a bush valley of mottled yellows and greens. To mark the spot, Lawless and Daniel made a cross from saplings, and Lawless carved:

Swiftie Lochran
matey
1832–1853

Daniel said a prayer, and Lawless laid a bunch of tiny white wildflowers on the grave.

Before they continued on their way, Sam looked to Alan and asked the question they all wanted answered. "What will we do now, guverner? I mean, we'll always be hunted men. How can we be stayin' free? And how will we live?"

At the time, Alan stood with his good arm around Lawless's shoulders, looking across Swiftie's grave down to the bush below. As he listened to Sam's question, he turned around to face the morning sun.

There was resolve in the very way he stood. His handsome mouth was set in a grim line, and the expression in his eyes was suddenly hard and uncompromising. They had never seen him like this before. He appeared almost callous, and it surprised them. He was thinking of Swiftie, left here on the hillside. His death was the price they had paid for their freedom. All that lay ahead of them was danger. There was no sanctuary for escaped convicts.

He looked slowly over the three faces turned toward him. "We *will* stay free, as long as we are careful and keep to ourselves. How will we live? There is only one thing we can do. Only one thing escaped convicts are qualified for. We will become bushrangers."

Sergeant Eric Dobbs was court-martialed at Brisbane barracks on March fifth, 1853.

It was ascertained that his attitude toward his prisoners and his men had been responsible for the attack upon himself which removed him overnight from his place of duty.

He was stripped of his rank and sentenced to one year's hard labor in the military prison at Brisbane barracks.

Fifteen days after the escape, Evan Evans and Peter Biggs stole a boat from the Brisbane River and were shipwrecked on Stradbroke Island. They were found four months later and resentenced.

SIX

John Stuart

1863

The mail coach swung across the almost treeless plain on the flat, dusty road that led into Bathurst, a sturdy little settlement of wide, unpaved streets and mostly wooden houses, named in

1815 after Henry, third Earl Bathurst and His Majesty's Principal Secretary of State for the Colonies.

The vehicle was now on the verge of the township, and after a long, wearying, hot ride, the passengers inside were looking forward to a cooling bath at the Royal Hotel, where they would spend the night.

A light evening wind had risen, and as the coach trundled by, it lifted leaves from a lonely silver gum tree. They hung in the air as if for a moment they could determine their next movements, then, in swirling, spiraling patterns, descended to the fields below. Some skimmed across the top of the passing coach to find their resting places in a tangle of morning glory. Three farmer's children played among the pretty vine, threading the soft blue-purple, cone-shaped flowers through the buttonholes in their pinafores, and running along trailing azure streaks of blossom in the wind.

Inside, a man with an angular face turned from the cheerful view of the children and spoke. "So, as I have said, I'm here to do something about them. Ah yes, to help Sir Frederick Pottinger, though he's made a few asinine moves, in my opinion." The speaker liked to talk, and he had been loquacious all the long way from Sydney town. Newly appointed by the government of New South Wales, Sir Rutherford Blake was a famous criminalist from London. He was what had recently been termed a "detective policeman," and had brought to justice many who had evaded capture for years. Sir Rutherford had been invited by a troubled colonial government to advise and guide on their ever-compounding problem, the outback outlaws, the "bushrangers."

Although Sir Frederick Pottinger was the police inspector of the western district, Sir Rutherford Blake was autonomous, liaisoning directly with the chief secretary of the colony and the inspector general of police in Sydney. He was presently directing his extensive knowledge at John Stuart Wakeman, who shared the coach.

John Stuart Wakeman.

His very name was a byword for wealth and grandeur. He was of the new breed, the landed gentry of Australia. His father, though originally but a surveyor from a country family in Sussex, England, had founded the estate of Mayfield on the banks of the Lachlan River in 1826, where John Stuart now lived in splendor.

John Stuart had listened carefully to Sir Rutherford's opinions for over one hundred miles, listened and, in the main, agreed. He liked the tenacity and the vigilance that he recognized in the other. He knew Frederick Pottinger, and it was his opinion that the man would have trouble keeping up with the subtle, sharp mind that was Sir Rutherford.

A serious expression appeared now on John Stuart's handsome, sun-browned face as he clasped his hands around his knee and lifted his black burnished boot from the floor. "Yes, Sir Rutherford," he replied. "Unfortunately, here in the West, the bushrangers have grown into a menace these last few years. There seem to be more and more of them all the time."

The other passengers, Timothy, John Stuart's valet, and Mr. David Elrington, a young crown prosecutor and Sir Rutherford Blake's assistant, nodded vigorously in agreement.

Sir Rutherford's eyelids almost closed as he leaned forward to John Stuart in friendly fashion. He had only been in New South Wales two months, but he spoke with knowledge and authority. "It's a sign of the times. People are loose these days. Ah yes, we had only the odd bushranger until the start of the sixties, all escaped convicts, bolters the lot. But now, these 'wild colonial boys,' just uncaught criminals is all they are. Ah yes, I've spent every waking moment since I landed engaged in learning about them. You could say I already *know* many of them intimately, and I'm ready for a few field trips."

John Stuart smiled.

Sir Rutherford Blake returned the smile, his face contorting to show an expanse of gum above his top teeth. "Ah yes, since the infamous gold robbery near Eugowra last June, the records show that the number of travelers stopped on the roads has burgeoned to where it is clearly a state of emergency to my way of thinking."

"But, too, there seems some sympathy for them. The bushrangers, I mean," spoke up David Elrington, his freckled face attentive, "though I cannot understand it myself."

Sir Rutherford now turned his attention to his assistant. "Ah yes and that is because you are law-abiding and, brought up as such, Mr. Elrington. It is the middle-aged who are former convicts themselves, who sympathize. They carry an innate resentment for law and the police."

"True," agreed John Stuart, "and, too, the city-bred often exacerbate the problem by their attitude. They mistakenly associate the bushrangers with gallantry. We country-born know better."

"Ah yes, definitely." The expert nodded grimly. "And my motto has always been 'Break those who break the law,' and I shall continue to live by it."

Local children ran and shouted alongside the vehicle as it neared its journey's end. The arrival of the coach always excited great interest, and the youngsters accompanied it the last hundred yards or so and waited, wide-eyed, to see the passengers, people who came from far-off, romantic places like the Blue Mountains and Sydney town, places the children had never seen.

It was the Tuesday before Easter, the thirty-first of March. At five minutes past the hour of four in the afternoon, John Stuart Wakeman stepped down outside the Royal Hotel in William Street, followed by Sir Rutherford Blake. As his foot touched the street, there was a welcome freshness in the evening brought by the same wind of the fields that had entered Bathurst in tandem with the carriage. To the local folk, it was consolation after the solid heat of the day.

"Why, it be Mr. Wakeman of Mayfield!" one of the children cried, an intelligent lad who knew many of the landed gentry by sight. There were yelps of delight at this news, for to them, his name was synonymous with bright threepenny pieces.

At this announcement, a few tradesmen came out into the street to look. It was not often they got to see the master of Mayfield. Although everyone had known he was coming soon, for his own coach had been sitting in the coaching house being polished for the best part of three days, waiting to carry him the nigh on eighty miles to Mayfield House.

John Stuart was returning from a cattle drive and business in Sydney. Thirty miles west of that capital was the railhead township of Penrith, where he had driven a herd of fattened Herefords and sold them at market. He had traveled on from Penrith to Sydney for a few days' business. It was the first time he had ever led a drive without Joe Larmer, Mayfield's manager and John Stuart's confidant and trusted adviser. A week before the drive was to begin, Joe had broken a bone in his foot, and his place had been taken by Jack Hennessy, Joe's second-in-command.

In Sydney, John Stuart had stayed at Government House with Sir John Young, the governor. It was there, in the capital, that he had been introduced to Sir Rutherford Blake, and circumstances had led them to make the long journey into the West together, over one hundred miles. They took leave of each other, in the hall of the Royal Hotel, and agreed to meet later for a meal.

Alone in his room, the best the hotel offered, John Stuart bathed off the dust of travel in the large hip bath carried up for him on the shoulders of two burly youths. The late afternoon sun streamed through his window and reflected in the long mirror as he put on the fresh clothing laid out by Timothy.

He descended the stairway into the front hall, where he received obsequious attention from the publican and his wife, a rotund pair who thrilled to the importance of their guest. Seemingly oblivious to their care, he passed out into the street, where he found Timothy and a growing group of children who waited, hoping to see the ''fairy-tale'' person.

He did not disappoint them. John Stuart was tall and wonderfully handsome, with thick, dark hair, serious brown eyes, faultless features, and an expression that verged on brooding. Even the children who clustered around him recognized him as distinctly out of the ordinary.

He chatted with them good-naturedly though briefly. Then, as was his habit, Timothy took the youngsters' attention with four shining threepenny pieces temptingly held between his thumb and forefinger. ''Now, leave the master be. These are for the winners in a game of marbles.'' And with the toe of his shoe, he drew a ring in the dirt, and the children, their eyes wide with expectation, left John Stuart and came to Timothy.

John Stuart proceeded along William Street, the main street of the township. The town's business had ceased for the day, and the street was quiet except for a happy buzz issuing from the bar of the Empire Hotel. He turned left on George Street where he watched the too bright sun descend in a cloudless evening sky, before he crossed to the parkland, a square of trees and gardens. Part of his mind was leisurely contemplating the onward journey. Today was Tuesday. He would start early and be in the township of Blayney by nine o'clock in the morning, where they would change horses. A brisk ride would see him in the small community of Cowra by midafternoon, and home at his beloved Mayfield before dinner. He breathed deeply, wishing he were home already.

He walked toward the setting sun, enjoying watching the glint of its dying rays and the strong breeze that caressed his face and caught at his coattails. Around him were dozens of great, deep green pines, so dark and European here in this southern land of gray-green and brown. Planted by the townsfolk to remind them of ''home,'' they stood in neat rows silhouetted against the rooftops of the sprawling settlement.

He made an intriguing figure in the waning light. He had changed his elegant traveling suit for a mixture of city and country wear. His fashionable, impeccably cut jacket and shirt were from David Jones's store in Sydney, and his shining knee-high boots were imported from London. But his trousers were serviceable country wear from Thelma's needle and thread, with a reinforced seat for sitting a horse days at a time. Thelma, Joe Larmer's wife, still did much of his sewing after all these years. She had always been there, ever since his mother had gone away when he was three years old.

John Stuart almost never thought of his mother, and so it was odd that she momentarily came to his mind now as he strode on beneath the pines into the anonymity of their deep purple shadows. A wistful look appeared for the space of a second on his features before his mouth turned down disconsolately.

He paused in the twilight gloom where it was difficult to separate his outline from the dark mass of the tree trunks. As he moved to face the north, he frowned with interest. A woman was coming toward him. She had appeared suddenly like some ethereal creature rising out of the hedge at twilight, moving quickly, gracefully, swinging in her right hand a small crocheted bag on pink strings.

It was obvious she took pleasure from the strong movement of the evening breeze on her face, for she stopped as she gained the inside of the hedge and took off her bonnet. Then she continued, her curls blowing away from her face, revealing the high color in her cheeks. Her lips were slightly apart as she breathed deeply, radiating vitality. She wore a light gown of floral cotton, open at the neck, and it seemed to him that the skin of her throat shone faintly golden in the setting sun.

John Stuart Wakeman stood and watched her move forward, draw near, come level, and pass by. There was a quick swell of feeling within him. He thought he had never seen anyone to equal her. She made her way through the park, unconscious of his attention, though she had come to within a few feet of where he halted. As she gained the far side of the park, she stopped; she had dropped her bonnet and she bent to retrieve it. Then she turned and looked back the way she had come. To him it seemed as if she looked straight at him there in the shadows of the trees. When, in a few seconds, she continued on her way, to his surprise, he followed her.

She was some distance ahead as he came after, his eyes held to the pale dress and the moving bonnet, softly illuminated in the closing darkness. She continued until she turned in to Russell Street, a thoroughfare of small stone cottages and wooden houses. When she reached number twenty-two, she passed through a fence covered with the dead blooms of a wisteria vine, and entered the house. In spring and summer, wisteria hung in masses of color from fences, sills, and eaves, staining the dusty community with a pastel loveliness.

Long after the lamps glowed into life through the windows of the town on this last day of March, John Stuart stood on the roadway some yards away from the small house. He could hardly believe he had followed the woman home. He knew many women: daughters of politicians vied for his attention on his visits to the capital, and many an affluent grazier's daughter had tried to "catch" him. There was no bachelor more desirable in the entire country, for not only was he immensely wealthy, but he was exceptionally good-looking. Until now, he had avoided any serious romantic attachment. He disliked women who threw themselves at him, and had been content to be master of Mayfield. If he had thought at all about a wife, it had been in terms of someone he had not yet met, a woman who was beautiful, virtuous, dignified, pure. In short, he sought perfection. As he stood in the darkness of Russell Street, he was confused by his reaction to the woman he had followed, but one thing he could not deny: she had captivated him. The moon was up and the stars had appeared before he finally left and returned the short distance to the Royal Hotel.

An hour later, he dined with Sir Rutherford in a private room. He did not mention the woman, and the two new friends parted after a hearty meal.

John Stuart slept fitfully and woke early. During the night, a light rain had fallen, and the day began under a cloudy sky. When he came downstairs, Deke Edwards, his coach driver, and Leeroy Barton, the guard, were waiting in the front hall. Deke, his sun-weary face mottled with creases and lines, smiled at him. "We be waitin' for ye, sir. The coach be shinin' ready to go, as soon as ye be wantin' te leave."

The master of Mayfield frowned. "I'll not leave until after luncheon, Deke. We can travel into the night. We've done it before."

"That's right then, sir, just as ye say."

John Stuart left the hotel and walked down to the livery stables. An hour later he tethered his horse to a tree at the bottom of a solitary hill on the plain that surrounded the Bathurst settlement. He climbed to the crest, swinging his riding crop at the flies that thought him new and agreeable game. He loved the clean smell of this sunny land, even more distilled today after the slight rain of the night. He breathed deeply, then bent and picked up a handful of dirt, which seeped through his fingers onto his polished boot.

A crow cawed in the sky above. He watched as it came to land some twenty feet distant from him. Its mournful cry filled the air. He felt the loneliness of the mighty country around him. It was possible he was the first man to ever stand in this particular spot. The enormity of that held him for many minutes. John Stuart was both highly literate and thoughtful; and although he was hidebound by the morality of the times, he mistrusted religious dogma and always searched for a rationale in reaching conclusions about life. Consequently, he was sympathetic with the freethinkers of the time. His peers were strictly religious, which made him unique for a squatter and Australian country gentleman.

He looked up at the dispassionate sky where his companion, the crow, had now risen. He thought of Mayfield. As always, when he reflected on his home, contentment and joy enveloped him.

Abruptly a picture of the woman he had followed the evening before disturbed his tranquility. He knew she was the reason he was still here, but who the devil was she? How could she have affected him this way? He had not even spoken to her. He wished Joe were here, he really did.

The expanse of country beneath him, which had filled him with such composure and happiness a mere minute before, had lost its power. He returned down the hill in great strides, mounted his horse, and was soon riding swiftly back to Bathurst.

It was no coincidence that, once he was in the settlement, his direction took him along Russell Street. Bringing his horse to a walk, he passed by number 22. There, attached to the front wall, was a brass sign, which had been concealed in the dark of the night before.

Miss Evelyn May Herman
Piano Lessons
Apply Within.

John Stuart registered ''Miss.'' He made a decision. He would not leave this afternoon. He must learn whether his woman of mystery was the miss designated in the sign. He had to know more of her, must ask someone about her, but whom?

Just then, a little girl carrying a satchel ran into the street from a house a few doors down. She was not exactly what he had in mind, but she might be able to answer his questions, and without the curiosity an adult would have. He called the child to him.

"Yes, sir?"

His smile was immediately duplicated on the little face gazing up at him.

"The lady who lives at number twenty-two, there with the mullioned windows." He pointed with his riding crop. "Does she live alone?"

The little girl was happy to supply the information. "Why, surely, sir. She's the piano teacher."

"You say alone. No one at all lives with her then?"

"No sir, I . . . I don't think so. She's the piano teacher." The child repeated the last statement as if it supplied all reasons for the lady's solitary existence.

A bright sixpence soon gleamed in the small hand, and she ran off with a smile of positive bliss on her freckled face.

John Stuart returned to the Royal. He called Timothy and gave instructions to cancel their onward journey, and he refused lunch. Timothy took these two changes with equanimity. A good valet never questioned his master's motives.

By midafternoon he was on his roan mare again, riding down Bentwick Street toward the Macquarie River. He must meet this woman. But there was a part of him that delayed his next move; intermingled with his desire to see her again was a fear that in the darkness of the previous dusk, he may have imagined grace where there had been only ease of movement, and beauty where there was but a pleasing look.

In the midst of his thoughts, a woman turned the corner and came toward him. A hot feeling rose inside his throat, and he felt as if his neck were expanding; his shirt collar was choking him. As he watched her, she stopped and touched a climbing rose on a trellis above one of the fences. There she was again, another beautiful picture encapsulated like the vision of the evening before.

He pulled his horse back to a walk as she advanced. It was by now after three o'clock, and the sun was behind him. The bonnet she wore had practically no brim, and he could see her face clearly as the light fell upon it. Relieved, he saw he had imagined nothing. There was a virtuous, dignified freshness about her that he had never attributed to any other woman. It was obvious she was not in her teens. This pleased him, too; he disliked very young women, found them awkward and trivial. Her features were regular, almost refined, except for a little fullness of her mouth, and he liked that, too. No, he had imagined nothing.

When she passed, he could not help but speak. "Good afternoon, Miss Herman." His voice sounded loud to his ears.

"And good afternoon to you, too, sir," she replied. The sound of the *a* vowel and the rounded *r* were most unusual. He fancied the accent similar to Irish, but he was not sure. Herman was hardly Irish.

She raised her hand to protect her eyes as she looked to see who had greeted her, but the sun was too strong, and he appeared only as a silhouette on a horse. He rode on by and did not look back. If he had, he would have seen her turn to watch him.

Three hours after the meeting in Bentwick Street, he stood opposite number twenty-two in Russell Street, just as he had done the night before. As he watched, the front door opened and a small boy carrying sheets of music came running at high speed from the house, as if released from captivity. He swung his body over the broken fence and went racing down the street.

John Stuart felt the breeze on his back, and at the same time the lace curtains in the bay window of number twenty-two lifted, ballooned, and danced a little. They glided forward through the opening and were blown about, flickering back and forth, pointing like white lace fingers at the neatly lettered brass sign attached to the wall. Moments later she came to the very window and leaned forward to retrieve the offending curtain. She looked in his direction. He smiled, nodded his head, and tipped his broad-brimmed hat to her. She returned a slight nod, but quickly and firmly drew in the curtain, closed the window, and pulled down the blind.

He stood another few minutes there in the twilight before he walked slowly and contemplatively back to his hotel.

Inside the small front parlor, Eve stood in thought.

She had returned from the window paying little heed to the gentleman who had taken her eye for a moment. She had hardly registered him.

She sat on the piano stool and closed her eyes. She was pleased to see little David Dean leave. The child hated learning to play. Some lessons were so different, really enjoyable, especially with the girls at All Saints' School, where she taught.

She felt tired. Thank goodness tomorrow was Maundy Thursday, when the Easter holidays would begin. She stood, and catching her reflection in the mirror over the mantel, sighed as she pushed back a fallen curl from her forehead.

There was a poise about Eve now. It was not merely the fulfillment of that promise seen in the seventeen-year-old girl of Sydney town. It was a combination of things. She was at peace. She did not need to apply the solitary strength that she had so relied upon in her teen years. Too, she had learned to check herself, and her tongue. She had dropped "blazes" and "devil" and "damnation" from her vocabulary under Father's tutelage, although the undaunted spirit that inspired those words still remained. She smiled gently at the thought of him. She could trust and depend upon him; with him there was security, the single most important thing missing from her life after her parents died.

She moved through her parlor by the picture of Queen Victoria, the parian bust of Lord Melbourne, the antimacassars, and the ruby glass, all representative of the niche she had found for herself here, and she thanked the Lord every day for finally having brought her here in February 1858, five years ago.

It had been like a miracle to rediscover Reverend Billings and to settle into a new life with him and Mrs. Billings. The rector was her mentor, her friend, and her surrogate father. She even called him "Father," a tradition rarely used in the Church of England, and having the other connotation for Eve. It felt right for both of them. So, too, a natural progression had occurred over the years, and his wife, Lillian, had encouraged Eve to call her "Mother."

From the first day she had ever seen Reverend Billings at Hastey's Auction Rooms there had been an affinity between them.

The money she had made from the sale of his watch had enabled her to rent Sully Tompkins's shed and start her sewing business. At first it had been very difficult to get clients, and she had spent many weeks trudging the streets of Sydney town from door to door. The first year had been one of hardship, long hours, and parsimony, but she had forced herself to be strong and remain determined. She had constantly encouraged Clare, who sometimes wanted to give in, until finally the orders began to come regularly. From then until she had closed the business in February 1858, they had been able at all times to make ends meet and to be independent.

There had been only one young man in Eve's life: Sully Tomkins's son, William. Sully, an alderman of Sydney, owned two successful haberdashery shops. William was learning the business. He was well educated, temperate, and considerate, and very deeply in love with Eve. While Eve was very cautious, in time, she came to have a real affection for him.

Clare had been involved with a succession of men, and at age nineteen, unmarried, she had given birth to a stillborn son. William's parents had been mortified and forbidden him to see Eve because of her sister, but "Billy," as Eve called him, had stood up to them and continued to call on her.

Clare was beautiful, addicted to pleasure, skeptical, and yet at the same time, gullible. She had always believed in every handsome man who said he loved her. So, while it hurt Eve, it did not really surprise her when she found Clare's note on their little mantel shelf one October morning in 1856.

> *Darling,*
>
> *Forgive me, but I have gone with Harry to Adelaide. He has acquired a most commendable position with the newspaper there.*
>
> *Do be happy for me as I am for myself. He has promised to marry me, Evelyn. I know you have never really cared for him, but he is good to me. I believe it is all very auspicious and that everything is for the best.*
>
> *I have taken most of the money we had saved, but you, sweetheart, will understand, I know. It won't take long for you to earn more, you are so very capable and clever.*
>
> *I am truly happy, and I shall write to you the minute we have lodgings.*
>
> *Your loving sister,*
> *Clare*

Within two weeks of Clare's departure, Billy asked Eve to marry him.

Eve thought about it. Clare was gone. She was alone. Billy gave her compassion and care and love. In her solitary moments, she admitted she did not return his love, but he was such a dear man and she liked him immensely. He had the ability to make her laugh and to lift her spirits. He was proper and reputable, and at his side, she would be accepted and respectable.

She agreed to his proposal, and six weeks later, they became engaged, much to the chagrin of Mr. and Mrs. Tompkins. They had been engaged for ten months when Billy went with a group of young men on a day's outing. It was unseasonably hot that September of 1857, and they decided to go for a swim in a creek outside Sydney. Within a week, Billy was dead. He and two other young men had caught diphtheria.

Eve was distraught. She had to see her sister. She closed the shop temporarily and went to Adelaide, only to find things had not worked out between Clare and Harry, and that Clare had been living with another man since the previous January. Eve spent ten days in Adelaide trying to convince her sister to come back to Sydney. Clare was living in tiny rented rooms with her new man, but Eve did not meet him, for he had gone briefly northeast to the Barossa Valley. In truth, Clare was pleased, for she feared Eve might say something to her friend that would spoil things with him. "It is better that you don't meet him, darling; you never like the men I like, anyway."

The last time Eve saw her sister, they met at the small tavern in Rundle Street where Clare worked and walked together down South Terrace to the path along the Torrens River. It was a gray afternoon. Eve took Clare's lovely tapering fingers in her own. "Why cannot you come back to Sydney with me?"

"Evelyn, darling, please understand. I truly love Nathaniel. I want to stay here."

Eve had shaken her head. "Oh, Clare. When in Hades are you going to learn? He hasn't married you, has he? Just like the others: Grayson, Larry Hutchins, Donald Blainey, Harry, and now this . . . Nathaniel, whoever he is. You've had as many men in as many years; more, if I know the truth. Damnation, Clare, I have followed you because I want you to come home."

Clare's eyes filled with tears. "I can't."

Eve turned away in frustration. There were leaves drifting by on the river current. She thought how like her sister they were, without direction or will of their own. Yet she loved Clare. She sighed. "I miss you, Clare."

"And I, you, darling. Stay here. Now, there's an idea. You stay here."

Eve turned back to face her sister. "What? And work in a blasted tavern again like you do?" Springing to Eve's eyes was the old anger with Clare. "No, that is the one thing I've promised myself I'll never do again. Never! I have a business in Sydney, which even now I am neglecting. I am returning tomorrow, and I beg you to come with me. Give yourself a chance.''

Her sister did not reply.

"I am leaving from Victoria wharf at eleven o'clock in the morning. Please be there.''

"Evelyn, you just don't understand.''

"No, I never have, and, my dear sister, I never will. The next man who holds me, holds me in the marriage bed.'' Eve looked in despair at the lovely face opposite, then she hugged Clare tightly and left her standing there.

The following morning, Eve departed from Adelaide alone.

Back in Sydney, she spent many hours walking in the domain encircling Government House, and down the gentle slope of the Botanical Gardens to the shore of peaceful Farm Cove along by Fort Macquarie. She wandered, and sat looking across the water, missing Billy and his laugh, and missing Clare. She thought how distant she and her sister had become, how different their needs. She felt sad for Clare, the way her life was, and yet she knew Clare did not want pity. She had made her choice knowingly. Eve wished she could get away to somewhere fresh and new, start again, but that seemed impossible.

Then on Christmas Day she read the advertisement that altered her life. She had just come home from St. James Church in Macquarie Street. In her small living quarters, she made tea and perused two recent copies of the *Sydney Morning Herald*. Her eyes ran down the "Situations Vacant" columns, and she drew in her breath in sharp surprise as she read:

SITUATION VACANT

There is a vacancy for a Pianoforte Teacher at
All Saints' Church of England School,
Bathurst, New South Wales.
Students are girls between the ages of seven and fourteen,
all from paying families in and around the Bathurst district.

The applicants must be prepared to play the church organ
(gratis) for services on Mondays, Thursdays, and Sundays, and
take sewing classes with children of most tender years, all
under the age of nine.
The successful applicant should be a genteel, unmarried lady

with an earnest attitude and a sedate, willing, and pious
nature who enjoys the country life.

Church housing can be arranged. And wages will be explained
by return post to those ladies making serious application.
Apply to: Mrs. Hazel Wiggers, Headmistress,
All Saints' Church of England School,
William St.,
Bathurst.

The advertisement was for the very church that, she remembered, "her clergyman" belonged to! How often in the past years she had thought of him, the wonderful man who had given her the gold watch that day in the street in Walsh Bay.

She had written to him after she had taken lease of Sully Tomkins's shed, thanking him for helping her. She had been painfully disappointed when he had not replied, for she had really felt a kindred spirit with him in their two brief meetings. Little did she know that her letter had never reached its destination. Instead, it had been thrown in the bracken by the Sydney roadside, having been on a coach that was robbed near Katoomba in the Blue mountains.

She wondered if the cleric was still at the church in Bathurst.

The situation advertised was one she could fill quite ably, even down to the sewing. Why, she could take her sewing machine with her! She was not exactly sure about the "sedate, willing, and pious" part. She had a little laugh at that. It was the thought of a country life that appealed greatly to her. And to be able to play piano again would be heaven.

Everyone she cared for had left her, and while she still believed in herself, her strength and resilience, there was nothing holding her in Sydney now. What was a business without someone to share it? She brought her hands together. "I'll do it!" she said aloud. "Nothing ventured, nothing gained." She went back inside and wrote two letters. One was to Mrs. Wiggers as the advertisement suggested, enclosing a letter of introduction from Canon Robert Allwood of Saint James's Church, and once again, she wrote to Reverent Billings.

This time, to her delight and surprise, she received a letter back from the parson within a week. It assured her that he remembered her and urged her to come to Bathurst immediately. She closed down her business and moved her life.

It was not until she finally met with Reverend Billings that they both found out about their earlier letters, which had gone so fatefully astray; and in their hearts, they both thought it a miracle that they had discovered each other again.

All the years, she had continued to correspond with Clare, but these days her sister's address was a post office box at the general post office in Adelaide. A letter had come only a few days ago, and Eve read it again before she went to sleep on this first day of April. It was short and cheerful, as usual. Clare was still in Adelaide, still working in a tavern, and still living with some fellow. Eve could always be sure that her sister would have a man. "Tall and handsome" was Clare's description. "Naturally," Eve said aloud.

It was not until later, when she was in that semiworld between yielding to sleep and actually sleeping, that she recalled the man who had stood across the street from her house in the dusk. Odd that he had been looking at her home. Who was he? What had he been doing there? Her thoughts floated over the scene. He had been well dressed, far too refined for the Bathurst streets, and dark under his wide-brimmed hat.

When she did sleep, she dreamed of strange men, tastefully dressed and wearing hats that hid their faces. John Stuart, on the other hand, hardly slept at all. He spent much of the night thinking.

His position in the colony was of unmistakable importance. Mayfield was enormous, hundreds of square miles, the largest property in the colony and in the country. He was powerful, and earnest about his power, and tried to embody in his own behavior the highest socially acceptable standards of morality. In this reign of Victoria, it was acceptable for a young man to introduce himself to a lady he admired, even after seeing her only once in the street or the field. But for John Stuart Wakeman, such was not the case. He pursued the "proper" social code, which did not encourage him to introduce himself to a female. This made it all the more remarkable that he had actually spoken to Eve in Bentwick Street. For all his freethinking, his personal behavior was formal.

If he had been less taken by Eve, he might have judged a Bathurst music teacher unworthy of his attentions, but as he lay sleepless that night, he had no interest in her station. He thought of her in the most physical way. She was different from other women, he was sure of it. He had convinced himself she was chaste and pure of heart and mind, but physically, she aroused and attracted him. He wanted his hands on her silken skin, and his face in her hair. He wanted to breathe in the scent of her, to taste the wetness of her mouth. He had to know this woman, know her and have her, but at the same time, he desired to protect and comfort her. When finally he slept, it was just before dawn broke over Maundy Thursday with a brilliant sun, and the promise of another hot autumn day became a reality.

Eve woke not long after John Stuart at last had slipped into sleep. She was going to spend the day with Father and Mother Billings at the parsonage. As she left her house in Russell Street, it was with the happy expectation of a carefree day in their company. In truth, they would have liked Eve to live with them, but they were wise enough to realize her need for independence and so had not pursued the matter even though some folk deemed it odd that a young, unmarried woman lived alone. She did not know, but she was often referred to as "the pretty piano teacher" by those of the population not given to envy, and as "that American woman" by those who were.

It was a short distance from her home to the parsonage. She wore a light blue cotton dress and a straw hat. As she crossed the street to enter the whitewashed wooden gate of the rectory, the vendors in the fruit, vegetable, and poultry market opposite turned to watch her.

In the last five years, a number of suitors had courted Eve, but she had not responded to any, and each, in time, had given up and married others. She could not help it; she wanted someone of distinction whom she could love and admire, someone like Father, an intelligent and well-bred gentleman. All that tiny Bathurst had to offer were local tradesmen or clerks or farmers. All her friends were married, except for one other teacher at All Saints', but still she did not care. She had the stability of Father and Mother now, so she could wait.

Mother opened the front door to greet Eve, and as she drew her into the hall, she wrapped her arms around her. "He's expecting you, my love, and as usual, he is being particular about what I feed you for luncheon."

The two women laughed affectionately, and together they passed arm in arm down the long hall to the study.

Father Billings rose as they entered, his face lighting up in a broad smile as he took Eve's hands in his. "Good morning. How bright you make the day, Eve." She returned his greeting and kissed him.

His earnest eyes softened as they rested on the two women. These were the flowers of his flock. The one he had been married to for forty years; he loved quietly, a balanced and harmonious love. The other, who had come into his life five short years before, he loved with exquisite intensity; she was the precious daughter bestowed when all hope of such a one had long been abandoned. At times she still reminded him of his beloved sister, Josephine, but now he knew *her*, and loved her as Eve, for herself.

"My dears, I am looking for some misplaced church funds at the moment. Now you are here, Eve, you can help me."

Mother smiled dotingly. "You two are to be in the back garden, at one o'clock sharp, for luncheon." And she left them to themselves.

They worked through the morning, happy in each other's company, comfortable and familiar. Once or twice he called her "Evvy," his pet name for her, and she smiled up at him from the pile of papers around her.

Before luncheon, the two of them took their customary walk, arm in arm, through the grounds of All Saints', but they followed orders and were in the back garden under the big jacaranda tree on the dot of one o'clock. During the meal, Father was brought a note by Mistress Lottie Thatcher, the housekeeper at the parsonage. She was a comely country woman of a height and coloring similar to Eve's, though older and with the unequivocal, direct gaze of the bush folk. She was unmarried and had been devoted to Father and Mother for seventeen years. She stood watching Father dispassionately as he read the message.

Father handed the paper back to her as he stood from the table. "Thank you, Lottie. Excuse me, my loves, but a gentleman wishes to see me. I hope the intrusion is not long." He strode across the lawn and into the house, followed closely by Lottie in her swirling brown skirt.

In the front hall stood John Stuart Wakeman.

The Reverend Billings had not seen John Stuart since his father, Sir Arthur Wakeman, had died over seven years before, though he read about him regularly in the Sydney and country newspapers. The cleric had been a friend of Sir Arthur and had visited Mayfield on occasions in the past. He knew the son did not inherit the father's good opinion of the church and had noticed that the generous yearly donation had ended after his friend's death.

John Stuart had changed little since the cleric had last seen him. The only differences the elapsed years had brought were more maturity and a dark mustache. He would be over thirty now, had always been a good-looking man, similar to his father, except his eyes were brown where his father's had been light blue. His bearing was the same, unmistakably that of a Wakeman, but he was taller than his father by at least two or three inches. The clergyman held out his hand. ''John Stuart, what brings you here after so long a time?''

For a second or two, it was possible to think an expression of irritation appeared on his visitor's face. Then the look was submerged in an affable nod of the head and an open smile. ''Good to see you, sir, good to see you.''

''Thank you, son. Are you here in Bathurst for long? Do come into my study, where we can talk more freely.''

When John Stuart had bent his long frame into a rosewood chair, and Father had done the same, the clergyman looked inquiringly at him.

He coughed. ''Sir, I've come to approach you on a delicate matter, and to ask you for your . . . help.''

''If I can, my boy, I will.''

The ticking of the large ormolu clock on the mantel shelf seemed loud. John Stuart appeared unsure of how to proceed. He wished Joe Larmer were with him. He took a breath, and his mouth turned up into a half smile. ''You see, there is a lady in this town. I saw her first the day before yesterday, in the park. She . . . well . . . she exemplifies everything I regard as desirable in womankind.''

For some incalculable reason, the reverend had an uncanny feeling that he knew exactly who she was.

''The matter which I wish you to attend to, sir, is that of an introduction. Now, she may not be one of your parish, but I hope you will accommodate me.''

Father passed his hand across his eyes. It was an uncomfortable gesture. ''This lady . . . You wish to meet her with a view to spending time in her company when you pass this way?''

John Stuart did not reply for fully half a minute. His dark eyes closed. When he opened them and focused them on the preacher, they held a resolve that echoed the determination in his voice. ''Sir, my desire is to marry her.''

The older man suddenly looked very weary. At that moment, the future with all its absurd contingencies seemed revealed to him. He felt as if he were in a flooded river, inextricably washed along. He knew the answer to his question even as the words came from his lips. ''And who is this lady? Do you know her name?''

"Yes. Her name is Evelyn Herman. She lives in Russell Street. Do you know her?"

At this very moment the heavy study door opened and Eve breezed in. "Father dear, I have been sent to find . . ." Her words trailed off as she caught sight of John Stuart in the chair.

Both men stood in unison.

John Stuart looked in amazement at Eve. "But this is the very lady. . . . How is it she is here and calls you 'Father'?"

The clergyman did not reply. It was as if he could not speak. He was a capable man. Chance events normally did not disconcert him, and he could understand any man wanting to marry his Evvy. She was a beautiful prize in his eyes. But the declaration by John Stuart had taken him quite unprepared.

Eve advanced to his side, swiftly answering for him. "I call the Reverend Billings Father because we both prefer it." She looked questioningly to the pastor.

He put a protective arm around her shoulders and, with an almost visible effort, said, "Eve, my love, this is John Stuart Wakeman of Mayfield. He has wished to meet you after seeing you in the park on Tuesday."

John Stuart, evidently entranced by her arrival, bowed. "How do you do, Miss Herman."

Eve had heard of John Stuart Wakeman. Who in the colony had not? She was quite fascinated to meet him. She stretched out her hand, which he took. She felt a tingle of pleasure as he held it until she extricated it. Then suddenly a look of recognition came into her face. "My goodness!" she said. "I know who you are! You're the man who stood across from my house last night, aren't you? Of course, and the man on the horse in Bentwick Street yesterday. I . . ." She turned to Father with a baffled smile.

Father looked questioningly. "What does Eve say? Did you stand opposite her house last night?"

John Stuart's eyes were intent on every small detail of her, even as he answered the reverend's question. "I'm afraid it is true. And I confess, I stood there the night before as well, only that time she was unaware of me." He continued looking into her eyes. "My admission extends. You see, I followed you home from the park on Tuesday night."

She laughed a small, surprised laugh. This was so unexpected, she was taken off guard. "Oh," she said. "I did not realize it." She could not help being flattered by John Stuart's obvious attraction to her. She thought him quite the best-looking man she had ever seen. A pleasant lunch with Father and Mother had turned into something much more exciting. She looked up at Father. "Mother sent me to find you. She will wonder whatever the delay is. Why don't we invite Mr. Wakeman to lunch? We've only just begun, and there's so much food."

The lunch was an exceptional success for John Stuart. The feeling between these two people was evident. He was openly captivated by Eve, and she was unmistakably interested in him.

She compared him with the men she knew. This was no plain Bathurst man; he was a man of authority and station. He spoke lucidly about the colony, its inadequacies, its achievements, and its future. When she mentioned her homeland, he expressed his wide knowledge of her own country and the Civil War that now gripped it. He even enlightened her on the series of recent victories for the southern army in Virginia, in particular the northern defeat at Fredericksburg on December 13, and how it appeared otherwise on the Mississippi, where the northern army had badly damaged the southerners. She listened to him gravely and marveled at the range of his information.

The look of confusion that lingered in the older man's eyes that afternoon did not disturb Eve, for she did not notice it. Her attention was on the eminent guest.

His distinguished air attracted her.

His assertiveness attracted her.

His physical appearance attracted her.

After his departure, she remained in the back garden alone for a time, an expectant expression in her lively eyes.

SEVEN

Cataclysm

On the Saturday after Easter, a horse and chaise stood to the side of a dirt track two miles from Bathurst. Near the vehicle grazed two saddled horses, and a hundred yards away, under the shade of a large wattle tree on the bank of the Macquarie River, four people sat on a blanket eating sandwiches.

Eve's eyes twinkled as she swallowed a mouthful. "I really enjoy picnics."

Father smiled, and Mother waved a tea cloth at a party of insistent flies. "I would, except, for these little wretches."

John Stuart lifted his handkerchief and joined their efforts to shoo away the pests. He had remained in Bathurst, at the Royal Hotel, since Maundy Thursday. His obvious attention to Eve Herman had become the talk of the entire four thousand souls of the borough. On Good Friday he came to the parsonage after church service, and he and Eve had sat for a long time talking in the garden. On Easter Saturday he arrived for tea, and again after church on Easter day. On Monday, which was a holiday, he invited Eve and Mother to dine with him at the Royal. During the work days that followed, he met Eve after school, and they took tea in the garden of the rectory under the poinciana tree.

Eve was doing a lot of thinking. Although she was usually clearheaded, discerning, and watchful where men were concerned, to find herself in the position of having John Stuart in attendance was something out of a dream. She had never been with anyone so scholarly, so worldly, so sophisticated, and so handsome. Nor had most of the population of Australia, for there were few John Stuart Wakemans available. He was articulate and could speak fluently on almost any subject. She could not help being flattered at his interest in her opinions. They talked a great deal about music, and she often played piano for him.

He had a certain way of watching her that at times made her feel a little embarrassed, but in the most exciting, womanly way. She thought he represented everything that was strong and manly.

As the days went by, and John Stuart remained in Bathurst, Father had confided to his wife what had passed between himself and John Stuart in his study. Mother had been delighted. "Really? But that is wonderful, Leslie dear. Oh yes, what a perfect couple they will make."

Father had taken up her hands in his. "Ah, my love, I suppose you are right, but I have the feeling that John Stuart is so captivated by our darling that he will take her from us very soon, if she agrees." Then he added quickly, "Not that I want to keep her when she can have a home of her own. It's just that I think all this goes too swiftly."

"It doesn't matter, if they are right for each other," his wife answered. Father had nodded and looked pensively into the distance. His face held the same expression now as Eve and John Stuart stood to go for a walk along the riverbank.

Eve smiled down at him. "We shan't be long, my dears."

"Don't worry about us," Mother replied. "Enjoy yourselves."

John Stuart held out his arm, and Eve slipped her hand around it. For a little time they walked in silence. It was a warm afternoon, and they kept to the shade of the casuarina trees, commonly known as she-oaks, that grew along the water's edge until they rounded a bend and came upon a stand of eucalyptus trees. Eve stopped to watch a koala bear asleep in the hollow of a gum tree, while John Stuart spent most of the time watching her. Finally he asked, "What is it that you would like more than anything else in the world?"

Eve turned to him and laughed. "Oh, my goodness, that's hard to answer."

"Well, try."

"More than anything in the world?"

"Yes."

A grave look rose in her face, and she pursed her lips in reflection. "I think that I would like people to be kinder to each other, and to know that there was no more cruelty, and that poor girls could be delivered from being deceived by the lies of certain men. Yes, and that the world did not judge as harshly as it does or that horrible disease did not kill people before their time, and that poor little children did not have . . .'' She stopped short, for John Stuart had begun to laugh. A deep frown of disapproval lodged between her eyes. ''Why are you so amused?''

He took up her hand and kissed it. ''Evelyn, I fear you have been too long with the parson. All these wishes for mankind are wonderful, and lofty dreams, no doubt, but I was meaning what do *you* want more than anything in the world for yourself.''

There was stubbornness now in Eve's brown eyes. Her mouth tightened just a little as she turned from him and walked on. ''I have just told you,'' she said.

The amused look remained on John Stuart's face for a second or two before it faded. ''Please wait,'' he called, hurrying after her. ''Evelyn, I'm sorry I laughed.''

She did not look at him, but continued on in silence.

''Eve, please, believe me; I'm sorry, truly.''

''You do not take me seriously. The world needs changes.''

He took her hand and stopped her from walking on. He turned her solemn face to his. ''All right, I admit I was frivolous. I apologize. You have told me, and I accept what you say. I am in awe of you and your altruism, Miss Herman.'' He lifted her hand to his mouth and kissed her fingertips. ''So will you indulge me in my disgrace and allow me to tell you what *I* want more than anything?''

She sighed, but she smiled, too. ''All right, tell me.''

''You.''

She drew her breath in sharply.

There was no mirth in his eyes now, only sincerity. ''Eve, you must realize why I have remained in Bathurst. I am in love with you, Evelyn May Herman and I want to take you home to Mayfield.'' His expression was soft, caring. ''I want you to know Mayfield as I do. Eve, I am asking you to be my wife.''

A thrill of excitement was running all through her. ''John Stuart, I have only known you nine days.''

''What does that matter? I love you, have loved you from the moment I saw you in the park. Say yes, my darling. Please.''

He stepped closer and slipped his arms around her back and drew her to him. He was looking into her eyes as he brought his lips down upon hers and slowly kissed her. At the contact, Eve felt a shiver, sharp and tantalizing. His mouth was delightfully wet and warm as he enclosed her lips inside his. She was conscious of his hands through the material of her dress as they moved over her back, and down her spine. The pressure of his firm body against her breasts aroused her. Gently he forced open her lips, and she felt the shiver of excitement extend through her body as she tasted his mouth for the first time.

She felt warm and womanly and wonderful.

When he drew away, his hands lingered on her bare arms. A hot breeze lifted her skirt and blew it forward to brush his knees. They stood there in silence, both aware of the response in the other.

"What do you say, my darling?" he asked at last. "Will you be my wife?"

She moved away to look across the river. Her emotions were in a wonderful sort of confusion. As she stood there, she felt his hand on her shoulder. It moved slowly across to the naked skin of her throat in caressing, gentle movements. She felt another sensual thrill at the touch of his fingers. His face came close behind her, his lips in her hair. "Eve, say yes. Then we can be married soon and go to our home." He sighed. "You and Mayfield, both beautiful, both my life."

Eve's heart was racing. She turned around to face him. He looked so solemn now, his flawless face so earnest and imploring. "Please, Eve, answer me."

She took a deep breath. "Just give me some time to think."

He leaned forward and kissed her, again stirring up the jumble of emotions within her.

"All right," he said, "I'll wait, but promise me you will tell me tomorrow."

She stood looking up at him. A cockatoo somewhere in the scrub screeched loudly. He smiled. She loved his smile. It was a little crooked at times, and for a second or two she thought she saw "the boy in the man," making him seem vulnerable. That surprised her; she had thought there were no insecurities in John Stuart's personality. She lifted her hand to the collar of his shirt and touched it affectionately, almost possessively. "All right, I'll tell you tomorrow, but we should get back to Mother and Father now, don't you think?"

He nodded; he could wait until tomorrow. Taking up her hand, he tucked it inside his arm, and slowly they made their way back along the river.

That night, Eve stayed at the rectory, as she often did on weekends. She hardly slept at all. She tossed and turned, and by the dawn light she rose and was washed and dressed and in the garden sitting under the poinciana tree before six o'clock. She was completely absorbed by John Stuart's marriage proposal. This was marriage; this was permanent; this was the thing men never offered Clare. What would life with John Stuart be like? Did she really love him? Did she want to marry him?

She leaned down from where she sat and brushed the dew on the grass with her fingertips. Through her mind ran the words that she had been recalling all night long, the words her mother had said to her when she was dying.

How clearly she recalled her beautiful mother, wasted and gaunt, in the big mahogany bed in San Francisco. Ada had asked to see each of her daughters separately, and when it had been her turn, her mother had taken her hand. She had drawn Eve down to her and then whispered, "Do you remember Matthis . . . that day in Boston . . . and what she said?"

Eve did remember and nodded gently. "Yes, Mumma, I do."

"I knew you were there and must have heard the letters she spelt out, M . . . A . . . Y . . . F. They will mean something of great importance . . . to you . . . and only you. . . . There were others, but Matthis could not see them all. . . . Yes . . . great importance . . . Remember them always." Then Ada had tried to lift herself a little and put out her hand to touch Eve's face. "And you will be loved, greatly loved. . . ." She had begun to cough then, and her father had come in with the nurse.

Eve had never told anyone about the prophecy. But from the hour in the back garden of the parsonage when she had met John Stuart, it had been on her mind, for the letters M-A-Y-F were the beginning of Mayfield.

"Darling, you are up early." Father's voice broke into her thoughts.

She turned on the seat to see him coming down the steps from the kitchen. "Yes. I want to come to early Communion this morning."

The Communion service ended at a quarter to nine o'clock, and when Eve and Father returned across the back garden from church, Lottie met them near the kitchen door. She pointed back through the house. "Mr. Wakeman is on the front veranda. He waits for you, Miss Evvy."

Father looked inquiringly at Eve. "He's here early."

"Yes." She dropped Father's arm. "Lottie, please tell Mr. Wakeman I'm coming." When Lottie had gone, Eve turned to Father. "John Stuart wants to marry me."

Slowly Father nodded. "Yes, my darling, I know."

"I had better go and see him."

Father smiled. It was a reassuring smile, full of love and tenderness and understanding. "Evvy, I want you always to be happy. You know that, don't you?"

"Yes, I know that."

She walked away from him to the steps, and mounting them, turned back to him.

"I'll always love you," she said.

"I'll always love you, too," he answered.

When Eve came to John Stuart, he stood facing away from her and turned at the sound of her footsteps, the crystalline brightness of the morning light reflecting a gaudy brilliance on the sheen of his silken coat. Suddenly she saw him differently, beyond his polish and handsome features. It was as if all her soul searching had culminated in this moment. As she crossed the veranda to his extended hand, her smile was one of welcome and trust; and as she watched him bow his head to touch the back of her hand with his lips, she was overwhelmed by the need to be with him. By the time he asked his question, she was certain of the answer.

Eve awoke with a start. For a few seconds she lay there gathering her thoughts and examining the green canopy of the bed above her. She was in her usual bedroom at the rectory. It was five weeks from the day she had met John Stuart, and it was her wedding day.

She smiled languidly and snuggled more deeply into the bedclothes. Then into the warm glow of her mind came thoughts of Clare. She sat up, a frown on her face. She had written to her sister the day after she had agreed to marry John Stuart. Of course, letters took weeks to get from Sydney to Adelaide, and she knew she would not hear from Clare before the wedding, but she truly wished she could have shared this day with her sister. A guilty little shiver ran through her, for she had not yet told John Stuart about Clare. She was not sure how John Stuart would react.

The only people in Bathurst who knew about Clare were Father and Mother. A few days ago, Father had counseled Eve to tell her future husband everything, but instead, she had been adamant that it was the wrong time, that when they were married, she would find a quiet moment to explain. It would be easier then. Father Billings had acceded to his darling's point of view against his better judgment and let the subject lapse.

Eve took a deep breath; it would be all right, she knew it would. She sighed just as the door opened and Mother bustled in, saying, "Eve, my love, time to get up. Our Lottie's here with the hot water for your bath."

Behind her came Lottie, struggling with a large jug. "And Jennie's got another, as well, Miss Eve, coming right away."

She climbed out of the big, soft bed and into Mother's embrace.

Later, left alone to bathe, she did something she had not done since girlhood. In front of the large cedar wardrobe, she stood, and untying her nightdress, let it fall to the floor. Her naked reflection stared out of the mirror.

Slowly she lifted her right hand and, studying each part of herself, traced an imaginary line down her nose, across her mouth, under her chin, over the little hollow at the base of her neck to her breasts. She traced around her nipples with her forefingers. They hardened to her touch. Lifting her left hand, down across her belly she flattened her palms into the curly pubic hair below. A tremulous movement lifted the tight spirals out from her body, and they sprang back from her fingers. Small erotic shivers of wonderful expectation trembled through her at the thought of intimacy with John Stuart. He was everything she had ever dreamed of in a man. Her eyes closed as she remembered the feel of his lips tracing across her neck and around to her mouth the night before. Oh yes, she did love him. She could hardly wait to be in his arms.

Eve was not a person given to great vanity, but as she opened her eyes and focused again, she enjoyed the look of the woman in the mirror. Her body was slender and free of imperfections. She smiled and turned away to her toilet.

Mother and Lottie spent the next hour helping her to dress.

The ceremony was at half past the hour of nine, and it appeared the whole borough of Bathurst had gathered outside All Saints'. Children had climbed the four casuarina trees that grew on the footpath, and some hung precariously from limbs, shouting excitedly to one another.

Eve looked through the window at the crowd as the time of her wedding drew near. Thoughts raced through her head. She knew everything had happened quickly, perhaps a little too quickly for Father. Nevertheless, once she had agreed to marry John Stuart, he had convinced her that waiting was futile. "I want to take you home, to 'our' home, Mayfield."

She was going to be Mrs. Wakeman. To be mistress of so

much and married to John Stuart as well was like a blessing ultimately bestowed by her guardian angel. She knew she was the envy of every young woman in the colony, and she wanted so much to be worthy of him, to be a good wife. This was not merely respectability; this was prestige, honor, prominence, of the most inordinate kind. But in her heart, she believed in herself, just as she always had. While he brought wealth and rank and station to her and the fulfillment of many of the dreams of Eve, the teenager, she, too, brought things to him. She was loyal and caring and competent. She looked forward to learning about the property and believed she could help him with the people who lived and worked there. She wanted to learn, and be involved with his life; to be his partner, his lover, and his friend.

When she finally passed from the rectory to the church door on Father's arm, she was exhilarated. A long, white veil hid her face, and her white silk dress and train were covered in hearts decorated with seed pearls. They had come by special courier from Sydney town. On her finger was the ring encrusted with diamonds and rubies that her husband to-be had placed on her finger a week ago. Highly aware of the throng, she held tightly to Father's arm. It was hard for her to believe that they were here to see her. As they neared the church porch, the crowd pushed forward, and clearly she heard the voice of Miss Macdonald, the old crone washerwoman, saying, ''Good on ye, Eve gel, ye be gettin' the pick of the whole ruddy colony.''

All Saints' was brimming with major dignitaries. The governor of the colony, Sir John Young, shared the front row with Thelma Larmer, Joe's wife, and Daydee, his seventeen-year-old daughter. The premier, Mr. Charles Cowper, sat with the colonial secretary, the speaker of the legislative assembly, and a number of the elected from Parliament. The mayor of Bathurst, Mr. Richard Young Cousins, bestowed his broad smile to right and left. Some rows back was Sir Rutherford Blake, arms folded in front of him, with his assistant, Mr. Elrington, at his right hand.

John Stuart's side of the church far overbalanced the left, for while Eve's friends numbered Lottie and Jennie and Mrs. Wiggers, the headmistress of All Saints' School, the other teachers, and some married friends, John Stuart had scores of guests.

Joe Larmer and Mother were standing for the couple, and they waited at the altar rail with John Stuart. When Eve had met Joe Larmer, she quickly realized that Joe was not only proud of John Stuart but loved him deeply. It was evident that the feeling was mutual. They were like father and son, and she recognized that there was no one on earth closer to the master of Mayfield than his manager.

When Thelma and Daydee arrived three days before the wedding, Eve responded warmly to Joe's wife, a motherly person of about fifty-five, who wore her long hair tied severely back in a bun, a style that accentuated her wide forehead and large, sincere, hazel eyes. It was apparent to Eve from the start that Thelma's was a simple, unaffected soul. She had taken Eve in her arms and hugged her affectionately. Her daughter, Daydee, a slight, dark-haired girl of seventeen, dressed in cream silk, was less enthusiastic, only taking Eve's extended hand after being prompted by her mother, and then without meeting Eve's eyes, although her greeting to John Stuart was almost excessive. She threw herself into his arms, saying, "Uncle John Stuart, I've missed you terribly. Why, what with the cattle drive and everything, you've only been home thirteen days in the last fifty, for I have counted them!" And John Stuart had laughed indulgently, half lifting her off the floor as she embraced him. Eve had watched the display, not sure what to make of it.

The inside of the church was resplendent, the work of Mother and Thelma, who knew each other from the days of Arthur Wakeman. There were beautiful flowers on every available flat surface, and decorated horseshoes, the old Irish tradition for luck in marriage, hanging at the end of the pews.

Outside, the noise grew, rising even above the sound of the organ. As John Stuart turned and watched his bride come toward him, Martin Carlyle, the church warden, could be heard at the door shouting, "Please, be quiet! In the name of God!"

Eve relinquished Father's arm to take John Stuart's hand.

Father was not in essence a selfish man. In fact, he was as charitable as men of his calling are supposed to be, but where Eve was concerned, he was cautious and protective. In the whole country, he could not have chosen a better partner for his dearest Evvy. But the Reverend Leslie Billings was not interested in looks and material success. He was concerned only with real happiness for his "daughter." If in the beginning he had thought the marriage too hasty, he had soon asked himself if he were merely prejudiced because he was losing Eve, and he answered that he wanted only the best for her, and soon had come to terms with the speed of the union. Still, his heart was beating rapidly as he looked from one to the other. "I now pronounce you man and wife."

When the ceremony was complete and the papers signed, the couple walked back down the aisle to the strains of one of Mozart's motets lifting from the organ and the musicians John Stuart had hired. The minister turned back to the altar and offered up a prayer to God. The prayer was short and passionate and full of benefits for Eve. Later, there were times when the good man thought his God had not been listening.

A peal of bells began as the bride and groom issued forth from the church and passed through the crowd of well-wishers and curiosity seekers, into the morning sun where the Mayfield coach waited for them.

The long journey would take them at least twelve hours, so they had decided to forgo a formal wedding breakfast. Their guests were to be entertained without them at a most elaborate feast for much of the remainder of the day. Even the ordinary townsfolk were to enjoy the celebration, as Joe had seen to it that pies, cakes, and drinks were to be made available to them in the park.

They retired for twenty minutes to the rectory to make their farewells. Tears filled everyone's eyes as Eve held onto Mother and Father in the entry hall of the parsonage. Father took John Stuart's hand and said, "Take care of our daughter." Eve hugged them all in turn, and Mother whispered, "God bless you, darling, God bless you." Lottie fussed about, making sure Eve's traveling dress was straight.

Yet it was Daydee who cried the most. She and her mother were staying on in Bathurst for a week with Thelma's cousin, and the girl clung to her father and John Stuart in unison as if she were to be separated from them for a decade. As her eyes found Eve's over John Stuart's shoulder, Eve was mystified by the hard edge of scorn reflected in them.

And so Mr. and Mrs. Wakeman departed in the shining coach with the Wakeman blazon upon the door, and Bathurst, in one voice, cheered the fairy-tale couple.

Father thought later, he had seen nothing in his long life to equal the beauty of his Eve's face that morning. He spent much of that day in the chapel, his favorite place to meditate. His good and understanding wife left him alone, and when he returned home after evening prayers, they sat silently, close together on the old sofa in their big, homely kitchen. Mother said, "Ah me . . ." and patted the back of her husband's hand. He answered, "Yes, Lily, my love, our daughter is gone," and they looked at each other, a significant look, comfortable and secure in their own abiding love.

It had been a wrench for Eve to leave Father and Mother and her secure life with them, but once she had, she looked forward to her future. She glowed, her skin shone, and when she looked into her new husband's eyes, her heartbeat quickened. "You are beautiful, Mrs. Wakeman," he repeated, many times turning to her in the bumping carriage and kissing her lightly on the lips or lifting her hand to his mouth. Eve laughed, a lover's laugh, in anticipation of what was to come.

The road ran through virgin bush, where now and then sparrows in flocks flew overhead. To left and right was a land of olive greens, grays, and soft browns, the colors of the iron bark and stringy bark gums. Much of the country was flat, with occasional long, undulating hills, and a few miles before their arrival in Blayney, a big buck kangaroo left its herd and kept pace with the coach, impressively leaping gullies and scrub, its massive hindquarters lifting it effortlessly into the air. Her husband explained this was not uncommon. There seemed to be something about a moving vehicle that fascinated the big kangaroos, and Eve leaned out the window, entranced.

John Stuart smiled at his wife's delight. When he did so, he exposed two rows of even white teeth beneath his dark mustache. He looked so boyish that Eve felt a sharp and sudden sympathy for him, though she knew not why. She bent toward him and took his hand. He squeezed hers in return, and with his left hand he took out the fine gold timepiece he carried in the fob pocket of his waistband. "Well, my darling," he said, "we've made splendid time, even though the road is bad, like all the damned roads in the colony. My six Mayfield beauties are averaging a good seven miles an hour. I think we'll be at the Albion Hotel in Blayney by three o'clock."

They were, and there they rested briefly while the horses were changed for a new team brought north from Mayfield. As they were leaving the hotel to rejoin the vehicle, an odd thing occurred.

Joe was already mounted and sitting beside Deke Edwards, the driver, when Eve and John Stuart came out across the wide dirt footpath toward Timothy, who held open the coach door. Eve was a few paces ahead of her husband, and as she neared the coach, a woman came toward her. She was poorly dressed and bonnetless, her slight frame burdened with an infant and some awkward parcels. She halted to let Eve, dressed so elegantly, pass by. As she paused, the woman dropped one of the items she was carrying, and Eve turned to her, saying, "Just a moment, I'll get it for you." A brief smile of gratitude broke across the woman's thin face, but before Eve could bend to retrieve it, John Stuart had leaped forward and almost bodily lifted Eve away toward the coach.

"I'll do it, Eve. You get in the carriage!" His voice was so agitated and his action so extreme that Eve unhesitatingly complied. He turned back to where the woman was now bending to the article herself. She was awkward and unsteady under the weight of the child and her other packages, and with his face deliberately averted from her, he steadied her with his right hand until she stood up again. There was unmistakable distaste on his face, and when she moved away, he unconsciously wiped his hand in a cleansing motion on the skirt of his jacket. The movement was so automatic that he did not know he had done it, but his bride, who watched from the coach, did.

As the vehicle gathered speed, Eve looked questioningly at her husband. "Who was that woman?" she ventured.

He turned toward her and took her hand. "Eve." He spoke almost condescendingly. "You are my wife. There are some people . . . people with whom you should never have contact. She is one of these, and—"

"But, John Stuart," Eve interrupted in defense of the woman, "she looked quite harmless to me, the poor thing."

A note of exasperation crept into her husband's voice. "She should not walk the same street as you. She's a damned whore! Everyone in the West knows! Let it be enough for me to tell you she has been in two de facto relationships and is now onto her third. The waif she carried is the offspring of God knows who!" He took a deep breath. "She's disgusting!"

The thought of Clare rose within Eve, and a chill started at the back of her neck and prickled down her arms and spine. She had avoided telling her husband of his sister-in-law and, now she was faced with John Stuart's severe, if not abnormal, reaction to the sort of woman that people would say Clare was. Eve was startled and concerned. She made a halfhearted defense of the poor woman in Blayney. "But, John Stuart, dearest, we don't know the circumstances that have brought her to this end. She may not be to blame."

"She's to blame, all right. That's unquestionable," came his obdurate reply. "She's like my mother was. They make the choice, these women. They are detestable."

Eve was aware that her husband's mother had returned to Scotland when he was only three years old. Father had told her there had been an affair, a scandal, in which an army officer was involved. It appeared she had been sent away. That John Stuart held a grudge against his mother, Eve learned early, for when she had mentioned her in the first week of their acquaintance, he had silenced her by saying, "Eve, my mother has not been in my life since I was a baby. Please do not speak of her, ever again. She is nothing to me, less than nothing."

Now he had referred to her again, in direct comparison to the woman in Blayney, and for the first time, Eve began to see that he was disgusted by any female he judged unworthy. It was a disconcerting revelation for her, and the more she thought of Clare, the more she wished she had told him before.

Even so, it did not take John Stuart long to forget the incident. Within a minute or two, his good spirits had returned. To him, what had happened was just an unfortunate occurrence. It was not so easy for his bride to dismiss, and it took her a little longer before she pushed the uncomfortable notion from her mind, promising to find a way of telling him when the time was right.

He had relinquished her hand and now he took it again from where it lay in her lap and kissed it. They turned to each other, forgetting the recent disturbance in the newness of their passion and their love. Eve ran her fingers through his hair and smiled up into his eyes, a playful, mischievous smile, beckoning her handsome husband-lover. He took her in his arms, and she lay across his body, her legs upon the seat. She touched his lips with her fingers, and he took a fingertip into his mouth. The wetness on her skin was deliciously inviting, and the thought of soon being loved by him sent sensual shivers trembling through her limbs. She knew it and welcomed it. He pulled her close, and she felt his muscular chest beneath the softness of his shirt pressing into her breasts. His mouth came down to hers, his arms enfolding and caressing her. The taste of him was heady, thrilling, exciting.

He thought he held a piece of Heaven, so soft and wonderful did she feel. He had seen her, wanted her, attained her, and as each minute passed, this bumpy, swaying vehicle was bringing him closer to the consummation of his ultimate desire. He drew his mouth from hers. "You tempt me to love you right here, my darling, but I fear we would be covered in bruises. Perhaps we should watch the bush for a while."

She smiled, moving gently away from him. "Yes, darling, I

think we should; this carriage lurches quite dangerously at times.''

So, for the next two hours the newly marrieds were light-hearted. They chatted with each other, laughed with each other, touched each other, and were happy with each other.

The day was closing. The golden glow of evening radiated from the orange ball on the horizon, and the long shadows heralding twilight reached across the road. As they came around a sharp bend, suddenly there was a shout from Joe above and abruptly the coach pitched to the left, skidding on its wheels. Loudly straining in all its joints, it slewed sideways into the bank at the roadside, sending dirt and dust high into the air.

There was a scream from Timothy as he toppled from his seat, dragging Deke with him, still clutching the reins tightly in his hands. They fell off the coach onto the earthen bank, and Joe was tossed facedown onto the footboard. The horses reared and whinnied plaintively as they were brought to a sudden, jarring halt.

''What the hell?'' came Joe's shout across the uproar.

Inside, Eve was thrown against the carriage door, and John Stuart fell on top of her. His chin came down sharply on her head, and for some moments they were dazed.

The vehicle righted itself, shaking and groaning, and John Stuart, disentangling himself from Eve's skirt, called, ''What the devil is going on?''

The answer came in Joe's now controlled, deep voice as he lifted himself up on his knees. ''Road's blocked, m'boy.''

In the middle of the road not twenty yards from the coach was a barricade of solid gum branches.

John Stuart hurriedly helped Eve to the seat, and seeing she was unhurt, jumped down from the coach. Eve, in the act of following him, halted at the next words she heard.

''Bail up! I say! Stand and deliver! Don't move or we'll shoot!'' The words came from behind the foliage that lay across the road.

''What in damnation . . .'' began John Stuart, who was interrupted by the calm tones of Joe. '' 'Fraid we've been held up, m'boy.''

''Bloody bushrangers!'' spat out Deke, who only now was rising, covered in dirt, with blood on his lip.

''Oh no!'' exclaimed Timothy, who brushed the dust and grime from his previously immaculate outfit.

''That's right,'' called the disembodied voice, ''so don't ye

be givin' us trouble or ye'll be sorry. And drop the gun, mister!
I can nail ye from here, quicker'n a flash!'' The last statement
was aimed at Joe, who, holding his rifle, had jumped down from
the carriage and moved protectively in front of John Stuart, who
said, ''Drop it, Joe. It's not worth it. Don't be a hero.''

From the branches the mocking tones of the same voice called,
''That's right, Joe, be a good boy and drop it. Don't be a *dead*
hero, Joe!''

Shrugging, Joe dropped the weapon in disgust. As the rifle
hit the ground, three men emerged from behind the debris. All
carried guns and had coverings over their faces. At the same
time, two others led three riderless horses in from behind the
coach. They, too, had their faces hidden behind handkerchiefs.

Although Eve's heartbeat had quickened a little and she was
concerned for John Stuart, somehow she did not really feel
frightened. She watched from within the coach as one of the
men on the ground came forward.

He was strikingly different, dressed in gray with black knee-
high boots. The covering on his face was black, and light brown
hair touched his collar under his dark hat. The shape of his
faultless body somehow showed even through the layers of his
clothes. He moved with a fluid action, and his sun-browned
hand motioned to Joe's rifle on the ground.

One of the men behind him, a small, ferretlike individual,
retrieved it, saying in the same voice that had spoken previously,
''Yeah, guverner, we could do with this.'' He patted the barrel
lovingly. ''Why, it's a Whitworth! My Lord, didn't think there
were any here. It's a beauty!''

One of the horsemen dismounted and came to meet the three
men on foot. He was slim but well built with solid shoulders,
and walked with a slight limp. He carried a Colt pocket pistol
in his right hand, which he waved in the direction of John Stuart,
Joe, Deke, and Timothy. With his eyes on the man in the gray
clothing, obviously the leader, he asked, ''What do ye make of
this lot, guverner? They look a rum team to me. Wouldn't be
givin' ye much for the big one. Overdressed for the back country.'' He pointed with the firearm at John Stuart. The other
bushrangers, who now stood covering the captives, burst into
laughter.

John Stuart, who had been silently bristling with anger, spoke.
''This is outrageous! Don't you know what coach this is?''

The man with the limp stopped chuckling. ''We don't stop

coaches without knowin' what they are! It's the monthly payroll inside we be interested in, not the Mayfield crest on the door.''

John Stuart took a step forward. ''Yes, this is a Mayfield coach, you fool! But it carries no payroll. I'm John Stuart Wakeman. You'll be sorry for this.''

There was silence for some seconds while the disguised men looked at one another. Then the man who wore gray spoke for the first time. Unlike the speech of the two before him, his was refined, the voice of an educated man, and pleasant to hear. It came as a great surprise to his captives, and to Eve, listening from inside the carriage.

''Wakeman, you say? And this is not the payroll coach? Can we have made a mistake, lads?'' He gave a short, cynical laugh. ''On the other hand, perhaps Mr. Wakeman does not remember the ninth commandment, which deals with the telling of lies. We will have to see for ourselves.'' He moved swiftly toward the door of the coach.

John Stuart lunged forward, raising his fist in a futile gesture. ''Stay away from there, damn you!''

A rifle was pushed quickly and keenly into his rib cage with such force that he staggered backward. ''Stay where you are, Wakeman, unless you're sick of bloody livin'.'' This was the fourth man on the ground speaking. He was larger than any of the others, broader and taller even than John Stuart.

John Stuart groaned slightly and recovered his balance. ''Stay away from that coach, I tell you! There is no payroll. It contains nothing but my wife!''

The leader, who now was at the coach door, turned back at this statement. He stood there, his spare frame covered in gray, his black boots polished to gleaming. He was not so tall as John Stuart who stood six feet one, but he was perfectly proportioned with a physical harmony about him, rarely, if ever, had John Stuart or Joe seen anyone more charismatic. A figure not belonging to the tales told of the unkempt robber of the bush roads. His eyes looked skeptically above his mask at the property owner.

''Your wife, Wakeman?'' He laughed the same short laugh as before. It was a disconcerting laugh, unreal, as if it came ''from'' him but not ''of'' him. ''I shall just make sure of that.'' He reached for the door handle.

His men all laughed loudly, and John Stuart, anger, pain, exasperation, and embarrassment welling within him, cried, ''Damn your eyes! I'll see you all hang for this.''

"Shaddup, you, or I'll blast you right now, I will!" retorted the big man who held the gun in his ribs.

"Calm, m'boy," came the steady voice of Joe as he laid a restraining hand on John Stuart's arm. "Stay quiet. She'll come to no harm."

By this time, the leader had opened the coach door.

Eve sat motionlessly as his eyes lit on a soft brown leather shoe and moved up over a dark green skirt to a white bow and the face above.

As his hard blue-gray stare encountered her soft, light brown eyes, Eve felt the oddest sensation. It was almost as if he had touched her, as if there had been physical contact. There was an absurd feeling that time slowed down and that reality distorted and dissolved, that the material things around her, the coach, the gum trees, the men and horses, faded away. She was conscious only of the steely, blue-gray eyes into which she stared, spellbound. She thought she saw suffering, and then tranquillity, as if the suffering were illusion.

"Don't touch her, you scum!" came another shout from John Stuart, and once more he was told to "Shaddup, Wakeman!" and was jabbed in the ribs with the rifle barrel.

The man at the coach door looked away from Eve, and casting a glance around the empty interior, turned abruptly from the coach. Eve experienced a most disturbing feeling, a kind of ebbing of herself after him. It left her disconcerted, confused, and dismayed.

The man with the limp broke from the group and came toward the leader. "Well, guverner, what is it? What's there?"

The bushranger answered. "No money, lad. It seems he speaks the truth."

"Oh no!" said the other as he moved past to the open door. "Well, blast me!" He looked Eve up and down. "Only his woman after all. No payroll! No wonder there was but one guard!"

A general groan of frustration sounded. Then the large man who held the gun on John Stuart shouted, "Well, I'll be buggered if we leave with nothin'. This bastard must have somethin' on him!" With that he pulled on the gold chain hanging from John Stuart's fob pocket and abruptly tugged out the watch. "And this'll do for a start!" He handed his gun to the little man beside him and began to go through the prisoners' pockets while John Stuart and Joe's eyes met. Joe's silent look told his companion to accept and do nothing.

There was a slight lifting of spirits when the bushrangers found ten guineas, four gold sovereigns, and some silver in John Stuart's wallet. And after emptying all four of their captives' pockets, there were seventeen pounds two shillings and six-pence on the ground before them.

Then the man who was still mounted spoke with an Irish lilt. "While it's not a payroll, at all, it'll help us poor unfortunates of the bush to pay our rent!"

Sounds of mirth broke again from the outlaws.

The big man who had just counted the money turned, and lifting his bounty in the air, called, "Well, we've got this, but what about her in the coach, boys? Married to this bastard, she'll have a diamond or two. Bring her out here and let's take a look!"

The leader held out his arm, checking the man's move toward the coach. "We are not down to robbing women, lad. Let her be!"

"Oh, boss! Why not? She's fair game," began the man, looking around sharply, but he did not continue with his complaint, and falling silent, turned moodily back to his prisoners.

"Do like the guverner says!" called the one with the limp as he walked to the horses.

Eve, fascinated, had moved to the open coach door. The man in gray had not once looked back toward her. He now came to a halt in front of her husband. Together, they were somehow overwhelming. They were both imposing, both sun-browned, both ideal physically, both seemingly inflexible; the one dark-eyed, dark-haired, in brown velvet and silk, the other lighter-eyed, lighter-haired, in gray and black. But there was more than their material actuality for Eve; there was an inconceivable "oneness" about them, an immense significance in their being side by side. For the fleeting moments these two men stood together, she was unnaturally alert. Her every sense seemed intensified. It was uncanny. Or was it ridiculous? What was going on? For the second time on her wedding day, a cold chill crept up across her body until she shivered almost uncontrollably. She felt as if she were suspended in a waking dream.

Beneath the mask, the intervening years had made scant change to Alan's face. He was as memorable as ever. The passing of time had drawn his cheeks a little, but there was no marked difference in him. His clean-shaven face was remarkably clear of lines for his years and forever inherent in his expression was the same disturbing mixture of the noble and the simple that had been there in the Southampton courtroom so long ago.

John Stuart examined the man who now stood in front of him. To his surprise, the eyes held no malice. Instead, there was a candor and integrity that he had not expected. Disconcerted, he felt his own anger subside a little.

Alan spoke to him. "Mr. Wakeman, I am sorry to have put you to this inconvenience. I assure you, I would have much preferred your payroll coach to yourself." He began to move away, then suddenly he turned back. "Nevertheless, methinks your priorities need a little readjustment. Four heavily armed guards for your usual pay coach, and only *one* for your wife!"

John Stuart endeavored to control himself, but the anger tumbled out. "The damned roads could be traversed without any guards, if it weren't for the likes of you and your rabble."

Joe stepped forward and broke in quickly, "Now you have our money, will you not leave us in peace?"

Alan glanced at Joe and gave a curt nod of agreement before he turned back to John Stuart. As their eyes met again, John Stuart felt his annoyance subside, for while he knew it was ludicrous, he could not help almost liking the expression he observed. Without speaking, as if he changed his mind about something, Alan turned sharply on his heel and walked to his horse. "Let's go, boys."

The bushrangers climbed into their saddles.

"Yeah, we'd best be goin'; I promised me mum I wouldn't stay out after dark," the big man shouted.

The others all laughed.

Alan mounted his horse, a fine gray stallion sired by the one he had escaped from Moreton Bay upon; and Goya-like, the animal rose up on its hind legs in relief against the shadowy bush.

"Be careful on the rest of your journey, the country's full of bushrangers." And he and his band faded into the rapidly descending night.

Eve moved to the carriage step, watching them depart. John Stuart ran to her. "Are you all right, my love?"

"Yes, darling, perfectly, thank you." She stepped to the ground beside him.

He took her in his arms and kissed her forehead. "What a thing to happen! Where the devil is Sir Rutherford when one wants him?"

Breaking across their thoughts came Deke's voice. "Second time I been held up, it is. Gettin' used to it. First time, it was

Old Joe Daily. This time, I'm for thinkin' it must have been the Hall gang. They be cheeky beggers, right enough.''

John Stuart shook his head. ''No, that was not Ben Hall, of that I'm positive! The leader spoke like an aristocrat. You know, Sir Rutherford mentioned them all, and I'm sure he said one was born into wealth and position, but I'm damned if I recall his name.''

Joe took John Stuart's arm. ''Yes, m'boy, I have heard tell of a gang led by a man they call 'the governor,' and I think we just now had an introduction to the fellow.''

''That's right, they called him 'the governor' right enough, they did,'' muttered Deke, nodding his head in agreement with himself.

Then Timothy spoke up for the first time. ''Mr. Wakeman, sir, I remember what Sir Rutherford said. The bushranger from a rich family was called 'Alan Fletcher.' ''

Eve shivered, and John Stuart's arm went protectively around her shoulder as he replied, ''Yes, Tim, you're correct. Alan Fletcher. I, too, remember now. Well, the roads should be free of them. Damn thieves! I'd like to see them all launched into eternity.''

Joe and Deke grunted approval, but Eve found herself startled at the suggestion. ''John Stuart, how harsh a judgment of them.''

John Stuart squeezed her closer, ''No, my darling, not harsh, just. You are innocent of the ways of the world. One must meet fire with fire.'' Although as he said these words, he remembered the look of benevolence he had recognized in the leader's eyes, the expression he had actually liked, and he added softly, ''I truly wonder what brings them to a life of crime.''

''Yes, I do, too,'' his wife agreed with a faraway look in her eyes.

EIGHT

Mayfield

Eve had been sleeping fitfully for some hours, lying along the length of one of the carriage seats with her head on John Stuart's lap, when he gently woke her. "Darling, wake up. You can see Mayfield House in the distance." His voice was filled with excitement, and the strains of the day had disappeared from his face.

Eve sat up and followed the direction of his hand. They were on high ground, and she noticed the coach was no longer bumping. They had been inside the Mayfield boundary for over two hours, where the roads were known to be the smoothest in the colony. Some were even macadamized. John Stuart had seen this form of road building on a trip to England when he was twenty-one, and being a student of things scientific and new, he had brought the method home.

John Stuart pointed through the window. There, far in the distance on the left, she made out a building, palely illuminated in the night light. "That's it; do you see it?" The pride sounded in his voice.

"Yes, I see it. It shines. It's beautiful."

The master of Mayfield nodded. "I estimate it's well after midnight, though I can't be sure." The oblique reference to his stolen watch caused him to think again of the robbery, but he was soon distracted by the significance of being home, and the enjoyment in pointing things out to Eve.

Soon they passed through two large stone pillars with glowing lamps set in alcoves, and along between an avenue of huge trees. She thought she saw hedges and lawns to right and left.

"Is it a park?" she asked, and John Stuart, smiling, replied,

"Yes, it is. It's almost half a mile in diameter, and Mayfield House sits in the middle."

Eve drew in her breath with surprise. The carriageway was smooth, and as they rolled along, she watched in enchantment, for there were lanterns hanging in the trees, and people lining the drive. "John Stuart, all these people, who are they?" Her voice lifted with excitement.

"They have come to welcome you," he answered, waving through the window to a group of folk who called congratulations loudly as the coach crept by. "It appears a great many have stayed up. Good show!" He was smiling now.

And then the house loomed in front of them. She was amazed at its size; even in the moonlight it was enormous. It reminded her of the Boston mansions of her childhood, only larger, and the whole place seemed to be lit inside and out. She was startled. Everything was so grand . . . the people, the lanterns, the gardens, the house. Suddenly came the awareness that she had married a man whose wealth and position she had estimated quite inadequately. Nothing had prepared her for this magnificence.

As the coach came to a halt, she calculated there must be close to two hundred people gathered to meet them, and it was the middle of the night! The door was opened from outside. John Stuart jumped to the ground and helped her down. As Eve descended, a cheer went up, and a small, sleepy-eyed boy handed her a beautiful bouquet of flowers.

"Why, I . . . thank you."

Her husband took her hand and they ascended to the veranda. There they turned back to face those who had collected to greet them.

John Stuart motioned to Joe to mount the steps and stand closely behind him.

Eve watched her new husband, who seemed happy and composed, make his speech. All the faces were turned toward him expectantly.

"My wife . . ." he touched Eve's arm with a proprietorial movement, "and I have traveled this day from Bathurst, a long journey, as you all realize." There were murmurs of agreement. "We appreciate your patience in waiting until this late hour. That you have done so has made us both proud and grateful, and although we are tired, nothing can spoil the joy of being back home." A cheer greeted these words. Then a change came over his face. Those gathered seemed to notice it, for the cheer was followed by total hush.

"This land of mine . . . of yours also," he said more quietly, lifting his arm in a sweeping motion, "is where my heart lies. I quote my father, Sir Arthur, who used to say, 'Whenever I am away from Mayfield, I am not quite whole.' " For a second or two after this, he did not speak. Then, as if gathering himself together, as if he had shown too much of himself, he finished in the strong voice of the John Stuart they knew so well. "So to one and all I say, sleep well and content, knowing that Mayfield at last has a mistress worthy of it. Tomorrow evening we shall finish our work early, for Mr. Larmer tells me there is to be a general celebration on the lawns, and you are all invited. Good night to you all."

His concluding remark was drowned in the deafening sound of cheers. Then he took up his wife's hand and ushered her through the huge white cedar doors.

Once inside, Eve met Mrs. Smith, the housekeeper, a small woman with a straight back and a severe expression, except when her eyes rested on her master, for then they softened noticeably. She and Mr. Baines, the butler, had seen to it that a marvelous supper was laid in the small dining room, although none of the travelers ate much.

Joe soon bade them good night and left for his own home, a brick house standing at the edge of the park, north of the west gate and built for him in Sir Arthur Wakeman's day.

John Stuart's mind was on their marital bed. The stress and exertion of the day had at last assailed them, but by the time they finally found themselves between soft, luxurious sheets, desire had revived them.

While John Stuart was determined to be a careful lover to his pure, delicate, and good wife, his desire for her was ardent and demanding. As she came to him at the bedside in her white lace gown, he smiled his half smile, and Eve's heartbeat quickened, for he looked like a faultless statue of David come to life in the lamp-glow. She thought him beautifully made, with his perfect features, his wide shoulders, his hard muscles of chest and stomach, and his firm, long body with bronze skin and patches of dark hair. He held out his hands and took hers, bringing her to him and holding her close to press kisses on her forehead, her eyelids, her lips, her neck. She tingled with pleasure as he pushed the lace gown from her shoulders. It slipped cooperatively down. His voice was thick with urgent emotion as he looked at her breasts, her belly, her thighs, in the flickering light.

"You are beautiful, Eve."

He drew her down upon the bed beside him, and his wet mouth passed from her lips down the side of her neck to suckle her hardened nipples. As his hands moved over her skin, fondling, exploring, wanting, needing her, she murmured gentle, willing sounds. She was ready to give herself to their union. When he opened her legs, he whispered, "I want you, I love you," and she replied, "Yes, darling, yes, I love you, too." And as he penetrated her, a tiny murmur escaped her lips and she kissed his mouth, his neck, his wide, smooth shoulders, as he moved within her. He moaned with sweet passion at her surrender, and his pleasure soared.

There was no climax for Eve that first night, but her body had responded fervidly, passionately, to his, and she knew she was falling deeply in love with this wonderful, noble man. Yet for a long time afterward she lay sleepless and disturbed, for once during their lovemaking the memory of the bushranger flashed through her mind. It had been only a second or two, but guilt-stricken, she felt that in some way she had violated their union. And when she finally slept, she was troubled by a dream of a masked man somewhere at hand, whose steely eyes kept finding hers in a swirling mist.

Even though it was cattle that had made Mayfield famous, many square miles were used for farming, so that the property sustained its tenants. There were wheat and cornfields and orchards running along the banks of the Lachlan River. A large dairy sat on the northern bank, and all manner of vegetable crops grew to the south, irrigated by a series of small aqueducts built especially for the purpose by John Stuart, who was constantly reading his scientific journals, and from them, introducing new methods and tools to employ on Mayfield. To sow, he had stump-jump plows; to harvest, the latest reapers with mechanical rakes that swept the cut stalks from a platform to the waiting workers.

Mayfield's northern border was some twenty-five miles long. No other land owned by a single family was even a tenth of the size. The country was good for raising cattle and sheep, and John Stuart and Joe had been the first squatters, as the landowners were known, to sink artesian wells for drinking water for their animals. However, John Stuart, like the cattle barons of the Americas, scorned sheep, though his father had not.

Arthur Francis Wakeman, the founder of Mayfield, had been born in 1798 in England, in the serenity of the Sussex countryside. The graceful village of his birth, Mayfield, sat on the high weald, and from almost any part of it, there were sweeping views down across the serene green woods and farmland.

Arthur loved this place of his boyhood, the tranquillity and beauty of his surroundings. He played in the grassy banks and hedgerows and lay on his back in the meadows, watching skylarks high in the heavens, on the long evenings of midsummer.

His father was a small freehold farmer, his mother the daughter of the village tailor. Arthur, the youngest of three, was a thoughtful boy who liked his own company. He would often wander alone through the yard of the village church, St. Dunstan's, after a day spent in the church school. He read aloud from the tombstones in a deep and somber voice and sat musing for an hour at a time under the dark old yew tree in the corner of the yard.

It was here on his fifteenth birthday that his second cousin, Millicent Baker, found him. His serious, young face lit up, for he liked his cousin. During their conversation, he read the nearest tombstone to her. "Here lyeth the body of Thomas Sands who was buried May the 15, 1713 aged 72 years." The two 7's had been carved backward and Millicent, finding it amusing, began to laugh. Soon Arthur's face lightened and he smiled at her. "You know Millicent, that is exactly one hundred years ago, as it is May fifteenth, 1813 today and I am taking it as an omen."

His cousin looked at him in wonder. "An omen?"

He became grave again. "I love this village and the peace of it and this church yard. But there is more out there. Even beyond London . . . far away." He waved his arm in a wide arc. "There is something in me telling me not to live out seventy-two years here as old Thomas Sands did a hundred years ago."

Her happy eyes clouded over, for what he said frightened her. No one she had ever known had gone further than London. "But where will you go, Arthur?"

"I don't know yet. But I know I'm going to leave Mayfield. My brothers seem content to stay here, but not me. All I know is I am going across the seas. It is 1813, Millicent, and the world is large."

At the very moment he spoke, in a land thirteen thousand miles to the south, three men, and their company, were trudging across tall wooded "Blue Mountains" finding the pass to the plains beyond; finding the pass over which he, Arthur Wakeman, would journey in less than ten years from this day, to his "Mayfield of the southland" and his future.

He took his schooling in Tunbridge Wells and London, and he qualified as a surveyor in the late summer of 1820, when he was twenty-two. In October of that year, he sailed to the colony of New South Wales, as a crown surveyor, under the new governor, Brigadier General Sir Thomas Brisbane.

He landed in Sydney town, and during the following January, he crossed the pass over the Blue Mountains. For the next three and a half years he surveyed much of the land southwest of the tiny settlement of Bathurst. There were only 114 people in the district, including 75 convicts. His field trips were mostly made from a small convict settlement north of the Lachlan River.

He was a thorough and competent young man, and his ability was obvious. His work soon drew the attention of his superiors, and for services rendered, the outgoing governor granted him two thousand acres of the land he had surveyed. Arthur Wakeman called it "Mayfield" after that other part of the earth he felt was his. With a few assigned convicts and ticket-of-leave men, as convicts granted partial freedom were called, he successfully ran some sheep and grew crops. But it was during the office of the next governor, Lieutenant General Ralph Darling, that he expanded his claim. He bought another two thousand acres of Crown land at five shillings an acre on the southern bank of the Lachlan, opposite the land he now owned.

As his enterprises flourished, so did he benefit, and by 1826 he had been granted another, larger, tract of land to the south.

Subsequently he ventured into cattle. By now, it seemed that Arthur Wakeman had the golden touch. In 1827, with a few other squatters, he opened a bank; and in that same year, he married Caroline Barnett, the youngest daughter of a Scottish nobleman. The marriage had been arranged between the two parties with the help of the governor, who saw the prosperous young Wakeman as his protégé. In March 1828 John Stuart was born, and his father continued expanding his claim to the south and the east. By 1830, Mayfield had became the largest property in the land, and was still developing.

Arthur Wakeman had grown to cherish this Mayfield, where a man could ride all day and still be unconfined, just as he did the memory of those emerald meadows and dales so far away. There was a tenderness in his heart as he watched the sun set behind the grand white house he was building on a hillside a mile north of the river.

Arthur Francis Wakeman, at the age of thirty-two, had become a man to be reckoned with. Wealthy and influential men fostered friendships with him. He was a force in both the economics and the politics of the colony. But, as fate has a way of disregarding achievement, it was in this year that the two great catastrophes of his life occurred.

He had planned to bring his mother and father from the sleepy English village to reside with him in the grand style he now could offer them. The ship that was to bring them arrived at Sydney Quay in August without them. Instead of his parents, there was a letter from his father informing him his darling mother had died in the winter, and that he, Arthur's father, could not envisage the long sea journey without her.

To sublimate his grief in the months that followed, he toiled alongside his men, branding, farming, building, fencing, and running roads across the miles of Mayfield.

Then came the second blow: his marriage failed. There had been an affair with an army officer. Perhaps Caroline had been left too much on her own; whatever the cause, the result was her departure. In August 1831 she returned to her family in Scotland, leaving her three-year-old son behind with his father. She had had no choice in the matter. Arthur Wakeman was the powerful one, and he wanted his son.

Thus it was a new, and even more determined, Arthur Wakeman who looked on New Year's Day 1832. From then on, it seemed he was endowed with second sight in matters material. With his influence, he expanded Mayfield even more and was able to buy land to the south and west in enormous tracts.

At this time he went into the exporting of red cedar to England and the Cape Colony, proving exceedingly successful, and by the late 1840s his ability and efficiency had made Mayfield fabled. He and his growing son could afford to live in the style of European noblemen.

He never communicated with his wife again. Neither did he see England, though he thought it necessary to send John Stuart, in the keeping of Joe Larmer, on a visit "home," as he called it, when the boy was twenty-one.

Arthur Francis Wakeman was knighted when he was forty-five years old and died of pneumonia at fifty-seven, after insisting that he participate in a cattle drive which drove into wind and rain for four days on end. To his son, he left his greatest legacy, Mayfield. John Stuart was determined to follow in his footsteps.

NINE

Clare

The first months of Eve and John Stuart's marriage passed peacefully. They were days of discovery for Eve about her new home and those who inhabited it. As mistress of Mayfield, she was enthusiastic and earnest, finding her new role stimulating and exciting, even daunting at times, when she realized what the extent of her responsibilities could really be. But she was determined to accomplish all she could, and she spent weeks learning how the huge property functioned. At first, when she would arrive back from having watched the herding of cattle, or men fencing, or the harvesting of crops, or visiting the stockmen's wives, John Stuart would smile indulgently. But he gradually saw that the days she passed in these ways, and the time she spent studying inventories and assisting Mr. Oldfield, his secretary, were not an indulgence. Eve was serious about being mistress of so much and so many.

She was also serious about her role as his wife. In their intimate moments, she was passionate and loving to him, giving herself freely and responding to him with a vibrancy and ardor he took delight in sharing. He was proud of her, certain in his view that she was unequaled by others: unadulterated, good, charitable, and tender, and she was proud of him, and deeply impressed by his abilities: his organized mind, his skill with animals and with men, his intelligence, his scientific knowledge, and his kindness.

If ever a stray thought of Clare or the disconcerting memory of the bushranger found their way to Eve's mind, she would adroitly block them from her consciousness, so determined was she to hold the peace of these days. She had this power over her waking hours, but when she slept, too often her dreams were frequented by the outlaw. She was disturbed by this, so she finally examined her feelings about the bushranger, and realized she was so in love with her husband that she dismissed any sensations she had felt for the other man as superficial fascination for an outlaw.

One Monday morning in winter, Eve was taking her usual walk. She had always liked walking, and now, with so large a property at her disposal, she did so almost daily. Sometimes Thelma joined her, or she took Stephanie, her personal maid, a sweet-natured girl of eighteen, but Eve enjoyed walking swiftly and so often preferred to take her exercise alone. One of her favorite paths was along the Lachlan to the east from Larmer's Crossing, as the tree-trunk bridge over the Lachlan was known. While it was cold, it was a pleasant morning, for the sun was mounted in a cloudless sky and there was no wind.

Eve looked across the river to where the married workers' cottages stood. The first of them was about a hundred or so yards away from the bank, beyond clumps of vine, scrub, tall grass, and wildflowers.

A spot of blue was moving in Eve's direction, about thirty yards across the Lachlan. It was a little girl, no more than two years old, wobbling happily through the grass. Eve's eyes scanned the bush, but there was no one about. The child was alone. What was she doing down here? A chill ran through Eve as the infant came toward the opposite bank, heading straight at the river. The Lachlan here was not deep, but there was a current, and it was about four feet to the bottom.

Eve had learned all the children's names, and she knew each one. It was little Laura Dale who ran so merrily toward danger.

"Laura, stop!"

Then the child appeared to see Eve, and laughing more, accelerated.

"Go back, Laura. Stop! No! No!"

But the baby was oblivious to what lay ahead, and on she came to the water's edge.

Eve continued to cry out even as she threw off her shoes and ripped off her jacket and skirt. Laura, heedless of her peril, plunged over the side of the bank into the Lachlan. Laura's cry sounded, plaintive and shocked, before she sank, and Eve jumped in the bitterly cold water. Reeds caught at Eve's arms and pantaloons as she fought through the river, but her whole being was focused on getting to Laura, who was struggling beneath the water. Eve used every ounce of strength she had to wade, push, and strive. She felt her foot hit something sharp, and pain seared up through her leg, but still she urged herself forward.

The icy water was taking her breath away, and Eve realized with horror that the current was beginning to move Laura downstream. She attempted to throw herself to the baby, even as Laura's body turned in a swirling movement away from her. With a last, violent effort Eve forced herself forward, arms outstretched, and she felt her fingers contact the material of Laura's dress. She grabbed hold with every ounce of strength she had.

She was gasping and choking, but her grip remained fast, while her other arm came around. She took the baby in her arms, and lifting her head up above the water, staggered to the bank and up onto dry land.

She was shivering; her teeth chattering, and her foot hurting but all her attention was on Laura. The child did not seem to be breathing. Oh Lord, what to do? She stopped herself from panicking and tried to think. John Stuart had told her about a method of reviving people when she had described to him the boat accident in Sydney Harbor. You had to push the water out of them. She looked in Laura's mouth, and it was empty. She turned the baby over on her tummy, putting her tiny head to the side. Then, gently, she began to push on the child's back, praying fiercely all the time.

Push . . . push . . . Come on, Laura, please. Oh Lord, please let her live, please let her live. Push . . . push.

Then a tremor of delighted relief ran throughout Eve's whole body, for the little one gave a gurgle and a cough and began to breathe again.

Mrs. Dale's eyes widened in absolute astonishment when she answered the insistent knocking on her back door. There stood the mistress in her pantaloons, with blood on her foot, holding Laura in her arms, both soaking wet, and looking bedraggled and half-drowned.

"Good Lord have mercy!" the woman exclaimed, and gathered up her child in relief as she heard what had happened.

That very afternoon, Eve went to see Jack Hennessy, Joe Larmer's able second-in-command, who had his offices close by the stables. Her foot was bandaged where she had cut it on the rock in the river, and as she limped into his office, he stood quickly from behind his desk. She came swiftly to the reason for her visit.

"Mr. Hennessy, this morning a baby almost drowned in the Lachlan. I want to make sure that such a thing cannot happen again. If a fence were to be built along the southern bank of the Lachlan, the children would be safe. I would like to know how long it would take and how much it would cost."

Jack Hennessy looked thoughtful. "It would depend on the length of it, and what sort of a fence it was."

Eve unfolded a map she had drawn. "Mrs. Larmer and I have measured the distance and I think it should go from here," she said, pointing to Larmer's Crossing, "and run for, say, four hundred yards."

Jack Hennessy nodded. "Are we speaking of a wooden fence or a stone wall, Mrs. Wakeman?"

Eve thought for a minute. "Whatever is most effective, I suppose."

He stood. "Then I'll just get Stephen Watson in, Mrs. Wakeman. He is the one who knows exact costs of this sort of thing."

That night, when John Stuart came home, he was surprised and upset to hear of his wife's adventure.

"Darling, you were wonderful. But it concerns me to think that you were all alone when such a thing occurred. Not only was the child in danger, but so, too, were you."

"No, my love, I was not really, for the Lachlan is not deep there. It's only that there is a current." Then she took him by the arm. "Now, please come and sit down, for I have something I wish to discuss with you."

She guided him to a sofa and began. "I want to make certain that no other of our Mayfield children can wander into such life-threatening peril again. So, my love, with your permission, I would like to have a fence built along the southern side of the river." She brought out her map and traced along it for him as she had done for Jack Hennessy.

John Stuart smiled tolerantly at her. "Eve, a fence down there might be unsightly. We've deliberately not built anything there, to keep the look of the bushland near the cottages. And in any case, this is something for Jack Hennessy or Stephen Watson. I don't know if we've got the men or the time to do it, and we would have to know the cost."

She nodded and unfolded another piece of paper, starting to read. "If the wall were stone, it would have to be quarried, and that is time-consuming and expensive. So the best fence seems to be a wooden one, along which we could plant creepers and vines. Within two summers it will be covered so densely, it will look like part of the bushland. A team of twelve men will put up a wooden fence four feet high and three hundred and fifty yards long in seven to ten days. Mr. Hennessy has assured me he can spare the men." She handed her husband the paper. "I have detailed costs of everything here."

John Stuart was looking at her with a strange expression on his face. "You have been to Jack Hennessy with all this already?"

"Yes, this afternoon."

Sometimes he did not know what to make of his vivacious, vital, determined wife. Each day she surprised him in some way or other. She was conscientious and caring and so very dear to him. He shook his head in obvious admiration. "It seems you move with great speed when you have an idea in your head, Mrs. Wakeman."

She smiled with satisfaction. "So, dear Mr. Wakeman, do we have the master's permission to put up the fence?"

He laughed, drew her to him, and kissed her. "How could I refuse?"

The fence was up by the time Eve's birthday approached, and one Sunday afternoon John Stuart and Eve went over to inspect it. As they returned toward Larmer's Crossing, they passed some workers coming from church in Cowra, which was close to eighteen miles from Mayfield House. Fortunately, ten of those miles were within the boundary of Mayfield, where the roads were sealed. Even so, it took the faithful the better part of the day to make the pilgrimage.

That religion was indispensible to most people was a fact that John Stuart tolerated and did not try to change. He employed Protestant and Catholic alike, and would have employed Jews had there been any, but there were few in this Christian land. His money and influence allowed him to hold his unconventional views without penalty. Nevertheless, his often-repeated statement "Priests are parasites, whatever their color" did shock his wife, and she answered him quite sternly with an energetic defense of Father and all those like him of all religions. To this he simply nodded and gave her his beguiling half smile and she begged him never to say it in front of other people. "I have said it to Joe," he replied. "Yes," she answered, "but Joe would let you blaspheme at the Lord Himself, so much does he care about you. Please promise me you will say it to no one else." The people Eve had known in her life were all of some religious faith or other, and she had never really thought about rejecting Jesus or debating belief in God, she respected her handsome, intelligent, articulate, deeply philosophical husband for coming to his own conclusions about life and the universe. It never occurred to her to judge him.

As Eve rode with him now along the path toward the river, the churchgoers waved. Eve looked to him. "I miss Sundays at All Saints'; it was such a part of my life with Father and Mother."

Her husband turned in the saddle to face her. "Mmm, I know. But after all, you do go to service in Cowra every other week with Thelma."

"Yes, and I appreciate that you realize how important it is to me, for I know you are a heathen." She sighed, then teased him. "And I know now why you were over thirty before you married."

He looked quizzically. "Oh, and why is that?"

"It was your fear of having to go inside a church!"

John Stuart burst into laughter, then took her hand.

"Ah, Eve, my father was a godly man, but I fear he lacked discipline with my religious training. All my tutors were men of science, thinkers. I was taught to be rational." He smiled in recollection. "And there was not a religious establishment between here and yours at Bathurst when I was growing, I'm glad to say. So there you are. You are lucky I let you drag me just the once to an altar."

She laughed, "John Stuart, you are incorrigible!"

They rode on in silence for a few minutes, John Stuart on Diomed, his chestnut stallion, Eve on Moonlight, one of her wedding gifts. He still held her hand, and squeezing it, he asked, "What is it you would like most for your birthday? It will be upon us in three weeks. How would you like to spend the day? Shall we grant a holiday like the queen does on the twenty-fourth of May?"

Eve smiled. "No, my love, I do not consider myself in quite the same class as Victoria." A small frown appeared on her brow. "But there is one thing I would enjoy more than anything else."

"And what is that?"

"I would like you to invite Father and Mother here to celebrate it."

John Stuart let go of her hand and rubbed his chin. "Damn it, Eve, you have the better of me. Now I must agree. It seems

I must have religion under my very roof to sup with me, now that you are my wife.''

''It will do you good. And thank you for consenting to my request in such an enthusiastic manner.''

He gave his hearty laugh again, then leaned back in the saddle.

''I'll race you back to the stables for a—'' Before he could finish, she had sped Moonlight forward over the long grass toward the river. ''Cheat! Cheat!'' he shouted. ''You did not wait to hear my wager.''

She beat him to the stables by a head, and they dismounted into each other's arms, laughing and teasing with unrestrained enjoyment.

Nineteen days later, Father and Mother Billings arrived in the Mayfield coach, which had been sent for them. John Stuart was a man who did not overmuch like houseguests, whoever they were. They threw off his routine and robbed him of his precious hours on his land. Only once a year, at Christmas, would he grudgingly ask some of his friends, including the governor, down for a week.

Because the parson and his wife were staying, however, John Stuart had decided to make a celebration of Eve's day and had arranged a dinner party. A string and woodwind octet would play, and a singer would entertain. John Stuart had invited twelve in all: Thelma, Joe, and Daydee would be there, of course, and an ebullient middle-aged couple, Stanley and Myrtle Ford, graziers who owned a property on the western side of Cowra. They were coming with their twenty-five-year-old son, Roy, a gentle young man, who was extremely fond of Daydee.

John Stuart's friend, Sir Rutherford Blake, was in Cowra at present with his assistant, five police troopers, and Sir Frederick Pottinger. They were interviewing victims of Old Joe Daily's, a bushranger who had been carrying out holdups on the Sydney road north of the township, so Sir Rutherford and Mr. Elrington would make up the company of twelve. The latter five would stay overnight.

Eve's birthday was, in the main, a happy day for her. The only moments that marred it were when thoughts of Clare came to her mind and the old dissatisfaction with herself for not having told John Stuart about her sister rose within her. But she quashed these reflections as she always had before. She, Mother, and Thelma spent the morning arranging dozens of magnificent flowers that had appeared overnight, while Father, trying to read the latest *London Times*, looked up at them indulgently every now and then from behind his spectacles.

Later, he and Eve rode for two hours along the Lachlan together. They had missed each other and spoke those inmost private things that they had been unable to say for many months.

Eve told him how she was settling into life on Mayfield. "This place is so easy to love, Father, and I feel such a part of it already. John Stuart jokes that 'Mayfield' is written on his heart." They both laughed. "He is so kind and generous. And what do you think? He knows every single man who works here by name, though there are hundreds. He quite amazes me. I'm so lucky. And, if it's possible, each day I am falling more in love with him."

That evening, around half past the hour of seven, when all were dressing for the birthday party, John Stuart was passing through Eve's sitting room carrying his silk shirt, his collar studs, and his necktie. Suddenly one of the small studs fell from his fist and landed in an open trunk. The trunk had only arrived the day before with Mother and Father. It contained the last of Eve's personal goods, mainly sheets of music that had been at the rectory in Bathurst.

"Damn," John Stuart said as he saw the tiny thing disappearing into the piles of music. Kneeling, he put the other items on the floor and, lifting a stack of sheets out of the trunk, burrowed down into the papers searching for the stud. When he found it, he began to replace the music that had now splayed out onto the floor. As he did, his brows drew together. He had noticed the name "Clare Herman" written on one of the sheets. He lifted it and looked more closely. It was Eve's handwriting. Now he saw a few others with the same name.

Who was Clare Herman? He knew Eve's mother's name had been Ada. Then he nodded to himself; more than likely another relative, a cousin or aunt. He straightened the heaps of sheet music in the trunk and closed the lid.

By the time his wife entered his dressing room five minutes later, he had forgotten the incident and was tying a bow at his throat and thinking about the cornfield Joe had a mind to plant a few miles to the east. Eve had donned her gown, a shimmering pale pink silk that was cut wide at the neck and embroidered with masses of deep pink beads down across the tightly fitting bodice. Her curls hung loosely over her shoulders. "Do you want some help with your bow, my love?" she asked.

For answer he stopped what he was doing and smiled.

She came to him and began to tie the bow. In the lamplight, the rounded tops of her breasts showed a creamy gold, and the perfume of her drifted seductively up to John Stuart's nostrils. "You are so beautiful, my lovely Eve."

She looked up. "And so are you."

His half smile played on his mouth. "Men are not 'beautiful.'"

"You are," she answered, standing on tiptoe and kissing him lightly on his mouth as his arms slid around her.

"Now I have you," he laughed. "You cannot slip away."

She smiled. "Perhaps I don't wish to."

Their lips reached for each other. The kiss lasted a long time. John Stuart whispered into her curls, "We have to meet our guests downstairs in less than thirty minutes."

She kissed the side of his neck as she whispered in reply, "I know."

His tongue touched the lobe of her ear. "This is silly," he murmured.

Again she whispered, "I know," playfully running her fingers through his hair.

"We should stop," he replied, kissing the side of her neck.

"I know we should," she answered.

In one movement, they snaked slowly down to the thick Axminster carpet, the bow tie so recently tied, untied, and the silk shirt cast on top of it. While the series of hooks at the back of Eve's dress cooperated with John Stuart's fingers to enticingly deliver her breasts to him.

They rolled together, in that delicious hunger called desire, until Eve parted her legs to feel the exquisite strength of her husband push in and drive down inside her, and the two beautiful, naked bodies fulfilled their need.

"I'm wrong," he said, when at last the final vibration of pleasure rippled through them, and he came to rest upon her. "This is not silly at all."

She laughed up at him. "I'm glad I hadn't done my hair."

The host and hostess did in fact keep their guests waiting, but only briefly. They made their entry hand in hand, Eve radiant, and John Stuart debonair.

John Stuart sat at the head of the mahogany table, which could seat twenty-six when fully extended. Behind him hung a portrait of Sir Arthur and himself at sixteen, painted by Conrad Martens, one of the very few portraits this early leader of the Australian school had ever done. Martens had been parliamentary librarian and painting in his spare time when Arthur Wakeman had met him in Sydney.

Sir Arthur had fostered colonial art' and he had remained a patron of the colonies' painters all his life.

The dining room was reminiscent of the regal rooms in the royal houses of Europe, and tonight's handsome inhabitants were lit by four magnificent chandeliers hanging from the sixteen-foot-high ceiling. On Eve's right was Father. On John Stuart's right was Joe. The meal progressed. The food was splendid. The wine flowed. The musicians played softly. The conversation sparkled.

At first, Daydee spoke little. Roy, who was obviously keen to talk with her, worked hard to get any acknowledgment. She sat rather sedately, until John Stuart directed some questions specifically to her. To these she replied eagerly with an animated smile. From then on, she brightened visibly and began bestowing a sweet smile on Roy, who glowed with appreciation. Only once after that did her eyes lose their merriment: when John Stuart stood to propose a toast to his wife. As everyone turned to their host, she looked back down the table to Eve, and her eyes narrowed with hate. The expression spanned scarcely a second, and Eve was oblivious. Her mind was elsewhere. The guests rose and drank to her health, and when she in turn stood to reply, there was a flush of pink in her cheeks as she spoke to them. It was as she sat down that Clare rose uncomfortably in her mind. Clare, Clare, beautiful, loquacious, enchanting. Who are you wasting yourself upon tonight? I wonder where you are. If only you were here. Her head dropped slightly and her face became grave. Suddenly she was aware of Father holding her forearm and saying in a quiet voice, "Eve . . . Evvy, what is wrong?"

She looked up into his eyes. "Oh, nothing, Father dear, nothing."

He smiled gently. "Come, my Evvy, no painful thoughts tonight," he whispered.

The birthday cake arrived, a grand three-tiered arrangement with an exquisite white marchpane house, representing Mayfield, on top, and iced yellow roses trailing down the sides. The words HAPPY BIRTHDAY DEAR EVELYN were written around each of the tiers, and the candles burned brightly.

She had never seen a cake like it. It was exquisite. She closed her eyes and made her wish. Clare, I am so happy, and thus my wish is for you. I want you to have peace and happiness wherever you are.

At the end of the meal, John Stuart called for Mr. Free, who, in the European manner, liked to be known as the "chef," and everyone applauded his work. Then the ladies retired to the drawing room to await the men who continued to sit some twenty minutes or so, as Victorians did, and discussed those subjects, which in delusion, they believed women should not hear.

When they rejoined the ladies, the singer entertained them, and Daydee recited, at John Stuart's request, "Ode to the West Wind."

Eve circulated among the guests. She was speaking with Mr. Ford when Sir Rutherford joined them. She thought him good-looking in an austere fashion, his sharp, aquiline features reminding her of a hawk.

"Mrs. Wakeman," he began. His heavy-lidded eyes looked penetratingly at her. "We have spoken little this night. I've heard you were the victim of a robbery by these damned bushrangers, and on your wedding day, no less. Ah yes, well I can assure you that if any man will stamp them out, he stands before you now."

"Hardly a victim, Sir Rutherford. They took nothing from me."

"Surely your husband's loss is yours, madam?"

Eve was saved from replying by Mr. Ford's interjection. "There is too much of it. Far too much of it. The roads used to be safe. But one's not sure anymore."

Sir Rutherford nodded enthusiastically. "Ah yes, Mr. Ford, it is my task to bring your roads back to safety. As I was saying to Mr. Wakeman over dinner, this idea of controlling the police force entirely from Sydney is a foolish move. It's allowing these 'wild colonial boys' full reign. But then, the force has asked for my expertise, and in that, they have offset their mistake. The outlaws are becoming cocky, almost arrogant. Only a month ago, the police magistrate in Wagga Wagga—what a quaint name that is—was held up by a fellow I'm sure was this damnable Dan Morgan. Ah yes, I'm working on a trap for him right now. Have posted two hundred and fifty pounds reward on him, and though Frank Gardiner has disappeared, we've not heard the last of him. Just between us, he's gone north, if I've guessed correctly."

Eve did not like this subject. More and more, bushrangers were the topic of conversation, and while she could not explain the reason, it unsettled her.

She had been delighted when John Stuart had seated Sir Rutherford next to him, far away from her, at dinner, for Sir Rutherford's whole raison d'être seemed to be to annihilate the bushrangers from the earth. She wanted desperately to forgo this conversation and was looking around to escape when her husband joined them and lifted her arm through his, blocking any hope she had of leaving.

The saturnine Sir Rutherford smiled at John Stuart. Even when he smiled, he seemed somber. "Mine host, we are discussing the bushranging vermin again."

"Having experienced a holdup, we are all for ridding the country of them, aren't we, dear?" John Stuart looked down at his wife. Eve attempted a smile.

Sir Rutherford's keen gaze passed from one to the other of his three listeners. "Do not worry. These characters will all make mistakes in the end, and I'll be there when they do. As for pardoning the devils, like they did with Martin Cash in Hobart town just last June, damn foolish, encourages people to break the law. 'Break those who break the law,' that's my motto. And as for printing letters written by them! I must say the *Lachlan Miner* has much to answer for. To have truck with such as 'Darkie' Gardiner, and to print his boastful reproaches, now, that is plainly foolish." His voice had been filling the room, and Daydee, Roy, and David Elrington moved closer to listen.

"Ah yes, it is mostly greed that leads them to become outlaws. Yet they all believe they've been forced into it. More often than not, they simply have grudges against society, which they translate as griefs. This Ben Hall blames the world for his wife's running off with another man, so he becomes a bushranger. And Dan Morgan's another one, a thief who loses a finger in a prison quarry and holds it against the police. Then Frank Gardiner, 'Prince of Tobymen,' as he so pathetically calls himself, has aboriginal blood he can't forget. Ah yes, 'Darkie.' Not only is he illegitimate, but he holds it against his mother for being a half-caste it seems, so he takes it out on decent, law-abiding folk."

"That is terrible," Eve said.

"What, dear?" asked her husband.

"Frank Gardiner's holding a grudge against his mother because of her aboriginal blood."

Her husband nodded thoughtfully, while the police detective answered, "You are right, madam. It is terrible. But with a man like him, if it were not that, it would be something else. Ah yes, they've all got their excuses."

Eve listened uneasily. She was thinking how positive Sir Rutherford was of his own judgment. She wished she could be as sure of *anything* as he seemed of *everything*. There was little doubt that he was highly intelligent, of course, but she wondered at the reasons for his staunchness on this subject.

Daydee stood next to John Stuart, and in an attempt to gain attention, she tossed her hair back over her shoulder. "What of the gang who robbed Uncle John Stuart? At dinner you agreed it was Alan Fletcher; tell us more about him."

"Ah yes, Miss Daydee. Now, that damn blackguard, he and his men have been on the run for ten years. Made his way south from the Moreton Bay area a decade ago, but he is a different case. He was a convict, ah yes indeed, a 'lifer,' a killer! But he is educated, runs his men like an army. He will be harder to take than the others, but they all make mistakes in the end."

He now turned to Eve, alight with excitement at the information he passed on. "Do you know, Mrs. Wakeman, he was from a viceregal family? His mother's father was a Braintree. Spent years in Lahore as governor of the Punjab. What a scandal it was, his grandson a murderer. And his father was old Sir Graham Fletcher, a squire in Somerset, knighted for his work with the public hospitals, a philanthropist. Ah yes, Alan Fletcher would have inherited the lands and farms, some of the richest in England. He'd had a ship of his own in the navy, he was someone in society. What a disgrace it—"

"Excuse me, Sir Rutherford," Eve broke into his sentence, "but I . . . have left something in the dining room. Please excuse me."

She turned from the group and walked away.

Her husband's eyes widened in surprise, and the detective policeman watched her for a few seconds, an expression both puzzled and curious on his face, before he turned back to his remaining listeners.

Fifteen minutes later, they had all retired to their rooms, and Mrs. Smith and her staff were tidying up. It was close to half past one o'clock in the morning, and the night had been a huge success.

John Stuart turned to his wife as he took off his shirt. "Evelyn?"

"Yes, dear."

"The way you walked out on Rutherford . . . Well, darling, it was a little rude."

"Oh, sweetheart, I am tired of all his talk of bushrangers. The man eats and sleeps them."

Her husband smiled. "Well, yes, he does at that. Nevertheless—"

She came to him, and placing her hands on his naked chest, looked up at him. "Darling, please let's not talk about this anymore."

"All right, my love, you are right, I suppose. He does go on a bit." He bent down, and enveloping her in his arms, kissed her and immediately forgot about Sir Rutherford.

"Perhaps," she said as he lifted his mouth from hers, "I could ask you for one more gift?" Her eyes invited him; her half-open lips allured him; the pressure of her breasts against him tempted him.

"I gave it to you before dinner," he replied with a smile. Then as his mouth found hers again, he murmured, "But as it's your birthday . . ."

Afterward, John Stuart fell quickly to sleep, and by the hour of two, Mayfield House was quiet.

The guest of honor, however, lay awake as the hours passed. Alan Fletcher . . . Alan Fletcher . . . Why did his eyes rise out of the blackness around her? Son of a knight! Grandson of a governor! Born to wealth! But a convict. A killer! No, he could not be! She did not want him to be. She felt cold. She felt hot. She could not get comfortable. What had happened to her that afternoon at the coach door? Or had she imagined it all? The man had only looked at her, for heaven's sake. She must forget him. This was madness! With a murmur of frustration, she nestled closer to John Stuart, and turning her thoughts to him, finally she fell asleep.

The next morning, she went down to breakfast nearly two hours later than usual. She found that Sir Rutherford and his assistant, Mr. Elrington, had left hastily after news had been brought early by messenger that Ben Hall's gang had made a daring raid on the town of Orange forty-eight hours before. The same night, patrons at a ball in Forbes had been bailed up.

The Fords acquainted her with the news as she arrived in the hall outside the breakfast room. They had already eaten and were about to return to their rooms to pack and take their leave.

John Stuart had ridden out to his day's work long before. He was supervising fencing over an hour's ride from Mayfield House, in the northwest corner of the property, so Eve found only Mother and Father in the breakfast room. They had obviously eaten at a leisurely pace, waiting for her arrival.

Father looked as if he, too, had not slept well. He seemed pensive and quiet. Mother, in her passive, calm way, also seemed more than usually thoughtful.

When finally the serving girl and Baines, the butler, left the room, Eve asked, "My two loves, what is it that makes you so preoccupied this morning?"

The cleric looked apprehensively at his wife. She nodded in reply to his unspoken question, and reluctantly he began, "Darling." His pale eyes were lit with concern, and he leaned across to where she sat, and touched her hand. "There is a letter. I have been carrying it since we arrived, but didn't want to give it to you until after your birthday. Let us meet in the garden when you have finished breakfast."

Eve now looked thoughtful herself. "Yes, dear, of course. We shall go to the garden bower, by my rooms. No one will be there. Will you come, Mother?"

"No, I have promised Thelma to go with her to the mothers' sewing bee this morning, and it is better that you and Father have the time alone. I must hurry or I'll be late." She kissed them and left.

"What is the letter, Father?"

"I do not know, my love. It is from Adelaide. I shall get it and meet you in the garden in five minutes."

When he came to her, she was waiting for him. As he descended the few steps from the veranda and walked toward her, she looked so lovely, he felt a funny little tremor in his chest, and he stood perfectly still for a few seconds looking at her. She was sitting on a wooden seat, wearing a warm mustard-colored gown and matching shawl. The early-blooming wattle tree beside her had brought forth the first of its golden buds. The morning sun filtered through the branches onto the soft fairness of her hair. To his eyes, the scene had an unreality about it, as if it were a painting where the artist had completed his picture, then covered his canvas in gold. He sighed as he touched the letter in his pocket and walked to her.

She moved to make room for him to sit, and as she did, he withdrew the envelope from his pocket, large and official-looking.

"It came a week ago, Evvy, and as I knew I was coming here, it was timely for me to bring it. It is marked Adelaide General Hospital and Sanitorium. I have not opened it."

"But, Father, what can this mean?"

A look of apprehension came into Eve's face. She turned the letter over in her hands, not wanting to open it. She heard the wild, harsh call of a crow somewhere over the house, and the barking of the dogs down across the park carried clearly to the garden. It was very quiet here under the trees, and when Father gave a small cough, it sounded loud to his own ears.

Eve tried to smile as he patted her arm, saying, "Perhaps you would rather read it in private, darling." He began to rise.

Eve stayed him with her hand. "Please, Father, no. I'd much rather you were here with me."

It was addressed to Miss Evelyn May Herman. Her hand trembled a little as she opened the envelope. There were two pages, and as she read them, she made small sounds of disbelief, and her eyes blurred with tears. When she turned her distraught face to Father, she tried to speak, but the words caught in her throat.

"My dear, dear, Evvy, what is it?"

Silently she handed the papers to him.

The first was on official paper from the superintendent of the Adelaide Hospital. It was dated September 9, 1863, and it read:

Dear Miss Herman,

It is with great reluctance that I find it my sad duty to inform you of your sister's death.

Sarah Clare Herman passed away in my hospital on this day of our Lord, September 9, 1863. The cause of her demise is listed with the Crown Coroner's Office as pulmonary consumption. Miss Herman was admitted to the care of this institution only one week ago.

She was beyond medical help, and only through the painstaking nursing of my staff did she endure these seven days.

She named you as her only kith and kin, and what possessions she brought with her are here for you to claim.

Yours faithfully,
Thomas Greer, Superintendent

The second page was a short letter from the Reverend Albert Durst of St. David's Church of England, River Road, Adelaide. It had been written three days later, and it read:

Dear Miss Herman,

Allow me to offer my deepest sympathy to you on the sad passing of your sister.

Your sister, Sarah Clare Herman, requested, and was given, a church burial according to the last rites of the Church of England. She lies at rest in the East Cemetery, Adelaide, C. of E. section, grave no. 245. God rest her soul. There were funds enough to cover her burial, but very little else, I am sorry to inform you.

I knew her not, but deemed it my responsibility to inter her as one of the flock after conversing with her in the Adelaide Hospital, where she took Communion shortly before she passed away.

> *Yours sincerely,*
> *Albert Durst,*
> *Rector, Saint David's Parish,*
> *Adelaide*

When Father had finished reading, he said quietly, "God Almighty, suffer the soul of Clare Herman to reside with you in Paradise this day, in the name of the Father and of the Son and of the Holy Ghost."

Then he turned to face the pallid woman beside him. Her lovely face was streaked with tears, and they continued to run in a stream down across her cheeks. Some fell from her chin, staining the mustard gown. She looked pathetic and childlike in her grief. He opened his arms, and she flung herself into them, the misery and the confusion and the pain she felt for Clare all bursting from her.

He held her safe and patted her hair and whispered words of comfort that parents say to their suffering children, and yet she cried on.

She sobbed for all that had been Clare. She sobbed for the wayward little girl, mischievous, fickle, yet captivatingly lovable. She sobbed for the beautiful, willful young woman, full of spirit and defying social standards. She sobbed for the frivolous grown woman who had continued to use her sexuality as her only resource in a man's world. And then, at last, she sobbed for her sister, the soft, sweet, disillusioned Clare, whom only she, Eve, had ever known, blood and flesh of the same womb, her alter ego, herself.

And so they sat on the bench in the sunlight. Eve suffering, and the man who held her suffering for her.

When ultimately her tears ceased, they sat silently together for a long time, drawing a kind of solace from each other.

Finally it was Eve who spoke. "Oh, Father, I still have not told John Stuart about her. How right you were. I should have told him before our marriage! It has lain like a shadow over me, and now . . . now she is gone."

He looked at her lovingly. "My child. At last she is at peace. Now there can be no shadow. Why is it that you have never told John Stuart?"

Haltingly Eve recounted the story of her wedding day and John Stuart's reaction to the poor woman in the street in Blayney. She told him that she realized John Stuart held a very low opinion of most women, and she knew he would be outraged to have a sister-in-law like Clare. She did not doubt that he hated his mother for the sort of woman she had been, and he would consider Clare the same, perhaps worse. Thus, for the months since her marriage, she had kept silent. "For I have been terribly afraid that he would somehow see it as a reflection upon me; that I would lose his love."

When she had finished, he put his arm around her shoulders. Occasionally she still shuddered with sobbing, and he spoke quietly but firmly. "Eve love, you are no doubt correct about John Stuart. But you are his wife. He married you. Not the poor woman in Blayney or your sad departed sister . . . but you. He loves you. Promise me you will now tell him of Clare. She is gone. Not even John Stuart's pride can be injured by the departed."

Eve's eyes brimmed again with tears. He dabbed them with his already wet handkerchief. "Cry no more, my love. She is in Paradise. No matter what Clare did here, she will be in the arms of the Lord now."

Eve then looked pleadingly at this man she loved and admired so much, and asked for reassurance like a child. "Do you really think so? Will she be with the Lord? Really, Father?"

"Undoubtedly. Don't you remember that our Lord forgave and loved Mary Magdalen? No, my child, dear Clare will not be judged in heaven as she was on earth."

Eve smiled for the first time since she had read the letters, a small, quivering smile. "Oh, Father! If only she could have known you. I think her life would have been so very different. All those times you wrote to her and asked her to come and live with us."

"Yes, Evvy, but her last letter to me showed that she was firm in choosing the road she trod."

Father had received a note from Clare in February in which she had thanked him for his missives over the years, and pointed out she was not dissatisfied with her lot, and she had a new "friend" now, whom she could not leave. She thanked him for his charitable attention. She asked him to take care of "her dearest Evelyn," and to understand that she was able to take care of herself.

Eve nodded. "Yes, I know, but if only she could have met you and Mother . . ." She broke off, and the tears welled again in her eyes.

"Perhaps. Thank you for the faith in us, my Evvy."

A tortured sigh vibrated through her as she rose from the seat. "I think I will go for a ride on Moonlight. I feel I want to be out in the bush, by myself, alone with the wind on my face. Do you understand?"

Father stood up beside her. "Yes, Evvy love, I understand. I will walk down to the stable yard and have a chat with Jack Hennessy, and then wave you off on your ride."

She hugged him again. "I will see you there."

She left him and walked away toward her bedroom, passing close to the bole of the beautiful poinciana tree that dominated the garden. It was an umbrella of bright green, dotted with the first of the buds that would become brilliant orange-red flowers within a few weeks.

He looked after her. Then, folding the two pages he still held in his hand, he put them in his pocket.

Father had been in Jack Hennessy's office for about ten minutes when Eve joined them. She had changed her mustard gown for a warm jacket and a flared brown riding skirt. She wore a small, dark hat tied beneath her chin with a red ribbon.

"Morning, Mrs. Wakeman."

"Good morning, Mr. Hennessy. I am taking Moonlight out for a ride."

"Very well, m'lady, and are you accompanying the mistress, Reverend?"

Eve shook her head, and Father answered, "No, Mrs. Wakeman prefers to ride alone today."

Jack Hennessy would have preferred her to have an escort, but he offered no argument and gave orders for Moonlight to be saddled.

Father helped her to mount. She rode astride as she always had.

"How long do you think you will be, my love?"

"Oh, I'm not sure. John Stuart is out building a fence near the bluff to the northwest . . . Daisy Ridge. I may ride over there and join him. Perhaps even take luncheon with him. Don't wait for me if I am not back by one o'clock."

Father was pleased. He hoped she would go to her husband and tell him of Clare. "Good. So do you think you will spend the entire day in his company?"

"Oh no, he shall be too busy for that; I will ride back directly after eating. I'll be home by three o'clock."

She bent down from the saddle and touched him on the shoulder. She smiled bravely at him. "Thank you, Father dear, thank you for everything. Words cannot express my gratitude." Then she turned the skittish Moonlight out of the stable yard onto the path that led to the road and down to the Lachlan River.

Father watched his darling ride away.

The road took her over Larmer's Crossing. She rode steadily for a long time, stopping now and then to go through gates in fences that separated the huge paddocks and fields. When at last she met a gate in a fence that kept cleared land from the bush, she dismounted to open it. The wind plucked at her skirt as the sun was suddenly covered by cloud. She looked up. It appeared that it could rain. Yet she did not consider returning, but led Moonlight through to the far side and closed the gate behind them. She stood deliberating for a few seconds before she nodded to herself in decision. Then remounting, she turned Moonlight's head in the opposite direction to where her husband would be fencing and rode at a goodly pace southwest toward a large escarpment, that was beyond a series of hills some miles away, on the other side of the valley.

She had resolved not to find John Stuart. She needed some time to adapt to her sister's death. To remember her sister and their years together. To recall Clare's happy, impetuous ways, her laughter and the days of her high spirits, the good and dear things about her. She didn't want people and talk and explanations. And that's what it would be if she joined John Stuart. No, she did not wish to do it now. Tonight . . . Yes, she would explain Clare tonight.

She let Moonlight have his head, and her hands went a little slack on the reins as she rode in the quickening breeze.

Tears rose to her eyes. But remembering her promise to Father, she tried to hold them back. He and Mother were the only people she had told about her sister. At first, she had been apprehensive and simply metioned that her sister lived in Adelaide, but later when she knew them better and realized the extent of their compassion, she had told them everything. That was when Father had begun to write to Clare.

She tightened her hands on the reins and looked up. Clouds chased the sun across the sky. The day was turning colder. It looked like rain to the north.

Down toward the Boorowa River she went. Near the bank rose several small mounds alive with black ants. She steered Moonlight away from them and entered the water. On the other side, she quickened the pace over the undulating ground, her red ribbons trailing from under her chin over her shoulders in the wind. The nimble-footed horse pounded through the tall paspalum grass, his white tail flying behind in unison with her red ribbons. On and on she went, her mind freeing itself of the pain and the sadness of the morning.

When at last she came to the far side of the valley, she checked Moonlight and looked about. She had been riding for over two hours southwest. She knew approximately where she was, for she had been brought this way a few times before, and she understood she was under the cliff that ran some miles along the valley and formed a natural portion of the western Mayfield border. The clouds seemed to sit upon the clifftop as she looked up and suddenly she wanted desperately to be there, above the world, looking down. She remembered that there had been a rough track leading up the side of this cliff somewhere. Eager to find it, she rode south for another half mile or so, examining the steep rock face.

Then she saw it! Her heart pounded, for it was a sharper ascent than she had remembered. She knew if she continued on for a few miles, the ridge yielded and met the valley in a much gentler incline. But today she felt like taking risks. Yes, she would go up the face of the escarpment. Taking a deep breath, she urged Moonlight forward and up onto the uneven ground. For the next fifteen minutes, they picked their way along the trail. Once or twice she faltered where the trail was nearly impassable, the drop to her right almost sheer, but finally Moonlight brought her to the top. The wind blew more fiercely up here, and the sense of being alone excited her, stimulated her.

She supposed it must be almost luncheon time. Oh well, her

darling husband would not miss her. He had no idea she had considered joining him, and Father and Mother would not concern themselves, for they would think she was with John Stuart. She felt quite pleased knowing that she was at liberty for hours yet. Even so, she must turn back soon to be sure of being home by the hour of three.

A bandicoot scampered around a dead branch to her right hand and disappeared into the scrub. She jumped and then laughed in surprise. Moonlight snorted beside her and lifted his head, sniffing the wind. She hugged his thick neck and remounted, heading through the bush and scrub that ran along the ridge toward the long, easy slope to the low ground.

To left and right, the green-gray of the scrub was highlighted with the crimson of the first waratahs and bottlebrushes pushing out of the undergrowth. She could smell the penetrating odor of the lemon-scented eucalyptus on the air. It was fresh and clear. The sun had come out from behind the clouds to offer a mild warmth through the cool wind. She sighed a small sigh and smoothed Moonlight's long white mane. He gave an answering whinny of pleasure.

Abruptly the picture of the bushranger flashed into her mind. She could envy him in a way: his life in the unrestricted bush-lands, his freedom. But then, of course, he also lived in constant danger. He was not really free at all. Who was? Weren't there always restrictions and rules and obligations for everyone?

She shivered. She must stop reflecting this way. She took Moonlight forward. Her pace needed to be a little quicker or it would be late by the time she got home. The horse moved easily into a fast trot.

Her course took her between the towering gums. Birds flew from their hiding places, and the smaller bush animals departed at the sound of the advancing hooves. Mostly the ground was even, but here and there it was striated, and dead branches and small rocks occasionally blocked clear passage. Unerringly the stallion avoided these. He moved up into a canter. Eve's ribbons trailed once more in the wind. She rode well and the horse responded. She could feel the surge of strength under the saddle as the animal accelerated.

Even the unfaltering Moonlight could not sense the approach of the big, red kangaroo that had been startled by a falling rock down a narrow gorge to their right, and now came leaping in fear and panic toward them.

On and on came the powerful animal, well over two hundred pounds of it, in giant strides, sight unseen.

On and on came the woman and the horse, moving at a steady pace, hidden from the kangaroo.

And so, inescapably, their paths crossed.

At the last moment, Eve saw what was happening, but too late. She tried vainly to pull back on the reins as the enormous animal jumped directly into Moonlight's path, smashing with all his force into the horse's forelegs and breaking them instantly.

There was a terrible sound and Moonlight reared up in shock. His head was thrown back, and his mane hit Eve in the face as she lost hold of the reins and was lifted up and out of the saddle. Her right foot caught momentarily in the stirrup, and she was dragged forward and upward by the rearing horse. Her hat flew off and landed in the bracken. Her body twisted in midair, and her head caught the trunk of a silky gum. Then her foot dislodged, and she fell heavily to the ground.

As the kangaroo shot past and crashed into the scrub, continuing on his way, Moonlight's shattered limbs collapsed under his body. The last thing Eve remembered before she lost consciousness was the sound of him, so like a human scream, high-pitched and piercing, expressing his pain.

Both Eve and Moonlight lay in crumpled heaps on the bush floor. The poor animal continued to whinny in shrill suffering and terror.

His mistress lay still and silent, the blood oozing from the wound at the back of her head turning the collar of her dark jacket a murky red.

TEN

Bush Meeting

It had been an early morning for Alan Fletcher.

He had taken a watch on top of Nelson's Boulder looking down from Treehard Hill as was sometimes his way when he woke before the sun, a habit from his shipboard days.

There was a chill wind blowing up the valley, and the day had broken with lemon rays across a cloudy sky. Just after dawn, Daniel, wrapped in a greatcoat, came to call him to his breakfast. They sat together in the kitchen, and Alan ate the hot oatmeal Dan had prepared while the others slept. Daniel was always the early riser, mostly up before six o'clock. He was the self-appointed cook, and his meals were plain but palatable.

Treehard Hill was "home." It had been Lawless who said, "Let us call it Treehard, mateys, for it's covered in trees and hard to find." Years had passed before they had fashioned the sturdy wooden house that nestled now on the flat natural tree-covered plateau between the wall of rock and the sheer drop of hundreds of feet to the valley floor. There were four rooms: two bedrooms, a large kitchen, and the fourth for storage of their clothes, saddles, and equipment.

It had been hard but pleasant toil to build a home, and it had made a goal for the men to work toward during the long, weary weeks between deployment. They had stumbled upon Treehard Hill almost four and a half years before. Alan had been searching for just such a natural stronghold for years. By accident they had made their camp near the thicket of trees that hid the entrance to the narrow tunnel through sandstone boulders. They had been there for over a week before Daniel, wandering deeply in through the trees to find firewood, had discovered the well-hidden en-

161

trance. In those early days after finding Treehard, they had camped out until they had built the first roughly hewn structure.

Even now a shudder ran through Alan whenever he remembered the hundreds of tarantulas that had lived in between the slabs of bark that were the hut walls. Of all the insects and animal life of the bush, and there were many, some deadly, he found tarantulas the most distasteful. Still, they had been constant companions. Masses of them had nested within inches of their heads as they slept, and no matter how hard they fought them, they could not clear the spiders from the bark. But since he had replaced the bark with weatherboard, and they had at last lined the rooms, the hairy, unsightly creatures rarely troubled them. Of course, there were the ever-present hazards of living in the bush, such as the death adder snake that had killed Lawless's wife, Patricia June. It was always possible on a hot night to see a length of scale slither across the doorstep. But the danger of one falling on a sleeper had gone since he had made the dwelling weatherproof.

Alan's latest refinement was to begin to build a proper veranda along the front of the kitchen, and he had plans for an additional outhouse where they would bathe, and a real stable for the horses.

He was thorough and imaginative. Other bands of bushrangers simply played cards, gambled, and became irritable and bored in their hideouts, but Alan's men were not idle. They had their relaxation, but it was in the evening time, like normal working folk, and they enjoyed it all the more, as it seemed a natural pattern of life.

How often Alan had heard of other bands disintegrating because of ill temper, drink, and women. He could control the first two, but could do nothing about the third. Daniel and Sam were not interested in women. Indeed Daniel was happy to simply take care of the cleaning and cooking at Treehard. And Sam? There were times when Alan wondered if females had ever occupied Sam's mind. With Lawless it was different; he had loved Patricia June with the energetic passion of a young man, and when he lost her on Christmas Day 1858, he had mourned her a long time. But recently Alan had noticed he was once again enjoying the company of women on the odd times they were all together. Yet it was only Jordan who made a priority of tarrying in the ''safe houses,'' the wayside taverns and inns where the owners were sympathetic to the ''wild colonial boys.'' Jordan O'Day, who had come among them because of his sister, Patricia June.

Alan finished his breakfast, pushed his plate away, and stood from the table. He was going hunting for fresh food. Daniel followed him out into the yard as he saddled Freedom, his gray stallion. Daniel handed him the reins of the second animal, Waterloo, Lawless's horse, which he took to carry the game.

''How long will you be, son?''

''We are low on provisions, Danny. Perhaps the best part of the day.''

''I'll not be easy until you're home,'' his faithful companion called as Alan waved, disappearing around the house and passing between the walls of the dwelling and the corrugated iron tank that held their water. His voice came back, ''Keep the boys working on the veranda, Danny.''

Eight yards from the back of the house rose the first huge limestone boulder. He circled it and entered the narrow passage. It was broad enough for a man on horseback to pass and was the only opening that led from their two-hundred-yard-wide ledge to the outside world. At the end of the passageway, he rode through the thicket of eucalyptus, white cedar trees, and scrub.

Daniel had followed partway down the sandstone passage to the rocky lookout they called Nelson's Boulder, from which he had a clear view across the hillside. He watched Alan until he vanished into the silent bushland.

Frost had settled overnight, covering the lower glades in a fine gray carpet, and Alan turned in the saddle to see the double line of prints left by Freedom and Waterloo. He smiled to see them, the only telltale sign that this lonely place had been disturbed.

Alan was a lover of the bush, just as once he had been a lover of the sea. He rode with the dexterity of one who has ridden from early childhood and both he and the horses blew little white clouds in the air with every breath. He was dressed in a durable sheepskin jacket, and as he lifted one sun-browned hand to turn up the collar, it made a dark line across his cheek, setting off his striking profile against the advancing day.

He and his men were forced to live mostly off the land. They ventured into towns only when grain, ammunition, or information was needed. Many of the bushrangers were foolishly imprudent, and in cavalier fashion, took little precaution. Some, like Dan Morgan and Johnny Gilbert, carelessly disdainful of the police, allowed too many people to know their whereabouts. Alan thought it could lead to their downfall in the end.

The Fletcher band's operations were kept absolutely secret. The single individual Alan trusted, apart from his band, was their proven friend "Bluey" Williams, and from him they received information about troopers' movements. But even Bluey did not know the location of Treehard, as much for his own protection as theirs.

The morning advanced. By ten o'clock he had three rabbits slung across Waterloo's back, and by noon he had added a wild boar. They were extremely dangerous animals and had been known to kill men, but they were delicious eating, and Daniel would be delighted with it.

Daniel . . . Alan's face softened in thought.

He was sixty-nine now, and the hardships of convict life and living out in all weather had taken their toll on him. In recent years he tired quickly and was sometimes out of breath. Alan smiled as he visualized his dearest old friend singing Irish ditties and going about his daily routine at Treehard Hill. When his thoughts came back to the present, he reined in Freedom and took stock of where he was. He had ridden a little farther than usual, in fact, some miles farther. He was in bushland leading up to the bluff that overlooked one of the valleys of Mayfield.

A lone kookaburra on a broken branch to his left laughed. It was a mocking sound, and it struck him like a jeer. He turned to look up at the bird before he urged Freedom forward up the slope. He would complete the ascent to the top, then would strike west and return in a ring to Treehard. He had painstakingly studied this part of the country, and his judgment in direction was unerring. He read the signs of the bush as well as he had once read the wind and the sea.

He cantered uphill and along the ridge. The wind still blew, although the sun had come out from behind the clouds where it had hidden most of the morning. He was about to turn and head west when he heard the crashing noise of an animal in the scrub to his right, and reining in the horses, he saw a huge, red buck kangaroo bounding in mighty leaps through the trees. Of course, he knew some of them grew to seven feet in height and often had tails of four feet and more, but this one was perhaps the largest Alan had ever seen.

Suddenly through the trees came another sound, faint yet discordant . . . not a bush noise. He nudged Freedom forward into a walk, and Waterloo, whose reins were tied to the back of Freedom's saddle, moved automatically. All the instincts of the hunted man, repressed until now, became alert. His right hand dropped the reins and found his rifle. He tensed in the saddle, and his mind cast about for the fastest route of escape. Then he gave his full attention back to the cry, for that was what it was, high-pitched and excited. It was coming from in front of him, directly north. He realized it was a horse in agony.

Traps for bushrangers were set in the most bizarre fashions.

"Be ready Freedom . . . Waterloo," he said. "We may have to run for it."

He turned the horses in a full circle, all the while scanning through the trees. He saw nothing and the pained cry continued. He sensed there was nothing to fear, so he urged Freedom on toward the sound. A minute later he saw the stallion, a beautiful, white creature writhing on the ground. And, almost instantaneously, he saw the figure of a woman beyond, lying facedown at the base of a gum. He dismounted and led his horse forward. He peered through the trees again in every direction. No one in sight and no noise of riders. What was a woman doing out here alone? Something had happened to make the stallion throw her. Her hat hung crazily in the scrub nearby, its red ribbons blowing in the wind. There was blood in her fair curls.

Delicately he turned her over. John Stuart Wakeman's wife!

He felt warm breath from her mouth, and a sort of relief shot through him. For a moment he had dreaded that she was dead. Her pulse seemed normal, although she was unconscious. He took off his jacket and covered her with it.

Then he turned to the unfortunate Moonlight. The horse's dignified head moved up and down in pain, and his continuous whinny was loud in the wind. It was obvious that both his front legs were broken.

Alan spoke quiet, soft, soothing words to the animal, and as he spoke, he leveled his rifle and shot Moonlight through the brain. The explosion brought a strangled noise from Freedom and a sound of returning consciousness from Eve. He moved back, and kneeling beside her, positioned her so that she lay against him. There was dirt down the side of her cheek and in her hair, but it was the wound that concerned him. He wiped some of the blood away with his handkerchief as she moaned again.

He felt the cold through his cotton shirt, yet the sensation was as if it belonged to someone else, for his whole attention was given to the woman.

As the blackness receded, Eve felt someone holding her. Her

head throbbed and there was pain in her arms and legs. "Can you hear me?" a voice said. "How do you feel?" She opened her eyes and began to focus. It was then that she recognized the eyes above her, and a shocked sound escaped from her lips. She drew away from him, and yet at the same time she registered the wonderful look of him, the sun-browned face, the face she had actually dreamed about. She shuddered as he replaced the handkerchief against her wound.

There was alarm in her voice. "You! It is not possible! How can you be here?"

"You have cut your head," he said quietly, disregarding her question. Then taking her right hand and placing it upon the handkerchief against her head, he added, "Here, hold this. I must bandage it."

She could feel her heart thumping. Vaguely she was still aware of pain in her head and soreness in her limbs, but the astounding reality of his presence overwhelmed her. She knew she had begun to tremble, but she was unable to stop.

"You fell from your horse," he was saying. "Hit your head on this tree, no doubt. You are fortunate. The wound is not deep."

Then, for the first time, she remembered Moonlight. She looked around but could not see him. Alan had placed himself in the way.

"Moonlight? Where is Moonlight?"

His tone was gentle. "If it is your horse you speak of, I'm afraid he had smashed both his forelegs. He was suffering badly. I'm sorry, lass, but I had to put him down."

Oh no! This was too much! Her princely Moonlight had gone! Her eyes filled with tears.

"There, lass," he said quietly. "He is better off. He could not be mended."

He stripped off his shirt and tore it in pieces. She feebly protested when she realized what he was doing, but he wound bandages around her head until he had encompassed the handkerchief and checked the bleeding.

The early afternoon sun, gaining some mastery over the day, shone down through the straggling clouds and brought a capricious warmth to the two people. Fallen leaves blew by them in the grass, and bush birds watched from the scrub. To Eve it seemed as if he were studying her, looking down into the depths of her. Unnerved, she averted her eyes.

"Is the pain bad?" he asked.

"No, not bad. It throbs a little."

"Sit still." He rose, and she noticed the L-shaped scar exposed on his left forearm. It looked an old wound, and it was the only imperfect thing about him. Somehow it heightened the symmetry of the rest of him. She felt light-headed, intoxicated. She stared at him as he walked from her to his horses, her eyes riveted to the rippling, muscular nakedness of his back.

With relief, she realized she had ceased to tremble, but in struggling to assess the sensations she was experiencing, she was able only to acknowledge the confusion that this man stirred within her. She was flooded with guilt.

Could it have been as recently as last night that Sir Rutherford had been discussing him? It seemed so much longer.

He turned back to her. She watched him cross the space between them, carrying a bedroll and a water bottle. His arms came down to her. She was highly aware of his hands pressing through her clothes as he lifted her to where she could lean against a rock.

She drank a little from the water bottle, and with shock she noticed the thought filling her mind was not that the water refreshed her, but that his mouth, too, had covered the opening of this bottle.

Her heart was still beating rapidly. She observed him silently as he placed the blanket over her and retrieved his jacket. He put it on, and she focused on that brown part of his chest that the jacket did not cover, beneath the hollow of his neck.

When he had buttoned his coat, he bent down, half kneeling, right knee on the ground, resting his left elbow on his left knee and surveying her. "Is there anywhere else that gives you pain? You will be bruised in many places."

He was so refined, everything about him extrinsic to the type of man Sir Rutherford described as a bushranger. Son of a knight, from a viceregal family, naval captain, convict, killer, lifer. It was all fantastic. She replied to his question. "My ankle hurts, too, I think."

He moved over to her. Gently he took off her riding boot and looked at her leg. It was swollen, but it moved back and forth without great pain.

"I would guess there is nothing broken. Probably badly sprained." Then his face broke into a smile. "Although you'll not dance on it for a few days."

It was the first smile she had seen from him, and suddenly

her aches and discomfort dissolved in a feeling of well-being. She smiled involuntarily back at him.

He began to ask a question. "Were you . . . ." And to their surprise, both of them completed the sentence in unison. "Riding alone?" they said.

"Yes, I was," she finished.

"What happened to make you fall?"

"It was a kangaroo, an enormous one. It seemed to come from nowhere. Moonlight reared, and I fell."

"Yes, they can be dangerous, the big ones." He guessed it was probably the huge buck he had seen in the bush moments before he heard her horse's cry.

Returning to his former position, he sat facing her.

She looked down at her hands. "How is it you are here?"

"I was hunting, as you can see." He pointed to the bounty on Waterloo's saddle.

Often in the months to come, when her mind drifted from the daily routine of her life, she would sit again on this bush floor, here with him.

Freedom lifted his head from where he was chewing grass some ten yards distant and whinnied. Waterloo answered.

Immediately Eve thought about Moonlight again and tried to look in his direction. The man opposite shook his head. "Don't think on it, lass. He is gone. There was nothing else that could be done."

The tears came again. "Yes I know. It's just that he was so . . . beautiful."

Then he said the thing she somehow did not want to hear. "I must get you home. Won't people be looking for you?"

"What time is it?" she asked.

He lifted his hands to shade his eyes and looked up at the sky. "Between one and two o'clock; closer to two, I think."

"I must leave soon, but I would rather rest a little longer here." Then she added, "If . . . you don't mind."

"That I do not."

She dropped her eyes lest he should see what she was thinking.

"My head does not hurt as much, but I must look a fright," she said.

"That you do," he replied.

She looked up quickly to see if he meant it, and there was amusement in his eyes. "You have the startling appearance of a female pirate after battle; your hair tied in a bandanna made from the shirt of a victim, no doubt. All you need is the eye patch!''

She laughed then. And he laughed. And above them, a kookaburra laughed.

He seemed to be studying her. ''Why is it that the mistress of Mayfield rides alone and so far?'' he asked.

''I sometimes like to ride alone. But I have never been this far before; I . . . wanted expressly to be alone today.'' She looked up into his eyes again, and now she felt no fear of him at all. How was it possible for this man to be a killer? There was no killing in him!

They sat in silence again for a short time. Then she sighed and said, ''I wished to be by myself today because I had some terrible news. Sad news. My only sister, she is dead.'' Tears came again to her eyes and clouded her vision.

He looked compassionately at her. ''We all must die, lass. And I'm sorry you are so sad. Perhaps you must experience the pain of her loss keenly now to rid yourself of much of the grief.'' Briefly a distant look came into his eyes. ''I have known those who lived daily with grief . . . and that is not living.''

For a few moments neither of them spoke, until Eve said, ''She was so misunderstood, so very misunderstood.''

He nodded. ''If you say so, no doubt she was.''

Then she felt a prevailing need to exonerate Clare. She did not know why, but she wanted to explain to the bushranger. She was aware it was ridiculous. And yet, from somewhere within her mind came the bewildering knowledge that this man would understand and that she truly wished him to know the truth.

''Don't upset yourself more. You have a head wound and have jolted yourself badly. You need rest and care.''

''But I honestly feel all right and . . . I would like to tell you about my sister. That is, unless, of course, you must leave now?''

He regarded her some moments. Was that a hint of a smile? ''No. I have no need to leave.''

Eve told the story of Clare to Alan, sitting on the ground in the bush, surrounded by the cold of a September day. He listened, calmly and impartially, with great attention, to what she said.

She related their childhood in Boston and their three years in San Francisco; Clare, erratic and loving, spoiled and sweet, always an enigma. She explained how her mother's illness, the coughing and wasting disease, followed by her death, had changed their lives. How her father had made the decision to bring them to New South Wales, only to die on the journey.

When she told him of her arrival with Clare in Sydney, alone in a strange land, he nodded thoughtfully. She spoke of the Magges and the Ship Inn and the sailors; of Father and the gold watch and the sewing business. And when she came to recount the morning Clare had left, she halted a moment and looked up to the sky. The old sadness and the hurt filled her, and now she felt the soreness in her limbs and the pain in the back of her head.

He leaned toward her just a little. "You have told me enough. I understand."

But she had said so much, she wanted to finish. In him she felt she had found a sympathy that perhaps not even Father could equal. Her voice was tentative. "Yet I . . . I feel as if I must go on."

"Then you must," he said in his disarming fashion.

So she told him how Clare had gone with Harry to Adelaide, how he said he would marry her when they got there, which he never did. "Clare's was a malignant star," she said. "Men were always *promising* to marry her. And now she is gone. From consumption, they said." She bent forward and held her head in her hands.

Quietly he moved to help her to her feet. "Come now, lass. You were the best of sisters, I have no doubt."

She stood with his help. "But it was all wrong! The last time I saw my sister, she was working in a barroom again! Clare, identical to me in so much, and yet so unlike me. There she was, elegant and graceful, in a tavern; it broke my heart."

He stood looking down at her. "Now, lass, it was her life. In the end, was not she responsible? Let her rest in peace now. For my part, I cannot judge her." He gave a sound like a laugh in his throat, but there was no humor on his face. "It would be presumptuous . . . indulgent," he finished.

"Yes, perhaps," Eve replied in a faint voice. "But there are those who don't quite understand, and who would judge harshly."

"I claim no close association with the Bible," he answered. "But 'Judge not, that ye be not judged.' My mother used to say that . . . a thousand years ago."

She looked intently at him and wondered about his mother. What would this man's mother be like? Did she know what had become of her son? And what had really happened to bring this cultured, urbane man to bushranging?

An impetuous anger rose within her toward Sir Rutherford and all like him. Suddenly she was positive that Alan Fletcher was good and incorruptible and fearless, no matter what they said about him. Yes, she knew this, with an unquestionable certainty, and it brought her heart to racing again. She was filled with a torrent of confusing sensations as she stood there looking up at him, and she realized, with a terrible surge of guilt, that she would always remember the intimacy of this strange afternoon.

"We must leave now," he said abruptly, as if he had to force himself to say it.

She looked over to where the lifeless Moonlight lay.

"I will return and bury him," he assured her.

Relief flooded her face. "Will you? Thank you . . . oh, thank you. Good-bye, Moonlight. I am so sorry, so very sorry."

Alan took her arm and steered her toward Waterloo. "Can you ride alone?"

Now that she was standing, she felt very dizzy and was conscious of the aching in her limbs. "No, I am afraid not."

"Then we shall ride upon Freedom." He took Waterloo's reins and tied them loosely to a small tree. "You wait here," he said to the animal. "I will come back."

"Does he understand?"

"Better than some humans."

He helped her upon Freedom and he mounted behind her.

"Thank you for listening to me," she said tentatively. "Somehow I feel a completeness about Clare's life now. I know I must have appeared . . . That is, I hope you didn't think me impertinent."

Then she thought she sensed him laugh, and a flush rose to her throat as he replied in her ear, "Impertinent? No, I did not think that."

They moved off through the gray bush at a walking pace and he said, "Sometimes we need to tell our inmost feelings, and perhaps it is easier to tell such things to a stranger."

At these words she felt sorrow catching in her throat. The feeling bordered upon injury. The reason she had told him was she had *wanted* to tell him. Him. Because she knew in her heart he would understand. She knew it was outrageous, but she did not think of him as a stranger. She did not *want* to think of him as a stranger! Yet all she answered was, "Perhaps."

Her head hurt badly now and she wondered if she would ever learn the truth about his life. She thought about John Stuart and how she loved him and how hurt and horrified he would be to know what she was thinking. This made her head throb even more. She considered as they rode the next few miles, then finally took a deep breath. "I know who you are. I know you are Alan Fletcher. And there is a man, a tenacious, brilliantly clever man, Sir Rutherford Blake. He was at Mayfield only last night. He is working with the police and is out to capture you. You and all the others!"

She was mounted in front of him; his body lay at her back, and his arms were around her holding the reins, so she could not see his face. He was silent for some seconds as if deliberating, then he replied, "Yes, I know of him. He wishes to be the nemesis of the bushrangers."

She was again alarmed at herself, but could not help saying, "I am afraid of that."

"Don't be," he said.

An hour later, they were crossing the valley floor in the biting wind. They had been traveling steadily back in a northeasterly direction.

Alan had been watching the dark and threatening horizon and could see that it was raining some miles in the distance, although for the present there was no sign of it here.

He held Freedom still for a moment, his eyes covering the landscape.

Neither had spoken for a long time, and recently she had begun to feel alternately giddy and sick. At the beginning of the ride she could not help but be excited by the closeness of him, but after all the emotion, her head throbbed badly, while the aching in her arms and legs now extended to her back.

"We are within Mayfield," he said at last. "I see a gate up ahead, although it will be some hours before we get to the homestead."

A sharp thought hit her through the haze of her distress. "We?" she began anxiously. And then she admitted to herself that she was afraid for him; that he was in danger inside the Mayfield border. Her fear for him brought her to say what she truly felt. "But you must not come into Mayfield. It is not safe for you!"

"I will take you home."

She felt too weak to argue, but she summoned up her strength. "What is the time now?"

"Around four o'clock."

"Then they could be out looking for me. You must leave me if you see riders. Simply set me down and ride away. I will be all right. It is not safe here for you." She sat up a little to be forceful, but began to sway. She felt him steady her as she continued. "You will do as I ask, won't you? You have been so . . . kind. I do not want you in danger. Please?"

"Fear not, I will take no risk," he replied to calm her.

At last her feelings overcame her; she lost her composure and now she was stammering. "Y-You see, th-they will t-take you prisoner. Th-They do not understand. It is too d-dangerous."

They had come to the gate in the fence, and he gave a few commands to Freedom, who knelt slowly down. As her guardian lifted her out of the saddle and placed her delicately on the grass, Eve was becoming incoherent, mumbling something about Father being the only one who might be sympathetic. Alan opened the gate and led Freedom through, returning for her inert body. This time he lay her across the saddle so that she rested in his arms, her head upon his right shoulder. He feared she was becoming delirious, but all he could do was to continue on toward the Mayfield homestead.

There would surely be a search party out for her by now. Alan supposed they would have a black tracker at Mayfield who would inevitably be following Moonlight's path.

He looked skyward. Fortunately it appeared the rain was not coming toward them but holding to the north. He rode with Eve in his arms for another hour. He forded the Boorowa River in the chill, bleak twilight and continued to talk softly to her, trying to keep her awake. He asked her questions about Mayfield and about who might be out looking for her, but she had slipped into complete unconsciousness half an hour before. He was very concerned. He had seen enough men with head injuries to know this could be very dangerous.

The last time she had spoken, she opened her eyes briefly and looked up at the blurred face above her. She had fought to bring him into focus. "Alan Fletcher . . ." she said as she drifted into nothingness.

He looked down at her, and for a few moments he was not on Freedom's back in this bleak, cold dusk, but elsewhere, elsewhere with this woman in his arms. His eyes clouded wistfully, but he shook his head, and he resolutely accelerated Freedom forward in the wind.

Suddenly he reined up and peered through the darkness. He

had heard unusual sounds, almost inseparable from the bush noises themselves, but sounds of a different nature. They were the sounds of horses and men! Ahead and to the right were two, maybe three riders.

They would be Mayfield men. No one else would dare ride this far inside the boundary when the homestead was sited only miles away.

He pulled Freedom's head toward the newcomers. The wind whipped by as he rode forward, and so tightly did he hold the reins that the knuckles of his right hand turned white.

The three men who appeared in the twilight each rode about ten yards apart and scoured the country as they came. The one who saw Alan first carried a telescope in his right hand and the reins in his left. He shouted and spurred his horse forward and the other riders followed. The man was Joe Larmer.

Freedom stamped his feet as they waited in the lee of a large boulder, while Joe skirted a gully between them. It was now that Alan recognized him. This was the man who had ridden shotgun on the Mayfield coach five months before. He must be careful.

As soon as Joe had seen the lone rider, he hailed him and rode forward to investigate. They did not allow strangers on Mayfield land. They would question him and then face him smartly around to the nearest boundary. It was not until Joe was avoiding the gully that he saw there was a blanketed figure in the arms of the rider.

Joe came straight to Freedom's side. It was then he saw Eve's face.

"Eve!" he said. "Thank God! Do you realize who you carry, man? This is Mrs. Wakeman."

Alan did not reply.

"Is she badly hurt? What happened? Where did you find her?"

Avoiding Joe's eyes and in a quiet voice, Alan answered briefly. "She fell and hit her head. She is unconscious now. I found her some time ago." He waved his hand in a vague fashion behind him to indicate the possible direction.

"Where's her horse?" Joe continued.

"Dead. He had two broken limbs. I shot him."

Later, when Joe was composed, he would analyze this encounter and recall that he had been given very little information. But now he was too filled with relief to notice.

He turned to one of his companions. "Fire the signal, Barnes."

The man so addressed fired two rifles, one after the other, into the air. Then, on the count of ten, he fired two more. Eve did not flinch during the explosions.

Joe turned back to the man who held her. There in the wind he caught the man's eyes. He had the uncanny feeling that he was being seen through, and that he had experienced this once before, but he had no time to think it over, and the sensation passed. He held out his strong, solid arms for Eve. "Give her to me."

When Alan lifted Eve's inanimate body over to Joe, a mysterious thing happened. Out of the unconscious woman's mouth came a single word. It was loud and clear, and all the horsemen heard it plainly. "No!" she said.

Joe was startled into thinking she was regaining consciousness and began to speak to her. "Eve! Eve! Are you all right?" But then he realized she was insensible. "Well, I'll be darned!" he exclaimed, and shook his head.

Then, anxious to be away, he said to the stranger, "I know Mr. Wakeman will want to give you a reward for finding Mrs. Wakeman. If you call or write any time to Mayfield House, there will be something there for you. Meanwhile, here . . ." He took from his pocket two gold sovereigns and a guinea. "It sure isn't much for getting the mistress back, but it's all I have on me."

For a moment, contradictory expressions seemed to vie for supremacy on the stranger's face. Then he spoke quite softly. "Just get her to care as fast as you can." And he negated the offering with a wave of his hand and looked directly at Joe again, just for a heartbeat. Then, after dropping his eyes another second to Eve, he turned Freedom around in a brisk movement.

Two galahs lifted from the branch of a gum and, swooping low, flew almost in unison with his retreat across the intervening country, until he was lost in the cold of the murky, swiftly falling night.

On the ride home, Joe thought of the stranger again and again. He could not get rid of the feeling that he knew the man. Joe was vexed with himself. There was so much more he should have asked the man. He didn't even know his name. But at least they had found Eve and were taking her home to Mayfield.

ELEVEN

Returned

It was well past three o'clock before Father rode down to the Lachlan to see if he could find his darling returning from her ride. Instead of Eve, he met John Stuart and the fencing party coming back from the northwest.

The clergyman told John Stuart of his wife's ride; how she had left that morning a short time after ten o'clock and had not yet come back. "She said she might take luncheon with you, and that is why I did not worry until the time had passed the hour of three." But he did not reveal what had prompted Eve's departure, or in what state of mind she had been.

"Damn!" replied John Stuart in the manner of a preoccupied businessman. "Eve should have more sense than to ride a long way alone." But when they arrived at the stables and found she was still not home, he became concerned for her and convinced that a search should be mounted.

At fifteen minutes to five o'clock, more than six hours since Eve's departure, the search party rode out. They had to rely on spreading a net of men in the general direction Eve had taken. Unfortunately, they were minus the aborigine, Charlie Lightfoot, Mayfield's best horsebreaker and black tracker, who was away in the southern hills with a team extending one of the connecting roads.

The men divided into groups of three. Father, John Stuart, and Richard Lane from the dairy rode together. John Stuart would have preferred to ride with Joe, but understood that the experienced men needed to be separated.

John Stuart was worried. Nightfall was advancing, and the

wind had intensified. The horses' tails danced in the cold air as the men drew their coats more firmly about themselves.

It was dusk when they heard faint gunshots. The prearranged signal on finding Eve was two shots followed by a ten-second interval, then two more. They held silent for the second volley. After ten seconds, it sounded.

"Praise be to the Lord!" Father said.

John Stuart coughed, then turning in his saddle, shouted, "Let's go, so we can be there waiting when she's brought in."

They rode, until at length their horses' hooves rang out on Larmer's Crossing and they sighted fires in the night near the buildings on the other side.

An hour later, fourteen groups had returned, all without Eve.

It was a little after nine o'clock, when Father went and sat by John Stuart in the glow of one of the fires. It was still cold, but blessedly the wind had dropped and the fires could burn unhindered.

John Stuart examined the man beside him. It was a concentrated look and it lasted many seconds. Then he spoke. He spoke from the heart. "I know you love her," he admitted. "And so do I, with all my being. I don't know what I'll do if she's badly hurt or . . . You see, she's the purest, most special woman. I knew it the moment I saw her in the park in Bathurst. She was ethereal, chaste, not like other women." He turned his head away and stared into the flames.

"I understand, John Stuart, I understand," the older man said, placing a hand on his shoulder. "Yes, she is a good woman." He sighed, and moving slightly closer, added, "Do not think I take a liberty when I say, simply love her for herself."

John Stuart's eyes came back around to his companion's. For a moment Father read indignation in them. Then, to his surprise, they altered almost to entreaty.

"Whatever do you mean? Do you not think I love her? For herself?"

For the first time Father felt sorry for John Stuart, and with the sorrow came affection. For all his wealth and grandeur, master of so much and so many, he was as all men are, in need of confirmation, of support, even of advice.

"Son," he answered. "I do not suggest you do not love Eve. In fact, I now believe you do, and deeply. All I say is to love the essence of Eve, which I know is remarkably good. Do not weave a dream about her."

In the flickering firelight, the two sat quite close looking at each other. John Stuart recognized the conviction in the older man's eyes, but he was now convinced that even the cleric did not really see Eve properly, though he undoubtedly loved her. No, it was only he, John Stuart, who knew her for the unparalleled woman she was.

He smiled at Father Billings. "I do not weave a dream about her," he said.

Father sighed and nodded, his face ruddy in the glow of the fire. He patted John Stuart's shoulder. "Let's ride over the river and wait there. It will give us something to do."

In the darkness they rode over Larmer's Crossing and waited together until at last they heard the unmistakable sound of horses from the southwest, and they rode toward it. It was Joe's party. John Stuart hailed him, "Is she all right, Joe? Do you have her? What happened?"

"I have her. She fell from Moonlight, m'boy. She has a head injury and is unconscious. Methinks I should hold her steady until we get to Mayfield house. Best I carry her the same way I have these past hours until I place her on a bed."

"Yes, yes, of course," agreed John Stuart. "You carry her, Joe!" The master of Mayfield was filled with anxiety. He had his darling wife back, but she was hurt. He followed Joe up to the house, feeling very helpless.

Dr. Bell, from Cowra, had been sent for when the search parties had gone out, and while they waited, Mr. Oldfield brought a large, gilt-bound medical book from the library. He read about "unconsciousness" and "brain concussion" to them. It informed them about how to dress the wounds and how to keep a fever down with cold compresses.

"Shame she went to sleep. Best to be keeping them awake when it's concussion," Mrs. Smith declared to Thelma in the hall later.

Dr. Bell corroborated the medical book's advice, but he did have a medicine which he instructed to be mixed with water and to administer once she was conscious. When he examined her, he found her ankle swollen, but ascertained it to be unbroken. The head wound itself, he deemed superficial, which was a good sign, although the fever could be dangerous. He assured them that as long as they kept the fever in check and there was no brain damage, she would be "as good as new" in a week or so.

"How in hell do we know there is no brain damage?" John Stuart interjected.

"We don't yet, sir," replied Gordon Bell, a sensitive, inventive medical man for the times. "Not until she wakes."

"We shall get our own doctor," the master of Mayfield declared to Joe when they had moved out of the bedroom. "In emergencies such as this, we need our own man here."

"I shall see to it," the other replied calmly.

"And where did you find her, old man?"

"It was not me who found her, m'boy."

"What do you mean, not you?"

"A stranger found her. We came across him well inside the Mayfield boundary. He was some miles this side of the Boorowa. He rode a fine gray, and he was carrying Eve. Said that Moonlight had thrown her."

John Stuart looked amazed. "But what of Moonlight?"

Joe shook his head. "The fellow had to shoot him. Two broken legs."

"What could possibly have happened?"

Joe shrugged. "I don't know. I'm disgusted with myself. Didn't even request his name."

"No!" John Stuart was firm. "You did correctly. Bringing her here without delay was critical, and you did that, old man. Thank you."

Then Joe was thoughtful. "You know, m'boy, I had the oddest feeling about that man. As if I knew him. Eerie, really!"

The night passed with Dr. Bell often at the bedside and John Stuart either holding Eve's hand or sleeping fitfully in a large armchair near her. She rambled softly now and then. But for the most part she seemed to sleep deeply.

When morning broke, the news was better, as it always seems to be in sickrooms when, with the coming of the day, comes optimism. The doctor said the fever had almost passed.

Soon after, Eve fell into a calmer, more rhythmic sleep. The doctor felt she would probably awaken soon, but she slept most of the morning away. John Stuart, Thelma, Father, and Mother were all in the room when she at last gave signs of returning consciousness. As she moved slightly beneath the covers and murmured, Dr. Bell spoke. "If Mrs. Wakeman is coherent when she wakes and remembers what happened, then there is no danger of her brain being harmed."

Perhaps half a minute later, she opened her eyes. She saw her loved ones around the bed, concern on all their faces.

The doctor came and lifted her wrist to take her pulse. "Is there any pain, Mrs. Wakeman?"

"My head is sore . . . and my leg. My back hurts a little, but I think that is all."

John Stuart knelt and took her hand, the frown of worry that had been a fixture since last night deepening as he spoke. "Eve, Eve love, what happened?"

She did not answer immediately. Then she remembered. "I . . . Oh, Moonlight. Poor Moonlight. It was awful . . . a huge kangaroo."

"What kangaroo, dear?" queried Father, who was leaning forward toward her.

"Why, the kangaroo that jumped in front of us. Moonlight . . . oh, poor Moonlight! He threw me. He could not help it." She closed her eyes as tears welled up in them. "He broke both his forelegs. It was too terrible!"

"So that was it. A kangaroo," John Stuart sighed. "My poor darling." He leaned across to kiss her forehead, and she lifted her hand and stroked his hair.

"The patient seems normal enough to me," spoke up Dr. Bell.

She smiled. "I feel a little hungry," she said, to the delight of them all.

That night as the grandfather clock in the hall outside her room chimed seven, Eve lay propped up by masses of soft down pillows. Stephanie, her maid, was administering her medicine, and Thelma sat tatting a doily in the lamplight.

Eve was thinking of Clare. Poor Clare. She had promised Father she would tell John Stuart. Oh dear! She did not feel well enough now. It would be best if she waited until she was well. She needed all her strength to make him understand. Yes, she would wait. . . . In a week or so.

The door clicked and John Stuart's frame filled the opening.

Stephanie and Thelma departed, and Eve put out her hand to her husband, who took it and sat on the side of the bed. He smiled at her. "Darling, there are some questions I would ask you if you are not too indisposed."

"Yes, sweetheart," she replied, her eyes standing out against the paleness of her face and the pillows.

"Reverend Billings told me you had proposed to ride out to find me yesterday. Why didn't you?"

She looked down. "No real reason. I thought you would be busy fencing and I might be in the way."

"I see. And the accident, where did it happen?"

Here she hesitated a moment. "On one of the ridges across the Boorowa."

"Which one, sweetheart? There are a number."

"Oh, darling, I don't know the country like you do."

"No, that is true," he agreed. "Were you inside or outside of our boundary?"

"Outside, I think. Why?"

"Oh, Eve!" he reprimanded gently. "You should never ride outside the borders. As if there is not enough of Mayfield for you to ride upon. There are some tribes still living in this area."

"Now, John Stuart," Eve answered, mildly reproving. "The aborigines are harmless; you know that."

"Yes, perhaps." He took her hand and kissed it. "But there are other dangers. I want your promise that you will never ride alone again."

"Without Moonlight, I don't think I want to ride at all."

"Yes, poor Moonlight. And that brings me to the man who had to shoot him. He carried you on his horse until you met Joe?"

"Yes. He was very kind."

"I am so grateful to him. Were you conscious when he found you? Do you know who he was?"

Eve gently removed her hand from her husband's and drew it across her eyes. This was her husband, the man whose life she shared. She wanted to be honest with him; she was already withholding the fact that she had a sister. "Yes, John Stuart, I do. He was the man who stopped our coach when we were coming here."

For a moment John Stuart was so amazed, he could not speak. He just sat there looking at her. Then he stood from the bed and the outburst came.

"Well, I'll be damned! The bloody bushranger! I can't believe it! This is too much! The bushranger!"

Three weeks later, on an October day, Eve and John Stuart sat on the veranda, looking south, enveloped by the warm spring sunshine. They had finished luncheon, and before returning to work, John Stuart was keen to show his wife a plan he had detailed to shift water from the Lachlan to the farthest orchards on the southern side of the river. He spread out the plans on the table in front of them.

She wore a sweet tiny posy of flowers attached to the bodice of her dress, which John Stuart had pinned there. Since her fall, no matter how busy he was, her husband had always arrived back at the house between noon and one o'clock, and they had taken luncheon together. He often brought her a small bouquet or a posy, as he had today, and during the first week of her convalescence, he had come to her with a boyish smile sitting charmingly on his face, and a covered basket tied with a red ribbon in his hands. Upon lifting the cover, Eve had found the most beautiful tiny, white kitten. It had big green eyes and fluffy fur, and she named it Velvet. The little fellow had become her constant companion, and lived mostly in their rooms and the garden outside them to avoid John Stuart's dogs.

John Stuart was tracing an imaginary channel across the paper with his long, sun-browned finger. "I want to move water through here. The pump I am using, a type of hydraulic ram pump, can move the volume I need without difficulty, but I'm concerned about the length of the channel I'll have to cut to feed the new field." His eyes lit up when he mentioned the pump. He reveled in things scientific. He moved his finger along the edge of the orchards, pointing out where the channel would need to go. "Unfortunately, it will have to be pretty long, and it will be expensive. I wish I didn't have to run it quite so far."

Eve was watching earnestly. Suddenly she had a thought. "But, darling, does the new field have to go there?" She tapped on the plan where he had pointed.

"Yes, I think so. It's the soil. Joe and Jack say it's the best there is for miles."

"You haven't planted it yet, have you?"

"No, we haven't; Joe will start next Monday."

She touched the plan. "Would the branding yard here, west of the orchards, have the same sort of soil?"

He nodded. "I expect so."

"Then, sweetheart, I have a thought. I know I'm not as knowledgeable as you and Joe about crops, but it seems to me if you put the new field here—" she pointed to the branding yard beside the existing orchard "—and not farther south, the water channel wouldn't need to be half as long."

John Stuart bent forward thoughtfully, his eyes on the drawing.

Eve moved her finger across in front of him. "And there is a gradual rise there, so the water would flow down easily across it, wouldn't it?"

Her husband did not reply but continued studying the plan. Finally he looked up and smiled. "Darling, I think you're right.

The orchard could go where you say. It will be even better on a gentle rise. We could take the branding yard down on the other side of the corn storage sheds, where it would still be close to the river and then we would avoid the need to pump water along a lengthy channel.'' He folded the plan and put it under his arm. ''Eve, you continually surprise me. Wait until I tell the boys who thought of this. Thank you, my clever girl.'' He kissed her lightly on the lips and bounded across the veranda and down the steps to where Diomed waited.

An hour later, Eve and Thelma were in the park taking an afternoon walk. They came to a stone seat, under a row of tall beeches that Arthur Wakeman had planted twenty-five years before, and just as they went to sit, a large goanna lizard ran from beneath it. They exclaimed in fright and then began to laugh as it disappeared under a hedge.

Eve settled onto the seat. ''The creatures of this novel land will always fascinate me.''

''Now, that is truly odd,'' exclaimed Thelma.

''What is?''

''What you just now said. It is exactly what Sir Arthur used to say. I can see him standing in this very garden saying, 'The creatures of this novel land will always fascinate me,' and it is the very expression you used this minute.''

Eve shook her head in surprise. ''Why, that is indeed odd. . . . You know, I do sometimes wonder about him. John Stuart seems to have worshiped him.''

Thelma made a soft affirmative sound in her throat. ''Oh, that's true enough, and he's like him in many respects. Arthur Wakeman was not afraid to work side by side with his men to see Mayfield rise, and neither is John Stuart.''

''Yes,'' agreed Eve. ''He does work long and hard. No doubt he is like his father in that. You know, I like the look of Sir Arthur in the paintings of him, the one in the library particularly. There is something in his eyes, a fanciful expression, as if life amused him.''

The other woman looked thoughtful. ''Ah, that painting was the last to be done, not six months before he died. That is the older Arthur Wakeman. He had changed, indeed he had! There was a mildness about him then. Not weakness, but composure and contentment. And yes, it's possible to say life could have amused him. I'm not sure.'' Here Thelma closed her eyes in recollection and frowned. ''Though life did not amuse him in his youth; of that I'm absolutely certain.''

"How do you mean? Was it because of John Stuart's mother?"
"Yes."

"Once or twice I have asked John Stuart about her," Eve
said. "He was very abrupt. Said she had left when he was small,
that really you had brought him up and he did not wish to speak
of her, for she was nothing to him. He has no respect or affection
for her at all as far as I can gather. Any mention of her disturbs
him, so I don't speak of her."

Just perceptibly, Thelma nodded, sadness and regret settling
into her face.

Eve noticed the expression. "Father said John Stuart's mother
had left years before he'd ever met Arthur Wakeman, that there
had been a terrible scandal and she had returned to Scotland."

"Mmm, that's right." Thelma considered a moment, and
then went on. "Perhaps I should have told you before, but because of the way John Stuart feels, we avoid the subject. Oh,
his mother was a beauty, right enough." Thelma's mouth pursed.
"Caroline Barnett. Arthur brought her out from Scotland. All
eyes and hair, she was, dark eyes, just like John Stuart's really.
Well, she was from the landed gentry, youngest daughter of a
laird up Fort William way, near Ben Nevis. The property is still
there, I suppose. Arthur married her in the late twenties after
he had been granted land here years before. The beginning of
Mayfield." She made the last statement wistfully, and Eve realized for the first time that Thelma was imbued with the love
of this place, just as John Stuart was, as all those who lived on
Mayfield seemed to be.

"John Stuart arrived eleven months after the marriage. We
were not here then, didn't come until late thirty when Arthur
went into breeding cattle. Gosh, but Joe and I were just young
things, you know, lucky to get the job. Well, pretty soon after,
you could tell things between him and her weren't working.
Why, we weren't here more than six or seven months when she
left and went back to Scotland." She paused. Eve did not speak,
and Thelma took up her narrative. "In those days, there was a
convict settlement near where Cowra is now. You wouldn't know
that, being from America and all. Well, there was an army major
in charge. Joe said he was a ladies' man, right enough, and he
was."

Thelma paused. "I suppose, what with him being the only
proper company for eighty miles, the major, I mean, Arthur
Wakeman invited him here to Mayfield quite a lot. Too much,
as it turned out. Caroline Wakeman and the major . . . It went

on a long time before Arthur realized. I remember she seemed so frustrated with everything, so unhappy. She used to say how she 'hated' this country and the heat and the flies, and perhaps she did, coming from Scotland and all. Yet I used to get the feeling that she put it on for our benefit when she knew she was to be sent back. Poor Caroline. I got to know her, and she loved John Stuart dearly. Still does, I'm certain. What mother wouldn't? Broke her heart to leave him, yet he doesn't know it or want to.

"Well, she went back to Scotland, sure enough. I'll never forget it. Seems like only yesterday. It was early morning in May, an overcast day, a dreary day, you might say. Young John Stuart was just over three years old. Arthur Wakeman stood up there." Thelma waved her brown hand in the direction of Mayfield House, then her face crinkled with sadness. "I watched from the window. It was a smaller house then. He held John Stuart in his arms as she mounted the coach. Well, she never once looked back. Her back was stiff as a ramrod. I could feel the tension in that woman, though I was yards away, through the window.

"Then as the door of the coach closed, Arthur Wakeman held John Stuart out, close to the window, as if to let his mother see him for the final time. I wept for them all, all three of them." She sniffed softly as if she were weeping again for them, there in the sunny afternoon, over three decades later.

Thelma took Eve's hands in hers and was quiet for a few moments before she shook her head disconsolately and finished her account. "So there you are. A proud man was Sir Arthur Wakeman. And that, Eve love, is why John Stuart will not speak of her. He is deeply offended by what she did to his father, and beyond that, he feels she abandoned him, scorned him. Although I'd say she had no choice but to leave him. Fact is, I know she didn't, poor thing."

Eve nodded. "Thank you for telling me, Thelma. I understand John Stuart a little better now. It is natural that he feels as he does, yet I wish he could speak of it and settle it within himself."

Thelma patted Eve's hand. "Perhaps you are right. I am only a bush woman, but it seems to me that somehow he cannot. You see, he has held this sort of mental penalty against his mother for all these years. I don't suppose he's about to stop now."

Eve nodded. She wondered if these feelings he had caused him to insist that his wife be more perfect than other women.

He glorified her, idolized her, or at least his illusion of her. How she wished he could love her for herself, imperfect as she really was, the way she loved him. For she did love him and never wanted to hurt him. Never. But she had not been honest with him, though he was her partner, and there should have been no secrets. Honesty was, after all, a measure of the trueness of love. She determined to steel herself and tell him that very night about Clare.

After dinner, she sat with her husband in the blue room, a lovely parlor decorated in varying shades of blue and violet, with an eastern aspect. Eve was waiting her opportunity to speak. There had been none at dinner, for the servants kept coming and going. Now, as Baines served coffee, John Stuart spoke. "Darling, Joe and Jack were impressed with your idea for the new field. I told them you are getting to be an expert about Mayfield, and they agree."

She smiled, and Baines, who was pouring out the tea, murmured approvingly.

John Stuart took up a sweetmeat. "When you said today that the branding yard was on a gentle slope, however did you know? I hardly recalled that myself."

"Oh, I was there yesterday. Remember, I accompanied Thelma to the picnic for all the wives and the smaller children?"

"Yes, now I do."

"Do you know we have twenty-nine married couples here on Mayfield now?"

John Stuart grinned. "Yes, I think I was aware of the number."

"We went up on the hill behind the corn storage sheds where the jacaranda trees are; its lovely and shady up there. One of the small children wandered away, and there was great fear that she may have found her way to the Lachlan, especially after little Laura Dale's experience. Thelma and I happened to go down to the branding yard looking for her. That was when I noticed the incline."

"I see. Did you find the child all right?"

"Oh, yes, she was picking field daisys over near one of the sheds."

Eve was waiting for Baines to leave. When at last the door closed behind him, she swiveled around on the sofa to face John Stuart. "Darling, I have something I want to tell you."

At the very same moment, John Stuart asked, "Who was the child?"

"What was that?" Eve replied, her mind engrossed in what she was about to say.

"I said, who was the child who wandered away from the picnic yesterday?"

"Oh. Mrs. Kinnock's little daughter, Katy."

John Stuart's face clouded. Muttering a sound of censure, he rose to his feet. His mouth tightened in disapproval and a frown lodged between his eyes. "Her? Kinnock's wife? She's trash. Kinnock's leaving at the end of the month, I'm pleased to say. What the devil was *she* doing at the picnic?"

A spasm of dismay ran through Eve. "John Stuart, dear, she's the wife of one of the stockmen. We do not discriminate between them. What's wrong with her?"

"Forget it, Eve." He turned from her and placed his coffee cup on the table.

But Eve was sick with apprehension. She had to know. "John Stuart, please, what is it about Mrs. Kinnock that vexes you?"

He moved back and sat down beside her, placing his hands on his knees and sighing. "Oh, Eve, I do what I can to keep Mayfield a green and pleasant land for those who live here, as my father did before me. And I try to find the best of men—decent, moral men, with good and faithful wives—to be my workers and my stockmen. But sometimes a man brings a woman here who does not fit, who is . . . like her. A bad type." He lifted his hands up to hold them over his face momentarily, then he turned to look at her. His eyes were pained, and he blinked as if to remove the expression from them. "Anyway, Kinnock's leaving soon, so let's say no more about it." He stood. "Now, why don't we have a gentle walk through the park before bed?"

Eve felt prickling sensations up and down her spine. She had been about to explain Clare to him. Now this had happened. "John Stuart, why do you feel this way?" she found herself asking.

A rumbling sound of frustration escaped from John Stuart's lips. "Eve, Eve, these women are all alike; they bring only pain. Kinnock is a fool. When he came here, it was to make a bit of money; he's on his way to Queensland, to start afresh. Joe and Jack felt sympathy for him, and so I agreed. But the woman was to keep to herself, and now I hear she's out at a picnic, with you. It's common knowledge amongst the men that the child you went searching for is not Kinnock's. It was born down in Yass, before she married him. I don't know any more than that, nor do I wish to. All I do know is, I am angered and affronted that you are forced into company with such low-class trash. The sooner she leaves Mayfield, the better.'' He moved a few steps. ''Now, please, are you coming for a walk or not?''

Eve stood. She felt quite lifeless. Automatically she put her hand on the arm he extended toward her. Out of the parlor they went, into the front hall and across the veranda in the lamplight, where the luxurious scent of the first jasmine blossoms of the spring floated headily all around them. As they passed down the stone steps her husband asked, ''Darling, did I hear you say you had something to tell me earlier?''

And Eve responded, ''Something to tell you? No, sweetheart, I don't recall anything.''

TWELVE

Chance Meeting

It was the twenty-third of November, and Joe and John Stuart were riding in, tired and dust-covered, after a hard day of mustering and counting two of the eastern herds. Their topic of conversation was the menace of the bushrangers, as it was in most of the West these days. The previous Saturday, bushrangers had held up a group of Roman Catholic churchgoers at a church fete in Cowra.

John Stuart shook his head. ''It is fortunate Eve is not Catholic, for she might have been there.''

''True, m'boy. At least no one was hurt.''

''Perhaps this raid will deter her from running to Cowra to church services with Thelma every fortnight.''

''It might.'' Joe looked doubtful.

John Stuart said no more but leaned across to Joe and patted him affectionately on the shoulder.

When they neared the stables, Jack Hennessy, followed by

Stephen Watson, waylaid them with the news that there had been a raid on David Campbell's small, sheep station at Goimbla, thirty miles from Forbes, a tiny township to the northwest.

"Campbell was attacked last Thursday by the Hall gang. Set fire to a barn, we're told. Terrorized them, by all accounts, though the homesteaders put up a good fight, for one of the Hall gang was shot and killed!"

"Pity more of them weren't shot," remarked Joe. "The whole countryside seems alive with the rabble. Sir Rutherford has his work cut out, that's for certain."

That night Eve and John Stuart sat at dinner in evening dress, as was the tradition of the upper classes. They were in the small dining room, adjacent to the breakfast room. She talked of many things pertinent to Mayfield. She had spent the day with the new doctor, Gerald Douglas, whom John Stuart had insisted on hiring after her fall. Eve had organized his cottage and surgery and had been working as his helper since he arrived, although he was also training Stephen Watson's sister, who showed a great aptitude for medicine. John Stuart had been reluctant to agree to Eve's helping to nurse the sick, for it meant tending the children and the general staff, and he argued she was not really back to health herself. He had been adamant at first, but Eve had persuaded him, for secretly, he was quite proud of her.

Toward the end of the meal, Eve's fingers reached out across the pristine linen tablecloth to lift John Stuart's hand. His features flattened in an indulgent smile. He was so in love with her: her beauty, her simple purity, her abilities, her virtue.

"John Stuart, I will have to go into Bathurst to do a little more Christmas shopping for the workers' children and the staff. Also I must order medical supplies for Dr. Douglas. While I am there, I would like to stay a few days with Father and Mother, if you agree."

John Stuart frowned and removed his hand from her grasp. "Certainly not, darling. While I understand you wish to work with Dr. Douglas, I still think you've hardly recovered from your fall, and after what's been going on in recent months, I should think you would want to stay off the roads."

"Oh, John Stuart, now, you know I am absolutely well again. Young Betty Watson is learning so fast with the doctor that I feel quite happy leaving for a week, and as to the roads, there have only been a few isolated incidents."

John Stuart shook his head. "Isolated incidents! Evelyn, we

hear of someone being robbed or harassed by bushrangers every other week. And this latest business of attacking a homestead, small and ill protected as it was. It's awful!''

Eve sighed. ''John Stuart, there must be more to the Campbell raid than we know about. It's probably some kind of feud. In any case, there aren't enough bushrangers to be on every road in the colony. I am not concerned.''

Her husband was unconvinced. ''Your mathematics are at variance with mine. There is danger in traveling, and I don't like it. And you choose to go to Bathurst, when it was Bathurst that was raided only last month. It is not a town to be visiting.''

A determined look came into Eve's eyes. ''On the contrary, my darling, it is more than probable that Bathurst is the safest town west of the Blue Mountains for that very reason. Anyway, it is the *only* town that has decent shops.''

''And it's coincidence only that a certain cleric and his wife abide there, no doubt.''

''Yes.''

He did not speak but returned to eating.

She watched him briefly. ''Oh, John Stuart, you exasperate me. After all, I will be in a Mayfield coach, thoroughly well guarded.'' She had almost added, ''damn it,'' but had caught herself in time.

He did not look up. ''You are too much of an emancipated spirit, my darling. That is how you came by trouble the day after your birthday and found yourself in association with such company.''

The indirect reference to Alan Fletcher brought disquieting memories. Her husband had not mentioned him since the night on her sickbed. She fell quiet.

After a little time, he broke the silence. ''You see, Eve, I am not pleased that my wife has had two encounters with a wanted man, a notorious outlaw.''

She took a deep breath. She knew John Stuart was only concerned for her welfare, but she did not like the tone of reprimand in his voice. ''I am desiring to go to Bathurst to shop, order medical stores, and to visit some loved ones, not to have an encounter of any kind with any outlaw.''

''Enough!''

He said it so sharply that she started in surprise.

''I will not have you speaking in this way. It is too flippant.'' His voice was rising. ''You are my wife. It is not fitting that you have been in the company of such a man, unconscious for most of it or not.''

Her chin lifted and she returned his gaze. There was the veriest note of defiance in her tone as she reminded him, ''He did me a kindness. Even more, he probably saved my life.'' She was thinking how alarmed John Stuart would be if he knew that she had been conscious for hours in his company; that she had held a long conversation with him; that she thought him honorable and moral and benevolent.

John Stuart's fist came down on the table in exasperation.

''Oh, Eve, you try me! All right. You go on the conditions that Thelma and Daydee accompany you and that you are in Bathurst no longer than a week.''

Eve agreed readily, although the idea of Daydee's company was not attractive.

Yet, on the following Monday, the Mayfield coach carried all three of them. Daydee had been enthusiastic to make the journey, for a close friend from her school days now lived in Bathurst. As the vehicle rolled across Mayfield toward the outer world, she leaned in the corner reading *The Moonstone*. She gave her attention to the two women intermittently, passing from petulant to gay, moody to talkative. Eve was well aware that Daydee disliked her. She had made many overtures toward the girl in the previous months, only to be rebuked in one way or the other. This did not concern Eve, for Daydee was difficult with many people. She was a spoiled girl with little on her mind except reading and painting and indulging in genteel pastimes. She was like all wealthy graziers' daughters, doing very little once their schooling was over, living in a sort of hiatus between schooling and marriage. Eve thought it understandable that the girl was infatuated by John Stuart. She had plenty of time to indulge in fancies. Consequently, Eve dismissed most of Daydee's attitude toward her as girlish jealousy, and assumed that in time it would pass.

They made the journey in easy stages and by nightfall were in the settlement of Blayney, where they stayed the night at the Albion Hotel, in the main street, the only street. Mrs. Osmond, the proprietor, waited on them herself. It was an honor to have Mrs. Wakeman under the roof for a whole night.

During the evening meal, Mrs. Osmond carried in a sweet tray, and as she put it down, she spoke, ''Excuse me, madam,'' she began, her pronunciation derived from the cockney, a distinctive pattern set to become the Australian accent in another generation. "There be a gentleman stayin' under our roof who says he knows ye. He is desirous of taking tea with ye after the meal, if ye would be so generous as to favor him?"

Eve looked inquiringly up at her. "Really? And who is he?"

"He says to give to ye Sir Rutherford Blake's compliments."

Sir Rutherford Blake! Oh dear, he would only make her feel uncomfortable. She felt inclined to refuse.

Daydee's face, however, had lit up at the mention of Sir Rutherford. "Oh, good, it would be ever so nice to see him! Maybe he's caught a bushranger!"

Eve motioned to the woman at the door. "Could you wait outside, Mrs. Osmond? We will just be a moment."

When the door closed, Eve turned to Thelma and Daydee. "I had thought to retire early, as we have the trip on to Bathurst tomorrow. I'm feeling rather weary. What do you think, Thelma dear?"

"Oh no," interrupted Daydee.

"Quiet, Daydee, please," her mother remonstrated. "Eve, I don't really know what to think. What would John Stuart want you to do?"

Daydee interrupted again, "Uncle John Stuart would expect us to see him, of that I'm sure! Why, Sir Rutherford is a friend of his."

Thelma looked skyward and shook her head, but Daydee's point had sailed home and ten minutes later, the police detective made his entrance. He wore a fashionable dark blue frock coat, a checked waistcoat, and a spotted cravat tied in a bow at his throat. His lean features took on an almost cheerful aspect as he said, "Ladies, ladies, a pleasure." He bent over their extended hands.

He soon ascertained where they were going. He tapped his finger on his saucer. "Bathurst. Ah yes, it's been getting a little attention lately from the lawbreakers. Well, I'm to be giving the township some attention of my own. I will be setting up my headquarters there in the new year, ladies, with an assignment of two dozen troopers."

Daydee was full of interest. "Why have you chosen Bathurst, Sir Rutherford?"

"The telegraph, missy, the telegraph. The line ends there. It allows me to be in communication with the inspector general in Sydney on almost a daily basis."

Then he smiled one of his mirthless grins. "I can honestly

say I'm not concerned about your entourage, Mrs. Wakeman. In the Mayfield coach with the four sturdy guards I saw downstairs in the bar, you'll not be troubled.''

Daydee's eyes were wide. ''Oh, do tell us, Sir Rutherford, what is the latest adventure you've had? What did you think of the church fete in Cowra being robbed, and the Campbell station raid?''

Eve shivered. The conversation in its entirety would be of bushrangers, just as she had dreaded it would.

''Ah now, missy.'' Sir Rutherford drank from his cup and clinked it down in his saucer. He dabbed his mouth with the napkin and rolled back his eyes. ''The three things you have asked me are all one. The latest adventure of mine has been on Campbell station itself. I've been there to scrutinize the scene, you might say. They put up a good fight, you know, the Campbells. Shot dead John O'Meally! The Hall gang is disintegrating. Micky Burke's dead. We got him in October, and I have John Vane in custody, surrendered in Bathurst the very day of the Campbell raid. Leaves only Benjamin Hall himself and 'Flash' Johnny Gilbert. Ah, yes, the facts are such that I'm feeling confident about taking the two surviving rascals. But your other question of the Catholic church fete.'' He coughed. ''I'm on my way to Cowra now to discuss the matter with the victims. I think it must have been Old Joe Daily or Dan Morgan. I'm sure it wasn't Alan Fletcher, for he acts quite differently.''

Eve's cup rattled loudly in her saucer. All heads turned toward her.

''Oh, do excuse me,'' she said as she leaned forward and with both hands placed her cup down on the table.

''Of course, madam,'' Sir Rutherford answered. He pursed his lips in thought before he went on. ''Although one never knows. It was not the sort of job Fletcher does. The women were robbed, and he doesn't rob women. And I've never known him to rob a church or the needy. In fact, it's more the government he goes after, or sporadically, the very wealthy.'' He looked directly at Eve. ''As you would be aware. Ah yes, now, he is so interesting.'' He was warming to his subject. ''Operates in various parts of the country, hard to track, has strategy.'' He gestured with his elongated middle finger toward Daydee. ''Now, always in my experience, outlaws, pirates, brigands, bushrangers, call them what you like, operate from a central point. He has acted as far north as Wellington, as far south as Young, as

far east as Bathurst and Crookwell, and as far west as Forbes.
And the center of those places is—''

"Canowindra!" interjected Daydee.

He turned almost a smile to the girl. "Ah yes, excellent ge-
ography. Months ago, I combed the plains around Canowindra
for ten, fifteen miles, but there is no sign of a hideout there,
young lady. No. Alan Fletcher is clever. What is more, his men
are devoted to him.''

Daydee was leaning forward, her face attentive, her small
mouth an O of excitement. "And who are his men, Sir Rutherford, do you know?''

"Ah yes, missy, I know. There are five in all. Three escaped
with him from Moreton Bay back these ten years. Samuel Cooper, Lawless Drake, and Daniel Dwyer, convicts with Alan
Fletcher to a man. The fifth member of the band is Jordan O'Day,
a horse thief, as so many of our 'wild colonial boys' are.''

He had opened his mouth to continue when Daydee spoke
again. "But you don't know, Sir Rutherford! Aunt Eve fell from
Moonlight on the day after her birthday, and it was Alan Fletcher
who found her in the bush.''

Sir Rutherford's eyes seemed to bulge, so large did they
grow. "What? What is that?" He looked to Eve for verification.

Eve steeled herself. "I cannot tell you much, Sir Rutherford.
The man found me after my fall, and returned me to a search
party led by Mr. Larmer. That's all.''

"But, my dear lady, there must be more. It is invaluable information to me. Anything about that man is. I am anxious to
hear, excited to hear. Please tell me all. What does he look
like?''

A prickling sensation ran across her shoulders. She gathered
herself and looked in his eyes. "I'm sorry, Sir Rutherford, but
I was injured at the time. I cannot tell you.''

He was looking at her with disbelief. "Cannot? But you were
with him. Actually with him! Why . . . ?''

"I repeat, sir, that I was injured. I was unconscious.'' Her
voice was cordial but uncompromising.

Thelma took Eve's hand, and in doing so, took her side. "Yes,
Sir Rutherford, Eve was unconscious; she had a head wound.
You would do better to talk to my Joe; he saw him, too.''

Eve stood. "I'm sorry, Sir Rutherford, but we are continuing
our journey tomorrow, and a good night's sleep would be welcome. I don't mean to seem ungracious, but if you will excuse
us.''

"Mrs. Wakeman!" her guest exclaimed, rising to his feet. "I've been unmannerly. I become so zealous given opportunity to learn about these ruffians, I forge ahead. Forgive me, madam. Please."

Daydee's mouth turned down. "Oh no, don't stop. I'm enjoying it."

Thelma broke across her daughter's words angrily. "Please, Daydee, have some manners."

Daydee looked peevishly at her parent, but said no more.

Eve extended her hand to her visitor. He bent over it formally. "Your servant, Mrs. Wakeman, and as your husband has been good enough to invite me to Mayfield for the Christmas week, I will be in your delightful company again very soon."

Eve had not known of this, but she covered her surprise with a polite smile.

He took Daydee's hand. "And we will continue our conversation then, missy."

He bowed to Thelma and walked to the door, turning back to say, "I certainly do hope you are entirely recovered from your fall, Mrs. Wakeman."

The door closed and Thelma rounded on her daughter. "Daydee! You really are the rudest girl. How dare you dispute Aunt Eve. Apologize!"

With half-closed eyes she looked from her mother to Eve. "I'm sure Aunt Eve would not want me to apologize simply because I was enthusiastic."

For a few seconds, Eve returned the girl's gaze, then patting her on the shoulder, replied tolerantly, "No, Daydee, I would not."

Outside in the corridor, Sir Rutherford hesitated. It was astounding that the woman had encountered Alan Fletcher. Almost too hard to believe! And her reluctance to speak of it. Fact was, she was not simply reluctant, she had refused. He shook his head in thought and continued on to the barroom.

The next morning, the Mayfield coach passed out of Blayney like some gilded, shining, precious thing, at which ordinary folk could but stare. The two women passed the time by reading the women's periodicals that arrived twice yearly from Scotland for Thelma, and Daydee was her usual incommunicative self. They arrived in Bathurst by thirty minutes past eleven o'clock in the morning.

Eve had been in Bathurst five days before Father mentioned Clare.

He brought up the subject when they had been into the church to set up the altar for evening prayer. As they came out onto the church porch, he turned to her, his brow wrinkling in the afternoon sun. "Have you told John Stuart about your sister?"

She looked guiltily at him and shook her head.

"Ah," was all he replied.

Some seconds passed. Two sparrows flew in and landed on the beams of the porch above their heads. They perched close together, their small gray bodies almost touching as they performed a sort of kissing action with their beaks. Eve looked up and seemed to be watching them as she replied, "Oh, Father, I cannot find it in myself to explain to him. He will never be able to accept her as I would need to tell her."

Father still did not speak.

She drew her eyes down from the birds. "Whenever I have been going to tell him, there is always something that prevents me. Would it be better if you told him?"

Father considered what she had asked before he answered. He was deeply concerned for her and understood her fears, but it would be wrong to intercede in this way. "No, it is for you to do, my Evvy. It is your responsibility. And one you must acknowledge. My intervention would not be a kindness to you. He cares deeply for you, and I believe he will accept what you say. Delay no longer, and when you have told him, I would like you to let me know."

Eve managed a smile she did not feel. She knew he was perfectly right. He was not letting her down. He never had, never would. She was accountable. She had the strength. It must come from her. She was John Stuart's wife and must live up to that, not have Father interceding. But she knew in her heart what her husband's reaction would be.

She nodded and took his arm, and they walked in silence to tea.

The following morning, she went to inspect the twenty small cloth dolls she had ordered from the seamstress on Rocket Street. The day after would see the week in Bathurst gone and they would make the return journey to Mayfield.

Mother and Thelma accompanied her to the shops. She was now much less of a spectacle in the settlement. A week had satisfied the inquisitive. She passed through the streets almost as Eve Herman would have done. Where George and Lambert streets joined, they separated. They would meet again at Mrs. Ayres's Tea Room, a cozy little shop run by Bathurst's premier cook, a friend of Lottie's.

Eve waved them away and proceeded diagonally across the road to enter the park. Her destination was on the far side. Her mind lazily surrendered to the warmth of the day. She remembered that this was where John Stuart said he had first seen her. She smiled at that, feeling the heat of the sun on her face and the back of her hands. Her gait slowed languidly.

The park was empty. Usually there was a mother and child, or a stockman in Bathurst for the day, resting under the trees, but as she looked around, she saw no one. Then suddenly, over to her left, a man issued through the trees, carrying a box of ammunition upon his shoulder.

Instantly she halted. It was as if someone had hit her hard in the stomach. There was no mistaking that form, that walk. Alan Fletcher! Here in the middle of Bathurst. But how could it be?

The memory of their afternoon together burst into her mind . . . his face, his eyes, his body. The warmth of his arms encircling her as she slowly slipped into unconsciousness. Gone was the lassitude of a few moments before. All the sensations of that time with him rose inside her, even the guilt, the terrible guilt. What was it John Stuart had said? "I am not pleased that my wife has had two encounters with a wanted man." And she had replied she was not coming here to have an encounter of any kind with any outlaw.

Seconds passed. He had not seen her. He walked on. She must turn away and leave. Let him go. It was best.

But was it? There was a panicky feeling in her chest. How badly she wanted to call out to him.

Then as she watched, he glanced sideways through the trees. With a reckless, exciting anticipation, she saw him catch sight of her and halt.

Ever so slowly he turned around to face her.

It was her! Daily he had hoped she was unharmed. Although in a sense he had never wanted to see her again.

For a moment he thought to tip his hat and continue on to where Lawless waited with the horses. But then, perhaps this was providential. He had been reminded too often of John Stuart Wakeman's wife in recent weeks. This was his chance to dispel the emotions he was beginning to associate with her.

He began to walk toward her in his easy way.

Eve's heart raced. A small vein in her neck pulsated visibly as she took a deep breath to calm herself. She even looked quickly to right and left as he advanced, but there were still only the two of them in the empty park.

"I am surprised to see you here," he said, tipping his hat.

"And I, you," she replied.

She watched him smile faintly at her. It was an odd smile. There was something in it that made her uneasy, and as he smiled, he asked, "How is it you are here in Bathurst?"

"I am visiting the rectory for a few days. The Reverend and Mrs. Billings are like parents to me. But you, why are you here?"

"Supplies of ammunition cannot be bought in the same store too often in my trade, else the shopkeeper might ask too many questions. Hence, we often travel far afield."

She nodded in understanding. "But is it not dangerous here?"

"Lass." He spoke the word from deep within his throat. "There can be danger in the most innocent of places. It is not something I dwell upon. But danger aside, I am pleased to discover you are well, with no apparent ill effects from your fall."

"Thank you. Yes, I am quite well again."

As they stood together in the middle of Bathurst town, they were unaware that they were being observed.

Daydee, on her way to her friend's house, had crossed Lambert Street and entered the park behind Eve, just in time to witness the meeting.

She stopped and watched across the bushes. At first, there was mere interest at the sight of Eve speaking with a strange man. But then her small, dark eyes narrowed. In the attitude of the two before her, there was something, a certain quality, intangible although it might be, that heightened her curiosity.

She began to advance across the grass toward them.

Eve was speaking. "For a few moments, I felt that perhaps you did not wish to see me."

"And perhaps you were right. It may have been better if I had not, but as I have, I am not unhappy about it."

She smiled at these words, delighted, confused, and mystified by her feelings.

He still held the box of ammunition on his shoulder, and he swung it down to hold it under his arm.

"We have so much ammunition at Mayfield, I wish I could give you some," she heard herself say.

The intimacy that had been in his expression died.

He seemed to withdraw himself from her, though he still

looked straight into her eyes. There was hardness now. He took a step away. "Yes, no doubt you have many things at Mayfield. And Mayfield is where you belong. I must leave now. It would have been better if this meeting had not taken place. You speak and act as if it were commonplace. But lest you've forgotten, I am a bushranger, Mrs. Wakeman."

The statement found her quite unprepared. She felt a stab of pain, and the smile faded from her mouth. Her hands hung awkwardly in the air. She stared at him in bewilderment.

At that very moment, Daydee's voice exploded at her shoulder. "Hello, Aunt Eve!"

Eve started and turned toward the girl. She said nothing. There was a dazed expression in her eyes, and she seemed to stare right through Daydee.

Eve's appearance only served to make Daydee more suspicious. She turned from Eve to Alan, inquiringly.

Alan's voice was raw and hard, with the tones of a bushman, totally unlike his own. "Why, thankye again, ma'am. I reckon I'll be able to find my way now." He tipped his hat and bent forward in a half gesture of a bow.

Automatically Eve turned, white-faced, to watch him walk away.

"Who on earth was he?" asked Daydee sharply. "I don't think I've ever seen such a man. His eyes are just . . . wonderful."

Eve's confusion was obvious. She did not answer but moved off in the opposite direction.

"Aunt Eve," the girl began again, following along, "I said, who was that man?"

This time Eve replied, though she did not look at her. "I don't know. He just wanted some directions."

Daydee had missed little. "Then why is it you were so upset when I came along? To me it looked as if you knew him well, as if he had told you something that distressed you."

"Daydee, please." Eve was trying desperately to sound normal. "I have told you what happened. I do not know him, and he did not upset me!"

The girl was watching her as she spoke, watching the telltale flush on Eve's throat and noting the agitation beneath the imposed calm.

"Where did he want to go, then?"

"What?"

"Where did he want to go, then? The man. What directions did he want?"

Eve stopped walking. When she answered, there was excitement and anger in her voice, which she tried unsuccessfully to quell. "Daydee, you really are the most inquisitive pest. I do not have to explain myself to you. Don't you have your friend to meet?" And with those words, she left the girl standing there.

On the far side of the park, Alan mounted Freedom, and with Lawless, who had been waiting for him, rode out of Bathurst town.

Three hours later, Eve sat alone in the back garden of the rectory, on the grass under the jacaranda tree where she had lunched with John Stuart on the day of their first meeting. Her head lolled forward, and her hand rested on her chin. Among her disordered thoughts ran many of her husband, and between them, intermingled with them, many of Alan Fletcher.

Why was he so significant to her? Why was she so instinctively drawn to the man? Why? Why? Why? Her head spun; she felt ill. This feeling she had for him was wrong, unseemly. Even *he* had so much as said so. It was deceitful. She was being false to John Stuart.

John Stuart.

She knew him so much better now.

Seven months at Mayfield had given her many insights into her husband. He was a complicated man, wise and often surprisingly kind, and always generous. He worked hard, too hard; twelve or thirteen hours a day were not unusual for him. From the top managers like Jack Hennessy and Stephen Watson, down through the ranks to the foremen and ordinary workers alike, he was held in high esteem. In fact, some almost revered him. So did she. So much so that she still could not bring herself to tell him about Clare.

His personality was complex. He hated what he considered loose or immoral behavior. He had been irreparably wounded by his mother's conduct, Eve was positive. There was no doubt that he placed her, Eve, above all women, but she could never live up to his saintly estimation of her. If only she could. It would remove the guilt that rose within her every time she thought of Alan Fletcher.

She closed her eyes. Her head was hot, she felt feverish. "Oh God, how to do that, how to stop thinking of Alan Fletcher? Please, please, let me think of him no more." Still with eyes closed, she stretched out her hands in supplication.

At that moment, Father came to find her. As he stepped from the back porch to the grass, he saw her gesture.

Tears rolled down her cheeks as she opened her eyes.

Father stood in front of her. "My love, what is it that troubles you so?"

"Oh, Father dear, you are back so soon; I was not expecting you yet." She tried her best to smile.

"I can see that, Evvy, love. Please answer me. What is it that troubles you this way?" He knelt on the ground in front of her.

Eve was about to reply, "Nothing," when the love and understanding in the eyes that looked into hers overwhelmed her, and she took his hands. "Father, there is something I must tell you. Something I do not comprehend at all. It is within me and overshadows many of my waking hours . . . my sleeping hours, too."

Father eased himself to the ground and sat beside her in the hot, dry afternoon breeze.

It was then she told him of Alan Fletcher.

She spoke of the first time she saw him, her wedding day. Of the inexplicable feelings she had experienced.

At first Father was clearly startled. Although he loved the woman beside him more than himself, he was a man of God. He had married this woman in the sight of his God, and now she was telling him of a strange and mysterious association with a known and wanted outlaw. He was amazed and frightened for her. He thought she must be hallucinating. But as the story progressed, and she told of the day after her birthday and the fall from Moonlight, he knew she meant what she said.

He did not interrupt her as so many of his counterparts would have done with remonstrance or argument. Instead, he listened, with all the calm and reason of his rare intelligence.

She came at last to the meeting that very morning in the parkland. When she told him of Daydee's intervention, he said nothing, but he did not like what he had heard. Father had summed Daydee up quickly, and though he was generous by nature, he could see little in her to inspire confidence.

Eve finished her story with the words "You see, no matter what men say, I know Alan Fletcher is not bad. I know he is moral and courageous and good, just as surely as I know that you are. But I am almost deranged. I feel as if there is a battle going on inside me. I am muddled and confused. I don't know why all this is, but it is. And it is not as if I don't love John Stuart. I do, with all my being."

And only then did he speak.

His fine brow wrinkled and there was concern in every nuance of his voice. "Eve, I have heard all you have said. And perhaps this Alan Fletcher is as you describe him. Nevertheless, no matter what you have felt in his presence, you are married to John Stuart, inextricably and forever. You say you love your husband. There is no future in thoughts or dreams. You must forget Fletcher! Even if he were not outside the law, any connection would be fantastic. You are Mrs. Wakeman. You must realize what that means, Eve. You are no longer the girl I met in Sydney, nor the determined teenager of the sewing business, nor the Bathurst music teacher. You have been elevated. There is no more important woman in the colony, not even the governor's wife."

Eve was watching him; her eyes shone, and she listened carefully. As he finished, she said, "Yes, Father, I know you are right. But it is as if there is an outside force reminding me constantly of Alan Fletcher. I have been in his presence in the most freakish of circumstances, and no matter what, it is beyond me to govern how I feel. Even if I never see him again, I think it will always be there." She looked imploringly at the man beside her. "Oh, I am so confused," she finished hopelessly.

Father spoke again, and now there was conviction in his voice. "Eve, what the bushranger said to you this day is beyond doubt. Even he sees the ridiculous nature of what has happened. Only you can divest yourself of these thoughts. It is up to you, no one else. 'Therein the patient must minister to himself.' I can only pray you will never see this Alan Fletcher again. Return to Mayfield and your husband. Work at your marriage."

As he completed his words, she sighed and murmured, "Thank you. Thank you for not judging me. I love you so."

His eyes glistened. "It is not for me to judge anyone, and where you are concerned, my Evvy, I *could* not judge. But ask God's help. Close your eyes now, and we will ask together."

So there on the lawn surrounded by the blue fallen blossoms from the jacaranda tree, they closed their eyes, and Father's voice softly began:

"In thee O Lord, do I put my trust: let me never be put to confusion.

Deliver me in thy righteousness, and cause me to escape: incline thine ear unto me, and save me.

Be thou my strong habitation, whereunto I may continually

resort: thou hast given commandment to save me; for thou *art* my rock and my fortress.

Hear our prayer O Lord, and give Evelyn May the help she needs to dismiss this man from her mind. Return her to Mayfield and happiness.

Hear our prayer O Lord. For thou art our hope O God. We ask this in the name of the Father and the Son and the Holy Ghost. Amen.''

THIRTEEN

Christmas

John Stuart missed Eve while she was away in Bathurst. His days were full and busy from dawn to dusk, but the nights without her were dull and lifeless. He had missed her laughter, the sound of her voice, her touch, and her sweet company.

Each evening, he and Joe ate together, two lonely men, lost without their wives. It was no accident that they were both working in sight of the road across the property on the ninth of December, the day Eve and Thelma were coming home.

By the time Deke Edwards brought his horses to a halt at the front steps of Mayfield House, John Stuart had arrived as well.

''My darling,'' he said as Eve stepped down into his arms. ''I've missed you so.''

Thelma smiled to see their delight, but Daydee's face was peevish, regarding the reunion with obvious unhappiness. When John Stuart at last turned from hugging his wife to greet her, she affected a pretty smile. ''And I have missed you,'' she said, looking meaningfully up into his eyes.

''Yes, it's good to have you all back,'' he answered, not noticing her earnest expression, and lifting her a little as he bent to hug her slight frame.

Joe soon arrived, and the Larmers departed. When John Stuart and Eve entered their home they were greeted by Mrs. Smith, Mr. Baines, and Stephanie. Then John Stuart turned to Eve and hugged her in front of them. Eve laughed, ''I see you truly have missed me, my love.''

While Stephanie unpacked for her, Eve and John Stuart walked down into the garden bower off their rooms. The poinciana tree was in full bloom; its glorious blossoms a sunshade of bright crimson above them, and the fallen ones, a carpet of glowing color beneath their feet.

''So tell me, darling,'' John Stuart said, bending down and breaking off a small cluster of chrysanthemums for her, ''what did you do in Bathurst?''

Eve took the flowers. ''Thank you, kind sir.'' They smiled into each other's eyes, and a little quiver of love ran through Eve as she was reminded how very attractive his genial half smile was. She replied, ''Oh, we were busy. It was lovely to be with Mother and Father. I helped with the altar flowers as I used to do. And Thelma and Mother and Lottie and I went to the church social evening, and we pottered in the garden and took luncheon under the jacaranda tree. Remember our first meal there together? We did all the things that we used to do.''

His mouth drew down in mock disappointment. ''I see, Mrs. Wakeman. You did not miss your husband at all?''

She threw her arms up around his neck. ''No, Mr. Wakeman, you are right, I did not miss you at all.'' And then she burst into merry laughter and ran from him.

He sprang across the space between them and, catching her up in his arms, pressed kisses upon her eyes, her cheeks, her hair. Then holding her face in his hands, he whispered, ''You tease me, Evelyn May, and it is not fair.'' He bent down and kissed her lovingly on the mouth, and the touch of his lips was wonderful.

They spent the remainder of the short afternoon together, and later, when they were dressing for dinner, they discussed their plans for the impending Christmas. When John Stuart mentioned the guest list, Eve told him of her meeting with Sir Rutherford in Blayney on her way to Bathurst; how he had taken tea with them and informed her he was coming to Mayfield for the Christmas week.

John Stuart nodded. ''Yes, darling, I'm sorry I didn't tell you. It slipped my mind; I should have. But I thought he and young Elrington would make a fine addition to our house party.'' Then he asked a most innocent question. "Did you run into anyone else you knew?"

A sharp chill ran across her shoulders and down her spine. Anyone else? Oh, Lord, yes, she had run into someone else. What should she do? Tell him? He would be so upset. She had thought a great deal about Alan Fletcher since her meeting with him in the Bathurst park, but, too, she had realized that Father's advice was manifestly right, and she had come home determined to reject the inexplicable feelings she had for the bushranger. Perhaps she should deflect John Stuart's question. There he was, the man she loved, looking at her with his dark, sincere eyes, so unaware of the import of his inquiry.

"Darling?" He wondered why she had not answered him.

"Yes, my love, I ran into a lot of folk I knew; after all, I lived in Bathurst five years."

"Of course." He turned into the dressing room to choose his jacket.

She felt quite sick. How desperately she wanted to be honest with him, about everything, always. She took a deep breath; her heart was racing and a flush had crept up her neck. "John Stuart?" Her husband turned around to her as she came in to him. "It is almost unbelievable, but I did run into someone else. Accidentally. I saw the bushranger, Alan Fletcher."

John Stuart's face became blank, totally blank. He stared at her vacantly, as if his mind had gone elsewhere.

She held her breath. She felt as if she would faint.

The seconds passed.

John Stuart had heard what Eve said. He knew he heard it, but it was as if he had not. His brain was refusing to acknowledge the name Alan Fletcher. It was obstinately rejecting that it was possible.

"John Stuart?"

With an obvious deployment of will, he refocused his eyes upon her.

"John Stuart, I know it's a surprise to you. It was to me; and of course, I was astounded to see him there . . . just as you are astounded to hear it."

"Astounded!" The word broke from his mouth with such force, she started. "Yes, I am completely astounded! How can this be? How in the devil's name can my wife go to Bathurst for a week with her parents and fall into company with that man again? It is not possible! What is going on in our lives?"

"Darling." Eve hastened to him. "It was the most unlikely

event. I was in the park, and there he appeared in front of me. I was amazed. I think he was, too. Our conversation was very brief. In fact, Daydee came up, and he lifted his hat and left.''

"Bloody hell, that you had any conversation at all is hard to bear, brief or not. He is a bushranger. Don't you understand?'' He moved away. "Are you stupid?'' A few seconds later he added, "Daydee? The child didn't realize who it was, I hope.''

"No. I said he was someone asking directions. It was none of her business.''

"Is that all?''

"Of course it is all! For goodness' sake, I left him, and heavens knows where he went.''

John Stuart was still in shock. He walked by her through to their bedroom and over to the window, where he stood leaning with his hands on the sill. For a full minute he made no sound. When he turned and spoke again, his voice was almost normal, but a strange expression lingered on his face. "So you were alone when you met him?''

"Yes, John Stuart, I was.''

"What did he say to you?''

"I think he said good day . . . and that he was pleased to see that I had recovered from my fall.''

"Bloody impudence. He's got a hide being in Bathurst. Up to no good, that's for certain.''

Even though the news had greatly angered him, Eve was relieved she had told her husband. She felt better for it. She sighed. "My dearest, I knew you would not like it.''

For some seconds he stood staring at her, then he moved swiftly and wrapped her in his arms. Her cheek was against him, and his voice sounded almost desperate in her ear. "No, I do not like it. I hate it. I hate to think of your having met and conversed alone with any man, let alone a blasted outlaw. Why, I am even jealous of Reverend Billings sometimes.''

"John Stuart,'' she retorted, her face pressed to him, "you are a silly thing.''

"I know,'' he answered, "but it's how I am.''

As he continued to hold her close, she looked up at him. "Come, darling,'' she said. "Please. Let's forget about it.''

Many of the inhabitants of the Australian cities were without work. Conditions in Sydney and Melbourne were poor, both more akin to shanty towns than cities. Despite available land, overcrowding was as bad as in Europe. Much of this was due to the rapid increase of population during the gold rush of the previous decade. Those who did leave the cities found it as hopeless to find employment in rural areas as in the towns.

But there were bastions of well-being and prosperity and perhaps the most flourishing of all was Mayfield.

Christmas Eve was hot and humid. Rain clouds threatened but did not deliver. Eve had been working with Dr. Douglas and Betty Watson consistently over the last two days, for there had been three stockmen injured curbing a stampede that had occurred near Daisy Ridge. Two were very ill and in need of constant care. Finally one of the dairy maids had come to relieve Eve but still she did not arrive home until after three o'clock in the afternoon, just in time to join the exhilarated party that made its way along the macadamized road leading from Mayfield proper across the river to the workers' cottages. The Christmas tree ceremony for the workers' children was to begin in half an hour with a concert on ''the green'' in the village. Among the party was Governor Sir John Young, who had taken a week off from his worries to come. He now laughed with his wife at some private joke as they rode side by side with John Stuart and Eve. Sir Rutherford rode with Daydee and the governor's aide-de-camp. David Elrington separated Mr. and Mrs. Stanley Ford, while their son Roy rode with Thelma and Joe. The rear saw John Stuart's barrister, Robert Robinson-Pike, in unison with the district's member of the legislative assembly, Mr. Stanley Payne, and his wife, Barbara.

Strapped to each lady's saddle was an umbrella, in case the menace of rain became reality.

The official party was welcomed with a cheer. Near two hundred were in attendance, not only married workers and their families, but single workers, too.

They all took their seats and the concert commenced. The last to appear was the eldest child on Mayfield, Jack Hennessy's son, Peter, a fair-haired boy of ten. He recited the first four verses of John Milton's ''On the Morning of Christ's Nativity.''

Then the children and their teacher presented themselves on the stage. There was a round of applause, and the gift giving began.

The excitement of the children was infectious. From a sea of Christmas paper and laughing, young faces, Eve, who was handing out presents, lifted her head to look over to her husband. There at his side stood Daydee. Eve frowned, but then she felt her hand taken by a small one and her attention was diverted to the children.

Daydee was on a mission. "May I sit a minute with you, Uncle John Stuart?"

John Stuart smiled up at the girl. "Of course, Daydee, sit down."

"We don't talk like we used to," she said, her dark eyes trained on him.

John Stuart laughed. "Well, my Daydee, it's a grown woman you are now. I can hardly swing you on my knee and banter as before."

Daydee sighed. "I didn't mean when I was little. I meant . . ."

John Stuart turned in his chair toward her. He brought her chin around to face him and looked into her small, intense face. He would have been horrified if he had known the joy she felt at the touch of his fingers.

"Ah, Daydee, now, don't be like a child. I am happy to talk to you, but I am a busy man, and now that I am married, things have changed."

"I know."

"Come on, give me a smile; it is Christmas Eve, you know. What about the famous Daydee Bronwyn Larmer smile?"

Daydee complied radiantly. She looked so young and virtuous that John Stuart bent forward and kissed her on her forehead. "Merry Christmas, Daydee," he said.

"Merry Christmas," Daydee replied, and under her breath said, "my love."

"Now, tell me," continued John Stuart innocently, "how did you enjoy your sojourn in Bathurst?"

A shiver of glee ran through her. John Stuart had asked the one question she had prayed he would. Her mind ran over what she had prepared to say. "Well, it was fun, really," she began. "I saw my friend Connie French every day, and oh, how we laughed about our days at St. Catherine's together. We had a grand time."

Just then, John Stuart's attention was taken by something else, and she fell silent until he turned back to her. "Now, what was that, Daydee?"

Her face brightened as she continued skillfully. "We all had a lovely time, actually. Aunt Eve is so fond of Reverend Billings, it was quite a delight for her to be back there, I'm sure. She no doubt caught up with many past acquaintances. Yes—" here she laughed a harmless, merry laugh ''—like that strange man she remained with for so long in the park that day.''

John Stuart frowned. ''What was that, Daydee? In the park? A man?''

''Oh, I don't know who he was. It was surely someone Aunt Eve knew extremely well, for they were standing ever so close as they talked. Although she swore she didn't know him at all. Funny, for they were so very familiar.''

John Stuart tapped on the side of his chair. Was Daydee speaking about the bushranger? This was not as Eve had told it to him. He was silent for some seconds, then he asked, ''How is it you know of this, Daydee?''

Daydee, pretending not to notice anything amiss, answered gaily, ''Oh, I chanced upon them. You would say it was amusing really, the way they didn't even know I was there until I came up and spoke. I'd been watching them for ages. They were sort of staring into each other's eyes.'' Here she gave another gentle, innocuous laugh. ''I daresay there were other friends with whom Aunt Eve reacquainted herself. Nevertheless, that gent did seem extra special, and he was so very handsome. I can't understand it really, when she swore she didn't know him.'' Daydee turned away as she finished her sentence. She was so intuitively artful that she allowed him to think she did not know his mood.

He coughed to cover his emotions. ''Ah, well, that's very interesting.''

Daydee smiled and let a little time pass before she turned back to him. ''I do so wish we could see each other like we used to; you never ride with me anymore, and our rides were such fun.''

''Ah, Daydee, you've turned into such a fine young woman.'' His hand went out and patted her hair absently. ''It is not me with whom you should be spending your time. It is the likes of young Roy over there.''

At that same moment Roy looked over and smilingly beckoned Daydee.

''Go on, my dear.'' John Stuart touched her shoulder. ''He dotes on you.''

''Silly old Roy,'' came Daydee's scathing judgment. ''He's such a child.''

''Don't be so harsh on him, Daydee. Off you go and see what he wants.''

''All right then, only because you ask me to.'' But she knew it was time to leave, and off she went.

John Stuart stood, and soon Robert Robinson-Pike, champagne in hand, joined him. While they chatted, John Stuart remained outwardly calm, but the information Daydee had given him aroused troubled thoughts. Of course, Evelyn had told him of the meeting. Naturally she would. She was good and chaste and honest, wasn't she? But little, innocent Daydee had seen the encounter as intimate, very intimate. *I'd been watching them for ages. They were sort of staring into each other's eyes.* The way Eve had told him, it was brief and dispassionate. Surely Eve would not lie to him?

At half past six o'clock, the children's refreshments began, and the Mayfield party mounted their horses and rode back to the big house. There, they were to dine in two hours, then exchange gifts.

The following day, Christmas Day, there would be a formal, traditional luncheon, and in the morning the Mayfield Chapel that Sir Arthur had built would be opened, and John Stuart would reluctantly attend while the governor would read a short service.

All John Stuart's guests knew in part his attitude on the church. They tolerated his views only because of his great wealth and personal charm.

From his earliest moments, John Stuart had been interested in the earth and the universe, fascinated by science and natural and physical phenomena.

His library was vast and carried much biology. On his visits to Sydney, he had lectured to the group of colonial amateur scientists who called themselves "Friends of the Royal Society." His last paper had been a treatise on Charles Darwin's *On the Origin of Species by Means of Natural Selection*, or *The Preservation of Favoured Races in the Struggle for Life*, which had been published four years before and had greatly affected John Stuart, and indeed the world.

But for all his logical thought, when the riding party returned to Mayfield House and retired to rest, bathe, and dress for dinner, John Stuart was preoccupied with strange, rankling thoughts.

Eve had noticed he seemed a little distant on the ride home, and as they entered their suite, she turned to kiss his cheek, saying, "Sweetheart, you have been very quiet. Is something wrong?"

Dejection and disappointment showed in his eyes. "When you told me about meeting the outlaw in Bathurst, you did not tell me you were in his company a long time."

Eve was taken aback. "What do you mean? Who has said I

was?'' Then she realized. "It's Daydee, isn't it? What has she been saying to you?''

He took her by the shoulders and gazed deeply into her eyes. "She said you were in intimate conversation. That you stood so closely to the man, you almost touched him. That she watched you a long time, and you were so engrossed with each other that you didn't even know she was at your side until she spoke. Evelyn, tell me she is wrong.''

Eve was disconcerted. That Daydee was trying to harm her was certain. Her husband looked so hurt. She felt terrible. "Darling, of course she is wrong. Daydee saw the astonishment I felt at running into the bushranger, and misinterpreted it. I was not going to explain myself to her; it was none of her business. Daydee is greatly overdoing the situation. She does that. Everything is dramatic with that girl. The whole thing was entirely accidental, as I have told you.'' She stood on tiptoe and kissed him. "John Stuart, don't you realize I love you?''

His peculiar expression faded. His hands slid down her back and crushed her to him; he hugged her so tightly, he hurt her. "Oh, darling,'' he whispered, "how could I doubt you for a single moment? What a jealous fool I am.''

After gifts were given to the staff, dinner was served, a splendid six courses.

During the meal, Eve became aware of Daydee watching her. Daydee was obviously eager to see any effect that her words with John Stuart might have had. She smarted at the peacefulness she saw between Eve and her husband.

Daydee hated Eve. It was a simple uncomplicated hatred. All her life she had played make-believe games in which John Stuart was hers. In her mind, John Stuart *did* belong to her.

When Eve smiled at her down the dinner table, she could not force herself to reply in kind. Instead she turned away and spoke to Roy, who sat beside her.

The gift giving afterward was an odd affair. Eve found it strange to exchange presents with people she hardly knew. She watched Sir Rutherford as he came over to her, carrying a parcel wrapped in shining silver paper. His footfalls were certain, firm, almost heavy. He was a man in charge of himself. She felt that he was an honorable man, a man with a strong sense of justice and of duty, but there was little humor in him. His laughter was never the hearty laughter of a man who knows joy. She wondered why that was, as he sat stiffly down beside her, and they exchanged gifts. Politely they thanked each other, and he moved away to speak to Lady Young.

Then Daydee came over. Eve looked up at her. For the space of a second, the eyes in the girl's face were icy. Then as Lady Young turned toward them, she said, "Merry Christmas, Aunt Eve," and dropping a box in Eve's lap, turned sharply away.

Eve untied the ribbon. Inside the package was a book, an atlas of New South Wales. A card lying on it said, "In case you are asked directions in the future. From Daydee." Eve put it down with a speculative expression.

Sir Rutherford had missed none of this. His usually reflective expression was even more so as he turned from Lady Young.

Suddenly a hand rested on Eve's shoulder and she looked up to find her husband standing beside her, his familiar, slanted grin lighting up his face. Her heart quickened, he looked so boyishly handsome.

He handed her a small package tied with yellow ribbon. She opened it with a beating heart. Inside was a miniature painting of Mayfield House. It was mounted in a gold and amber frame, and made into a brooch. It was exquisite.

"John Stuart, it's too beautiful."

"Nothing is too beautiful for you," her husband answered in one of his most serene moods. He pinned it to her breast, and she felt a swell of love for him.

Later, when sleep had descended on the many rooms of Mayfield House, its hostess lay awake, listening to the rain falling outside and reflecting on the day's events. When John Stuart had questioned her tonight about meeting Alan Fletcher, once more she had felt terribly guilty. He had made love to her tonight, aggressively, thrusting hard into her as if to somehow purge them both of the bushranger. She had not minded that. In fact, she had found it wonderful, erotic, and their orgasms had been long and intense. Their lovemaking was always good. His hand still rested on her bare stomach as she listened now to his soft breathing beside her. She moved and kissed his hair as he murmured in his sleep. She did love him, now and for always. Father was right. She must forget Alan Fletcher.

She was beginning to realize how much Daydee despised her. The girl was showing it increasingly. The reason was obviously John Stuart. The girl worshiped him. Had she grown up in such luxury, was she so spoiled and peevish, that she could not realize how foolish she was? Eve sighed. John Stuart certainly did not take the girl seriously. He was twice her age and thought

of her as a child. There was no point at all in her being jealous
of Eve. But the barbed message that came with the atlas had
drawn clear battle lines. Well, Eve would give her no satisfaction. She would not allow herself to be embroiled in a fight with
a spiteful teenage girl.

That night, Eve underestimated Daydee Bronwyn Larmer.
She was not simply a spiteful teenage girl. She was an insanely
jealous, viciously effective hand-to-hand combatant, who would
never forgive Eve for having John Stuart's affection. She was as
unyielding in her hatreds as the Moor, and self-interest was the
motivating force behind all she ever did.

Eve assessed Daydee with reason, and there was no reason in
Daydee.

After the rain overnight, the bright, cloudless sky of Christmas morning proclaimed a warm, dry day. The service was at
ten o'clock, and the entourage walked the three hundred yards
to the small chapel. Sir John Young read the service in a fine,
loud voice, and Eve thought of Father in Bathurst doing the
same. They sang one hymn only, "Hark the Herald Angels
Sing," to Mrs. Myrtle Ford's accompaniment on the harp, and
soon issued back into the sunshine.

On the return walk to Mayfield House, Sir Rutherford left Mr.
Payne's side and fell in step with John Stuart. Taking his arm,
he asked confidentially, "Have we time to take a ride across the
Boorowa and get up into the hills to look at where that blasted
bushranger found Mrs. Wakeman? Oh yes, I'd really like to see
that part of the country."

John Stuart turned his eyes to Sir Rutherford's. "I doubt it.
Those hills are well over two hours' ride. Tomorrow, yes, you
could. But today? I think not."

Sir Rutherford nodded. "Tomorrow is better, actually, for I
would like your wife to accompany us and show me the exact
place."

John Stuart's pulse quickened. He was not happy about taking
Eve along. He wanted to avoid any more connection between
her and the bushranger. The number of encounters she had already had with Alan Fletcher continually rankled and festered
in his mind. "No, Rutherford. I think not. I don't want her in
any possible danger."

"There will be no danger, I can assure you of that. What with
a few good men like Jack Hennessy and Mr. Larmer carrying
carbines, the danger won't be to us."

"Nevertheless, I do not want Eve reminded of it. I prefer she remains at home."

Rutherford was grave. "Just as you wish mine host. Perhaps, then, you will not mind if I question her. I will cause her no distress." He turned his head and gazed with narrowed eyes at the classical profile beside him.

John Stuart acquiesced. "All right."

When dinner was over and all had assembled in the drawing room, Sir Rutherford detached himself from his group and moved in long strides across the room to John Stuart. "So we ride up into the hill country tomorrow?" he began enthusiastically.

"Why, yes, Rutherford, that is the plan, is it not?"

Eve sat looking up at the detective policeman.

"And you, dear lady, while your husband wishes that you do not ride with us, I would, with your permission, ask you a few questions."

John Stuart patted Eve's hand. "Yes, sweetheart, Sir Rutherford wishes to ascertain in which area you were when you fell from Moonlight."

Eve answered as dispassionately as she could. "I don't want to disappoint you, Sir Rutherford, but it would be absolutely useless to question me. I have no idea where I was that day."

Sir Rutherford's face lost its expression of amusement. "Not even an idea of which way you went?"

She met his eyes, and for a moment he saw the real strength of character in them. "Of course. I traveled southwest across the Boorowa. But I have no recollection of my direction after that. Possibly because of the fall."

The expert on the bushrangers nodded slowly; Mrs. Wakeman was far more interesting than he had thought. "In that case, dear lady, I shall leave you in peace."

Eve felt cold even though the breeze through the open door was warm.

Her husband patted her hand again, before he rose and moved away in conversation with Sir Rutherford and Joe.

She pitied any outlaw who came within the police detective's grasp, and she found herself praying silently that Alan Fletcher would be spared, that he would never be caught and that no signs of his whereabouts would come to Sir Rutherford's notice.

Suddenly she realized that the detective policeman was watching her over her husband's shoulder. Looking at her speculatively, studying her with thoughtful eyes.

And just beyond Sir Rutherford, Eve saw Daydee. The girl was playing cards with Roy and David Elrington. She held her cards up in front of her, and above them, her dusky little eyes were maliciously trained on Eve.

Eve was absent when the riding party left the next day to search the hills. She was once more in the small surgery building they called "the hospital" down by the river. Two children, a brother and sister, had fallen from a tree that morning and had broken bones.

As the band rode down across the paddocks of long grass to the river, Eve was holding the little girl in her arms while the doctor set her leg, and as the riders crossed the Lachlan, she kissed the tiny, tear-stained face and looked up to see them through the window, and to watch them turn and pass the orchards before heading southwest away from Mayfield proper.

After the riding party had crossed the Boorowa River, they stopped to refresh themselves. The horses drank from the river, and the humans drank from leather water bottles. While they were having a bite to eat, Daydee found Sir Rutherford.

"And how do you enjoy the ride, Miss Daydee?" he asked sociably.

"Splendid. I find the whole notion exciting." She returned him a wide smile.

He tapped his riding crop on his shiny, brown boots as he studied her. "Ah yes, you are a gallant sort of girl. Unlike some other ladies, methinks."

"Unlike Aunt Eve, do you mean?" came Daydee's quick retort.

"Well now, I didn't exactly mean that, Miss Daydee."

Daydee's smile broke into a little laugh. "Oh, come now, Sir Rutherford, I understand much more than you think."

Sir Rutherford was looking quizzically at her. "Do you now, young lady?"

"It seemed odd to my way of thinking that she could not help you with your questions last night."

The police detective said nothing.

"Perhaps," said Daydee naively, "she sympathizes with them."

Sir Rutherford's eyebrows rose as he grinned down at her. "No. I'd not believe that, missy."

Daydee gave him one of her long, slow looks. Sir Rutherford

had never been the recipient of one before, and it excited his curiosity, so much did it convey.

"She certainly doesn't like to talk about them," she added, before she walked away.

He watched her very carefully as she moved through the men to her horse. So the girl wanted him to believe that Mrs. Wakeman commiserated with the bushrangers? He already suspected there was no love in Daydee Larmer's heart for John Stuart's wife, and now this. Ah yes, an interesting subject was Miss Daydee, and so, too, was the object of her dislike.

There was much laughter and jollity on the trail that day, but as for finding any indication of the bushrangers' whereabouts, there had been nothing. Even so, Sir Rutherford was not disappointed. For in finding nothing, he had found something, and this he pointed out to John Stuart as they passed along the ridge overlooking the river valley.

"For you see, my dear John Stuart," he said, "although we know the bushranger Fletcher was here on the day he found your wife, we have discovered nothing to explain *why* he would be here. No coaches run here. No gold passes from the goldfields here. No settlement or town is here. No farms are here. So why was he here? Well, there is one thing that *is* around . . ."

"Food," broke in John Stuart. "There is an abundance of game."

"Er . . . ah, yes," replied Sir Rutherford. "You are right indeed. I see you are abreast of me, and so you realize that Fletcher was most probably hunting. If I am right, it means he does not rest his head a very great distance from this spot. For even had he gone far afield from his hideout on that specific day, it is unlikely that he would ride more than a few hours to seek food. Also, I believe he is no longer nomadic. It is my view that the notorious Alan Fletcher dwells within ten or fifteen miles from us at this very moment. I am elated, my friend! Excited in the extreme! Ah yes, it is a start, a real beginning you might say."

John Stuart turned in his saddle to face Sir Rutherford and the question that came from him was filled with doubt. "That certainly sounds a rational deduction, but would it not be impossible to find his hideout in the vast sameness of this country?" He waved his hand in a wide curve at the endless forest of gum trees.

A hint of smugness crept into Sir Rutherford's look. "As I have said before, my friend, they all make mistakes in the end.

Ah yes, and each piece of knowledge I gather will turn into the completed patchwork quilt at last. Why, some public opinion is even with the beggars! But too many people have dealings with them, and in the too many will be one or two for me. One or two who will inform. That is why this first minute indication I have gleaned about 'the Governor,' as they call Fletcher in out-law circles, excites me. Up to this time, he's been like a phantom.'' He made a rumbling sound in his throat, and then he laughed. ''You know, I did not get much help from Mr. Larmer when I approached him for a description of Fletcher. Seems he was so happy to find your good wife that day, he took little notice. Ah yes, it was your man Barnes who was most helpful. Good man, that. Recalled Fletcher as slim and sun-browned, wearing a sheepskin jacket. Said he was what a person would call handsome. Strong jawline, light brown hair, penetrating gaze. Astride a gray stallion. Now, it's not as good as having seen him myself, but it is the first description I've ever had of the devil, for—would you believe it?—the old convict files could not be found. Typical,'' he finished.

FOURTEEN

Daydee and Lake

Daydee awoke from an exhilarating dream. She had been kissing John Stuart. The kiss had lasted a long time, and she murmured aloud and moved in her bed. She opened her eyes and sighed.

It was still dark. A cool breeze blew through the slightly open window, and she pulled the blanket up around her shoulders. If only her dream had been real! Damn Eve, damn Eve to hell! How she hated her!

John Stuart could have been hers, would have been hers, if

she'd had more time. She had only come home from school in November of '62. He had begun to notice her then, as a woman. If only he hadn't gone on that cattle drive in March of the following year, for he had returned in April to announce that he was getting married! She had been shocked, and had become so ill that she came up here and locked herself in and cried and cried.

Since he'd married, everything had changed. In the eighteen months since *she* had come here, she had ingratiated herself with all the Mayfield people. Even Mother, stupid Mother, thought *she* was wonderful. Daydee was so sick of hearing "how good," "how kind," "how thoughtful," Mrs. Wakeman was. It made her want to vomit.

Still, there was the odd time now and then when she did have John Stuart to herself, totally to herself. In recent months, just three or four times she had waylaid him on his way to the summerhouse, where he read his journals on Sunday afternoons, and he had allowed her to come and sit with him and read her own book. She pretended that they were married to each other and that *she* was not at Mayfield at all, that she was not even alive!

Now the most terrible thing of all was happening. It seemed that Father and Mr. Ford had been communicating, and they wanted her to become engaged to Roy. Well, she never would. No, never. Hot tears ran down her cheeks in the chilly night air. She had turned nineteen a month ago, and she wanted excitement!

She noticed how the hands watched her when she went riding or stayed down at the stables. There was unveiled admiration in their eyes. Mr. Watson's grooms stammered awkwardly whenever she spoke to them. Why couldn't John Stuart see how lovely she was? It was all because of *her*. All *her* fault.

Many of the men desired her, she was sure of that. Like that cheeky stockman about John Stuart's age. He had been sent up to the house to call her father out to one of the yards a couple of times. He was only a "short-timer," as they called men put on to help at busy times, but he had a way about him. He had looked straight at her with an impudent smile and said, "You're a good-looking woman, Miss Daydee." Of course, she had given him one of her "how dare you" looks and walked away. But she could not deny that there was something about him. He was truly handsome, and in some ways he reminded her of John Stuart. She had found out his name. Lake, he was called, Nathaniel Lake.

She swung her legs down onto the floor and into her slippers, and dragged the counterpane from the stool at the foot of the bed. Wrapping it around her shoulders, she made her way to the window. She looked out into a predawn September morning, then caught her faint reflection in the glass. Her dark hair hung in waves over her shoulders, and her small, pert face looked smooth and fresh. Her lips were a cupid's bow of deep pink, and her long eyelashes circled her eyes like a frame. As she rested her hands on the sill, her firm, young breasts pushed up enticingly beneath her warm, white nightdress. The grooms would stammer if they saw her now!

From her window, she could see the evenly planted windbreak of firs and beeches that lay along the side of the house. Through a gap in the trees to the southwest, she could make out the lights in the bunkhouses, a mile away down the gentle slope. She stood for a time looking toward them.

While she watched, men were tumbling out of their bunks and making their way to the good-smelling cookhouses, where breakfast was already being served. Early morning in the hands' quarters was a time of good-natured banter, and now at fifteen minutes past five o'clock in the morning, a longtime employee, Jason Fowler, in one of the washhouses, lifted an empty bucket into the air. "Damned if I can get these short-timers out o'bed. Methinks I'll be goin' and fillin' this bucket and douse me a few o'them."

"I'm a short-timer, but I'm up, old man," replied a handsome, sunburnt individual who looked up from a washbasin, his face dripping water.

"Sure ye be, Lake, but ye don't follow any pattern as I can notice. Never see'd a man who could drink as much as ye at night, and be gettin' up smooth as silk at cocky's crow, as I note ye've done once more, again."

Lake laughed and returned his face to the water. He was very popular with the other men. He was always ready with a quip or a joke, and never moody. He drank too much, he knew that, but it did not affect him. A long drink of water and five or so hours' sleep, and he was good as new.

This was the second time he had worked a spell on Mayfield. He had spent three months here in '58, six years before, on his way north from Adelaide. He liked his way of life, no ties to anybody, and only working when the money ran out. Another thing, you didn't get caught by one woman this way! Spread yourself around, that was what to do. Well, yes, there had been a few "ladies" he had tangled himself up with for a time. And one he had lived with nigh on a year, down in Adelaide. She had been a looker, right enough, but he did not like town dwelling and had moved on when the time was right.

The problem at Mayfield was a lack of good-looking women. The only available girls were the dairy maids and the staff up in Mayfield House. All the others in the cottages were married. They did not like anything "improper" going on here. At least the self-righteous Mr. John Stuart Wakeman didn't.

Now everybody said his wife was a beauty. Wonder what a woman would have to be like to catch old Wakeman? He was a good judge of "woman flesh" was "Lakey," as he called himself. He would give her points out of ten when he saw her and she would have to be pretty good to beat some of his women.

Well, if none of the girls here gave him any loving, there was always the publican's daughter, Elizabeth Jenks, in Cowra. On his way here, she had been real nice to him. Bit of a slut, and thick ankles, but nice eyes, and he had always been a one for eyes. Yes, he could put up with the ride into Cowra on his day off, if none of the Mayfield girls gave him what he wanted.

Nathaniel Lake had begun this day much the same as all the stockmen, with a bowl of porridge, thick, buttered toast and bacon, and a laugh. Then he and fifteen others had been sent over to the yards southeast of the river to begin branding baby calves. It was spring, and there were hundreds of "ready" cattle about to calve. Teams of men had been tending the mothers night and day for the last week. It was tedious work that left the men blood-soiled and tired. Lake was pleased he had the branding. He preferred that.

During the afternoon rest, when the billy was boiled and the men took a short respite from their backbreaking work, Lake and two companions wandered down and sat on the riverbank. They were joking, and Lake slapped his friend Larry Cadee on the shoulder. "You know, Cadee old son, these Herefords remind me of some women I knew on the goldfields at Sovereign Hill near Ballarat."

"Why's that, Lakey, old boy?"

"Well, they stand five feet high, got thirty-two teeth, they're stupid, and they take nine months to bear a young 'un."

This they found very amusing.

"Ye be a wag and no mistake, Lake," said Tillert, another short-timer.

"And you're a poet and don't know it," retorted Lake, which produced some more laughter.

The Lachlan River was not wide at this point, and a natural ford joined this side to the home pastures on the other bank, so it was no surprise when riders appeared in the distance and made their way toward the ford.

"Here comes Mr. Wakeman," said Tillert.

"And Mr. Larmer," spoke up Cadee.

"Yes, and that looks like her, Mrs. Wakeman, with them." Tillert pointed with his mug. "Fancy gettin' a visit from the mistress. Probably wanted to see the wee lambs, I'll be bound."

The men watched the riders come to the ford and begin to cross. Joe waved a greeting as he passed.

"Well, what da ya think o' the mistress, Lake? Mrs. Eve Wakeman, that's her. A real beauty, ain't she?" asked Tillert.

Lake did not speak.

"What's up, Lakey boy? Struck dumb by the lady fair, are ya?"

"Hey, Lake, ye be turnin' white as a ghost," said Cadee.

Lake make a strange, strangled sort of sound and then coughed.

"Are ya all right, Lakey?" inquired Tillert. "It's true ya do look a bit peculiar and all."

Lake took a couple of deep breaths and stood up. Finally he spoke. "Yes, yes, I'm just a little odd today. Might have been eating luncheon too quick. A bit of indigestion, I suspect."

Cadee nodded. "I been tellin' ya that ya eat too fast."

Just then they heard the call to resume work.

"Come on," Lake said, turning from his mates, "I'm all right. Feeling back to normal. It'll take more than eating quickly to stop old Lakey. Here, let me tell you a joke I heard on the Yuralga goldfields. . . ."

Eve was fascinated.

John Stuart had preferred that she not ride down among the cows, so she remained sitting on a tree stump on a knoll seventy yards away.

She felt so sorry for them. Even at this distance she could see the pain and the blood of birth, and hear the plaintive bellows in the air. They were two purebred herds of beef cattle: the black, compact Aberdeen Angus, and the red and white, low-set Hereford. There had been two other calvings since she had come to Mayfield, but this was the first time John Stuart had agreed to let her come. Before, when she had insisted, he had answered, "It's no place for a woman." *Why* it was no place for a woman, when women had been giving birth since the world began, she could not fathom.

Where there were cattle there were flies, and she spent much of her waiting time waving her hand across in front of her face and hitting at them as they came to rest on her. When one bit her on the arm, she struck out at it saying, "Go to blazes, damn you." Then she laughed, her brown eyes twinkling with mirth, for she had not said such a thing for years.

Over to the right, away from the calving, the branding was taking place. The calves that were healthy and strong were being marked and then returned to their mothers, before being loosed to graze.

When John Stuart returned up the hill in long strides, he was alone.

"Isn't Joe coming?" Eve asked.

"No, he will remain awhile."

As they rode away, one man looked up from where he squatted holding a branding iron over the fire. His body was tense with excitement. A hundred times during the past hour, he had looked up to where Eve waited on the mound.

"Well, I'll be damned!" he said to himself. "Imagine my finding *her* again. And she has set herself up as the mistress of Mayfield, nothing less. Calling herself Eve, eh? Fancy that!" He took his iron from the fire and repeated half-aloud, "Well, I'll be damned!"

It was only four days before the cattle drive to Penrith, over 150 miles away by road, was to begin.

Eve had risen early to have breakfast with John Stuart. She wanted to spend as much time as she could with him, for he was not coming straight home after the drive. He and Joe would continue on to Sydney, Melbourne, and Adelaide. Robert Robinson-Pike was accompanying them, for he had arranged land deals in Melbourne and Adelaide.

He and Joe would journey by sea and on the new railways between some of the towns, taking them away from Mayfield perhaps six weeks.

Eve came to the breakfast room just as John Stuart folded a newspaper and placed it on the table beside his latest scientific journal. "Eve," he said, pointing to the paper as she sat down, "there is much of interest to you here. There have been great battles in Virginia, and Grant closes around Lee's positions near Petersburg. The South is suffering badly. Your Northern blood should be pleased at that, my dear.''

"No, John Stuart. I'll be glad when my homeland is no longer at war with itself. Even families have been divided. It's awful.''

"Yes, I understand that.'' Her husband's expression was sympathetic. "And perhaps it will be over soon. Let us hope so. Here, you may read it for yourself, my darling.'' He handed her the paper.

After breakfast she did read the long article, and it left her heart heavy for her countrymen. Her thoughts were consistently of the tragic war all the morning during her household chores. After luncheon, she went down to the hospital and found Betty quietly sewing cloth arm slings for broken bones. She did an hour's work on the latest medical inventory before taking her daily walk. Since the incident the year before when little Laura Dale had almost drowned, John Stuart preferred that Eve have a companion on her walks, so that Stephanie or Thelma often accompanied her. But Stephanie did not enjoy the long walks as Eve did, so Eve did not always take her, and today Thelma was in Cowra. Thus Eve went alone.

She took a path that followed the meandering course of the Lachlan, and soon she was in a secluded part of the valley where the first blossoms of native heath were in bloom. As she often did, she gathered some clusters of the red, bell-like blooms, using the small silver scissors that dangled on a ribbon from her waistband.

As she bent to cut the stems, her mind played the trick that it often did, and flashing into her thoughts came the day she had been with the bushranger. Somehow, she did not feel as uncomfortable with his memory out of doors. She did not have so much of the sickening guilt out here. For a few minutes she stood holding the bunch of heath and remembering. So much had happened to the bushrangers this past year and she read the newspapers avidly for any account of them. She knew all of the well-known names: Ben Hall, Johnny Gilbert, Dan Morgan, Old Joe Daily, Lefty Dawson, Jake Crane. Lately a new one had appeared, a man from Queensland, James Alpin McPherson. Recently there had been some sort of a duel between him and Sir Frederick Pottinger, the police inspector under Sir Rutherford. Eve could not help smiling when she read that. Sir Rutherford would have been livid.

Mayfield had seen two brief visits from the detective policeman in the past six months. He had brought the news of the notorious Frank Gardiner's capture at Apis Creek in Queensland. There was no doubt he had been right about that. He had always maintained that Gardiner had fled to Queensland. Gardiner had been sentenced to jail for thirty-two years in July.

She lived in constant fear of hearing that Alan Fletcher had been captured. There had been a bank holdup in Goulburn in August, which at first had been blamed on Alan Fletcher, but later it was found to be "Flash" Johnny Gilbert. Gilbert and Johnny O'Meally had been the first men ever to rob a bank in Australia, a year ago in Carcoar.

Then, earlier this month, had come definite news about the Fletcher band. The government gold diggings at Theresa Town had been their quarry. The whole town had been held up, and government gold taken, and a Chinese thief set free. It was all the more notable, for Sir Rutherford Blake had been there and was held prisoner along with his troopers. All the gossip said he was made to look a fool. There had been no injury, except to Sir Rutherford's pride, she guessed, and a new reward of a thousand pounds had been posted for Alan Fletcher.

Yes, the world was a "very mess," as Clare had so often said. Her home country was at war with itself: men killing one another, sacking cities and pillaging. And here, in her adopted home, men used force and were given to hatred of their fellow man in just the same way.

She sighed. Men! No doubt it would be a better world if women ran it! She had proven in her own life that she could be self-reliant and plucky; many women she had known could have been leaders. Why, Clare could have, if she had been given the chance. But Clare lay in a graveyard Eve had never seen. Yes, she, Eve, was the lucky one. She had so much . . . John Stuart, a man so worthy, so upright and moral. She must be more mindful of him, more contrite, stop thinking of other things, of another man. How many times a day did she say this? Life was so difficult!

She turned to continue on her way. She had been standing so still in reverie that a platypus had come up behind her out of his burrow in the riverbank to rest in the warm grass. The water on his smooth, ebony, molelike fur glistened in the afternoon sun as his webbed front claws opened and closed. When Eve turned, the movement of her skirts brought him to life, and in seconds he was gliding swiftly beneath the water.

A short time later, she branched off the river path and headed up the wooded hill to a spot where she looked back. She always did this; it was such a pretty view through the trees to the Lachlan.

What she saw pushed all thoughts from her mind in amazement.

Not sixty yards away, down through the trees, she saw a man and a woman. His arms were encircling her waist. The woman was undoubtedly Daydee! The man pushed back Daydee's dark hair with his hand. He was much taller than the diminutive girl. Eve could not make out his features, but she could see he was a stockman and had a shock of dark hair falling to his collar. He was about the size and shape of John Stuart. As she watched, he bent forward and kissed Daydee on the mouth, lifting the girl from her feet into his embrace. Then he put her down and they walked away, hand in hand.

Eve turned on her heel and hurried along the path.

The two people behind, oblivious of her presence, strolled along by the river shallows.

"Well, you are the cheeky one," said Daydee. "When did I give you permission to do that?"

"Ah, permission now, eh? Is that what I have to ask for?"

He stopped and, turning to her, took her hand and bent over it, saying in mock servility, "Dear Miss Larmer, would you be so kind as to lend your lips to a passing wayfarer, as he has never seen any as beautiful as yours in his whole life." Then, from where he bent stiffly at the waist, he turned his head and, looking up at her, winked.

She began to laugh. "Oh, Nathaniel Lake, you are the joker."

He stood straight, and putting his hand over his heart, said, "Yes, ma'am, I cannot lie, I am. But I'm serious about your lips," and taking her again by the waist, pulled her to him.

After the kiss, she moved away. "How could you be sure I would meet you here today?"

"I couldn't be," he answered, leaning back on a rock and looking her up and down, "but it's a chance I had to take. I'll bet there are a few boys back at the quarters who should give a week's pay to be here in my place."

Then Daydee turned sharply back toward him, fear in her eyes. "You won't say anything, will you? You won't tell anyone about this."

This amused him. "Will you?" he countered.

"No, of course not."

"Then neither shall I. Come." He grasped her hand and

gently pulled her over to their tethered horses. From the back of his animal's saddle he took a rolled blanket, and placing it on a grassy spot secluded in the undergrowth, he motioned for her to sit. They spent half an hour on the blanket, and when the time came for Daydee to leave, he persuaded her to meet him again the following afternoon.

And so she did. She lied to get away as she had done the previous day. Down to Larmer's Crossing and over the bridge she galloped, past the orchards and around the river paddocks and along the cliff paths that ran high above the river. She rode swiftly, descending to the low path through the scrub and finally emerging at a shallow part of the river. Here she forded the Lachlan and found him waiting.

He kissed her many times, and between kisses, asked her questions about Mayfield House. Of course, she understood his interest, for the cattle and stockmen were rarely allowed past the great hedge boundary enclosing the big house.

The wetness of his tongue thrilled her. He ran it back and forth across her teeth and searched her mouth. The only thing she did not care for was his asking her to drink some brandy from the flask he carried. It had made her feel peculiar. But when he saw she did not like it, he brought fresh water from the river in his water bag. After she had drunk some of that and eaten an apple, she felt better.

The next day, she arrived before him. She sat waiting on a small rock on the edge of the river. She certainly found this Nathaniel Lake diverting. He was the first man she had ever agreed to meet, and it was exciting. At last, there was something of interest in her boring life!

She liked his talk and the way he made her laugh. He reminded her of John Stuart. They were both big men. She liked the way Nathaniel's mustache felt on her mouth. She pretended he *was* John Stuart. Oh, how she longed to be kissed by John Stuart. Suddenly she felt a terrible longing for him, and she clasped herself tightly around the waist as she bent forward on the rock.

She heard the sound of an approaching horse on the far side of the shallows. Nathaniel Lake was coming! She sat up straight and tossed her hair back over her shoulder. She could learn from "Lakey," as he referred to himself. Yet she would not go too far. Oh, no, she was not silly! She just needed to have some experience. Yet there was no doubt Nathaniel Lake was handsome, and he did make her feel like a grown woman. Yes, this sort of thing was amusing for its own sake.

He placed the blanket down, as he had the last two days, and they sat on it as usual. He did not have the brandy flask with him, and his mouth tasted fresh and wonderful. She was lying in his arms, and he was playing with the ribbon on her dress when he said, "I'll not be able to come tomorrow."

Daydee made a sound of disappointment. "Is it because of the cattle drive?"

"Yes, love, it's the day before it starts. Some of us will be on duty with the herd all night. Although the following day, now, that'll be different. We've already been told that once the drive begins at seven o'clock, those of us who worked the night shift will have the day off." He kissed the tip of her nose. "We can see each other a lot of that day for certain."

"How do you know you shall be one of the men who has the day off?"

He laughed and, leaning over her, kissed her on the earlobe, whispering, "Lakey will make certain of it, m'dear."

She put her arms up around his neck, and a tiny frown creased her brow. "Oh, darn it," she said. "That will be Monday, and I have two hours with Mrs. Cadman, who comes out from Cowra to give me piano lessons. She stays to lunch, the old crone. It will be well after two o'clock before I can get away."

"Never mind, I'll be here," he replied. "There is plenty of the day left after the hour of two. Where are you supposed to be now, by the way?"

She smiled at him. "Why, that is the best thing about having one's own horse. It has to be exercised, you know."

"Clever girl," he said, and he kissed her again, their firm bodies pressed together. She let him undo the ribbons on her bodice and her camisole to feel her breasts as he had done the previous day. And today she did not stop him when he pushed back the material and covered her nipples with his mouth. His hot, wet tongue aroused all sorts of amorous feelings in her.

During the final year at school, some of the girls had spoken about love and loving. It was always at night. They would gather on one of the beds and whisper about it. Daydee remembered how one girl's mother had said a man must never be allowed to touch a woman's breast, even with his hand. That it was profane. Well, if this was profanity, Daydee liked it. But later, when his hand strayed beneath the skirt of her riding habit, she sat up straight, saying, "No, Nathaniel."

"Oh, love," he whispered, holding her close, his voice thick with passion, "don't you like it? Don't you?"

"No," she said again, and pulled away from his embrace.

"All right, all right. I understand. But come on, girl, give old Lakey a kiss, if nothing else." He put on such a comic face of entreaty that when he came across the rug to her, she kissed him as he asked.

Later, he lay back with his hands behind his head and asked her more about Mayfield House. "So it was built by Mr. Wakeman's father, was it?"

"Yes. He began with one wing. Now it's the kitchens, sculleries, and pantries."

"And that is the side nearest your house, is it?"

"Yes, that's right. But why is Mayfield House so interesting to you?"

He gave her one of his special smiles. His face creased, showing the tiny dimple in his left cheek. "Well, love, to be honest, I was an architectural student before I took to this easy life, and that place is the finest example of design I have ever seen anywhere." He took a deep breath and rolled on his side to regard her. "So your house looks across to the kitchens and sculleries. I suppose the master and mistress live above the kitchens, eh?"

"Oh, Nathaniel, are you ever serious?"

"About you? Yes." He took his hands from behind his head and leaned toward her. "So tell me, then, what part of the house *is* theirs?"

"The wing farthest from our house. It was added at the time Sir Arthur was dying. I was only little, but I remember it."

"To me, it's like a U with a tail. The tail is their wing, eh?"

"Yes, that's right, I suppose. There is the walled garden all along to the front of the house. Only Aunt Eve uses the garden. It's private."

Lake did not miss the spite in the words "Aunt Eve."

"Don't you like her?"

"Who?"

"Come on, Daydee, you cannot fool old Lakey. Your 'Aunt Eve.' "

Then he saw the anger rise in her eyes, and she gave the habitual toss of her head. "No, I don't like her. It's different since she came."

"It would be."

"How do you know?"

"Let's just say I do," he replied enigmatically. "Now, tell me, they say she's from Bathurst. Is that right?"

Daydee did not want to talk about Eve; her answer was reluctant. "Mmm . . . she was a music teacher there."

Lake smiled, remembering how he had only heard her play a few times in pubs. But ah, how she could play! Her fingers had darn well skimmed across the keys. She had made the thing talk!

"And this was only last year, the boys tell me. Say he met and married her all in about a month."

Daydee's mouth turned down in distaste. "Yes, it's true. He met her at Easter time and married her five weeks later. And if you don't mind, Nathaniel, I did not come here to talk about *her*."

His arm went out around her, and he pulled her to him. "No, and nor did I." But he was thinking about her, the mistress of Mayfield, as he pulled little Daydee to him and kissed her again, long and hard, fondling her breasts with his right hand at the same time. His mouth was moving down to the girl's nipples again when she broke from him and stood. "It's getting late, I must return."

He drew the back of his hand across his eyes in disappointment before he clasped his knees and sat regarding her as she smoothed her riding habit. While she tied the bow on her bodice, he asked, "And so, my pretty Daydee, I'll see you here the day after tomorrow at two o'clock, eh?"

"It will probably be later than two o'clock, but I will come."

"Make a good excuse, so that you can stay a few hours."

"What will I say?" she asked him naively, sounding suddenly very childlike.

He looked closely at her. So youthful and innocent did she appear standing there in the gentle light of the dying afternoon that he almost told her not to come at all. Instead he heard himself saying, "Ah, Daydee, love, I have no doubt you will think of something."

When she had ridden away, he climbed upon his horse and crossed the Lachlan, deep in thought. If any one in authority here knew he was seeing Daydee Larmer, he would be thrown off the property; in all likelihood never get a job on any station or farm in the colony again. But God! hadn't he taken risks before?

Tomorrow the cattle drive would begin. Old Wakeman was leading the drive again, as he always did, they said. It was one of the things his men admired about him.

God! If it hadn't given him a start when he saw Wakeman's wife ride by last week. She had not noticed him, he was sure of that. She had been looking straight ahead, so high and mighty, too. Sitting tall in the saddle with the same straight back he recalled so well. And still as beautiful as she had been, what was it exactly? Six . . . seven years ago? Eighteen fifty-seven? Yes, that was it, 1857. Wouldn't she be fascinated to know he was here, working on Mayfield? Somehow, he might just have to let her know.

God, weren't women amazing?

He smiled broadly as he rode along the bank of the Lachlan in the dying day.

FIFTEEN

Mistake

It was the night before the cattle drive was to take place. Darkness had fallen when John Stuart returned to the house and his evening meal.

Eve had been a little tired for the last day or two. Sometimes the monthly change in her system affected her that way. So when John Stuart stood from the table to return into the night and make a final check on the herd, he had simply said, "You go to bed, dearest; do not wait for me. I shan't be late." He smiled at her, adding, "I must be up before dawn, anyway."

But Eve surprised him by answering, "It's a perfect spring night and I feel much better. I would like to come with you."

Her husband looked thoughtful. "All right. I'll be there only briefly, for Joe has everything under control, I'm certain. But, darling, are you sure? It's over two miles to the herd."

"Yes, John Stuart, I would love to come."

He sounded pleased. "In that case, I'll take the phaeton."

Half an hour later, Eve and John Stuart sat in the black, light carriage on the drive at the front of Mayfield House. Deke Edwards held the reins in front, and Jack Hennessy and Tommy Barnes were mounted on horses beside them.

It was a clear sky, and two large lanterns, attached to either side of the carriage, would give plenty of light to illuminate their way. Nevertheless, Jack Hennessy insisted on riding in front.

Out of Mayfield Park they went, around by the Larmers' front door, down across the incline of the valley.

Eve and John Stuart were silent for the first part of the ride. Her hand lay in his, and every now and then he would squeeze it gently. There was one moment when he leaned toward her and whispered, "I fear I could be away as long as six or seven weeks in all, and I shall miss you every day."

She turned to him and kissed his cheek in the darkness. She heard him say, "I love you, Evvy." He had never called her that before. A tingle of surprise ran through her, for it was Father's pet name for her.

"Yes, John Stuart," she replied gently in a voice so quiet that he bowed his head to hear her. "I do love you, too."

It was a balmy night, much warmer than the previous September. The stars shone above, and a breeze stirred softly in the trees. There was something perfect about this ride. For the moment, she felt no intolerance or possessiveness in the man beside her. He was the essential John Stuart, the kind and generous one, the noble one, the one she loved with all her heart. He moved in the seat and turned to her. Her eyes filled with tears, and as his mouth came down on hers, she kissed him and only him; there was no ghost of Alan Fletcher anywhere in the night around her. It was a long, loving kiss, and afterward she laid her head on his shoulder and was completely content. How she wished he did not have to go away, especially for such a long time. She would miss him awfully. She loved him deeply, truly, and forever.

"Talk to me, John Stuart," she said quietly. "Tell me more about your journey, about the land you will buy and the places you will go."

Eve listened carefully as he spoke and questioned him and attended his replies. There were moments when they laughed softly together, when they murmured intimate things and all the journey he had his arms around her, and three times more his mouth found hers before they reached the herd.

Then suddenly, over the brow of a hill, they saw the glowing dots that were the fires of the herdsmen. It was not until they were relatively close that the muffled, plaintive bellows of the cattle drifted to them.

"Why is it that so many steers make such little noise?" she asked.

"Cattle usually settle down with the sun," her husband explained, "and even though they are gathered here in a great number, they will be relatively peaceful until the morning light. Then, my darling, it will be a different matter."

As they approached, it was hard to make out the individual cattle, but Eve could distinguish the mass of bodies ringed by the fires of the men who watched them. The steers were held inside a large fenced area, nearly 150 yards square. Inside were other fences separating them into four groups. Some lay, others stood, and a few milled in circles. There had been grass here during the day when they had been mustered, but by tomorrow morning when they moved out, it would have vanished.

They halted about twenty yards from one of the fires near a huge silky-bark gum, and John Stuart alighted while his men dismounted.

As Deke tethered the phaeton's two horses to a small stringy-bark sapling, John Stuart leaned back into the carriage. "You wait here, darling," he said to Eve.

"But I should like to accompany you." She really wanted to be with him tonight every minute.

His boyish smile formed on his mouth. "Evelyn . . ." She could see, in the faint light, his slight amusement. "You *cannot* come down amongst the stockmen, I really cannot agree to that. Edwards will stay with you."

She watched him stride across to the fire, followed by Jack Hennessy and Tommy Barnes. The six or seven stockmen there stood respectfully as he spoke briefly to them and then moved on to another fire.

A few minutes passed. Deke Edwards was not a voluble individual, and when she asked him the occasional question, he answered monosyllabically. Soon she dropped into silence. She could feel the eyes of the men around the campfire looking up at her. There was a wealth of difference between a man and a woman in this world, and a chasm between "Mrs. Wakeman" and the stockmen. She climbed down from the carriage.

"Are you all right, Mrs. Wakeman, ma'am?" called Deke Edwards promptly.

"Perfectly, thanks, Mr. Edwards. I'm just going a few yards to look at the stars."

When she was beyond the radiance of the carriage lamps, she turned and looked back toward the men. One stood up slowly. He moved almost languidly, his back toward her. There was something familiar about him. He bent and spoke to his companions before straightening his long body again and detaching himself from the group. He moved outside the rim of light and did not turn around. Perhaps he was one of the stockmen whom she saw regularly. But, no, it was not that; he seemed familiar for another reason. Then he was hidden in the darkness beyond the firelight.

A breeze began drifting gently across the valley, and she thought she fancied she could tell the sweet scent of the yellow box and the faint, tangy smell of the tea tree.

A few minutes later, she heard John Stuart calling good night to the men at the fireside. When she joined him and the others at the phaeton, he hugged her. "See, darling, I wasn't long."

As her husband helped her up into the vehicle, she was observed by the ring of stockmen around the fire, but closest by the one who stood outside of the light.

"Now, I wonder if you noticed me tonight, 'Mrs. Wakeman,' my love?" Lake said softly to himself as he lit a cheroot.

God, she was a good-looking woman. Wouldn't he love to get at her again. Those firm breasts that Wakeman nuzzled these days . . . lucky bastard. If only . . . but there was no chance of that; he'd have to content himself with little Daydee instead. He sighed and drew deeply on his cheroot.

On Monday, September 12, the morning of the cattle drive, Eve and John Stuart had risen before first light.

Dawn was a beautiful sight. The whole valley was awash with tints of rose and gold. A single cloud hung in a vermilion streak along the horizon, and the trees behind Mayfield House were lit like sharp, yellow brushstrokes on the hillside.

John Stuart and Eve came thorough the front door just as their horses were being brought to the steps. Before Eve could mount, her husband took her by the hand and walked her southeast across the carriage drive and over the wide lawn still damp with dew. Then on through a thick screen of tall Norfolk pines and native shrubs to the summerhouse, which nestled by a trellis covered with climbing rose.

The sun was higher now, and the yellow glow that had bathed the house and its surroundings had turned to a vivid light.

This was John Stuart's favorite spot, where he read his scientific journals and the latest copy of the London *Times* so it was not unnatural that he would bring his wife here to say good-bye. Once inside, he turned to her and kissed her. He held her tightly to him, smoothing her curls as he kept her within his arms. "I hate to leave you, Eve. The other drives were soon over; this is not the same. I shall be away many weeks. Take care, my love."

Then he held her from him at arm's length and looked into her eyes. "It is hard for a man to say this, but I loved my father above all things, Evelyn, and when he died, well . . . I know I love Joe, for he has been the constant in my life, but it is not the same as my love for you. You are special, different from so many others." The tone of his last sentence grew slightly hard.

His words made her sad, so very sad. A feeling of shame shot through her for the moments when she had not been able to be honest with him. She took a deep breath and answered gently, "Do not make a saint of me, my dearest." She had said it to him so many times, but he never seemed to hear. A small shiver ran through her. She removed her eyes from his.

Then, to her surprise, he took a small velvet box from his coat pocket. "This is for your birthday. I am sorry I will not be here to spend it with you."

"Oh, John Stuart, you are always so generous."

He spoke softly. "I like to be, my Evvy."

The box had a small silver catch at the side. Inside lay the most amazing chain and pendant she had ever seen. The links of the chain were golden hearts, and the pendant was a larger golden heart covered entirely with tiny diamonds and dark red rubies. The rubies spelled out the words:

EVE
I'LL ALWAYS
LOVE YOU

It was so beautiful that it left her speechless. She looked from the sparkling heart to John Stuart's face and down to the heart again. "Why, I . . . I . . . ." was all she could say.

"Don't you like it?"

It was then she found her voice. "Like it? Like it? It is . . .

magnificent. I have never seen anything so perfect, darling. Thank you, thank you.''

He turned her from him and clipped it around her neck. She felt the cool touch of the metal on her skin, then his hands on her shoulders as he brought her back to face him. From inside his coat he took a small hand mirror. She could see it lying on her skin, gleaming.

''Why do you always spoil me so?''

''Because, my Evvy, I want to, and you must let me. You are my perfect love and thus you must wear perfect things.'' He smiled a quiet smile.

The sickness of guilt rose in her again. She wanted to cry, *No! Please don't say these things! I am wicked in my thoughts. I am not sinless and pure, as you say. I cannot put Alan Fletcher from my mind. I have hidden my sister's existence from you out of fear. God! That you could love me with all my faults!* But instead of saying these things, she smiled. It was a sad smile, but John Stuart did not realize it, for he was smiling happily back at her. Taking her arm in his, he led her from the summerhouse.

When they reached the herd, it seemed that all of Mayfield was there.

Of the thirty stockmen going on the drive, most were already in the saddle, but well over a hundred others had come to see them off. All around were men coming together and chatting and passing on, calling out to their mates and gesturing to one another over the incessant noise of the herd. Standing on the fallen needles beneath a clump of tall casuarinas were many members of the household, who had been brought over in drays. If there had been acrobats and some colored stalls, Eve could easily have mistaken it for a fair.

A little distance beyond the bustle of activity, sitting in a chaise on a rise covered with long grass, was Thelma. When she saw Eve riding up the incline toward her, she waved and beckoned her.

''Good morning, Thel; there's always something thrilling about it, isn't there?''

The older woman nodded. ''Always, my dear. I have watched them leave from this spot for nigh on thirty years.'' She laughed. ''It's above the dust; that is why I chose it.''

''You must have seen the size of the herds grow immensely,''

Eve remarked as she dismounted and tied her horse to the back of the chaise.

"Mmm, that's true. Do you know, in the early days, when I used to have John Stuart here beside me watching Joe and Mr. Arthur leave, we were the only ones to wave good-bye."

Eve laughed. "What a difference."

They spoke loudly, for the sound of the steers was almost deafening now. Eve thought the noise significantly like a protest, as if the cattle knew somehow what their destination represented. They were massive animals, all finished steers, solidly fat with brisket full and muscle firm down either side of their tails.

She climbed up beside Thelma just as the gates were pulled back and the cattle herd rumbled forth in an undulating motion.

From the left, around the exterior of the fences, John Stuart and Joe galloped over. There was a slight flush of enjoyment in her husband's face. It was plain he was stimulated by all the activity. He looked wonderfully handsome this morning, and her heartbeat quickened as Eve looked up at him.

"Good-bye, darling. Keep Mayfield beautiful for me."

"Good-bye, darling," she answered. "I will."

He leaned over from his mount and brushed her lips with his own. Then he took her left hand, raised it, and turning it over, kissed the palm. As his lips touched her she had the most unnerving sensation. She felt as if she were losing him. Last night had been so wonderful; why did he have to leave now? She wanted to stop him, to beg him not to go. A weight seemed to press on her shoulders. She felt horribly strange. As he lifted his face from her palm, she raised her right hand to touch his cheek longingly. He smiled his engaging half slanting smile at her and then moved his horse around the carriage to Thelma.

Eve watched him with heightened clarity. His perfect features, his dark hair under his hat, his olive skin and his irresistible smile, the sun-browned part of him where his shirt opened at the neck, the backs of his hands, with the oval fingernails, the gold buckle of his belt peeping from under his leather waistcoat, his shining brown boots polished to the highest luster . . . and then for a second he changed. The clarity was gone. He was without definition. She was staring at him . . . and imagining Alan Fletcher. John Stuart's face was Alan's face; his body, Alan's body. She gave a startled sound, but amidst all the noise, it went unheard. She closed her eyes and shook her head and refocused. Now, again, it was her husband she saw. He and Joe had said good-bye to Thelma, and now they were riding away. The older woman's eyes filled with tears. "It's a rare sight to see, isn't it?" Thelma said sadly.

"Yes," Eve replied, coming back to the present. "That it is."

It took the cattle a long time to disappear from the valley. So great were their numbers that they spilled over the sides of the narrow road, up the banks and down the gullies, a sea of black, russet, and white, surrounded by mounted cattlemen, who kept them in loose formation. When finally the din had died out and all that could be seen was a great cloud of dust in the distance, the onlookers began to retreat.

Eve saw Daydee riding around the fences. The girl had remained on the far side of the herd all morning, for she had no wish to be near her mother or Eve. When she had said her parting words to her father and John Stuart, they had hugged her, and she had clung to them both a long time as she always did. John Stuart had kissed the top of her head.

She did not catch sight of Nathaniel until half the cattle had departed. He was on the inner fence at the third of the yards, opening the gates for his section of steers to leave. He did not make any sign that he had seen her, but indeed he had. It had been harder for him to make out "Mrs. Wakeman," but finally he had spotted her in the chaise up on the far hillside. If only there were some way of getting to her, some way of being with her, some way of touching her, putting his hands on her flesh, making love to her again. He'd have to stop thinking like this; it was driving him mad.

As the cattle moved out along the valley, he and his comrades wandered around the outer fence and over to their tethered horses. They came closer to Thelma's chaise. He wished *she* would look his way and see him, but never once did she turn in his direction.

When Daydee rode up to the chaise, Eve spoke in a friendly fashion. "Did you enjoy the spectacle, Daydee?"

"It was like any other drive. No different."

"Well, now," her mother broke in, "back home to a cup of tea, Daydee, before Mrs. Cadman arrives for your music lesson."

"Yes, Mother, you needn't remind me. But afterward I'm going to take my paints and a picnic, and I'm going up to Chinaman's Hill to spend the entire afternoon."

Eve smiled amicably. "On your own?"

"Yes, on my own. I enjoy my own company."

Eve nodded. "But Chinaman's Hill is a long ride, Daydee, especially alone."

The girl's expression was supercilious. "You, of all people, shouldn't worry about that. After all, last year you rode so far that a bushranger had to bring you back."

"Yes, Daydee, but that was foolish of me, and I am very careful now."

"You still go for long walks on your own," Daydee argued. "I know you do."

"Don't be so rude," Thelma broke in. "How dare you speak to Aunt Eve this way! It's dreadful," She turned to Eve. "I'm so sorry, dear; forgive her."

Daydee sat sulkily on her horse, looking away.

"No, Thelma," answered Eve tolerantly, "Daydee's perfectly right. I set a bad example by riding out so far alone last year. But as for the walks, Daydee, they don't take me great distances."

Daydee's reply was a sullen glance, then she said, "Daddy agreed that I may go to Chinaman's Hill to paint. He gave me permission. It has the prettiest colors in the whole valley, and if he said I can, why should you stop me?"

Her mother eyed her skeptically.

"Then you should take one of the housemaids with you," Eve said slowly.

"None of them can ride," retorted Daydee quickly, "and painting is a solitary occupation. I could not bear to have anyone with me. I always paint alone."

"But you always paint in the park," her mother countered, "so the question does not arise."

"But Father said I could," the girl persisted, plaintively.

Thelma looked to Eve and sighed. "Ah, Eve, let's go home and have a cup of tea. My daughter plainly has a mind of her own."

It was half past the hour of two when Daydee rode away alone in the direction of Chinaman's Hill. She had won. She passed at a trot through Mayfield Park and the east gate. Because it was so surprisingly warm this September, she wore only a light riding habit and soft leather boots. When she emerged from the trees at the appointed place, she was delighted to see Nathaniel standing in the shallows of the Lachlan, his corduroy trousers rolled up to the knee. Of all things, he was fishing! He had a small branch of sapling with a line on the end. He stood there smoking a cheroot and grinning broadly, and looking so deliciously odd and agreeable that she laughed and waved as she approached him.

"Well, love," he called as she dismounted, "I had to fill in the waiting time somehow. Look at this." He pointed to a small boulder, and there on top of it was a minute fish; the poor little chap was hardly six inches long.

"My reward for an hour of toil!" he laughed.

"Oh Nathaniel, you are the one, you really are."

"Come in, get your feet wet; it feels wonderful," he tempted her.

She laughed again, then sitting on the bank, drew off her boots and stockings, and entered the water. He held out his hand and she took it. It certainly delighted her to have the cool wetness on her feet and legs, and she made little squeals of pleasure.

When Lake splashed her riding skirt, she took it off and laid it on the bank in the sun. Then she pushed her pantaloons up over her knees and went back into the river. They spent a merry half hour in the water, fishing and laughing and sitting on rocks and dangling their legs in up to their knees. Finally Lake said, "Daydee, love, would you go in totally?"

She looked at him questioningly. "What do you mean 'totally,' Nathaniel?"

"Well, it's quite warm, isn't it? With all your clothes off."

Her amazement showed in the soundless O her mouth made.

"Will you?" he asked quietly.

"No, Nathaniel, I will not," she answered, all imperious lady, and with that, she left the river shallows and put on her skirt.

"Shit," he said softly as he followed her.

They ate the picnic that had been prepared for Daydee and fought off the hungry flies. Afterward she painted some flowers and trees to take home with her, and she did a sketch of him. It was not a bad likeness really. She gave him the picture, and he folded it and put it in his saddlebag.

Later they took a walk along the riverbank, and Lake carried the blanket. In a shaded glen between some candlebark trees and some mint bushes where the soft scent, similar to the mint herb, pervaded the air, they lay down in the undergrowth, and he kissed and fondled her again. He was very aroused this afternoon, and he grew angry when she would not let him go further than her breasts. He was getting tired of this child's play.

He moved away from her sullenly and sat with his back to her, looking down at the river.

It was her turn to coax. She ran her fingers playfully through the hairs on his arm. She kissed him on the ear and told him to give her "some time to think about it."

"How long do you want?" he said moodily.

"I don't know, Nathaniel. It's something I must consider. I . . . I'm a little frightened," she confessed.

Then he turned back to her and took her in his arms, saying, "Oh, love, it's not easy for me to be with you like this. I want more of you. You are so beautiful, Daydee, and damn it, I think I'm . . . in love with you." He was looking straight into her eyes.

She felt a tingling sensation all over her body. No man had ever said such a thing to her. Well, not a real man, that was. Silly old Roy had tried to say it at Christmas time. She did not know what to reply. She knew she longed to hear John Stuart say it, but he was far away on the cattle drive, and Nathaniel was here, right here in her arms, and he was so handsome, so much fun, and she was enjoying how he made her feel.

Suddenly she realized that it was very dark in the glade. It must be nearing dusk, and a breeze had blown up. Her small face filled with concern. "Nathaniel," she said in a worried tone, "I have to go now. It must be very late."

"Oh, all right." His tone was resigned. "Come on."

As he bent to pick up the blanket, a thought occurred to him. His eyes half closed in deliberation. "Love," he said in a more cheerful way, "what time are 'lights out' at your establishment?"

"What do you mean, Nathaniel?"

He took her by the arm and led her toward the horses. "I mean, what time of night does everybody retire at your house?"

"Well, while Daddy's away, I suppose about ten o'clock or half past. Our manservant, Leith, goes to bed around that time, I think. And Bess and Rosy, the maids, and Beth, the cook, usually go to bed and read. Why?"

He was setting a goodly pace back to the animals now, and hurrying her along. "Saturday night, can you get out of the house and meet me? The nights are so pleasant lately. Not cold at all. I often leave the smoky bunkhouse and go outside at about the hour of eleven, and it's wonderful."

Daydee halted, and he almost shot past her.

"Hey! What's wrong, love?" he asked, turning quickly back to her.

Her small eyes looked at him knowingly. "Nathaniel Lake," she began in a severe tone, "*now* you are suggesting I meet you in the middle of the night."

Biting his lip, he returned her gaze, a hopeful expression in his eyes.

She wagged her finger at him. "Mind you—" her tone was milder now "—I don't say it's a bad idea; it should certainly be an adventure. I suppose I'd like to, if I can, for it's been very hard to keep coming here in the afternoons on my own. They are *all* so keen on chaperons *all* the time. It's a wonder I'm sane."

He sighed faintly and smiled. "Ah, but you are, love, and clever, too. Now, come on, let's work out things as we go."

They hurried on, and Daydee, excited now, reminded him, "We shall have to be careful of the night patrol. Mind you, if we meet inside the park, we'll be safe, for they only just ride through once about midnight. Yes, that's it. It will be easy for me once I'm out of the house, for we have a private gate from our back garden into the park."

They had arrived back at the tethered horses. He retrieved the paints and pictures from where she had left them to dry, and put them in one of her saddlebags. She mounted, and he gave her a significant look. "I'll meet you inside the park. I will wait near your gate in the hedge. I'll be there by eleven o'clock on Saturday night. Now, don't forget."

She bent down to him, and he kissed her.

"I'll see you Saturday night, Nathaniel," she called over her shoulder as she disappeared into the twilight. Her heart beat quickly as she rode back. She had stayed too long. God! What if they had sent Leith to find her? There would be the devil to pay! How she hated not ever being able to do as she liked. How she hated her mother and Eve. They forced her to this subterfuge. It was their fault!

Nathaniel had said he loved her! Did he really? He was so different from the others on Mayfield. He was handsome and well bred. Educated, too. Not like a common old cattleman. Of course, he was not as refined and wonderful as John Stuart, but then, who was? No, there was no man in the whole world like John Stuart. But Nathaniel was showing her things, and oh, how she was loving the way he made her feel. She thought of his kisses and the way he fondled her. Perhaps she ought to let him go a little further on Saturday.

Daydee saw them as she rode up to the house. They were down near the front hedge, waiting for her. She had ridden directly to the house, specifically to let them know she was all right. Did they have to stand there, accusingly?

She really did hate them. Her mouth pulled down, but as she came near and they could see her face, her expression changed completely, and she began to smile.

"I do hope I didn't worry you, mother dear," she began. "I was having such a good time, I didn't realize how late it was. I do feel sorry for having concerned you, really sorry."

Thelma shook her head in exasperation, and Eve answered, "Yes, Daydee, you have concerned us. But at least you are back now and safe."

"I'll not have you riding out alone again," her mother added. "I don't care what your father said. We've been so worried."

Daydee edged the horse away from them. "I shall be back directly, Mother; I had better take Boots down to the stables."

When Daydee returned over the field from the stables, it was almost dark. She was close to her front hedge when she saw Eve waiting for her. The girl started in surprise.

"Daydee, I want to speak with you."

"What for?"

"Ah, Daydee, dear Daydee," Eve said quietly, "whoever he is, he's not worth it."

"What do you mean?" the girl said, throwing her head back and tossing her hair over her shoulder.

"I mean, Daydee, the man you have been meeting. You were not at Chinaman's Hill painting today."

Daydee's look became defiant. "So you've been spying on me, have you? How disgusting!"

"No, Daydee, I have not been spying on you. I had no need. I knew you would not be there."

The girl's eyes were cold, contemptuous. She was looking at Eve with loathing.

Suddenly Eve realized the depth of Daydee's hatred, and the knowledge was truly frightening. This was not something she could continue to ignore. She went quite cold, so much did Daydee's expression impart. Never had she suspected the girl's antipathy was so malevolent. For those moments there in the dusk, Daydee Larmer was ugly. The hate inside, manifesting itself upon her face, actually altered her features. Gone was the dainty look, with the pert, upturned nose. Instead, her nostrils flared hostilely, and she looked coarse, pitiless, vindictive. . . .

Eve was alarmed; she had difficulty believing what she saw.

"What is it you want with me?" Daydee uttered belligerently. When Eve remained silent, the girl prompted, "Well?"

With effort, Eve managed to speak civilly. "Daydee, I . . . don't want to hurt you. I am trying to stop you from doing something indiscreet. Although the more I look at you, the more I wonder if you're worth it. I am not judging you, just warning you. If anyone learns that you have been secretly meeting this man, it will be the talk of Mayfield and beyond. You would be disgraced, and you would hurt your parents dreadfully."

"Will you inform on me?" the girl asked.

Eve shook her head. "No, I will not inform on you. Unlike you, I do not act maliciously. I'm not interested in telling tales to people. All I ask is that you consider what I have said. Think of the shame you would bring on those who love you."

Daydee's face grew so antagonistic that Eve finally shook her head in disgust and swiftly walked away.

"I shall do as I please," the girl's voice sounded after her. "Just go away and leave me alone, damn you! Oh, how I wish you had never come to Mayfield. How I wish you would go away forever."

All the following day, Daydee wondered how on earth Eve could have known she was meeting Nathaniel. Obviously Eve did not know who he was or she would have said his name. Daydee could only suppose that somehow Eve had guessed what she was doing. Eve's warning did have an effect: it made Daydee decide to be more cautious. This meeting at night was a far better idea. For a start, she did not need to make excuses.

As Friday passed, she became more and more alert. She was positively excited about it. Her walk, normally bouncy, was positively jaunty; and on Saturday, in expectation of the meeting, her disposition became more pleasant by the hour.

That night after dinner, Thelma announced that she was going over to the "big house" to play cribbage with Eve. It was all Daydee could do not to laugh with delight. She read a little, but her mind was not on the story. At twenty minutes to ten o'clock she put out her lamp and sat by the window, looking down through the trees to where Nathaniel would be. She heard the grandfather clock at the foot of the stairs chime ten times, and about fifteen minutes later, her mother's footsteps on the stairs.

She heard the rustle of her gown as she passed down the hall, then the sound of her bedroom door opening and closing. Good. She at least was out of the way.

The next half hour was the slowest of Daydee's life. She paced the room in a nervous excitement. She dressed in a sweet concoction of pink and white, with bows and ribbons. She brushed her long black hair and tied a double bow at the back.

Ten minutes before the hour, she took her shawl and opened her bedroom door. The house seemed still. She made her way down the staircase and crept toward the kitchen.

Suddenly she stopped, every nerve on edge. There was lamplight in the kitchen. God! Leith must still be up, damn him. She could not go out the back door now. What to do? Oh, yes, she could go out through the long French windows in the dining room and creep along the side of the house and around the hedge gate. Out through the long windows she went. It was a calm night, no wind, just a gentle, exhilarating coolness in the air. She slipped silently through the shadows.

The lamplight from the kitchen threw a wan beam across the back garden as she stole to the hedge gate. She opened it gently; it squeaked just a little. Through it she went.

"Nathaniel, Nathaniel?" she called softly.

"Over here, love."

She ran forward to him, and he enveloped her in his arms. But where she expected tender loving, she found herself repelled. She pulled back, an expression of distaste on her face. "You're . . . you're drunk!" she said in a loud whisper.

"No reproof, love," he countered, pulling her back to him. "Give me a kiss." His mouth covered hers. His tongue pushed deep into her. The sour taste of stale alcohol was so opposite to the sweet kisses of the afternoons. She was shocked; he was so different, so coarse. She was repulsed.

She drew her face away from his. "Don't, don't!" Her voice rose out of a whisper. "Nathaniel, I don't like it. I don't like you when you're drunk."

"Well, I like you," he replied, holding her more tightly in his arms.

"Please, Nathaniel, you're hurting me." She was scared, yet she did not dare to cry out. She was tugging to get out of his arms, but it was useless. She was so light and tiny, he easily pulled her down to the ground with him. His hand went beneath her gown, his eager fingers pushing up between her legs, his mouth searching for hers.

"God, Nathaniel, someone comes!" she said in a voice of fear.

He stopped and looked around in surprise. "Where?"

In the moment that he loosed her, she rolled away and gained her feet. She ran swiftly over the grass and the flower beds and through the gate, and was gone before the befuddled man realized it was a trick.

"You bitch, Daydee, you bloody little bitch!" He said it loudly.

He gathered his senses and moved quickly over to a bench and picked up his bottle of rum. Mustn't leave that here. As fast as he could, he went back toward the park gate. He was about to step out onto the gravel when the idea came to him.

What if he dared? He smiled widely there in the night. Daydee was only a bloody waste of time. He would go to *her*, up there in Mayfield House. She would have him. She had always been in love with him. She wouldn't change, not that one. She was just like him, always ready for a good time. He could still hear her saying, "Nathaniel, you're the one I'll always love truly." All he had to do was get into that private garden. It led directly to her bedroom.

And Wakeman was away. God, he could feel her heat beneath him already. Drunk, was he? Well, he might be a bit. But he knew exactly what he was doing. He knew exactly where to go to get the loving Daydee wouldn't give him. What damn good was a fucking virgin anyway? He laughed softly at that, "a fucking virgin," what a contradiction! How bloody amusing!

He moved through the darkness of the trees at the edge of the carriageway toward the pale radiance of the house. Lamps were lit on the veranda. How positively awesome it looked. So grand it was, and to think she was in there.

The three carriage-drives opened up into a large graveled half circle surrounded by lawn in front of the house. He kept to the line of trees until he crossed the roads, his boots crunching loudly. At last he stood beneath the stone wall that enclosed the garden. The top was only a couple of inches above his head. He could have climbed it, if he hadn't had a drink. He moved along the wall a little way. Now, blast it! What had that bloody Daydee said? Yes, that's right. She had said there was a wooden gate somewhere. Where the devil was it?

In front of him loomed a shape. Oh, only a tree. Now, that

was better. He could climb that if he had to. He moved on by, and yes, the girl had told him correctly, here was the gate. Latched on the inside! Bugger it! Back to the tree.

To his amazement, he climbed it easily. He had to drop down on the inside, and as he did so, he felt the rum bottle fall. His hands groped around in the grass. He found it, uncorked it, and took another swig.

It was bigger than he thought, this garden, and bloody dark, but soon his eyes adjusted, and he could make out the shapes around him. There were many small, trimmed trees and hedges. He found a path. Quietly, so quietly, he walked along it.

He halted under the only large tree in the garden. It was shaped like an umbrella. He took another swig of the rum bottle and ever so gently laid it at the foot of the tree. He leaned on the trunk, looking over to a wide veranda, where a kerosene lamp, on a marble table, threw a benign light across hanging baskets full of flowers and a climbing rose trailing along the railing. Fancy living in a place like this. God! Hadn't she come up in the world?

Then, as if the thought of her made her a reality, she issued through the long casement windows onto the veranda. She looked just as he had seen her so many times: her body covered with a film of a nightgown, a light shawl around her shoulders, and her burnished curls hanging down her back. Her forearms were bare. Her breasts looked lusciously full.

Ahead of her scampered a white cat.

Eve had said good night to Thelma at about ten o'clock. They had enjoyed a quiet, pleasant evening playing two-handed crib-bage, and after a glass of port and some sweetmeats, Thelma had gone home with Leith, who had waited for her.

Around eleven o'clock, Eve bade Stephanie good night. "As it's Sunday tomorrow, I shall sleep in a little, Stephanie, dear, so don't wake me early. And you sleep in, too," Eve added as the girl closed the bedroom door.

She had been reading for some time when Velvet ingratiated himself into the bedroom through the door from the sitting room. "Oh, Velvet, is that where you've been?" He stretched his long, supple limbs, arching his back, before he made his way to the casement windows and began to scratch on them.

"You are a nuisance, you know," she said playfully, climbing from the bed to open the casements, and let Velvet scamper through.

The night was still. She walked across the veranda to lean against the thin balustrade. In the soft lamplight, she noticed that on the lawn below, Velvet had hold of something in his front paws and was teasing it.

"Oh, no, Velvet," she called. "You naughty boy, what have you there?" She hurried down the stone steps and across to him. In his claws was a small lizard.

"No, no, sweetie," she said, lifting the cat away with one hand and rescuing the tiny reptile with the other. The lizard seemed stunned and Eve could feel its heart beating. Keeping Velvet behind her with one hand, she walked to a garden bed near the poinciana tree and, bending down, put the creature in among the flowers. "There you are, little man," she said softly. "Away you go."

Then she turned and lifted Velvet in her arms to keep him from following his prey. It was as she stood up with him that she heard the voice.

"Clare," it sounded thickly, "Clare, love, I'm here."

She was petrified with shock. She stood stock-still, unable to move. Velvet half fell, half jumped from her, dragging her shawl with him, as a hand took her arm and turned her. She looked into a face she did not know.

She was astounded. Icy cold fear shot through her limbs.

The mouth was on hers in an instant. She pulled back in automatic resistance, still in shock.

"Clare, Clare," he said again, "it's me, Nathaniel."

At last something like a strangled sound came from her throat. "No! Please . . ."

He pulled her tightly to him and kissed her again. The taste and smell of liquor was revoltingly overpowering.

He was staggering slightly. "Come on, old girl. What the devil's wrong? Too good for your old lover?"

She managed to lift one hand and push at his face. "No! No! Don't!" She turned in his arms and tried to escape. Her elbow swung sharply up into his ribs as she thrust herself away.

"Not you, too," he uttered angrily as she writhed out of his grasp. His hand slid down her arm as she pulled away, and grabbing at the flimsy material of her nightgown, took hold of it. At the same time, he lunged with his other hand, striking her shoulder as she moved away from him, knocking her off balance. When she fell, she felt her nightdress rend.

She was aware of her nakedness and then the weight of him as he fell on top of her. The fumes of alcohol were overwhelming, and he was mumbling, "Come on, love, come on." She rolled to the side, but he had his arm around her ribs and he pulled her back under him. She pushed at him, digging her fingers into his throat and twisting her body to slither from beneath him.

For a moment he hesitated, growling in anger, "What the shit? Clare, have you gone mad?"

Swiftly she squirmed sideways, kicking and reaching out to free herself, but he recovered and dragged her back down, flattening her with his body, his hands on her breasts, his hot, alcoholic breath continuing to fill her senses.

She tried to scream, but horror had made her dumb. There was nothing but blind panic in her now, and the only sound that issued from her throat was a gurgling sound of terror. His mouth thudded onto hers; the sweat from him mingling with her tears. Her thoughts reeling with shock and horror, everything she did was instinctive. She pushed his head back and hit at his face.

He yelped and rose slightly from her, giving her a chance to push at him and to lift her knee as she tried to turn and snake away from beneath him.

This man was not just angry now, his voice was crazily excited and urgent. "So you want to fight? Good, I love to fight," he cried, smashing a heavy blow across the side of her head and driving it round into the grass. The impact dazed her, but she knew he was trying to pin her arms to her side. She heard him call her Clare, over and over again, and through the blur of terror, she managed to force her right hand up out of his grasp to claw at his face, and draw her nails down across his cheeks. With a growl, his head jerked back. He was in a frenzy, stimulated by alcohol, aroused by her resistance, intent on fulfilling the need that had brought him here. He struck out with his fist, punching her in the face, and at the same time, pulled his legs up to straddle her. She lifted herself in an attempt to drag her body out from his, but he cuffed her across the face again, knocking her backward.

She was writhing, kicking, swamped by the appalling reality of what was happening. With all her will, she drove the top half of her body upright again, throwing her hands up to take him by the throat and dig her fingers deep into the flesh of his neck.

"You bitch! Want it rough, eh?" he growled, knocking her hands away and this time grabbing her wrists and pushing her arms down, down, back to her sides. He was plainly stimulated by the resistance in her. His desire heightened.

She was fighting for survival now, blindly, fiercely, her brain screaming for her to fight, struggle, kick. With a mighty effort, she forced one hand from his grasp, and thrusting it up to his face, found his lips, his nose, his cheeks. She tried to drag her fingernails across them again, but he tore her hand from his face as his body snapped backward and momentarily slid sideways.

"Clare, you fucking bitch!" he shouted as she shoved him from her as hard as she could. He lost his balance and for a moment his bulk was toppling, but his big legs were still encompassing her, and at the same time, his arms were already lashing back to grab her. She began to yank her body from beneath his, but he regained his balance, his determined hands reaching out and groping for her naked arms. She felt his long, thick fingers find her shoulders and take hold. He had her now, he was back on top of her, her body pinioned beneath him, his solid weight riveting her to the ground. He jerked her shoulders up toward him and then smashed her head down to the ground. Once . . . twice . . . He lifted her again, pounding her head into senselessness. Was he going to kill her? As she thudded backward, she knew she was trying to scream, but she had no idea whether or not any sound came from her mouth. There was a part of her violated mind that told her no one would hear her anyway; they were all far away in the other wings of the house.

As she plunged into unconsciousness, she thought she actually managed to say, "I'm . . . not . . . Clare!" The last thing she felt before her mind went completely dead was the force of him down between her legs and the brutal pain of his entry into her body.

She was insensible to his noises as he moved over her limp nakedness, panting and groaning. At last he was releasing himself, completing what he had come for. She was unconscious for the minutes he used her.

Awareness began to return to her just as he made a final, bestial grunt. She became conscious of the cessation of movement within her and his heavy body rolling away. His breath was coming in short gasps. He made strange sounds as he half rose. She saw his hand come back toward her, and she gave a sharp, terrified intake of breath. But his fingers only touched her mouth. It was absurdly like a caress.

"Oh God!" he said. "Who are you?"

She closed her eyes, and her only answer was her tears.

He made a hopeless attempt to cover her with the torn nightdress, then she heard him lurch to his feet.

"Damn you!" he said. "Why did you let me believe you were Clare? Look what you've made me do!"

She heard him move across the garden, mumbling things she could not understand. She heard him unlatch the gate, heard it open and close.

Then nothing, only the pitiful silence of the night.

SIXTEEN

Aftermath

As Eve rose and gathered her nightgown and shawl to her, her foot touched something cold. A bottle . . . alcohol. She took it in her shaking fingers and, gaining her feet, stumbled back to the veranda.

The clear sounds of the horses' hooves on the graveled drive drifted to her in the stillness. The night patrol were riding through. Was it only midnight? It seemed so long since she had climbed into bed between the crisp, white sheets.

She locked the casements and mechanically drew the curtain. She wrapped the tatters of her nightgown in an old petticoat. The numbness that was her mind told her tomorrow she must dispose of it somewhere.

She looked in the mirror. Two eyes looked back, glazed eyes. Clare's eyes? The woman in the mirror had blood coming from her nose and the edge of her mouth, and her lip was swelling. There were dark red patches and scratches on her face and breasts, and marks, which would turn into bruises, showed near her eyes. She bent her head. Some of the skin had been rubbed from her thigh, her knees, and her elbows. She could not feel any pain. Her body seemed as paralyzed as her brain.

She sat down to gather strength, then with trembling fingers she wiped the blood from her nose and mouth with a handkerchief.

Slowly, very slowly, she put on her dressing gown and, taking her pitcher from the washstand, made her way out along the corridor toward the small room where she could tap the water cisterns used on this side of the house. Fortunately, she did not have to go over to the kitchens and scullery. She passed along the corridor like a barefoot automaton, not feeling the rich carpet beneath her feet. She filled the pitcher and returned.

With deliberate movements, she bathed her cuts and bruises and put on fresh bedclothes, then once more she made the walk along the corridor to throw away the dirty water. She simply could have opened her door and poured it in the garden, but the irrational fear that he might still be out there filled her mind. She picked up the bloody handkerchief she had used. She would throw it away with the remains of her nightgown.

Now she began to feel things. Her joints ached, and a little muscle in her groin twitched uncontrollably. Her right hipbone and upper leg were tender, and her face and neck felt as if they had been twisted in a vise.

Finally she was between the clean sheets of her bed again.

How in the Lord's name could this have happened? That she had escaped this very act by her wits and wiles when not much more than a child at the Ship Inn, with no one to protect her, only to be assaulted here with dozens of servants nearby.

Her sobs, pitiful sounds of outrage and misery, filled her whole distraught being. She began to shake uncontrollably, and sinking her face into the softness of the pillow, she drew up her legs and curled into herself, until, at last, she drifted into blessed sleep.

Poor Velvet took the blame for the swelling on her mouth and the abrasions to her face. She was drawn into intimating he had accidentally tripped her on the veranda steps and she had fallen heavily to the ground.

Stephanie and the household were all compassion and concern. Mary Smith prepared an old herbal remedy to relieve the swelling and applied it to Eve's mouth, while Mr. Free cooked a special beef broth for her.

Eve had lain ever since she awoke thinking of what to do. There were moments when she burst involuntarily into tears, and others when she had an almost ungovernable desire to scream. It was unthinkable; sexually attacked in her own secluded garden by a man who had mistaken her for her twin sister. Firstly, no one knew she had a sister! If only she had told John Stuart long ago as Father had advised her. Everything now was so horribly complicated.

A woman in her position could not be raped. It would reflect on John Stuart; it would reflect on Mayfield. She had always realized that John Stuart would be appalled to learn of Clare. But now? How could he contend with the knowledge that his wife was the twin of a woman whose lover had found his way to Mayfield and assaulted her! It was a nightmare. How her head ached. What was she to do? Visions of both John Stuart and Alan Fletcher rushed simultaneously into her mind. How she longed to be held, hidden and safe, away from this ghastly reality.

But there would be no holding, no minding, for the one, even were he here, would have difficulty understanding; while the other, though he were understanding, could never be here. But perhaps she was wrong. John Stuart would understand; of course he would. When he returned, she would tell him everything. He would be as he had been in the phaeton the night before he left, so dear, so gentle, so loving. God in Heaven, why hadn't she told him about Clare then?

Then her confused brain screamed, no, she would never tell. She would remain silent. People looked up to her. She was "the mistress," and "the mistress" did not get raped. Only harlots and unfortunate girls in slums and poorhouses were raped. She had no choice. She must uphold all that she and John Stuart stood for; she must maintain the dignity of her husband and his position as master of so much and so many. No one must ever know. She began to sob again. Thank heaven Dr. Douglas was not on the station to examine her. He had accompanied the cattle drive and was attending an annual assembly of medical men in Sydney.

By midmorning the news of the accident was all over Mayfield. Thelma wasted no time in coming swiftly to the big house.

"Oh, my dear, my dear, I feel terrible," Thelma began as she entered the room. "Why didn't you wake the servants and send for me immediately? When did this dreadful thing happen?"

Smiling wanly, Eve replied, "Last night after you had gone." Eve avoided her friend's gaze, and now she lay back and closed her eyes. "I'll be perfectly well in a day or two. It looks much worse than it is, Thel."

"It looks terrible, more as if you'd been beaten than fallen." Thelma came over and sat on the edge of the bed, and in doing so, touched Eve's side. Eve winced.

"Why, you are hurt in your body, too?" Thelma said, surprised.

"It's nothing, dear. I must have twisted as I fell."

"Oh, Eve." The older woman's face creased in sympathy. "I fear you are in more pain than you say."

"No. No. It is nothing serious. I am sure."

Thelma looked skeptically at her. "My dear girl, I shall send to Cowra for Dr. Bell, and we'll find out."

Alarmed, Eve looked up quickly. "But it was only a fall." When she saw the older woman was not convinced, she began to panic. "Thel, please. If I am not feeling better in forty-eight hours, then definitely, yes, I shall send for him. But you must let me decide what is best. Please."

"I don't know what John Stuart will say, he only just gone, and this happening. I won't blame him if he holds us all responsible."

Eve gave a trembling sigh. She hated this subterfuge. She had an overwhelming desire to tell Thelma everything, but she could not do that. How unfair it would be to burden her good friend with such a horrible, shameful secret.

Thelma left to let her sleep, and at five o'clock Mrs. Smith arrived.

"Mrs. Wakeman," she began, "the gels have brought hot water, and I have a little remedy to go in the bath. It will help." She patted her apron pocket.

"Mrs. Smith, thank you. Please leave the remedy with Stephanie and explain its use. I shall be happy to try it."

"Very well, mum, ye know best."

Eve realized that Stephanie would see her body. As Eve's personal maid, the girl often saw her in the bath. She and Stephanie had spent a great deal of time in each other's company, and there was a bond between them. When the girl came in, on her big, round face was a mild, loving expression.

"Stephanie, you will need to help me bathe. You will see that I have other marks and bruises. It was a very bad . . . fall. I have not wanted to worry Mrs. Larmer or the household, so I'll ask you not to mention them to anyone. You understand?"

"Yes, ma'am, but, Mrs. Wakeman, shouldn't you send into Cowra for Dr. Bell?"

"No, Stephanie, my dear, I am going to be all right. I just want you to be prepared for what you shall see." But for all the warning, when the girl saw her body, she exclaimed, "Oh, no, Mrs. Wakeman! Oh Lordy me!"

It was not until twenty-four hours later that Eve learned what her attacker had been doing on Mayfield. When Thelma came to sit with her the following morning, she brought a pile of the women's magazines she received from Scotland. "Read these, love, when you feel up to it; they'll help to pass the time." The good woman stayed a few hours and chatted a lot. "You know, love, Mrs. Hennessy told me a strange thing this very morning. She brought over some pound cake, the dear, she do make that a treat, you know, the best cook on Mayfield, if you ask me. Well, it seems Mr. Hennessy had one of his short-timers just up and go the night before last. In the middle of the night, too, would you believe it?"

Eve stiffened.

"Well, now, it seems this short-timer was a real one for the women. Notorious in the bunkhouses, they say. Name of Nathaniel Lake, I think she said."

Thelma could see that Eve appeared to be paying attention, and so she went on enthusiastically. "As I say, my dear, in the middle of the night, he went and took his horse from the stables. Didn't take his wages, nothing. Mr. Hennessy says that for all his years on Mayfield, he has never known a short-timer to leave without his money. Says he's mystified. But Mrs. Hennessy and I say it's obvious, unfortunately. Only one thing makes a man run in the middle of the night."

Eve could not help herself. "And what is that?"

"That, love, is a woman. Sad but true. We have no doubt he's running from a Mayfield girl. Stands to reason. As Mrs. Hennessy said herself, 'There's some poor girl here on Mayfield as is in the family way, mark my words.' And you know, Eve, she'll be right. No blighter runs off in the middle of the night like that for nothing. To be sure, we'll find out who the poor soul in trouble is soon enough."

Eve's heart was racing.

Her friend continued. "We've had more than one marriage here on Mayfield as where a bairn has come before its time. Oh, yes, we've had a few seven-month babes; but that is one thing. When the man lights out and leaves the woman, it's another altogether. Remember when poor Sally Collins got herself into trouble?''

Eve shook her head.

"Oh, no, love, of course you wouldn't. You weren't here at all then. It was proper disgraceful. He was a Mayfield man, too, no short-timer! And he lit out as soon as he knew about the babe. John Stuart did right, I believe, after all. Yet I was a mind to being a touch more sympathetic to Sally at the time.''

"Why, Thelma, what do you mean?'' Eve asked, her voice sounding a little unsteady to her own ears.

"Well, the father had gone, as I mentioned, and the girl, Sally, she hid her problem until she was nigh on six months gone. Heaven knows how, for those girls often sleep two and three to a room. When John Stuart found out, he was more than a mite outraged. He doesn't hold with immorality, but I don't need to tell you that. None of us knows exactly what John Stuart said, but she came out of his study crying her heart out, nonetheless. Although he was more than kind, really. Many a man in his position would have been heartless and sent her away immediately, no pay, nothing, but she was allowed to stay on here until the baby was born. The child was removed from her at birth. She didn't lay hands on it at all. That's what I felt was a touch hard at the time, but you know? When I look back on it, I'm more of a mind to reckon it was kind, for she had no chance of becoming attached to it. And so the baby boy, for it was a boy, was taken from her the minute of birth. We kept it over at my house the first three weeks. Dear little angel, it was.''

Thelma closed her eyes in memory. "Then a minister, a Reverend Theodore, came and took him away. I asked John Stuart where he was going. You know, Eve, I remember his very words: 'It's not the poor infant's fault, Thelma,' he said. 'It's the degenerate pair that begot the child who are to blame. It would have been branded a bastard, but I have done the best I can by it.' He had found some couple somewhere that couldn't have a child of their own, and that Reverend Theodore, yes, well, he delivered it to them.''

Eve couldn't help asking, "And what of Sally, the mother?''

"Sent away as soon as she could travel. Oh, John Stuart made sure she was given plenty of money to tide her over until she could place herself somewhere again. But that was it. He was only concerned with the welfare of the child. That's the way John Stuart is. He has no time at all for fallen women.''

"No." Eve shook her head. "He hasn't." A sickening chill rippled through her.

When her friend had gone, she began to tremble. So Lake was his surname? Into her mind came the fearful memory of his voice. "It's me . . . Nathaniel." She even remembered which one of Clare's menagerie he had been: the very one Clare had been living with when she went to her in Adelaide in 1857. She had never seen him, but she remembered his name. Oh, God, the irony of it all. *Your* lover, Clare. And he had run away? Of course, he would. He didn't want to get lynched. At least he was gone, never to come back, and she had time to consider how to broach things when John Stuart came home.

Dr. Bell was never called, because she said she felt better each day, and by Wednesday morning, she had convinced Thelma and Mrs. Smith that she was well enough to leave her bed. It was uncomfortable to walk, but her lip was down to its normal size, and even though she had a black eye and abrasions, some of the soreness had left her limbs.

She wanted desperately to be normal, and in the morning she insisted on working with Mr. Oldfield in John Stuart's study, checking lists and supervising accounts, but by noon, she had left him and gone to her bedroom, where she washed herself all over. She lay on her bed seeing the horrible, mad images of Nathaniel Lake in her head. Suddenly an overwhelming anger took hold of her, and she sat up, consumed by indignation and resentment. She moved swiftly to the door and across the veranda and down into her garden bower. "Damn you!" she called aloud, smashing her fist into the indifferent trunk of the poinciana tree. "Damn you to hell!" Then, as quickly as her rage had risen, it died. She sagged forward, overcome now by guilt and fear. How she needed compassion, understanding, and love. But she was alone . . . alone, once more in her life.

When she was called to her luncheon, she forced herself to eat something so that the household would not be concerned, and she spent the afternoon taking gentle walks and resting on the veranda.

She thought of Father. If only he were here. Perhaps she should go to him, stay with him and Mother while John Stuart was away. Being with them would calm her, and she would find the strength to combat this. Yes, in a week or so she should be able to travel. The very memory of the two dear folk in Bathurst brought a small measure of cheer into her misery.

Suddenly, out beyond the Norfolk pines, something pink

caught her eye. It was a parasol bobbing up and down, and under it the jaunty walk of Daydee, passing through the grounds. The girl looked over toward Eve, and the realization struck like lightning.

Lake! Nathaniel Lake! He was the man she had seen kissing Daydee that afternoon by the Lachlan. He was the man who had stood up from the campfire on the night before the cattle drive and walked into the darkness. Another cold shiver rippled through her. He was the man she had warned Daydee not to see! It was like some fantastic, morbid jest being played upon her. She had to lean on the railing in front of her for support as every nerve end screamed. She felt physically ill.

Daydee, too, had learned that Lake had gone. Not that she cared! She was glad. She hated him for the way he had fooled her. How she had wept last Saturday night when she returned to the safety of her bedroom. She had been awake and worried all night because she realized she had left her shawl in the park! The next morning, she had sneaked out just after daybreak and found it, and a blanket. But she had learned things, too, from her experience with Lake, and even though she hated him, in some ways she was grateful to him. How she loved John Stuart, perhaps more than before, if it were possible. And now, as she passed through the park with her book, *Agnes Grey*, under her arm, she looked sideways and saw Eve on the veranda.

Daydee had a sense that all was not as it appeared with Eve. Goodness! She hardly knew what she thought. But it was to do with Eve and the fall and Lake. Lake had disappeared from Mayfield in the middle of Saturday night. Disappeared without a trace, no pay, no good-byes to anyone. She was positive he had not left because of what he had done with her in the park, unless he was worried she would inform on him. No, he would have known better. She would have disgraced herself by her own misconduct. It was something else that had made him run! She had this irrational suspicion. She had seen Eve up close, and the woman looked more like someone who had been beaten than someone who had fallen. But . . . even Nathaniel would not have dared! Drunk as he was. He was a mere working hand. *She* was Mrs. Wakeman. Nothing made sense. Yet the suspicion lingered. She must be watchful. Possibly she would find something out.

* * *

As the days advanced, Eve's bruises faded, her lacerations healed, and the soreness all but disappeared, yet she could not heal the wound inside or throw off the feeling of being dirty. She washed herself two and three times a day, feeling the horror and the shame of Lake's assault crushing in on her. She felt weighed down by guilt. If only she had told John Stuart about Clare, perhaps this would not have occurred. Could it be that the attack was some mysterious kind of retribution for her falseness?

She postponed her idea of going to Father and Mother; for as much as she desired to see them, something told her to wait here at Mayfield for John Stuart. Finally, after all her soul-searching and reasoning, she decided she must try to accept the degradation of it all and to tell him everything the moment he came home. She knew he would understand and help her. It would be a new start, no secrets or doubts between them. All would be right.

Once she had made this decision, she forced herself to begin walking again, with good-natured Stephanie trailing her over hill and dale, and with her belief in the future, her spirits lifted a little. She dreamed often about her husband and sometimes about the bushranger.

Occasionally she noticed an aching in her teeth and tenderness in her breasts, but she took little notice, thinking it was the aftermath of the trauma.

On her birthday, she had grown strong enough to have a small luncheon celebration with Thelma, Mrs. Hennessy, and Mrs. Watson, and while there were still moments of ungovernable depression, guilt, and misgiving, for a time her feelings became more stable.

Then, five weeks after John Stuart had left, a message came to say he would be delayed until at least mid-November. It seemed the buying of land was going so well, he wished to visit other places that interested him. From the moment the news arrived, Eve felt odd. It had nothing to do with the news itself; it had to do with her. As each day passed, the apprehension ebbed and flowed until the day came when she could no longer keep the feeling away. Though the aching in her teeth had gone, she could not ignore the soreness in her breasts, or the slight dizziness she felt now and then.

It was seven weeks to the day since Nathaniel Lake had bludgeoned into her life that she was sure she carried his child. Her cycles were always regular. This time she was weeks late and had awoken ill and dry-reached into the marble dish on her washstand.

No, not his child! It was too obscene. She had irrational thoughts. First, she thought to kill herself. Better to be dead than this! She would cut her wrists and be out of this appalling misery. But no, suicide was not the answer. Evelyn May Herman was stronger than that. Then she thought to brazen it out, pretend it was John Stuart's, but she could not do that either. It would be cruel, cowardly deception.

She began to spend more and more time alone. She ate solitary meals in the garden. She kept her appointments with Mr. Oldfield and continued to do those things that were her duty, but any social engagement, she tried to avoid with the excuse that she had been having headaches, which, indeed, was mostly the truth.

She still took walks, long walks, but always alone. When Stephanie asked why she did not wish her company, Eve was sharp with the girl for the first time. "I do not need a servant questioning my actions. Do not dare to interrogate me again." Stephanie, abashed, looked as if she would cry as she turned to leave.

Then, feeling immediate regret, Eve called, "Wait, Stephanie!"

The girl turned back, and Eve spoke wearily. "I'm sorry, truly sorry; I did not mean to speak so cuttingly. I am unwell lately."

She grew thinner, and the tiny lines near her eyes were more obvious. Her half-crazed thoughts led her to avoid Thelma. She made up excuses for not spending time in her friend's company, and when Thelma called by to pick her up to ride into church, Eve met her on the veranda with the pretext she was tired of the long journey into Cowra. Thelma stood at the bottom of the steps, one foot tapping the sandstone as she looked up at Eve with an expression of concern. "I see, love. I'm sorry you feel this way." Eve turned from her, and Thelma called, "Eve?" She looked back. "I shall stay home with you. The good Lord won't miss me."

"No, Thel," Eve quickly replied, "I don't want you staying home on account of me. Please, I insist you go." And she turned swiftly away and reentered the house.

Thelma's concern deepened. She knew there was something very amiss. She wished Eve would confide in her and tell her what was wrong, but obviously now was not the time. She shook her head sorrowfully before she mounted her gig and drove away.

One November morning, Mr. Oldfield came to Eve, holding in his hand a telegraphed message from the Mayfield man stationed in Bathurst. His young face was aglow.

"Mrs. Wakeman," he began as he opened the door, "I've some grand news."

Eve lifted her drawn face from the papers in front of her and asked with dread, "And what is that, Mr. Oldfield?"

"The master comes home at last. He wishes for the Mayfield coach to arrive at the Penrith railhead by December first. He will join it by the following afternoon and be home by the fourth. And Mrs. Wakeman," the young man went on zealously, "as today is the twenty-eighth, it had better leave straightaway to get there in time."

"Yes, yes, of course." She tried to smile, to inject some eagerness into her voice. "You will see to all that, will you?"

"I will indeed, ma'am, with pleasure."

When he had gone, Eve stood from her chair. So, within the space of a week, she would be reunited with her husband. She shivered. Now that his return was imminent, she could not help feeling the cold chill of fear. She had heard there were people who knew how to bring about miscarriages, but who were they and where could she find them? Even if she knew such a person, could she go through with such an act?

In the late afternoon, she decided to leave the house and go riding in the fresh air in an attempt to clear her troubled head. She rode to the north for twenty minutes or so, on Betsy, a smallish roan mare, steady and reliable. She reined in on a gentle slope, and for a time she sat down on the ground and looked at the tiny white flowers, wondering at the miracle of harmony that they were. She felt an overwhelming sadness for these beautiful things which would soon be dead, and for some minutes she sat and, in turn, touched each small flower within her reach with the tip of her finger, in some vain, pointless game, as if the ones she touched would not die.

She began to reflect on her life, recalling all the contingencies that had brought her to this day, and how she alone had been the one who could have changed it. A tear broke over her eyelid and ran down her face.

There was a large, gray cloud above that seemed to be like a human profile with a handkerchief across the face. Immediately, she thought of the bushranger. Where would he be? Did he ever think of her? And then, her brain did what it often did and across her thoughts of that man came thoughts of the other, and she imagined John Stuart, her husband, looking down at her with his irresistible smile.

She returned to Mayfield as the sun was setting. Thelma was waiting at the entrance of the stable yard. She felt a rush of sadness and guilt.

Thelma had been worrying daily about Eve. She knew there was something very wrong indeed. She had first noticed a change in Eve a few weeks ago when she had made an excuse not to go to the monthly mothers' meeting, and subsequently it had become obvious that Eve was avoiding not only Thelma, but others, too. Then, a few days ago, Thelma had gone to the big house to talk to Eve, and Eve had refused to see her.

Today Thelma had gone over to the big house again, only to find her friend not at home. She had been informed that Eve was out riding, so she had come to the stables to wait for her. After all, she counted herself as Eve's close friend, and if Eve was in trouble, as she certainly appeared to be, then Thelma wanted to help her.

"Hello, Thelma," Eve said as she dismounted. It was a reserved greeting.

Thelma's face crinkled in an encouraging smile. "Hello there, dear. They told me you were out riding, so methought I'd come and meet you. Walk home together. We've not done that for a week or two, eh?"

"No, Thelma, that's true."

Adrian, the head groom, took Betsy and they joined the path that led up toward their homes, walking in silence for half a minute or so, then Thelma said, "It's turned nice, hasn't it, after the heat today?"

Eve looked cautiously into Thelma's kindly eyes. "Yes, it's pleasant in the breeze. I like this time of day, the twilight, although it makes me sad, somehow."

They continued on a little further without speaking until Thelma took Eve's elbow and, steering her off on a side path that led over to a wooden seat, said, "Come on, love, let us sit here a minute or two and watch the sunset."

Behind the seat, a small clump of banksia grew, and above them two flame trees reached toward the sky. The seat was covered in red flowers, and Thelma bent to brush them away before they sat. Eve picked one up and sighed.

"I have just been up on the northern plain a little way. The ground there is covered with wild daisies. Flowers are miracles aren't they?''

"Yes,'' her friend answered, "wouldn't trust a person that didn't like flowers.''

They sat, and Eve waited as Thelma took her cold hand and held it between her own. "What is it, love? I have watched from afar for weeks now. Don't keep me at arm's length anymore. Please tell me what's wrong. Whatever it is, if I can do anything to assist you, I will.''

Eve felt terrible, hiding so much from her friend. "Oh, Thelma, dear Thelma, I know you will.''

But at that moment, they saw Daydee appear through the trees, from the direction of the river path. She was accompanied by Rosy, the maid; they had been to a painting class in the schoolhouse and were walking home. Rosy carried the paints.

Thelma smiled as they arrived. "Hello, girls. Shouldn't you be home? It's getting late.''

Rosy agreed, but Daydee asked, "Aren't you coming, too, Mother?''

"No, Daydee, we've things to talk over. I'll be along in a minute. Off you go.''

The girls went on by and were soon out of sight.

Thelma turned back to Eve. "Now, dear Eve, please tell me what troubles you.''

Eve had told herself over and over that she was strong and self-reliant, but now as she sat looking into the sympathetic hazel eyes of her friend, all she really knew was that she was confused, bewildered, and terribly alone.

"Ah, Thel.'' Her voice was thin and weary. "I know you are sympathetic and kind. . . . You are so much so that I wish not to burden you with my worries.''

"You are no burden. Tell me.''

Suddenly Eve could hold it in no longer. "You remember when you told me of the man . . . the man Lake, a short-timer who ran away in the middle of the night, the night I fell? You said that, no doubt, some poor, unfortunate woman was the cause of his flight.''

Thelma nodded, puzzled.

"I am that woman.''

Thelma's face dropped; her eyes grew large in her sun-browned face. She stammered, "But I—I—whatever . . . ? Eve, love, I don't understand.''

The leaves behind them rustled in the breeze. In the distance an owl hooted.

Eve shuddered a sigh. "Somehow, that man Lake got into my private garden on that night. I did not fall, you understand? He assaulted me. He called me . . . by another name. He mistook me for . . . someone else." She raised her hands, palms upward, in a gesture of hopelessness, then they fell heavily back into her lap. Even though she was relinquishing part of her dreadful secret at last, she still held back about Clare, for she was absolutely convinced that her husband must be the first to learn of her sister's existence.

"Oh, my dear, my poor dear," Thelma said, taking Eve in her arms and pressing her tightly to her breast.

"That is not the worst of it," Eve went on, bringing herself gently from her friend's embrace. She could not stop talking, did not want to stop talking. "You see, Thelma, I don't know what I am to do. What troubles me and makes me almost insane is . . . that I am carrying the man's child."

"Oh, dear Lord God in heaven!" Thelma cried. "You poor, poor girl, are you certain? Certain it's his?"

"I'm certain." She lifted her eyes to look directly into Thelma's. "For you see, the very time that John Stuart left me makes it impossible for the child to be his. It was during my period. It is not John Stuart's, and he will remember. He will know immediately, and he is due home within the week."

Thelma did not speak, she simply clasped Eve to her again. After a little while, she spoke gently. "Oh, darling, no wonder you were so badly hurt. And keeping this to yourself all this time. It's an outrage. He must be caught and punished. Why, oh, why, didn't you tell me before?"

Eve drew back to look at her friend. "I did not want to burden you. Oh, Thel, I was so confused, I did not know what to do. I still don't. God! It's just so awful."

"Eve, love," Thelma replied, patting her hand, "please do not be discouraged." Her face broke into a comforting smile. " 'A worry shared is a worry halved.' My old mum used to say that, and I believe it. I know how you must be feeling; the fear you must be experiencing. But you are John Stuart's wife. I know he loves you, and I'm certain he will know what to do. You poor child; fancy suffering all these weeks on your own. It makes me sick to think how you must have been feeling. But this is no place to discuss it. What say we go home? I made some fresh scones this very afternoon. We shall go and pick them up, then directly on to the big house for a good natter and a cup of tea. Dinner can wait."

"Oh, Thelma," was all Eve could say, but relief trickled through her, and there was the flicker of a smile on her lips, for at last she felt a small swell of hope.

Behind them in the dim light, the leaves of the banksia trees rustled again. The slight figure that had stood silently there and listened for many minutes turned and slipped speedily back the way it had come. It ran to get ahead of the two women. It darted across the path and into the wooded field beyond. It ran again, until soon, flushed and triumphant, it entered the front door of the Larmers' house.

"Is that you back, Miss Daydee?" called Rosy as she came downstairs.

"Yes, Rosy, pour me some tea, will you?" the figure said as it closed the door.

SEVENTEEN

Lake's Lie

The night passed as Thelma had promised. The two women enjoyed a few quiet hours, and Eve slept peacefully for the first time in weeks. Although with the coming of the day and the imminent return of John Stuart, she did not feel as calm as she had in her friend's company the night before.

The next days passed in the same way. When she was with Thelma, she felt sure that all would be well, and when her friend departed, her security left, and her fear fashioned dread.

"Tell him, love, without a moment's delay, as soon as he arrives," Thelma advised her. "He is a good man according to many lights. He loves you and is great and powerful and will know how to bring that evil man to justice."

Why was it she believed this when Thelma said it and disbelieved it later?

Just after twelve o'clock on Sunday, the fourth of December, one of the stockmen reined in his horse outside Jack Hennessy's office, shouting the news to alert the homestead of the approaching coach. It had been seen two miles from the property border and would make Mayfield House by half past the hour of one. Adrian was dispatched immediately to tell the household.

The feeling of expectancy that had pervaded the big house for the last few days expanded into excitement, and the large rooms echoed with the sounds of raised voices.

It was a hot, airless afternoon, and Eve changed into a pale rose muslin dress. She wore a crinoline, and she had Stephanie pull back her curls and pin them with a pretty olive-branch hair comb, that John Stuart had given her. When she and Thelma finally sat together on the front veranda with most of the household milling below them on the grass, and half a hundred wives, and children, and cattlemen beyond, she had calmed herself. But the moment the children called, "It comes! It comes," she stood up, all nerves.

Half a minute later, the coach came into view, swinging up the drive. Eve noticed a single, riderless horse tied to the side, but she did not give it any meaning.

Beside her, at the top of the steps, stood Thelma.

Before the vehicle came to a halt, a figure leaned out of one of the windows, his big hand raised in a happy salute. It was Joe, a broad grin on his face. People called and waved in greeting, and as the coach halted, Joe opened the door and jumped to the ground.

Eve waited for John Stuart to follow, but instead, the next figure to alight was a female. Eve was so surprised that it took a second or two to recognize Daydee, in a cream riding habit and neat, feathered hat, as she bounced down into her father's arms. She heard Thelma whisper at her side, "Daydee! So that's where you've been."

The girl looked happy. She turned all smiles to the carriage. "Come on, Uncle John Stuart."

A burnished boot followed, and the master of Mayfield unfolded from the coach. There, a few short yards in front of Eve, stood her husband, and the chill that she had felt so often recently settled down along her spine.

An hour before, while Eve had been dressing, the Mayfield coach was making solid progress along the sealed northwest road within the property. It moved along in the face of a hot breeze, and Deke Edwards, working to keep the horses at a steady eight miles per hour, called encouragement to his charges. The only hindrances were pauses to open the successive gates that divided some of the huge paddocks.

The weighty vehicle had just slowed in front of one of these, when Joe saw a horse cantering toward them from the southeast.

Daydee hailed them with a wave of her hand as she brought Boots to the other side of the gate where she dismounted and stood waiting with determination on her face and mean superciliousness in her smile. Her eyes were hard and scheming and her small gloved hand tapped the gate post restlessly as Leeroy Barton jumped down to open the gate. As her father and John Stuart alighted, an immediate change came across her features, and her small mouth broke into its widest, most innocent smile. Her eyes lost their meanness. The haughty air was gone. "Father dear, I have come to meet you both. I could wait no longer." She threw herself into her father's arms.

"Yes, it's been a long time, sweetheart, nine or ten weeks to be sure," her father replied, hugging his daughter.

"More like twelve, Dada. I have counted." She turned to John Stuart. "Oh, how simply wonderful it is to see you," she said, embracing him. "It's so good to have you home, Uncle John Stuart, so good."

He smiled affectionately as he disentangled himself from her embrace. "Yes, Daydee, it was too long to be away. Thank you for coming to meet us."

"Is it all right if I ride inside with you?"

Boots was tied to the carriage, and it ambled forward. Inside, Daydee laughed and chatted excitedly with her father and John Stuart about the events of Mayfield since their departure.

"And what of the calves? Any losses after we left?" her father asked.

"No, not a one, and you should see them now, great beasts they are growing into." She related a few other snippets of information before she said, "We have all been so excited since we knew you were coming. I went out to Nervy's Hill right after breakfast with the lookouts; we were positive you would arrive today, and when we sighted you through the telescope, I rode on to meet you." Here she turned to John Stuart, who sat beside her. "No doubt Aunt Eve would have ridden out to meet you as well . . . except for her condition."

John Stuart looked alarmed. "Her condition, Daydee? Whatever do you mean?"

Daydee's face registered surprise at the question, before she answered, "Well, I mean the baby of course. You must know, Uncle John Stuart, Aunt Eve's having a baby." Then she paused, and gave a look of concern. "But oh, I mean, you *do* know about the baby?"

For a few seconds John Stuart's face was expressionless. He and Eve had not planned to have children yet. What was this about? He was confused, but he smiled. "Ah, Daydee, I cannot say that I did, but it's good news all the same."

"Now, Daydee," her father said reprovingly, "you never were one who could stay quiet about things." Then clasping John Stuart's hands in both his own, he continued, "Well, well, congratulations, m'boy. What wonderful news."

The coach continued its steady pace, and so, too, did the conversation. But now John Stuart only half listened. He was considering what Daydee had told him. Sometime later, he asked, "Daydee, is Eve ill? She's not abed, is she?"

To which she replied, "Oh no, she is very well. Most days she goes out walking, or riding alone, goodness knows where, for hours on end."

A frown creased his brow, and it sat there on and off for the remainder of the journey.

Daydee watched him closely. And all went as she hoped; for by the time the coach reached Mayfield House, John Stuart had clearly remembered the day of his departure; he had remembered the time of the month; and he had realized that it was impossible for his wife to be carrying his child.

When he stepped down from the coach behind Daydee, the people gathered raised a cheer of welcome. He responded with a smile he did not feel. There was no telltale sign of his inner conflict as he mounted the steps and kissed Eve upon the cheek. She smiled at him, her mind so engrossed in her secret that she did not feel the lack of warmth in his touch. And when he turned back to his people and spoke, it was only Daydee who suspected he was troubled, even though his speech was a good deal shorter than it normally would have been.

"Thank you, one and all, for being here. You have waited for us in the hottest part of the day and given us a Mayfield welcome. I have looked forward to returning home to the very faces here gathered. Mr. Larmer and I have traveled a great deal since we last saw you, and we have seen much of this fair country, but nowhere has the landscape pleased my eye as much as it does here. Again, thank you, all.''

Another cheer, and John Stuart turned on his heel and entered his home.

Thelma caught her daughter's arm. "And now, miss, why did you not tell me you were going to ride on from the lookout to meet your father? I gave you permission to go to the lookout, not to waylay the coach.''

Daydee's eyes narrowed. "How could I tell you when I didn't know myself? I only decided to meet it when I saw it coming.''

Thelma sighed. What could she do with this girl?

"Mother, please don't be difficult,'' her daughter said as she pulled her arm from Thelma's grasp and moved away to her father.

Thelma shook her head unhappily. "Ah, Joe Larmer,'' she said aloud to Daydee's departing back, "we've truly ruined that girl.''

Once inside the house, John Stuart turned stiffly toward Eve. She moved quickly to him to enter his arms but to her amazement, he stepped away from her. It was now that she saw his uneasiness.

"Evelyn, please join me in the library in twenty minutes, will you?'' It was such a formal statement. "I wish to change clothes first.''

At that very moment, Mrs. Smith entered. "Sir,'' she began, "I have luncheon ordered for you. Will you eat now?''

"No, Mrs. Smith, I wish to bathe and change clothes. See to it, will you?''

John Stuart walked away as soon as Mrs. Smith had turned from them. Eve was amazed. What was wrong? She had so much to tell him. So much that needed a sympathetic, loving John Stuart. Not this strangely severe man.

As the minutes passed, she began to think that Daydee must be behind whatever troubled him. Daydee had traveled with him in the coach. What had she said to him? What *could* she say to him that would make him this way? Eve felt cold, she felt hot, she felt sick. Surely Lake had not told Daydee that he suspected she was Clare; surely Daydee couldn't know anything. But why was John Stuart so cold and distant? It was Daydee, she was sure of it.

Swiftly she returned to the front of the house and looked through the windows. The coach had gone and the people had dispersed into smaller groups. Joe and Thelma were still there, and so was Daydee, talking to Mrs. Hennessy. The bright sun lit up the girl's features as she threw her head back in laughter.

Disconsolately Eve toyed with the fringe on the heavy tassel of the sash securing the curtain. Then, coming to a decision, she hurried through the front door across the veranda and down the steps.

"Daydee," she said as the girl turned to her with a puzzled look. "I want to talk with you. Excuse us, Mrs. Hennessy." She took the girl's arm, steering her across the steps, up onto the veranda, and into the house. "Follow me," she said, crossing the hall and into the blue drawing room. Once inside, she closed the door and faced around. "What have you told my husband?"

Daydee feigned amazement. "What on earth do you mean?"

"Don't pretend, Daydee. You have told him something. I know you have."

"I have told him nothing. Why would I?"

Eve's eyes met Daydee's steadily. Once more she read the patent hatred in them. She knew the girl had caused her husband's strange withdrawal; it was obvious. "Daydee, your very demeanor proves that you have."

The girl's expression remained contemptuous.

A frown creased Eve's brow. "I fear you are much more evil that I could possibly have imagined. I have underestimated your wickedness."

Daydee's voice sounded smugly in reply. "Your opinion of my character means nothing to me." Then her eyes hardened as her violent hatred finally found release in words. "You make me sick. You don't belong here. You never have. You don't deserve him; he's wonderful, and you're nothing. I despise you."

Eve's heartbeat quickened as she forced herself to step a pace closer to the repellent expression trained upon her. "Daydee." She spoke slowly and deliberately. "You waste your time if you think you can ever take my husband's love away from me. You are a mean, selfish child." She saw Daydee flinch. "Yes, *child* is what I said, and that is how my husband thinks of you. He will never take you seriously; you are merely a joke to him."

Daydee's mouth opened in injury and rage. Tears of resentment sprang to her eyes. "I'm not a child. I'm a woman," she spat angrily as Eve turned away and walked to the door. "Damn you, damn you to hell!"

Eve opened the door, and halted. She did not look back. Her voice came steadily. "And you, Daydee Larmer, are not worth damning." With that, she closed the door and walked away, but rather than satisfaction, she felt the chill of fear increasing again, and with it, the lost and lonely feeling of the previous weeks rising like a net to cover her. John Stuart must listen to her: he must, no matter what Daydee had said.

She entered the library and stood behind one of the gold brocade Louis Seize chairs. The strain she was feeling made her concentrate intensely. Sunlight came through the windows in broad beams, and she noticed the dust motes dancing in them. For the first time, she observed the complicated bas-relief of small carved angels at the top of the bookshelves and how they were repeated as a pattern around the skirting board. Near the casement windows hung a portrait of John Stuart's father. This was the one she liked. A somewhat droll smile played around his mouth as if he saw that things were not so important as poor mortals made them. Ah yes, how she truly felt that was so.

The great walnut door swung back and John Stuart entered. He had changed from traveling apparel and wore a suit of dark garbardine, but he still wore his unhappy expression.

Eve thought to begin first, and she came forward to him, holding out her hands. "John Stuart, darling, I have much to tell you."

He raised his hand to stay her, bewilderment and confusion now showing plainly in his face. "Evelyn . . . is it true that you are with child?"

Eve started, and taken aback, she said, "But how can you possibly know?"

His face paled. "Then it's true?"

Eve was silent. Now she, too, was hopelessly confused. Daydee must have told him, of course, but how could *she* have known?

He waved his arms in a lost, helpless movement as his voice rose a little. "But how can this be? I have been gone for twelve weeks, and we both know the time of the month that I left. Eve, how is it possible that you are carrying a child?" John Stuart still could not believe that it *was* possible. He had been looking forward to seeing his wife for so long, his beautiful, pure wife, and to be told in the last half hour before joining her that she carried a child, a child that could not possibly be his . . . It had eaten into the core of him. His own mother had cheated on his father and made love with others behind his father's back. She had been immoral and despicable.

With terrible fear, Eve recognized the shock and horror in his face. Panic constricted her throat, but fighting desperately to keep her voice calm, she said, "Please, John Stuart, listen. You must listen to me, and let me explain. It is not simple."

"Simple?" He whispered the word, but it would have been better had he yelled it, so ominous and sinister did he make it sound. "What has been going on here? What has happened in my absence?"

"Dearest . . . John Stuart, this is not how I expected it. I don't know what to say. It's Daydee, isn't it? What has she told you?"

He moved forward and, pulling her to him, held her tightly. "Eve, please . . . what has happened? Answer me!" He seemed to be slipping out of control. She knew there was no hope of explaining, as she had planned, but she must try, she must. She lifted her hand, and touching him gently on the face, began to say as serenely as she could, "There was a man. Nathaniel Lake. He was hired, extra help, you know, a short-timer. He mistook me for someone else. . . . One night soon after you had gone, he . . . he was in our garden. . . . He attacked me . . . assaulted me. The child . . . I . . ."

John Stuart dropped her arms as if they were molten lead. The look in his eyes terrified her. "No! It cannot be." Now his voice was distracted, desolate, like someone else's. "It is obscene. Tell me it cannot be."

His eyes were begging her to deny it, but all she could do was to look back at him beseechingly. He was silent for many seconds. He stood looking at her in disbelief. She made small imploring sounds, which he did not hear, and then in misery, he cried, "The swine! I'll kill the swine! I'll kill him!"

She looked up at him and clutched him. "Please, darling, listen!"

Clearly bringing himself under constraint, he removed her hand, not roughly, but deliberately. There was a sick, malevolent look in his eyes. "Evelyn, where is he now?"

"I . . . I do not know. He is gone, gone from Mayfield."

He turned and left the room.

There was no sympathy in him as he strode down the corridor. He was past understanding. His mind was a blur with pain and the need for revenge. How he hurt as he smashed through the door and into the front hall. Oh, how this Lake had hurt him! How dare any man touch her! It was beyond endurance. He did not hear her cries to him as he stamped away. He did not hear her shout that there was more he must know. He heard nothing but the ringing in his ears of his own damaged pride.

Eve rushed after him. Down the long corridor she ran. As she came to the door leading to the hall, she heard a crash and the sound of broken glass.

When she reached the bottom of the wide staircase, he was already striding across the front veranda. Stephanie and one of the chambermaids stood on the stairs staring, their eyes wide with amazement, but Eve did not even see them. She hesitated. The glass of the locked gun cabinet in the hall was smashed, and two Enfield rifles were missing. There was blood on some of the shards. He must have used his fist. She went out onto the grass at the front of the house. She could see him in the distance striding swiftly away.

She must follow and explain everything. He was appalled and hurt, yes, but what could he do? Lake was gone. He would, of course, send immediately for the police, probably even enlist Sir Rutherford. They would find Lake, and he would go to trial, and all the sordid, ugly details would come out. Everything, including Clare and her liaison with Lake. Could John Stuart bear it? Could she bear it? She felt sick, sick to the pit of her stomach. "Come back, John Stuart, please, please. . . ."

At that moment Mrs. Smith ran from the house. "Mrs. Wakeman, Mrs. Wakeman," her high-pitched voice called. "There are all sorts of things being said inside: that the master is responsible for the broken cabinet; that you are upset. I have put them all sternly in their places, ma'am; don't concern yourself about that. A lot of busybodies, they are. Can I be of help to you?"

Eve turned back and began to speak, but Mrs. Smith spiraled into a dark shape as Mayfield House went black behind her, and the whole, giddy world spun up at her as she fell toward it. The housekeeper just managed to run forward and catch her before she hit the ground. Her cries brought others from the house, and Eve was taken immediately to bed.

John Stuart had stopped a rider just outside the park gates and taken his horse. When he reached the offices, Jack Hennessy was not there, but Stephen Watson was. He was Mayfield's confidential clerk in charge of records and correspondence. There was a grave look in his intelligent eyes, and his freckled brow dimpled with concentration as he answered John Stuart's questions, for the man could see his master was enraged, and he did all he could to reply helpfully.

"So you employed this man Lake for six and half weeks?"

"Yes, sir, he left as I told you, the night of the seventeenth of September, with pay owing to him. It's all here, sir, in the day-book." Stephen Watson tapped the ledger lying on the desk in front of him.

"Do you know where he went?"

"No, sir. But some of the boys might."

"Get his mates immediately. Send for them and bring them to me at Mr. Larmer's home."

"Yes, Mr. Wakeman, sir." He ran from his office, shouting loudly for Adrian and the grooms in the stable yard nearby.

When John Stuart arrived at the Larmers' front door, he did not wait for Rosy to take him into the parlor, but went straight past the girl and down the hall, calling for Joe.

Thelma had been all nerves since Joe and John Stuart had come back. On their way home across Mayfield Park after the gathering outside the big house, her husband had taken her arm and said, "Now, Thelma, love, isn't it grand that our boy is to have an heir? Wonderful, news, eh?"

And she had stopped walking in astonishment. "But how can you possible know?"

Then Joe laughed indulgently. "Ah, Thelma, love, you know our little Daydee can't keep a secret. Told us in the coach on the way here."

"Then . . . then John Stuart knew before . . . he got here?"

"Yes, love, I just told you our little chatterbox let the cat out of the bag."

Thelma had not said any more. She felt ill. How could Daydee have found out? Her daughter was such a troublemaker. She felt a flood of anger toward Daydee, and guilt and sadness when she though of Eve. She remained sick with apprehension, and when John Stuart arrived in her dining room, looking fit to kill a man, she was not surprised.

Joe stood from the table, his napkin in his hand and a look of consternation on his face. "Whatever is it, m'boy?"

"I'm glad you've eaten, old man, as we've a ride in front of us this day."

The ominous note in his voice was unmistakable, and Joe had not missed the violence in his look and the guns in his hands.

It was then Thelma saw the blood on his fingers. "What have you done? Let me bathe it."

"It does not bother me, Thelma," he replied, but she went to get hot water and a bandage just the same.

As soon as she left, John Stuart moved to Joe. "We ride to

kill a man, Joe. It's hard to believe or comprehend, old friend, but my wife was raped while we were away. It is not my child she carries. You and I ride to track down an animal called Nathaniel Lake, the cur responsible."

Joe shook his head, astounded, but he left immediately to get his gear together.

When Thelma came with water and bandage, John Stuart protested, but he allowed her to dress the ugly gash on his hand. As she tended his wound, she watched him from beneath her eyelids. She prayed to God that Eve was all right, but she said nothing. He, too, said nothing, though his pulse raced and pain gripped his chest as if a band of iron had been welded around his heart.

Soon Timothy arrived with the master's riding clothes, and he and Joe were waiting, ready to leave, when Jason Fowler rode up.

"Good day, Fowler," Joe began as the man raised his hat. Both he and John Stuart knew all of the Mayfield men by name. "I want you to tell me of Nathaniel Lake, a short-timer who disappeared a few weeks back. Do you have any idea where he would have gone?"

"Well, sir, I do and I don't."

John Stuart broke in sharply. "Then just tell us what you *do* know, man, and now."

"Yes, sir. Well, 'e might have gone to the goldfields. Always said 'e was goin' there after 'ere. But there be a mate of 'is, Larry Cadee, 'e might know more certin-like. 'E's tendin' the servicin' of the bulls down in the farthest of the river paddocks, sir."

"He's been sent for?" asked Joe.

"That 'e has, sir."

Jack Hennessy had arrived with the saddled horses and the spares before Cadee and a second man came galloping up.

"Afternoon, Mr. Wakeman; you wanted to see us?"

Joe answered. "Yes, Cadee. You and Lloyd tell me what you can about where Nathaniel Lake would have gone after he left here."

The two men looked at each other. Then Cadee spoke. "Why, it's hard to say, sir, but he said oftimes he was goin' on to the goldfields."

Joe continued. "Did he ever mention which one?"

"Well, not in so many words, Mr. Larmer."

"Is there anyone other than yourselves who would know?"

Both men shook their heads.

"Damn!" John Stuart exclaimed.

Then Cadee spoke up again. "Well, actually, sir, there is someone as might know, or as might hazard a good guess."

"Who, man, who?" asked Joe.

"She's the publican's daughter at the Fitzroy Arms in Cowra. See, he always said he was goin' to her for a bit when he left here. Mind you, he might not have as he went in a kinda hurry-like. But he was all for stoppin' with her awhile, at one time."

"Her name?"

"Elizabeth Jenks. She's the barmaid there."

John Stuart was already riding away as Joe turned back to Jack Hennessy and spoke quietly. "You'll manage things until we return, Jack?"

"That I will, Mr. Larmer," the man answered in the same quiet tone. "Haven't I been doing that very thing for the past three months already?"

"Aye." Joe nodded.

As they rode out, Daydee walked in the back gate with Leith. They had been out to the strawberry gardens, and they carried two baskets full of the bright red fruit.

Thelma stood watching the men leave.

"What's happened?" Daydee asked.

"Nothing that concerns you."

"Well, where are they going?" Daydee continued.

"I don't know," answered her mother, walking by her into the house, "but come with me; I want to speak with you."

She followed her mother reluctantly.

Inside, Thelma rounded on her daughter. "How did you know Eve was with child? Tell me the truth, Daydee. I am very serious."

Daydee was prepared for this. "I heard you talking together about it one day. I didn't mean to listen; I just couldn't help it."

Thelma was exasperated. "How dare you eavesdrop on other people's conversation, and then to go and repeat it to your father and Uncle John Stuart. It is just most horrible."

"Why is it horrible?"

Thelma looked at her in disbelief. "Oh, my goodness, Daydee Bronwyn Larmer, if you don't know the answer to that, there is no hope for you." She shook her head. "I don't think you are my daughter at all," she said angrily, before she turned and walked away.

* * *

Two and a half hours later, John Stuart and Joe tied their horses to the hitching rail outside the Fitzroy Arms, one of the two hotels in the tired township of Cowra. The summer heat rose up around the cluster of wooden huts and buildings. Semblances of life were few. A dog lay some ten yards away on what served as a footpath, and down the street a little way, dust rose in the air as Father Murphy swept the wooden stairs of the Roman Catholic church.

The Fitzroy Arms was a typical bush hotel, one story only of roughly hewn timber covered with a cast-iron roof. The wooden planking of the verandah squeaked as if the footfalls of the newcomers were some kind of invasion of the barren silence.

Inside, weary movement passed for activity. Three men played cards at a small table in the corner, and a couple of old-timers lolled spiritlessly at the bar. Behind the bar, a jaded-looking woman of perhaps thirty, her dark hair piled at the top of her head, looked up from washing glasses as the door swung open. She had an ordinary face. Her nose was not of a pretty shape, and her chin receded, but her eyes were large and striking. Her bosom was heavy, and beneath her gown, her legs were thick and unshapely, but she was still in the last stages of the appeal that comes with youth, and before it finally passed, there would be those who would find time for her. When she registered the presence of the two arrivals, a glimmer of interest showed in her face, for while she had seen him only a few times, she thought she recognized the master of Mayfield.

At the door, John Stuart sniffed the air as if he smelled something offensive, then crossing to the girl, asked, "Are you Elizabeth Jenks?" He spoke in the abrupt manner of a person used to immediate answers.

When she hesitated in replying, Joe said, "Come on, girl, what's your name?"

One of the men at the bar turned toward them, and in a mocking tone said, "She don't often get called 'Elizabeth.' It's a bit highfalutin' for ya, ain't it, Lizzie?"

"Oh, shuddup, you," the girl said, and turning her eyes on John Stuart, answered, "Yes, I am Elizabeth Jenks. Why is it of importance to you?"

Joe answered. "Can we speak away from here? Is there anywhere private?"

She pointed to an opening in the wall beyond the end of the bar. They passed through into a mean sort of sitting room.

As the woman entered, Joe began. "We believe you know a

man called Lake, Nathaniel Lake. We want you to tell us if you know where he is."

Her demeanor changed slightly. She swung her hips around to them, and with arms akimbo, looked knowingly from one to the other. "Why? What's he done?"

John Stuart viewed her with contempt. "Just tell me where I can find the man. I've little time to waste with you."

She stared back at them for a second or two, then, shifting her glance so that she did not meet their eyes, replied, "Tell me why you want him first."

John Stuart was barely containing his temper, but Joe intervened. "We are not going to tell you, so it's useless your asking. But here, this may help your memory." He handed her a gold sovereign.

She turned it over in her hand, and a grin passed across her face. "Do you have more of these, then? For I deem you want the information very badly."

John Stuart grunted angrily, but Joe calmly handed her a second gold coin.

She stood unmoving and looking insolently at Joe. Her arm was still extended, the two coins lying in her palm.

He dropped another beside them. "That's all there is," he said quietly.

Now she smiled and closed her fist around the coins. Then putting her hand inside the pocket of her dress, she clinked the three coins together. She had an exquisite feeling of joy as she felt the metal rub. "He was here for a few days in September. Worked for you before that, didn't he?" She looked at John Stuart, who averted his eyes. "Promised to marry me, he did." She gave a small, disdainful laugh. "Well, he's gone. Wouldn't say where he was going 'cept to say he'd try his hand at mining, so I'd say he's gone to the goldfields."

"We know all that, damn it," broke in John Stuart.

"Come on, girl," went on Joe calmly. "You've told us nothing we don't already know."

She considered a second or two, her eyes moving from one to the other. "Well, you won't know this. He left with a fella that I happen to know was going to the goldfields at Tanner's Rock. So I'd say, if you looked there, you just might find him."

John Stuart turned on his heel and left without further communication. Joe tipped his hat to her and followed. As they departed, the girl was still clinking the coins in her pocket. She stood there saying to herself, "Yes he did, said he'd be back and marry me . . .''

Tanner's Rock was a small goldfield, over seventy miles to the southwest, and John Stuart rode toward it with one dominating thought: to kill Nathaniel Lake. It was not as if he did not think of Eve; he did, although he was so blinded by his own need for revenge that he did not begin to comprehend her suffering. Yet he did think that perhaps he should not have left so hastily, that he should have told her not to worry, that everything would be all right. One thing he could not bring himself to consider was the baby. He must deal with this abominable man before he could allow his mind to come to terms with that.

They rode another four hours, through one of those hot Australian summer nights that almost stifles the thought processes. By the time they reached the small outpost of Mogongong, men and horses were exhausted. They slept on the verandah of the single dwelling, a tiny inn, and the next morning, they set off into the searing heat once more to ride the forty miles to their destination.

If it was possible, John Stuart's determination had grown with the passing of the night. Yes, he would be the judge and jury, and convict and kill this animal. No man in the colony would blame him! He would find Lake, wherever he was; he did not care if he had to ride around Australia.

Nathaniel Lake had ridden away from Mayfield a shaken man. Ever since he had seen her ride by at the ford that day, he had been absolutely positive the Wakeman woman was Clare. It was uncanny; the likeness was exact. He had been totally convinced, until he had her on the ground; then he had realized. He should have stopped of course; he had been a bloody fool not to. Still, what was done was done. But who the devil was she? He vaguely remembered Clare had once or twice spoken of a sister. She had come to Adelaide when he was living with Clare, though he had never met her. Could that be it? Were they twins? They had to be. God! The bloody bad luck.

He had ridden straight to Cowra and the Fitzroy Arms. Elizabeth, the old tart, had taken him in. He spent four really good days with her, at it morning and night, safe in knowledge that Wakeman was still on the cattle drive. Of course, he had moved on smartly before Wakeman returned. He knew that if the woman told what had happened, he would be a dead man one way or another! He'd have no hope against Wakeman. He'd be hanged.

But his strong belief was that she would remain silent. Lots of women did that, to avoid scandal. And what a scandal this would be! It would stagger the whole colony! Yes, being married to Wakeman, she would surely avoid the humiliation if she could.

Nathaniel Lake was, in essence, an indolent creature, and when he reached the goldfield and found women there, voluptuous, easy women, he stayed. At first he had been apprehensive, but when nearly two months went by without incident, his self-assurance had returned. Mrs. Wakeman had obviously stayed her tongue.

When Nathaniel Lake made his way in the gathering dark of this November night along the single, dusty street that was Tanner's Rock, he whistled a bawdy tune and walked with a jaunty step. His mind filled with the pleasures that awaited him later in the tent down the street. There was one there he really liked, Leslie-Jane, who was more skilled than the others and had big eyes and big tits . . . his type. He grinned. He had been relaxed for weeks now.

A touch of breeze had sprung up, giving some relief from the oppressive heat. He was heading to the tavern; he could see the lights in the bar ahead. This place was a pile of bark huts and tents that straggled along the thoroughfare. There were as many Chinese here as had been in the Victorian fields, a damned queer lot with odd habits. He had seen one of them combing his hair out this morning; down to his waist, it was. Fancy a bloody so-called man with hair to his waist! They were a clean bunch, though; he would say that for them.

He was within fifty yards of his destination when suddenly his name was spoken from behind. He stopped whistling and turned. "Yes?"

The blow to his mouth sent him staggering backward. In the darkness, he had not seen the man who hit him. As he recovered his balance, he realized there were two figures in front of him. It was then he discerned the guns. Fear clouded his mind as he tried to make out the faces of the two men. They were not police; he could see that. He held his right hand to his mouth as blood seeped from his lip where his tooth had cut it. "What the devil . . . Who are . . . ?" he began, then froze as he recognized John Stuart Wakeman.

"Mr. Wakeman . . ." After all this time. No, it couldn't be! Why? What had gone wrong? Even in the darkness, he could see John Stuart's eyes were wild.

"You swine," he heard John Stuart say, "I am going to kill you. I am going to execute you."

Lake's mind went blank. In horror, he watched the rifle being leveled at him. Then the thoughts came. Oh god, so she had told him after all. After so long. Why? He heard words come rushing from his mouth, extemporaneously, all uttered to delay the firing of the gun. "Please, you don't know what you're doing! There must be some mistake. Mr. Wakeman! Sir! Please, what have I done? Please! Why would you want to k-kill me!"

"My wife, you animal! For what you did to my wife."

Lake's mind raced, looking for something to say that would ensure survival. "What do you mean, did to your wife? I don't know what you're talking about, sir, please. . . . "

Then John Stuart hit him again, and this time the blow had such force that he fell backward, and tripping, dropped to the ground.

The menace in John Stuart's voice took on a new sound; there was killing in it as Nathaniel Lake, ice-cold with terror, heard him say, "You know exactly what I'm talking about. That an animal like you even touched my wife is not to be borne. But that you assaulted her is abominable! And for that, I am going to kill you, now."

Lake heard the hammer cock, and his body ached with terror. Instinctively he began to speak. He heard himself say, "I did nothing to your wife. Nothing she didn't want. She knew me well. She asked for it. I swear before God."

John Stuart's sharp intake of breath sounded loudly on the night air. In the weak light, his face tightened with consternation and the rifle barrel edged up just slightly. "What do you say? She knew you?"

Lake went straight on, "Look, I knew her long before she married you. She wanted it. She asked for it. She's that sort of woman; she led me on."

Joe spoke for the first time. "I don't believe it. John Stuart, he's lying. She would not do such a thing! She's a good woman."

Thoughts tumbled over themselves in Lake's racing mind; his head throbbed; impulsively he rushed on with the lie that preserved him. It was easy to say, and it had the ring of truth to it, and in telling it, even he was convinced, for he only had to imagine that woman in his mind to truly believe she was Clare.

"I'm telling the truth," he cried. "As God's my judge, I knew her in Adelaide years ago. She was my de facto. When I met her, she was with another bloke. Look, she knew lots of shady characters; shacked up with them, too, I swear. When she came to live with me, she called herself Clare Herman.''

As he said, ''Clare Herman,'' John Stuart blanched, the blood drained from his face.

There was just enough light for Lake to see the impact of his words on the faces of the two men above him. They were amazed, disconcerted; that was clear. Ah, sweet providence. He must cement their misgiving, and quickly.

He started to speak again, and as he did so, slowly raised himself from the ground to his knees and then stood, his arms open and palms out toward John Stuart. Now he could think more clearly, he spoke with the expertise of the congenital liar and it was all the easier, for remembering Clare, he could regard what he was saying as actual.

''Look, sir, I would never have told you that. Never! But you were going to kill me. It is not a thing that one talks about, sir. I realize how you feel, Mr. Wakeman. That is why I left May-field. After all, Clare is married to you now, and mistress of so much. I was only confusing her, bringing up her past. I . . . don't know how she told it to you, sir, but there was no assault. I swear it. There was no need for assault, if you know what I mean. I'm not saying Clare . . . ah, excuse me, Mrs. Wakeman . . . is a liar. I wouldn't. But I swear on the Bible, she was not opposed to it.''

John Stuart looked toward Joe. He lowered his gun and re-treated a step. There was shock in his face and a dazed look in his eyes; they implored Joe to help. He bent forward as if he had received a body blow, and somehow seemed much smaller than his six feet one.

Joe hated to see the suffering in him, but all he could do was to ask him, sadly, ''Do you know if she was ever in Adelaide, m'boy?''

''No, I . . .'' The words were lifeless. ''There's so much I don't know, it seems.'' Then his eyes returned to Lake, upright now with some of his former perky air returning. He was dab-bing the blood from his mouth with a handkerchief, and he watched them closely.

With a visible effort, John Stuart asked, ''This time you speak of in Adelaide. When was this?''

''Oh, some six or seven years ago.''

''What year? Tell me.''

Lake was quiet for a second or two, then answered, ''I sup-pose it was fifty-seven. Yes, it would have been fifty-seven.''

"And where had she come from? This Clare you speak of?"

"From Sydney," Lake replied, and then as a perceptively brilliant addition, said, "I think she went to live in Bathurst after we separated, taught music. She could play the piano like a dream."

The feeble light gave enough illumination for him to see John Stuart step back as if he had received another blow. He watched as the master of Mayfield turned his head slowly to Joe. "There is no more to be achieved here."

The two men before Lake stood silently, then John Stuart jerked into movement and began to turn away. Lake sighed, and the glimmer of a relieved smile started forming on his mouth when suddenly, like a whiplash, John Stuart rounded back on the man and smashed him another blow in the face that sent him reeling backward again.

Though there was a deadness in his look, there was anger and disgust still in his voice. "You're a parasite, a disgusting bloody parasite," he hurled before he turned again and walked away.

Lake, still in fear, watched them move into the night toward their horses. He stared until he saw with relief their distant silhouettes mount their horses. Then a smile of real satisfaction curled his profusely bleeding lip. He was free to go now, wherever he wished. While his heart was still thumping, he was taking charge of his feelings once more. Now he would make good his escape, get as far away from this bloody place as he could. Perhaps even get back to Sydney and hop a ship. He had heard there were things to offer a clever man in New Zealand these days.

He wiped his mouth as his smile widened. He had saved himself.

EIGHTEEN
John Stuart's Belief

John Stuart had left Mayfield in a passionate fury; he returned in a passionless self-possession.

In the three days since they had ridden away so hurriedly, Mayfield had been astir with gossip, from the scullery to the bedrooms, from the dairy to the orchards, from the cottages and living quarters to the stables and beyond. Those people in positions of rank, such as Thelma and the heads of staff, would say nothing and have nothing said in their presence, but they were a few mere mortals against the tide of common talk. The speculation was endless. That Lake had stolen something very valuable was the popular belief; what he had stolen varied, depending on who told the tale.

Mrs. Wakeman's swooning in Mrs. Smith's arms was something no one was really sure about. Some said Mr. Wakeman had blamed her for allowing the theft to occur, and she had collapsed in mortification. Others said she had run after her husband in such a temper that she fainted. Some even averred she must be with child.

Daydee soon found out that her father and John Stuart had gone after Nathaniel Lake. She and her mother were the only ones who knew of Eve's pregnancy. But neither knew about Clare. Had Thelma known, she might have been able to help the situation; had Daydee known, she would have been delighted, instead of merely happy. The girl's thoughts were filled with what must become the staggering scandal of Eve carrying Lake's child. Surely this would ruin the marriage? The marriage could be annulled. She had read about a marriage being annulled by the Archbishop of Canterbury. The husband had been

283

at sea for a year and had returned home to find that his wife carried another man's child. Well, this was like that, really, just like it. Daydee was so pleased, she went around singing to herself.

When Eve fainted, Dr. Douglas, the Mayfield doctor, had been sent for immediately. He had come from the bedside of a sick child over in one of the river cottages, and while she said she felt quite normal, he had insisted on examining her and had confirmed what she already knew. She asked him not to say anything to anyone about her condition.

He smiled gently. "Of course, Mrs. Wakeman, as you wish."

Eve was so ashamed for John Stuart. The knowledge of the child she carried would emasculate him in the eyes of the world, and worse than that, in his own. Again she thought to commit suicide. Perhaps that would release John Stuart. He had created the myth about her; he alone had made her a Lucrece. Should she kill herself as Lucrece had done?

When she remembered the agony in his face after he had learned of the assault, she cried for him. She would think of Alan Fletcher and his compassion that day they had spent together in the bush. If only John Stuart were more like him . . . together they would survive this.

Thelma continued to comfort her like the good friend she was. She hardly spoke to her daughter, so angry was she about her behavior, but that did not trouble Daydee.

So the days passed until John Stuart's return.

When John Stuart and Joe had left Lake standing in the street of Tanner's Rock, they had ridden ten miles back to a run-down tavern, standing alone, a single decrepit building, in an area known as Billabong Diggings. In this, they spent an uncomfortable night, surrounded by human flotsam and jetsam. The next day they rode on, and that night slept again on the veranda of the inn in Mogongong. There was little said between them, and when they did speak, it was of business and Mayfield concerns.

From Mogongong to Mayfield, John Stuart seemed to dawdle, halting for rests on the hour and riding slowly. His excuse was the heat, and although the day was enervatingly hot, it was no hotter than the previous days. It was as they reined in for one of these pauses, near a clump of mulga trees, that Joe decided to speak his thoughts.

Joe Larmer was a weather-beaten sixty-seven; he had spent

over forty years in the heartless Australian sun of the bush. He barked commands to the hands on Mayfield, as a general would to his troops, but there was an honest respect for him pervading the attitudes of all the men. There was no one more reliable in times of trouble; no one more knowledgeable about the hard country they sought to tame. He could converse in his objective, unassuming fashion with gentry or common man, and neither would take him for a fool . . . a man of his times, steady, moral, loyal to Mayfield, queen, and country.

Yet inside this modest discerning man lay an intensity of emotion completely alien to one so stable. Where his daughter and John Stuart were concerned, he was governed by blind love. They could do no wrong, and any who hurt them were his enemies. Consequently, all his feelings told him to hate Eve, as an immoral impostor. Yet somehow he hoped there could be an explanation. He wished this most of all for John Stuart's sake. John Stuart's pain was Joe's pain; it had always been so.

Ever since they had left Lake, he had felt sorry they had not dealt more severely with him. Unfortunately, you just could not shoot men for being animals. Joe sighed now as he spoke. "M'boy, I've a feeling you move at a sluggish pace because of what is ahead when we get home."

John Stuart turned his dark, morose eyes to Joe and slowly nodded.

"I know how plainly shocked you are. We both are. It's a blow few men could take. But there is something I would caution you to do, when at last you face your wife."

"Joe, it seems she was never wife to me."

"Now, m'boy, that's as may be, but what I'm saying is this. That man back there was scum, albeit he spoke like an educated man. And while he condemned Eve, there may be more in the explanation when she tells it."

John Stuart made a sad, scornful sound. His head ached from the heavy thoughts that sat in gloomy judgment there. "Joe, I recognize the man was worthless, but there were too many things he said that fitted precisely what I know of her. He said he knew her in Adelaide. That she had come from Sydney and that, after being his de facto wife in 1857, she went to Bathurst."

"Aye, lad, I'll admit that sounded bad, but he could have learned she lived in Bathurst from the men on Mayfield."

"But the date fits. He knew when Eve went to Bathurst, that she was a music teacher, and he knew the name 'Herman.' He

knew her maiden name, Joe. How do you account for that?''
John Stuart dismounted as Joe replied.

''Well, now, John Stuart . . .'' Joe was struggling to find a
reason. ''It's not impossible that again some of the Mayfield
hands knew her maiden name.'' He frowned in thought. ''Nevertheless, it was strange he would call her 'Clare Herman.' Why
wouldn't he just say 'Eve'?''

John Stuart tied his horse to a low branch, and stood with his
back to the older man. ''Joe, you did not realize it, but that is
the very thing that helped to damn her.''

He waited silently while Joe dismounted. When he turned
around, there was not a vestige of hope left in his face. Briefly
he leaned on Diomed's saddle, as if gathering strength. ''At one
time, she must have called herself Clare Herman.''

''Why do you say that, sonny? How do you know such a
thing?''

''Joe, I have never mentioned this, for at the time I thought it
unimportant. I think it was the night of her birthday. Anyway,
I remember I was passing through her sitting room.'' He told
Joe of how he found music sheets with the name Clare Herman
on them. He sighed as he completed his tale. ''The handwriting
was Eve's. Of course, at the time, I was so taken by her that I
assumed it was the name of a relative. Now I realize differently.
There was a time when she called herself 'Clare,' and I fear that
time was when she was in Adelaide.''

''Ah,'' said Joe, ''I see.'' His walk, too, was lethargic as he
came to rest by John Stuart in the sparse shade of the mulga
trees.

''And there is the other thing I omitted to tell you, Joe.''

''What is that, m'boy?''

''I have had much time to remember things on this ride, Joe,
and much has fallen into place that I would have preferred did
not. You will recall that when Daydee met us in the coach on
our way home three days ago . . . Was it only three days? She
said that Eve had been taking long walks and long rides alone
in the months we were away. Well, I have got to thinking about
those lonely walks and rides.''

''What do you mean, m'boy?''

''You remember when Lake said she had *known* a lot of shady
characters in her time?''

Joe nodded.

''Ah Joe, we both know the 'shady character' who held up
our coach on the day we married, and we both recall who it was

that brought her back to Mayfield the day after her birthday when she rode beyond the Mayfield borders.''

"Yes, we do, but what has that to do with things?''

"You recall she went to Bathurst a month or so before last Christmas?''

"I do, m'boy, with my Thel and Daydee.''

"She met the same shady character there, a third time, in the Bathurst park.''

An expression of amazement rose to Joe's face.

"Oh, she told me about it right enough. But I now fear that was only to put me off the track of what in truth occurred, for our own little Daydee, innocent of all that has been happening, told a vastly different story from Eve's.''

"What do you mean, m'boy?''

John Stuart brought his eyes to Joe's. "Eve's account of the meeting was brief. She said she ran into the bushranger accidentally, that she was as shocked to see him as he was to see her, that he asked her how she was and that was the end of it. I believed her; but now I am recalling little Daydee's version of the event, and I can tell you honestly, old man, it was entirely different. Daydee alerted me of the fact that Eve and the bushranger were in close and intimate conversation in the Bathurst park. She said she happened upon them, and they were so involved with one another that they didn't realize she was beside them until she spoke. She said they talked for a very long time.'' He sighed, a painful sound. "Why, I ask you, would straightforward little Daydee lie?''

Joe shook his head. "She wouldn't. She'd have no reason to.''

Darting back to John Stuart's mind were Eve's words, *I do not go to Bathurst to have an encounter of any kind with any outlaw.* It all seemed very devious now.

Joe's expression was melancholy. He put his hand out to rest it on his boy's shoulder. "The sum of all this is not good, is it?''

John Stuart's voice was lifeless. "Joe, the sum of all this is very bad indeed.''

When they finally rode through the gates of Mayfield Park and up to the house, John Stuart had decided on the course he must take. Before he dismounted, Joe leaned across and took his arm. "If you need me, I'll be waiting.''

"Thanks, old man.''

He stood on the threshold of his home. He did not enter immediately. He was still thinking. *I must not let her charm me. She is capable of so much that I still cannot believe it. She, whom I thought was pure, is corrupt, just as my mother was.*

He had dwelt much on his mother during the long ride home. He did not remember anything of her, yet he had hated her all his life. No, perhaps not all. When he was very small, he remembered crying into his pillow at night and wishing she would come back to him. But he had always known she was bad, even though his father refused to speak of her. Oh yes, he had always known that, from the time he was eight years old and he had heard the ticket-of-leave men discussing her. In those days, in the thirties, there had been actual convict servants and a lot of ticket-of-leave men on Mayfield, convicts who had been granted a form of freedom to work for themselves.

John Stuart had been playing alone in the foundations of Joe and Thelma's new house, where the ticket-of-leave men were doing the building. He had overheard them talking, and when they mentioned his father's name, he had stood still and listened.

"Yeah, I wuz here when Mr. Wakeman sent her away," one said.

"What wuz she like?"

The man had laughed. "A beauty, right enough, black hair, flashin' eyes, and big tits!"

They had all laughed at that.

"Yer cud see she wuz openin' her legs for that Major Jackson right from the start. Don't know how the master didn't cotton on to it for so long. I mean, we all knew she was whorin' with the major, all of us knew that."

"It's the kid what I'm sorry for," another voice had said.

"Who? Young John Stuart?" the original voice had replied. "Don't be sorry for him. Gawd! He's goin' to be ya landed gentry even if his mother was a whore."

John Stuart had not any idea what a whore was, but he knew it must be very, very bad. He had slipped away unseen and cried alone for a long time after that. It was three years later that he found the painting of her. He had been playing "dress-up," as he used to call it. At the time many old trunks and boxes had been stored at the top of the stairs above the east wing of the house. He had found some old clothes and had been rummaging through them when he came across a portrait brooch on an old velvet coat. A funny thrill passed through him as he looked at it. It was a painting of a beautiful lady with black hair to her shoulders.

Something told him not to take the brooch to his father, so it was Thelma he approached. He took it from his pocket, tentatively, and held it up to her. She took it and looked at it, then she hugged him. "This is your mother, darling. Perhaps you should give this to Daddy." But he had not; he had hidden it, and he used to take it out at night and look at it. It was then he knew she did not love him, just as she did not love his father, and that was when he had begun to really hate her and to wonder if all women were bad like she was.

He had grown up believing there had never been any word from her, but he learned differently after his father died.

He had found Thelma alone after the memorial service, and he asked her something he had wanted to since the morning they had found his father dead. "Thelma, on the night of his death, why do you think he wore the wedding bracelet my mother had given him?" He said it awkwardly, playing with the cushion at his right hand.

She shook her head before replying, and she plucked at her skirt, avoiding his eyes, but she gave him an honest, straight answer, right from her heart as she always had. "I think he knew he was dying, and at the last, he somehow wanted to have Caroline, your mother, with him. You see, the bracelet was all he had."

The gold marriage bracelet his wife had given him on their wedding day was inscribed on the inside of the band with the words "To my dearest Arthur from your own wife Caroline."

John Stuart was confused. "But I never knew he had such a thing. I thought he had disposed of everything that had been associated with her."

"Yes, that's what we all thought, but now we know otherwise, don't we? He had always kept that, her wedding gift to him."

"I don't understand it. She left us. She was bad. He hated her. Why would he want to wear her bracelet at the last?"

"Perhaps he didn't hate her after all."

"But he did. He would never speak of her, never. In all my life, we have never communicated with her, or she with us."

Thelma smiled a sad smile and leaned forward toward him. "John Stuart, what lies in the heart is sometimes different from what a body shows to the world. And she did communicate with you, although you never saw the letters."

"What do you mean?"

"I would never have told you while your father lived, but now perhaps you should know. Each year, for your birthday, a letter came from her, until you were about fifteen.''

John Stuart was amazed. "How do you know?''

"You may remember that before your father employed a private secretary, it was I as did such things for him. When I fell with Daydee, Mr. Arthur said it was too much for me. I'd had four stillbirths before her. We are lucky to have her . . . I suppose. Well, you are a grown man now, and until those letters stopped coming from Scotland, I handed them to Mr. Arthur myself.''

John Stuart stood up defiantly. "I'm glad he did not give them to me.'' His tone was angry, adamant. "Her behavior was such that appalls me, disgusts me. I wish no communication with such as she, and I am ashamed she was my mother.''

Now, pausing on the veranda of his home, all this returned to his mind, and he saw his mother and Eve as one. He stood there, his eyes cold and glassy, his mouth a grim line of anguish and bitterness.

When he entered the hall at last, Mrs. Smith stood patiently waiting.

"Good afternoon, sir. Welcome home. Is there anything I can get you?''

"No, thank you. Where is Mrs. Wakeman?''

"In your private garden, sir. I have sent a gel to tell her of your arrival.''

As John Stuart strode away from the housekeeper, he noticed the smashed doors of the rifle cabinet had been removed, and unconsciously he rubbed the cut on his hand. He passed swiftly through the house now, his lethargy gone. When he stepped onto the veranda, Eve walked toward him across the grass. She had been down on her knees planting some seedlings.

She had been thinking about him. The fact was, he was all she had thought about. Her love for him was strong. Surely his was the same for her. Couldn't they fight all this together? She had been planning to start afresh, to tell him of Clare, of everything, and he had rushed away from her in pain and anger to find Lake. She had analyzed his reaction over and over, and she sympathized with him; she knew he had been stunned to his very core. He could not help his Wakeman pride, and she truly understood the reasons that had taken him in blind fury from her. And now here he was back again, and whatever had occurred, she would right things. She smiled compassionately as she came forward to him.

He saw her as she came out of the shadow of the poinciana tree. She was in a white dress and a rose-colored apron. Her sleeves were rolled back to the elbow, exposing her forearms. She still held the small trowel she had been using. Her hair was tied back in a ribbon, but some stray curls had fallen forward. She was smiling.

He halted. His heart was beating rapidly. Why, oh, why, did she look so simple, so pretty, and so good? For a second he wavered. How could one who looked this way be bad? But then, had not his mother been lovely, too? Perhaps evil women were all beautiful.

They faced each other across the host of blooms that filled the garden.

She spoke first. "John Stuart, I'm glad you are home again."

As he came closer, she saw the remoteness in his face. But his distant expression hid the mad pounding going on in his head. *She was my de facto . . . de facto . . . knew lots of shady characters, shacked up with them too . . . called herself Clare Herman . . . shady characters . . . 1857. Yes, it would have been 1857.*

He did not answer her greeting; he simply asked, "Eve, when were you in Adelaide?"

"Why do you ask this?" she replied, coming closer to him. He was so different from the last time she had seen him. The pain and anger had been replaced by a dead sort of coldness.

"Answer me!" was all he said.

"Please, darling, tell me why you want to know."

"Eve!" his voice rose. "If you do not reply to me, I shall simply turn and leave, and will have no further conversation with you now or any other time in your life."

It was terrible, but there was no doubt he meant what he said. She did not know what to do. She had been awaiting his return with some trepidation, but she had brought herself to feel confident that things would be all right; she was not ready for this. For a second she faltered; then she said, "John Stuart, I *was* in Adelaide briefly some years ago. I know this has something to do with that man Lake. What is wrong? Did you find him?"

He seemed without emotion, like an automaton. "It is important that you answer me truthfully. What year were you there?"

She looked blankly back at him.

"What year?" he asked again, more loudly, yet his eyes seemed to look through her, to be trained on the garden wall.

"I . . . I . . ." she began. "Why does it matter? This is some sort of foolishness. I simply went to visit—"

"Tell me the year!"

"This is silly," she remarked.

"Your evasion reveals that what I have been told is true."

This frightened her, and in frustration she replied, "Oh, John Stuart, this makes no sense, but perhaps it was late 1857."

"Oh God!" he said.

She had never heard him say "God" in all the time she had known him. It was so alien to his whole persona that she froze with fear. She did not understand what was happening, but she was aware there was no time left. She must act quickly, say the things that needed to be said immediately, without hesitation.

She dropped the trowel she had held until now and stepped closer to him. As she did, he in turn stepped away.

"John Stuart, John Stuart," she began, "please, all this is a dreadful mistake. But there is much I have to tell you. Much you don't know. I should have told you things long ago, and I am truly sorry that I did not. But it is not too late. I am heartbroken that you have been hurt so, but I have been hurt, too, badly, and want to tell you now. Please hear me. You see, when I was born, I was one—"

He was not listening and he cut her off with the words "Yes, there is much I don't know! There has always been much. I have given you everything. Elevated you from *nothing* to mistress of Mayfield. Thought of you as purity itself, and all the time you were just like my . . . my filthy whore of a mother! Your own words condemn you. There is so much I know now; things have all fallen into place, things that I would have preferred to die before I knew. You lived with Lake. You are mean and depraved . . . just as *she* was!"

Eve was shaking her head as she heard his words, and she came toward him with her hands outstretched to touch him. There was a pitiful entreaty in her voice. "But that is not true; please believe me. It was not I who lived with him." She could see he found her repulsive. As she touched him, he pushed her away, and she stumbled sideways into an ivy-covered seat and only gained her balance because of it. Her face was white with despair, and the look of shock and fear that passed across it was to live in his mind.

"Please, please, listen, I beg you," she beseeched.

"Do not speak!" he commanded, the conviction of her immorality making him feel ill. His hand rose again as if to strike her. Then he checked his voice and kept it awesomely steady. "Listen carefully, woman, for I will never again repeat what I say this day."

She stood watching him now and shaking her head at his words, words that numbed her mind and chilled her heart, as if she stood in an arctic wind instead of the heat of this draining summer day.

As he spoke again, his eyes never left her face.

"I know you carry the child of your old lover. That he assaulted you I am now certain is a lie. One of the many lies I fear you've told me. Lies about your meetings, your associations, your liaisons. You must live with that, but I shall not. The vileness is yours; the dishonor will be mine. Until your child is born, you can remain here. I will move into other rooms today." He fell silent for a second or two, although his eyes still were locked with hers. The sick pain of what he now believed almost made him unsteady on his feet.

"I shall expect you to leave here as soon as you are able, after the birth. In the months ahead, I ask you to have the decency to avoid me." He took a deep breath, a breath that made a shuddering, echoing sound. "There will be no need for us to speak to each other again. Should there be reason for communication, then it will be through Mrs. Smith. I do not wish to see you. Do you understand?"

Understand? Understand? She understood nothing. It was like some monstrous nightmare. She stood paralyzed, looking blankly back at him.

"Do you understand?" he asked again, and when she did not reply, he paused no longer. "I assume you do," he said as he turned from her and walked away.

She was petrified. She could not think. Her eyes were the only parts of her that moved as they followed his departure. The seconds passed. Then suddenly she began to tremble uncontrollably. How desperately she had needed his love, his sympathy, his care, his understanding. Instead, she had received this. She was so stupified that when she opened her mouth to call out after him, only a strange shriekish sound came. And then as her whole body began to shake, she managed to force out the words "It . . . was . . . my . . . sister!"

He was striding up the steps of the veranda, his own pain singing in his ears, and just far enough away not to understand the words, though somewhere in his brain he registered the soulfelt agony of the cry. He never turned back, so he did not see the helpless shaking or hear her stammering like a child to explain herself to the empty garden. He did not see the hopeless gestures her hands made or the tears that broke from her eyes to run down her face.

And, too, there were things she did not see. She did not see the despairing misery that replaced the severity in his face as he left her. She did not hear his pitiful whisper, "Oh God! How I loved you . . ." and she did not see his tears, the first tears that had fallen from John Stuart's eyes since his father had died nine years before.

Three hours later, John Stuart dictated messages to each of the people he had invited to Mayfield for the Christmas week. He was canceling the invitations.

Mr. Oldfield sealed the letters and departed from the library without any show of emotion. His place was taken by Mrs. Smith, who entered as he left. John Stuart looked up from the papers he studied as, with sedate movements, the little woman came to him, her hands clasped behind her back. In her bearing was submissiveness. He was her master, and her devotion was complete.

"Sit down, Mrs. Smith. You have been here at Mayfield how long?"

"I came in thirty-nine, sir. Twenty-five years; twenty-six next March."

"Yes, you are an important part of Mayfield."

To this she gave a rare smile.

"You have been in the position of housekeeper for all of my adult life."

"Since forty-eight, Mr. Wakeman."

John Stuart nodded. "It is a position of great trust, and because of that, I have something to tell you. Something which causes me undeniable pain."

Mary Smith edged forward ever so slightly in the chair.

"It is impossible for me to relate this in the particular, Mrs. Smith, but you must now be told that while I was away, Mrs. Wakeman's conduct was such that dishonored me and her position as mistress at Mayfield. From this day forth, we will live separately. She will stay in the master suite. I will live here in the south wing."

As John Stuart continued, the first glimmers of emotion stirred in Mrs. Smith's sedate features.

John Stuart attempted to sound in control, but every now and then, his voice trembled. "Mrs. Wakeman should still be attended by the girl Stephanie, and yourself. I do not wish her to have general access to the rest of the staff. She is not to ride or to walk beyond the gates of the park. She is not a prisoner, you understand, and is quite free to move within the limits I have mentioned, but it would be best if she were not seen by the majority of Mayfield's employees, for there will be a child born, and after that, she will leave here."

The severity of Mrs. Smith's expression softened in sympathy as she listened. She was hurt and mortified for her master. How could such a thing have happened to this wonderful man? A child born, and obviously not his! It was too dreadful. She had loved Arthur Wakeman with a passion. He had taken her as a poor convict girl and had given her dignity, self-respect, and position. She had worshiped him with an undying loyalty, and his son had been the natural heir of her affections. She was honored by his trust, and she would not fail him. "And what of Mrs. Larmer, sir? They have been very friendly up to now."

"I would not restrict Mrs. Larmer's movements under any circumstances. She may come and go as she pleases." He motioned that the interview was over.

Mary Smith stood. "I understand perfectly, sir."

After she had gone, John Stuart sat with his head in his hands for a long time. Tears dripped through his fingers. When he stood at last, twilight had fallen.

He ate a solitary meal he did not want, and later he walked alone in the park. He slept little that night, and when he found himself awake at sunrise, he arose and went down to one of the river paddocks. He was already breaking horses when Joe arrived at seven o'clock.

As the hours passed, they worked side by side. At mid-morning when the men stopped for their tea break, John Stuart and Joe stayed apart from the others. They walked out of hearing range of the men to a rocky outcrop that arranged itself along the side of the paddock. As they gained the first of the boulders, Joe touched John Stuart affectionately on the shoulder. The younger man tried to smile, but his expression remained grim. There was a forced animation in him this morning.

"How are you, m'boy? I've been very worried."

"I'm all right now, Joe." He made an unhappy sound. "It was just as we thought, old man," he said in a small voice for such a big man. "She had been in Adelaide with Lake."

"I'm sorry, lad."

John Stuart put his mug of tea on top of a large, weather-worn stone, and looking back toward the men who rested from their work, he recounted what had passed between himself and his wife.

When he finished, Joe answered with resignation. "I truly would not have thought it of her, but we shall get by, m'boy. We always have."

"It's so hard to believe this is happening to me. You know, old man, I actually looked forward to an heir of my own someday, but I thought it best to have a few years alone with her first, just the two of us, before we shared ourselves with a family. How stupid I was." He laughed, a wretched sound. "And now—" his eyes closed "—all there will ever be is the poor bastard issue from her."

Joe nodded, leaning forward to hold John Stuart's shoulder. He spoke quietly. "You could get a divorce."

John Stuart did not answer for a few moments; it was obvious he had not thought of this. When he replied, it was slow and considered. "I think not, Joe. While I know there are men who have done it, divorce is long and difficult, and there will be enough malicious gossip attached to the Wakeman name. No, I must stay as I am, for now anyway. It is best."

"But, John Stuart, m'boy, there may be another woman somewhere, one who would make you happy."

He gave a melancholy smile as he answered, "No, Joe, old man. I would never trust another, not in this world."

Over at Mayfield House, Thelma had just come down the steps to join Eve in the walled garden. It was a hot, cloudless morning, and the sun's rays lit Eve's hair to a golden sheen, in contrast to the white, desolate face she lifted to her friend. She had spent a night in the depths of misery. After John Stuart had left her in the garden, she had stumbled to the steps and across the veranda to her bedroom. She could not believe what had occurred. Over and over again she pictured John Stuart's face, the look of cold, remote despair in his eyes and the loathing on his face. She sobbed for a long time alone in her room. Her life was shattered; nothing mattered anymore.

It was almost dark when she heard the gentle tap on the door, and she dragged herself to her feet to find Stephanie standing in the doorway, a look of concern on her face. She sent the girl away, saying that she needed nothing and preferred to be alone for a time.

Why hadn't her husband given her a chance to explain? Why

was he so ready to believe Lake? Did he really think that all women were deceivers? Yes, he probably did; that's why Lake could convince him. John Stuart could not help himself. She was shocked to her soul that he could believe something so vile of her. She was not like poor Clare. But then she had only herself to blame for not telling him ages ago of her sister's existence. But she was *not* responsible for the ease with which John Stuart fell a ready victim to Lake's lies. Did their love mean so little to him?

Then she thought of the bushranger, and suddenly she realized that John Stuart might have misinterpreted her meetings with him and concluded they were not accidental. With John Stuart's willingness to see all women as corrupt, he had condemned her without allowing her to speak, had rejected her before she could defend herself. How could he have so little trust in her? How angry she was, how hurt and dejected at his repudiation. How badly he had treated her when she needed him most.

Thelma came across the lawn to her and hugged her. "Oh, love," the good woman began, "whatever has happened?"

Eve sighed, a broken sound. "He believes I was Lake's woman and that I consented to lie with him."

Thelma looked baffled. "But that is impossible; you didn't know the man. How could John Stuart think such a thing?"

Eve slowly shook her head. "Seems he found Lake . . . somewhere. Lake said he had once lived with me. Swore that I was his woman, in Adelaide, years ago—1857. And it's true, I was there to visit that year, Thel, I . . . John Stuart would not listen to me. He seems to think I have had meetings, liaisons. Whatever Lake said, he convinced John Stuart, absolutely."

"Oh dear, this is terrible. I must go to him, tell him he's wrong."

Eve waved her hand tiredly, negating the idea. "No, Thelma, love, you must not. He will not want to hear what you have to say. He does not want an explanation. He hates me as he hates his mother."

"But I know you are innocent," Thelma insisted. "I must help you. This is too outlandish. How is it possible the man is so blind?"

Then Eve stood up from the seat and moved across the grass. She stood motionless, looking up into the stark brightness of the day. Should she tell Thelma the whole truth? For a few seconds she was truly tempted, for she was so very badly in need of help. The sunlight hurt her eyes and she squinted as she stood there thinking. No, it would not be fair to her good, true friend, not fair at all. It would place Thelma in a terrible position. She turned back to her friend, and now her inner strength shone in her eyes, and her chin tilted determinedly.

"I should honestly prefer you did not, my dear Thelma. He now believes that I am as bad as he once thought me good. John Stuart Wakeman's accusations and judgments are not all his fault. I see many things I did not see before, and somehow, now, I think it is better that he believes what he does. Sooner or later he would have found some other reason to condemn me, for I could never be as perfect a wife as he wants. He is a good man according to his own lights. It is simply that perhaps they are not mine."

For all Eve's resistance, Thelma could not let such a dreadful injustice occur. She had to defend her.

It took her twenty-four hours to find the courage to approach John Stuart, and her step faltered as she was given entry to him, for it was a long time since she had been alone with him. She had fondled him, nursed him, fed him, mothered him, until he was five years old. Then a series of nannies and tutors had taken him from her, although her influence had remained all during his childhood. But as the years had passed and adolescence had changed to manhood, he had slipped from her and passed from the candor of youth into the self-possession of an adult aristocrat.

He looked over as she hesitated at the door of the blue room. It was a hot, still night, and he sat in gloomy silence with his dogs. "Yes, Thelma, what is it?"

"I have come to speak to you on an urgent matter, John Stuart."

"Yes, yes, come in, sit down."

She did so.

"Well, begin; what is it?"

She took a deep breath. "I believe you have come to a terribly wrong conclusion about the delicate matter which concerns you and Eve."

"And why is that?"

"I was here. You were not. I saw her the day after the attack by that . . . that man. She was in a dreadful state, bruises and goodness knows what abrasions she had. Her eye was black and all. Face swollen. I don't know what that terrible person told you and Joe, but it was a lie. Eve is a good girl, she is innocent. Please forget all this and go to her and—"

"Thelma!" He cut in on her words. His tone was icy. "You speak from your feelings and you do not know the facts. You are being duped. I *do* know about the bruises she suffered from her fall. Mrs. Smith told me everything."

"But that is not so. It's Mrs. Smith don't know the truth," Thelma argued.

"No, Thelma." He rose to his feet, and his voice became louder. "This is all so distasteful; my tolerance is breaking down. She has told me a series of lies, lies you know nothing about, and in your good-natured fashion, you have been fooled by her. I have allowed you to speak because of who you are and your long association with me, which gives you certain privileges, but I will *not* tolerate discussion of this again, not from you, not from anyone. I forgive you only because you are not in full possession of the facts."

He turned away from her, signaling her to leave.

She stood. The insides of her hands were damp from the tension; he was intimidating her just as she had known he would. She was aware that she could not be successful, that all she was doing was aggravating him. She knew he wanted her to go, to hear no more, but she was a strong bush woman for all that, and so, with beating heart, she made one last attempt. She spoke to his unyielding back.

"John Stuart, you have made it clear that I have dared to speak when I should have held my tongue, but as that is so, I shall brave a little more. This is a terrible mistake. I do not share your view of Eve, no matter what evidence you believe you have. I will respect your wishes and will never mention it again, but one day you will see for yourself her innocence and the error you make, although I fear there will be much heartache 'tween now and then. There's none so blind as he who will not see. Ah, John Stuart, my heart is heavy for you both."

He did not speak.

He did not turn around.

She sighed and left him standing there.

There was a sick feeling in his stomach, and his chest felt tight. He walked out through the open doors onto the white-washed terrace. The strong scent of jasmine hung in the warm air about him. How he wished his life were different. How he wished he had never seen her that night in the Bathurst park. Oh, how good and pure she had looked in the twilight. But she was iniquitous. To think he had cared for her, touched her, kissed her, loved her. His mother and his wife . . . blasted whores! His bitterness rose to his tongue like bile, and he opened his mouth wide to breathe.

He looked about him into the darkness. And coming back to him, out of the night, was the mocking refrain of Lake's words, *When I met her, she was with another bloke. She knew lots of shady characters; shacked up with them, too, I swear. . . . Called herself Clare Herman . . . was my de facto . . . de facto . . . knew lots of shady characters.*

Poor innocent little Daydee, meeting those two in the Bathurst park, so unsuspectingly. Briefly he felt a flash of tenderness toward the girl. At that very moment he turned and walked over the doorstep into the sitting room to see the door to the hall open and a maid announce Daydee and Joe.

"Uncle John Stuart," Daydee began, "I have wanted to show you my paintings for ever so long, and at last Father has succumbed to my wishes."

Although he would have preferred to be alone with his melancholy thoughts, his recent reflections had left him feeling fondly toward the girl. He manufactured a smile. "Good, Daydee. I would be happy to see them."

She had a certain talent, and her watercolors of parts of Mayfield were quite well done. When John Stuart remarked favorably upon them, she preened. Later, while the two men talked of Mayfield matters, Daydee became engrossed in a pile of journals and newspapers.

After a time, Joe asked in a low voice, "Was that Thelma of mine here this night?"

"She was. She came to tell me that she did not share our view of Eve, but she shall speak of it no more."

"That's the trouble with women these days," Joe commented. "They've got minds of their own. I'm sorry, m'boy."

John Stuart shook his head. "No, it matters not, Joe. She has been deceived a little longer than we have, that is all. She knows not to mention it again."

A whistle from Daydee broke into their conversation.

"Now, that's a very unladylike thing to do," her father remonstrated, looking across to where she sat, newspaper in hand.

"Oh, listen to this." She lifted the *Sydney Morning Herald* in the air. "It's about Sir Rutherford and the bushrangers. 'At an interview with Sir Rutherford Blake, the New South Wales police adviser on the apprehension of bushrangers in the colony, he made it known that an act would be passed in the new year called the Felons' Apprehension Act, which would give police the power to shoot known bushrangers on sight.

" 'Sir Rutherford made it clear that there would be long jail terms for anyone known to have assisted or harbored an outlaw. He also said he had issued orders via Sir Frederick Pottinger, police inspector of the southern and western districts, for police to carry firearms even when off duty.' " Daydee lifted her finger in the air. "People say Sir Rutherford has little time for Pottinger."

"Yes," her father answered. "It'll be Sir Rutherford that will do all the catching, if you ask me. He is the bloodhound. I'd hate for him to be tracking me."

Putting the paper aside, Daydee stood and came forward to John Stuart's side. "Will he be coming again for Christmas, Uncle John Stuart? I do like him. He's so diverting."

Her father looked up hastily; he had told Daydee not to mention anything sensitive. But John Stuart did not look alarmed; he merely stretched his hand out to her, and she came quickly into the arc of his arm.

"No, Daydee, there will be no visitors, I'm afraid. Only us."

"Oh, that's perfectly all right," the girl said. "In fact, I would really prefer it."

NINETEEN

Alan and Rutherford Blake

Sir Rutherford Blake twisted in his chair.

"How extraordinary! How damned extraordinary!" he exclaimed aloud as he folded the letter that had caused the outburst and turned to look thoughtfully out on the unseasonally moody, wet December day.

The letter had been lying on his desk in wait for over two

weeks while he had been out west in the hill country reconnoitering where it was said Johnny Gilbert had been sighted. He had not found any trace of Gilbert, but he had caught a horse thief and made friends of many of the country folk thereabout, and that was tantamount to making enemies for the bushrangers. He regarded it as time well spent.

The letter was from John Stuart Wakeman, and the contents were shocking, to say the least. John Stuart was not to hold his customary house party this year. It would appear that there was some scandal involving Mrs. Wakeman. The innuendo was that John Stuart had been cuckolded! It seemed hard to believe, for while the woman had a comely body and fine features, he would not have thought her flighty or immoral. To him, she seemed to have an eternal disinclination to talk, but at the same time, he had received the impression that she was not lacking in inner strength. Nevertheless, the letter had informed him of John Stuart's shame and had asked him as a friend to understand the rescinding of the request for his company. He rubbed his thin top lip in thought.

Today was four days before Christmas, and he had been planning to leave for Mayfield early tomorrow. Well, now he would ride south to the town of Young before Christmas instead of afterward, as he had originally proposed.

There were times when he wished his headquarters were in the South somewhere and not in Bathurst; but the telegraph came only this far, and he needed to keep in touch with Sydney and the inspector general of police.

He had little respect for Frederick Pottinger. Bushrangers had slipped through their fingers more than once because of his incompetence. It was only because he, Sir Rutherford, had ridden long and hard, covering the territory, and making friends such as the parish priest Father McCarthy in the township of Carcoar, that they had ever caught the likes of John Vane of the Hall gang. The priest had talked Vane into surrendering, and when Sir Rutherford had promised that if Vane talked, he would not swing, he had kept his word. Things like that impressed the bush folk.

There had always been bushrangers. When the colony began, they had been, in the main, escaped convict scum, bolters. It was not until recently the class known as the "wild colonial boys" had developed; free malingerers with a grievance against the public. He had studied each of them in intimate detail, to find some sort of pattern in their movements. The amazing thing was, he thought he had! That was why he wanted to be well south of here and established with a force of police troopers in the heart of bushranger territory by the coming January. In all his research, he had noticed that each and every gang had made a major holdup shortly after Christmas, usually early in January. Ah yes, certainly they robbed in other months, any month! But the one month they all had in common was January! Perhaps it had something to do with the excesses of Christmas.

Whatever the reason, he had discerned that even as far back as the bushrangers Michael Howe, early in the century, and Matthew Brady, in the twenties, robberies always took place in January. He had gone to the archives to diligently trace the crimes of Martin Cash in the forties, and sure enough, there it was. So, too, with the others. In the fifties, Frank McCallam, who called himself Captain Melville, had made his notorious raids on the sheep farmers near Geelong . . . in January. Not one had bypassed the month.

In recent years, the very same had occurred, all south and west of Bathurst. And this year there had been three significant January robberies. Johnny Gilbert and a man called Collins at Goulburn coaching office; Dan Morgan at two homesteads outside Lambing Flat, now renamed Young after the governor; and Alan Fletcher and his gang at the magistrate's ball in Wagga Wagga. Ah yes, Alan Fletcher, the one who had been evading the law the longest, the one Sir Rutherford wanted the most.

He tapped his fingers rhythmically on the windowsill at his right hand. How many long nights he had sat by the light of the kerosene lamp here in his office, contemplating Fletcher. The man always took from the government, and was the sole one who operated that way. It was as if it were some sort of revenge. In a few weeks' time, he would have evaded capture for twelve years. . . . Amazing! He was unique. Since his escape in '53, he had held up government officials, police, and magistrates all the way from the Darling Downs in Queensland south in a rough spiral to the township of Orange. The last of these linked crimes appeared to have been in January 1859.

That is why he believed that Fletcher had found a permanent hideout. He was no longer on the move. Since '59, robberies accredited to him were all over the place, no pattern emerging. Ah yes, he had a feeling about Fletcher's hideout. He felt sure it was somewhere south of Cowra outside Mayfield's western border.

He looked over to the map of New South Wales that domi-

nated his wall. Months ago he had been given a passing fair
description of Fletcher from Tommy Barnes, but not good
enough to recognize the fellow in the street, and that had held
true until three months ago when he had the disagreeable, but
invaluable, experience of meeting Alan Fletcher. Now he knew
what most of the bushranger's victims noticed; it would be a
man of little observation who could look into those singular eyes
of Fletcher's and not recognize them a second time. Ah yes. But
now he knew the man's habitual movements, his height, the way
he held himself, the rhythm of his walk . . . all priceless. He
would most definitely recognize him if he saw him again.

Sir Rutherford could barely wait for the new year and the
outlawry act. The chief secretary himself had promised it would
be tabled and passed by Parliament early in the coming year.
Sir Rutherford was using his influence to get a twenty-year jail
sentence included in the act for anyone found aiding the bushrangers. That would check scum like Morgan from strutting into
inns and ordering drinks all around, and it would put a stop to
the safe houses. Ah yes, they all used the safe houses, even
Fletcher.

He lifted a paper from his desk and read the description upon
it. "Fletcher, Alan: About five feet eleven, medium-muscular
build, slim, light brown hair and brows, skin browned from the
sun, well-spoken, long fingers, blue-gray eyes." Beneath this
in pencil he had scribbled, "haughty, aristocratic, impudent,
also unusual eyes."

The memory of the day when he and Mr. Elrington and six
police troopers had been at the Theresa Town gold diggings
brought a flush to his face.

He had taken his men there on a lead to the whereabouts of
Ben Hall. There had been two robberies in six days just south
of Theresa Town, both by Hall, Gilbert, and an eighteen-year-
old delinquent nicknamed "the Jockey." The rumor was that
Gilbert was sweet on a girl at the diggings.

Theresa Town had a government mine in operation as well as
being open to public diggings, and soon after his arrival, Sir
Rutherford was informed by the police in charge that there was
a Chinese miner turned petty bushranger, who was robbing travelers on the road to the south.

"They say he lives in a cave three miles away and that Ben
Hall himself has been seen with him."

Now, the expert on the outlaws knew that this could be just
"bush gossip," but nevertheless he took Mr. Elrington and his

six police south from the diggings, disguised as miners. They separated and walked in groups. The plan worked. Sure enough, the Chinese robber, Foo Yong, held up the third group, and after a fierce struggle, during which the gun belonging to the Chinese discharged in the air, the police detective took his prisoner.

It was not long before Sir Rutherford realized that Foo Yong knew nothing of Ben Hall; nevertheless, he was one more lawbreaker in custody.

That night was the monthly miners' dance, and Sir Rutherford was guest of honor out of gratitude for the capture of Foo Yong. He had been proving somewhat of a nuisance to the miners and their suppliers.

Applause broke out as the police detective entered. He bowed from the shoulders in reply to the acclamation and stalked through the guests to his seat beneath a picture of Queen Victoria peering gravely down upon the raucous laughter and noise of her colonial subjects.

Beer was handed around, and the music, piano and fiddle, began. The entire European population of Theresa Town, all 215 of them, were here, spilling out of the bar over the veranda into the heat of the October night. The hundred or so miners who were Chinese kept to their tents on the far side of the hill and left the white men to their own entertainment. The twenty-three women in Theresa Town, dressed in their finery, spun from partner to partner upon the dance floor.

The merrymaking was in full flight when Sir Rutherford's sharp senses registered something odd. There was something wrong outside. It was intangible, but there was a difference. He stood from his chair and began to move to the nearest window. He had taken no more than two steps when the swing-arm doors of the bar slammed back loudly against the wall.

The music stopped. Everyone turned in amazement as two men, with faces covered and rifles leveled, thrust themselves to each side of the door and trained their weapons on the gathering. "Hold still, you lot!" Then a third masked man in dark clothing and carrying a gun entered to stand midway between the other two. "We're sorry to interrupt your gathering, ladies and gentlemen, but I assure you it is necessary, from our point of view. We will not keep you long." The voice had total authority, and the nuances of sound were of a class not usually heard in the outback.

He lifted his hand to keep the crowd quiet and then called

over his shoulder, "Inside here, everyone. I'm sorry you will have to be overcrowded for a few minutes, but please be patient."

The men who had been out on the verandas and in the street, under the encouragement of the rifles, filed in through the door. As they came in, the two who had stood to either side of the door moved through the crowd to the back of the room. One, whom Sir Rutherford carefully noted had the semblance of a limp, mounted the bar. The other, a very big man, pushed two chairs together and climbed upon them. From their strategic locations they menaced the gathering below with their rifles.

Now the leader called to one of Sir Rutherford's party who was moving away as the men from outside swelled the numbers inside. "Constable, you there! Forward here beside me, please." He pointed with his rifle through the swelling crowd to the other police near the bar. "And you others, over here beside me!"

"Move as ye're told!" shouted the man on the bar, brandishing his rifle.

In a few minutes the room was overfilled with the 215 souls of Theresa Town and the visiting troopers.

Then the leader turned his head and called out through the open door, "Send in the other members of Her Majesty's police force." And he moved aside as two constables, one who had been guarding Foo Yong, and one who had been guarding the shed of government gold, entered. Behind came two more armed men, looking dangerous. One moved close behind the leader, and the other held fast at the doorway with a view to the outside.

"Over with the others now, like good policemen," the leader said to the troopers as a titter ran through the crowd.

Sir Rutherford could be quiet no longer. "Blast you!" he shouted, pushing men aside as he advanced to within a few yards of the intruder. "This is an outrage! What the hell is going on?"

"Stand fast, you!" the stranger answered, taking a step forward and halting Sir Rutherford with a threatening movement of his rifle. "I shall do the questioning here, not you, whoever you are."

Sir Rutherford fell momentarily silent as he registered the warning in the eyes he beheld, but as the man turned from him to look over to his companions, he could not contain himself. "I demand to know what is happening here. This is a gross violation of the law, and I will not tolerate it!"

In contrast to Sir Rutherford's shout, the man's reply was quiet. He spoke with his back to the police detective. "I can only assume you are Rutherford Blake." Then slowly he rounded to face him. "The trooper guarding the prisoner said you were here. You act like one whose arrogance could at times cloud his clear thinking. You should control that part of your nature; it is not conducive to winning."

Sir Rutherford contained his ire. He wanted to strike the man. No one had ever dared to say such a thing to him. With a tremendous effort of will, he calmed himself, and his answer brought murmurings from the fascinated crowd. "I will remember what you say . . . Alan Fletcher!"

For a second, an expression of mild surprise appeared in the eyes of the stranger. The look was so fleeting that all except Sir Rutherford, who was close to him, missed it. Then he said, "I must ask you to join your men, here beside me." He motioned with his gun.

Sir Rutherford did not move.

It was then the small, wiry man next to the leader, who had mustered those from outside, spoke up. "Move, man, as the guverner says . . . now! Or I'll not be accountable for what me rifle does." He stepped forward agilely and cocked the trigger on his gun. Sir Rutherford concluded he was probably Cooper, and mindful of his safety, did as he was told.

"Now," continued the leader, "there will be one more here I had better be aware of. Which one of you is Elrington, the companion of Sir Rutherford? His secretary assistant, I fancy you are called."

All eyes turned automatically to look at David Elrington, who stood in the midst of those gathered at the front of the room.

"So you are the appprenticed 'police detective.' Over here, young fellow. I would like all vigilant law enforcers standing together."

"Yes, over here as ye are told, with yer mateys," said the small man, gesturing toward Sir Rutherford's group. "And now we'll be havin' that pistol I be noticin' in yer belt, son."

David Elrington gingerly took the gun from his waist and handed it to the speaker, who added it to the arsenal in his own belt. "Nice of ye other gents to come unarmed," he said as he looked back to the leader and winked.

The leader now moved back into the doorway. "Understand this. We are not here to harm any of you. Most of you are honest men hoping to find your fortune. It is with the government of this fair colony that today we are at variance."

Sir Rutherford's eyes greedily followed the man's every movement. He would remember everything about Fletcher. For he knew it was Fletcher, had been positive from the moment he saw him and heard his voice.

"There is a little matter of the shipment of government gold that is being held in the shed down the street. We come to alleviate you all of the worry of holding it here. Once it is gone, you will be able to sleep soundly, knowing no bushrangers will be coming to invade this little scenic spot, to take it away."

Some of the ordinary diggers laughed. They found it amusing that the government gold might be stolen. It gave them no pleasure to see the government working the mines they thought should be freehold.

"So," he went on, "I will have the key please, which my police guard informant—" he gestured to the man who had been at the gold shed, "—tells me Constable Boehm is holding. Forward please, Constable!"

Just then there was a clicking sound from the man behind him at the door; all heads turned as the leader asked over his shoulder, "What is it?"

"Looks like some Chink chappies peeking over the hilltop."

"The Chinese are an intelligent and sensible race," answered the leader. "They will look, but they shan't interfere." Then he turned his attention to Sir Rutherford. "Which constrains me to tell you of your prisoner. The poor chap looked a little indisposed. He was under some impression that you were going to hang him."

"He is a prisoner of Her Majesty, a criminal and a thief. Justice will be done!" Sir Rutherford broke in angrily.

"But not as soon as you would wish. You see, I have given him a horse and told him to put as many miles as possible between here and where he hopes to set up trade again. He has ridden off, assuring me he will follow my advice."

Now the police detective shouted, "Damn you! That man was in my custody. I'll see you hang as high as any of them, I will!"

Just for an instant, Sir Rutherford fancied he saw the leader stiffen with distaste before he replied, "My boys and I will continue to defer your pleasure as long as possible."

"Shut Blake's filthy mouth now, boss, with a bullet!" the big man on the chair called angrily.

"Constable Boehm," Alan said, "the key to the shed, please, or I shall have to let the more aggressive of my crew have their way."

The constable handed him a large lock key from inside his jacket.

"Thank you. So much better than chopping down the door." He strode out, followed by the man Sir Rutherford had guessed to be Dan Dwyer.

Sir Rutherford began speaking to the remaining three bush-rangers as soon as the others had gone. "Listen, you men, don't you realize the risk you run? If you will only listen to me, I will—"

He got no further, for the man on the chair swung his rifle in the air and discharged it into the ceiling. The crowd fell away in shock as bits of wood dropped down upon them.

"Now, shut up, shut up, I say!" he growled as he took a pistol from his belt and brandished it at Sir Rutherford. "I will not shoot the bloody ceilin' next time, I'll shoot you, Blake."

"Steady, friend, steady!" counseled the man on the bar.

"Just disciplinin' Blake, guverner!" shouted the little man at the door out into the inky street.

Sir Rutherford, realizing he was getting nowhere, decided that discretion was indeed the better par of valor, and fell into a bitter silence. Some six or seven minutes elapsed while the captive men and women murmured and sweated in the closeness and heat, and then they heard the leader's voice. "All right, lads, we have accomplished what we came for."

The bushranger on the bar waved his rifle in an arc over his head. "Right then, back up, ye lot, nice and tight, I say! Make a path. Now!" Then he jumped down, and he and the big man passed, back to back, along the opening to join the little man at the door. There they were met by the leader. Sir Rutherford thought he could perceive a smile beneath his mask.

When his men were all outside, Alan did a startling thing. He was holding a ten-pound bag of gold in his hands and had untied the string at the top. He bent and poured a line of nuggets across the doorway, saying, "I would like to share some of the govern-ment's gold with you, my friends . . . for your patience and good humor."

With that, the bushrangers left as a man and were on their horses and riding away within ten seconds, while behind them the pandemonium that Alan had counted on broke out as men scrambled to the gold, falling over one another and shouting in their haste.

Sir Rutherford grimaced as he remembered all this.

He had pushed the reward on Fletcher up to one thousand

pounds after Theresa Town. Oh, how badly he wanted him. Damn the man. Damn all the bushranging scoundrels!

A knock sounded on the door. It brought his head up in sharp awareness.

David Elrington entered, carrying a paper in his hand. "Sir, I have just now received this telegraph message. It is from Sir Frederick. He cannot meet you here today as planned. He will join you in Young after Christmas."

The expert on the bushrangers made a contemptuous sound. "Then we shall miss him, for we ride to Young tomorrow."

"But, sir, we do not go to Young until after our Christmas at Mayfield."

Sir Rutherford shook his head. "We do not go to Mayfield after all. Mr. Wakeman is having troubles of his own. Our Christmas there has been canceled. Instead, I am pleased to inform you, we will ride south tomorrow and get ourselves deep into bushranging country."

"But, sir, it is raining pretty heavily for a long ride."

"What's a drop of rain, man? You won't melt!"

As the door closed behind his assistant, he turned to the window, a preoccupied expression on his face, and his gaze on the falling rain.

TWENTY

Eve's Decision

Eve stirred.

The patter of rain sounded in her ears, and for a moment dream and reality blurred, then thunder rolled in the distance and the veranda door rattled in the wind and she was awake. She shivered. She was cold even though it was a little stuffy in the closed room. Ever since the assault, she had been afraid to open the windows at night.

What a strange dream: Alan Fletcher and John Stuart together, in the San Francisco of her girlhood.

The thunder rolled again. What a night to be out! She supposed some poor souls would be. That brought her to thinking of Alan Fletcher. Where would he be on a night like this? She wondered where he lay his head and if he were dry and comfortable. Could he hear the same thunder she heard just now? Sir Rutherford seemed to think he dwelt not far from here. Ah, but that was a year ago.

She rolled over and lay on her side. She would have liked to lie on her stomach, but that was not comfortable now. It, poor creature, grew within her. It was almost fourteen weeks old. Today would be the twenty-first of December, four days to Christmas. What a sorry Christmas it would be at Mayfield this year. The master and the mistress estranged. The whole property talking about it. What would John Stuart do? She knew he had canceled his invitations for Christmas. Dear Thelma had told her that. And the children's tree? Would he go to that putting on a brave face? Even though life hardly seemed worth living, there was yet a corner of her heart that was sorry for John Stuart. His dream had been shattered. How could their love and their lives have come to this?

She had passed two wretched weeks since her husband had returned, waiting to see if he would come to her, longing for him. But the days had gone by without his face, and the nights had stretched into long, lonely hours. Each morning she had awoken with the hope that today he would come and make amends. Yesterday she had even waited on the veranda, knowing the time of his return to the house. She thought that if he saw her, he would soften and come to her, that perhaps she could speak to him. Surely his love for her would overcome the horrible belief he had? When he had appeared on the carriageway astride Diomed, she had come down the steps toward him, lifting her arm in gentle greeting, but when he had seen her, he had stopped momentarily, then turned the horse around and ridden away. She had lost all hope after that. There was little doubt, he found the sight of her unbearable.

How very alone she was! Her eyes filled with tears, and she felt them run across her temple to fall into her hair. All her frustration and anger and pain and suffering raged through her again. For some moments she was back in the garden, on the ground being battered by Lake. The nightmare was still there, living in her head. She was sobbing, consumed by an awful, empty ache. How could John Stuart have believed that vile man? How could he have treated her this way? Finally she pulled herself up on the pillows and, wiping her eyes with a handkerchief, said aloud, "Come on, Eve, what are you going to do?"

Her future appeared as interminable months of day-to-day confinement. Oh, she would have Thelma; that brave lady had not let her down. And, too, she had the company of sweet Stephanie. But that would all end when the baby was born. John Stuart intended to send her away.

"No!" She spoke aloud in the darkness again. She would not allow that! How dare he? She would leave of her own volition, in her own time, and soon, when he would not suspect it.

Go to Father! Yes, that was it! Of course! Father and Mother would stand by her. She could deal with any scorn if she was by Father's side. She would be strong in the face of all the indignity that was to come. John Stuart did not want to know the truth. He probably never would be able to contend with the truth. Let him continue in his misbelief.

She had been sick again these last few days, had not been able to keep food down, but perhaps she would be well enough to travel soon. Yes, yes, she must be. She would tell no one. She would leave at night and go to Bathurst. But she must wait until after Christmas Day. Christmas Day was one of the two busiest days of the year for Father.

That was it!

She would leave in the early hours on Boxing Day when the house was asleep. She would ride to Cowra and be there to catch the mail coach at nine o'clock in the morning. It ran to Blayney every day of the year except Good Friday and Christmas Day; and from Blayney, she could catch another to Bathurst.

That was what she would do. She would stay here no longer. It was her decision, no one else's, and it was made.

Christmas Eve was a quiet affair.

There was an unseasonal chill in the air, and because of the rain they had been experiencing on and off for days, the children's Christmas tree was held in the schoolhouse and was a much smaller affair than usual. John Stuart made only a token visit for the concert and departed before the gift giving.

When he left the hall in company with Joe, Daydee followed

him out onto the veranda, disappointment on her face. "Uncle John Stuart . . ."

They had turned to her.

Her father spoke. "What is it, love? We are in a hurry."

"Oh, Uncle John Stuart, I . . . I just wanted to say, I think it's just wonderful that . . . that you came here this evening, and merry Christmas."

John Stuart smiled gently as he came the two paces back to her. He took her tiny shoulders in his hands and bent to kiss her forehead. "Merry Christmas, dear."

Her small eyes followed him longingly into the covered landau. Then as Deke Edwards, wrapped in leather cape and hat against the rain, urged his horses forward into the damp twilight, she blew a kiss after him.

When the two men left each other an hour or so later, Joe was concerned. "It looks like we might have some flooding on our hands if this rain keeps up, m'boy, although I would say we are only experiencing the edge of it. It's worse to the north and west. Bathurst is getting it bad, they say. Did I tell you we had a message from Cowra yesterday? It was the second day the northern mail coach had not gone through. Had to turn back before it reached Blayney; seems the Belubula River broke its banks, and the lowlands are flooded on and off for miles."

"No, Joe, I did not realize. In that case, we had better watch our Lachlan. It doesn't seem to be rising as yet, but it can happen quickly, and if it does, the river paddocks, the dairy, and the closest cottages would be in trouble."

Joe agreed. "Right. In fact, I might take a ride out in the morning, just check upriver a few miles, see what she's doing."

"I'll come with you," replied John Stuart.

When Christmas morning broke, it was raining only lightly. There had been a deluge during the night for many hours, and just after dawn, John Stuart and Joe had ridden up the Lachlan to where it joined the Boorowa.

The river was running at speed, not surprisingly, for it had taken a lot of water from the hills in the past days, and had swelled in some places enough to be in danger of breaking. If the rain stopped in the next twelve to twenty-four hours, probably all would be well, but if it did not . . .

It was close to noon when the two riders, in wide-brimmed hats and long leather capes, returned over Larmer's Crossing. Up the gradual incline they rode together, quiet in thought, and as they neared the stables, Joe broke the silence. "So, then, we will see you tonight, m'boy?"

"Yes indeed, we shall have a great dinner, I'm assured."

"You know, m'boy, it is not necessary."

"I want to have it, old man. I want to have the backbone of Mayfield at my table this night."

Joe smiled. "Very well."

After coming home from the children's Christmas tree the previous evening, John Stuart had made a late decision to have a Christmas dinner at Mayfield House even under the present circumstances. First thing this morning, he had dispatched messengers to some of his trusted staff. His guest list was going to be unusual, but certainly one his father would have approved. This year there would be no governors or colonial secretaries, no knights or members of Parliament or lawyers or officials. This year his table would be graced by Mr. and Mrs. Jack Hennessy, Mr. and Mrs. Stephen Watson, the three Larmers, and Mr. Oldfield.

When Joe returned home, John Stuart did not. He stayed the entire afternoon in the stables, grooming his own horses. It gave him satisfaction to be close to the animals. He even cleaned out the stalls, working so hard that while the temperature had dropped greatly, he still stripped to his waist. As it was Christmas Day, no one was there, so he was alone, exactly as he wished.

The married men were with their families, and the unmarried were having their own banquet in the recreation hall. Now, that was something he was very proud of. Mayfield had the best housing and facilities for working men in the entire country! It was one of the many ways in which Mayfield was unique, and those lucky enough to live and work upon it realized it.

Why hadn't the woman he had elevated to be its mistress proven worthy?

A sharp picture of her face, as he had seen it that terrible day in the garden, came to his mind. It made him feel uneasy. Unhappy and uneasy. He dropped the hoof-pick he had been using. Diomed and his stable mate whinnied as he moved out into the rain.

She had waited for him a few nights ago; he had seen her coming down the steps of the house toward him as he rode up in the dusk. She had waved, and he had steeled himself to turn and ride away. She was corrupt, he knew she was, yet he could not control that part of his mind which continued to recall her face and her voice. For some time he stood in the cobbled yard, wondering what she might be doing.

* * *

At the same time, alone in her room, Eve was standing in silent consideration. She, too, was thinking of him and what his reaction would be when tomorrow he heard she was gone. Would he be sorry? No, probably not. Perhaps he would not care at all.

Stephanie had told her he looked gloomy and sad. Strange, but to hear that had brought her no joy. How much she needed his love.

What a fool he was! And what a fool she, too, was! Why hadn't she told him long ago about Clare? How many times had she been over this in her mind? It would not have mattered anyway. It all would have ended in this fashion. She would have been assaulted by Lake. She would be carrying his child, and John Stuart still would not be able to contend with that.

He would need to be a different man altogether. Perhaps more like Alan Fletcher. Momentarily she imagined the two men standing on the bush road, side by side, as they had done on her wedding day, John Stuart and Alan. She made a small, sad sound, clasping herself around the waist, holding herself tightly.

Velvet brushed her skirt as she stood unmoving. She bent and lifted him to her arms. "I will miss you, darling boy, but dear Thelma and Stephanie will take care of you. You like Thelma."

There had been no service in the chapel this year, although it had been open for anyone to use. For the first year ever, none of the Mayfield folk had gone to church or mass in Cowra. The weather was too terrible.

Thelma had spent the morning here with her. Eve had been glad of her kindly companionship, for she had given Stephanie the day off to attend all the festive staff events. It was now close to the hour of four in the afternoon. What an awful Christmas Day. It was all unbearable, unbearable to her and unbearable to him. Well, she would be away from all of it tomorrow. Home with Father soon. The first smile for weeks hovered on her mouth.

Outside, the wind blew rain across the veranda. The smile left her face as she noticed it. She returned Velvet to the floor. What if it was raining when she left in the morning? Oh, please, God, let the rain stop! At a sensible pace, it could take almost four hours to ride into Cowra. The mail left at nine o'clock. She had better leave herself six hours, for some of the ride would be in the dark of night. Yes, to give herself plenty of time, she had better leave her bedroom before three o'clock in the morning. If it continued to rain, there was nowhere to shelter on the road-side. She would just have to pray that it did not.

If only she could feel more well. Her head was often dizzy and she felt sick on and off all day. At least she had not vomited for a few days now. That was a blessing.

"Ah, poor thing within me," she said aloud, holding her stomach. "I am truly sorry."

Rousing herself, she crossed to her dressing table. Out of one of the drawers she took a large jewel box. She opened the lid. She did not touch the important gems that John Stuart had given her. Instead, she lifted out a few simple pieces Mother and Father had given her over the years, and put them in a gilt trinket box that had been a gift from Billy Tomkins. She sighed. Poor Billy. Then she put the trinket box in the soft carpet traveling bag she would take with her. Her eyes returned to the diamonds, rubies, sapphires, emeralds, and gold, all fighting for supremacy. She lifted out the diamond heart with the ruby message EVE, I'LL ALWAYS LOVE YOU upon it. It was so exquisite, she sighed with that certain touch of pain that can come when beholding something perfect; and then, with an acute thought of the imperfection of the love of the giver, she returned it to its place.

Suddenly she had a short, sharp pain. She felt faint and a little squeamish. She crossed to the bed and lay down upon it. She must have fallen asleep, for she awakened to a light tapping upon her door. Thinking it must be Stephanie with her evening meal, she called, "Come in!"

The door fell ajar and John Stuart's frame filled the doorway. She sat up in surprise. She had expected to leave tomorrow without seeing him. Fear shot through her. What if he knew of her plan? Then he spoke, and she realized he knew nothing of her scheme.

"It is Christmas Day," he began, his voice low and controlled. "I believe you asked to be allowed to go to the chapel?"

It was true, she had asked Mrs. Smith this morning, but had been told that John Stuart was not at home, and since then, she had heard no more.

She lifted herself from the bed.

He noticed how thin she looked, and a small tremor of sorrow rippled through him. He had overheard Thelma saying she ate very little. He attempted a smile; his look was almost gentle. "I am sorry to have disturbed you."

"You do not disturb me. Yes, I did ask this morning if I could use the chapel, but I was given to understand you were away from home." She sounded polite, distant, but her pulse raced. How she prayed he had come to put things right.

He advanced a few steps into her room. He made an awkward gesture with his hand, explaining, "I was out riding along the river to see if it had risen anywhere. All the rain, you know . . . I must keep watch."

She nodded. "Of course."

"This afternoon I . . . worked down at the stables. I was unaware of your request until my return here this evening."

"It doesn't matter."

"Yes it does, and of course you may use it. Eve, I told you, you are not a prisoner here. The chapel has been unlocked all day for those who wish to go in. You did not need to make a formal request. You simply could have gone there. It is inside the park; you needed no one's permission."

"But I did not wish to embarrass you by visiting at a time when others might be there."

"Really?" he replied, and for a second, his expression softened. At the change, a ray of hope shot through her.

Then other thoughts rushed to his mind, and unable to help himself, he made a sneering sound. "I would have thought that embarrassing me was a knack of yours."

Her chest constricted. "Oh, John Stuart," she answered dejected, and closed her eyes.

There was silence between them.

He took another step into the room, and before he could check himself, was saying, "Do you go to pray for the forgiveness of your sins?"

She walked away from him around the bed to the far side of the room, where she stood silently looking out into the gloomy light. It appeared to have stopped raining.

Now he felt sorry he had spoken so hastily, and as she turned from him, he actually lifted his hand toward her. There was a sickening torment inside him; he wanted to take her in his arms, to hold her, to kiss her, even to forgive her, but his arm dropped without touching her, and she was unaware of his intention or that momentarily he had lifted his hand.

When she turned back to him, she looked tired and ill. What was the point in prolonging this? John Stuart hated her. It was obvious.

"I am tired, John Stuart, tired, do you understand? You seem to have come here simply to mock me. Well, this is your house, and as that is so, this is your room, and you can be here if you wish. But as for me, I was happy with the understanding that we would lay eyes upon each other no more."

"Yes, I can see you were." Now his voice was bitter.

"And as the chapel is open to me, and it seems you are not ready to leave this room, I shall go, and you may stand here as long as you like."

She came forward and picked up her pelisse, which lay on the end of the bed. As she did so, he said, "Why? Why have you done all this?"

She stood at the end of the bed facing him. Her eyes dominated her face.

The air was heavy with tension, yet for a moment both seemed to see wavering in the other's expression, like a breaking down of feelings, and for the space of a second, both thought they saw love and forgiveness. Then Eve thought she was mistaken, and she replied deliberately, "I have done nothing to be ashamed of."

"Nothing to be ashamed of?" he echoed her. "Nothing . . ." He shook his head. "Oh, Eve . . ."

She brushed passed him into the corridor beyond.

He moved to the door, intending to call, "Eve, come back!" But he only got as far as "Eve," and then in frustration he shouted, "Damn you!" smashing his hand upon the open door.

"And damn you!" came her answer, flying back to him from down the corridor.

He stood in the doorway watching her disappear. He was in torment. He smashed his fist into the door again, and into his head came Thelma's words, *Eve is a good girl, she is innocent. I saw her the day after the attack by that . . . that man. She was in a dreadful state. . . . I was here. You were not. . . . I don't know what that terrible person told you and Joe, but it was a lie. . . . I was here. You were not. . . . Eve is a good girl.*

With a sad, tortured sound, he strode away.

An hour later, when Eve returned across the lawn toward the western side entrance of the house, the rain was still falling, and so, too, was the night.

Only a few hours more and she would be gone, and what happened here on Mayfield would not concern her. It was then she felt a powerful pang of tenderness.

Mayfield!

Her eyes filled once more, but this time with sentimental tears for this beautiful retreat that had been her home. In the twenty months of her marriage, Mayfield had insinuated itself into her heart. Never had she loved anywhere like this. She walked back across the veranda and, resting her hands on the rail, looked through the rain over the magnificent lawns and neat garden beds that lay in geometric patterns in front of her, their magnificent summer blooms cheerfully tinting the failing light with color. She looked to the left where the rows of stately pines grew along the carriageway, and to the right, where above the park and over the cool, green beeches along the perimeter, she could see the black ranges in the distance. With the rain and the clouds, the whole scene, darkening swiftly as she stood there, had an energy of its own. The very atmosphere of Mayfield would move any heart. Oh dear, yes, she did love this place! It was no use to pretend she wouldn't miss it; she always would.

When she returned to her rooms, the lamps had been lit.

It was Mrs. Smith who brought her dinner. Eve was disappointed. She had expected to see Stephanie for the final time.

"Now, Mrs. Wakeman, ye yerself knew she was to have the day off."

Eve sighed. "Please, Mrs. Smith, I would like to see her. I have a gift."

Mrs. Smith yielded. "Oh, of course, then I shall send her to ye directly."

Eight minutes later Stephanie's gentle rap sounded on the door.

Eve rose and came toward her. "Merry Christmas, Stephanie." She handed the girl a small package.

"Oh, ma'am," she began as she opened it, "you shouldn't have."

Inside lay a velvet pouch, and inside the pouch, a delicate bracelet of jet and pearls inlaid with gold. The girl had never thought to own anything so lovely, and tears welled in her eyes. "Oh! I . . . It's so beautiful and . . . genteel."

In a spontaneous movement, she hugged her mistress, and Eve, glad for the opportunity to hold her, hugged her, too. Then, abashed, the girl drew out of the embrace, saying, "Oh, pardon me, Mrs. Wakeman, I . . . ought not to have done that."

"Fiddlesticks, Stephanie dear, I wanted to hug you just as much as you did me."

"Really?" the innocent girl asked.

"Really," said Eve. To prove it, she hugged her again.

"Would you like me to stay with you, ma'am? I'd be as pleased to be here with you."

"No, that won't be necessary. I would like to think you were enjoying yourself. What are the staff doing? You usually have a treasure hunt in the park on Christmas night, don't you?''

The girls eyes lit up. ''Mmm, yes, we do, and we were going to as well, except it's been canceled as it's raining again. Mrs. Smith got special permission from the master to use the ball-room, and we're going to have a dance and a party. It's about to start.''

Eve actually smiled. ''And there you were, my dear Stephanie, about to give all that up to stay here with me. I wouldn't hear of it. Off you go. Have a lovely time, and wear your new bracelet.''

Stephanie left smiling. She would miss Stephanie. The girl had been a dear companion.

Later Eve sat and wrote a parting letter to Thelma. She had desperately wanted to tell her friend she was leaving, but had decided against it. It was not a long letter.

Christmas Day 1864

My Dearest Friend Thelma,

I cannot stay here, estranged from John Stuart. The sadness of each day is such that I think I will die if I do. Instead I go to those others who love me.

Thank you for the help and care you have shown me. And thank you for believing in me. Seldom have I met a heart so true as yours.

Perhaps one day we will meet again. I do truly hope so, with all my heart.

Do not worry about me. I feel quite sure of what I do. I will always remember you with love.

Your friend,
Eve

She would place it on her pillow when she left.

She must wake before three o'clock. What if it was raining? Please, Lord, don't let it, she prayed. Her heart beat quickly. She looked across to the large ormolu clock on the table by the bed. It was well after eight. Six hours to go.

She slept fitfully, constantly waking to check the time, and on each occasion she listened for the rain, and gratefully sank back on her pillow when she heard none. She felt she was not strong enough to ride in the rain.

But she must get away, she must.

At twenty minutes after the hour of two, she rose, and walking to the doors, looked out into the night. She could actually see the moon filtering through restless clouds. It gave her heart.

She dressed, and soon she sat for the last time at her polished rosewood dressing table and brushed her hair in the lamplight. She studied her reflection for a moment. She looked older. Her face was much thinner, and the lines near her mouth a little deeper. Then suddenly thinking of what might be the reaction to her empty bedroom in the morning, she smiled. She looked better when she smiled, so she smiled again, determinedly. A moment later she rose and took up her pelisse and carpetbag.

She felt mildly unwell, but not as bad as she had so many times in the past weeks. Taking a deep breath, she went toward the door.

As she opened it, a whim took her and she turned back. Crossing to the dressing table, she took up a delicate gold and jade ornamental hair comb that lay there. It was the olive-branch pin John Stuart had given to her in the first days of their marriage. She often wore it in her hair when she twisted her curls up on top of her head.

Swiftly she went to her davenport, and taking paper, pen, and ink, wrote, ''John Stuart, I'm sorry.'' She placed it on her pillow alongside the note for Thelma, and put the olive branch on top of it. As her fingers left the hairpin, the hurt and sadness at John Stuart's rejection rose like something solid in her throat. She gasped and coughed, then took some water from the jug at her bedside.

She looked around. A tear welled over her lid as she spoke aloud. ''While I am leaving you, John Stuart, I did love you and I am sorry for all that has happened and I do wish you peace.''

In eerie fashion her words seemed to hang in the air after she had said them. The great long drapes over the windows, the massive bed, the tall pieces of furniture, the shadows between, all seemed to echo her words like living things. ''Peace,'' they seemed to whisper, ''peace.''

She took a last look at the room where her husband had loved her so many times, before she closed the door behind her, moved silently down the passage, and out of the sleeping house.

TWENTY-ONE

Rescued

Alan Fletcher was awake.

At the door of the solid wooden hut, he stood cross-legged, leaning against the frame. His arms were folded and he surveyed the night.

Above the treetops he watched a moody sky of rain-laden clouds pushed by a fast wind. It was cool tonight, cooler than it had been since the winter.

It was the small hours of Boxing Day, and he had found it hard to sleep, as he had for the last few nights. He had been restless and troubled. But then, Lawless had gone yesterday to visit Patricia June's grave, alone; Alan had always accompanied him before. It was a regular habit at Christmas ever since the girl had died exactly five years ago. No doubt, subconsciously, he was worrying about Lawless, yet too there had been discomfiting thoughts of her, the woman who was married to the richest, most influential man in the land.

He thought of her often, and he had lain awake thinking of her tonight, until, impatiently, he had risen, and not wanting to wake Daniel, who shared his small room, had donned a jacket and gone to meditate by the kitchen door. He stood now wondering about her. But why? He had no answer to that. On many recent nights she had walked in his dreams, with her soft brown eyes and tempting mouth. He dreamed that they rode together on Freedom and that he did not take her home but brought her here with him to Treehard.

He brought his hand up across his eyes as if to smooth away the thoughts. He could hear Sam and Jordan both snoring in their bunks, and he moved across the veranda to where his long fingers clutched the rail.

Tomorrow he and Jordan would ride down to Lyon's Tavern on the road south of Cowra, and there they would wait for Lawless to join them. Lyon's Tavern was one of the safe houses. It stood alone slightly off the main road in the area known as Wattamondara. Henry Lyon was an ex-convict, a big, good-looking, congenial man, who, like many of his ilk, disliked the "traps." He was a man of his word, and when he knew Alan was coming, which was not often, as Alan did not frequent the same places regularly, he would close his doors to other travelers. Alan had agreed to meet Lawless there for Jordan's sake. He was the youngest of them and looked forward to visiting the taverns, particularly Lyon's, for he was sweet on Bridget, one of Henry's three handsome daughters.

It was a rarity for an argument to occur at Treehard, and when one did, it was usually because Jordan wanted to go and meet a woman more often than the others thought was wise. When Jordan calmed, he would look over to Alan with his big eyes, so reminiscent of Patricia June's, as if desperately seeking his leader's exoneration, and Alan would invariably nod and smile and things would calm. After all, Jordan was young; it was understandable.

When they did visit a safe house, it was one of a very few that Alan knew had a reliable owner, one like Henry Lyon.

In early 1859, when Alan's band were making their way south, he and Lawless, alone out hunting, had come upon two men screaming fit to bring the gum trees down around their heads. It had been at the bottom of the Sugarloaf mountains. They had rescued both men, and in the years since Henry Lyon and Edmund "Bluey" Williams had become their friends.

Thus, Alan had arranged to visit Lyon's Tavern tomorrow and to drink of the spirit of Christmas with the few trusted folk who would be there. Nevertheless, these days there were more and more troopers abroad, and it was a concern to him that he had to frequent safe houses at all.

Daniel and Samuel never accompanied them on these visits. Both preferring to stay in the seclusion of Treehard. Daniel, at seventy, was as sprightly as ever, and his mind was as keen as when they had met, but he caught chills easily and had a chronic cough.

Alan folded his arms and moved slightly against the railing. Straight ahead of him were the stable and the outhouse currently

under construction, and behind them towered the tall iron-bark
gums, which dotted the top of Treehard Hill to the edge of the
escarpment, where the land dropped dramatically away to the
valley floor. For perhaps another fifteen minutes he watched,
before rain began to fall, and giving a final glance to the gloomy
scene, he returned to bed. It was to the sound of Daniel's voice
that he awoke.

"Come on, sonny. Breakfast is on the hob, and tea's made to
your liking. It's nearly the hour of six, and you are to meet our
Lawless by half past nine of the clock."

As it was a ride that could take close to three hours, he rose
immediately.

"I'm coming, Danny; I'll be but a minute."

Half an hour later, Alan and Jordan, wearing leather capes
and wide-brimmed hats, mounted their horses, which Samuel
held steady in the lightly falling rain.

Daniel sat watching on the veranda. He was feigning offense
at not going with them, and called merrily, "So it's an old man
I am now, eh? Leave me home with me keeper and all, is it?"
He pointed to Samuel.

Samuel laughed. "No, old man, it's not that. It's ye be too
unfit to go out in the rain."

Daniel stood in mock insult, arms akimbo. "What's that?
Unfit to go out in the rain, is it? I'm telling you, Sam, my man,
I'm from Ireland. I was weaned on rain."

"All right, Dan," his small friend called, stepping away from
the two riders, "and we'll have more fun here at Treehard with
our bottle of rum than they will have with the like o' foolish
women botherin' them down at the tavern."

"That's true enough," agreed Daniel. "And you two, remember, if you are coming home tonight, be back by nightfall,
otherwise we will understand that Bridget has enticed Jordan,
in which case we shall see you definitely by nightfall tomorrow."

"Don't expect us tonight, mateys!" shouted Jordan as he entered the passage behind Alan.

Samuel laughed.

"I'll not breathe easily until they're back," said Daniel to
himself as he turned and entered the kitchen.

The riders wended through the trees, undergrowth, and scrub
outside the secret passage and soon were riding down the long
slope to the Cowra road. The track was slippery and muddy in

parts, but it was mostly a moderate incline, so water did not lie on their path.

As they gained the road, Lawless was already on it, but some sixteen miles to their north on the near side of the township of Cowra, heading toward Lyon's Tavern at Wattamondara. He had skirted Cowra, even though it was early morning on the Boxing Day holiday. It was second nature to him to take no risks. He, too, wore a flowing leather cape as protection from the rain and wind. Waterloo, his horse, was making slow progress up a long, muddy incline, where rainwater lay in the unsealed road. He was looking forward to reaching Lyon's. The guverner would be there, and they would enjoy the indulgence of a shot of whiskey in their stomachs, and their feet resting in a warm, dry room.

He hated to leave Alan, even for a day. Alan was the voice of sanity in his life. He was like his mother, father, and own best friend. And to think the guverner was gentry! Yes to think that he, a child of the London slums, could count such as the guverner as his life-long friend. He often thought there should be a better word than "friend," for Alan was so very much more.

Always before, the guverner had accompanied him to visit Patricia June's grave. That was the guverner all over! But somehow, this year, Lawless wanted to go on his own, and he had decided this would be the last time he made his Christmas pilgrimage. For yesterday, as he stood in the lonely valley named Coral Way where she lay, he had experienced an odd sensation. He felt he heard her saying, "Lawless, love, ye do not need to stand over a pile of dust and pretend it is me. I am livin' in yer heart, love, that's where I am. Remember me, but let me go; don't mourn." And he had nodded and replied aloud, "All right, Patricia Junie, I understand."

Yet he was pleased to think she had a proper resting place, and he smiled sadly as he thought of the inscription carved on the tablet of stone.

> *Patricia June Drake*
> *Sweet Wife of Arnold*
> *Sister of Jordan*
> *1835–1858*
> *"O for the touch of a vanish'd hand*
> *And the sound of a voice that is still"*

Alan had given him the lines of poetry; they had been written by someone Alan had actually met at home in England. Lawless had carved the inscription lovingly, for it said what he felt so exactly.

And to think they had gone and found Treehard only a few months after her death! How she would have loved Treehard. Just as Swiftie would have! He missed Swiftie, too, and yet it was twelve years soon since he had gone.

And dear old Daniel and Sam, what true mates they had been for so many years, like brothers, they were really . . . and Jordan. He sighed as he thought of Jordan. After all, he was Patricia June's brother, and he was part of the family now.

And so Lawless mused on such things as he rode along, his wide-brimmed cabbage-tree hat tilted forward against the wind-blown rain. He had met no other traveler on the road since he had left Mike Dunphy's safe house at dawn, and so it was with surprise that he lifted his eyes to the brow of the hill to see a single rider coming down the gradient toward him. Always cautious, he reined in his horse and looked right and left and then behind the way he had come.

No one in sight. He moved Waterloo forward at a walk.

The lone rider was perhaps a hundred yards away. It looked as if the person leaned forward in the saddle. Then he realized with surprise that it was a woman! She wore a rain-sodden cape, and her hood had blown back to reveal her wet face.

They drew abreast and he hailed her. ''Good morrow to ye, mistress. Where are ye headed on such a terrible day as this? It be no weather for ridin' out, I'm sure.''

The woman focused weary eyes upon him, a glazed expression in them. Her sodden hair fell limply to her shoulders, her whole demeanor one of fatigue. She replied in a voice that held a soft accent. For a moment he thought she was Irish, then he realized it was a sound he had never heard. He wondered about her. Somehow, he fancied he had seen her before.

She tried to sit up straight as she replied, ''Good morrow to you, sir. Can you tell me how far I've yet to ride to reach the village of Cowra?'' She sagged slightly forward again as she finished speaking.

''Ah, ye be almost there, m'lady. It's less than a mile straight ahead.''

''Thank you, I must get there soon. My journey has taken me longer than I thought. I must . . . catch the nine-o'clock mail coach north.''

"I'm sorry, but ye won't be catchin' the mail coach north, mistress."

"Why . . . yes . . . I must."

"But it has not run for days, ma'am. The road is greatly flooded just south o' Blayney. I know this, for I've been north of Cowra myself, since yesternoon. The mail has not been goin' through these three or four days since, and they don't know when it will be runnin' next again, for there's heavy rain continuin' to the north, and floodin' in many places."

Now the woman did sag completely forward. Then she rallied, regaining herself, and slowly forced herself upright.

It was at that moment, Lawless recognized her. Mrs. Wakeman!

He had seen her only once in his life, but he was sure. What in heaven's name was she doing here alone, and bedraggled like this?

"Oh no!" she whispered.

Lawless did not know what to do or what to say. She looked so ill. He felt he wanted to console her somehow. Involuntarily he put his hand out to her and almost touched her before he withdrew it, and said, "Mistress, you seem unwell. You need help. Go on and find the doctor. There is one in Cowra."

She was frightened now and sick. But she must rally, must go on. She had to find strength. She looked at the traveler; he seemed kind. It was good just to be with someone after the hours of lonely riding in the night and wind and rain. She forced herself to think clearly. "Can . . . you tell me then . . ." she began falteringly, "if the afternoon coach runs? The one that goes south to the township of Young? Does the flooding affect that one, too?"

Lawless did not know for certain, but he thought there was no flooding yet to the south, so he replied as best he could. "It might be runnin', mistress, for there's no floodin' there, as I know of, yet ye'll recall that the southern coach only travels but three times in one week. I fear ye shall not be findin' it runnin' today."

"Oh dear," she began. Her alarm was obvious. "I must get away. Perhaps there will be someone I could pay to take me where I need to go. Yes, perhaps."

In this, Lawless knew he could help her. "If it's private transport ye be wantin', mistress, why, old Ronald Richards will carry ye in his dray, I'm sure; for a shillin', he'll take ye to the moon, they say. But he will be unable to take ye north; there's no hope o' that.''

"Oh, thank you. Where will I find this man?''

"All in Cowra knows him. He lives in an old place hard by the food and grain store.''

She lifted her eyes to meet his. Even in her tormented state, she could recognize the sympathy in the man's face.

"You are very kind. Do I know you?''

"No, m'lady, but I know who ye be. And it's strange and all for the mistress of Mayfield to be abroad in such a sorry state.''

"Yes, I suppose it is. Thank you. The man's name was Mr. Richards?''

"Yes,'' Lawless called after her as she edged her horse forward. "Ronald Richards, but do see the doctor first, Mrs. Wakeman.''

He watched her for a minute or so, wondering if he should accompany her. If he did, he would be late, and the guverner would worry. His loyalty was to Alan, not to some rich woman in trouble.

He urged Waterloo forward and continued on.

Christmas night had passed slowly for the master of Mayfield. He had eaten his dinner and conversed with his guests and smiled good night to them on the veranda, then seen them to their vehicles in the wet air; all this with his mind elsewhere. When his guests had driven away, he remained unmoving in the darkness.

Since seeing Eve that afternoon, he had experienced conflicting emotions. The fact was, he had been feeling the conflicting emotions since that ghastly day in the garden bower, and this afternoon had only increased his torment. He had been startled this afternoon to see how sick and pale Eve looked. He had not expected that. It worried him.

And he had recalled many things. Today when he had said to her, "Why have you done all this?'' she had replied, "I have done nothing to be ashamed of,'' in the firm, deliberate fashion of the guiltless. He had not meant to say things to her in the way they had come out of his mouth. He kept seeing her drawn face, and he felt sorry for her. But there were other things that disturbed him greatly, and for well over a week, he had been reflecting upon them.

Lately he had spent many long, unhappy hours looking out on the December night skies and remembering.

When he had been convinced by Lake, he had come home a changed man. He had confronted her in the garden only to condemn her. The sick import of what Lake had told him and his recollections on the homeward ride had festered inside his head until he was consumed by belief in her guilt. But enough time had passed now for him to analyze Lake's words. To analyze Lake.

When he tried to remember what Eve had said in her defense, he realized he had allowed her to say little, and that which he did remember concerned him more and more. On that terrible day, his hurt and rage had rung in his ears so that he didn't allow himself to really hear; but now he thought he recalled some things like, ''John Stuart, all this is a dreadful mistake. . . . It was not I who lived with him. . . . There is much I have to tell you. I should have told you, long ago.'' It all danced crazily around in his mind. And there was something else, but he could not recall it at all. It floated at the edge of his awareness, but he had not listened. That was the part which troubled him most.

So he stood alone near the veranda railing, deep in thought, hardly feeling the dampness or the chill. Finally he sighed unhappily and turned with leaden footsteps to enter his home.

He was sitting in the long drawing room, staring at a painting of his father, when the watch rode through in the rain at midnight. He could hear the music drifting from the ballroom. He smiled wanly. The celebrations of his Mayfield folk were still going on.

A minute or so later he heard sounds on the front veranda. He stood and walked to the hallway door. The ornate white cedar front door opened, and there stood Joe in a wet leather cape and hat. He removed them before he crossed the threshold.

''Joe, what brings you back?''

''You, m'boy.''

John Stuart looked at him questioningly.

''I am troubled. What is going on in that head of yours?''

''Ah, Joe, how well you read me.'' He turned, and the older man followed him back into the drawing room, where they sat facing each other. It was a full minute before John Stuart spoke, and Joe sat watching him, arms folded on his chest.

''I have been thinking, old man, constantly thinking, if the truth be told. I am confused and unhappy.''

''I know.''

''Joe . . .'' He lifted his hand in a weary gesture. ''I remember your words when Lake accused Eve. You said, "He's lying. She would not do such a thing. She is a good woman."

The older man nodded. "Yes that is so, but now . . ."

"No, Joe, that's just it. *Now* I find I feel differently from *then*. I have deliberated over and over on it, old man. I am . . . that is . . . I find I really want to believe that I have made some sort of . . . mistake."

"Dear boy, there is no doubt that Lake was a no good."

"Yes, he was."

Joe unfolded his arms and leaned forward. It was time to remind his boy of those things that had convinced him. "But what of the 'proof,' m'boy, the things that pursuaded you at the time? What of Eve's meetings with the bushranger?"

Once again, John Stuart fell silent for a long time. They could hear the wind on the veranda outside, and the sound of the last waltz at the Christmas party floated from the ballroom through the corridors to them.

"I saw her this afternoon, Joe, and while I don't understand any of it . . . I do know how . . . I feel about her. I want things to be all right again. I want to believe the meetings with the bushranger . . . were accidental, Joe."

"And what of Adelaide in 1857—the year she said she was there?"

"She said she went there to visit only."

"And Lake's words that she encouraged him to make love to her?"

"I do not want to believe them."

"And the name 'Clare Herman'?"

"That I do not understand, but now . . . tonight, I realize I want to hear what *she* has to say about it."

Joe was silent for a time. He was studying his boy, thinking and studying. "And what of the baby? What of that?"

Again, John Stuart did not reply immediately. He sat looking at his hands, deliberating. When he brought his eyes up to Joe's, he answered, "I don't know, Joe. I am so confused."

The older man bent forward to pat John Stuart's arm, a furrow of concentration between his eyes. "Look, m'boy, you need answers, and the only person who can supply them is your wife. We should sit here no longer. It is clear how you feel. Go to her now, this minute."

"No, old man. When I saw her this afternoon, I was shocked. She was so pale and sickly. It is far better she sleeps the night through."

"Then go to her first thing tomorrow, and I shall bide impatiently to hear what happens."

An hour later, John Stuart was still awake, peering through his window at the restless clouds tossing the milky moon in the sky. He drifted briefly into sleep and was awake again to hear his turquoise and enamel bedside clock strike thirty minutes after the hour of two in the morning. Some time later, he drifted once more into a heavy sleep. It was in that last moment, before he slipped into his dreams, that he imagined he heard a door open and close somewhere in the house. . . .

He awoke to a gentle tapping on his door and a bleak Boxing Day morning of wind, chill, and rain; he sat up in bed.

Timothy entered. "It is a quarter to eight o'clock, sir. Are you all right?"

"Eight o'clock!" He jumped out of bed. "Great heavens, Timothy, I have never slept in so late in my entire life."

Five minutes later, he strode down the corridor to the bedroom he had shared with Eve. There he hesitated. Momentarily all the considerations rushed through his mind again . . . his mother's actions, and how in Eve he had seen her . . . all of Lake's arguments . . . Eve's meetings with the bushranger . . . the name Clare Herman. But the overriding feeling that swamped all these things now was his love for her. Oh, yes, he loved Eve Herman Wakeman. Loved her with a deep, abiding passion. He wanted to hear what she had to say, wanted to believe in her.

He knocked gently and opened the door.

"Eve? Eve."

The big draped bed was empty.

Swiftly he went through the dressing room to the large sitting room beyond. "Eve?"

Would she be outside? Surely not, it was raining heavily. Nevertheless, he went out onto the veranda and down into the walled garden. Where could she be? She would not be out walking in the park in this weather. A feeling of apprehension rippled through him.

He returned to her bedroom. It was then he saw the things upon the lace pillow. His face went white. There was the olive branch hairpin he had given her, and underneath it a paper with "John Stuart, I'm sorry" written on it, and an envelope addressed to Thelma.

He stood there rereading the words. *John Stuart, I'm sorry . . . John Stuart, I'm sorry.*

He ran down the corridor and through the massive hall out onto the veranda in some vain hope that perhaps he would see her in the park, but all was quiet except for the constant pattering of the rain. Down the steps and across the park he ran, leaping small flower beds and avoiding bushes. He threw open the Larmers' back gate and bounded up the steps and into the kitchen, calling, "Joe! Where are you?"

Leith looked up in amazement from where he knelt on the hearth lighting the fire, to witness the master looking like a bedraggled Neptune dripping water onto his clean slate floor.

"Mr. Wakeman?"

"Quickly, Leith, where is Mr. Larmer?"

The man sprang to his feet, and was soon calling, "Mr. Larmer, come quickly, sir, the master is here."

Joe had been up since five o'clock, when it had begun to rain heavily again. Shortly before the hour of seven, he had ridden down to the Lachlan. He had come home and changed and was about to go up to the big house to tell John Stuart that the river was rising around the crossing. He had just put his foot on the top step to come downstairs when Leith shouted to him. He came swiftly down and was met by John Stuart at the foot of the stairs.

"M'boy? What the devil is it?"

Leith diplomatically withdrew.

"Joe, Eve is gone!"

Joe listened calmly as John Stuart explained what had occurred.

"Ah, m'boy, this is serious."

"She left this for Thelma." He withdrew the envelope from inside his wet corduroy jacket. "Where is she?"

"She is just now dressing, what with it being a holiday morning. I shall get her."

As Thelma came down the stairs, she saw John Stuart. "Oh, my Lord, you are soaked. Please change your clothes. I shall get Leith to—"

"No, Thelma, that can wait. Read this, please, if you will."

She opened the envelope and read the letter. With a deep sigh she handed it to John Stuart. "You read it for yourself."

He did so. He lifted his eyes to Joe's and shook his head as he handed it to the older man.

"So there we have it. She goes to 'those others who love her,' the Reverend Billings?"

"Yes, m'boy, I would guess so."

Thelma said nothing. She could see that John Stuart was distraught. It was patently obvious that he had changed his mind about Eve, and she thanked God for that.

"Now, m'boy," counseled Joe, "Eve could not get far in this dreadful weather. What do you wish to do?"

"Ride after her, of course. I must bring her back."

His bewildered eyes found Thelma's as Joe's arm went around his shoulders. "All right, son, we shall find her."

When Lawless rode into the backyard at Lyon's Tavern, he smiled. Freedom and Jordan's horse were tethered there. He dismounted, and before he gained the threshold of the door, Alan was there to meet him on the small veranda. Their hands met and held in a sustained clasp.

"Journey go well?"

"Aye, guverner. The ride up was wet on and off, but the ride back has been wet all the way."

"Come on then, lad, inside and warm yourself; Mrs. Lyon has provided us with dry shirts and an excellent toddy that no doubt shall interest you."

Lawless extricated himself from his water-soaked cape and hung it on the pegs alongside the others, then he took off his boots and followed Alan.

Inside, a ring of happy faces greeted them.

"Good on yer, Lawless!"

"Happy Christmas!"

"Gudday, Lawless. Sit 'ere. We've kept the seat dry 'specially for ye."

Soon Lawless, in dry shirt and stockinged feet, sat down next to Alan. Opposite sat Mr. Henry Lyon, side by side with his wife, Edna, a pretty-faced, corpulent, middle-aged woman with gray hair, and beside her, their old ostler handyman, Felix. Behind them, near the bar, stood Jordan with his arm around Bridget Lyon, a small girl with a voluptuous body and wide mouth. They were in conversation with her two sisters, Christina, who was tall and captivating with smooth olive skin and long hair, and Marilyn, who was slender with dark, sensuous eyes and a teasing smile.

"So this is the company then?" asked Lawless.

Henry shook his head. "Not quite; we're expecting Bluey."

Bluey Williams's real name was Edmund, but in colonial fashion he was called "Bluey," an inexplicable but accepted nickname for red-haired men. Edmund "Bluey" Williams was of that remarkable ilk whose word is their bond, and who remain loyal to those they care about all the days of their lives. Bluey not only owed Alan his life, but idolized him. He was an itinerant odd-job man, who plied between Bathurst and Young and lived in a wooden hut a mile in the bush to the north. He had the knack of making people laugh, although he was an imaginative and thoughtful man. It was through Bluey that Alan learned about police movements, information that had kept himself and his men out of harm's way in the last few years. He was also a trusted go-between.

"Good," answered Jordan as he squeezed Bridget. "It's a while since we've seen old Bluey, isn't it, boss? I'll be glad to see him."

Alan nodded, and Christina said, laughing, "Me, too." She was Bluey's girl.

Henry Lyon patted his wife on her massive arm. "How about some music, my sweet? Get the party started."

She nodded, and soon the first chords of "Paddy Finley" rang out on the piano. Jordan and the girls joined her and began to sing.

Lawless sipped his toddy and settled back in his chair. "It was a long ride I made."

"Indeed," agreed Alan, "it was, and it's good to see you here. I do not like your making any long journey alone."

"Aye, I know that, guv." Then a thoughtful look passed over Lawless's face as he took another drink. "I had a strange meetin' on my way here, guverner."

"And what was that?"

"Oh, no trouble or nothin'. It was real odd, though. I was comin' up the long, slow rise that leads to Fagin's Pass just south of Cowra, ye know the place, when I see a woman, alone on horseback, ridin' toward me from the other way. She was all wet and she looked mighty tired and sick. She stopped by me and spoke with an accent I've scarce been hearin' before. Now, she wants to get to Cowra and the northern mail coach. I told her it wasn't runnin' because of the floods, and she carries on all upset-like. Then I realized who it was, guverner. I mean I was truly amazed and all, for it was Mrs. Wakeman, Mr. John Stuart Wakeman's wife. Well, I can tell—"

"What?" broke in Alan. "She was alone, you say? And ill?"

"Aye, that she was. Talked like she had to get away from somethin'. Quite queer and all, really."

Edna Lyon was playing another boisterous tune on the old

upright piano. Jordan, Bridget, Christina, and Marilyn were rocking in time to the music, and Felix was beating his hand on the bar. Henry Lyon, whiskey in hand, had joined the merry-making.

Lawless looked up in surprise when Alan took hold of his arm. "Lawless, lad, you say she was going to Cowra? Are you sure? Are you certain she was alone?"

"Why, yes, guv. I told her to be seein' old Ronald Richards, said he might drive her where she wanted to be goin'. But I don't understand what it means to ye, guverner. What does it mean to ye?"

Alan dropped his friend's arm and confounded him now as he said, "Fagin's Pass and into Cowra. Yes, all right. It's rain-ing, the roads are slow. If I leave now, possibly I'll be there in an hour and three quarters . . . two hours."

Alan stood, and so did Lawless . . . in bewilderment.

"What is it, guverner? What's wrong?"

For reply, Alan took his friend's arm again and led him out onto the back veranda. The others were all enjoying themselves singing and laughing. Marilyn's deep hazel eyes were the only ones to notice them leave. Outside, the rain was still falling and the air was still chilly.

"Lawless." Alan looked him in the eye. "Listen carefully to me. This is of great importance. I have no time to explain to you now, but I will, lad, I will. That woman is . . . it is hard to tell it simply. Suffice it for me to say that she means something to me. That I have seen her . . . more than once since we held up the coach. I did not tell any of you, for I believed it could have no meaning in our lives. But now . . . tell me again. You are sure she was alone and sick and she seemed to want to catch the coach north?"

"Aye, that is so. I saw no one at all but herself all the way here."

Alan bent down and began to pull on his boots.

"In that case, I be comin' with ye."

"No, Lawless, it is a celebration in there. Jordan has been looking forward to it for weeks, as no doubt the others have. You must stay and wait for me."

Rarely had Lawless ever questioned a decision of Alan's, but he did so now.

"Guv, this lot here are goin' to have a fine time whether I be stayin' or no. But where ye be goin' is dangerous territory. Now, I don't understand all this ye be sayin' about the woman, and that's as may be. What I do understand is she belongs to May-field, and she'll be drawin' more attention than a bushranger at Government House. There may well be all sorts out lookin' for her now, for all we know. Maybe even police involved. Ye'll be needin' a second string to yer bow, goin' chargin' off like this. And me, I'm that second string.''

Alan smiled. ''You are right, of course, Lawless, and I thank you.''

Just then, Marilyn's soft voice sounded from the doorway. ''Oh, no, Alan! You are not leavin'. You just got here.''

''Sorry, lass,'' Alan replied. ''But there is something we must do, and immediately.''

''What?'' she asked, looking up at him with ill-concealed affection, her hand on his arm.

Alan touched her gently on the chin. ''Now, Marilyn Lyon, you know better than to ask such a thing.'' And with that, he moved inside.

Edna stopped playing as Alan approached the piano.

Jordan looked down at Alan's boots. ''Going somewhere, boss?''

''Yes, Jordan, though it doesn't concern you, lad. You stay here and enjoy yourself.'' He looked around their faces. ''Lawless passed a traveler on the road who is an old friend of mine and might need help. We are going to ride out now and assess the situation. We will be back.''

Jordan had never before heard the boss mention any ''old friend,'' but he was too taken up with Bridget to consider it for long. He squeezed her to him and kissed her cheek. ''No need to hurry, boss.''

''Take no notice of him, Alan,'' said Marilyn, looking provocatively up at him. ''I'd like you to hurry.''

Alan smiled at the girl and touched her hand in farewell.

''You wait here, Jordan. We will return for you, understand?''

''Absolutely.''

''And bring Bluey back, if you see him,'' instructed Christina.

Henry Lyon came close to Alan. ''Sorry ye be leavin', mates. Is there danger in this?''

Alan shrugged. ''It is best you know nothing, Henry.''

''Aye,'' agreed the publican. ''Now, that's true. But be careful.''

They made good time to Cowra, considering the doggedly falling rain and muddy, sodden roads. When they entered the wide, deserted street of the township, it was fourteen minutes before noon.

On the way north, Alan spoke little. He had thought to explain himself to Lawless and then changed his mind. Time enough to do that if they found her and it became necessary. How dearly he had wanted to see Eve Wakeman again. How often she slipped into his mind and made him yield to reckless thoughts of her, sometimes so rash that he could almost feel the movement of her against his body in the wind. It was absurd. Any feeling for her was absurd, and he had told her so that day in the Bathurst park. Not only was she married and beyond his reach in every way, he was a bushranger; yet here he was now, this very minute, riding north in wind and rain to find her.

They crossed the decrepit wooden bridge that lay over the Lachlan and soon were riding up the gentle slope of the main street of Cowra. There was little to see. After all, it was the Boxing Day holiday and it was raining. They soon found Ronald Richards's small dwelling, but no one answered their knock.

Alan looked at Lawless, a frown between his eyes. ''She would have reached here hours ago, but let us go to the coaching office anyway.''

''Aye,'' agreed Lawless, ''but in a township this small, there's nary a person who won't know she's been here.''

''Keep a ready eye on the street; we don't want to be surprised by men we have no wish to meet.''

The search began and ended at the waiting room of the coaching office, for as they mounted the steps to the interior, they saw figures moving inside. Umbrellas were open and dripping near the doorstep, and three small children played noisily at flicking the water on one another. Two men and two women stood with their backs to the door, while a fifth was kneeling down in front of a woman lying along the wooden seat.

As they entered the small, dank room, they could hear some of the conversation.

''Oh dear, she's out to it. What will we do now?''

''We shall just have to carry her to my place in this rain and all.''

The people turned around, sensing the presence behind them.

Alan saw immediately that it was Eve who lay upon the bench. He felt his pulse quicken as he swiftly estimated the situation. He spoke immediately. ''Ah, there is Mrs. Wakeman. We have come for her. Ridden on ahead. The carriage comes behind.''

His educated voice made them all regard him with respect. One of the men stepped forward, and Alan noticed the reversed white collar of a priest. The brother's face broke into a smile. "Oh, good," he said, "we are so pleased to see you. So, er, you are Mayfield men?"

Alan did not reply but came forward to the group. Obviously Eve was unconscious. He moved through them, and lifting her in his arms, turned back to leave.

The priest looked alarmed. "Now, now! Surely, er, Mrs. Wakeman must wait for the carriage. She is unconscious, has fainted. It amazes me how she got here in the first place!"

But Alan was already moving to the door.

"Hey, wait!" shouted one of the men. "Where is Mr. Wakeman?"

"He follows in the carriage," Alan called over his shoulder, not stopping but continuing out of the building and down the steps.

The group inside followed. It was still raining, which kept the women and children back, although the priest and the two men came out. "Earlier we sent to Mayfield for Mr. Wakeman," the priest called. "Andy Leeman rode out. Did you come across him on your way?"

Alan passed Eve to Lawless and mounted Freedom. Then Lawless lifted Eve up into his arms, and he enclosed her inside his cape, protecting her.

"Hey, did you see Andy Leeman, I said?"

Looking down, Alan called, "No, he must have gone by the north fork."

"Gawd, guverner," said Lawless quietly, "what the devil does that mean?"

At that moment, one of the women called from the door, "Mrs. Wakeman's purse bag!" And Lawless was already running back for it.

"Hey, er, steady on," called the priest, coming across the footpath. "I really don't think this is proper. Mrs. Wakeman should wait for the carriage. She is obviously quite ill." Now his voice was stern. "What sort of instructions did, er, Mr. Wakeman give to you?"

By this time, Lawless had moved around to Waterloo, and Alan answered, "Don't worry, sir. You can be sure we shall take care of her."

Lawless had now mounted.

The brother opened his mouth to speak again, but without waiting for further consultation, Alan spurred forward.

Brother Michael turned to his companions. "Now, er, what on earth do you make of that? I do, er, wish Mr. Wakeman were here."

But they were not to see Mr. Wakeman until well after one o'clock in the afternoon, in company with Andy Leeman, whom he had met on the way into Cowra.

A few hundred yards south of the rustic Cowra bridge over the Lachlan, the road turned left and ran through a dense growth of white cedar trees; their ancient limbs almost touching across the road. There was partial shelter beneath the thick arms of the boughs, and below the widest, Alan brought Freedom to a halt. Lawless reined in beside him.

Eve's face had been exposed to the falling rain, and it had served to revive her. She moved slightly in his arms and opened her eyes. In her weakened state she could not believe that it was Alan who held her. She thought she must be dreaming. Tears broke over her lids and ran down her face to mingle there with the dampness from the rain.

"It cannot be," she whispered.

"Ah, lass, don't weep, please," he said gently. "Listen to me. Listen carefully. We found you in Cowra, and now we have a long ride ahead of us, no matter which point we travel toward, but there are some questions I must have answered."

"I don't understand . . . I've been . . . all alone. How can it be you?"

"We found you in the coaching office. You had fainted. I don't understand how you come to be alone and ill in Cowra. Should you not be at home? Am I now to return you to Mayfield once more?"

"No! Oh no!" she answered, gathering her strength. "It's *away* from Mayfield I've ridden all through the night. I was on my way to . . . to Father in Bathurst. I must get to Father."

He was in a dilemma. Nothing was clear.

"Do you mean the minister?"

"Yes . . . Father. Reverend Billings. I must go there. I must."

"All right, lass, I see you are spent and ill. Worry not. You can tell me all about it later. But I must repeat, should I not return you to your husband and your home?"

She moved in his arms and turned her face to his. "Oh, no,"

she said again, "you are . . . my friend. Do not do that. I will not go. Oh, please, I will not."

"I cannot take you to Bathurst, lass. The roads are covered with floodwater, and there seems to be no abating in the weather. We may not be able to make that journey for weeks."

Her voice became a little stronger, more resolute. "Then . . . then I will stay with you until I can get through."

Alan did not answer straightaway. He was deciding his next move.

Lawless looked across to him, and there was doubt in his eyes. "Are ye thinkin' to take the mistress home to Treehard, guverner?"

"I don't see we have an alternative, Lawless. We cannot leave her here. Would be best if we could find a doctor."

Understanding the situation, she straightened a little in Alan's arms. "I do not want a doctor. I can make the ride." She looked over at Lawless and seemed to see him for the first time. "Why, it is the traveler I met on the road."

"Aye," answered Lawless, "it's me. I'm Lawless, yet my real name be Arnold, and when I told the guverner here we had met, it was promptly we were on the road again to find ye."

Vague comprehension dawned, and she managed to smile. "Bless you, thank you."

Alan put out his hand. "Give me your blanket, lad. We had best move on, but first we shall protect her face from the rain."

"Where are we heading, guverner?"

"We will head for Bluey's. It's a long ride for her, but it's the nearest safe place."

As they rode on, she settled in his arms. She did not feel ill anymore. She felt almost euphoric. Some prodigious marvel had brought her to him, and that was all that mattered.

John Stuart had mobilized swiftly and ridden in haste from Mayfield with Joe and Jack Hennessy by half past eight in the morning. Joe was worried about the Lachlan rising, and he and Jack Hennessy were concerned about their return ride, when they might be unable to get through the lowlands around Cowra and back to Mayfield, but they knew that Eve was the most important thing on John Stuart's mind.

The ride into Cowra was slow and difficult, much harder even than when Eve rode through a few hours before, for the constant rain had brought down mud slides in places. And while John Stuart pushed them hard, and even harder after they met Andy

Leeman, it still took them five hours. As the sodden group made their way through the mud to the coaching office, John Stuart's heart was beating swiftly. She was here. Thank heavens for that. Now he could talk to her, let her know how he felt, take her home.

They dismounted and leaped up the steps into the waiting room.

Empty.

Andy Leeman pointed down the street. "They probably took m'lady to the doctor's home, sir. They waz discussin' doin' that when I left here."

They made their way along to Dr. Bell's home. There were no Cowra-ites on the street, for the rain was coming down in sheets. Outside the wooden cottage covered in climbing vine with a small sign over the door reading, GORDON BELL, M.D., they reined in. Mrs. Bell was in the parlor, and through her front windowpane, saw the arrivals. She hurried to the door. Her small veranda was crowded with the frames of the four riders.

"Oh, my Lord! Mr. Wakeman, sir. What brings you here?"

"Isn't my wife here?"

The woman looked mystified. "Oh Lordy. I . . . But isn't she with you by now?"

Joe took off his rain-soaked hat and stepped a touch closer. "Mrs. Bell, we have been of the understanding from Mr. Leeman here that you were taking care of Mrs. Wakeman."

"Well, we were, sir, down in the coaching office, until your riders came in and took her away."

Joe and John Stuart looked at each other in amazement. Joe responded, "Riders? What riders?"

Now the doctor's wife was completely perplexed. "You mean you didn't send them?"

"What the devil . . . ." began the master of Mayfield.

Joe lifted his hand to John Stuart's shoulder; it was a calming gesture. "Mrs. Bell," he said, "could we come in? And perhaps you can tell us what exactly has occurred. Is there anyone else who knows anything?"

"Oh, why, yes, Brother Michael was at the coach waiting room, too, and Dick Barovill and—"

Joe turned to Jack Hennesy. "Get the priest and bring him here, Jack."

Ten minutes later, they had heard the entire tale from Brother Michael.

John Stuart sat in silence, his brow furrowed, his right hand up to his chin. He had asked no questions during the interview and had left it entirely to Joe. To Mrs. Bell and the priest, he appeared quite calm, but the truth was that his heart thumped crazily against his chest, and his mind was in sick turmoil.

Joe reiterated, "And so they rode out to the south, you say?"

"Yes," Brother Michael agreed.

"And the man that did the talking was educated?"

"He was. Spoke like nobility, you might say. Not fancy or—priggish, mind, but upper-class. Now, that was really why we let them take Mrs. Wakeman." He looked to John Stuart. "We, er, could not stop him, really. He just whisked her away."

John Stuart's expression did not change, except for the subtle hardening of his mouth.

Joe went on, "You have not exactly described what the man looked like. Would you please do so now, Brother?"

Brother Michael peered seriously at them from behind his spectacles. He was the lonely representative of his church in Cowra, an outlying district of the parish, and very small. He was a kind, principled young man, and while he accepted that this was none of his affair, it all confounded him. He answered Joe's question, seeing again in his mind's eye the man who had taken Mrs. Wakeman away. "Well, he was taller than me, perhaps five feet ten or eleven, clean-shaven, firm jawline, sun-browned, and er, Dick Barovill, who was with me, pointed out that he had singular eyes."

John Stuart stared straight ahead, expressionless.

Joe nodded thoughtfully. "And the man with him limped, you said?"

"Yes, he did. I noticed that; didn't you, Mrs. Bell?"

"Oh, yes, I did."

"And Mrs. Wakeman was unconscious the entire time, you say?"

"She, er, certainly was; she had fainted before they came in the door."

It was at that point that John Stuart rose from the sofa and extended his hand to Brother Michael. His pulse was still racing and his mind was leaping from strange conclusion to strange conclusion. "Thank you." He turned to the door.

On the small veranda with the rain pattering loudly on the corrugated iron roof, they joined Jack Hennessy, who pointed to the horse tethered to the railing. "We found Betsy, sir."

Joe nodded and faced around to John Stuart. "What do you make of all that, m'boy?"

Now there was real pain in John Stuart's face. Both he and Joe were thinking alike, thinking of the description, thinking of the only man they knew who fitted it. Neither of them spoke his thoughts aloud; after all, Jack Hennessy was standing there. But both knew what was going on in the other's mind.

"What do you want to do, son?"

"I must follow. They've got my wife! Let's go."

"But, m'boy, that was two hours ago, and with the heavy rain, we have little hope of—"

"Joe, I must."

Joe said no more. They jumped down the steps and rode into the rain.

It was over two long hours later on the road south of Cowra, in the mud and slush, that Joe put up his hand and halted. "M'boy." He turned to John Stuart, rain dripping off the brim of his hat. "I am now very concerned for those at home. This rain is constant. The bridge at Cowra was close to overflowing when we rode over it hours ago. We need not cross it again to get home, but it was a sign of how quickly the Lachlan is rising."

"What are you saying, Joe?"

"M'boy, we have seen nothing to indicate that Eve is still on this road. She could be anywhere." He leaned over and took hold of John Stuart's arm. "I do not want to be the one to say we are riding in a futile search, but . . ."

John Stuart looked at Joe. The older man was waterlogged but ready to persevere. He turned in his saddle to Jack Hennessy, who sat in the rain, water running in rivulets down his cape to flow onto the mud below his drenched horse's body. The horses were obviously tired, and while they had been fed and watered in Cowra, it had been a long, difficult ride. Of course, these two men would continue on with him, he knew that, but it was unfair to them and unfair to those who depended on them at Mayfield. But, by all that was sacred, his wife had been abducted.

"Perhaps I should go on, and you should turn back."

"I will not allow you to go on alone, m'boy."

He was torn. He had a pressing duty to those at home. He looked up at the leaden sky. This downpour would certainly continue. And Joe was right, Eve could be anywhere. Anywhere. And he knew exactly where those others were to whom he was also responsible.

He felt a nauseating lurch in his stomach. When he spoke, his voice quivered slightly. "We return to Mayfield," he said, pulling Diomed's head around.

TWENTY-TWO

On the Ride to Treehard Hill

Edmund "Bluey" Williams's eccentric little two-room shack could be missed easily by anyone who didn't know it was there. It stood well back from the road through a thicket of small trees, its rickety veranda nestling against a clump of shrubbery. Beyond it, an outhouse for the horse and dray leaned on an angle against part of a picket fence covered in vine.

For the first few miles of their ride from Cowra, the heavens had shed only light rain, but now, as they arrived, it was falling heavily.

Lawless climbed down first, calling, "Bluey! Bluey!" as he did so. There was no reply. He came around Freedom to help Eve down. Then Alan dismounted. His arms were stiff from holding Eve and he rubbed them now as Lawless helped her onto the veranda.

Eve, weakened by the strain of the last twenty-four hours, leaned heavily on Lawless. "Bluey? Bluey?" he called again.

Alan walked ahead and pushed on the front door. It swung open, although there was obviously no one at home.

"No doubt he's at Lyon's," Lawless decided.

They divested themselves of their capes and boots and helped Eve inside, where in a number of places Bluey had placed large buckets to catch the water from the leaking roof.

As Lawless returned outside to shelter the horses, Alan gently steered Eve to a chair. "You must take off your damp clothes and lie down while we are here."

"I . . . but . . ." she began, looking up at him, embarrassed, even in her lethargy.

"Come on, lass, your shoes are sodden, and the rest of your clothes are damp; it's no time for modesty." He knelt at her feet as he spoke and relieved her of her shoes. Then he began to unbutton her jacket. She rallied and, pushing his hands away, said, "I'll do it. You are right; I must lie down."

As she undressed, he turned away and found an ancient kettle and some firewood. He busied himself building a fire and putting the kettle on to boil. When he turned around, she was lying under the blanket on Bluey's iron cot with her eyes closed. "Good girl," he said, taking her clothes close to the fire to dry.

There was a gentle knock at the door, and Lawless entered. He crossed to the fire with their waterlogged boots and stood them near the grate.

"A cuppa, guverner," he said, looking across to Alan. "That's what we all be needin', a sweet, strong cup of tea."

"You are right, lad, that will help rejuvenate us."

Lawless managed to find some salt beef and damper that had been put safely away from the ants, and they ate some of it when the tea was made. Afterward, Eve lay back down and fell quickly into a deep slumber. Both men, too, were fatigued. They had ridden hard and long in cold, wet weather, and they soon fell asleep also.

Bluey's hut became silent, the only sound, other than the rain on the iron roof, the steady breathing of the three fugitives in the shelter of the interior.

An hour later, Alan awoke and noiselessly crossed to where Lawless lay on a blanket by the primitive hearth. He knelt down and touched him softly. Lawless's eyes opened instantly, full of the alarm of the hunted man woken, but it disappeared as he focused on Alan's composed expression. "Nothing to worry about, matey," Alan said quietly. "All's well. But one of us will have to ride to Lyon's to tell Jordan and inform Bluey we are here."

"I'll go," said Lawless, rising. "I'm ready."

"I would not have you go, lad, except that it is probably better I stay here with her."

"I reckon, guverner." Lawless smiled.

Alan continued in an undertone. "There is no need to bring Jordan back here. I've decided to bide here the night, and he will be happy to stay where he is until tomorrow."

"Aye, he would be counting on that, I'd say."

"And you stay there, too. Don't bother to come back in this weather. Just make sure you are both here by eight or nine o'clock on the morrow."

"I'm not concerned about that. I'll take the news to Jordan and Bluey, and I'll return to ye here, guv."

Once more Lawless attired himself in his long leather cloak and wide-brimmed hat, and pulled on his damp boots.

Alan walked with him onto the veranda. It was time to be honest with his faithful companion. "Lawless, lad," he said, taking his arm, "it's now I should explain to you about her."

"Orr, guverner, it isn't necessary. I be seein' for meself, ye be attached to her."

"Yes, Lawless, that is true, but you have a right to know more, for it seems we will be in company with her for a time."

He took a deep breath and began to speak of the complexities he did not understand himself.

When he had finished, he said, "It would have been wrong to burden you with any of this before."

"Now, since when could anythin' ye say be a burden to the likes o'me? Ye be the rare one and all, guverner."

Alan pulled affectionately on the brim of Lawless's hat and smiled. "No, rare is what you are, my dear, true friend. Rare is what you are."

He watched Lawless mount up and leave, a strong, capable bushman, the sun-browned color of health. As Alan lifted his hand in a wave, he remembered the bone-thin young man with pallid complexion who had been sentenced for pilfering a meager living in the London slums. The horseman, who now disappeared among the trees, held no resemblance to that street youth of long ago.

Alan sighed. Life was not just; he knew that. Life was mysterious, and rarely just. If there were equity, the mild, steadfast man who had just ridden away would have been born of happy parents in a prosperous English town, made a career for himself, and sired sturdy sons, never knowing the shock of prison or what it was to run a hunted man.

And the others?

Diminutive Sam would have lived an even, settled life, a farmer on the Surry Downs. Swiftie would not have died, shot in the back at twenty years of age, but would have turned his wit and sensitivity to some lucrative trade. Daniel, dear Daniel, would never have been pushed to the brink in times of poverty.

His sweet Audrey would have lived, and they would have grown old together in tranquillity. And Jordan? Fate had dealt harshly with him, too. If he had not lost the farm his parents had worked all their lives, he never would have held the grudge that led him to horse stealing, and thus placed him outside the law. And he? Alan Fletcher? If life were fair, where would he be? He would be at Long Moss House surrounded by the daily chores among his tenant farmers, embroiled in the pleasant destiny of English country life. In his peaceful moments, he would be writing of the sea and reading his books. But if the truth were told, he would rather be here, living this strangest of all existences, with the knowledge that trust and faith flourished in the hearts of the men who were his comrades, and yes, here . . . with her asleep inside.

The only thing he would change would be the deaths of Swiftie and Patricia June.

He turned and went back inside. She still slept. Her face was drawn and tired, there were shadows under her eyes, and her pale, full mouth looked almost too large in her thin face. He wondered what had happened to make her look this way. The blanket had slipped down from her shoulders, exposing her hand, which lay across her breast. He lifted the blanket back, and as he did so, noticed a cut on her forefinger. He was touched with tenderness for this woman whom he felt he knew. He smiled down at her.

The fire had gone out. The hut was chilly again. He stacked more wood in the fireplace and relit it. Then he sat at Bluey's table considering what his moves should be over the coming days. The sound of the rain on the iron roof was soothing, mesmerizing. All was peaceful when into his thoughts came noises, distant noises heralding riders.

He looked sharply up and across to Eve. She still slept.

His hand went automatically to his rifle as he rose and moved swiftly to the door and on to the verandah. Through the wet trees, he could discern the shadows of the coming figures. They were riding very fast, almost too fast, in the thick scrub. It appeared to be only two: Lawless and Jordan. What was Jordan doing here?

"Trouble, guverner!" shouted Lawless as they reined in.

"We'd best get out of here, and fast, boss!" added Jordan.

"What is it?"

"Bloody countryside is crawlin' with traps," answered Jordan, dismounting and arriving on the veranda in one leap.

Lawless followed, enlightening Alan as he came. "There have

been two robberies, guverner, one in Warraderry yesterday at Christmas noon, the other at the Redley station, near Lansdowne, this morning. They be blamin' Dan Morgan for the one in Warraderry—''

''And the bastards are blamin' us for the other,'' broke in Jordan. ''Seems they wore masks, and a policeman was shot dead. They've called in every bloody mounted trap for forty miles. The troopers are headed this way. Bluey thinks they might come here.''

''All right, lads, now calmly,'' answered Alan temperately, ''let's have the story as best you know it. How did you hear of all this?''

''From Tinker, guverner, Bluey's mate. He came precise at the time I arrived at Lyon's. Isn't that right, Jordan?''

''Yes, he'd been in the tavern north o' Greenthorpe this afternoon when five troopers rode in and surrounded the bloody place; seems somebody told the traps *we* were supposed to be there celebratin'. They questioned everybody, and then Tinker left, ridin' the eight miles cross-country on the back bush track by Gorman's farm to Lyon's.''

''Right, then now we have it,'' answered Alan calmly. ''I gather Bluey didn't come with you in case the troopers were here first.''

''I reckon he don't want to be caught up in it,'' reasoned Jordan.

''And neither he should be. He is a first-rate friend, and we are fortunate in that. So they are laying the blame upon us for shooting a man?''

Lawless grimaced. ''Aye, and we have never done no such thing; it's disgustin'! What'll we do, guverner?''

Alan's mind had been racing. He was thinking of her, inside. Where could he leave her so she would be safe? The bush was sodden and cold, with no prospect of improvement on this day. Troopers might ride abroad to catch a bushranger in the dusk of a warm, starry night but he did not know of a trooper in New South Wales who would be willing to chase a bushranger into the inky blackness of a chilly, wet night, but night was still a couple of hours away. In any case, they had best move out.

''We will depart from here as soon as we can,'' Alan answered as Lawless and Jordan extricated themselves from their capes.

Then Lawless looked to Alan. ''I haven't told old Jordan about the mistress, guv. For there were no time, ye see. He bein' ready to hightail it over here as soon as Tinker dropped his news.''

Jordan looked to Alan. "What's that?''

Alan unconsciously stepped back to bar the door. "A friend, a lady you met once before, is in the hut, Jordan. Mrs. Wakeman."

Disbelief spread across Jordan's face. "What?''

"It's a tale I'm not going to relate to you now, lad," Alan went straight on. "It's enough to say she is exhausted and sick, and I find myself accountable for her. I will explain it all to you when we arrive at Treehard."

Jordan was confounded. His mouth dropped open. Mrs. Wakeman of Mayfield? The boss had gone completely bloody mad!

He looked to Lawless to have this absurdity contradicted, but all Lawless did was to nod his head.

Jordan's arm went out to move Alan aside to see for himself, but Alan stayed him. "She's asleep. I am going now to wake her. Then we shall wait out here while she dresses. After that, we make the ride to Treehard. Is this all clear to you, Jordan?''

"No, it isn't, boss, not bloody clear at all."

"It will have to be sufficient for the time being."

"Come on, then, Jordan, matey," said Lawless, putting his arm around the big man's shoulders and dragging him back a step. "We'll wait here and give the horses a drink, eh?''

"Bloody strange!" commented Jordan as Alan went inside and shook Eve gently.

"Lass, wake up now. I'm sorry, but we must depart this place."

Coming out of her slumber, Eve felt weary and her bones ached, but seeing his face above hers brought a smile to her mouth. "Why, it's you," she said, trying to remember how it was they were together.

"It is possible we may need to ride on soon," he said quietly. "Are you well enough?''

She nodded.

"Are you sure, lass? For it's raining outside, and I cannot promise you a comfortable ride."

"I'm sure!" she said with more determination in her voice than she felt in her heart. She sat up. "After our last meeting, I had feared we were no longer . . . friends."

He looked searchingly at her for a moment and shook his head. "Ah, lass. Yes, I remember. But that had naught to do with whether we be friends or not. Don't you understand?''

"I . . . I think so."

He smiled at her reply. "I shall stoke up the fire and leave you to don your clothing."

"Where are we going?"

He had already moved to the hearth, and responded with his back to her. "To my home, the place we call Treehard, in the hills some hours ride from here."

She was holding the blanket up to her breast. "I fear it is not proper," she said softly.

He heard, and after a heartbeat, turned around. It was anything but proper. She, a married woman of the gentry, going with him, a wanted outlaw, to his hideout in the hills.

He had really known all along it could not happen.

He would send Lawless and Jordan on home ahead; that way, he would not endanger them. He would take her to Lyon's Tavern. After all, it was an inn, even though one of dubious reputation. At least that had overtones of propriety. He would not tell her of the police in the district.

"You are right, lass," he answered; there was the tiniest hint of disappointment in the sound. "It is quite improper, and I am more the fool for ever suggesting it. Forgive me."

"What do you mean?"

"There is a tavern but a mile or so down the highway where there are rooms for travelers. I will take you there, and you can wait for the flooding on the roads to subside. Afterward, you can continue your journey to Bathurst. It is more seemly."

Fright rose in her. He was thinking to abandon her! "Do you not want me with you? Am I too much trouble?"

"Ah, lass, you confuse me. No, I am not thinking anything such. I want you to keep your reputation. This way, I believe you can. It is more discreet."

She gave a small laugh. "My friend, there is much of which I have to apprise you. I have no reputation to keep." Sadness crept into her voice. "But if you prefer to be without me, then of course, I shall go to this tavern. I would not have you in peril for my sake."

Alan came back the few short feet between them, and there was a note of severity in his tone. "Now, lass, I would not deposit you at any tavern and leave you to yourself to ease complication in my life. I am ready to do whatever you wish, but you must not trifle with me."

"Oh, I do not! I do not!" she repeated adamantly. "Forgive me, I do not trifle with you. You see, I cannot go back to Mayfield. There is much I must explain. My marriage is over. Dreadful things have happened. I thought to go to Father and Mother, for I believe that being with them is best . . . in some ways. Then the rain and . . . I cannot believe that you found me. It is a miracle.'' Here she hesitated and dropped her eyes from his before adding, ''I feel greatly comforted. I hope you do not think me bold.''

For answer, he smiled and shook his head.

She took a deep breath and expelled it along with the words that now rushed from her. ''Please take me to this Treehard. Do not leave me alone in a strange tavern. When the floods go down, I can make the journey to Bathurst; you need but get me to a mail coach. I would not add to your worries for any length of time.''

She had said what she truly meant, and he knew it.

''As that is your decision, you must prepare to ride on at once. My men and I have knowledge that police troopers are in the district.''

''Oh no!'' she said.

''I will leave you now. When you have dressed, we will journey on.''

As he closed the door, she rose promptly. She still felt weak and very light-headed, but better than she had when they arrived here.

Her clothes were dry and she was just pulling on her bodice when a sharp, stabbing pain seized her. It took her breath away. She bent forward, grasping herself, and made a small, moaning sound. This was not good; they were in a hurry. There were police in the district. Oh dear. She must hurry . . . but the pain. She eased herself onto the bed. Oh dear! Oh dear! Come on, Eve. Half a minute lapsed and the pain passed. She righted herself and pulled on her dress. To think he had been going to take her to the inn, with police in the area. . . . The risk to him, the terrible risk! She was buttoning the dress across her breast when a knock came at the door, followed by his voice above the constant sound of the rain. ''Are you prepared in there now?''

''Yes, please enter.''

He came in, followed by Lawless and a very big man who looked at her intently, disbelief in his eyes.

Alan waved his arm in the direction of the fire. ''Jordan, Lawless, but a minute by the flames to warm yourselves, then we shall douse it and be on our way.''

As the two men moved the short distance to the hearth, he

spoke again. "Mrs.—" there was just the slightest hesitation after this word "—Wakeman. You already know Lawless. I would like you to meet Jordan O'Day."

"How d' you do?" Jordan said.

"Pleased to meet you," Eve replied.

Alan lifted her small bag of possessions. "We must ride in tandem again, and it will be cold and wet for the next few hours."

He smiled to reassure her, and once more she experienced the inexplicable happiness that came over her in his presence.

On Bluey's worn and pitted table, Alan left two gold sovereigns.

As they moved to the door, the wind gusted with such force that the tin roof rattled and the water came through the leaks in streams.

Outside, Jordan hesitated. "The night's goin' to worsen, boss. Do you think the stinkin' traps will be searchin' in this weather?"

"It depends who leads them. Most wouldn't, but a man such as Rutherford Blake would, if he thought to capture us. Until nightfall, there is some risk."

"Aye," spoke up Lawless, "Batty Blake would ride on in the rain as well. He's got a score to settle with us."

"You are right, Lawless," agreed Alan. "And unfortunately there will be mud slides on the old trails we would normally use, so we must ride by the open road a little way."

As they came up to the road through the gloom of the bush, Alan called, "we will need to keep sharp watch both in front and behind. You, Jordan, lad, ride ahead until we reach our track and keep a lookout. If you see anyone, return to us immediately. You, Lawless, keep a constant watch behind us, for I cannot turn in the saddle as you can."

The rain was steady, enduring and perpetual. The temperatures were the lowest for a summer day ever in the colony of New South Wales. The sodden band rode on. They covered the mile to the turnoff near Lyon's Tavern without catching sight of any other travelers. As they passed the corner that turned down toward the inn, Jordan scouted ahead warily, but all was deserted.

"I bet they're having fun down there," he grumbled to himself. "And here I am, out in bloody weather as is not fit for a dog!"

Jordan had been lying with Bridget in the little room behind the bar when Lawless and Tinker had arrived, and he was not one who suffered well interruptions to his lovemaking. He got to do precious little of it as it was. Blast the traps! And now, being blamed for a raid you didn't make! And hours of this riding in the cold and wet. Christ, what a man had to put up with! The bloody injustice of it all.

And what the devil was going on with the boss and this Wakeman woman? Now, that was something unbelievable. Takin' her to Treehard, no less! Oh well, no doubt the boss knew what he was doin'. Anyway, he hoped so. Seemed like nothin' but trouble to him.

He rode on, his thoughts tumbling over one another. No doubt that was why he did not see the troopers until they came out of the dip in the ground not a hundred yards in front of him: five police on horseback pushing their mounts at a goodly pace through the mud and pebbles of the road, in the moody evening.

He froze, pulling back hard on the reins of his horse.

Alan and Lawless were behind him back around the bend and could see nothing yet. Too late to ride back and warn them!

This was the first time in his life outside the law that he had ever been taken unawares. Alan had always delivered him from such as this.

His mind went blank. He could not think. And so he panicked. With panic came frantic, startled movement. He pulled his horse's head sharply around and plunged into the bush. The animal jumped forward and almost lost its footing as it staggered on the waterlogged brushwood of the bush floor. But it righted itself, and with Jordan holding on for dear life and spurring him hard, the horse crashed through to the trees beyond.

The troopers had not expected to see anyone on the road this late in the day. After all, it was Boxing Day, and raining. They were tired and had been riding for many hours in fruitless search for the Fletcher gang: first in the bush around Landsdowne and then in a raid, without result, on the inn north of Greenthorpe. Sergeant Samuel had pushed them on through the tiny community of Koorawatha, promising that they would lie up for the night at Kiddley's place, one of the only two inns between here and Cowra, on the Sydney road. And at last the inn was not far ahead, and there they would sleep for the night. They could already taste the rum heating their throats, and they smiled at the pleasurable thought, swallowing it in their imagination, and bringing a little solace to the chilly damp eating through them.

Then, suddenly, as they plodded up over a rise, they saw a man on horseback on the road in front of them, perhaps a hundred yards ahead. To their surprise, at sight of them, the rider brought his horse to a violent stop and then pulled the animal around and lunged into the bush. Sergeant Samuel was the first to gather his wits. "After him, boys!" he shouted at the top of his voice. "Forward!"

Their horses rallied to the touch of their spurs, and his troopers shot forward at as fast a pace as the water-drenched road allowed.

"Halt!" shouted one of them to the swiftly disappearing Jordan and the sergeant lifted his rifle from beneath his leather cape and fired into the air.

The discharge sounded exactly as Alan and Lawless came around the bend into view to see troopers charging toward them.

"Oh Gawd!" exclaimed Lawless. "Oh Gawd, guverner!"

Eve sat bolt upright at the noise of the gunshot, and she felt Alan's body tense.

The four troopers charging through the mud saw the newcomers, and two of them halted while the others continued off the road into the scrub after Jordan.

Alan took it all in immediately. He looked across to Lawless. "Ride forward at the same speed," he said. "We are farmers; I will do the talking. We have been to my parents for Christmas day." He thought swiftly of two names from his past. "Lawless, you are Anthony Miller, my farmhand, and I'm James Trent." His arm tightened around Eve. "Don't be worried."

Seconds later, the two troopers barred the road in front of them while the sergeant, who was some yards behind, rode forward.

"Hold there!" cried one of the police. "Who are you and where are you going?"

In the voice Eve had heard him use in the Bathurst park when Daydee had surprised them, Alan answered, "Afternoon, sirs. We be travelin' south to our farm. Bin to me mother's for the festivities, yet we are thinkin' we ought to have bided home, the weather bein' so blasted sorry."

Sergeant Samuel arrived as he finished speaking. "Who do we have here, Crystal?" he asked one of the troopers.

"They say they be farmers, Sarge."

"Farmers, eh? Well, what the devil are they doin' ridin' out on a day such as this?" He looked hard from Lawless to Alan. "Explain yerselves!" Then he noticed Eve. "Oh! Good afternoon, madam. Such dreadful weather to be ridin' out in, I'm sure."

"That it is," she replied softly, her pulse quickening.

In the silence that followed, Alan spoke. "We bin to my mother's," he explained again. "This be . . . my wife, and my farmhand Anthony." He nodded toward Lawless.

"Gudday," said Lawless.

"And who are you?" asked Sergeant Samuel.

"James Trent at your service, sir," answered Alan.

"Did you see a rider ahead o' you at all? For a man just dashed off into the bush at sight of us."

"Well, I saw your troopers just this minute goin' into the bush. Chasin' a man, eh? Now, I thought at one stage I be seein' a rider, and then ye understand at another stage, I wasn't certain. Did ye see a rider, Anthony?" Alan asked.

Lawless sat staring ahead.

"Anthony!" Alan repeated, turning in the saddle and raising his voice. "Did ye see a rider ahead of us?"

"Oh!" answered Lawless, recognizing his name. "Er, well, in this rain, ye cannot be sure of such a thing; it's hard to tell, and that's definite."

"Ride on carefully, then," continued the sergeant, "for I've reason to believe it's likely he was a bushranger. I hope they catch him. It's gettin' so it's not safe on the roads."

"Aye," said Alan, "terrible an' all, I know. We often say how terrible it be."

"We've been chasin' our tails all day," went on the good-natured sergeant. "The Fletcher gang robbed Redley station early this mornin', and we've been on wild-goose chases all day since. Mind you, this here fellow takin' off into the bush like that gives me heart. Maybe we are closer to them than we thought."

"True, true," said Alan.

"Y'know, madam—" the sergeant looked to Eve "—seein' a lady such as yourself out ridin' so close behind what could have been a robber, now, it's a worry, it is."

Eve smiled. "Yes."

"For weeks we been settin' up for Sir Rutherford Blake to arrive, and then low and behold, the rain. He's stuck in Blayney until the floods subside, and we're down here with all the worries. Ah well," he sighed.

Alan dearly would have liked to know more of Rutherford Blake's impending arrival, but he was concerned that at any moment the two troopers might return with Jordan in their charge. He could not take the chance of being here with Eve if that happened, and if Jordan were actually taken, he could work out some plan to help him afterward.

"We'll be gettin' on, then, Sergeant," he said. "The wife's a little poorly, and this blasted weather be no help in the matter."

"Oh, I'm sorry," answered the sergeant, moving his horse to let them by as he added, "Where did you say it is? Your farm?"

"Down well past Bendick Murrell," replied Alan.

"Oh," spoke up the trooper called Crystal, "near Fetteringham's hut then."

"Farther south."

Before another word was spoken, a gunshot sounded through the trees.

"Hope that was one o' our boys gettin' the lout," said Crystal, looking toward the noise.

Alan edged his horse by them. "Well, good-bye, Sergeant."

"Yes, best you get on," said the kindly policeman. "And get home out of this flamin' weather. Never known so much rain." He looked to Eve and half saluted. "Good evenin' to you then, Mrs. Trent."

"Good-bye, Sergeant. Nice to meet you."

They rode past at an even pace, leaving the three police in the middle of the road, and Eve marveled at how calm Alan and Lawless had remained during the questioning. They were soon out of earshot, and yet no one spoke. It was not until they were two hundred yards away from the troopers that Lawless said, "That blasted Jordan, why the devil didn't he see them comin'?"

"Yes, I wonder," answered Alan.

"And actin' up like that and rushin' off into the bush. He might have been shot! *We* might have been shot."

"No doubt he panicked, but let's hope he was not hit. That would be bad."

"Aye, it would."

"But don't judge him yet, Lawless. We all make bad decisions sometimes. Let us hope he is home and safe when we get back."

"Yes, so I can punch him in the mouth," said Lawless angrily.

"No, lad, I shall do the disciplining. Now, let us hurry on to the track. The sooner we are off this highway, the better."

It was over three hours later when they found out about Jordan.

They had avoided mud slides and continued on through the

merciless downpour, the damp chill biting through their capes. For the last mile uphill toward the entrance to Treehard, they rode in almost total darkness.

Alan was very concerned about the woman in his arms. She was breathing in a labored way and making soft moaning sounds against his chest.

A hundred and fifty yards in front of the trees and rock face that hid their home, they reined in. Lawless tilted back his head, the rain falling in his mouth, as he gave a high, piercing call, indistinguishable from the screech of the parrot. In the distance, two calls came back in answer, to which again he replied.

"All's well, guverner. That was Sam's answer and no mistake."

"Aye, and it makes me think Jordan is already there, for it seems like Sam was waiting for us."

Sure enough, Samuel was waiting inside at the end of the rock passage as they came through in single file. He held a large umbrella in one hand and a hurricane lantern in the other. With his sharp features, lit in the glow of the lantern, he looked like some mischievous goblin. He followed as they rode around to the front of the cabin, shouting above the wind and rain. "Thank heavens ye be here safe. Jordan arrived as bedraggled as could be. He's had the devil of a fright and was not able to tell us what had become of ye. Says we been blamed for a holdup. Daniel and I been worried sick. It's more than a body can take, ye've no idea. And what's all this about a woman?" he scolded.

"Now, now, Sam, hold the scathin' tongue; a lot has happened," Lawless explained as he dismounted.

Alan handed the semiconscious Eve down to Lawless, who then carried her up the steps to Daniel on the veranda.

"Thank the good Lord Jesus, I see you both safe and sound with my own eyes," Daniel said, holding out his arms to help Lawless and Eve.

Sam shook his head as he led the horses away, clicking his tongue and mumbling to himself. "That's all we need, I'm sure, a sick woman. Oh, and not just any woman! We but must be pickin' on the most notable in the colony."

Eve was too weary to help herself. She was aware that she was undressed and put to bed. Her whole body was fatigued, and there was a dull ache in her pelvis, but when the blankets covered her, the warmth of the bed made her rally a little, and she opened her eyes. A sort of strange peacefulness rippled through her, for there was the bushranger, looking down at her. It all seemed quite fantastic, like a dream.

"Will you be able to take a little hot broth, lass?" he asked quietly.

"I will."

When he brought her the soup in a cup, she raised herself enough to drink it. He waited silently. When she finished, he asked, "How do you feel?"

"Weary."

"Then sleep. There will be time for talking later."

He smiled at her, and the sensation of well-being ran through her again. Soon she drifted into slumber.

When Jordan had arrived back to find Alan and Lawless still away from home, he had avoided explaining to Daniel and Sam what had happened. While they had questioned him, all he would tell them was that there had been a robbery for which they had been blamed, that they had run into troopers on the road, and that he had become separated from the others. To their consternation, he added that Mrs. Wakeman of Mayfield had been traveling with them. About that, however, they would have to "ask the boss."

Since arriving at Treehard, Alan had not spoken to him, and he had kept to the room he shared with Sam and Lawless.

When Alan at last ascertained that Eve seemed quiet for the night, he requested that Jordan come from his room, and gathered his men around the kitchen table in the light of the fire and the oil lamp.

"You be needing something warm to eat, Alan," Daniel protested. "Jordan and Lawless have partaken, but you have not."

Alan shook his head. "No, Daniel, food can wait. There are many things I must explain to you, and I will do so. But first there is something else which concerns us all."

Jordan sat surveying his leader, the thick forefinger of his right hand tapping on the scrubbed wooden surface of the table.

The rain drummed loudly on the roof as Alan spoke. "We shall keep our voices low because of the woman. I would prefer to have this talk elsewhere, but there is nowhere else to go. We were on the main road south of Cowra this afternoon when a sergeant and four troopers appeared. You were riding vanguard, Jordan. Why is it you did not warn us?"

Daniel and Sam reacted with surprise.

Jordan's eyes narrowed as he looked down at his hand. He had been waiting for this to come, and it really wasn't fair. When he had left the road in panic, some of the troopers had followed. He charged through the bracken and the branches that caught at him, threatening to bring him down. Luckily, there had been some open country of sedimentary rock after about a hundred yards, and he had made good speed across it. In a sense he knew where he was, whereas the troopers did not. One had discharged his rifle at him. It had near blown his flamin' ear off! He knew he had lost them when, half a mile or so later, he no longer heard their shouts. But he had been mighty scared all the way to the valley that led to Treehard Hill.

And now the boss was angry! Well, Jordan was sorry he had panicked, and doubtless it had put the boss in an awkward position, but Alan had got through, just as Jordan had suspected he would. So what was all the fuss about? No harm had been done.

He raised his big, soulful eyes. There was silence in the room.

Lawless looked accusingly at him.

Samuel looked unhappily at him.

Daniel was not looking at him. His eyes were directed to Alan.

Alan waited. "Jordan?"

"Well, it's easy for you to be blamin' me for what happened, and I'm sorry. But none of you nearly had your bloody head blown off like I did!"

"Serve ye right, indeed," Lawless spoke up, leaning across the table in anger. "Ye damn near had us taken, ye bugger."

"Not so loud, lads. Keep it down." Alan's tone was even. "But Lawless is right, Jordan. The only thing that saved us from a hopeless situation was our companion." He gestured toward the room in which Eve lay. "We said we were farmers, and if we had not been with a woman, I doubt we would have passed by the sergeant so easily."

"But you did," Jordan defended himself. "You're here and unharmed, and I have said I'm sorry." His voice had risen again.

Lawless brought his fist down on the table. "How can ye disregard what ye did? Of course ye should be sorry; ye were supposed to warn us, damn ye!"

"I couldn't help it! You would have done the same!" Jordan cried, standing up.

"I would not!" countered Lawless, jumping to his feet.

"Silence!" Alan's voice was hard. Silence fell.

"Now, sit down." Alan's voice was even again. "I will only say once more for us to keep our voices down." He looked from

Lawless to Jordan. "This is an issue that you, Jordan, seem to be taking too lightly. It is very serious and affects each of us. If we cannot rely on one another, our very existence is placed in even more jeopardy."

Jordan spoke sulkily. "Damn it, boss, I panicked; can't you understand?"

"Yes," Alan said, raising his hand to silence him. "I can. We all make mistakes. You have no monopoly on that. It is not about the panicking that I am speaking. It is quite natural. What I am talking about is reliability. Your job was to watch the road ahead, to miss nothing, and you managed to miss five mounted police until they were nearly on top of you."

Jordan opened his mouth to speak, but Alan went straight on. "Enough has been said. As you earlier observed, we are all here and safe, so this can be the end of the matter. But it *must* not happen again. Understand?"

Jordan nodded.

"Ye be too easy on him," Lawless mumbled.

"Now then," Sam spoke up, leaning forward and patting Jordan's forearm, "come on, me old sod, let's have a tot o' rum."

"A minute, Sam." Alan restrained him. "There is just one more thing I want to say, but before I do . . ."

He stood from the table and went to the door of the room where Eve lay. He opened it gently and looked in. He could see her face in the lamplight. Although her breathing was still labored, she was deeply asleep.

When he returned to his men, his face was solemn. He stood at the end of the table, holding the back of the chair in front of him, considering them for some seconds before he began speaking.

"I will tell you about Mrs. Wakeman."

Eight eyes were trained on him.

"She will stay until the floods on the northern roads subside. Then I shall put her on a mail coach to Bathurst, where she has friends. As you have seen, she is sick. I do not wish to speak at length about my association with her, but you all should know that I met her twice after we stopped the Wakeman coach. Once in the bush some months later, when I was hunting. Enough for me to say, I spent some hours with her and came to know her. I think of her as . . . a friend, and as you must all be aware, she regards me in that fashion also."

"But how is it that she comes to be with ye at all?" Sam asked.

"For some reason, she has left her home . . . and her husband. I know nothing of that, except that it is patently obvious she has no intention of returning. Lawless came upon her on the road on his way to Lyon's. It was sheer chance. We rode back to Cowra and found her."

Lawless nodded. "Aye, she was ever so pleased to see the guverner. She wanted badly to come to Treehard; there's no mistake about that."

"So there you have it," said Alan. "I hope it will not inconvenience any of you."

"Won't inconvenience me," Lawless replied quickly.

"Me either," said Daniel. "Nice to have a lady about for a bit."

"Hope we can trust her," murmured Sam.

Jordan did not speak.

Alan sat down. "Now, where is the food you spoke of, Danny? And that rum of yours, Sam? Let us have them." Then he smiled over to Jordan. "Come and sit by me, Jordan," he said.

TWENTY-THREE
Womballa

The skies were dark when the bedraggled troop of John Stuart, Joe, and Jack Hennessy wended their way into Mayfield Park. They were met at the front door of the big house by Thelma, who had kept watch from the long window in the west drawing room. Tonight, in the wind, rain, and inky blackness, she had seen nothing until the menfolk had ridden right by the window.

"Thank God you are home. Where is Eve?"

"Not now, love," her husband replied. "We could not find her. Let's leave it at that for the present."

Mrs. Smith and a number of the staff materialized to remove their soaking capes and hats and to see to the horses. The weary riders crossed the threshold into the hall to find Stephen Watson and two of the foremen waiting.

"Sirs," Stephen began, looking around their faces, "we fear the Lachlan is rising on both sides of Larmer's Crossing."

As the Cowra road led directly west off the property and Larmer's Crossing was to the south, they had not come home near the river.

Joe answered. "Is there likelihood of it breaking tonight?"

Stephen shook his head. "No, but more'n likely by tomorrow noon, she'll go."

John Stuart looked to Jack Hennessy. "The river cottages?"

"Aye, we'd best evacuate at first light. I'll be getting home there now, Mr. Wakeman."

"Right," said Joe. "It's first morning light we evacuate. Good night."

When Alan sensed there was something amiss, it was during the small hours of the morning. They had all retired early after the anxieties of the day.

Eve was in Daniel's bed, so the older man had set up bedding for himself and Alan in the small fourth room of the cabin, the utility room where they kept guns, saddles, and equipment.

Alan had fallen almost immediately to sleep, but awoke with a start. He lay listening to the rain falling loudly on the roof. What had woken him? He slid down from the makeshift bed on one of the wide shelves that housed the saddles. Daniel slept soundly nearby.

Swiftly he pulled on his trousers in the darkness, and feeling for the lamp that rested on the floor at hand, took it up and went through to the kitchen. In the glow from the dying embers, he lit the lamp. The light revealed Eve's blanket-draped figure in the doorway. She leaned against the frame, gasping and doubled over in pain.

"Oh, lass," he said, coming swiftly to her, "what is it?"

He caught her as she began to crumple to the floor.

"I . . ." She faltered.

He lifted her in his arms, and as he did so, he felt the dampness of her. She was covered in blood!

"Eve!" he exclaimed, using her name for the first time in his shock. "What is wrong?"

He carried her back to bed.

She sobbed now and began to tremble. Her words came almost convulsively. "Baby . . . baby . . . I fear it's . . . miscarriage. . . ."

"Oh, lass," he whispered as he laid her down. "Oh, lass. Is the pain bad?"

She was breathing in gasps, and her words came between the gushes of air. "Yes . . . bad . . . now." Beads of sweat covered her forehead.

"Stay still, please do not move."

He passed quickly into the room where Daniel lay. Shaking the older man from his sleep, he said, "Danny, my friend, the lass is with child, and I fear she is miscarrying. Help me. I need hot water and cloths."

Daniel was awake instantly. By the dim beam of the lamp from the kitchen, Alan saw his eyes grow wide in amazement, but he was up and pulling on his trousers in seconds. "By the good Lord God in Heaven above, another calamity!" Then he asked in an undertone, "Should I be wakin' the boys?"

"No," Alan replied as he turned away.

In his life, Alan Fletcher had faced many fears. Faced them, and in the main, conquered them. His was a natural instinct to accept the untoward, but this plight of Eve's compounded his emotions. Recently, when he had thought of her, he had longed for her physically, and he had deliberately put from his mind her intimacy with John Stuart Wakeman.

But now as he tended her, cleaned the blood away, heard her moaning, barely able to suppress the cries that rose inside her, he was forced into catharsis, confronting all that he had suppressed. And in doing so, he saw that it had no significance.

It was *his*, Alan Fletcher's, hand she held.

His eyes she looked up into.

His strength she drew from.

And, finally, *his* name she cried with the coming of the shapeless fetus.

Her single cry had woken Sam, although Lawless and Jordan had not heard it. He rose and found Daniel in the kitchen heating water.

"Did I hear that woman call Alan's name?" he asked, his eyes bleary with sleep.

"Aye, Samuel, and I'm to be taking this here water in now, for there have been things amiss this night."

"Oh?"

"It seems the mistress was with child."

The frown line between Sam's eyes deepened as Daniel poured hot water into a dish. "And but a few minutes ago, she lost it. Now, excuse me, matey," he said, moving by his friend toward the door, "for I'm helping Alan."

At last, Eve slept.

Daniel had brewed tea, and now, as his leader issued from the bedroom, he handed him a mug.

"You look a tired, laddie."

There was strain on Alan's face and tension tightening the corners of his mouth. "I'm concerned for her, Daniel, my friend. She's as weak as a kitten and has little stamina left to fight."

As Alan sat, Daniel smiled sympathetically. "Ah, lad, I know. She has been through a great deal, and 'twould seem obvious that there was worry and stress in whatever it was that took her away from husband and home." He sipped his tea, then pursed his lips in thought. "Son, this woman may bring trouble upon us. Is she worth it?"

Alan looked hard at his old friend before he answered slowly. "She is worth it to me, Danny."

"Then she's worth it to me," the older man answered. "She reminds me in a way of Patricia June. Now, there was the sweetest angel of a creature. Why the good Lord God in Heaven thought to take her and be leaving some of the ones he has . . . Well, I'll never understand it." He sighed. "Now, this lady we tend has a singular interest for you, my son, and that is why I pray the Lord has the notion to save her for you." His eyes closed momentarily.

He took a deep breath and stretched out once more to cover Alan's free hand with his own. Alan put down his mug and placed his other hand over Daniel's. Finally Daniel added his free hand on top.

There they sat, hands on hands, and no more words were necessary.

For the remaining few hours of the night, Alan slept fitfully in a chair by Eve's bedside. Dawn entered through the cracked windowpane as a melancholy light, revealing Eve's drawn, gray face. He moved to her bedside and felt her pulse. It was feeble, and her hands were clammy. She lay motionless as he felt her forehead. That, too, was moist and sticky. As he knelt there, she opened her eyes. They were bloodshot and glazed.

He remained on his knees, motionless, as she lifted her hand and touched his face. It was a touch of love, unconstrained, and he felt it. There was a tremor in his chest as he noticed the tears run from her eyes.

She saw him through a haze. "Alan Fletcher," she said, and his name was a caress between them.

He whispered, "Fight, lass. Fight. I want you to."

He was not sure, but he thought she said, "No . . ." as she closed her eyes.

And now fear rose in him. He could hear Daniel moving once more in the kitchen. He was always the first to rise, no matter how little sleep he had. Alan guessed it was about six o'clock. He came to a decision. There was nothing else he could do for her. His heartbeat quickened. It was evident, she had been so physically spent before he had found her that now she had no endurance left. She appeared to be drifting into death. There was only one man he knew who might be able to help.

Daniel looked around from the hearth as he came into the kitchen. "How does she come along?"

"Worse, Dan. I think there is little hope unless I can persuade Womballa to see her."

Daniel closed one eye in thought. "But aren't they on the move? Last time I saw any of them was months ago."

"When they are around here, they invariably camp over on the high plateau. I'm going to ride over to see. It is all I can do."

Daniel shook his head. "I doubt that he will come here, even though he thinks the world of you. It'll be the devil's own job persuading him."

"Perhaps, Danny, perhaps not."

An hour later he rose onto the southern plateau, riding as swiftly as conditions allowed.

The man he sought was an aboriginal elder of the small Welba Welba tribe, one of the religious leaders. Alan had stumbled upon the camp four years before while out surveying the territory around Treehard. The aborigines had seen Europeans but had studiously avoided contact with them. They greeted Alan's arrival with shock and fear.

He remembered how Womballa had stood in front of Freedom, shaking his spear in defiance and shouting. When he had not thrown the spear, Alan had sensed his curiosity and for a long time had not dismounted. Long enough for them all to realize he was alone and for some to come from behind the trees where they had run in fright.

Alan had seen aborigines in the settlements. Poor desperate creatures neither Europeanized nor in their natural state. A few others worked on homesteads as stockmen, and they were often used by the police to track down runaway convicts and the like, for they were magnificent bushmen and could follow signs that white men could not see.

Womballa's tribe still existed in the same condition as their ancestors had for five hundred generations. They had come to terms with their environment as no European could ever hope to do. Alan saw them as the great Captain James Cook had seen them almost one hundred years before, ". . . living in a tranquillity which is not disturbed by inequality of condition . . . coveting not magnificent houses but sleeping as soundly in a small hovel as the king in his palace. . . ."

That first day he had been with them, Alan gave them some honey he had collected from a yellow box tree. It turned out to be a most acceptable gift, for it was a favorite delicacy of the aborigine. He remembered how Womballa had marveled at the jar that held the honey, and was as happy to have the container as the honey itself. In the years since, Alan visited the tribe whenever they were nearby, and he continued to bring them gifts. They were seminomadic, but being territorial, they returned to the same plateau two or three times a year. Womballa always remembered him, and so did the others.

Alan had learned much about this ancient race, even though he could see their social and religious disciplines were complex. They were fascinated by ornament, and he noticed that when they were preparing for a ceremonial occasion, the men painted themselves in a diversity of design. In hot weather, both sexes went naked, but in the cool winters, they wore cloaks of kangaroo or opossum skin.

Womballa had learned a smattering of English words and could make himself understood, albeit haltingly, and one of the children, a boy called Odoono, picked up phrases quickly and could chatter away in English quite well.

Womballa's face broke into a grin, showing broken and blackened teeth, whenever he saw Freedom approaching. He and Alan had formed an attachment for each other although his culture was stone age and he had no way of understanding Alan's world. He was an artistic, peaceable old man in touch with the harsh land and the elements, and Alan rode to him now because of the old man's skill with tribal medicine.

Perhaps he could save Eve.

As Alan brought Freedom through the trees toward the place where the camp should be, he felt his heart quicken with hope. A minute later in the weak light, he saw through the drizzling rain the gunyahs that were the bark dwellings of Womballa and his people.

Coming to a halt on the edge of the encampment, he heard the familiar tones of Odoono calling, "Fletcher, he come! Good you see, Fletcher!"

A few pensive faces peered at him from beneath the scant protection of the gunyahs.

Odoono and another boy of nine or ten braved the rain to run excitedly toward him. "Oh, Fletcher," Odoono gabbled, "good plenty, you come, hey?"

Alan dismounted and took the children by the hand.

"Where Womballa, hey?" he asked.

"You come, you come," the boy called excitedly. Then he shouted in his own tongue as he brought Alan toward a lean-to where smoke curled up around the edges. All the gunyahs were on rocky ground slightly higher than the floor of the plateau, so rainwater could drain away.

Alan bent and entered beneath the sheets of thick bark and branches that formed the defense from the rain. In the center of the shelter, Womballa sat by a small fire, smoking a wooden pipe made from a hollowed-out branch. He wore a hat that Alan had given him. His black eyes, under thick, dark brows, welcomed his friend. He blew smoke out of his wide nostrils and nodded, smiling. "*Orana,* Clever Fletcher."

Beside him sat his wife, Datta, who, as was the custom of the Welba Welba, had come from another tribe. She was now an old lady, although Alan suspected that both Womballa and she were actually only his age, possibly even younger. The harsh rigors of their existence aged them quickly and dictated their life span.

Some of his children, with their spouses and children, clustered around him. One of his daughters, a girl of about fifteen, sat clutching a newborn in her arms. She was particularly lovely. Her jet black hair hung in tousled curls across her forehead; her long, black lashes swept her cheeks as she blinked. Her nose was broad but was in complete symmetry with her high cheekbones. Her teeth gleamed white against the deep purple of her ample lips. Whenever Alan saw her, Gray's lines ran through his mind. "Full many a flower is born to blush unseen,/And waste its sweetness on the desert air."

She smiled at him now in welcome, as they all did.

Alan knew some of their language, enough to explain that he came for help.

Interest flickered in Womballa's eyes. Perhaps he found it intriguing that his "Clever Fletcher," as he had designated Alan, would be in need of help, particularly his own. Alan said how Womballa made "good medicine," and Womballa nodded his craggy head in agreement.

Alan explained that in *yargunyah* he had a very sick woman, perhaps near to dying, and that Womballa's medicine was the only way to save her.

Womballa seemed to consider Alan's predicament. He puffed silently on his pipe, then to Alan's surprise, came the question, "This woman your woman?"

"Does it make a difference?"

Womballa studied Alan impassively. Then he handed his pipe to Datta and, folding his arms, said, *"Paluna."*

Alan's heart pounded. "Then she is my woman," he replied.

The old man nodded. "Womballa bring medicine Clever Fletcher woman."

The other elders of the tribe were called, and soon Womballa's body was being painted ritually, while the stones on the floor of his gunyah were also painted with mythological designs.

Alan wished they could leave and be on their way, but he knew the significance of these rites, so he sat waiting in the dwelling of Gumulu, one of the other tribal elders, while the chanting drifted over to him through the sound of the rain. In actuality, Womballa's medicine had already begun, for the ritual painting and chanting were part of it.

An hour later they left. Alan had known the rites to take much longer, and wondered whether Womballa had used his influence to shorten them. He was never to know, for discussion of the myths and ritual of the "dreaming," as it was called, was taboo to outsiders.

Womballa would not ride. He walked and ran beside Freedom in company with one of his sons, Mulgatta, who came to "guard" the elder.

As they neared Treehard, Alan explained that he must give a bird call to his friends to let them know who came. He made the parrot sound as Lawless had when they came home with

Eve, and the replies sounded, telling him all was well and to advance. Womballa and his son burst out laughing at the sound of the cries, for, to their subtle hearing, the noise was nothing like a true parrot call.

The rain had almost ceased on the journey to Treehard, but now as they passed through the hidden passage, it began in force again.

Alan had explained to Womballa that there would be other white men present he had never seen before, as well as Daniel, whom he knew. Womballa pulled on his beard and hung back as Alan dismounted. Sam, in his customary long cape and umbrella, took Freedom.

Daniel waited on the veranda and signaled a welcome to Womballa and his son. The two stood together in their kangaroo-skin capes, their long, thin legs painted with white ocher, their mysterious faces painted blue and white. Water dripped from them, merging the colors. Men out of a timeless place, coming fearfully into modern culture, to help a friend.

"Come please, Womballa, come please, Mulgatta," said Alan, mounting the steps. But only Womballa came.

Mulgatta had come as far as he intended. He had accompanied his father to "Fletcher *gunyah*" as he had been told to do, but nothing would induce him to enter the place.

"Now, the boy cannot be standing in the rain," said Daniel. "It's not proper. He's come so far."

Alan shook his head. "I'm afraid he won't come in, Danny."

Daniel looked grave. "Well, I'm not having him getting wetter than he already is; he looks waterlogged now, he does." And with that, Daniel came down the steps and went to Sam, who was tending Freedom in the stable lean-to. He took Sam's big umbrella, opened it, and advanced toward Mulgatta. "I know you don't understand me, laddie, but I want you to hold this," he said, and placed the handle in Mulgatta's right hand. The boy, quick to comprehend, stood under it.

Inside, Lawless and Jordan had gone to their room, reasoning that Womballa may be afraid to be surrounded by so many white men. And there was no doubt that Womballa did enter the building with trepidation. He even trembled a little to be inside such a construction. He looked upon the furnishings with awe, but even as misgivings rose within him, Alan spoke and thanked him for his friendship and his courage, and the old man managed an unsteady smile.

"This way, my *waminda*," Alan said.

Eve lay as she had when he left her, the dark circles under her eyes even more pronounced, the bones in her shoulder exposed above the blanket.

Alan gestured to her as he explained, "There was a child come. The child was dead."

"The magic strong," replied Womballa, looking around the small room.

"Can you help?" Alan asked.

Womballa did not reply. Instead, he sat on the floor and unwrapped a piece of folded leather he had carried from his camp. Inside were five or six different substances. Alan recognized a small amount of manna, the sugary matter from insects that collected on the leaves of the candlebark tree. There were three large waratah leaves, and what looked like two black bean pods and two dead flowers, which resembled blooms from the hakea shrub, plus a few small samples of things Alan did not recognize.

The craggy old face looked up at him from the floor. "*Nabilla* . . . water . . . need water."

Alan returned to the kitchen, where the worried faces of Daniel and Sam greeted them.

"Womballa wants some water."

"Hot or cold?" asked Daniel.

"Cold, I imagine."

When Alan returned with the liquid, Womballa was bending over Eve, observing her. "Bad *ungawilla*," he stated.

Alan knew the term meant black magic, and he watched in silence.

The aborigine's large hands felt the veins in her neck, then he put his hand under the blanket and felt her stomach.

He took the dish of water that Alan held out to him and returned to his position on the floor. On each of the waratah leaves, he mixed a number of the substances together with drops of water that he made by putting his hand in the bowl and letting the water drip from the ends of his fingers.

Alan moved to the bedside and he lifted Eve's inert arm, with the intention of taking her pulse. Womballa reacted. "*Tauo!* No! Fletcher no touch. Clever Fletcher heart close with woman heart. *Awulla adina*. Womballa take badness."

Alan moved away from the bed.

"If badness go," he added simply.

Womballa rose with two of the waratah leaves in his hand. He lifted back the blanket and placed one on Eve's navel, the mixture against her skin. The two seeds that looked like black bean pods, he had broken open, and these he put in each of her armpits. Then he lifted her head up just enough to feed her from the other leaf.

She moaned but did not open her eyes.

His gnarled old hand pushed the mixture into her mouth, but in her semiconscious state, she did not swallow. Alan noticed that Womballa put pressure on a spot in her neck, and automatically she did swallow. He did this until she had taken all the mixture, then he returned to his position on the floor and began a chant.

Alan stood watching. His mind turned to all the formidable events that had occurred in his life. He was sure that the outcome of this one was more important than that of any other. He did so want her to live. He knew now that whatever happened, this was his greatest wish. Last night he had finally admitted to himself that he loved her, as she so obviously did him. He acknowledged it had begun for him the day he had found her in the bush, inexplicable though it was. He had thought to live out his life without admission of their feelings ever passing between them, but the touch of her hand on his face during the night had been her confession, and the saying of his name, her embrace.

Eve had believed she was dying. She could feel the coma of death begin to wash over her and had brought herself to show her love. Alan did not know what to make of it, or what to do about it. All he knew was that he wanted Womballa to make her well.

After a long time, the aboriginal elder stopped chanting and rose and went to the bed. Eve was perspiring profusely, and the blanket was wet. He removed the two pods from beneath her arms. The waratah leaf on her stomach, he replaced with the remaining one he had not yet used. He glanced sideways at Alan. "Leaf stay on woman one dark sky." Then turning to face his friend, he said, "Womballa go now. Medicine *nguldin*. Clever Fletcher woman hot like fire. Good. Some badness go."

Alan smiled anxiously. "Will she live?"

Womballa did not respond immediately. He seemed to think about the question. Then he said with finality, "Spirit leave . . . going skyworld. It come back, she live. It no come back, she die."

"How will I know, my friend?"

Womballa concentrated, again finding the English words.

"Woman live two dark sky. She come back . . . speak with Clever Fletcher."

"Thank you, my *waminda*."

They returned to the kitchen.

Womballa was the most intrepid of his tribe, and perhaps the most intrepid of all his race. He passed with Alan into the kitchen, where Daniel and Sam sat waiting. He looked at them with interest, his coal black eyes intense as he regarded them. He had done all he could to help the woman. His son waited for him outside, but he was here, in this wonderful dwelling, where Clever Fletcher and his "father," for that is how he thought of Daniel, lived. He wished to look at the possessions of the white man, for he would never again be able to do so. If he had known the word, he would have regarded it as an *opportunity*.

He walked slowly around the small room. He touched the table and, to the amazement of Alan and the others, sat down on the edge of one of the chairs and placed his hands flat on the tabletop. He sat this way for perhaps half a minute, looking around. When he rose, he went to the old wooden dresser in the corner. He lifted the cups and plates in curiosity and turned them over in his hands. He even clinked two of them together, smiling at the noise. The pots and pans, he touched and rubbed, then stood in front of the hearth to watch the fire and the iron cooking plate, on which the billy was now heating. He took up the poker and felt the weight of it.

There were other things to see: wooden shelves beside the door, and on these, towels, books, newspapers, containers, scissors, even a small pendulum clock, which had belonged to Patricia June. Finally he turned back to the wall of the room where Lawless and Jordan were concealed. On this wall hung a decorated shield he had given to Alan. It obviously delighted him to see it so displayed. His face broke into a wide smile. He slapped his thigh with pleasure and said, *"Numurkah!"* the word for "war shield." Then abruptly, as if he had decided he had seen enough, he walked out onto the veranda.

Alan followed him. They stood facing each other silently: the ocher-painted, time-worn, Aboriginal tribesman and the sea captain aristocrat, the bushranger, Alan Fletcher.

Beyond them, in the drizzle, Mulgatta sat on the tree stump used for chopping wood; he was still holding Sam's umbrella.

Alan took off the leather coat he wore and handed it to Womballa. "For Womballa, my *waminda*." As Alan helped him to put it on, Womballa's face lit up with pleasure. Sam and Daniel watched enthralled through the unshuttered kitchen window. Then Alan took off his belt, to which was attached his hunting knife in a sheath. He had given the tribe knives before, and it was something he knew they used and highly valued. He fastened the belt around Womballa's waist.

"Thank you," Alan said.

The aborigine scrutinized him, his head to one side. Then with the guileless logic of the innocent, he said, "Woman die . . . gifts come back Clever Fletcher."

"Womballa," Alan answered, "I give in friendship. I do not want them back."

"*Tauo!* Woman die, I bring. Woman live, I keep," came the conclusive reply. It was not to be argued with, and Alan nodded.

As Womballa went down the steps to his son, Samuel called through the window, "Tell the boy to keep the umbrella. I'll get another somewhere."

Alan went to the end of the passage with his friends, and there took his leave of them. His eyes met Womballa's in farewell, and soon the two dark bodies were lost in the thicket of trees.

While Jordan and Lawless had been alone in their room, little had been said for a long time.

Then, after about an hour, Jordan said, "How much longer is this farce goin' to be, I wonder?"

"Now, Jordan, what is the meanin' of that?"

"I can't understand the boss bringin' a flamin' black here to try and cure her. She will either live or die without him and all his mumbo jumbo. And what bloody well happens, I ask you, if she does die? Mrs. Bloody high-and-mighty Wakeman dead in a bushranger's hideout."

"Jordan," replied Lawless, looking up at him from where he sat on the floor cleaning his saddle and boots. "Ye be a . . . what is it? A 'pessimist,' that's it! Now, first and foremost, if the Guverner thinks that Womballa can save the mistress, then that's bein' my opinion too. And as for what happens if she dies, no doubt we shall face that if it comes upon us."

"And him," said Jordan, pointing out to Mulgatta, who had taken up his vigil on the tree stump, "look at him. Too flamin' stupid to come in out of the rain."

"Ye be a hard man, Jordan O'Day."

"Ah, there's no point in discussin' it. Your mind's clouded with the opinions of the boss. You've no mind of your own," Jordan said, taking up a book to read.

Lawless shook his head. "That's not true, but were it so, it would not be the worst thing to happen to a body."

His companion groaned.

The rain continued relentlessly. The air was dank and cold, yet Eve perspired so much that in the first twenty-four hours, she soaked three blankets. Over and over, Alan wiped her brow and her cheeks and her neck. Her features etched themselves on his memory for all time as he sat and watched her: the shape of her mouth and the gentle curve under her lower lip, the tiny creases at the corners of her eyes, the long lashes like her mother's, the fine line of her eyebrows, the delicate shape of her nose and chin. Sometimes she would murmur, and his heartbeat accelerated hopefully, then a violent tremor would run through her, and his hope would sink.

Time passed, and Danny drifted in and out, a comforting, helpful aide. Finally a wan, misty light filtered through the rain outside the window, and it was the following morning. He removed the waratah leaf and the mixture from Eve's navel and noticed that it had changed color. When Womballa had placed it there, it was a pale, muted yellow. Now, as he removed it, it was a deep orange-brown.

The next twenty-four hours were slow to pass, but Eve murmured quite often and began to move. Now Alan's confidence rose. Shortly after dawn broke on the second morning following the two "dark skies," she opened her eyes and spoke.

It had been exactly as Womballa had predicted, and Alan praised the old man in silent thanks.

By the hour of eight in the morning, the rain had stopped. It was the twenty-ninth of December, and there were pockets of blue sky in the clouds.

It had been the greatest deluge in New South Wales since the colony's founding in 1788. All the rivers for nearly one hundred miles had broken their banks: the Macquarie, the Belubula, the Lachlan, the Boorowa, the Campbell, and the Fish; and what had been water holes had become great lakes. All over the countryside, there was devastation. In the low-lying areas, homes had been flooded and water lay across the roads. Telegraph poles and wires were down, so that communication was lost. Some towns even had water several feet deep in the streets, and rescuers rowed in boats through the thoroughfares to save stranded householders. Trees were uprooted, and livestock went swirling by in raging currents. Bridges gave way, and men and women had been drowned.

But at Treehard, there was no destruction.

Hundreds of feet high, clinging to the top of the escarpment, it had been remote from the ravages of the floods. The only thing to overflow had been the water tank, and the nearest they had come to water damage was from leaks that had appeared in the roof.

And now Eve was awake.

She was weak and infirm and would need many weeks of convalesence, but she was alive! She was remembering many things, things that a week ago would have embarrassed and abashed her. She was sipping broth, lying back on a pile of pillows in the man's undershirt she had found herself wearing when she awoke.

Somehow she had not died, and she had been so sure she would. *He* had saved her.

Suddenly she remembered the child, the poor creature of her womb. It was gone. She put down her broth as she was overwhelmed by the loss, even though she admitted she had not definitely wanted it. "I'm sorry," she whispered. It had been forced on her in a most savage assault, but now she realized it had been part of her. There were so many anomalies in her emotions. Tears welled over her lids, and she wept for it, the poor little person who would never be anyone.

Some time later, she became conscious of what was around her and she began to notice things. The sun streamed through a broken and cracked window to her left. She was in a proper bed, a wrought-iron one with all manner of design in the bedstead at her feet. There was another in the room, but it was just a wooden stand with a mattress and blankets, without framework. It was a neat room, painted white with pale blue around the window frame. Clothes hung from a wooden clothes horse in a corner, and there were shelves along one wall, with many books and papers upon them. Beside both beds were small tree stumps, polished and smoothed to pass as tables, and beside the bed in which she lay was a chair with a yellow pillow on the seat. She knew this must be Alan's room, and he obviously shared it with someone.

The door opened. She looked around. He entered, closed the door behind him, and stood looking at her.

She had difficulty finding her voice after her days of silence. "Thank you for making me well," she managed to say.

He shook his head. "It was not my doing but the skill of a

great friend of mine. His name is Womballa. He is a native of this land.''

Eve marveled at such a thing. "It is hard to believe."

"Nevertheless, it is so, although I fear it will be many weeks before you are truly over your ordeal and able to travel."

The circumstances of her presence here rushed to her mind. "Oh yes, I see. . . ."

A grave expression settled on his face as he moved to sit in the chair beside her. "I do not wish to tire you, lass, but there are things I must understand."

"Perhaps now," she interrupted, "you could call me Eve, for I know I have called you Alan."

"Perhaps," he answered quietly, before he stood and moved to the window, where he turned back to face her. "As I was saying," he resumed, "to the world it will seem as if you disappeared. You were in Cowra, and two men came and whisked you away. There could be a search mounted. Your husband, with all his resources, will be a hard man to avoid if he decides to find you."

"He will not," she replied simply.

"And how is it that you are so certain of this? For you have maintained that point of view."

Then she explained to him. Beginning with her failure to tell John Stuart about her twin sister, and afterward of her fear to do so when she realized his attitudes. The mistake Lake made in her identity and the rape, and John Stuart's reaction, followed by his pursuit of the man; of Lake's lie that she was Clare, and John Stuart's belief in the lie; of his censure and his ultimatum to her.

"Of course, I should have told my husband about Clare before we married. Afterward I was always too afraid, and holding silent has brought me to all this."

"I see," he answered.

She was wondering what he was thinking as he leaned on the windowsill gazing at her. After a few seconds' silence, she said, "At least I will bring no more shame upon him or Father and Mother. Now the world can only say I left my husband. There will be no poor, innocent infant who will suffer."

"Yes, that is true." It hurt and angered him to know how she had been used and how she had suffered. He thought her gentle and beautiful and resourceful and resolute. Her husband appeared proud to the point of insensitivity, yet he would not be judgmental about John Stuart Wakeman. He was obviously a complicated man. The one thing Alan Fletcher was grateful for was the miracle of her presence.

He listened as she finished in a weary voice. "So you see, I left but half a year before I was to be turned out. Our marriage is finished. John Stuart will not give chase. I *know* he will not."

He came back to her and sat down on the chair beside the bed. "What of the others, the Reverend Billings and his wife? You were going to them. Will they not worry when they hear of your disappearance?"

Eve's face became troubled. "Oh yes, they will be distraught, and it will be so long before I can . . . travel to them and tell them what has happened. If they hear before I can tell them, it really will be too dreadful."

He tapped his lip in thought. "You must rest now and not concern yourself, for I know a way to appraise them of your whereabouts. Tomorrow, when you are not so tired, I will discuss it with you."

She closed her eyes and smiled. She felt so warm and secure here. "You seem to be able to do anything," she murmured. She heard the door close gently behind him, and soon she drifted into a comfortable sleep.

Alan spent the day working side by side with Lawless, sawing wood and hammering nails, while Samuel tended his water-logged vegetable gardens, helped by Daniel. Jordan, up on the roof, checked for places where the water had leaked through. In the evening after a meal of damper, vegetable soup, and eggs, Alan gathered them all together out on the veranda in the pleasant night air.

"Gentlemen," he began as he arrived at the kitchen door.

Lawless sat on the stone steps looking at the sky. Daniel was moving gently to and fro in the rocking chair that Lawless had made for him a Christmas ago. Samuel stood leaning on the rail, smoking an old wooden pipe, and beside him, Jordan lay full length on a bench, feet up on the rail, smoking a cigar. Their leader stood in the doorway, lamplight behind him.

"You all know I go to the height near Camara's Creek, for the arranged meeting with Ben Hall, a fortnight this day. Thursday the twelfth of January, to be exact."

"Lor, I'd forgotten," spoke up Lawless.

"I remembered," said Jordan between puffs of smoke. Jordan never forgot a chance to visit a safe house, and they would be stopping at one or two on the long ride to the appointed place.

"I shall keep the appointment. After which I will continue on to Bathurst to let the Reverend Billings, who has been a father to the lass inside, know that she is all right."

"Gawd, boss, how do you know you can trust him?" asked Jordan.

"The little I know of him is enough to convince me that I can."

Sam clicked his tongue. "Don't like that at all, guverner. Ye ridin' into Bathurst."

Lawless shook his head, "Nor I."

Sam continued, "And this meetin', is it not with blasted Morgan and some of the others? The ones with a price on their heads?"

Daniel spoke up. "Yes, that is what Bluey said when he gave us the message. It's to be a meeting of all the 'leading' 'rangers."

"But we've never been 'afore," argued Sam. "Ye've always refused to meet with them when they've asked 'afore, guverner."

"I know, Samuel, and I would not go this time but that Hall has arranged it. In him I see qualities lacking in the others. Besides which, lads, it's the right time. The newspapers are full of this coming 'Felons' Apprehension Act.' Perhaps the time is right to discuss it with the other bands."

Jordan swung his legs down off the railing and sat up. "Do you think they'll make it law to shoot us on sight, boss? Like the papers say?"

"Probably, Jordan, and then at last you will understand why I have maintained our disguises all these years. Why I do not even like such as Henry Lyons and his family knowing what you all look like."

"Aye," agreed Lawless. "It'll be hard to shoot a man on sight, Jordan, if the troopers don't know what he looks like."

"Yes, yes," agreed Jordan, "I understand."

"What else do you think they'll put into this act, Alan?" asked Daniel.

"I only know what I've read, Danny, but the mood of the people has changed a little in the last six months. There was still sympathy abroad when they brought the heavy sentence down on Frank Gardiner last July. But since, what with Gilbert's shooting of Sergeant Parry and the mad way Dan Morgan's behaved, killing two police in the last six months, not to mention those he has wounded . . . opinion is changing."

Samuel clicked his tongue again. "And now we know there was another shot on Boxing Day, which we've been blamed for!"

Alan stepped down onto the veranda and walked to the railing to stand beside Sam. "Yes, Sam, so the Apprehension Act will make it mighty hard on those folk associating with bushrangers. I think they will get jail sentences, and heavy ones."

Lawless looked up quickly. "Then why is it exactly that ye've agreed to go and meet with the others, guverner?"

"Because I have an idea that could lead to our survival for many years yet. I will put it to them at the meeting."

"And then ye shall go on to Bathurst?" asked Sam, looking sideways at him and puffing on his pipe. "As I say, that I do *not* like."

Lawless nodded vigorously. "Yes, Bathurst's a hotbed of troopers now that blasted Blake has his headquarters there, guv."

Alan nodded. "I have decided it is my responsibility to inform the clergyman in any case. And as Camara's Creek is within twenty miles of him, I have made the decision to combine the two."

"Decided, then, is it?" remonstrated Sam, standing up from beside Alan where he rested on the rail and looking straight at the leader. "Decided indeed? I see, and what if somethin' happens to ye, Alan Fletcher? Eh? What about that?"

Alan laughed. The sound rang mirthfully on the night air. "Ah, Samuel Cooper, your sharp tongue hides exemplary sentiments, which I do not pass over lightly." Then he put his arm around the little man's shoulders. "I promise, I shall take whatever care is necessary not to leave any of you orphans."

At that, they all laughed. All except Sam, who puffed furiously on his pipe, mumbling about people "not listenin' and takin' foolish risks."

The following day, Eve sat propped up on pillows, her eyes closed, when the door opened and Alan came in. She opened her eyes and smiled as he came forward and sat once again on the chair before her bed.

"I must go close to Bathurst thirteen days from now."

She looked concerned. "But I fear I shan't be well enough by then. It is a long journey. . . . A week or so more . . ."

"No, you misunderstand me. It will be three or four weeks before you should consider traveling. I go because there is to be a meeting between Ben Hall and myself."

Now she looked surprised. "But, he has killed people," she whispered.

Alan shook his head. "No, he has killed no one. It is those he has kept company with who have done the killing."

She was lying back on the pillows watching him. The reality of what he had to do . . . the people he knew . . . how he survived . . . struck her. She was looking at a fugitive, a man who met and spoke with criminals, who took things at the point of a gun. And yet, she knew as incontrovertible what seemed a perverse truth, that he was just and honorable, and that there were few men who had ever lived who were as good. A lump of sadness settled in her throat; she swallowed and quickly looked away, holding back tears.

He continued speaking. "The meeting is to take place on Thursday the twelfth of January some twenty miles from Bathurst and your Reverend Billings. I will deliver a message from you to him. It is unlikely that word about you will have reached him by then, as the floodwaters will take a week to subside."

She looked back at him. "But won't it be dangerous? Why must you meet this Ben Hall?"

"Because I said I would." His mouth twisted in a grim sort of smile before he added, "And after that, I will let the minister in Bathurst know that you are safe." He stood to leave. "I go now to my friend Womballa to tell him of your recovery."

"I should like to thank him myself."

"Sometime you shall." He turned to leave.

"Before you go," she said, holding up her hand to his back, "there is something I must say."

He turned around. "Yes?"

She had been wondering about this for twenty-four hours. "You do not think the less of me, do you? For what I related to you yesterday?"

Then he smiled broadly. "Hardly, lass." And he bent and touched her hand before he left the room.

On the way to the Aboriginal camp-site, he found himself thinking back through his life. It was a long time since he had done this; he was not a dweller on the past, although he recognized there were moments from it that he cherished.

He was not a fatalist, although with his experiences it would not have been surprising had he been. He believed in individual responsibility and self-determination of the course of one's life. Yet he accepted that external influences sometimes left a man little choice. He saw the arrival of Eve in his life like this. When by all that was logical their first meeting should have been their last, it had not been.

Yet the fact remained she was married to John Stuart Wakeman.

He considered the master of Mayfield, remembering him. Alan did not think him vainglorious but it had been obvious that John Stuart Wakeman was perhaps too proud. It now appeared he was uncompromising when he had made a value judgment. But also, Alan admitted he had recognized principle and strength of character in him that day during the hold-up. He shook his head. It was not comfortable for Alan to think of John Stuart, just as it was not comfortable for John Stuart to think of Alan.

He brought Freedom to a halt, looking at the rain-soaked bush, the trees bright green and fresh with recent moisture. The world sparkled and smelled sweet to his nostrils.

The woman he loved was alive and at Treehard. For how long mattered little. It was this way now.

TWENTY-FOUR

After the Flood

Eve sat in Nelson's Boulder watching the riders disappear. She strained her eyes to catch the last glimpse of the gray figure that was Alan as the bush enveloped him. He and Lawless and Jordan were going to meet with Ben Hall, and then Alan was to ride into Bathurst to tell Father and Mother what had happened.

She was feeling much better, and each day in Alan's company had been like a revelation. There was a tranquillity here at Treehard unlike anything she had experienced before, and it stemmed from Alan Fletcher. Security and calm emanated from his very presence, and all those who lived here felt it. The only times she had felt this sort of peace before were now and then when walking across the great, open spaces of Mayfield.

She sat staring at the patch of gray-green bush that had enveloped Alan, feeling an emptiness now that he had gone. Ever since she had awoken in Daniel's bed after her miscarriage, he had been there. Each day had brought his face and his smile and the look of care in his unforgettable eyes. When Alan's gaze lingered on hers and when he touched her in the course of their daily lives, she knew pure joy.

She also thought of John Stuart and beautiful Mayfield, for even after everything that had happened, she could not erase the feelings she had for him; but they were different now, and there was deep pain attached to them. She had given vows before God to love him and cherish him. Her heart raced when she thought of that, for there was so much about him that was worth loving and cherishing, but he had rejected her and scorned her. She felt guilty, and yet at the same time, set free.

Now she recognized that while she had truly loved John Stuart, she was "in love" with Alan Fletcher, had been ever since their eyes had met at the carriage door on her wedding day. She was sorry that John Stuart had spurned her, that he hated her, but his actions had created the circumstances that had delivered her to Alan. Perhaps there would always be great confusion in her heart about John Stuart, but there was no confusion about her feelings for Alan, none at all.

While no mention had been made of their love since she had thought she was dying, she knew he did love her; it was apparent in all he did.

In the two weeks since he had brought her here, he had tenderly nursed her back to health, and she thought she would be well enough to travel in another week or two, then she would go to Bathurst to Father and Mother. She knew that she dearly wanted to stay with Alan, yet it was not fair to him and to those with him to remain here. They were wanted men, no matter how harmless they appeared to her, and her presence was merely one more problem in their lives. She must leave, but until she did, she intended to assist those who lived here, to justify the help they had given her. They were strangely diverse characters, but each, in his own way, appealed to her.

Daniel was a caring man, the father figure. She liked the way he hummed Irish ballads as he went about his work. Samuel had a veneer of severity, but beneath the arrant chiding Eve had soon realized he was the softest, most good-hearted of men. Lawless was as agreeable a man as she had ever met, sunny-natured and cheerful. Jordan was the youngest, boisterous at times, introspective at others. And she suspected he badly desired Alan's approval.

She took her eyes from the sea of bush and looked down at the rock surface where her hand rested. Tiny black ants were running backward, forward, and around in circles, meeting one another, stopping, and going again. There seemed no pattern in their movements, but they looked mighty busy. She smiled. That's what she should be, busy. Then perhaps she would not miss Alan so much. Besides, she would feel better working; it would take her mind off all the disturbing memories living in her head.

She stood up, and with a last, longing look down across the hill where Alan had disappeared, she left Nelson's Boulder and climbed down the stone steps that led to the passage back into Treehard.

John Stuart wiped his brow with his handkerchief, then flicked it at the flies that buzzed incessantly around him. The heat of the sun was intense. He lifted his arm to rest it on Diomed's saddle. Suddenly he flinched and withdrew his hand as it came in contact with the metal studs, burning hot from hours of exposure to the sun.

He was waiting for Jack Hennessy and Stephen Watson, who were advancing toward him up the mud-dried slope from the pile of bricks and wood that had been the dairy. The smell was vile down here, where the water had lain and everything that had been mud-covered delivered up stench.

It was two weeks since the rain had stopped.

After their return home on the night of the twenty-sixth of December, the Lachlan had broken its banks and continued rising for over seventy-two hours, even after the rain had stopped, so much water had come down from the upper reaches. Where the Boorowa and the Lachlan joined had swelled to a lake almost half a mile wide. Fortunately that was many miles from Mayfield proper although they had taken their share of destruction here. Floodwaters spilled into the Mayfield community just after midday on the twenty-seventh as Stephen Watson and his foreman had predicted, but never had they been ready for the ruin the raging waters had brought.

As the water rose swiftly to inches beneath the bridge of Larmer's Crossing, all the families in the river cottages had been evacuated and taken over and housed in the recreation hall.

Early that same morning, they had begun moving the live-stock to high ground, but even so, there were cattle drowned, and now as John Stuart looked about him, his nostrils quivered as he recalled the days when he had worked side by side with his stockmen in the cloying mud to bury the carcasses.

Over to his right across the now normal Lachlan, there were men working on the river cottages that had been underwater. They were rebuilding and still cleaning away the debris deposited by the flood.

The rushing water had wreaked havoc on the cottages and the dairy, and had annihilated much of the orchards. Most of Eve's fence along the Lachlan had been swept away, and trees had been torn up along the banks and been brought down to lodge against the bridge of trunks that was Larmer's Crossing. Finally the bridge could hold no longer, and it had been washed entirely away.

There had been only two human casualties, and for that, John Stuart was grateful, although it saddened him to think of them. One was a married worker called Shaw who had become separated from his group while leading a team of steers to high ground. He had disappeared, and they still had not found his body. The other was young Peter Hennessy. John Stuart had blanched when he received the news. Unbeknownst to his parents, the child had gone back to their cottage after they had been evacuated, perhaps to get a precious possession, as children might. He had been caught by the rising water and surrounded. When the waters finally receded, they had found his little body lodged in the hallway of their half-demolished house. His mother had fainted when they told her.

They buried little Peter beside the Mayfield chapel.

John Stuart sighed as he watched the child's father walking up the hill toward him now. Watson and Hennessy stopped momentarily to discuss something, and Stephen Watson lifted his hand in a wide arc, expressing some point of view. It was Stephen Watson whom John Stuart had sent to Bathurst.

Oh, he had really known in his heart it was a wild-goose chase, but he had sent him, nevertheless. When John Stuart had decided to stop his search in the deteriorating weather on Boxing Day, he had kept the forlorn hope that somehow Eve had gone to Bathurst and that he would find her with Reverend and Mrs. Billings.

Immediately after the floodwaters had gone down and a man could ride through to Bathurst, John Stuart had sent for Joe, but the older man had influenced him not to leave his property and his people. ''M'boy, we suspect Eve left Cowra in company with the bushranger. I do not believe she will be in Bathurst, as much as I would hope the opposite. We must be having services for the dead child and Donald Shaw, and with all the rebuilding to do, the Mayfield folk need to see you, the master, *here* with them.'' He had lifted his arm and placed it around John Stuart's shoulders as he finished, ''But do send a trusted man to Bathurst to see if, by some strange chance, Eve is with the reverend.''

So Stephen Watson was sent and had returned with disquieting news.

In fact, he had not even needed to go into the little township to see if Eve were with the minister, for he had met Dr. Marcus Walker at a crossway six miles out of Bathurst. Stephen Watson had grown up in Bathurst and knew the medical man.

''Dr. Walker, good day to you, sir.''

''Hello there, Stephen, my boy. What brings you so far from Mayfield?''

Now, Stephen was a loyal Mayfield man, and he was told not to discuss his reason, so he merely answered, ''I am come from Mr. Wakeman to see how some in Bathurst fared during this great flood we have experienced.''

''Oh, yes, dreadful, wasn't it? I've had many sick from the effects of it. And some have died. Why, two of Bathurst's best were taken, wonderful women that they were. Mrs. Jackson, the alderman's wife, went on Christmas night, died in childbirth stranded in their homestead, and Mrs. Billings was drowned on Boxing Day in Clearfield Creek, which rose without warning.''

''What?'' said Stephen. ''Mrs. Billings of All Saints' Church?''

''Yes, Stephen. She and the reverend were out helping the farmers when they were caught. She drowned, and I'm sorely afraid he did himself such harm in bringing her to the bank that he will soon follow.''

''Oh, my Lord, how terrible.'' Now Stephen thought he would ask a question. ''So the reverend is very ill, you say. Is anyone with him?''

''Yes, good Mistress Thatcher is taking care of him; I was only just attending him before I rode out here this very morning.''

Stephen thought to ask another question. ''Then he has not had a visit from anyone?''

''Actually, he has had many visitors; all the town is worried about him.''

''But there is no one staying with him? Other than Lottie Thatcher, I mean.''

Dr. Walker looked quizzically at this. "What do you mean, 'staying with him'? There's nobody in that rectory other than himself and Mistress Thatcher . . . oh, and young Jennie, who is soon to leave, I believe." Now the doctor looked stern. "What on earth are you talking about, Stephen?"

Stephen realized his journey was at an end, for the one thing that Mr. Larmer had impressed upon him was to be discreet. He did not need to go into Bathurst town now. He doffed his hat to the doctor and thoroughly astonished him by saying, "Well, sir, I'm sorry, but I cannot say more. You have supplied me with the information I sought. Forgive me for not explaining. It is grand to see you again, but I must be moving on." And he turned his horse's head around.

Thus, Stephen had returned to his master with the news that not only was Eve not with the minister, but that Reverend Billings was gravely ill. John Stuart was saddened by the news. He was sorry that Mrs. Billings had been drowned, and sorry, too, about the clergyman. He truly hoped the man would live.

Eve. There was a nagging ache through him whenever he thought of her, which was almost all the time. Why had things gone so dreadfully wrong?

He moved away from Diomed to greet his men. "Hello, boys." He looked to Jack Hennessy. "How is Mrs. Hennessy?"

The furrows in the man's brow deepened as he positioned his feet and folded his arms. "Well, sir, she's taken it hard. Peter was her firstborn, and there was something special about him. I find her crying when she thinks none see. Yet we have the other two, and they are a solace. She's a real Mayfield woman and strong. She will rally." He took a deep breath and added, "Now, me? Work is my cure."

John Stuart's eyes met his. He gave the suggestion of a nod. "Work is my cure, too," he said very slowly.

The two men looked sharply at him.

It was the first time John Stuart had ever referred to his own situation in front of anyone other than Joe. This was John Stuart's deliberate offering to his faithful employee. The statement proposed kinship, and Jack Hennessy recognized his master's gift. The man did not speak; instead he smiled in empathy, and in appreciation he tipped the wide-brimmed hat he wore.

John Stuart nodded gently, and the moment passed.

They began to talk of other matters.

* * *

When John Stuart arrived back at Mayfield House, he left Diomed hitched to the veranda railing and strode up the stairs into the house just as Daydee was exiting the blue drawing room. He was unaware that she had been waiting there, watching for his arrival.

"Uncle John Stuart, what a nice surprise. How are you?"

"Passably well, Daydee, considering everything; and yourself?"

"Oh, I'm happy enough, thank you, although everyone's been so busy since the flood, there's so much to do."

"Work never hurt anyone, Daydee."

Daydee did not agree but smiled at him anyway.

He patted her on the shoulder and moved down the corridor.

The encounter had been far too brief for Daydee, and with a yearning look upon her face, she watched him depart. She was thoughtful for a moment, then decided to find her mother. She wandered down the tall corridors looking into the open doors of the rooms, but nowhere did she see Thelma. She was about to turn and go back when she had an idea. Smiling to herself, she hurried down a side hallway into the corridor that led to Eve's rooms. Outside the bedroom, she hesitated, then ever so gently she turned the knob. It was not locked, and opened to her touch.

The sun's rays came through the heavily draped windows to light up the interior. It was a beautiful room, and Daydee sat upon the white lace bedspread and looked around. Oh, to be John Stuart's wife and to sleep here with him. Sighing, she reached forward to caress the pillow with her small hand.

Then she swung down from the bed and passed into the dressing room, where two massive walnut wardrobes stood in state. Gingerly she opened one of the mirrored doors. Inside were all the beautiful gowns that Eve had worn. Standing on her tiptoes, she reached up and lifted out a black silk gown with embroidered sleeves. She held it in front of herself, smiling all the while.

Then her features tightened in hatred. She knew that John Stuart had ridden out to find Eve on Boxing Day. Even now, her father said he wanted her back. How could he? She threw the dress from herself to the floor in fury. "God, how I hate you! You are so ugly!" she said aloud. With aversion lingering on her face, she went into the sitting room, where Eve's books and music and other personal possessions lay as she had left them.

To her right hand was a wicker table on which dozens of sheets of music lay. Daydee rifled through a few of them and found

"The Meadow Green." Her expression changed to delight. She had been trying forever to get a copy from Sydney town. She picked it up and turned to leave with it in her hand, then her smile died as she drew in her breath in shock. "You . . . you . . . startled me!"

"And what is that ye be holding there?" asked the somber figure of Mrs. Smith, who stood eyeing her from the doorway.

"Oh . . . it's music . . . 'The Meadow Green.' I have been wanting it ever so long. I shall take it."

Mrs. Smith's face hardened with disapproval. "*Miss* Daydee, what are ye doing in these rooms? And what is the meaning of that?" She made a severe gesture to the black silk gown lying crumpled on the floor behind her.

Daydee stood her ground. "I don't know."

Mrs. Smith did not approve of Daydee, always dressed in silks and lace and acting as if she owned the place. She was a spoiled brat, to the housekeeper's way of thinking. "Now, I was in here earlier, and there were no dress lying in a heap on the floor and no wardrobe door open."

"Well, I know nothing about it."

Mrs. Smith's expression called Daydee a liar, but she said no more; instead she pointed to the sheet of music in the girl's hand. "And now tell me who has given ye permission to take that."

"No one, exactly," argued Daydee, "but I know Uncle John Stuart should let me have it if I asked him."

Mrs. Smith flicked her hand at the girl. " 'No one, exactly,' eh? So, *Miss* Daydee, ye had best be receiving permission to have it very quickly indeed. For I'm under instructions from the master himself to lock these rooms, and that means what's in them stays here. Put it back."

Daydee's face was full of fury, but she dared not take the music. After all, Mrs. Smith was the housekeeper, and the old witch was a favorite of John Stuart's. Her chin shot forward aggressively as she faced the woman across the room. She put the sheet down slowly on top of the pile.

"I shall get permission," she said with deliberation, "and I would not lock up with too much haste if I were you." Then she turned on her heel and left the room. "The witch! The old witch!" she kept saying to herself all the way down the corridor.

Fortunately, John Stuart was at home for lunch; at least she knew that. But how to disturb him? She must, for she badly wanted that music, and she badly wanted to beat that old biddy at her own game. As she headed toward the kitchens, Baines came along carrying a silver tray with a single covered platter upon it.

"Is that for the master, dear Mr. Baines?" she asked.

Baines looked down his long nose to the girl barring his way. He liked Miss Daydee: she was such a pretty girl and had a charming turn of phrase.

"It is, Miss Daydee. He eats alone in the morning room. Just a few vegetables is all it is. I do wish he would eat more."

"Oh, Mr. Baines, it is so important that I speak to him. When you go in, would you please ask him if I could but have a brief word with him? Please?"

Who could refuse the bright young face turned up to him? "All right, Miss Daydee, come along behind me."

He was not long. "Miss Daydee." He smiled. "The master says go in."

"Oh, thank you, Mr. Baines; you are so clever."

"And what's so urgent, Daydee, that it has occurred since I saw you in the hall?"

"Dear Uncle John Stuart," she began, "it's but a mere pesky happening and I would not have troubled you, but it is urgent, you see."

He smiled tolerantly at her.

"There's a piece of music, 'The Meadow Green,' I've been waiting on it for simply ages to come from Payne's music store in Sydney."

"Mmm."

"Well, just now I saw a copy of it. Mrs. Smith is in the east wing, and . . . I . . . popped in there. 'The Meadow Green' is on a table among a lot of music. I know Mrs. Smith is right to refuse to give it to me, but it seems a shame to let it lie there when I would get so much pleasure from learning to play it." She looked down at her hands. "Especially as Aunt Eve is no longer here to play it."

John Stuart closed his eyes for a brief moment. No, his wife was no longer here. But he was leaving her room and her belongings exactly as they were in the hope that one day she would return to them . . . and him. Nevertheless, it seemed unreasonable not to let little Daydee have a piece of music.

"Did Mrs. Smith stop you from taking it?"

"Yes."

"Mrs. Smith is only doing her duty as she sees fit."

Daydee's face dropped.

"But at the same time—" he smiled "—she is often strict."

"So I may have it?"

He nodded thoughtfully, replying in an undertone, "I'm quite sure that Eve would like to know her music was being played. So yes, you may, and if there are one or two others you especially like, I think she'd want you to take those, too."

She had won, as she had believed she would. She broke into her loveliest smile.

"Now, you go and get your music, and I'll explain to Mrs. Smith."

Ten minutes later, Daydee was sitting on the floor in Eve's sitting room sorting through the music when Mrs. Smith returned from the master. The girl lifted her head and, tossing back her hair over her shoulder, smiled with open satisfaction at the woman. Mrs. Smith did not look at her, but as she swept by, said, "Be swift with yeer choices, *Miss* Daydee. I want no delay. This room is to be cleaned and locked before the afternoon is out."

After Daydee had sifted through the stack of music on the wicker table, she noticed more on a shelf below. She continued on through these. Some had no name written on them at all; some had "Eve" or "Eve Herman" on them; others had "Eve Wakeman" in neat writing. But her eyes widened in surprise as she came to one sheet that had "Clare Herman" written on it, in the same hand. So, Eve's other name! Or at least the one she had used when she was with Nathaniel Lake in Adelaide.

Oh, Daydee knew all the story of Eve calling herself Clare and living with Lake in Adelaide! Her father had told her and her mother about it when he and John Stuart came back after finding Lake. Her mother had not believed it and maintained that Eve was good and respectable; but then, her silly mother's opinion did not matter.

It seems Lake had convinced her father and John Stuart of his intimacy with Eve, and that the baby was a result of their lovemaking. That was why Daydee could not understand the reason John Stuart ran after Eve on Boxing Day. Why had he changed his mind? It made no sense. And no wonder Nathaniel had always been so interested in her! All those questions he had asked. All the time he had known her!

Daydee was now certain that Lake had gone from her to the big house the night he was drunk in the park. She was also sure that he had assaulted Eve, although she was telling no one about that. In the state he had been in, he was capable of assaulting anyone, past lover or not. It had almost been her in Eve's place! How Daydee hated them both, Eve and Lake. She had always suspected there was something to know about Eve, yet, she had never for a moment considered that Eve was playing false to John Stuart. It just went to show how devious people could be! Especially *her*.

She was so happy that Eve had gone, even though her father told her John Stuart would continue to search for her. She prayed that he would not find her! As time passed, he would forget her. Yes, please, Lord, let him forget her! How badly she wanted him for herself.

She took the piece of music that had the name "Clare" upon it and added it to those she had chosen. Then she picked them up in her arms and passed again through the empty dressing room. The black silk gown still lay where she had thrown it. Huh! She was not going to pick it up. Let the damned servants do it.

She caught her reflection in the mirrored door and stopped to look at herself. She bent down and put the pile of music on the floor, straightening up to swirl around and admire herself. She made a few haughty faces and imagined herself as the mistress.

It was as she bent again to retrieve the music that her eye caught something lying just beneath the wardrobe. It had obviously fallen there unnoticed. She reached under and lifted it out, a gray cover with silver embossing. She had only ever seen a few of them; they contained photographic likenesses. Her mother and father had obtained one of themselves in Sydney a few years before, and they had taken it out of the cover and placed it in a frame on the mantel shelf, over the fireplace in the drawing room.

She opened it.

Her mouth dropped open in shock at what she saw. She knelt on the floor, holding in front of her a picture of two girls, two *identical* girls . . . twins, of about thirteen or fourteen. Underneath was written, "Evelyn and Clare, San Francisco, 1852."

Oh Lord! Eve had a twin sister. This was Clare! Suddenly she understood so much more. Nathaniel had mistaken Eve for her twin sister. It was Clare he must have lived with in Adelaide. He had gone to Eve that night thinking she was Clare. Eve was the innocent victim after all! And where was this Clare? It was obvious John Stuart knew nothing about her.

For some reason, Eve must never have mentioned her twin. How strange. Or perhaps not so strange. For it was scandalous, living in a de facto relationship. It was something only harlots did! Daydee was wholly enthralled. Her eyes darted this way and that in concentration.

"What are ye doing there on the floor, *Miss* Daydee?" The clipped tones of Mrs. Smith sounded behind her.

Startled again, Daydee grabbed up her music to hold it against her body and to hide the photograph. "Nothing, nothing," she said as she stood.

Mrs. Smith looked suspiciously at her as the girl backed out of the room, saying, "I'm going now. I've much to do this afternoon."

Ten minutes later, Daydee sat in her room with her door locked. She had taken a metal dish from the scullery as she came upstairs. She placed the photographic likeness in the dish and took out of her pocket one of the long matchsticks and a piece of stone that Leith used to light his pipe. The matchstick ignited as she rubbed it on the stone.

She was so intent that her hand shook ever so slightly as she touched the flame to the sepia photograph. Then her black little eyes gleamed meanly, and her face filled with satisfaction, as she sat and watched it burn until it was a small pile of ashes in the bottom of the dish.

Twenty minutes before the hour of three o'clock, John Stuart sat behind a large mahogany desk in the west drawing room. Fifteen drawing room chairs in the Regency style had been placed in three rows in front of it, and in front of them, an armchair for Joe. He had called a meeting of the leading men of Mayfield to discuss with them the aftermath of the flood and the details of rebuilding and repair. His right hand toyed with an inkwell decorated in colored flowers and gilt.

He was thinking of his wife. The words she had written to him and left on her pillow, and the gold and jade olive-branch comb, were both in his jacket pocket. Ever since he had found them, he had carried them there.

He must find her, he told himself. It was driving him to distraction. How dare the bushranger ride into Cowra and . . . remove her, up and away, just like that. Rutherford was not the only one who wanted Alan Fletcher now. John Stuart Wakeman wanted him, too. He knew it was the bushranger who had abducted her, had been absolutely convinced since he had spoken again with the priest who had come to Mayfield to hold a service for little Peter Hennessy. Mrs. Hennessy was Catholic, and young Peter had been christened in her religion.

He shivered and stood from the desk.

It had been only two days ago, a stiflingly hot afternoon, and after the service, Joe had brought the priest up to Mayfield House.

John Stuart had gone ahead and waited for them. He had decided to take tea out on the veranda, where the confining heat of the day was not as bad as inside the stuffy, airless house.

They sat facing each other on white painted chairs with lattice backs.

Brother Michael did not approve of gossip, and yet the whole story of Mrs. Wakeman's disappearance with the two strangers had been as much a topic of conversation as the flood. It was turning into a scandal, and he could not help thinking that a number of strange events must have occurred here to account for Mrs. Wakeman's "running away" to Cowra, as everyone termed it.

Brother Michael still did not know what to make of Mr. Wakeman. No doubt he held unorthodox beliefs. Perhaps that was why the man had not invited him inside to tea but instead had served him here on the veranda. Well, that didn't matter. He could turn the other cheek, just as the good Lord had done.

Joe broke the silence. "When we spoke to you in Cowra, you said Mrs. Wakeman had arrived wet, tired, and ill."

"Yes."

Joe nodded. "And you tried to persuade her to stay and see the doctor?"

"Yes, indeed. She, er, had some idea she was waiting for Ronald Richards to appear and to, er, take her somewhere in his dray."

"And then," resumed Joe, leaning back and folding his arms, "you said that Mrs. Wakeman fainted, and the two men turned up and carried her away, pretending to be Mayfield men."

"You are right. They were so forceful. That is, the one who carried her off."

John Stuart's expression did not change, but Joe sensed him stiffen.

"The one that carried her off was well educated, you said. Would you repeat his description to us?"

"Well, he was taller than me, perhaps five feet ten or eleven. I recall he was clean-shaven, firm jawline, sun-browned, and I think he had light brown hair. There was a real authority about him." Here he looked to John Stuart. "As I think I told you at the time, that is why I believed he was, er, one of your men."

"And his eyes?" Joe prompted.

"Er, yes, his eyes. Dick Barovill thought they were unusual. Penetrating, I think he said, bluish sort of color."

There was silence for a few seconds, during which time Brother Michael built up courage to ask a question of his own. "Do you know who they were?"

John Stuart spoke at last. He uncrossed his legs and stood up. "We have our suspicions," he said. "I am grateful for your help."

The priest smiled. "I, er . . . It must be a terrible worry. Yes, sir, I can quite understand how you must be feeling."

John Stuart stood holding the back of the chair he had just vacated. He looked down into the cleric's eyes as he said quite deliberately, "On the contrary, Brother Michael, I do not think you have the remotest comprehension of how I feel." Then he bent forward and offered his hand to the startled young man, who took it in an automatic reaction as John Stuart finished. "I am indebted to you. Good-bye."

John Stuart sighed now as he moved to the wide window of the drawing room. It definitely appeared that the bushranger had carried his wife off somewhere. Where, oh, where? The torment he went through when he thought of that! How in the devil's name had Alan Fletcher been in Cowra on Boxing Day?

Eve, where are you? Damn it! Damn and blast it! Where in hell are you? I must find this bloody bushranger and bring you home.

At the same moment that John Stuart prepared to meet his staff, one of the subjects of his recent thoughts, Alan, sat on a boulder on the flat top of a sandstone hill near Camara's Creek, three miles from the Bathurst road. He was waiting for Ben Hall and the others.

The arrangement, made through Bluey before Christmas, was to meet at this spot, at four o'clock in the afternoon, on Thursday the twelfth of January, 1865.

Alan, Lawless, and Jordan had spent the previous night under Bluey's roof in his little hut and had risen before dawn to make the ride here. Bluey's robust voice had followed them through the bush as they rode away. "Let me know the outcome, governor, my ally," he had shouted. "And don't turn your back on mad Dan!"

They had arrived at the meeting place an hour early. Alan had met with some of the bushrangers on this very hill in '62, when Frank Gardiner was plotting the Forbes gold escort robbery.

Ben Hall had been lucky that time. For, although he had been taken by the police in an initial rounding up after the robbery at Eugowra, they had been unable to prove his involvement, and he had been freed.

As they waited, Jordan looked over to Alan. "Boss, there's somethin' I still don't quite understand."

"What is that, lad?"

"You've always maintained that we didn't need to mix with the others. That the likes of Dan Morgan and Johnny Gilbert and Lefty Dawson are to be avoided. That their killin' need never have happened and you found them offensive."

"Yes," answered Alan.

"Then I'm not clear on what we're doin' here."

"First, Jordan, we have been asked here by Ben Hall, who does not kill, and whom I classify slightly differently, although he sleeps in tainted company. Second, even though Morgan, Gilbert, and Dawson may be impetuous fools, we need them to agree to what I shall propose today."

"And what's that?"

"An overall plan, which you will hear when they all arrive."

"What time is it?" asked Lawless, who stood above them, atop some rocks that gave him a vantage point over the plain below.

Jordan took out the gold fob watch and chain he had taken from John Stuart almost two years before. "It's near to twenty-five minutes past the hour of three now. There's more than half an hour to the appointed time."

Lawless nodded. "Oh well, if I be rememberin' correctly, it was Benjamin Hall as was early when we met here before. It was dead Henry Manns and live Johnny Gilbert as were the tardies."

"Yes, Gilbert was very late," laughed Jordan, "maybe that's why he never robs coaches these days, you have to keep to a schedule to do that, don't you boss?"

Alan nodded, smiling.

Lawless took a small telescope from his belt and scanned the countryside. "Well, Jordan," he said, "Gilbert be ahead of his schedule today, for I reckon it be he and Hall comin' through the trees down there now."

Alan and Jordan stood up.

"Is it only two, Lawless?"

"No, guv, I'm wrong, another comes behind. It be three, but the third, I've never seen before. He looks pretty young from what I can see of him."

"Johnny Dunn isn't it?" said Jordan, climbing up beside Lawless to look.

"This'll be the fifth or sixth of Ben's partners who've been called John, won't it, boss?"

Five minutes later, the newcomers stood facing Alan and his men.

Ben Hall was one month off twenty-eight. He was a man of medium height and walked with a limp from a broken leg he had suffered years before. Johnny Gilbert stood beside him; slight, thin, and good with a gun; one might say *too* good. The third man was indeed the new recruit, Johnny "the Jockey" Dunn.

"It's been a few years," Alan said, offering his hand to Ben Hall.

Hall enthusiastically took Alan's hand in both of his. "Yes, it has."

"This is 'the Jockey' Johnny Dunn," introduced Hall.

"How do you do," Alan said.

Johnny Dunn's eyes were wide open, and that was something of a feat, for Dunn had tiny eyes that in their natural state were half closed. He was actually facin' the famous Alan Fletcher! The Guverner. Strewth! The man was a flamin' legend. Why, they said that he was of flamin' noble birth, a cousin of the Queen yet, and had been an Admiral in the navy, and the old-timers said there was a certain look from his eyes that could affect a man's bloody breathin'. Johnny Dunn, finding his voice, replied, "All right, thanks."

Ben Hall was looking hard at Alan. In truth, Hall was almost as much in awe of Alan Fletcher as young Johnny Dunn, but not for the same reasons. Hall was a thoughtful man who was lost in admiration for one who had kept himself and his men free from capture twelve years, when most who took to the road were imprisoned or dead within a quarter of the time.

He was appraising Alan now. Fletcher did not appear as old as they said he was. Hardly looked much older than himself, really.

Everything about Alan Fletcher fascinated him. No one knew where his hideout was, for a start. It was suspected to be south of Cowra. The story was that Jordan O'Day had said so when in his cups one night at a safe house. It was told that he had been an intimate of the Prince of Wales, was of gentle birth, had been very rich.

Hall had despatched the message to Fletcher through Bluey

Williams. He had sent communications before, but Fletcher had always rejected his proposals. So, when Bluey had returned this time with an affirmative answer, he had been very pleased and surprised. He was deeply impressed by the man opposite him, and he stood looking at Alan now, as if by scrutiny he might learn how to be like him.

"Who else will be here?" Alan asked.

Gilbert replied. "Dan Morgan said he'd be 'ere, and we got an answer that James McPherson would, too. Do ya know 'im?"

"We do not."

" 'E's all right," Gilbert said.

Alan smiled.

"And Old Joe Daily will be here, and Lefty Dawson said he'd come."

"What about Crane?" Alan asked.

" 'Aven't ya heard?" broke in Gilbert. " 'E's bin shot. Bloody Rutherford the Rat took 'im near Flat's Creek a week ago."

"Shit!" said Jordan.

Alan looked to Ben Hall. "Where is that, Flat's Creek?"

"Just south of Orange."

" 'E was caught there in camp with his girlfriend, a darkie, just after midnight," Gilbert explained. "Seems they surrounded 'im and shot 'im dead. No sign of his partner, Billy Dunken."

Ben Hall nodded. "There was some talk that Rutherford Blake tried to ride south before Christmas with a pack of traps but was held back by the flood. When it subsided, they turned west for some reason and caught Jake Crane."

"We reckon Billy musta informed," stated Gilbert.

"It sounds likely," agreed Jordan.

No one spoke for a few seconds, then Lawless's voice announced from above them, "Here comes dangerous Dan, with two young fellows in tow, and if I'm not mistaken, there be horses ridin' in from the west as well."

By ten minutes after four o'clock, all the bushrangers had arrived. James McPherson was the only one who came alone. All the others had one or two companions each.

The meeting place had been chosen because of its uninterrupted view on all sides to the plain below.

Lawless was asked to stay in his position as lookout with clear vision to the north, east, and west, and one of Joe Daily's men took up a station where he could see any movement to the south.

Both were well within hearing of the conversation that took place in the inadequate shade of a few straggling gums.

They sat sharing two fallen trunks and various small rocks and boulders to form a rough circle.

A checkered group they were.

Directly below where Lawless kept lookout sat Dan Morgan with two teenage boys as cohorts. He eyed the group morosely from where he hid behind his long, black beard. Next to him was Ben Hall, quietly dressed like a farmer, sharing a tree trunk with "the Jockey" and Johnny Gilbert, who had dressed for the occasion, wearing a flamboyant red shirt and knee-high boots. Over from them squatted James McPherson, who called himself "the wild Scotsman," his lean face pensive, his hands clasped around his knees. Beside the Scotsman, settled on the other trunk, was Old Joe Dailey, pipe in his mouth, nicknamed "old" because his hair was pure white, although his age was only twenty-nine. Beside him was one of his partners. Next to them were Alan and Jordan. Jordan's blue shirt was unbuttoned to show a yellow kerchief tied around his thick brown neck. Making up the circle were Lefty Dawson, a big, lumbering man in a cabbage-tree hat, and his brother Kenny, smoking a cheroot.

It was to be the last and the largest gathering of bushrangers ever on the Australian continent.

Exactly one month later, James McPherson would be captured, only to escape and be recaptured a year later and sentenced to fifty years' imprisonment. He, in fact, would serve only eight.

Within three months, Dan Morgan would be shot dead.

Within four months, Ben Hall would be shot dead.

In just over four months, Johnny Gilbert would be shot dead.

Within nine months, Lefty Dawson would be caught and within twelve months hanged, and his brother would be jailed for fifteen years.

Before the year was out, "the Jockey" would be caught and within eighteen months hanged.

One year later, Old Joe Daily would be captured and subsequently sentenced to thirty years' imprisonment. He would, in fact serve sixteen.

But on this hot, humid January day, they were all very much alive, and they sat weighing each other up as the minutes passed.

"Tell us why we be here, Ben?" Old Joe broke the silence. "It was from ye that I received the message."

"I asked you all to come," Hall replied in his quiet voice,

"but I'm not sure why 'cept I thought perhaps we might be able to help each other, as it seems the traps closin' upon us, under this mongrel Blake." He stopped speaking and looked to Alan. "Is there not usually a 'chairman' or something when there's a meeting?"

"Yes, usually," Alan agreed.

"Then it had best be you," suggested Hall deferentially.

"Yes, boss," agreed Jordan.

"That's right." Daily nodded, pointing with his pipe. "Ye do it, governor, 'old boy.' Ye be the one who has had the experience with genteel matters like chairmen and all."

Everyone laughed except Dan Morgan, who moved uncomfortably and repositioned himself on the rock.

"Well then," Alan said, "is there something you would all like to discuss?"

"Yeah," said Gilbert, "I'd like to discuss how to shoot bloody Blake. That'd get rid of our biggest problem straight off."

There was general amusement at this recommendation, and a few lewd suggestions about which part of his anatomy the bullets should remove.

"No, come on, fellas," called Ben Hall over the noise, his expression solemn, "we're not here to talk about Blake's balls. Let's talk serious."

Kenny Dawson dug his brother in the ribs. Lefty Dawson responded by saying, "What about this here act that's becomin' common talk. That sounds bloody serious to me."

"Yeah, what about that," asked Gilbert. "Ominous, I'd call it."

Alan bent forward, elbows on knees. "Yes, I believe much will change when Parliament passes it. What Lefty refers to is the Felons' Apprehension Act. No doubt you have all read about it."

"I can't read," spoke up the Jockey.

"Shaddup," replied Gilbert.

Alan continued. "It is an extreme measure, an outlawry act dating back many centuries. I assure you, if they bring it into force, it is because they see the present state of affairs as an intolerable threat. The government cannot allow us to continue as we are."

"Yeah, the bastards are afraid of us," spoke up James Mc-Pherson.

Alan nodded. "I think you are right, but men in fear do not behave moderately." He looked around the ring of faces. "We may find that 'safe houses' will no longer be safe, and men we have all trusted will no longer be trustworthy.''

"Why do ye say that, guv?" asked Daily.

"Everything I've read points to heavy jail sentences for helping outlaws, and worse for harboring. Fear alone will close their doors to you."

"But some say such an act is a long way off," declared McPherson.

"Na," retorted Gilbert, shaking his head, "they'll pass it soon, the bastards."

"It won't make no difference to my mates," said Lefty Dawson. "They'll stand by me."

"Mine neither," spoke up the Jockey. "They'll be true blue."

McPherson agreed. "Yes, I can count on the blokes that've helped me in the past."

"Gentlemen!" said Alan.

They fell silent.

"You don't seem to understand. There may be a sentence of fifteen or twenty years for these 'mates' of yours, if they so much as point you in the direction of water. To make matters worse, many outlawry acts make it legal to shoot outlaws on sight. If that becomes law it will be a different world."

"Holy bloody hell!" the Jockey exclaimed.

Alan looked grave. "Thus, Ben Hall was right to call us here to see if there might be any way to prolong survival."

"Do you think there is?" asked Hall, looking hopefully at Alan.

"Yes, do ye believe there is?" repeated Daily in the same way.

"Possibly," answered Alan.

Quiet descended.

A slight breeze had sprung up, taking some of the steaminess out of the hot summer air. It blew in tranquil change across the company on the hill. The horses snorted and moved their hooves in enjoyment of the difference.

Gilbert removed his hat, and his long, wavy hair lifted gently back over his shoulders.

Alan looked around the strange group. "I think there *is* a way we might avoid Rutherford Blake's net, but we all must agree on it. We know that the police force is centrally controlled in Sydney."

"Do we?" asked the Jockey.

"Shaddup," ordered Gilbert.

"The police districts are often too large for the numbers of police to enforce the law properly, and even Rutherford Blake is not autonomous. He has to get his plans agreed to by the inspector general in Sydney. Now, all that is time-consuming, and while he has the telegraph system, Blake is hidebound much of the time to Bathurst, for the telegraph ends there. Hence, he forays into the countryside only when he seeks to get one of us, and that is usually after a major raid.''

''What the devil's the point ye make?'' thudded the heavy voice of Dan Morgan, who had held silence until now.

''The point is this,'' Alan continued, looking now directly at Morgan. ''If we used an agreed-upon stratagem, we—''

''What the hell is that?'' Morgan broke in again.

''A plan, a scheme for obtaining an advantage,'' explained Alan. ''We can divide the colony up into districts similarly to the way the police have done, and we each keep to within our alloted areas.''

Ben Hall was listening closely, his face earnest with concentration. ''Go on,'' he prompted.

''Then, don't you see, we would keep the police divided. Blake simply would not be able to mount the large search parties he has in the past, for we all would be operating at extreme distances. Let me give you an example. Although we all have acquaintances who pass on news to us, our own 'bush telegraph' if you like, it is not always as swift or as reliable as we need it to be. If I had known that you—'' Alan motioned to Ben Hall ''—had done two robberies near Theresa Town last October, I would not have ridden quite so casually into the goldfield to remove the government's gold. It was a little disquieting to find eight troopers in residence instead of two, as well as Rutherford Blake himself. Now, I'm not saying our raid was not successful. It was. But perhaps a raid elsewhere would have been safer for my men.''

Hall was absorbed in Alan's words. ''I see what you mean.''

''And so, too, if you, Dan Morgan, had not done the Cootamundry racetrack robbery four days before you, Old Joe, held up the Cootamundry mail, or vise versa, then you, Joe, would have four men in your band today instead of three.''

''True.'' Old Joe nodded. ''Ida never done the bloody coach if Ida known there was traps around lookin' for ye, Morgan.''

''Yes,'' agreed Ben Hall, ''I *do* see what you mean.'' He turned to Lefty Dawson. ''That goes for us as well. We wouldn't have done Dry Flat if I'd known you'd been there a couple of days before. Traps almost took us there.''

"Yeah. Bloody bullet actually grazed me," said Gilbert, holding up his hand to show the mark.

"So . . . if we each took a division of land, and the areas are quite huge enough for all of us, and kept our own efforts within them, the large raids would be so separated that such incidents as we have just discussed could never happen," argued Alan. "And Blake's force would be so divided, he would have real difficulty maintaining any sort of pressure upon us."

"But, boss," spoke up Jordan, "there are always the petty thieves, and they will still be robbin' all over."

"They do not mount police search parties for them, lad. We are the ones they want. There is not a man here who doesn't have a price on his head, and Rutherford Blake wants us all. This is the one way I believe we can make it hard for him."

Every eye watched Alan. He turned his smooth, sun-browned face away from the assembly to look up at Lawless. He was a prepossessing figure meticulously dressed in dark gray with boots brought to a lustrous shine. He had spoken well and articulately, exactly as Ben Hall had hoped he would.

There were mutterings of agreement.

"Yes, I like it," said Ben Hall, "and so what sort of areas do you think we should—"

He got no further, for suddenly Dan Morgan jumped to his feet in a blind fury, and pulling a revolver from his belt, fired it indiscriminately in the air.

The explosion reverberated through the bush stillness.

Lawless, who stood at lookout on the rock above him, yelled in fright as the bullet shot straight past his face.

Alan started as the others jumped to their feet in amazement.

"What the fuck . . ."

"Shit!"

"Christ, man, are ye mad?"

"Bloody 'ell!"

Dan Morgan stood violently shaking his revolver in the air.

Alan had recovered quickly; there was resignation in his voice. "Have you something to say, Morgan?"

"Too bloody right!" Morgan screamed. "I'll not sit 'ere and be told by a bloody upper-class dandy where and when I may go abroad. I've been doin' all right the way I am. Ye'll not point at a map and tell me where to live. Ye're a bastard!" he yelled, waving his revolver at Alan. "And no doubt in this carvin' up, ye've saved the best for yerself!"

"Drop the revolver, Morgan! Or I'll be puttin' a bullet through yer mad dog's brain this second!'' shouted Lawless, who had regained his senses and now trained his rifle on Morgan's head.

"He means what he says, Morgan!'' Alan's voice was icy now. "We don't hold with killing, but we can make an exception.''

Morgan was panting with fury. Saliva ran from the corner of his mouth to lodge in his thick, black beard. He looked resentfully around their faces. "Bastards!'' he exclaimed, dropping the revolver to the ground.

"I gather you don't agree with our proposal,'' Alan said quietly.

Ben Hall shook his head. "You're a fool, Morgan, a bloody, stupid fool!''

"I'll not be told what to do!'' Dan Morgan answered, shaking his now empty hand in the air. "Not by ye or any fuckin' man. Arrogant arseholes! Now, I be ridin' out o' here, and me boys with me.''

"Then walk steady, fellas,'' called Lawless loudly, "and mount real, real slow. I can make a proper mess of each one of ye at this range.''

Morgan and his two associates moved to their horses.

Alan picked up the revolver and emptied it of its bullets.

"I'll die game, I bloody will!'' Morgan stated as Alan handed him up his empty gun.

"No doubt,'' answered Alan.

A few seconds later, Morgan spurred away down the hill to meet his fate.

Old Joe Daily watched his retreating figure. "No wonder they call him 'Mad Dog.' ''

Ben Hall spoke almost to himself. "He's a mindless fool, and we will all pay for his stupidity.''

"For a minute I thought we was goners,'' philosophized the Jockey.

"Yeah, he's bloody mad enough for anythin'!'' commented Lefty Dawson.

McPherson came back a few paces from where he had watched Morgan ride away. He hesitated before he spoke. "Look, you blokes, it's not that I'm in agreement with Morgan, for he's an odd bugger, no doubt about it, but I'm a bit of a free spirit meself. I work alone, you see. It's the Scot in me.'' He smiled. "Like to keep the rewards for meself. Now, I prefer to cover great distances, and if the truth be said, although your idea is a sound one, Fletcher, I'm not denyin' that, actually . . . I'd rather not be a part of it.''

Kenny Dawson looked speculatively at his brother. ''Yeah, he could be right, Lefty. Might still be better to work the way we have been, I reckon.''

Ben Hall sighed loudly, a very dejected sound.

Fifteen minutes later, the hill was quiet. The bushrangers had all departed.

When Alan said good-bye to Ben Hall, they were both on their horses, ready to ride away. They looked at each other in silence a few seconds.

''It was a brave idea you had, Ben Hall,'' Alan said.

''Yes,'' he answered, ''and it was a good and feasible plan you had.''

''Be careful,'' Alan said, leaning forward and offering his hand.

Ben Hall took it in both of his as he had done earlier, but this time he held on to it for a long time.

When at last he let it go, he said, ''Thank you.''

TWENTY-FIVE
Father

The following evening, close to the hour of six, Alan was riding cross-country toward Bathurst. In his breast pocket was a letter from Eve to Father.

It had been another hot day with sun searing down from a cloudless sky, so opposite to that of a few weeks before. All around him on the plain grew the purple Patterson's curse. It had burst into bloom after the flood, and Freedom thudded now through a sea of deep violet flowers.

He came to Reverend Billings at night, for he was very aware that as Bathurst was the headquarters of Sir Rutherford Blake, there could be as many as twenty or twenty-five troopers billeted in the town at any one time. On entering the township, he avoided the police paddock at the end of Russell Street, where the troopers kept and trained their horses, and made his way to George Street. Opposite the park, where he had met Eve and where John Stuart had first seen her, he dismounted and hitched Freedom among the twenty or thirty horses collected at the side of Buckle's Ale House, a large, popular place, which stayed open until late.

"Wait here, my beauty," he said softly, and the animal, in answer, gave the gentlest of whinnies.

Bathurst was a straggling settlement. Like any country town of the time, there were no lamps in the wide, unpaved streets, and any illumination came only from the moon and the indirect light from the buildings. The streets were all but deserted, yet the ever pervasive smell of dust and horses hung in the night air.

All Saints' Church and parsonage were in the next block to the jail, but rather than walk by it, and the policeman at its entrance, he took a circuitous route and came back toward his destination from the opposite direction. He was some hundred yards from his objective when a door not far ahead opened in a stone wall and two men came out in front of him and turned toward him. Alan instantly saw the police uniform one wore but continued on at the same pace. As they passed, the man nearest Alan, who wore mufti, greeted him.

"Good evening."

"Evenin'," Alan replied, recognizing Rutherford Blake.

To gain the parsonage, Alan had to cross the road and turn the corner, but he dared not go toward it. Instead he continued straight ahead.

Meanwhile, Rutherford Blake had stopped dead and turned to watch Alan's receding figure.

"What's wrong, sir?" asked Constable Crystal, his thick eyebrows rising.

"Now, who is that man? He's not a local. Where have I seen him before?"

"Dunno, sir."

Alan did not accelerate, although every nerve in his body strained to do so. He concentrated on reaching the corner and turning it.

Sir Rutherford's mind was calculating his dark form and the way he moved.

By now Alan had almost gained the corner.

Suddenly Sir Rutherford remembered. "Halt!" he called loudly. "You there! I wish to speak with you!"

As he shouted, Alan reached the corner, and turning it, ran as fast as he could down Russell Street away from the town.

Sir Rutherford was now certain of his identity. "Damn it, Crystal! That man is Alan Fletcher! Quickly, this way!"

They raced to the corner in time to see Alan leap a fence and run across an open paddock toward the backs of the houses in the next street.

"Stop! Stop!" both Sir Rutherford and the constable shouted in unison as they ran after him and jumped the fence in pursuit.

Alan's figure could be seen reaching the side of one of the houses some fifty yards away.

"Give me your revolver, man!" shouted Sir Rutherford, who was one of the best small arms' marksmen in the colony.

Constable Crystal handed the revolver he carried in a pouch at his waist to his superior, who took aim in the poor light, steadying his right wrist with his left hand. The gun exploded as Alan disappeared down the side of the house and was lost in the trees.

"Did ye hit him, sir?"

"I'm not sure. Come on."

The noise of the discharge brought people out of their homes, and as Sir Rutherford and the constable raced along the side of the house where Alan had gone, people appeared at the front.

"There he goes," called the constable, pointing as Alan crossed the street and leaped a fence.

"Stop, thief!" shouted one of the men who had come out into the street in time to see Sir Rutherford charging after Alan.

Others appeared at the front of the house across the street to see what all the noise was about. They carried a lantern, and as Sir Rutherford and the trooper ran up to them, in the light of the lantern, they saw blood on the whitewashed fence where Alan had leaped over.

"Ah yes," he cried, "see that? I have winged him."

Alan could hear the hue and cry after him. The bullet had ripped through his jacket and shirt, opening the flesh at the top of his arm, and continuing on to lodge in a tree trunk. He ran, all his senses intensified, as he vaulted fences and careered down streets and lanes.

Sir Rutherford was loudly deputizing as many of the townsfolk as he could to search for the bushranger. The shouting and screaming seemed to come from all directions.

It was almost impossible to keep track of where he was. On he ran, trying to attend the buildings he passed and always moving away from the noise of pursuit. Finally, when he could no longer hear yelling and shouting, he took stock of where he was. With relief, he realized he was in the lane behind the hay and corn market, which was only a block and a half from All Saints'. Luck had brought him around in a circle. He ventured to the lane's end. Down the street some few hundred yards to the right, he could see figures in the night holding lanterns, but they were moving in the opposite direction.

Stealthily he crossed the uneven road and walked on. He turned in to the small street that ran in front of the church and the parsonage. All was silent.

He was breathing heavily and he moved inside the church grounds and came to rest in the church porch. He stood a minute to regain his breath.

He put his hand inside his coat and felt the letter he carried. Then he took a handkerchief from his pocket and wrapped it as best he could around the wound, knotting it with the use of his teeth and his right hand. As he crossed the churchyard, his boots crunched on the gravel between the gravestones. He looked to right and left.

No one in sight.

He jumped the small stone wall that divided the churchyard from the rectory. As he did so, Martin Carlyle, the church warden, closed the side door of All Saints'. He had been in to return the altar silver, which his wife polished at home once a week. The warden saw the dark shape bound across the stone wall, and he watched it move noiselessly into the shadow of the trees at the side of the parsonage. Curiosity led Martin to hurry to the street in time to see Mistress Lottie having conversation with the figure.

She had come to the door when Alan knocked. "Who is there?"

Alan replied, "I come on urgent business to see the parson."

She opened the door and saw the stranger. Her face grew stern. "What business can ye possibly have with the reverend?"

"I must see him, lass."

Lottie looked at him keenly. "Where are ye from? Ye are not from hereabouts."

"No, I come from far afield to carry a message to Reverend Billings. It is imperative that I speak with him now."

A rueful expression came to her face. "Then ye don't know?"

"Know what?"

"The Reverend Billings is very ill; it's not but ten minutes since the doctor's been. So I cannot allow ye in, and that's all there is to it." She went to close the door, but Alan held it open.

Lottie could look formidable when she chose, and she chose to now.

Alan looked into her eyes. "Now, please, lass, I entreat you to stand aside, for it's imperative I see the clergyman, ill or not."

There was something about the man that made Lottie waver. "Why?"

"I bring a message from Mrs. . . . Wakeman."

Lottie's mouth opened in surprise. "Oh! In that case, come in."

As she closed the door behind him, in the light from the hall lamp, she saw the bloody handkerchief wrapped around his left arm. With a sharp intake of breath she said, "Oh, ye are hurt!"

Alan shook his head. "It is but a graze. Unimportant. It is seeing the cleric that's important. Is he able to speak?"

Alan saw now that her eyes were puffy from crying and that she was full of sorrow.

The woman nodded and tears rose to her eyes. "Though Dr. Walker says it's but a day or two he has left. He is . . . dying." Then she regained a little of her severity. "Ye have not come to atrouble him, have ye?"

"No." His voice was sympathetic. "Can you tell me what happened?"

"Oh, it were all too dreadful. Ye see, in the flood, Mrs. Billings and the reverend were out atrying to help folk as was homeless. . . ."

Here tears brimmed over her lids, and Alan said gently, "There, lass, I'm sorry to distress you."

She sighed deeply. "They got . . . caught in a flooded arm of the Macquarie. Mrs. Billings drowned, ye see. Oh, it's terrible, and the good reverend, in atrying to save her, harmed himself so greatly that he took mortally ill. Oh, it's too terrible."

Alan patted her on the shoulder. "Take me to him, lass."

Down the corridor that Eve had passed along so many happy times, they went.

"Ye won't disturb him too much?" she asked as they halted outside his door.

Alan shook his head. "I hope not, and I will be as brief as my message allows."

"I will tell him ye be here. What is your name, sir?"

"Just tell him I come from Mrs. Wakeman."

Lottie looked intently at him again.

"Please, lass."

She sighed with resignation and went in, shortly to reappear. "I will await ye in the hall. Go in."

Alan entered and closed the door behind him. The room was lit by two lamps, one on a table by the bed, the other on a mantel shelf on the far side of the room.

In a four-poster bed lay the man Eve called Father. He was propped up on pillows, and his face was gaunt. Beads of perspiration covered his high forehead. His look was troubled as he brought his eyes up to regard the intruder.

Alan came close beside the bed. "Reverend Billings?"

"Yes?"

"I bring a letter from the one who regards you as her father. Are you able to read it, sir?"

"Eve . . ." He said her name like a prayer. He spoke with great difficulty and his breath was labored. "Yes, I can read, if it is from my darling. But I do not understand who you are and why you come to me."

"She is no longer at Mayfield, sir. Please read the letter; it will explain."

Father pointed to the spectacles that lay on the table in the lamplight. Alan picked them up, and as he leaned to place them on the sick man, Father lifted his hand and took hold of Alan's arm. "And who are you?"

"I am Alan Fletcher, sir."

"I thought as much," uttered Father with a quivering sigh. "And I see someone has been shooting at you."

"Rutherford Blake. It is merely a flesh wound, though it bleeds freely."

Then he opened the letter and held it for Father to read. It said:

*Written at a place of safety,
January 11th, 1865*

My Dearest Father and Mother,

You may or may not know that I no longer live at Mayfield. If you have heard of this, then I am truly sorry to have worried you. If not, herewith is the truth.

I left Mayfield of my own free will. I am sadly alienated from John Stuart. I am with a friend who is the bearer of this letter. He is an honorable man, who, as luck would have it, found me alone and ill in Cowra on Boxing Day.

You will know him, Father, for he is the man we spoke about as we sat beneath the jacaranda tree in your back garden, when I visited with you in November 1863. Understand that he is my dear friend and comes to deliver this letter at great personal danger to himself.

I am not yet fit to travel, but I will come to you some weeks hence, and then I will explain everything, my dear ones.

For the meantime, remember that I am well and safe. I trust my life with the man who brings this dispatch.

I miss you both and I love you very dearly,
Evvy

Father closed his eyes. "Ah, that it has come to this."

He opened his eyes and tried to raise himself and contemplate the man who stood at his bedside. A second or two later, he sank heavily back upon the pillows.

He reminded Alan of an old lion he had seen on the veldt, inland from Natal Bay in the Cape Colony. The lion was alone and dying, and as he and his companions approached, it raised itself up on its front paws and shook its craggy head defiantly.

Alan could see that the clergyman was close to death.

"My darling says . . . she will come to me a few weeks hence. I fear she will come to a graveside. Can you . . . possibly understand what that means to me, Alan Fletcher?"

"I am not sure, sir."

"Then I must make you sure. My Evvy writes of you . . . as moral and good. Is that how you would describe yourself?"

Alan said nothing for a few seconds and then he leaned down toward the clergyman. "That is how she sees me, and for her sake, I would be that."

Father regarded Alan steadily. His life was ebbing away, and he was so conscious of his responsibility to his darling Eve. This was the bushranger, the outlaw, the felon he had heard about, read about. And yet this same man, his Evvy said, she "knew" to be fine and good.

Something terrible must have occurred at Mayfield, something that had driven her from her home and husband. Yet did the letter not say she was "well and safe"? And if that were so, it was due to this Alan Fletcher. Father needed to rally, to find the strength to converse. He prayed to his God to give him the capacity.

"I had two loves, Alan Fletcher," he said at last, "Lillian, whom I made my wife, and . . . Evelyn May Herman, who was my long-lost daughter."

Alan stood silently listening.

"The one who was my companion is gone. The other writes to me, to tell me things . . . that perhaps I would rather not read."

"I understand that, sir."

"Yes, I believe you do." Father stopped speaking, and his labored breathing lasted for a long time.

Once again, he raised himself a little with an obvious effort of will. "You see, I am but a man. A broken, tired old man. The Lord has seen fit to take my Lily, and thus, I, too, must go, for what am I without her? For Evvy, I wish I could stay, but that is not . . . to be."

"I am sorry, sir."

Father nodded. They looked at each other for some seconds without speaking.

"I want you to know, sir . . ." Alan began, and stopped short, for the sound of raised voices in the hall outside carried to them.

It was the voice of Sir Rutherford Blake arguing with Lottie!

"I must see the man who is with the parson!" came his shout.

"The parson is very ill," answered Lottie's voice, raised in irritation. "Ye must not go in."

"Let me by!" sounded Sir Rutherford's voice again.

"No!" came Lottie's high-pitched answer, followed by a scuffling sound.

Apprehension fleetingly crossed Alan's face. He looked quickly around the room.

Then Father spoke. "Move, get behind me . . . behind the drapes at the back of my bed."

There were long, heavy brocade curtains hanging from a canopy above to the floor at the back of the bedstead. Swiftly Alan moved behind them just as the door opened and Sir Rutherford Blake burst into the room.

He was followed closely by Lottie, expostulating on how she had tried to stop him. Out in the hall stood Constable Crystal and another trooper.

"Where is he?" Sir Rutherford demanded as he entered, looking speedily to right and left.

Father raised his hand. "What do you mean . . . by this intrusion?"

"Oh, excuse me, Reverend," Sir Rutherford apologized. "I

am sorry for the use of force, ah yes, but I am told you had a visitor whom I believe is a wanted man."

Father's ailing eyes could still flash, and so they did now. "Sir Rutherford, this . . . is unforgivable!"

The detective policeman was slightly taken aback, and for a second or two said nothing. When he again spoke, it was in a quieter, more even tone. "Reverend Billings, I should never have been so brash as to intrude in this manner upon one so ill had I not been told by your own church warden that he saw a man enter the parsonage who fitted the description of the man I chase. You see, sir, at this very minute, my men are searching the town for the bushranger Alan Fletcher."

Father closed his eyes. "I see."

"Ah yes, I hope you do, sir. For it is very important that I apprehend him. I am led to believe there has been a man who fits his description in here, that is, in the parsonage. I must ask you if he has been in this room with you."

"There was a man here, but he has gone."

"I hate to bring any unnecessary stress upon you, Reverend, but I must ask who he was."

"A friend, who brought me a letter . . . a very important personal letter."

"You are a man of God, sir!" declared Sir Rutherford. "Do I have your word the man was not Alan Fletcher?"

Father opened his eyes. He looked directly into his inquisitor's face.

"You do," he said.

Sir Rutherford almost groaned in disappointment. "Then I believe you. The warden must have been mistaken. Accept my apologies for disturbing you."

Lottie had stood silently in the background, tense with horror. She had been watching a bloodstain on the brocade drapes at the back of the bed. Watching it widen!

Sir Rutherford moved back from the bed, and as his eyes lifted in the direction of the blood, Lottie's voice sounded unnaturally loudly in his ears. "This way, Sir Rutherford! Come along, I will see ye out." With a theatrical wave of her hand, she ushered him to the door.

The door closed, and some twenty or so seconds elapsed before Father said, "It is safe. You can come out."

The brocade moved and Alan came to the bedside. "Thank you, sir. I don't know how to express my gratitude for what you did just now."

Father looked up into Alan's face and met his eyes. "I did it for Eve."

Alan nodded.

"Tell her . . . there is a small estate for us to leave. . . . It is now hers. Tell her to see Mr. Lees, the solicitor here. There is a matter of some three hundred and fifty pounds, mostly dear Lily's from her parents before her."

"I will, sir."

"And give her this." Father pointed to the leather-bound Bible lying on his bed.

At the same time, there was a gentle knock on the door. Startled, Alan turned toward it.

"Do not worry," said Father. "It is Lottie."

His body tense, his hand on the revolver in his belt, Alan watched the door open and the woman enter.

Father lifted his hand in a weak gesture. "Lottie . . . you have perhaps guessed who our . . . visitor is."

"I have," she answered, "and the sooner he be aleaving, the better."

Father beckoned her closer. The exertion had taken its toll, and he spoke now barely above a whisper. "Dear Lottie, this man is our friend. . . . He is a good man. He brings news of Miss Evvy. She is in . . . his care."

Lottie looked up at Alan and considered him. She was a bush woman, and she took this news in her stride. "I see."

"You must . . . bathe his wound . . . help him to leave Bathurst . . . make sure he gets away safely, dear Lottie . . . I beg you." His voice faded.

"You be tired, sir," the good woman said. "Leave it all to me. Get some sleep now, dear Reverend Billings." She tucked the sheet in at the side of the bed.

Father lifted his hand again. "Alan Fletcher . . ."

Alan moved closer. "Yes, sir."

Father took his hand. "I don't know how it is so, but I know you have all the . . . qualities that my Evvy says, and I believe . . . you will look after her."

"I will keep your trust," Alan answered.

The dying man closed his eyes as Alan followed Lottie from the room.

"Ye be lucky there's only me here," she scolded as they went down the corridor. "There used to be two of us maids, but Jennie, the other, has gone just yesterday, to look after the new

parson.'' She pursed her lips before she added, ''I doubt ye
could have trusted her.''

''Then I'm fortunate indeed that it is you who are here,'' Alan
replied as they entered the kitchen.

As she heated some water to bathe his injury, Alan noticed
all the blinds were drawn.

''Take the shirt off, please, Mr. Fletcher.''

''You have a great affection for the reverend, I see,'' Alan
said as she bathed his wound.

''He is the best man God ever saw fit to place upon the earth,
as was the mistress the best woman. Why the Heavenly Father
has chosen to take them is beyond a mere body like mesel'.''
Tears welled in her eyes again and Alan comforted her.

''Don't be too sad, Mistress Lottie. He will be remembered
with love and affection, and that alone is the most remarkable
of achievements.''

She bound his wound, and he stood from the table.

''You are a kind soul, Mistress Lottie, and I thank you. I shall
leave at once. I would not have you or the parson at any more
risk for me.''

She looked alarmed. ''But that is not what I've been told,''
she declared. ''The reverend was particular that I *must* help ye,
and aputting ye out of doors to be surrounded by the troopers is
not ahelping ye, I'm sure.''

''I do not want you in any more peril; I can make my own
way now.''

Lottie pulled herself up to her whole height and put her hands
on her hips, and in what reminded Alan of Samuel, she pressed
home her point. ''Now, Mr. Fletcher, I do not know aught of
ye but what I've read. The *Bathurst Times* says ye are a fearsome
robber, while such as the *Katoomba Advertiser* writes that ye
have never robbed any but the government and the exceeding
rich, which I approve of. *The Plainsman* paints ye as romantic
and brave, while the Sydney newspapers say ye be a blackguard
and a devil.'' She sighed. ''So who do I believe? The Reverend
Billings, that's who! And he says you are good and our friend,
and that I must be ahelping ye out o' Bathurst. Now, ye must
wait here until those that do the searching are sure they can find
naught. Where's the animal ye came to Bathurst upon?'' she
finished disconcertingly.

Alan smiled. ''In George Street, near Buckle's Ale House.''

''Very good, for that lot in there will be staying adrinking for
hours yet. Now, if ye be our friend, Sir Rutherford is not. Thus,

it's the two of us, Mr. Fletcher, who will be walking the streets o' Bathurst arm in arm in a few hours' time, for the troopers will be looking for a man alone, not one with a female on his arm."

"You are a forceful woman, Mistress Lottie." Alan smiled again.

For the first time in weeks, Lottie smiled back. "It's thanks to the Lord that I be just that."

Three hours later, as midnight fast approached, Lottie and Alan left the sleeping Reverend Billings and made their way through the churchyard to the street on the far side of All Saints'.

Alan had gone into Father's room before he left and stood a few moments in silence looking down at the sleeping man, now withered by his mortal illness. What pain this death would bring to her who waited at Treehard. He was sorry he had to bring more grief to her, for she had suffered enough already.

When they left the house, Lottie was dressed in her darkest gown, and Alan in some of the Reverend Billings's clothes, including a pair of eyeglasses. They made their way arm in arm down William Street, onto Lambert, and finally onto George. A large dog came out and barked as they passed the Empire Hotel, and Lottie's hand tightened on Alan's good arm as she said, "Oh Lord, I do hate big dogs!"

A lamp lit the windows of the alehouse, still as noisy as ever. In the hitching yard, they found Freedom, and on him they returned to the churchyard. This time they passed two police. One carried a lantern. The men looked up at them, but registering the skirts of a woman, they simply said, "Good night."

Down the side of All Saints', they rode, and around to the back of the church. After they had hitched Freedom to the reverend's sulky, Lottie returned inside. When she came out, she carried Father's Bible and a small portmanteau of silver.

"Mistress Lottie, you are as brave as any man I know. I thank you for what you have done."

"As it happened, Mr. Fletcher, there was no danger at all."

"That there could have been was where the courage lay."

He took her hand. "I fear the good Reverend will not last many days. But be not too sad. He wouldn't want you to mourn; I am sure of that. Where will you go, Mistress Lottie, when that time comes?"

"The master has taken care o' me. I am to engage in the cleaning of the church for a small annuity, and I'm to work two days a week for Mrs. Ayres in her tea shop. Mrs. Ayres is a sweet and generous soul, and will look after me. Truth is, I'm the lucky one, for there be six tiny cottages belonging to the church down by the river. The reverend has seen to it that one is my home whilst I live. Noble is what he's been, Mr. Fletcher.''

"I understand that, Mistress Lottie. I know he has also left a legacy to Eve.''

She nodded. "Yes, that's as what the reverend told me.''

"Can I ask you to do one more thing?''

She smiled at him again, and now there was approval in her expression. "You can.''

"It will be a long time before Eve is able to travel here and claim her bequest. If a letter were soon to come to you, would you take it privately to the solicitor Mr. Lees?''

"Of course I will, certainly.''

"Thank you, Mistress Lottie.'' He pulled himself up onto the vehicle with his good arm.

She smiled up at him. "Please be passing my love to Miss Eve.''

He looked down at her, and in the dim light their eyes met in a silent good-bye. Then he took the sulky forward into the night.

As she watched him leave, she could not help saying aloud, "Oh, please, do be ever so careful, Mr. Fletcher,'' before she turned away and hurried inside.

In a short time, Alan came to the edge of town. Ahead of him he could see a lantern standing on a barbed wire fence post. In its timid light, two troopers spoke to two riders on horseback, while a third trooper lounged nearby. They waved the horsemen on, and all turned at the sound of Freedom's approach.

"Halt!''

One trooper blocked his way, and the other two came forward. "Who are ye and why are ye abroad at such an hour?''

"I am Thomas Drew, salesman of fine silver.''

He looked down through the spectacles in haughty fashion. "I am upon the road at this unfortunate hour for I needs must be in Lucknow before breakfast, my friends. There, to make a sale of the finest silver this side of the Blue Mountains.'' Alan leaned down, waving one of the reverend's goblets in front of their noses. "Would you be interested in buying some yourselves?''

"No, no,'' replied the trooper with the rifle. "Methinks ye fellows would sell to yer own mothers. Write that down, Simmons,'' he said over his shoulder to the policeman with the book, "Thomas Drew, silver salesman.'' Then he looked up to Alan. "Lucknow, ye say? That's to be yer destination?''

"That's right."

"Write that down, too, Simmons." He waved Alan by. "On yer way."

The three constables were looking for a bushranger, on a single horse, who had been hit by a bullet, not an uninjured, smartly dressed silver salesman in a gig.

Three hours later, Alan arrived at the North Star. Sitting wide-awake on the front vernada, he found Lawless. The rest of the house had long gone to bed.

"I been worried sick, guverner," Lawless admitted, looking in amazement at the sulky.

"I knew you would be, lad, but there was little I could do about it." He put his good right arm around Lawless's shoulder. "I shall tell you all about it in the morning. Let's get a few hours sleep and be on our way home."

At the same time that Alan and Lawless entered the North Star, an alert Sir Rutherford roamed his office in the lamplight. David Elrington sat watching, a frown of preoccupation between his eyes.

The police detective shook his head. "We've definitely lost him. Too many hours have gone by, Mr. Elrington."

"Yes, sir, I'm afraid so."

Sir Rutherford turned to his assistant. "Mr. Elrington, how long ago is it since I sent to England for the transcripts of his trial?"

"I suppose it must be four or five months."

"Is that all? Then it's unlikely that they could be here before another four or five. Damn!"

"Let's hope we've caught him before then."

"Ah yes, Mr. Elrington, I like your optimism, but the man has avoided the arm of the law for twelve years. It seems quite feasible that he may continue to do so."

"Yes, he's a jolly sight more clever than the average bush-ranger."

There was an expression of bemused admiration on the detective policeman's face as he replied, "Mr. Elrington, he is a jolly sight cleverer than the average *anything*."

Some hours after the evening meal on the following night, in the typical enervating, still Australian summer heat, Eve sat on the Treehard veranda with Daniel and Samuel in the pale moonlight.

It had been twenty days since she had arrived at Treehard. She felt almost well again and was mentally preparing herself to leave this place. Somewhat wistfully, she looked at the two men and the scene around her now.

She remembered Alan's words of some days earlier. "We do not complain," he had said. "Society must have rules for the good of the majority, and although there are miscarriages of justice and harsh sentencing, which we at Treehard have all experienced, the British system is still probably the fairest in the world. It is some of the men who work within it that I would change."

It seemed absurd that these two inoffensive men sitting with her under the stars had bounties on their heads.

They sat quietly, speaking their thoughts now and then. Eve's reflections were mostly on Alan. She pictured him looking at her with his concentrated gaze. How she hoped he was all right, that he had met with Ben Hall and seen Father and that all had gone well. She lifted her eyes up to the stars and heard the rustling bush sounds and the noise of the hot breeze in the trees. Suddenly she had the feeling that he was quite close, and to her surprise, within seconds, out of the still night came a parrot call.

Sam jumped to his feet and ran down the steps and around the side of the dwelling to the tunnel mouth, where he cupped his hands to his lips and replied twice. Back came a call in answer.

"Thank the good Lord God above in His Heaven," cried Daniel, "our boys are back."

A couple of minutes later, Alan and Freedom issued out of the mouth of the passage, followed by Lawless and Jordan.

"At last," said Samuel, "and not a minute too soon. We've been worried sick! I'm tellin' ye. Good grief, what's this?" He pointed to Alan's bandaged arm.

"A flesh wound only, Sam. I'll tell you all about it shortly."

Daniel looked concerned. "Well, come in, and I'll put the kettle on."

"Whiskey for me," answered Jordan, dismounting. "It's been a hard ride and a hell of a stinkin' hot night." He turned to Alan. "Hasn't it, boss?"

"It has, Jordan."

Sam led away the fatigued horses, and the travelers turned toward the steps of their home.

Eve moved to Alan as he came behind Lawless and Jordan. Her face glowed with the pleasure of seeing him, but she was alarmed to learn he was wounded. "I'm so glad you have returned safely. But I fear you have been in danger."

"We are through it and safely here," he told her calmly. "That is all that matters. However, I have news for you, and it is not good. I am sorry." He stood beside her now, and there was sympathy in his eyes.

A chill ran through her, and a look of apprehension crossed her face.

"Come inside, lass." He pointed through the door. "It is best I tell you in private."

Her eyes begged for reassurance, and he steeled himself. How to tell her? Tenderly he took hold of her arm and guided her across the veranda. His touch somehow strengthened her, and they passed inside together. She realized something must be wrong at the parsonage, but nothing could have prepared her for what she was to hear.

When they came to her room, he spoke immediately. "Lass, there is no way to tell you gently. Mrs. Billings was drowned in the flood, and the reverend, in trying to save her, did himself great injury. When I saw him, he had but a little time left."

She felt an icy coldness run through her. "Oh, no!" she cried, shaking her head. "It can't be true."

"I am only sorry that it is."

"But they . . . they cannot *both* be . . ." She turned away in shock, trembling, hugging herself. Her darling Father dying. "I must go to him."

"It would be too late, lass. I fear even now he is gone."

She brought her ashen face back to him. Father gone! Mother gone! The security of life with them gone! Dead! Dead! Mother and Father both dead! She stood looking up at him. His face was blurred through her tears. Blindly she put her hands out toward him, reaching, searching, and then she stepped forward into his arms.

Tears streamed from her eyes and she clung to him as if he, too, might leave her. She was the lonely, unhappy teenage girl again. She sobbed against his chest, and he held her close.

"Now . . . now," he said tenderly. "It will be all right." He swallowed hard as her curls brushed his lips. Every fiber of him yearned to turn her face upward and to kiss her mouth, to kiss away the tears, to alleviate her pain. He cradled her close and stroked her hair, and when she looked up to him with her puffy, red eyes and tearstained face, he thought it was the most perfectly beautiful sight he had ever seen.

"There, lass, weep no more. They were the best of humanity, and you were blessed to be one of those they loved. Think of their benevolence, and the way they enriched the lives they touched. That is a thought to bring joy, not sadness."

"Yes, I know you are right, but . . . ."

He continued to hold her. "Try not to be sad. I will take care of you."

She attempted to smile, and the veriest sound of resolve came to her voice. "But I do not want to be regarded a burden . . . not by you, or the others."

"You could never be that."

His words had the effect of composing her. She believed him as a child believes, as a woman believes the man she loves. She wiped her face and looked up at him with determination, but then her mouth began to quiver and her eyes filled with tears again. "Oh, how terrible it is to think I'll never see their darling faces anymore."

"I understand," he added softly. "But please don't worry. Everything will be all right."

Some five miles to the southwest, in a wide, sweeping valley beside a swiftly running creek, two men sat in the tent they shared together.

They had eaten their evening meal around the campfire with their twenty-four companions, and afterward some of them had told "tall tales" and sung bush songs that echoed along the creek bed in the immense stillness of the endless trees. At around ten o'clock, they drifted off in twos and threes to bed in their own communal tents.

Now, in the vague illumination of the hurricane lamp that sat on a collapsible table between their two stretchers, the two men talked.

"Well, m'boy, how far have we come from Young in the five days?"

John Stuart lifted his eyes from the map he studied and drew his hand across them wearily. "I reckon we've covered an area six miles wide by fifteen long."

"How long do you figure it will take us to investigate the stretch between here and Cowra? There are a lot more heavy woods and scrub to the north, you know."

"I do, old man. If we keep the same pace, it will be another eight days or so."

"Mmm. This searching the bush is all very well, and I am happy to, don't misunderstand. But what if you get to Cowra and we have found nothing?"

John Stuart sighed. "Then I must search farther in from the road. Rutherford is positive the Fletcher hideout is this side of the Sydney road, between Cowra and Young."

Joe nodded. "M'boy, that will see us well into the month of February. Remember, there is rebuilding to complete at home, as well as the lambing in March and the drive in April."

"Yes . . . yes, I know. I realize my responsibilities, and I will not avoid them, but I *have* to do this. I must find her." He lifted his right hand to his forehead as if it were in pain. "Joe, Joe, I am at a loss to understand all this. I am shocked, I am angry, I am affronted, and damn it . . . I *miss* her so very badly."

There was something very tender in the older man's expression as he reached across to touch John Stuart's knee. "I know you do, m'boy, I know you do."

TWENTY-SIX

Sir Rutherford Remembers

Sir Rutherford Blake stood from the small table where he had taken a cool drink, and after doffing his hat to Mrs. Ayres, who was standing behind her cake counter, he strode to the shop door.

It was a day when the sun beat down from a cloudless sky with unforgiving intensity, one of those oppressive Australian days when the heat lies like a eternal woolen blanket over the country. Sir Rutherford, sweating profusely, ached for the moderate summers of the northern hemisphere. Nevertheless, his swift stride was not slowed by the heat and in another minute, he was across the wide dirt street and opening the door to his office. Simultaneously his inner door opened and David Elrington entered.

"Letter just arrived for you, sir. It has the Wakeman seal on it."

His assistant left him as he took it and picked up his long ivory and gold letter opener. His face tightened in concentration as he read.

> *In camp, by the Lachlan River,*
> *Just south of Cowra,*
> *24th January 1865*

Dear Rutherford,

I write this in my tent just after dawn.

I am halfway through a search of the countryside, the like of which, to my knowledge, has never been undertaken before. I, along with Joe Larmer and twenty-four Mayfield men, began in Young on January 8, and investigated the entire country in a six-mile-wide strip running along the Sydney road north as far as Cowra. I am about to turn around and do the same on the inner stretch of six miles, making the width from the Sydney road twelve miles, and touching the Mayfield border in some places.

I know you adamantly believe the bushranger Alan Fletcher has his hideout in this strip of country, and I believe you will be surprised when I say that I search for it. But I think you will be even more surprised when I say I do this to find my wife. Yes, Rutherford, I have reason to believe the outlaw has my wife at his hideout!

Eve left Mayfield on Boxing Day and went to Cowra. There she took ill and became unconscious. I learned that somehow the bushranger found her around eleven o'clock in the morning and that he kidnapped her. There was a second man with him who walked with a limp.

I am assuming that the deputization of myself and Joe Larmer, made when we rode into the hills beyond Mayfield to search for signs of the outlaw, is still in force. My wife's leaving home is something I deeply regret, and I will explain the many contingencies which bring me to this oddest of quests when I next see you.

I live in the hopes that my search will have ended soon and that I have the person dearest to heart with me again. And, too, that I can deliver up to you, at least, information about the bushranger.

*Forgive the ambiguity of this missive. I repeat, I shall ex-
plain the details of this most mixed affair when next we meet.*
                                              Your friend,
                                              John Stuart

Sir Rutherford reread the letter to be sure he had understood.
It was astounding! Mrs. Wakeman kidnapped by Alan Fletcher
in Cowra on Boxing Day! What the hell was this all about? It
was very hard to believe. What the devil was going on? Suddenly he dropped the letter and brought his hand down hard on
the desk. ''Of course!'' he said aloud. ''I see it now!''

Rapidly he passed out into the small corridor and over into
the records room. Soon he was perusing the report lodged by
Sergeant Rodney Samuel on the events that took place north of
Bendick Murrell on the Sydney road on Boxing Day. Samuel
was a good policeman and thorough, and the report was well
detailed. He found the description of the event on the Sydney
road between Koorawatha and Cowra, on the twenty-sixth of
December 1864.

''. . . Two of my constables gave chase into the bush after the
suspect while I and the other two rode forward to meet an on-
coming trio. There were two men and a woman, by name Mr.
and Mrs. James Trent, farmers, and their farmhand, Anthony.
James Trent said his farm is south of Bendick Murrell.''

Sir Rutherford read on eagerly. ''. . . continued to rain during
interview. Mr. Trent said he had been to Christmas with his
mother. His wife was poorly. I let them pass. . . .''

Then Sir Rutherford found the descriptions of the people.

Anthony: No last name given. Occupation, farmhand.
Age: mid to late thirties.
Wore cabbage-tree hat and leather rain cape over clothes.
Sun-browned, clean-shaven, long side whiskers, pale eyes.
Neither a large nor a small man, but muscular.
Mrs. Trent: Farmer's wife.
Age: Late twenties?
Spoke little. Looked tired, even ill. Thin face, fair curls,
pretty.
James Trent: Occupation, farmer.
Age: Probably older than farmhand, Anthony, but uncer-
tain.
Wore bush hat and leather riding cape covering clothing.
Sun-browned, clean-shaven. Light to brown hair, what could

be seen beneath his hat. Probably well above medium height.
Spoke like a bushman, yet troop remarked he had a quality
of authority. An imposing man. From memory, his eyes were
not dark. I think light blue or gray.

Sir Rutherford's lips stretched back across his face in a distorted smile. Ah yes, it *was* Fletcher. Now he was sure. Fletcher
and the Wakeman woman! Riding south. And their companion?
From the description, it was most likely Drake.

The point was, John Stuart and Joe had only mentioned two
men. Perhaps the third who ran at the sight of the police was
not with the trio at all. Even so, he was sure now of the two
with the woman. Of course, he would ascertain whether there
was a James Trent farming south of Bendick Murrell, but he
already knew what the findings would be. He would get Sergeant
Samuel in first thing tomorrow and go over the meeting with
him.

So Fletcher had been heading south of Cowra on the main
road! Yes, John Stuart searched in the right place. He was absolutely certain of that.

He returned to his office and moved across to the map on the
wall. How often he studied it. He ran his finger in habitual
movement down from Cowra past the western borders of Mayfield, and this time stopped on the hamlet of Bendick Murrell.
He had planned to go down south to Wagga Wagga the day after
tomorrow, anyway, after Mad Dan Morgan. That meant he had
to ride through Cowra and Young. With a bit of luck, he might
run into John Stuart. He really should talk to him. Perhaps he
should get going tomorrow.

He turned from the map with a sigh and sat down at the desk,
staring in deep concentration. His mind searched into the night
of January 13, when he had chased Fletcher through Bathurst
town. Suddenly he sat bolt upright. "Ah yes!" he said aloud to
the silent room. "At last, I see much more." He brought his
fist down so heavily on the desk that the lamp that sat to his left
hand wobbled.

It *had* been Fletcher whom the church warden had seen here.
Martin Carlyle, nosy Parker that he was, was reliable. Alan
Fletcher had been here to see Reverend Billings! And it was
something to do with the woman. She was as a daughter to the
clergyman. Alan Fletcher had been in her company since Boxing Day! Had he brought a message to the parson from her?
Fletcher had been there, perhaps even in the room with the dying

man. And on his deathbed, Reverend Billings had lied to save the bushranger. A spasm of shivering ran through him as he remembered how the minister looked him directly in the eye and said it was not Alan Fletcher who had been there. It was hard to believe that the priest had lied. Why? For the woman's sake? Ah yes, most certainly.

Sir Rutherford shook his head.

Mistress Lottie Thatcher had been in it, too, up to her eyeballs in it. God! It was incredible! All was clear at last. When his men had blockaded Bathurst that night, they had given him a list of thirty-nine people they had stopped leaving the town, and there had only been one man they had been unable to trace, a silver salesman on his way to Lucknow, one Thomas Drew by name. Thomas Drew? Silver salesman? Ah yes, Thomas Drew alias Alan Fletcher, was the fact. Sir Rutherford himself had visited each and every homestead and farm in and around Lucknow, and no one had been expecting a silver salesman. Yet his constables had said the man had been dressed in a suit, carried fine silver, wore spectacles, and gave no sign of being wounded. And even more convincing, Thomas Drew had driven a sulky. The parson had died the following morning, so there had been no more conversation with him, but when the new Reverend Cornish had moved into the parsonage, the sulky belonging to All Saints' had been discovered missing.

No doubt it was Mistress Thatcher who had helped him escape. She would have bound his wound and given him the clothes and the silver, too. Ah yes, his reasoning was faultless, he was sure of that.

But what was Mrs. Wakeman's involvement? He recalled her attitude whenever bushrangers had come into the conversation. In retrospect, it was an aversion to discussing them. He recalled the Larmer girl's destructive words. *Perhaps she sympathizes with them.*

When Sir Rutherford called for his assistant and gave him the news, the young man's reaction was one of total bewilderment. "I cannot for the life of me come to believe it, sir. That Mrs. Wakeman is at Alan Fletcher's hideout? It's bizarre, sir."

His superior nodded sagely. "Yes, it is, but so much is clear now that was murky before, eh? It's a pity the Felons' Apprehension Act is not yet passed, else we could put the clever Mistress Thatcher behind bars."

The young man sucked in his cheeks in habitual movement as he thought. "Perhaps, sir, we could go to her, question her about it. She might admit to something. She lives down in one of the church cottages by the river now.''

''And warn her that we know something? Mr. Elrington, that idea is not worthy of your distinguished intelligence.''

His assistant looked abashed.

''There may come the day when Mistress Thatcher helps us unwittingly, providing she does not know we suspect her. And things may change, now that the bushranger has the Wakeman woman with him. Ah yes, Mistress Thatcher was an intimate of hers for years at the parsonage. One never knows.''

His senior stood from where he sat at the desk, and appraising his companion, asked, ''So what do we do, Mr. Elrington?''

''I imagine we will keep a vigilant eye on Mistress Thatcher.''

''Exactly,'' said Sir Rutherford, smiling almost fondly at him.

It was three months later that Sir Rutherford sat in his office and patted the *Sydney Morning Herald* of Tuesday, April 18, with an air of satisfaction. It had taken two days to come from Sydney, and it was worth waiting for. He was smiling. It was a smile of real mirth, even elation. For the newspaper beneath his hand carried the banner, WILL BUSHRANGERS SURRENDER? And underneath: ''All bushrangers are ordered to surrender to the jailer at Goulburn jail by April 29th or be aware that they will be declared outlawed. Hence from May 8th, 1865, it will be legal to shoot known bushrangers on sight.''

In March the long-awaited Felons' Apprehension Act had been passed, and while he had argued long and well for a twenty-year sentence for any who aided the outlaws, the members of the government had seen fit to make it fifteen. Well, he was not unhappy about that. Fifteen was more than enough to scare off the sympathizers. In the main, it had already stopped the safe houses from functioning. The scum had nowhere to hang their hats in safety now.

He turned back to look with gratification at the map of the colony of New South Wales. There were a number of small black and red crosses dotted here and there upon it. Each of the black crosses represented a dead bushranger and the place he had died. The red ones were for captured bushrangers, and the places they had been caught. There were sixteen crosses placed upon the map in 1864; most of them were red, for un-important names, but there were a couple of black ones for Johnny O'Meally and James Jones.

This year was proving gratifying. Early in January, he had

added a black cross for Jake Crane. Billy Dunken, Crane's ex-partner, had informed on him, and he had been taken in his camp south of Orange. Unfortunately, Crane had been shot dead. Sir Rutherford felt a touch sorry when his troopers shot and killed. It wasn't the way he liked to do things. It was untidy. He preferred to take them alive and let them face justice.

Then in February, he had added a red cross for James Mc-Pherson, the wild Scotsman. Thirty miles from Forbes, in his lonely camp, they had surrounded him, and taken him without a fight. A good old black tracker had led him to that one.

The most recent cross, he had added not two weeks since. He had drawn it in with mixed feelings: a black cross and an arrow pointing down from the New South Wales border toward Wangaratta in Victoria. It represented Dan Morgan. Sir Rutherford was greatly comforted to have Morgan on the map, but he felt cheated all the same. Once again, it had been his own ingenuity that had really caught the bushranger, for he had maintained his vigilant search parties in the south where he knew him to be. It was in desperation that the criminal had crossed the border into Victoria, where a crack shot called Wendlan had apparently shot him through the throat. Thus, the Victorian police claimed Dan Morgan's head, although Sir Rutherford knew it morally belonged to him and his men.

There was a sort of irony in claiming Morgan's head. It had, in fact, been severed from the bushranger's body shortly after death and placed on his chest for the local folk to file past and view. Sir Rutherford thought the action more than a trifle extreme. His mouth drew down in distaste now, as he thought of it.

In the same week Morgan had been shot, the news had broken of the death of Sir Frederick Pottinger. In March the man had finally been dismissed as police inspector of the Western District. He had been traveling to Sydney to appeal against the sacking when, at a coaching stop in the Blue Mountains, his revolver went off, shooting him in the chest. He had died a month later. When Sir Rutherford heard, he could not help but wonder if Pottinger had committed suicide. Whatever the truth, the man was gone, and Sir Rutherford was not hypocrite enough to pretend he had not wanted him out of the way. Still, he had not wished the man dead, not at all.

Now there was much to be done, and a law enabling his men to shoot bushrangers on sight gave him the advantage he needed. Most of them had cavalierly let their faces become well known.

It was only the Fletcher gang who had not made that mistake. Yet good fortune had given him the close look at them that night in Theresa Town. Ah yes, of them all, Fletcher was the one he wanted most. An aristocrat who had allowed himself to become a cohort of convicts and outlaws. It was an outrage! Sir Rutherford almost took it personally.

He left his desk and walked to the window, where he stood staring out into the street. Across his sight walked a lively figure. His mouth set rigidly as he watched the slim back of Lottie enter Mrs. Ayres's Tea Room. He sighed. Ah yes, Mistress Thatcher, I know you helped Alan Fletcher once. Just try to help him again, and I shall see you in jail for fifteen years!

Behind him, the door opened and David Elrington came in. He looked around to the bright young face: it wore a troubled look as he came forward to his superior.

"I have the report you requested on the movements of the Hall gang and the Fletcher gang, sir: those between January first and April twenty-second."

"And?"

"There were six Hall gang robberies, sir. On January nineteenth and twenty-sixth, February sixth and seventeenth, March sixteenth, and April tenth. Deaths were two. January twenty-sixth, Constable Nelson shot dead. March sixteenth, Constable Kelly mortally wounded, died three days later. Wounded were two: February seventeenth, Constable Wiles, and March sixteenth, Mr. Donald Blatchford, JP. Gunshots were fired in each deployment, sir."

"And the Fletchers?"

"No activity recorded in January or February. Robberies on March twentieth and April eleventh. Each done by three masked men, thus assumption was the Fletcher gang. Both robberies successful, and no gunshots fired."

"And what were they?"

"The government claims office at Bushman's was robbed of bank notes, and cash and troopers escorting supplies to Goulburn jail were held up; six rifles, Terry carbines, were taken." The young man handed the papers he held to his superior. "There is much more detail on all the raids here, sir."

"Thank you. Sit down, Mr. Elrington."

David Elrington sat, and Sir Rutherford sat opposite him.

"I have been studying the cases of the two robberies on Christmas Day last and have now closed the case on the Warraderry picnic holdup. We know conclusively it was Dan Morgan. But the other . . .''

"The Redley station raid?"

"Mmm, the Redley station raid," repeated Sir Rutherford. "Ah yes, then let us see how my instruction has served you. At first it was laid at the door of the Fletcher gang. And what is it that we have noticed time and time again about the Fletcher holdups?''

David Elrington frowned and sucked in his smooth cheeks in meditation. He was, in fact, a voracious learner, and listened avidly to his leader. He was intelligent and articulate, and all lawbreakers affronted his fastidious sense of fair play.

The years ahead were to prove him one of the most famous and let it be said, fair-minded, judges of the Supreme Court. But for now, he was learning his trade and he took a deep breath and said, "Well, sir, the thing that has stood out, with the exception of Redley station, was that the Fletcher gang had never killed anyone; in fact, rarely had they ever fired on anyone.''

"Correct, correct. And yet on Christmas Day, we note that a trooper was shot and killed in a most perfunctory manner. Ah yes, and that the reason the eyewitnesses thought it was Fletcher was that the raiders wore masks.''

"True," agreed his protégé.

"Now, we know there were four men in the gang that day, and that is odd for Fletcher, is it not?''

"It is, sir, for they work in three or five, mostly three. Since being joined by O'Day, we do not think they have ever worked with four.''

"Ah yes, good, Mr. Elrington, and is there anything else that makes us doubt that it was Fletcher?''

David Elrington was silent for a few moments, then he suggested, "That they have never robbed anyone other than the government, sir . . . or very occasionally the vastly rich.''

"Excellent, Mr. Elrington." Sir Rutherford beamed at his protégé. "Ah yes, and more often than not it is the government, eh?''

"It is," uttered the young man, looking respectfully at the older, "and Mr. Redley is neither the government, nor is he in any way rich, sir.''

"I am proud of you, Mr. Elrington," Sir Rutherford said, standing and moving to the window, where he stood, hands clasped behind his back, looking out onto the street. "Ah yes,

I am. And there is a final clue that suggests the Redley station raid was the work of another gang, though I will not blame you if you cannot tell me what it is.''

David Elrington looked puzzled. He thought very hard. He looked at the palms of his hands and then turned them over to study the backs of them, but the answer was not written there. "I'm afraid I cannot tell you, sir,'' he answered, a trifle deflated.

Sir Rutherford turned to face him. "Never mind that you cannot tell me, but listen well, and remember.''

The young man leaned forward in concentration.

"It was ill planned. Ah yes, Mr. Elrington, they *never* do anything that is ill planned. Thus, their holdups are always successful, but the Redley station raid was not. All of which leads us to what conclusion?''

"That it was not the Fletcher gang.''

Sir Rutherford nodded. "So you see, Mr. Elrington, as much as I would like to believe that Alan Fletcher is beginning to make mistakes and that he did make the unsuccessful raid on Redley, I know it is not so.''

"Yes, sir, that is evident now, and I shall go immediately to the file and change the record.''

As David Elrington stood, he looked at his notepad. "Oh, by the way, sir,'' he added, "just before I came in, I received a message from the Royal Hotel. Mr. Wakeman and Mr. Larmer will be expecting you for dinner in their rooms tonight at eight o'clock.''

"Ah yes,'' replied Sir Rutherford, "of course. Looking forward to seeing them.''

Sir Rutherford had not seen his friends since he had met with them in Young in February, after John Stuart and his pack of Mayfield men had rigorously examined 480 square miles of countryside looking for the Fletcher hideout. Well, at least that is what the people of Mayfield and the West had been led to believe, that they were deputized to help Sir Rutherford. It was only Sir Rutherford and Joe Larmer and a handful of trusted Mayfield men who knew that he searched for his wife, whom Fletcher had abducted. If any others suspected the truth, it had not reached the ears of the master of Mayfield and his intimates.

When they had been in Young together, Joe had been the one to explain to Sir Rutherford the story of Nathaniel Lake and the consequences. It had obviously been a strain for John Stuart even to listen to, and Sir Rutherford had felt acute sympathy for his friend. He remembered when Joe had finished the account, how

John Stuart had turned to him, a terrible sadness in his eyes, and added, "So, Rutherford, unlike my futile search, there may come a time when you *do* find the bushranger, and if Eve is with him, she will be with child."

Ah yes, John Stuart had been disappointed in his search for his wife. In all their long ride, they had found nothing. Joe had related their fruitless search to the police detective. "Between Young and Cowra, there is virtually no habitation, no farms or stations, only two inns, and perhaps two or three huts of odd recluses. Other than that, we saw two aboriginal campsites, which were deserted, and that's all. Yet you have always been adamant that the Fletcher hideout is in that territory."

"Yes," Sir Rutherford had replied at the time, "and while you have found nothing, my friend, I still do believe it."

John Stuart had shaken his head, desperation sounding in his voice. "Hell, Rutherford! We have just spent weeks in minute examination of the very area, and it has been futile."

Later, Sir Rutherford had told them of the night he had chased the bushranger in Bathurst. He would have spared John Stuart if he could, but felt the man should know.

Joe had remained calm. "At that time, we were three days into the search down here, when all the time the outlaw was in Bathurst."

"Yes, Joe." Sir Rutherford had nodded. "But he was alone; I'm sure of that. Mrs. Wakeman was not with him. From what we know, I'd say she was kept at his hideout as you have believed." He looked to John Stuart. "May I say how very sorry I am, my friend, ah yes, that this should have been in the stars for you."

John Stuart had said nothing. He had simply covered his face with his hands.

And tonight Sir Rutherford was to be reunited with his two friends once more. Ah yes, it could be valuable to see John Stuart again.

John Stuart and Joe had arrived in Bathurst in the midafternoon and were staying overnight at the Royal Hotel. They were returning to Mayfield after the first of their twice yearly cattle drives. Neither of them had been in Bathurst since Eve had disappeared, four months earlier.

The purpose of the sojourn overnight was to see Sir Rutherford. And yet, there was another consideration that John Stuart did not quite admit until he insisted on their taking a turn around the town in the late afternoon.

He did not care for Bathurst these days. He found it, like its counterparts, an ugly, dusty country settlement of wide, sprawling dirt streets and straggling houses, many of them not more than wooden cottages. He would be glad to be on his way tomorrow.

He directed their footsteps to the graveyard of All Saints' Church of England Church, as Joe had suspected he would. It was easy to find the burial place they sought, for the parishioners had erected a substantial marble tablet above the resting place of the reverend and his wife. It had come all the way from Sydney and only been positioned the week before. The words were painted in gold.

Here lies
The Very Reverend Leslie Billings,
Late rector of this parish
October 9th, 1794–January 14th, 1865
His devotion an inspiration
His very passing caused by his dedication
to the people of this district
Always remembered
The Lord is my light and my salvation

And his good and faithful wife, Lillian
June 26th, 1800–December 26th, 1864
Lost doing God's work
for the members of this parish

A heart true in all she did
Thy will be done O Lord

John Stuart removed his hat and stood silently. He had confused feelings.

He looked past the mint bush at the side of the grave, over the fence to the back garden of the parsonage. He could see the jacaranda tree where he had lunched with the clergyman and his wife and Eve. The event seemed so long ago, and yet it was only just over two years. How briefly she had been with him. He wondered where she was, as he did every day of his life. Was she safe? Did she ever think about him? He glanced sideways to Joe, who was looking straight ahead.

Where are you, Evvy? Where are you?

As he and Joe turned to walk away, he said, "Would you see this new Reverend Cornish in the morning, old man? We will pay for a plaque to be attached to the walls inside All Saints' in honor of Reverend Billings. Let it speak of him as the good and responsible man he was. Deflect them from making it too religious."

On their return walk to the hotel, they did not speak. They were comfortable together in silence.

Later they met in the parlor for a drink before the arrival of Sir Rutherford. John Stuart had bathed and changed into a brown velvet jacket and trousers. He wore a soft silk shirt and a dark bow tied at his throat. If it were possible, he looked even more handsome these days, for there was a distant look in his dark eyes concealing his melancholy, and somehow heightening his attractiveness.

The older man looked with pride at the younger as he entered. "How well you look this evening, m'boy."

"Thank you, old man, and so do you."

When the barmaid brought their sherries, she stared with unabashed admiration at John Stuart, who gave her a brief half smile. It did Joe's heart good to see it, momentary though it was, for it had not sat often upon his boy's mouth in recent months.

John Stuart looked over his wineglass and asked, "Are you and Thelma still keen for Daydee to marry Roy Ford?"

Joe shook his head. "Ah, m'boy, it's not pressing or compelling that she marry at all. It is just that the Fords and Thelma and I have always had a sort of understanding that we would like our two children to join together. It is Daydee who is the dissenting voice."

"Yes, I understand that," answered John Stuart, remembering back to the day only a week or so before the cattle drive when he had met Daydee in the front hall at Mayfield House.

It had been Sunday afternoon, and he carried his scientific journals under his arm. He had thrown himself into his work after he had been unable to find any sign of his wife in all his long searches and expenditure of time and money. He had always been innovative, trying labor-saving devices and time-saving theories on Mayfield, and in one of the scientific journals he was carrying was the story of the French chemist Louis Pasteur, of his work on the mysteries of germs and the rejection of spontaneous generation. It was Pasteur's marvelous process of heating to kill germs that John Stuart was eager to apply on Mayfield. He was heading in the direction of the summerhouse to read it all when Daydee appeared from the corridor leading to the kitchens.

"Good afternoon, Uncle John Stuart." Her mouth was turned down at the corners.

"You do not seem happy, Daydee."

"I'm not."

He moved to pass her, but he hesitated and asked, "Why?"

She did not meet his glance but instead dropped her eyes to her hands, which she held clasped tightly in front of her. "Well, it's a mite personal, but I am being pushed in a certain direction, and I've no one to talk to, for it's Mother and Father who do the pushing."

John Stuart succumbed. "Daydee, come and sit with me awhile and tell me about it."

Happy now, she followed him through the hall and out into the day.

When they reached the summerhouse, they sat opposite each other.

"Now, what is this terrible thing your parents are doing?" he asked.

She moved on the seat and crossed her legs, bouncing her tiny foot up and down and watching it as she replied, "It's that Roy Ford. They suggest that I should·become engaged to him. Oh, but he is such a dreary, I hate him."

"I think that particular emotion a little strong, Daydee. He always seems a nice young man to me."

She scowled, "Ah, there it is. Nice, nice, that's what Mother says about him. Oh, Uncle John Stuart, what is 'nice' tires me."

"Yes, Daydee, I think it does."

"I will never like him," she said definitely. "He is not the type of man I like."

Then he looked at her with interest, and she felt her pulse quicken ever so slightly as he inquired, "And so, Miss Daydee, what sort of man is it that you do like?"

She lifted her eyes to meet his. Her heartbeat accelerated.

"A perfect man. One like you."

He said nothing for a second or two, then he shook his head. "You flatter me, Daydee; but look not to a man such as me, for I made the worst mistake a man can make." As he made mention of his personal situation, he found himself wondering why.

"But it was not your fault," the girl insisted.

He did not want to continue with this. "I point it out to you only to make you aware of the foolishness of looking for perfection in another human being."

Daydee dared to persist, for this subject, of all things, was dearest to her heart. She spoke softly. "But now Aunt Eve has gone, cannot we all live as we did before she came?"

He looked at her. To him she appeared unworldly, innocent, and virtuous, her youth expressing itself in her simple statement. "Daydee," he said, "as time passes, you will learn that it is difficult to ignore strong emotions. Eve . . . is gone, yes. Indisputably so. In fact, she seems to have run away . . . from . . . me. No, I will never be as I was before she came here. It is impossible."

And then, even though she feared to ask the question, she did so, there in the summerhouse with the sun shining on her jet black hair. "D-Do you think she will ever come back?"

She sat looking at him, an elfin creature with an intense look on her face. The child whom he had known since birth was growing into a woman.

The only person who knew how he really felt was Joe. No one else would be audacious enough to ask him about Eve. No one but this fairy opposite him. He would have repulsed others, put them swiftly in their place, but to Daydee he answered, "She has been gone for over three months, and I have not been able to find a single trace of her. No, dear Daydee, I do not think she will."

He did not explain any of the intricacies in the torrent of feelings that he had for his wife. He did not say he was still confused by Lake's story and the incidents that had led to his mistrusting her. He did not say that he wanted, more than anything in the world, to see her and hear her explanations. He did not say that he was hurt and angry with her and himself. He did not say that he had finally admitted to loving her, whether she was good or bad. He said none of this, for he assumed he spoke to an inexperienced, naive young woman, and consequently, the plain answer sufficed for the proper one.

But Daydee had heard what she wanted to hear. Eve would not be back. Daydee smiled at him, a heavenly smile.

John Stuart changed the subject. "Now, this business with Roy," he said seriously. "Why don't you give the young man a chance? It would please your parents, and you may in time find you do not hate him after all."

"I don't think I will. You see," she explained, "there is nothing about him that appeals to me."

"Daydee, your parents only want what they believe is good for you. They are the best parents in the world. They would not harm you."

Daydee did not quite see it the same way, but she did not differ with him. Then pushing her hair back over her shoulder and smiling at him once more, she asked, "Please, may I stay and read the journals with you, if I'm quiet?"

"Yes, if you are quiet."

John Stuart's mind returned to the present and Joe's grave face opposite him. "Mmm," he said, "perhaps you should give Daydee more time. The Fords are not pressing you, are they?"

"Not in any real sense, but Roy is twenty-seven. I had a letter from Stan before we came on the drive. Roy is in love with Daydee at present, but he only sees her four or five times a year. Now, we know Roy to be earnest and hardworking and a good character; besides, he shall inherit a tidy sum eventually. He is exactly the type of man I want for my Daydee."

"Yes, I think he is a refined young man, but perhaps it is better not to mention it to her for a little while."

"She is always reading those novels. Too much fantasy. Doesn't see life as it is," her father complained.

Just then Sir Rutherford entered, ebullient in his greeting. "My good friends, it is grand to see you both."

John Stuart and Joe rose to shake his hand.

As the three friends sat, the police detective could not help observing how well John Stuart looked tonight: ah yes, well, but not happy, sort of smoldering, brooding. He had been quick to notice the looks the serving girls were giving the master of Mayfield. No doubt he was most attractive to women.

By now it was generally known throughout the colony that Mrs. Wakeman had departed from Mayfield; it was the scandal *célèbre*, and John Stuart's name was on everyone's tongue.

The detective policeman sat back in his chair. "One week from Saturday, I must be at Goulburn jail to see if any of our 'wild colonial rabble' do, in fact, surrender."

Joe asked, "Do you think any will?"

Sir Rutherford actually grinned. "No, I don't. That mob don't go in for surrender. Now, had it been amnesty, it would have been a different matter. No, it was merely a step in the legal process and had to be announced."

The meal progressed and the conversation turned to the cattle drive.

"Did all go well in the capital?" Sir Rutherford inquired.

Joe smiled. "Always does. Though this time, we saw to something in particular." He put his hand in his inside pocket and withdrew an official envelope.

"Rutherford, it seems that my wife has disappeared off the face of the earth," John Stuart said.

"Yes, it does. Mind you, if she is in Alan Fletcher's hideout, that is understandable."

"Because I am so sure she is, and the Felons' Apprehension Act is about to become a reality, I had to do something to protect her. For, even though in the first place she was abducted, she has not reappeared." He pointed to the envelope Joe held. "In this is a declaration signed by the governor, the premier, Mr. Cowper, and the inspector general of police. It states that if you or any of your men do apprehend Fletcher, or any of his men, and she . . . Eve, is in company with them, that she is a Crown exception from the Felons' Apprehension Act and is not to be arrested."

"I see." Sir Rutherford put out his hand for the envelope. "She is a very lucky woman."

"Yes, and a pity she didn't know it," Joe replied, before he had time to think.

John Stuart half suppressed a sigh and shook his head at the older man. Joe was so loyal, but what had transpired was not Eve's fault. The whole mess was so complicated.

Sir Rutherford took the envelope, his aquiline features shining in the lamp-glow. "If I find her, what do I do with her?"

John Stuart looked to Joe's eyes and took strength from the compassion there. "She should be taken to a place of safety . . . without delay. To a magistrate would be best. The magistrate should take care of her until we can come for her. It's very important that we should be alerted the moment you know, or have any suspicion of where she is."

Sir Rutherford prided himself on his ability to judge the caliber of his fellow creatures. He had never estimated Mrs. Wakeman as a woman of loose morality, no, not at all. Even so, while she had been "kidnapped" in the first instance, it appeared she had remained with Alan Fletcher for months now. What could one possibly think? He watched his friend sitting across the table. John Stuart's eyes were despondent, dark. Ah, yes, people were very strange indeed . . . and fascinating. He smiled. "Of course."

TWENTY-SEVEN
Days at Treehard Hill

As the three friends sat in the Royal Hotel in Bathurst, the moon filtered pallid light through the tall gums at Treehard Hill down upon two figures walking back along the neat path from the escarpment edge toward the little wooden house.

"So will you be gone the entire day tomorrow?" Eve asked.

"Yes, it's over a thirty-mile ride to the store near McGorman's mine where we shall get the provisions this time," Alan replied.

It was now fall, as Eve termed it, and the nights were cool and soothing. Even the days were almost pleasant. It had been the hottest summer in living memory.

She had remained at Treehard; there had been nowhere else to go once Mother and Father had gone. Besides, she had wanted desperately to remain, and the wonderful thing was that Alan had wanted her to as well.

She turned to face him. He halted beside her. "Alan," she said softly, "will you ever leave Treehard Hill?"

"Leave? Perhaps. The 'climate' in New South Wales is changing toward bushrangers, lass, and a time may come when we have no alternative but to leave." He was looking down at her, his eyes reflecting the moonlight.

She nodded to him in the darkness. He was so discerning and courageous. Being with him was a continuing enrichment in her life. "The future is always uncertain, isn't it?" she said.

"Yes, uncertain for all of us. The future is something I must think about, though I try not to dwell on it."

"Are you ever—" she hesitated "—afraid?"

She thought a brief smile flashed across his mouth. "Afraid of what, Eve? Of being caught?"

"Yes . . . no. Of the possibility of leaving here, of the future that you mention. Life here is so easy, so happy, and yet I feel my hold on . . . this happiness is tenuous." As she finished, she looked away.

He made a tender sound in his throat, and he took her shoulders to turn her toward him. His touch ran a shiver of pleasure through her. He did not touch her often, although his eyes met hers a thousand times each day, and he was always completely natural with her. If their hands or bodies met during the course of their daily chores, they both felt it was normal and spontaneous. He was caring and warm toward her, but he held himself back, she knew he did, and she knew a great part of it was out of consideration to her, for what she had been through.

Now his hand came up to her chin and he looked down into her eyes. "Eve." He elongated the *e*, and the sound was wonderful to her ears. "If I am afraid of anything in this life, it is that these days with you may end." All his love and empathy for her filled his words, and somehow, magically, they echoed ever so slightly in the night air. Her heartbeat quickened. His head seemed to come down toward her. Momentarily the moonlight disappeared, the world was black and exciting, and tremors of delirious expectation ran down her limbs. Then his eyes left hers, his hand dropped from her chin, and taking her hand, he lifted it through his arm and moved her forward.

She had been so sure he was about to kiss her that she felt let down. She knew herself now, knew her own strengths and resources and, yes, her vulnerabilities, all the things she should have done and had not. She had made mistakes, but now she saw them clearly and hoped she had learned by them. The months here at Treehard had given her time to examine her life, her losses, and her griefs: Lake and all the pain she had suffered because of him, the rape and the aftermath of her miscarriage. Recently she had realized a new sense of strength; she now could accept what had occurred as part of the fabric of her life. It had been months since Lake had attacked her, and the animosity and the guilt and the fearful shadow in her mind had dissipated.

As they walked together, the lovely contours of her face yielded to a delicate, tender expression, for it was all because of the man here beside her, his compassion and understanding and gentleness and love. All her experiences had prepared her for this. She knew she was ready now, ready to be loved by Alan Fletcher, whom she loved, had loved, always. From all the lives of human time, from the beginning, Eve Herman had loved Alan Fletcher.

Her frustration seemed to be manifested in the very air, for a breeze came suddenly up over the cliff face, blowing her dress sideways to hover around his knees, as if linking them together. She knew her hand was vibrating on his arm.

Alan's voice sounded a little unsteady when he spoke. "Danny will be waiting to brew us tea before retiring; it's time we went inside."

"All right," she answered softly.

The next day, as the new dawn's sun gave forth the brilliance of a flawless morning, Eve stood on the Treehard veranda with Danny and watched Alan, Lawless, and Sam ride into the tunnel. Jordan was still asleep; he was remaining at home with Eve and Daniel.

The hours of the morning dragged. She groomed the two remaining horses, a job she had begun since her convalescence, and one she enjoyed. Then she trimmed the vine that grew up the front of the little house and wound along the railing of the veranda. The small, white blooms had died weeks ago, and now it looked straggly and leafless. She knew Sam had been meaning to trim it, but he had so much else to tend with his gardens and paths and lawns. She remembered how she had seen Thelma do this very job on her own porch at Mayfield where a wisteria wound up to the roof. She often thought of Thelma, her dear, good friend.

Early in the afternoon, Eve went gathering native flowers. It was hard to find blooms, for the summer flowers had mostly gone. By the time she had a reasonable bunch, she found herself at the very edge of the north corner of Treehard. She remembered how she used to do this same thing at Mayfield, and unconsciously she looked out over the escarpment across to the northeast where the property lay. Momentarily she imagined John Stuart riding toward her upon Diomed. She wondered how he was; the months away from him had soothed her anger and despair with him. And yes, she had loved him deeply and in many ways been proud of him; not the same love or pride that she felt for Alan Fletcher, but it would have been enough to last her lifetime, had his distrust and rejection of her not driven her away. For a moment she pictured him smiling down at her, and she felt so sad, for in many ways her marriage had been wonderful. She always felt as if something were incomplete when she thought of John Stuart, as if there were a place of sorrow in her soul. Perhaps there was and would always be.

She was sure John Stuart would be all right. He had Mayfield, and he loved the property with all his soul. It was odd, for often thoughts of Alan brought thoughts of John Stuart, or vice versa.

In reality, she thought, she should be grateful to John Stuart; it was his action that had brought her into Alan Fletcher's life. She smiled a peculiar smile, somehow cheerless.

Through the bush to the south, she could see Jordan cutting branches from trees close to the cliff face. He looked over and noticed her, lifting his bushman's hat high in the air in greeting. She waved. Soon she was back along the path near Sam's tool shed. A large bottlebrush grew here, which Sam carefully tended, and it had some late blooms on it. It was so top-heavy that it had drooped, and Sam had attached it with thick twine to the roof of the shed to hold it up. She cut one of the last few red bottlebrushes to add to her bouquet.

When she came back to the house, Daniel was chopping chips of wood for the fire. His features broke into his customary broad smile.

After she had fed the chickens and swept the small front veranda and drawn water from the tank for their use that night, she made tea and took a mug out to Daniel, who now was in the stables.

"I shall take a mugful over to Jordan as well."

Along the orderly gravel path she went and found Jordan on top of a wooden ladder, sawing through a branch, his tall frame bent forward. He wore nothing on his upper body, and his brown, muscular chest and arms shone in the streaming evening light.

"I have brought you a drink."

He completed cutting the branch, and it fell to the ground.

He appreciated the tea, warm and sweet, and gulped it down, his big, expressive eyes watching her over the rim of the tin mug. He still could not get over the reality of her being with them, at Treehard. The mistress of flamin' Mayfield bringin' flamin' Jordan O'Day a drink! Whole thing was bloody amazin'. She was mighty pretty, really, great mouth, and even though she was a bit skinny, a bonzer figure, yeah, real bonzer. He smiled. "Nice breeze now, coolin' the evenin' down."

She pointed to the stack of branches. "Have you removed all these already?"

He nodded. "Once I get started, I work fast." He grinned proudly. "Yeah and I'd best get back to it. It'll soon be dark." He turned from her and strode over to the tree he had been working on. It was ready to bring down; he had cut off all the large branches on the cliff side of it so it would fall the right way. He looked back to see if she were watching him lift the saw.

She was still there.

He smiled and put down the saw and picked up the large ax they used for cutting down the trees. To Eve's surprise, he swung it back in a wide arc and began to chop into the trunk about two feet from the base. A man alone could accomplish the cutting off of branches, but felling a large tree single-handedly was reckless.

"Stand back!" he called to her. "I'm bringing this one down."

"Jordan, don't! It's dangerous alone! You should wait for tomorrow with Lawless."

Either he didn't hear or he preferred not to answer, for he continued hefting the blade high in the air and driving it with all his might into the tree. Minutes went by, and then with a tearing, cracking sound, the trunk began to break forward in her direction.

Jordan jumped back, throwing down the ax, beads of perspiration on his temples and a triumphant expression on his face. But the expression died as his eyes widened in fear, for the tree did not continue to fall straight; it skewed sideways as it came down, and even as Eve shouted a warning, one of the remaining limbs clipped him hard on the shoulder, knocking him backward. He lost his balance and staggered a few steps, then righted himself momentarily, but his left boot caught between two stones, and to Eve's horror, he catapulted backward across the few feet to the cliff top. His big hands grabbed at the air as he screamed and disappeared over the edge.

For a second, she could not move. Then, white-faced with dread, she ran to the cliff and looked over.

To her amazement, he was dangling ten feet below, clutching a dead tree stump that jutted out from the escarpment face, his legs hanging in nothingness like a frantic marionette. There was blood on his arms and forehead where they had hit the rocks.

He was terrified.

She was terrified.

"For Christ sake . . . get Daniel!" His voice was desperate.

But even as she went to move, she saw the tree stump begin to tear away from the surface of the cliff.

"Oh Jesus!" he screamed. It was an appalling sound.

She looked wildly around. There was no time . . . no time. It was all heightened in her head . . . the dreadful sounds of terror from over the cliff, the ladder on its side, the pile of branches, the fallen tree. No rope . . . nothing to use.

What? Sam's shed.

She ran the forty yards without knowing she had.

String . . . useless . . .

Where is the thicker cord? The one he uses for holding up the bottlebrush? Where? Ah, thank heaven, here it is. Will it be strong enough? No time. It must be.

Back to the cliff top. The stump was cracking now.

Stay calm . . . double the twine . . . tie it around a tree . . . knot it . . . back to the edge. Ignore the cracking sound of the tree stump . . . throw the cord down to Jordan. Yes, yes, Jordan had it.

She watched in hideous fascination, the muscles of his arms expanding like sails in a wind, as slowly he climbed toward her, his veins appearing like laces of purple string across his deep brown skin.

He groaned in terror as his foot touched the tree stump he had been clinging to, and it broke noisily, ripping from the surface entirely and falling down the sheer drop to the ground below. His eyes were on hers, pleading, begging to be saved, as he inched his way to where she could take hold of him and help him up over the edge of the cliff.

"Oh God!" he kept saying. "Oh God!"

They were both trembling as he lay panting beside her.

When at last he staggered to his feet with shaking legs, he mumbled, "Thanks, I was a goner without you."

They made their way back to the house, and Jordan went to his room. He remained there, door closed, until the sun went down.

The three of them ate the evening meal together, and afterward Jordan smoked his cheroots and whittled silently on the form at the small veranda's end.

Eve and Daniel cleared away the dishes and washed them. As Dan put the last plate away, he turned back to Eve, resting his worn, brown hands on the back of the nearest chair. "Our Jordan owes you his life. It was a brave and marvelous thing you did today.''

"Oh, Danny, I was so lucky the twine held.''

Dan nodded before he passed through the door to sit a little way from Jordan in his rocking chair.

They all waited on the Treehard veranda in the comfortable night, all with thoughts of their own, until close to ten o'clock when they heard the bird call of their returning companions.

Within minutes, Eve was enjoying the happy laughter and excited voices of welcome return. They all helped to bed down the horses and carry in the sacks of grain and supplies, and soon the kitchen table was covered with provisions for weeks to come.

Eve moved to the leader's side. "Any trouble, Alan?''

"No, lass, nothing untoward. But I have something of interest to us all.'' He took a newspaper from out of his saddlebag and, making room at one end of the table, spread it out. It was the *Sydney Morning Herald* of Tuesday, April 18, and the banner it carried said, WILL BUSHRANGERS SURRENDER?

He pointed to the words underneath. "You will see here that we are ordered to surrender to the jailer at Goulburn jail by April twenty-ninth or be declared 'outlawed.' ''

Lawless gave a short laugh. "Funny that, and here I was thinkin' we were outlaws already.''

"Let's see,'' said Jordan, breaking his long silence and looking around Alan's shoulder. "Oh, bloody hell,'' he continued as he read. "So it's come at last?''

Then Sam spoke up, for he and Lawless had already read the newspaper. " 'Fraid so, Jordan, matey. Yep, the rotten act's goin' into force. It'll be legal to shoot us on sight from May the eighth.''

All of a sudden, the little kitchen fell silent. The apprehension was like a living thing. It was as if the minds there all realized the dreadful import at the same moment and somehow reached out to one another for security; the six figures were rigid in the candlelight, the only noise the crackle of the fire in the hearth.

Eve became aware that Alan made the first move; he stepped very close to her as his dispassionate voice filled the space with reason. "That part does not matter to us. The few who know our faces will not shoot us.''

The fatal twenty-ninth of April had come and gone. Eight days had passed since all bushrangers had been called upon to surrender to the jailer at Goulburn.

Alan and Sam had ridden off before dawn to cover as much territory as possible to find out how the people felt about the act, which would be law tomorrow.

Through the tall Treehard gums, Eve's figure moved, gathering firewood not far from that part of the cliff face where she had saved Jordan's life. She was about to bend down to add to her bundle when she heard her name called.

It was Lawless striding through the trees toward her. He had been digging a new garden bed for Sam. She thought him quite charming. She enjoyed his quiet company; they often conversed, and it was from him she had learned, at least in part, the stories of the lives of the others. He was much more discerning than people would at first perceive, and he could estimate men and situations accurately. It was from him she had heard the story of Alan's arrest and sentencing. He had looked at her and said, "Fancy bein' duped into believin' the guverner could kill in cold blood! Can you imagine it, Mistress Eve?" And she had returned his look and answered, "No, Lawless, I cannot. Some people will believe anything."

He was kind and sensitive, never a man of moods, and had become her friend.

"Hello, Mistress Eve." He gave an amused chuckle and leaned on the shovel he had been carrying. "I was just thinkin'. This weather is so balmy and nice after the heat of the summer. Do you know there was a time in my life when I had never felt hot . . . no, not at all. The closest I came was bein' warm occasionally. It was a hard life in the Rookery when I was a boy, hard and cold."

Then he shook his head. "Though I'm not complainin', now. One of the first things the guverner taught us was . . . . the way things are is the way things are. If ye be in a situation ye surely cannot change, then that's the way of it. Ye must accept it, and I be happy enough with the way of things."

"I know you are, Lawless, and it is something I admire in you, admire in you all. The way you have made a life for yourselves through all the adversity. The way you have kept truth in your lives, truth and dignity."

"Why, Mistress Eve," he answered, looking searchingly at her, "now, that's a real nice thing to say."

She smiled at him, and he returned the expression. She was totally comfortable with Lawless, always had been. Lawless and Danny had welcomed her from the start, and since that dreadful experience when she had saved Jordan's life, Jordan's view of her had changed. She was now treated as an equal who belonged at Treehard.

She turned from him and bent to pick up her firewood.

Suddenly, without warning, she was hurtling sideways, knocked off her feet by his body crashing into hers. She screamed as she fell, shocked and startled, to the ground. Then she saw his arms come down across her, smashing his shovel into a brown snake, even now poised, head up, mouth open, fangs exposed, to bite.

"Oh, my Lord, Lawless!" she cried as he measured out a second blow, severing the head of the stunned creature. Perspiration stood out on his forehead, and his face had changed color. There was anguish in his look, where there had been gladness a few seconds before.

As she regained her feet, he took the two pieces of the reptile on his shovel, and walking the fifty or so yards through the trees to the edge of the escarpment, threw them over the side. When he returned to her, he was shaking his head. "Ye cannot be too careful," he said quietly. "Although they are worse in the summer, the creatures can be around any time of year."

"Oh, I know, Lawless, and usually I have my wits about me. I am so sorry."

"The brown snake is deadly . . . deadly." He repeated the word, emphasizing it bitterly.

"Thank you for . . . saving me." She was still agitated.

He sighed deeply, a sigh that came from the depths of him. "Ah, mistress, I am but pleased I was here to do so." Then he looked away as he added, "There was an occasion once before when I was not in time."

"I don't understand, Lawless."

Then, looking carefully about him, he took her arm and sat her down on a log. He placed the shovel at his right hand as he knelt down beside her. "Ye have heard me speak, perhaps, of my Patricia June?"

"Your wife who died? Yes, I have."

"Brown-snake bite," he said softly, looking straight ahead.

"On, no! I am so sorry."

He seemed to concentrate steadily on the silky-bark gum in front of him. "She was my sweet angel, saw nothin' but good in me." He gave a sad smile. "Why, she even found my limp charmin', she did." He was silent a few seconds. "We met her and Jordan—as ye be aware, he was her brother, though they be different as chalk and cheese—north o' Millthorpe in fifty-seven, accidental like. They'd lost their parents' farm, taken from them by the law. They had debts they couldn't pay. Jordan's never got over it, but Patricia June didn't hold grudges. Weren't in her to be that way.

"I'd say we fell in love right there and then, beside that billabong. The guverner is a wise man and clever. He was quick to ken I couldn't go on without her. Well, he kept us in that district nigh on eight weeks, and I'd be sayin' it was to see if our feelin's died. I suppose he hoped it would, but no, there it was, me meetin' with her every day. Well, what with Patricia Junie knowin' about my way of life, Jordan cottoned on. Now, he was all for joinin' with us straightaway. No doubt the guv did a lot of thinkin', and finally he sent for Jordan and interviewed him, like."

"And he let Jordan join you?"

"Truth to tell, I do believe it were because of me and Patricia. He knew I wanted to marry her, and the only way to keep us all tight-knit was to agree to let Jordan join with us."

"I see."

"And she would never have left him behind," rejoined Lawless. "Fact is, she doted on her brother." He sighed again and shifted slightly around to face her. "For the very words the guverner spoke to me about my Patricia June were high compliment, and I'll never forget them. He said, 'Lawless, it's no life for a woman, bein' on the run, and I've always said I wouldn't allow it, but I note that your Patricia is different. She is strong and gallant and has that superior quality of dependability. If we can find a priest or a clergyman who will marry ye, then I believe it should be done." Lawless lifted his eyes to look straight at Eve. "The guverner were right about her, just as he always is where character be concerned."

"Yes, Lawless, I'm sure that's so."

Lawless dropped his eyes, and there was the edge of anger in his voice. "Well, we never did find a priest or a clergyman to marry us. No, none o' them ever would. My Patricia were distraught. How they stood in judgment on her and brought tears to her eyes."

"Oh, dear, I'm sorry," said Eve gently.

"No, don't be—" his voice lightened significantly "—for we *were* married, all real and proper like, in the sight of God by one o' the best representatives the good Lord has ever had on this poor earth."

"Who?"

"The guverner, of course!" he answered proudly. "He was the captain of a ship in Her Majesty's navy. He had the authority, ye see, the authority, and Patricia June was so merry when I told her he would do it. As for me, tell me, mistress, what's another man o' the cloth to me? But the guverner marryin' us, now, that had meanin', that did. For even though he told me he had lost his rank, and that the marriage would not be recognized by society, it mattered nary a bit. Givin' Patricia June a weddin' was what mattered, and we were married in my eyes and the eyes of Heaven." He smiled in remembrance, falling silent.

Eve thought how touching it was that this unaffected, ingenuous man beside her was revealing all this. Watching his tender smile, just for a second she was reminded of her own marriage in All Saints' Church. A sad feeling brought a sigh to her lips.

He, too, sighed, as he had done often during his tale, and took up his story once more. "Well, we had been husband and wife for close on one year when the darlin' told me I were to be a father. Happy day. That were when Alan said we had to find a proper hideout, a real home. But she was never to see it. She had been carryin' our child for just four months when the brown snake bit her. It were Christmas day and all, 1858. Don't seem right, does it, that an angel would be taken at Christmas? We were camped in a dry creek bed not two miles from the Warraderry Inn. Dan and I'd been gatherin' wood for the fire, while the guverner, Sam, and Jordan were out gettin' us a square meal. I can see her now, staggerin' toward us and cryin', 'Oh God, Arnold, it were a brown snake . . . not three minutes since. . . .' and holdin' up her darlin' wrist for me to see the puncture marks." He did not speak for a few moments, then he wiped his hands across his eyes as he finished, "She was dead in my arms within five minutes more. Both of them . . . dead."

Eve said nothing. She just sat looking at his profile. His teeth were clenched together and his eyes were wet. She could feel his suffering; she knew what it was to lose those you love, and she wished she could say something to alleviate it. She put out her hand on his forearm and held it there.

"Lawless, the two of you were blessed beyond most others with the love you shared. I do not think that Patricia June would want you to be sad."

He turned to face her. "Now, Mistress Eve, ye be speakin' the truth there and no mistake. That is why I try to keep a cheerful heart . . . for the memory of my angel, and for Alan, too, in a way. It is only in the speakin' of it all that I have become melancholy, and I thank ye for the sentiment ye have shown me.''

"You're a fine, good man, Lawless, and I am honored that you saw fit to tell me.''

He was moved by her words, and for a short time they sat without speaking.

He broke the silence. "I'd been visitin' her grave when I met ye on the road.''

"I see," she replied softly.

"Well, mistress, we had best be gettin' in . . . luncheon time.''

They bent in unison and picked up her firewood. As they stood, he cleared his throat and spoke again. "You're a fine, good woman. Never truly thought there'd ever be a woman good enough for my guverner . . . but ye are.''

"Oh, Lawless, thank you. It warms my heart to hear that.''

The afternoon dragged, and so did the night. It was close to eleven o'clock, after Daniel had been pacing the Treehard veranda for hours, that they heard the bird call and Alan and Sam returned.

Daniel stood near the entrance, relief appearing in his face. He cried out happily, "It's grand to see you, that it is! What with the day passing like a slug over silt, it's been a wearing time, I assure you.''

The leader's gaze lifted to the veranda where Eve stood on the top step in the reflected light from the kitchen. She had combed her hair down, and it lay in masses of soft curls over her shoulders. She was wearing her good dress, the one she kept as special. Her face radiated happiness, and there was a vigor in her that made her skin glow and lent effervescence to her smile of welcome.

She thought it a miracle that it was he who dismounted below and smiled up at her. He thought it a miracle that she stood on his doorstep smiling down at him.

Alan's feet had hardly touched the ground when Daniel was asking, "Well? Well? What did you determine? How is the lie of the land? What is it that people are saying?''

"Steady, Danny, my friend,'' Alan replied. "It's a grim tale, but the short answer is that Ben Hall has been shot dead, and the general feeling predicts little good for us.''

"Oh no!'' uttered Lawless.

Daniel sighed. "Ah me. Ben gone, eh? God rest his soul.''

Lawless and Jordan asked simultaneously, "When? Where?''

"Now, ye two, leave the guverner be!" chided Sam. "We've been on the road since dawn and ridden nigh on eighty-five miles today. We be tired, and the horses be exhausted."

When the horses had been fed and watered, they all assembled in the kitchen.

Alan related the day's events. "We made for the Canowindra district. There are more inns in that part of the country that we have not frequented, and, too, I thought to get the opinions of farmers and itinerants as well.

"In a tavern south of the goldmine near Idolwood Creek, about fifteen or twenty miners were congregated. Sam brought up the question of the act after we had been there ten minutes or so, and the mood of those men was that it was about time something was done about the safety of the bush roads. When Sam and I, at last, rode into Canowindra it was after one o'clock in the afternoon. We had visited some six or seven inns, and everywhere the general feeling was for the act and against the bushrangers. Very different from a few years ago."

"Why," spoke up Sam, "one young blood said he couldn't wait for the morrow when it became legal to shoot us on sight. I felt like hittin' the sod in the mouth, but I restrained m'self. All I said was, 'Would ye be knowin' a bushranger if ye looked one in the eye?' And he reckoned he would, makin' him a liar, as well as bloodthirsty."

"Gawd!" said Lawless. "Ye've had a day of it, all right. What else, guv?"

"We hadn't been in Canowindra more than a few minutes when we realized the whole town was afire with the news of Ben's death. He was shot yesterday morn at daybreak. Seems he was staying in a hut of a friend called Mick Connolly."

"I know him, boss," Jordan broke in, looking to Alan. "He's a half-caste, mother was an abo, used to live in a shanty near Billabong Creek, northwest o' Forbes."

"Yes," said Alan, "that is the place Ben was caught."

Jordan's eyes narrowed in contemplation as Sam's fist came down on the table in front of him. "Sounds suspiciously like Connolly ratted on him to me."

"Aye, me, too," agreed Lawless.

Alan shook his head. "Whatever the truth is, and we've heard a number of versions today, Ben Hall is dead. Gilbert and Dunn were not with him. Apparently he was alone in the hut when a black tracker called Billy Dargin led the troopers in. He died in a hail of bullets."

"Yes," Samuel added. "Some of the blokes were sayin' there were more than thirty bullets counted in him!"

Lawless shook his head. "Gawd!"

Eve shivered.

It was Daniel who spoke first. "No doubt we'll be learning soon enough if this Connolly informed. If he did, he'll not need to be living in a shanty by a creek; the reward money will see to that."

The others murmured in agreement.

"Ben was not a bad bloke really," stated Lawless in his straightforward fashion.

"Yes," said Alan thoughtfully, "he was a cut above the rest."

Eve shivered again. Rutherford Blake was having his day.

Later, when Treehard was quiet with all the occupants in bed, Alan lay thinking. His responsibility was to keep safe the five people under his roof. He did not fear for himself—fear had never been Alan's companion—but he felt concern for them. Things were changing in New South Wales. Perhaps if they were careful, as they had always been, the act would have no effect on them. No one knew the whereabouts of Treehard Hill, and very few law-abiding citizens knew their faces: fewer than ten in the whole colony. That was, except for Jordan; some knew him, for he had grown up in the bush, farmed in the bush. And Jordan, unfortunately, would still want to go abroad. The lad needed the outlet of female company, and Alan understood that; they were natural feelings. But he would have to make sure that Jordan did not see the same girl too often from now on. He would have to talk the boy into lessening his visits to Bridget at Wattamondara.

For a long time he had been thinking of making a run for Western Australia. There was pastoral land opening up north of Perth, and no one was looking for them there, over two thousand miles away. They would all like the farming life, especially Danny. But now that he had Eve to take care of, he was not so sure, for it would be a very hard life, and the danger of one day being discovered would always dog them. The men were used to being on the run; Eve was not. With Eve there really was no place to hide in Australia; the settlements were tiny and far apart, and strangers were noticed. It would be best if he could get them all somewhere truly safe. A thought was taking shape in his head, for today he had seen something that had stimulated a fresh idea. By the time he drifted into slumber, the idea formulated into a new plan. One of vision . . . one that would give them a life of real freedom, far from New South Wales.

The very next morning, Eve came to Alan as he was shoeing Freedom. He looked up at her and smiled. "You want me, lass?"

She had a quivering feeling around her heart as she smiled and replied, "I do. Will your friend, Womballa, be back on the plateau yet?"

"Yes, I think by now they will all have returned."

"I wish to thank him for saving my life."

"That's a fine idea. I'd like to see the old fellow again myself."

They went riding in the tranquil autumn afternoon. Alan rode Waterloo, for Freedom had carried him the immense distance of yesterday. Eve rode Milford, Daniel's mare, a horse with a compliant, amenable nature. They traveled south through the bush for perhaps twenty minutes and then began slowly rising toward the plateau. They rested briefly on the tableland, and about fifteen minutes later, came to the area of the Welba Welba.

Eve had never been to an aboriginal camp, so it was with interest and a little trepidation that she saw, through the trees ahead, six or seven dark brown bodies appear as if out of nowhere. They had recognized Alan and so made themselves available to him. He lifted his hand, and two or three signaled back. Then, leaping and shouting, came a child of ten or eleven.

Alan laughed. "It's Odoono," he explained, turning in his saddle toward Eve. "He is my little friend and companion during my visits here. He is a quick-witted lad and speaks some English."

No sooner had Alan said this than the babbling voice of Odoono reached Eve over the rugged terrain. "Fletcher! You come! Good! We no see long time." The child came running to the side of Waterloo in fearless fashion. He looked with interest at Eve and pointed at her as Alan leaned down and took the willing boy up into his arms and placed him on the saddle.

Through the trees, silently to the right and left, Eve saw people, all naked, making pace with the horses as they rode by. Some had never seen a white woman up close, and there were disconcerted looks and much mumbling.

When Alan dismounted and lifted the voluble Odoono to the ground, the tribesfolk crept forward from behind the trees and the closest gunyahs to look. Their dark eyes were round in wonder, and only after Alan had called to many of them by name did they come within a few yards of the curiosity that was the European woman.

Then there was a loud shout! A hail of welcome! The closest bodies fell back and separated, and Eve looked into the face of the man who had saved her life. He gestured welcome, his thick lips parted in pleasure, his white beard resting on his chest. He was a wonderfully eccentric figure, wearing the hat Alan had given him, with the hunting knife strapped around his waist above his long, thin legs. Three or four of his family were clustered behind him.

Everyone watched as he came swiftly forward, hand outstretched. "Ah, Clever Fletcher, again you come, *waminda*."

Alan took his hand and shook it in the English manner. "Womballa, my *waminda*, I come to bring you the woman you make well with good medicine." He turned to the other aborigines and praised Womballa, saying that Eve had been very ill when the rains came and that the tribal elder's good medicine had saved her. "*Elginbah* when *paamburra pakaderinga* come, now no *minga*. Womballa, *murumba wallamurra*."

The old man smiled broadly, showing his line of broken teeth. The members of his tribe may be timid in the presence of this woman, but not he; had he not been with her spirit in the "dreaming"? There was a gleam in his black eyes and mirth in his face as he said, "*Merinda*, Clever Fletcher, *merinda*."

Alan smiled and answered, "Yes." For Womballa had called Eve "pretty."

Then the the old man beckoned Alan and Eve to follow him.

The whole tribe, having been given the example, came along in unison to Womballa's gunyah. Alan was always a source of enjoyment to them, and they were realizing that the white woman was not to be feared.

Outside Womballa's gunyah, Alan and Eve sat on the ground beside the old man and the other tribal elders, while Datta and Mulgatta and Womballa's other sons and daughters, and their husbands and wives, made a rough circle. The rest of the tribe looked on, Odoono standing proudly behind Alan.

There was movement behind them, and something that looked like a long, thin hollowed-out tree branch, covered in all manner of design, was handed through the throng and given to Womballa. He raised it to his mouth. Eve looked questioningly at Alan.

"It's a *didgeredoo*, a musical instrument," he whispered.

Womballa filled up his cheeks with air, until they were like two round balls, and he began to produce the most amazing stream of rising and falling sound. Eve listened, fascinated, while all the tribe began a soft chant that ebbed and flowed with the moaning of the *didgeredoo*. After a minute or two, the dark, naked bodies began to sway. The performance lasted perhaps five or six minutes and came abruptly to an end.

Eve automatically began to applaud. Then she stopped, for there was total silence. They were all staring at her, their wide faces filled with interest. Never had they seen anyone clap hands in these circumstances before. A few pointed and gestured. Alan explained as best he could that what Eve had done was a display of appreciation and gratitude, and Womballa nodded in understanding.

Later, when Alan took the six pots of honey from his saddlebags and gave them to Womballa, the old man took them and handed them to Datta and Mulgatta before he turned back to Alan and clapped his hands. Alan, surprised, smiled with pleasure. Then the whole tribe began to clap, and in thanks, he dipped his head to them all.

To say farewell, Womballa donned the leather coat Alan had given him. They walked beside each other to the edge of the encampment, while all around milled the tribe. Enthralled, Eve watched the two friends say good-bye. There they stood together on the rocky ground of the plateau, the most incongruous of friends, and yet the most compatible. Alan took Womballa's hand in the European manner, saying, "Good-bye, my dear *waminda*."

Womballa shook Alan's hand as he had learned to do, and then he said, "Clever Fletcher, *yanniwan*. You watch day and night. Stay safe."

Eve stood in wonder as he lifted his dark, callused hand and gently touched Alan's face. The movement was tender, even loving, and she fancied that the tribal elder's black, inscrutable eyes clouded over for a moment or two.

Alan drew his eyes away from Womballa's and shook hands with the other tribal elders. Then he took Datta's hand and held it as he said good-bye. The old woman giggled with amusement.

Odoono, leading Waterloo by his bridle, had kept up his volatile chatter all the while. He tugged upon Alan's coat. "You come back soon, Fletcher. You come back soon, bring honey! Yes."

Eve stood awkwardly, uncertain what to say, and Alan encouraged her. "Say *apo*, lass; it means 'good-bye.' It is all that is necessary."

But she wanted to say more. She looked into Womballa's eyes, making a conscious effort to remember them. At the same time, she put out her hand, and he shook it as he had done with Alan. She did not let go, but grasped it in both of hers, and he, quick to new ways, grasped with both of his. Later, when she thought on it, she was honored to have touched him, to have held the hands that had saved her life. She said, "Thank you, thank you, Womballa. I will remember you always, all my life. *Apo*, thank you."

Womballa unhesitatingly answered, "*Apo*, Clever Fletcher woman."

Alan ruffled Odoono's hair affectionately before they mounted their horses and rode away, waving to the cries of *"Apo!"* that sounded after them.

As they crossed the densely wooded plateau and began the gradual descent to the valley, Eve was thinking. A short time ago, she had rescued Jordan from falling to his death, and only yesterday, Lawless had delivered her from the brown snake, and now, twenty-four hours later, she had met the man who, only a few months ago, had saved her from dying. Life could be extinguished in a moment. *In the midst of life we are in death.* She looked over to Alan. The thought gave an exquisite urgency to her love for Alan. How long would they have? These wonderful days they were spending together . . . How long would they last?

They had not gone far when Alan turned Waterloo onto a natural track that led through the thick bush to the east.

"Where do we go?" called Eve.

"Follow; it is worth seeing."

Five or so minutes later, the track ended against what looked like dense scrub. He dismounted, and she followed. He tied the horses loosely to an enormous banksia.

"Where are we? What mystery is this?" she asked expectantly.

He motioned for her to follow and led the way on foot over the rough ground. They had to scramble across a few small boulders, through undergrowth and trees. Then as they rounded some rocks, quite suddenly the bush opened up. She stood still in delight, surveying what lay before her. It had appeared like some conjurer's instant illusion, a beautiful, grassy glade.

The plateau towered above to her right, a vast, rocky image.

Down its face a small waterfall trickled into a creek, a few yards from where she stood. The water was so clear, so transparent, she could see vividly the diverse browns and yellows of the smooth stones at the bottom. The last of the summer wildflowers grew here, determined, tiny, blue blossoms dotting the scrub all around. The scent of the mint bushes was strong in the air. Here was an atmosphere of harmony, of serenity. It made her feel released from care, and she laughed with pure pleasure. She turned around in a circle, looking all about. "What a truly beautiful place it is. I don't think I've seen anything quite like it before."

"Yes," he agreed. "There is almost a sense of Nirvana if one remains long enough." Then he smiled in remembrance, a moving smile, before he added, "Although here it is more rugged, it reminds me of a part of my father's land by Long Moss House. A green, mossy hill towered there, just as the tableland does above us now, and a stream ran down the hillside into a clear, rocky pool where I used to play."

She was watching his face. "England must be beautiful," she remarked softly.

"It is."

He turned away and looked down the creek. "But England is my past. This land is my present."

"And the future?" she questioned his back.

"Who can answer that?"

She ached to touch him then, to move to him and to hold him. She wanted to say all manner of things. Positive things about the future, their future: that now she did not care about convention or what was deemed proper; that she wanted to be with him always, whatever the future held. It was exquisite agony, this being alone with him, this wanting desperately to hold him and love him. She moved closer to him and spoke softly. "Perhaps the future will be kind to us. The fates have seen fit to bring us together. Who would have believed, a year ago, that I would be with you now?"

He turned back to her. There was a coldness in his expression. A tingle of fear passed through her. She was reminded of the day in the Bathurst park when he had rejected her.

"Alan," she said quietly, "what is it? What is wrong?"

"We should not be alone together." There was an edge to his voice. "It was wrong of me to bring you here."

"But why? It is so beautiful, and I *want* to be alone with you."

"That is the very reason, don't you see?"

"I don't understand."

His tone was distant. "You are another man's wife, Eve, and you always will be."

She thought of John Stuart then and briefly she felt odd, yes, and guilty, just as she used to at Mayfield when she thought of Alan.

They were standing no more than two feet apart, their eyes locked. The seconds passed in silence, the only noises the sound of the bush and the running water. He was contemplating her in the way that made her feel he could see inside her. She felt wonderfully uncomfortable.

Then she lifted her hand to his face, and when he did not draw away, she said, "I cannot help what has happened in the past. While I am responsible for many mistakes, and I acknowledge them, all I know is that I love you now . . . and have loved you since the moment I first saw you."

The late afternoon sun was filtering through the trees. As the sun descended, the light in the glade seemed to intensify momentarily, and for a few seconds, the two still figures were caught in relief against the shimmering verticals of the sunbeams through the trees behind them. There was something unreal about the moment. Dreamlike. Eve felt as if the bush around them disappeared. She was aware only of Alan and the radiating light around them. In his eyes, she saw the longing, open, obvious. She lifted her other hand to his face and drew down his head. "You hold back for many reasons, and I know them all . . . and I love you," she said, covering his mouth with her own.

For a second or two, it was her kiss only; he still withheld.

Then, as if his response to her traveled through his veins like a stream of lava, his restraint of all the months was gone.

At last . . . at last . . . She felt his hands moving down across her body, demanding, greedy, wanting her. He was holding her so tightly pressed to him, she could feel the rippling tension of desire in him, as if he were melding, merging with her, body into body. A powerful rush of elation churned through her. She had never been more aware, more alive, than now. This was what she had dreamed of, waited for, longed for. The feel of him down along the length of her, his arms, his body enveloping her. The wonderful smell of him, the clean, bold smell of the bush, of courage and sunshine. Her hands were in his hair, on his neck; her mind was blurring. There was a cosmos of intense pleasure, and she was the core. Her lips opened to the pressure of his, opened gladly, hungrily. His tongue tasted the inside of her mouth, searching, meeting. Know me, Alan, know me, love me.

She made a joyous sound in her throat, an earthy, voluptuous sound of desire, of urgency and victory, and he echoed it from deep within his soul. This was what she had known and yet not known. Had there ever before been passion like this? Sweet sensations exploded in her breasts, and her nipples rose inside her dress in wanton expectation.

Then, as suddenly as he had taken her in his arms, he broke away from her. His eyes were clouded with yearning, and his voice was thick with the need of her, but he resisted. "No. We must leave this place." Suddenly he grabbed her hand and, turning immediately from her, pulled her after him back toward the horses.

She was cognizant only of him and his hand drawing her behind him. She was oblivious of the rocky ground, the scrub, the birds calling in the trees; nothing but Alan filled her consciousness. She was hurt, thwarted.

They rode home in silence, and when he lifted her down to the ground from Milford, he still did not speak.

"Well, good morning, my son." Daniel greeted Alan with a wide smile as he entered the kitchen a little before half past six o'clock the following day.

"Good morning, Danny. Is anyone else awake?"

"No, they all be abed still, but I will wake them soon."

"Then before you do, I want you to hear something. Come outside, will you?"

Daniel followed out onto the small veranda, where the morning autumn sun was steeping Treehard Hill in a flood of yellow. The trunks of the great eucalyptus reflected a lemon light all around, and rays of sunshine made golden stripes between the trees.

"Ah me," exclaimed Daniel, "that does my old heart good to look upon."

Alan patted him gently on the back. "Danny, when Sam and I were in Canowindra the day before yesterday, we learned something of great use. The mail coach was about to depart, when the driver turned to the guard and said, 'My God, what with the news of Ben Hall's death, I clean forgot to get the pay slip.' The guard must have been new to the route, for he didn't know what the driver meant. The driver gave him a long explanation. He was authorized to pick up at the Bathurst bank the pays for the fifty police, forty troopers, and all the magistrates, prison and government officials, and employees stationed in the Central, Western, and Northwestern districts. They do this six times a year: in January, March, May, July, September, and November. The money is held in Bathurst over the first weekend in those months, and then distributed. His run is Bathurst Orange. All the money and two more guards are picked up in Bathurst on the Monday morn, and delivered to Orange for noontime. Evidently in Orange the pays are divided and go to all the other settlements in the North and West.''

Alan's eyes met Daniel's, and he smiled at his friend. ''All those government pays,'' Daniel mused. ''Two months of pay for how many?''

''Perhaps two hundred.''

Dan calculated for a minute. ''It could be sixteen hundred pounds. A lot of bank notes, Alan, son.''

''Yes, Daniel, and added to the gold left from Theresa Town, it will be a surfeit for six passages to America and freedom. For that's the destination I'm contemplating. From what I read in the *Lachlan Miner* in Canowindra, the Confederate armies have all but lost the war. It shall soon be over. It means a new start for that country, and we can all have new starts along with it.''

Daniel sucked in his breath in surprise. ''Oh, Alan, son,'' he whispered. Then he repeated, ''Oh, Alan, son.''

Alan leaned forward and took the older man by the wrist. ''That's my plan, Danny. To take the coach in July when it makes its next run.''

''Aye, lad, it sounds a good and workable idea. And to take from the government again, as is your way. But it'll be dangerous, as always.'' He sighed and looked down at the backs of his hands.

''Daniel, my old partner?'' Alan said softly.

Dan raised his eyes. He could not disguise his apprehension, although he truly tried. Alan was looking deep into the pale eyes in front of him, and he continued to hold Dan's wrist.

''I ask you this without the others present, for the journey will be the hardest on you. You *will* make the journey with me, won't you?''

The older man found it hard to answer. He swallowed. ''It will break my heart to leave Treehard.''

''I will not go without you.''

Daniel sighed. "Ah, then I must come with you, my son, and that's the way of it."

TWENTY-EIGHT
After the Felons' Apprehension Act

Alan looked up from the map on the kitchen table. It was a detailed drawing of a section of the road between Bathurst and Orange. His finger rested on the spot where a wooden bridge, only the width of a carriage, had been built across a stream known as Kettle's Creek. At the same time, beside him, Samuel's head lifted from poring over the map.

The strains of singing coming from across the yard drifted in to them.

> *"To Jack Robertson we say,*
> *You've been leading us astray,*
> *And we'll never go afarming anymore,*
> *For it's easier duffing cattle*
> *On a little piece of land*
> *Far away from the Eumerella shore"*

Alan smiled. "Sixteen years since we were brought to this land, and now our lad from the Rookery sings political songs in the Australian bush."

"True, true, guverner," Samuel agreed. "Lawless knows more of this land than the one that bred him."

"That's right, Sam, my friend, and when our plan comes to fruition, there shall be Eve's homeland for him to come to know."

A stern expression asserted itself on Sam's face, and he rapped with his fist on the table. "Aye, guverner, what ye say is all very well, but it's this job ye must be doin' first, and I don't like ye doin' it with just three. I should be along.''

"Sam, don't grumble. It's very important to me that you remain here. You see, my dear friend, if anything does go amiss, then I know I can rely on you to take the gold and get Daniel and Eve on board a ship to America. I cannot stress this too strongly. Don't you see that, my friend?''

Sam's chin wrinkled and his mouth grew tight. ''All right,'' he admitted at last. ''I do. But if anything goes wrong with ye and the lads, do you really think I'd have the heart to go on?''

"I would be relying on you.''

Sam's answer was unequivocal. ''Life would have little meanin' without ye in it, but I would do what ye wanted to the best of my ability, as ye know full well I would.''

At that moment Daniel came in through the kitchen door, followed by Eve and Jordan, both carrying .31-caliber Colt pocket pistols. Daniel had been watching them shoot targets at the southern end of Treehard. Lawless was the last to enter; he had taken a quick look down over the hill from Nelson's Boulder and now joined them at the kitchen table.

When the meeting began, Alan explained that after much deliberation, he had decided to take the government payroll coach. He described a plan that was methodical and precise. The coach was due to leave Bathurst at eight o'clock on Monday morning, the third of July, and should reach Kettle's Creek sometime after nine o'clock. On a Monday morning, there was little doubt it would be the only vehicle on that road.

Alan had chosen Kettle's Creek because there was a backwood's track not far from the creek running three miles south through the bush, a fast getaway. The location was within ten miles of Bathurst, and Alan did not like to be so near to the headquarters of Rutherford Blake, but the bridge was unquestionably the ideal place to bail up the vehicle. The coach would slow down almost to a crawling pace to cross the narrow bridge, and immediately beyond, the land rose in a long hill, allowing no acceleration. Alan and the others would circumnavigate a huge rock formation twenty-five yards from the crossing and come up directly behind the coach, surprising the guard on horseback. Providing the others were not heroes, it would be relatively simple to take them as well.

"As always,'' he said, ''our argument is with the authorities, not individuals. We shoot at no man unless we have the need to defend ourselves, and even then, we fire to wound only. We

carry arms to cause submission, not to use. We have never yet
resorted to violence. This time must be no exception.''

For the next weeks, Alan went over the plan daily with Lawless and Jordan, until at last came the Thursday evening before
their departure.

Daniel had prepared a special dinner of pigeon pie and dump-
lings, and to follow he had made a bread pudding with fresh
milk, a real treat at Treehard. Jordan had brought the milk home
two days before, after he had been down to Wattamondara with
the intention of spending the night with Bridget. His visit to
Wattamondara had been a cause for some dissension in the Treehard household, for Alan had not wanted Jordan to go. He had
finally allowed it, but only after Samuel had taken up Jordan's
cause.

''The boy is twenty-nine, guverner,'' Sam had said after seeking Alan out in the confines of the stable, where he was polishing
his saddle. ''He has not been with a woman since you came
back from Goulburn in April, and he has not been with Bridget
since March. It's near to four months!''

Alan continued working. ''Samuel. Samuel. Four months?
We have known men of his age who went without a woman for
four years, even fourteen, so what argument is four months?''

But after Samuel had promised to deliver Jordan to the tavern
himself and straight back the following day, Alan relented.

Sam had grinned. ''Thanks, guv, the lad will be right happy,
he will.''

But Jordan had returned unhappy. In fact, he had come home
abashed, solemn, and hurt. Things were no longer the same at
Wattamondara.

''The only good thing to come out of this here visit is the
fresh milk they got, and that's a fact,'' Daniel said later.

Lawless's opinion was a little stronger. ''He should not have
been goin' down there, and we all know it. He be a selfish
perisher at times, and Sam be wrong in takin' his part.''

Eve decided to say nothing, for while she agreed with Lawless
that Jordan seemed to do as he pleased at times, she could understand how he wanted to see the girl he cared for; it was a
difficult situation.

Jordan would not recount what had occurred. He communicated very little. It was Sam who told the story.

When they had arrived at Wattamondara, it had been a cold,
gray day and was settling into dusk. Sam remained on horseback

at the side of the inn while Jordan went around the back. During his wait for the all clear, Sam's eye was taken by a number of posters nailed to a new billboard under the awning.

He felt a tremor in his chest as he read, WANTED DEAD OR ALIVE! The reward for Alan's capture had gone to two thousand pounds. Each of the rest of them, one thousand, and the same for the "Jockey," young Johnny Dunn. A man Sam had never heard of, Frederick Ward, alias "Captain Thunderbolt," was posted at five hundred pounds. Old Joe Daily and Kenny Dawson were there at twelve hundred, and a couple of others for smaller sums. But the principal surprise was that such a notice board would be attached to the wall of Henry Lyon's Watta-mondara tavern. Slowly he had ridden Milford back to Jordan's horse.

Suddenly he heard yelling and shouting from inside the inn. He jumped down from Milford and came rapidly through the back door in time to see Jordan holding a chair above his head. Another lay broken against the wall where Jordan had thrown it.

There was only one drinker in the barroom, and he was watching the display apprehensively.

Bridget was standing with her father behind the bar. Henry Lyon was speaking. "Blast it, Jordan, things are different now. Can't you see Bridget doesn't want you here?"

Jordan brought the chair heavily down in frustration. It clattered loudly and fell on its side. "You tell me!" he shouted, pointing at the girl. "You tell me yourself, Bridget!"

Sam's head did not come as high as Jordan's shoulder, but he moved speedily forward. "That's it, Jordan, laddie. Settle. Ye've naught to gain with force."

"Stay out of it, Sam!" He shook Sam off like a nuisance fly and strode to the bar.

"Speak to me, damn it, Bridgy! Please. Too bloody good for me now, eh?"

"Jordan, I'm sorry." Bridget burst into tears.

The young man leaped around the bar, and Henry Lyon barred the way between the bushranger and his daughter.

"Don't, Jordan, cut it out, she's confused," the publican pleaded as the big man thrust him backward. "Don't you see what you're doin' by just bein' here? If the bloody traps learn of this . . . fifteen years' jail! You're a menace. Go away and leave us alone, for Christ's sake!"

"Jesus!" cried Jordan in desperation.

For a few moments there was silence, broken only by Bridget's sobs coming from behind her father. Then Jordan lost control and smashed his fist into the publican's face. The man dropped to the floor, and Bridget screamed.

Jordan made a loud, frustrated sound, and the drinker, who until now had stayed at the bar, hurried out.

Simultaneously Henry's wife came running in from the next room, followed by Christina and Marilyn, both wide-eyed and frightened. Edna Lyon shrieked when she saw her husband on the floor.

Sam knew it was time to take charge. He lifted his rifle up over the bar and pushed Jordan back away from Henry with the side of the barrel. "That's it, Jordan. Move out, laddie. We've done enough damage here."

Jordan, tired at last of the scene, did as he was directed.

"I'm real sorry, Henry . . . Edna," Sam said.

"Just go, Sam, and leave us alone!" Edna Lyon pleaded.

The last thing Sam heard Henry call after them was, "Tell Alan we're sorry, too, but it's different now. Everything's different!"

They mounted their horses, and as they passed the front of the tavern, Jordan looked over and noticed the milk urn on the veranda steps. He dismounted.

"What the devil are ye doin' now?" Sam asked in agitation.

Jordan did not answer. He took his water bottle from his saddlebag and dipped it into the urn and filled it with milk. Then, wrapping it in his large handkerchief, he remounted and rode off.

They arrived back at Treehard in the dark of the cold winter's night.

When Sam had explained everything, Alan took Jordan aside. "Jordan lad," he counseled, "don't brood over what has happened. Henry and his daughter are not to blame. Circumstances are now beyond their control. They act out of fear."

Jordan's mouth turned down. "Yeah, and you knew it. How is it that you always know things?"

Alan took Jordan by both shoulders. "Laddie, I don't. But I have had a longer time to observe the way men comport themselves under trying circumstances."

"It's not fair, boss. It's just not bloody fair."

"Life isn't, lad, so let us leave it there. We have much to accomplish in the days ahead." He smiled encouragingly. "Just think, if all goes well, there is a time coming when you will be free of the scourge of being a bushranger, and you will be able to make whatever friends you like.''

Jordan nodded thoughtfully and attempted a smile.

Since then, there had been a flurry of preparation for the departure to Kettle's Creek and Thursday had been spent in making sure everything was ready.

The day had been cold, the evening was colder, winter having begun; there was a bitter wind whipping up the valley, pushing wispy streaks of cloud across a waxing moon in a deep rose sky.

Alan's preparations were finished, and now he was in a clear patch of grass between the trees, doing his calisthenic exercises. It was a practice he had developed in his naval days when the confines of a ship had checked his riding and walking.

Eve was standing on the veranda. She could not see Alan, but she knew exactly where he was. Behind her in the kitchen, Danny lifted his pigeon pie from the hob, the aroma floating appetizingly in the air around her. The others, she could see through the stable door, moving in the lantern light. She tapped her fingernails on the railing. She was here, and he was here, and tomorrow he would be gone, into terrible danger. She hurried down the steps and across the yard.

Out of the corner of his eye, Daniel watched her go, a tiny, knowing expression appearing at the edges of his mouth.

Alan, in his cotton shirt sleeves, warm after the exertion, saw her coming toward him. She was wrapped against the wind. If only he had known; his reaction was similar to the one John Stuart had experienced when he first saw her in the Bathurst park.

She walked swiftly through the gums. She was thinking about the afternoon in the bush glade, and she knew the titanic struggle that had gone on inside him that day. During their walks since in the soft Treehard twilight, he had never referred to it, and she knew why. Oh, Alan, what does it matter? I love you. I'm sure you love me. This whole human life is so uncertain, so precarious. I only need you. I am ready. There is no need to hold back in consideration of me; I don't need that. If I have beaten the ghosts of Lake and the miscarriage, and the frustrations of a ruined marriage, why can't you? Why cannot you just love me?

She came up to within three feet of him, her ardent brown eyes regarding him. ''Alan . . . I . . . There is something I want to say. You go tomorrow. It will be terribly dangerous.'' She dropped her gaze to her hands. She twisted her fingers and rubbed her nails. Then she lifted her eyes back to his, and as her words came slowly, deliberately, he recognized again, with a ripple of love, the indomitable strength living in her soul. "Father once said to me that there was a time for truth, and that the recognition of it brings a freedom tantamount to flying with the angels. He said other things that I try to live by, but the truth, I think, I have often evaded." She took a step closer to him. He did not move away, but his look asked her not to come nearer.

"Why are you saying this?" he said.

"Surely you know."

"Eve." His voice was cheerless, and he elongated the *e* sound as he sometimes did. "What is this truth you talk of?"

"The truth that is us," she answered.

"I do not intentionally misunderstand, but what do you mean?"

She took a deliberate step closer and took hold of his arms. He did not move. "Tomorrow you go to take a payroll coach, while I wait here powerlessly. I know you will have it no other way. . . ."

"You are right, I will not."

So I am forced to bide here, until you come back . . . or do not come back."

"I always come back."

"Yes, yes, that has been so, and I hope with all my heart that the same is true this time, that you come back, and we all escape to America and freedom. But if you do not, in case you do not . . . I must tell you."

"What?" The light in his eyes somehow intensified, reflecting the last rays of the departing day, and the wind, which until now had not found the little clearing, whistled in the trees.

Eve shivered and suddenly her eyes welled with tears.

His voice was tender now. "What must you tell me, my Eve? That you want me to hold you? Kiss your mouth? That you want me to love you physically as I do mentally? Because if I do not do these things, and I do not come back to Treehard, our love will not be complete?" He looked at her . . . into her, and she could contain the tears no longer.

"Yes," she said as they broke over her lids. "I want all those things, for you are the truth in my life, and the truth is love." She continued to hold his arms as if never to let him go.

He lifted his hands, and now he, too, held her arms. "Eve," he answered, "don't you realize how much I want these things you want? But not now. Not yet. Not here. I *will* come back. I will take you away from Treehard, and when we have left these shores, I will love you as I have craved to love you, from the day I found you in the bush.''

''Then kiss me . . . as you kissed me in the glade.''

''No . . . not as I kissed you in the glade.''

His hands slid beneath her jacket, around her waist, to nestle in the small of her back. Her world filled with his eyes, his thick, sun-lightened hair, his brown skin, and the feel of him as he leaned down to meet her. Slowly, like the dew settles on the petals of a flower at sunrise, he touched her mouth with his, covering her lips with his own. Seconds passed in vague glory as the all-encompassing pledge of love flowed from him. It was for her and only her, this tenderness, this benevolence, this pure love. Never had she received anything like this, never had she known there was anything to receive like this. A sensation of ethereal tranquillity that left her somehow dazed with perfect peace spread through her entire being.

When he lifted his mouth from hers, he said, ''Now, dry your eyes, my love.''

She smiled gently, coming back from the supreme, blissful infinity. ''I have heard what I wanted to hear, and felt what I had no idea I could feel.''

As night descended, he drew her arm through his, and they walked in silence back through the trees.

The following morning, Alan, Lawless, and Jordan left Treehard.

It was an optimistic farewell, all talking of the future and their lives in America. Dan hugged Alan close, his time-worn arms wrapped tightly around him for a long time, so long that Alan could actually feel the beat of the older man's heart. Dan's expression was of deep and lasting love, admiration, and trust. When he stepped back to look at Alan, his eyes were wet, but his words were confident. ''We will be expecting you back, sonny, sometime during the night on Monday. I'll have the fire going and a billy on the boil.'' He mustered a smile.

An uncomfortable shudder ran through Alan as he answered, ''Yes, Danny, my dearest old partner, I'm sure you will.''

''I will miss you every moment,'' Eve said when Alan turned to her.

''And I, you,'' he replied. Then, for the first time ever, he touched her intentionally in front of the others. He stepped forward and held her a few seconds in his arms, as his lips brushed her fair curls.

Samuel slapped them all on the back and was giving stern instructions even as they rode away. "Now, mateys, remember, on Monday I shall be up in Nelson's Boulder from twilight onward. Call loudly, Lawless, and for heaven's sake, make good time home, as I dinna want to be in that cold hole all night!"

Soon they had all entered the tunnel, and Sam turned away.

"Aren't you going to the lookout to watch them down the hill, Sam?" Eve asked.

"No, I'm goin' to the garden for a while. I'll go to the lookout later."

"Well, as for me, I'm for watching them now," Daniel said, turning to Eve.

"Yes, Daniel, I'm for watching them now, too."

Dan took Eve's arm, and together they walked into the tunnel to Nelson's Boulder.

TWENTY-NINE

Decision

Jordan rode behind Alan and Lawless in silence as they made the long descent down the hill to the valley. His mind was in turmoil.

He was still hurt over the events of Tuesday night. He had been so looking forward to that soft bed in the back room where he had lain many times with Bridget. The smooth touch of her skin and her dark, full nipples pressed against him. He could almost taste the wetness of her mouth now. He sighed. The bitch, turning sour on him just because the bloody traps had her and her family scared. It wasn't fair! A man's whole life was changed.

God! They could shoot now; anybody could shoot a bushranger on sight! It was awful. If only he weren't an outlaw!

His eyes rested on Alan's back. The boss. So flamin' forgivin' all the time. If only he had never met him. Then he would still be a man with no price on his head. The others were all convicts, for God's sake! It was natural for them to be outside the law, but he had never been in jail. It wasn't right that he could be shot on sight. It wasn't right his women were turnin' against him.

Sam had said that there were two thousand pounds on the boss's head now. Imagine that, a bloody fortune! On Monday next, the whole payroll wasn't goin' to be that much. Two hundred men's wages for two whole months, and it wasn't to be as much as the price on the boss's head. And the rest of them? Lawless, Sam, Daniel, and himself worth a thousand pounds each! God! The lot of them were worth six thousand pounds!

Jordan rode on, feeling dizzy just contemplating the amount.

That night they made camp on a small tributary of the Belubula River some twelve miles south of the pretty township of Carcoar, where, in November 1863, Jonny Vane of the Hall gang had talked to Father McCarthy and been induced to accompany the priest and give himself up in Bathurst.

They slept well, for the wind dropped with the coming of the night, and the temperature climbed marginally.

They were in "the middle of nowhere," as Lawless put it, so there was little need for a watch. Nevertheless, Alan mounted one to keep the fire burning and an eye out for anything untoward. Snakes were unlikely on a winter's night, but there was still the slight chance of a bush animal blundering into the camp. He took first duty from ten o'clock to one o'clock; Jordan the second, from one to four; and Lawless, the deepest sleeper, took four o'clock to sunrise, around the hour of seven.

Alan woke a little after three o'clock, feeling cold. The fire had gone out, and Jordan, who was on watch, was deeply asleep. Alan woke him and stoked up the fire.

"I couldn't help it, boss, really," the young man argued. "And in any case, we're in the middle of bloody nowhere."

"Jordan, listen to me. I know we are far from any settlement and there is no chance of discovery here, but that is not the issue. We keep watches for other reasons, and you know them well. Now, turn in, and I shall stay until it is time for Lawless to take over."

Saturday morning was cold, and a fine film of frost covered the grass in the low-lying areas when they stoked up the fire to boil the billy for breakfast.

"Where will we camp tonight, guv?" Lawless asked, sipping his tea.

Jordan raised his head from his plate of damper and grinned. He had regained his humor and forgotten the incident in the night. "I reckon we could be bold enough to camp right at the spot, boss. There'll be no one around on a Sunday."

Alan smiled. "Yes, lad, we probably could. But we shall take the precaution of removing ourselves a mile or so."

They made gradual progress, and by four o'clock, Alan had chosen his campsite for the next two nights, on the Bathurst side of Kettle's Creek, approximately a mile south of the bridge. The creek was very shallow at this point, and the bank lifted in a moderate slope to a small, flat area where a clump of young, red cedar trees, with their grayish-brown, scaly bark, grew in a loose half circle. To one side, a mound of rocks reached twelve feet into the air. The area between the two afforded a sheltered space. A gully ran at an acute angle from the creek and cut through behind the rocks, an ideal place to tether the horses.

In the hour before dark, they raised the tent and built the fire. The wind dropped a little, but it was hard work to keep the fire going, and they slept fitfully, for it was a very cold night.

"The only bloody good thing about this frost and cold is the fact that it kills the flamin' flies," Jordan remarked as he rolled up his bedding the following morning.

"Aye, too right, old son," agreed Lawless.

They rode to the bridge at Kettle's Creek, where they rehearsed the operation. Only once did they have to retire to hide in the bush, when David Elrington and four troopers rode by.

Lawless's observation was a mutual thought. "Boy, I'll be glad when this job is over and we be back at Treehard, mateys."

When they returned along the creek to the camp, they bathed in it while the sun was still out, and at dusk they lit a fire.

Alan regarded the two men with him in the flickering firelight. Lawless was now as fine a man as any who made the laws of the land. He was proud of Lawless; the lad was an example of the enduring good in the human spirit.

Jordan, still young and impetuous, nevertheless had stood his ground as well as any hardened old salt in the British navy on more than one occasion, and doubtless would again.

He closed his eyes and imagined Eve at Treehard in her cotton dress, with her hair tumbling in curls over her shoulders.

And then he thought of diminuitive Samuel, a lion heart, faithful and humble.

And Daniel? At seventy, the kindest, truest friend a man could have, who had been father to him for sixteen years. For just a moment as he pictured Daniel, his pulse quickened ever so slightly. He moved uncomfortably before he stood and moved out of the circle of firelight. He walked down a few steps toward the creek and looked up at the night. Suddenly, he saw a falling star. He felt odd. He was not concerned about tomorrow morning, for while any job could be dangerous, he knew he had planned things as well as possible. It was something else . . . something intangible.

"Guverner!" Lawless called from the fireside.

"Yes, Lawless, what is it?"

"Do we keep the same watches? It fast approaches ten o'clock."

"Yes, lad, I'll look out until one o'clock. You, Jordan, take three hours after that, and wake Lawless to watch until sunup. I want to be in position by just after eight o'clock."

It was about fifteen minutes before midnight when Jordan sat up and came out of the tent to find Alan putting another log on the fire.

"What is it, Jordan, lad?"

"I don't know, boss, can't sleep tonight, though Lawless is out to it for certain."

"Would you like a cup of tea?"

"Yeah, that's an idea," the young man said, putting on his greatcoat.

After Alan had boiled the billy, Jordan made the tea. They sat and drank, in the stillness of the vast, black silence.

"You may as well turn in now, boss," Jordan said, putting down his mug. "I'm really wide-awake."

Alan looked across at him. He seemed to weigh Jordan's offer. "All right, lad, I will. Good night." As he moved toward the tent, he stopped and turned back. "Jordan," he said softly.

Jordan looked up from the fire.

"There is a flat rock just up there." He motioned to it. "It is a vantage point that gives you a clear view of us in the tent, and the fire, while at the same time allows you to see through the cedars up the line of the creek."

"Sounds good."

"And if you feel at any time you are dropping off to sleep, wake me, Jordan, for I want a lookout all night tonight, you understand?"

"Yeah, yeah, boss, all right."

Jordan stayed seated. Trust the boss to bring up the other night! Well, he wasn't goin' to fall asleep this time, no sirree. The trouble with the boss was, he was so bloody perfect; never made a mistake, and had to remind others when they did. And he was always bloody right, the boss; look at the way he'd known beforehand how Bridget and her father would behave.

He poured himself another mug of tea. That bloody Bridget. Too good for him now. He wondered what she would have done if the boss had been there. He always had the feelin' she was sweet on the boss. He knew for certain her sister Marilyn was. Why was it the boss had that way with people? Why was he so bloody irresistible?

His face grew hard in the firelight. He stood up and put more small branches on the fire. He could hear the regular breathing of the two men in the tent. He lifted his rifle, a breech-loading Enfield he had taken from one of the police at Theresa Town, and moved in the direction of the rock that Alan had pointed out. Suddenly he stopped. Why should he do what the boss ordered? Automatically go and flamin' sit on the flamin' rock because the boss said he should. If the boss was so damn clever, how come he had two thousand pounds on his head? God! What a man wouldn't give for two thousand pounds! It would set a bloke up for life, that sort of money would. It was a fortune!

An idea flashed to his mind.

He looked back involuntarily to the tent. No, no, forget it!

His eyes moved rapidly back and forth. Why should he forget it? He never should have been a bushranger. It wasn't his fault. He wasn't one of them. Not really. Never had been. And bloody Lawless had never liked him, right from the start. Well, there was a way out; the way to a free life and stacks of money as well. What he could do if only he had money! Bridget would be all over him then. All the women would be! Yes, don't be afraid . . . do it. What about all the talk of Mick Connolly goin' to get part of the reward money out on Ben Hall and Johnny Gilbert! And when Bart Smithers informed on Ruggy Dick, he got half the reward, they reckon. All that money. And Billy Dunken; now, he had turned . . . what was it? Queen's evidence. Against Jake Crane. Heck, Bart Smithers and Billy Dunken had both been pardoned and got reward money, too!

He looked back again to the tent. All silent.

No, he wasn't really one of them, never had been . . . not really. A pardon, yes, that's what he could get.

Buck up, Jordan. It was now or never!

He was less than ten miles outside Bathurst. Less than ten miles from Rutherford Blake. This was the best chance he would ever have. The *only* chance he would ever have. Now was the time! He would show the boss who was the cleverest after all. Yes, yes, he would do it.

Stealthily he crept back and put a solid log and some branches on the fire. He waited a short time to see they took light, his heart pounding in his chest and perspiration dampening his shirt even in the wind. Then he picked up his saddle and moved away around the rocks into the gully, where he untethered his horse. He even untied the two packhorses and Freedom and Waterloo in the vain hope that they might wander away. Freedom stamped his hooves and gave a gentle whinny.

"Quiet, Freedom boy, quiet."

He led his horse until he was well away from camp before he mounted and followed the creek to the bridge.

Soon he was spurring his horse and riding as fast as he dared in the moonlight toward Bathurst township.

Sir Rutherford shifted in his chair.

He pulled the lamp a little closer as he pored over the map on the desk in front of him. He ran his index finger back and forth over a spot on the paper and then leaned back in consideration. It was the same area that he always studied. Where the hell was the Fletcher hideout? John Stuart and a troop of Mayfield men had minutely investigated the whole countryside, and he had taken his own men there more than once, but they had found nothing. Why, last month, the master of Mayfield had gone far to the south and even searched the farthest reaches of the Boorowa River, to no avail. Could the hideout be inside the Mayfield border? No, that was impossible. John Stuart seemed to know every nook and cranny of his property, enormous though it was.

Poor John Stuart. The disorder, let alone the dishonor, that had been brought into his life by the Herman woman. He should never have taken her for his wife. That is what happened when one married out of one's class.

Flashing to Sir Rutherford's mind came the unhappy image of a girl in black dress and white apron. She was laughing, her merry hazel eyes regarding him. She tilted her elfin face, and her auburn hair fell to the side. She was lifting her dainty hand up . . . up to him. It touched his face. Ah yes . . . Coralea, you were truly beautiful, and how you loved me! So clearly did he see her among all the other indistinct memories from his past.

He shifted awkwardly in his chair, and for a brief time his severe features yielded to an uncharacteristically wistful, sentimental expression. Why was she still here? Living in his head, able to haunt him? He had come all this way to forget her. Still . . .

"No!" he said aloud as he ran his hands across his eyes. Hadn't he done what was right and proper? She was a servant in his father's house. He could not have married her. He was the heir to a marquisate. She was beneath him. No one should step down out of his class. He stood from the chair and walked to the window to disperse the memory.

Ah yes, and that was another reason among the many why he hated Alan Fletcher. The man had disgraced his birth. Sunk to murder and the dissolute life of a bushranger. The others were born scum, but Fletcher had made the conscious choice.

He put his hand in his fob pocket and drew out his watch. It was after half past the hour of one in the morning. He should retire. There was no more he could achieve tonight.

He was about to turn away from the window when a figure crossed his vision, and to his astonishment, there was a loud hammering on the door.

"Sir Rutherford Blake, is that you? I must see you!"

He opened the door, and a large man loomed in front of him.

"Yes, I am Rutherford Blake. Who the devil are you, and what do you want?"

Twenty-five minutes later, Sir Rutherford's office was crowded with troopers, mostly half-asleep and groaning. While his men had been sent for, Sir Rutherford had questioned Jordan O'Day. He now knew where Alan and Lawless lay sleeping.

"How can you guarantee they will still be asleep, O'Day? The earliest we can make their camp will be after three o'clock in the morning."

"I cannot, of course, sir. But Lawless sleeps real deep, and he would never wake on his own. And it's much warmer tonight, so I'm sure the boss won't stir. He was pretty tired."

Sir Rutherford looked skeptical. "I pray that your opinion is correct."

When Jordan had drawn the position of Treehard Hill on the map, Sir Rutherford brought his fist down excitedly on the table. "I knew it! I knew it! All my instincts told me it was somewhere there. Once more, I am proven right!"

"You would have no hope of findin' it, even knowin' where

it is,'' Jordan replied. ''The entrance to the tunnel is hidden.
You would ride straight by. It's a sort of natural fortress.''

''But we *will* find it, won't we, O'Day? For you will show it
to us.''

''Not without your guarantee that I'll be pardoned, I won't.
And I want half the reward money, like Bart Smithers got for
Ruggy Dick Middleton.''

''Listen, you scum!'' Sir Rutherford rounded on his prisoner.
''You will do exactly as I say. You will show us where Fletcher
is. You will show us where this . . . this . . . 'Treehard Hill' is,
and then, ah yes, and only then will we talk pardons and reward
money.''

Jordan, undaunted by his barrage, lifted his head and looked
defiantly at the detective policeman. ''But am I Queen's evidence? I'll do nothin' if I'm not Queen's evidence. I'm not afraid
of you.''

Sir Rutherford sighed. ''You aren't such a thing at present.
You cannot be; it's a legal term. But yes, Jordan O'Day, I'll see
to it that you will be.''

The briefing of his troopers had been short and explicit. ''We
will ride to Kettle's Creek. There, I and ten of you will surround
Fletcher and Drake. Meanwhile, O'Day shall take the rest of
you, led by Mr. Elrington and Sergeant Samuel, on to the hideout at Treehard Hill. O'Day will show you the secret entry, and
you will capture Dwyer and Cooper.'' He waved his hand toward the door. ''Now, fall in, men, and mount up and be ready
to ride.''

As they went from the room, Sir Rutherford took David Elrington aside. ''Now, we are relying on O'Day's word. There is
nothing else we can do. He says that Mrs. Wakeman is at their
hideout.''

His assistant's eyebrows rose in censure. ''So she *has* been
with Fletcher after all.''

''Ah yes, apparently. And as you know, she is a Crown exception to the Felons' Apprehension Act. She must be taken
expeditiously to the nearest magistrate's house.''

''That would be Mr. Finimore's in Young, sir. Though it's
near to a twenty-mile ride.''

''Yes, it is, but that is where she must go.'' He handed the
young man an envelope. ''And send this with her. It explains to
the magistrate that he is to take good care of her until her husband arrives for her.''

''Is it true what is being said, sir?''

Sir Rutherford looked questioningly at the young man. "What is being said?"

"That Mr. Wakeman wants her back at any price."

The expert on the bushrangers inhaled deeply. "While it is none of your concern, Mr. Elrington, yes, it would appear so. Thus, as you pass the Mayfield turnoff, have trooper Boehm withdraw and report to Mr. Wakeman. He has asked specifically to be alerted of such an event without delay. Boehm is a good man; I shall tell him what to say." Then, as the police detective's assistant moved outside to join the troopers, Sir Rutherford said softly to himself, "John Stuart's search must have taken him very close to Fletcher's hideout."

When he joined David Elrington outside, the young man's voice barely held back his excitement. "And you, sir? After you have taken Fletcher and Drake, what then?"

Sir Rutherford actually smiled. "I will send them under heavy escort to Bathurst jail, and I will ride swiftly on to join you at the hideout. I want to see this place for myself. I've thought of it night and day. Make sure you leave a man on the road to show me where to turn up the valley. And wait at the hideout with your prisoners until I arrive."

"Yes, sir. And, sir, if they put up a fight?"

"Just make sure you don't kill the woman. It would be more than Mr. Wakeman, or the government, could abide."

In the cold, dark street among the hubbub of the troopers and a few gathered townsfolk, the leader mounted his horse. Then raising his hand up in the style of the military, and signaling them forward, he shouted, "It might be two o'clock in the morning of a winter's night, but it's to be a day of glorious victory for us, so onward we ride!"

Two miles outside the settlement, they came to the Orange turnoff.

"Now, O'Day," Sir Rutherford said, "when we come to Kettle's Creek, Fletcher is a mile along from the bridge to the south, you say? On this side?"

"That's right."

"And we can reach the place by following the course of the creek?"

"Yes. They are on a rise near a clump of red cedar and a pile of rocks. You will see the tent and the glow of the fire."

Sir Rutherford addressed David Elrington and the sergeant. "Keep up the pace even though you have a ninety-mile ride ahead of you. Commandeer fresh horses in any place you can.

You have a full moon during the dark hours, which is a real blessing. Ah yes. Godspeed!''

The noise of those departing soon was lost, and Sir Rutherford was leading his body of men along the road toward the creek. At the bridge, they turned off the road and followed the watercourse. When they had gone half a mile, he halted them.

''We cannot risk their hearing us. So dismount and tether your horses. We go on foot from here. No speaking until after we have them. And remember, if you must shoot at Fletcher, shoot low, to wound only. Understand? I want him alive to interrogate. Drake doesn't matter.''

Along the bank they crept in the chill of the night air. The scrub caught at their clothes, and one or two stumbled, but they moved silently enough. After a few minutes, an owl hooted above them, and some of the men gasped, startled. Sir Rutherford, enraged, whispered, ''Silence, you fools.''

After five minutes more, they could see the glow from the embers of the fire up ahead. When they were some forty-odd yards away, Constable Ward and three others moved out at Sir Rutherford's signal and rounded the hill. The rest spread out to each side of Sir Rutherford, who started up the incline from the creek, heading toward the tent.

All was motionless. He could see the tent flap open, and he thought he made out two forms sleeping within.

Ahead of him and beyond the camp, he watched the dark figures of his four troopers coming through the cedars. When they were ten yards from the tent, he lifted his arms in the moonlight, and the two men with him dropped to the ground. He, too, went to his knees as his voice broke the silence, sounding harshly in the still morning. ''Alan Fletcher! Give yourself up! You are surrounded! Do not try to escape or you will be shot!'' There was a tingling sensation throughout his whole body, and his hands holding the rifle in front of him shook slightly. His heart was beating rapidly now and he called again, ''Come out with your hands in the air!''

But nothing moved.

The tent flap still hung open and all was silent.

Sir Rutherford stood and advanced, his troopers at his side. He was wary, ready for a trap, and his eyes darted this way and that. Still nothing moved.

''Come out, Fletcher! Or we shoot!''

Silence.

He dropped his hand, and the men with him fired into the top of the tent. The rifle blasts ricocheted loudly in the night. He moved swiftly forward and pushed his rifle in through the canvas opening. But even as he did so, he knew he had been thwarted. He knew there was nothing here but a pile of blankets. In frustration, he smashed his fist into his rifle butt.

"Damn!" he exclaimed. "Damn and blast the bastard!"

Alan had fallen quickly to sleep when Jordan had taken over his watch, and for a time he had slept deeply.

Perhaps it was the indefinable feeling of apprehension he had been carrying; perhaps it was that he felt the chill as the fire died; or perhaps it was the loud hoot of the owl in the night. Whatever the cause, he woke suddenly with a feeling of alarm. Lawless was fast asleep at his side. He sat up, and taking his greatcoat, moved out of the tent to find Jordan.

Jordan was not by the fire. It had gone out and was now bright cinders.

Surely Jordan had not fallen asleep again.

He moved swiftly to the flat rock he had mentioned, but he could see no sign of the young man. He looked down through the trees.

"Jordan!" he called softly. "Jordan, where are you?"

It was then he turned to face the gully, and in the light from the moon saw only four horses. Jordan's had gone!

His mind raced.

He looked up at the night sky. It must be close to three o'clock.

Where had the boy gone? And how long had he been gone? For a few seconds he tried to think of what could have taken Jordan away; but he soon realized the futility of that. A bushranger did not take his horse and disappear into the night, away from his mates, unless he had one thing on his mind. To inform!

Why, Jordan? Why?

Alan leaped down from the rock and woke Lawless. Lawless's eyes opened wide with shock as Alan said, "Jordan's gone, lad. Don't know how long since! Quickly . . . we must leave now without a moment's delay. We must get back to Treehard and warn them."

Lawless assessed the import of Alan's statement immediately. "Gawd, guverner, the bloody little rat!"

Alan was already lifting his saddle as Lawless came out of the tent, putting on his overcoat. "Bring your saddle, lad. Simply take your guns and ammunition and anything of value you have here. There is no time to waste."

"Will we take the packhorses, guv?"

"Yes."

Rapidly they saddled the horses.

"Ready?" Alan asked quietly.

"Ready," answered Lawless.

"Wait here." Alan turned and ran across the gully and up between the rocks. He climbed agilely to the flat rock and looked down through the cedars. There, coming along in the moonlight less than a hundred yards away, were dark figures carrying guns.

Hastily, soundlessly, he retreated.

Lawless was upon Waterloo.

"They come," he whispered. "We will cross the creek here at the bottom of the gully and get away into the bush on the far side. Courage, lad."

The horses moved down the ravine as if they knew to be quiet. They crossed the stream and were in the bush on the far side while Sir Rutherford and his men were still thirty yards from the camp.

Exasperated, Sir Rutherford kicked at the coals of the fire with the toe of his boot.

"What now, sir?" asked Trooper Ward.

"Well, we don't know how long they've been gone. It could be ten minutes or it could be an hour. By the time we get back to our horses and make the road, there is little doubt we will be the last in the race."

"What shall we do with their effects, sir?" Ward asked.

"You, Himsworth, and Fox stay behind and confiscate them. I'll examine them on my return to Bathurst."

Trooper Ward's face dropped. He had hoped to continue on to the hideout.

"You three return to town. We need some sort of representation of the force there now as things have turned out. The rest of us will go on and take a look at this blasted Treehard Hill."

"Yes, sir."

"Ah yes, and one more thing," added Sir Rutherford as an afterthought. "Remember to keep an eye on Mistress Thatcher now and then."

Constable Ward saluted.

"Shouldn't we look about the near countryside first, sir?" spoke up Constable Fox. "Fletcher and Drake might be hidin' around 'ere somewhere."

Sir Rutherford looked with disdain at the man. "Good Lord,

do you know so little of those you chase, Fox? He is loyal to his men. That means he will ride posthaste to warn those he has left behind of the danger. All we can pray is that Mr. Elrington is well ahead of him.'' He coughed. It was cold out here near this blasted creek. Bloody cold! He pulled his greatcoat more tightly around him, and heading back down the hill, shouted, ''We shall breakfast first in Carcoar, then ride as swiftly as we can to Fletcher's hideout.''

THIRTY
Nightmare at Treehard Hill

Thelma looked up to see the burnished leather boots in her vision. Her eyes lifted. ''John Stuart!'' she said in surprise, standing from where she knelt nursing Velvet. Eve's cat spent more time with her these days than in the big house. ''What brings you over here?''

''To speak with you. Do you have time to spare?''

She was mystified. John Stuart never spoke to her alone; Joe was always present. What on earth was happening? ''Of course. I was about to take luncheon. . . . Shall we go indoors?''

''No, let's sit over here.'' He motioned to a wooden seat in her back garden, out of the wind and in a ''sun-trap'' between the garden wall and a hedge. When they were seated, she turned to him questioningly.

He held silence for a time, and Velvet came and rubbed up against his boot. Unconsciously he stroked the cat's tail. ''Thelly,'' he said, and a short, sharp thrill rippled through her, for it was the name he used to call her as a child. She had not heard him say it for over twenty years. ''I want to talk to you about Eve. I know you have always maintained that she was not in any way involved with that Lake person.''

"I have."

His brow puckered. "I knew he was bad. Yes, I knew it at the time. But I just kept seeing in her the image of . . . my mother. It confused my thoughts."

Thelma clasped his arm in compassion. "Oh, John Stuart, I know that and I am so sorry."

He turned his head to look at her, to stare at her. "Thelly, did she ever love me?"

Thelma's eyes filled with tears. "Oh, my dear, dear boy, yes, she did love you. She just could not stay here when she thought all love had been removed from her; when she saw condemnation all around her. She *needed* your love."

He sat up, uttering a bitterly sad sound. "But perhaps she needs it no longer."

"John Stuart, what makes you say that?"

He turned to face her, his dark eyes a misery, his striking features clouded with regret. "There is something you don't know. That only I and Joe, and a few others, know. . . . When Eve was in Cowra on Boxing Day, she was carried off by two men."

"Yes, John Stuart, we all know that. She was abducted. That's why you've been so worried and all. It's more than a body can stand all these months."

John Stuart attempted a smile, but it failed to mount his mouth. "Ah, but, Thelma, I *know* who those men were."

The good woman looked amazed. "You do?"

"It was Alan Fletcher, the bushranger, and one of his men." Thelma's face dropped in disbelief.

"So you see, I have lived these past months in utter torment." He bent forward, elbows on his knees, head in his hands.

Thelma placed her hand gently upon his back. "John Stuart, are you sure?"

He continued to hold his head in his hands as he answered. "Yes, we are positive. So positive, in fact, that I have prevailed on the governor and the premier to make her a Crown exception to this Felons' Apprehension Act."

"Oh, my Lord above!"

It was at that moment Rosy's voice called. "Mrs. Larmer, where are you? Mrs. Larmer!"

John Stuart sat up.

Thelma met his eyes. "I shall send her away." She stood up. "Rosy, not now! I'm with the master."

The sound of Rosy's shoes clattered along the path. "Oh,

there you are, ma'am. Why, it's the master and all they are looking for.''

John Stuart sighed. "They can't leave me alone even for a few minutes, it seems. I am coming, Rosy.''

"Very good, sir," the girl said, turning back to the house.

They stood looking at each other. Thelma felt closer to him than she had in two decades. "Thank you for coming here today like this, and for telling me. Do not give up hope, my dearest boy.''

He took up her hand and brought it to his lips, then he left her standing there. She watched him walk away and she unconsciously lifted the hand he had kissed, and she held it to her heart. Confusions of thoughts ran through her mind. Eve, the bushranger . . . What did it all mean? How she hoped dear Eve was safe, and how she hoped by some miracle she would return to John Stuart. It pained Thelma to see him so disillusioned.

Inside the Larmer household, Timothy waited. "Sir, there is a trooper over in the big house. He has a message for you from Sir Rutherford Blake.''

When John Stuart came to Constable Boehm, he stood immediately from where he had sat awkwardly on the edge of one of the Louis XVI chairs in the morning room. "Mr. Wakeman, sir. A message, sir.''

"Yes, trooper, what is it?''

"Sir Rutherford's compliments. He says to tell you, sir, that we know the whereabouts of Alan Fletcher's hideout, and that the object dear to you will be in Young by tomorrow morning, waiting for you at the magistrate's house.''

Eve looked around at the sound of Daniel's voice.

He was with Sam, moving through the trees near the stables. "Mistress Eve, come and look at this. If this doesn't beat all.''

She pulled her coat more closely around her before proceeding down the steps of the veranda toward them.

It was afternoon, the sky was a clear blue, and while it was a cold day, there was warmth in the sunshine.

The two men continued to beckon her, and Sam put his finger to his mouth to indicate silence. She followed them through the trees a little way, and there, in a nest beside a fallen log, was a baby spiny anteater, and a foot or so away, its mother, a roly-poly body of bristling spines clutching a branch in its four claw-tipped paws and licking it clean of termites. Eve looked at the baby with delight. She was enthralled by the strange little creature, with its long nose and round, fat paws for legs. The quills of its coat were just beginning to sprout, and it was struggling to leave the nest and mount a small tree limb nearby.

"Oh, the darling," she whispered.

The two men with her smiled, enjoying the spectacle. "Thought ye'd like this," Sam said quietly.

The baby's long, probing tongue kept popping in and out. They watched as the mother moved back to her infant and deftly pushed him down from where he doggedly tried to climb up the branch. They remained a few minutes longer, then they quietly moved away.

"I've never seen a baby porcupine before," Eve said. "Aren't they the dearest, quaintest things."

"True, mistress, and ye be lucky to see a grown one, as they burrow in the earth and hide as a rule," Sam informed them. "It's a real surprise to see a babe in winter like this. But they'll be here until the little one's prickles grow long enough, so we could look again tomorrow, eh?"

Eve smiled. "Yes, we certainly will."

"Well, now, I think I'll be goin' to the lookout and have a peek down the hill," Samuel said as they walked by the stables.

Daniel shook his head. "But Alan and the lads cannot possibly be back before late tonight, Sam, no matter what."

"True, I know," the little man answered. "But I just fancy I want to be lookin' down the hill; that is all there is to it, Daniel, my man." And with that he mounted the veranda and picked up his tranter revolver, which lay on a shelf of the old walnut whatnot. He loaded it and stuck it in his belt as Eve and Daniel, noticing, looked at each other.

Eve pointed to the gun. "Why do you take your tranter, Sam?"

"I just fancy I want to, Mistress Eve. I just fancy I want to."

As Sam's figure disappeared into the entrance of the tunnel, Daniel shook his head. "It's a real change for him to be as nervous as me."

Eve said nothing; she felt the same way.

It was about half an hour later that Sam's head appeared around the veranda rail, and looking into the kitchen, he hailed them.

Eve came to the door. "Anything to see, Sam?"

"No, nothin', but I'll pop back up to Nelson's now and then. Just feel I want to keep an eye on the outside world today." He turned away, and she watched his small figure cross over to the stable.

Daniel pursed his lips in thought. "I wonder if dear old Aggie or Red have given us the treat of an egg today?"

Aggie and Red were hens that Bridget had given Jordan as chicks. They roosted in a wooden coop away in the trees on the kitchen side of the house.

Eve nodded. "I shall go and see for you, Danny."

Before she went to collect the eggs, she looked for Sam in the stable; he was sweeping out the stalls. The broom was as tall as he was.

"Sam, I've just come to tell you that after I've gathered the eggs for Dan, I shall accompany you to the lookout and sit awhile, before I groom Milford."

He smiled at her as he looked up from his work. "Why, goodo, Mistress Eve." She turned to leave, and as she did so, he asked, "Is America like this country at all?"

She came back toward him a few steps. The little man's expression was earnest.

"Now, Samuel, they speak English, which is a great similarity for a start."

"But what about them red Indian folk? I heard a few strange tales about them," he said, putting aside his broom.

"There are none in the cities, Samuel. And yes, they can be savage, but they are no more so than most men. I fear they are like any people who react in panic when a more advanced civilization descends upon their lands."

He scratched the side of his nose. "True, I suppose. I reckon the guverner could make friends with 'em. Look at the way he's a crony with Womballa's crew over there on the upland. There's somethin' mighty uncommon about our guverner, there is."

"Yes, Samuel, there is."

He was looking at her with one of his faintly stern expressions. He hesitated, then he took a deep breath and said, "Ye're not the only one what loves him, ye know. . . ."

Eve put her hand on his arm and smiled gently. "Oh, Sam, I know that."

He sighed and dropped his eyes, his lean face wrinkling with emotion. Then he coughed. "For sure, I won't mind goin' to America. Though no doubt there'll be drawbacks, for nothin' worth havin' in this life comes easy. It'll be goin' home for ye, won't it?"

"Yes, it will, Samuel. Yet I have found happiness in this country, you know."

"What? With the guverner?"

"Yes, and with others."

He turned his eyes up to hers. He spoke very quietly. "Would us lot be in them others?"

She smiled at him. "In truth, Sam, you lot would be."

He gave a strange, comic grin and looked away, then picked up the broom and began to sweep again. The scar on the back of his left hand shone as he gripped the handle. It was where the bullet had gone through his palm so long ago, during the mutiny. Eve noticed it now and wondered about it, but she did not mention it. She simply said, "I'll see you very soon then, Samuel."

Before she got to the door, he called, "Mistress Eve . . ."

She turned back, "Yes, Sam?"

He swallowed and took a step toward her. "I don't mind tellin' ye, it's real nice havin' a lady such as yeself here, and I'm lookin' forward to America, I am."

"Samuel, how lovely of you to say such a thing. Thank you. And I am looking forward to America, too. With all of you."

A happy expression broke across his face, and he went back to his work as she walked away. He liked Mistress Eve. She was a right good sort o' gal, really. A feeling quite mellow overcame him, and he began to hum an old song he had learned as a boy on the Surrey Downs. It had not been in his mind for years. His grandmother had taught it to him. His voice lifted into song as he came to the last two lines.

"And a hey and a ho my darlin' love did sing,
And a hey, and a ho, dorry oh."

He stopped singing and put down his broom, a frown lodging between his eyes. There were unaccustomed sounds of movement in the yard. "What's that?" he said, coming quickly out through the stable door. His mouth dropped open in amazement as he saw a mass of troopers, rifles at the ready, coming straight toward him.

For a second he was frozen, then coming to life, screamed, "Traps, Daniel! Traps!" as he pulled his revolver from his belt.

The volley of shots that met his shout actually lifted him in the air before he could pull the trigger. He was dead before he hit the ground, blood spurting from the eight gaping holes in him.

Daniel in the kitchen heard Sam's scream and the thunder of the gun blasts.

"What is it, Sam?" he cried in shock, rushing out to his friend. His eyes grew wide in horror as he registered Sam's bloody corpse, grotesquely twisted on the ground.

"Oh, Lord God!" he cried.

At the same moment, three troopers reacted to his appearance. They had seen something in his hand and mistaken it for a gun. As the bullets hit him, he groaned, "No . . ." before he toppled forward down the steps.

Too late, David Elrington shouted, "Don't shoot, he's unarmed!"

As Daniel fell, the wooden spoon he held, which he had been using to stir the stew, dug rigidly into the ground and stood upright like some absurd, erroneous marker beside him, as he shuddered in death.

At the first volley of shots, Eve, who had been sauntering back through the trees with three eggs in her apron, stopped in fright, the eggs dropping to the ground. At the sound of the second discharges, she ran forward in terror. Her heart was beating wildly as she called, "Samuel, what is it? Danny, what's wrong?"

In terrible fear, she ran back toward the sounds, and when she broke through the trees into the clearing between the house and the stables, David Elrington screamed, "Don't shoot! It's Mrs. Wakeman!"

For a few seconds, she was hopelessly bewildered. She could not understand the scene in front of her. She looked wildly around the faces of the men with guns. Then she saw the two bodies on the ground, and the appalling reality of what had taken place hit her.

"Oh, dear sweet Jesus!" she exclaimed.

There were men bending down to the shattered frame that had been Sam, and others moving over to Daniel on the ground near the steps.

She screamed, "No, don't touch them! No!" as she ran to Daniel and, dropping to her knees, took him in her arms and cradled his head to her breast. She was hysterical now, tears running down her face. Sobbing, "Daniel, Daniel, no . . . no . . ." she rocked him back and forth, cradled to her heart, his blood soaking into her apron and her dress.

It was not true. They could not be dead.

Oh, God, why?

They were going to America. All of them together. They were all going to America!

She looked up at the killers, and to her astonishment, she saw a face she recognized, and then another. Her mind was so blank with horror that for a few seconds she could not place them. Then she realized one was David Elrington, Sir Rutherford's assistant. . . . And the other? Jordan O'Day, white-faced, his eyes wide with dismay. What was Jordan doing here? He was with Alan!

Suddenly it registered, thudding into her brain.

"What have you done?" Her voice was so soft, it was almost a whisper, but every man heard her. "What have you done? These men were your brothers . . . your family. They trusted you." Her eyes grew large in her distraught face as she remembered the day on the cliff top. "Oh, God in Heaven! I saved you, saved your life, for this! For *this*!"

He turned away and could not look into her eyes.

Then cold terror took hold of her, and in alarm her voice rose as she clutched the body of Daniel more tightly in her arms. "Alan, Lawless, oh no!"

David Elrington's clipped tones sounded impersonally in her ears. "Mrs. Wakeman, we hope Sir Rutherford Blake has the criminals you mention in captivity. In the meanwhile, please take hold of yourself, madam! This is not at all seemly."

After that, she heard nothing. Her mind was a blur of misery. The world was mad.

Danny dead. Sam dead. And Jordan O'Day was alive!

She just knelt there sobbing, in a blind sea of tears, clutching Daniel.

They had to drag her away from his body in the end.

THIRTY-ONE
Womballa's Good-bye

"Mrs. Wakeman, I have come to ask you to please collect your belongings. You are to be escorted away," said David Elrington, standing at the door to Eve's room.

"Whatever do you mean?"

"What I say, madam. It is not . . . proper that you stay here. I have orders to transfer you to the magistrate's house in Young."

Eve looked confused. "But that is a twenty-mile ride from here. Why?"

David Elrington sucked in his cheeks as he appraised the woman in front of him. He certainly did not approve of her. He was perplexed by her. His superior had mentioned long ago if they ever found her, she would be with child or would have delivered one. Well, there was no baby around here. Anyway, that was none of his concern. She had been the mistress of the fabulous Mayfield; yet here she was in this place, the consort of bushrangers.

"Mrs. Wakeman, I have my orders, and I must ask you to prepare yourself to leave here immediately. You will be in good hands, I assure you. You don't need to worry. You shall spend the night in the police camp at Bendick Murrell and be taken on to Young in the morning."

She stood up and faced away from him. So they were sending her to a magistrate. Probably they were going to charge her. She asked without looking around, "Am I then to be charged with a crime?"

He sighed. He found it very difficult conversing with her. He had no orders to tell her anything. All he had been told to do was to make sure she was not killed, and that she was transferred without any delay to Mr. Finimore's in Young. "Madam." His voice was strained. "I must ask you please to organize yourself so that you can be on your way."

She was feeling very unsure. "Why am I being taken by escort to a magistrate?"

"Mrs. Wakeman, I find this all distasteful. The magistrate's house has been chosen for your welfare. Now, if you would be so kind, I want you to leave within fifteen minutes."

Drawing on all her resources, she took a deep breath and met his eyes. "You are certainly a good apprentice of Sir Rutherford, but let me tell you something. Things are not always as they seem. The two men your troopers killed this day were harmless men forced into this life simply for survival. You have no right to stand in judgment upon them."

He was a little taken aback by this spirited defense of the dead outlaws. "I have done what I was ordered to do."

"I suppose you think that exonerates you."

He turned to leave, and she stopped him with the words "Do you know where Alan Fletcher is?"

He faced slowly back to her. She really was shameless. "Mrs. Wakeman, I do not know, and even if I did, I could not tell you." He saluted and left the room.

When, ten minutes later, she came out of her room, the house was full of troopers marking things and noting them down, collating and counting. They had all been astounded by Treehard Hill. They had never seen anything like it. As one trooper remarked, "It's better'n many a squatter's homestead, let alone a bloody bushranger's hideout."

On her way through the kitchen, she came upon Sergeant Rodney Samuel, the man who had stopped them on the highway on Boxing Day. He lifted his eyes to hers as she passed. Of course, the man had obviously recognized her and put the pieces together, but unlike David Elrington's, his tone was gentle. He stood up as she came by him and doffed his cap, saying, "They are ready for you outside, ma'am." His earth-colored eyes were full of compassion.

His was the first sympathetic expression she had seen. She acknowledged it gratefully. "Yes, sergeant, thank you."

David Elrington followed as she went down the steps to halt where Daniel and Sam had lain. Their bodies had been removed, though the ground where Sam had fallen was stained with blood. The wind whipped across the backyard now. The sun was behind the clouds, and the afternoon was gloomy and cold, like the desolation in her mind. She knew the eyes of the few troopers in the yard followed her, and she heard their mumbling and the soft, crude laughter among them. She turned back to David Elrington before she mounted Milford. "What will you do with them? Where will they be buried?"

He looked so confident, so convinced of his position as a bringer of justice. His face was smooth, and the freckles on his nose made him look even younger than his twenty-four years. He was a picture of arrogant, youthful inexperience. She felt ancient by comparison. He smiled. She found it bizarre that he could smile.

"Oh, that will be up to Sir Rutherford to decide. We are expecting him here sometime tonight. These are Constables Dorando and Peters. They will see you safely to Young." He handed Peters an envelope. "Give this to the magistrate. And treat Mrs. Wakeman well. Good-bye, madam."

She turned away to mount Milford, and as she did so, saw Jordan watching her from inside the stable door. He was shaking his head, and his big shoulders drooped despairingly. She felt sick at the sight of him and deliberately averted her face. When she was astride her horse, Sergeant Samuel came to her side. She looked down into his kindly eyes.

"Mrs. Wakeman." He patted the back of her hand holding the reins. "Good luck, ma'am."

David Elrington looked sharply at him, but he made no comment. Instead, he stepped up close to Milford, and looking up at Eve's profile, said, "A question, madam, before you leave. How many years have you known Alan Fletcher?"

She did not know whether to answer or not. Her head ached. She felt very lonely. She was still in shock, sick at heart and troubled, but she could not . . . would not, let him know. She continued looking straight ahead. "Mr. Elrington, not as many as I would have wanted."

David Elrington watched her ride away. "Kidnapped"? Sir Rutherford said she had been kidnapped. He did not believe it. She certainly did not behave like someone who had been taken forcibly.

Minutes later, she was riding southwest, down through the trees to the road, leaving the place that for six months had been a haven. Her mind was dazed by the events of the last hour, and she rode in a lifeless fashion. Every now and then she would rouse herself and try to think. She continued saying prayers for the safety of Alan and Lawless, but she felt empty and drained.

Meanwhile, from a different angle heading uphill toward Treehard in a southeasterly direction, Alan and Lawless continued uncompromisingly to push Freedom and Waterloo. The two pack animals had tired when less than halfway home, and Alan had left them within sight of a small sheep station. Now, as they covered the final miles, Freedom and Waterloo were also all but spent. Their breathing was labored, and they sweated profusely in the chilly air, lifting their hooves listlessly.

All Alan hoped to do was to get to Treehard and remove his loved ones. He did not know that David Elrington was in front of him.

Alan and Lawless had left the highway shortly after Koorawatha and taken one of their shortcuts, thus they had not seen the trooper stationed on the roadway at the bottom of the valley in readiness to alert Sir Rutherford. They had watered their animals at a small stream and were pushing on over the undulating hills up the gradual rise of the valley when suddenly, in front of them, they saw through the trees Womballa standing with Mulgatta and two other tribesmen, Gannawarra and Goodool.

"Hey, guverner, that be your matey Womballa and his son Mulgatta, isn't it?"

"Yes, lad, it is, and they are a long way from their usual habitat. I've rarely seen them north of the plateau."

Womballa was signaling with his spear for Alan to stop.

"Womballa, my *waminda, booralla* to see you," Alan said. "I am sorry I cannot stop to talk." Then he explained to Womballa that they must hurry to Treehard, for there were bad men following. "*Murrunmil yanniwan* Treehard *langunyah, thulga jerribong warreyin.*"

"No!" shouted Womballa with such force that Alan, bewildered, asked, "What is it, Womballa? What is wrong?"

The old tribesman shook his spear in the direction of Treehard. "*Thulga jerribong no warreyin. Thulga jerribong noondha* Fletcher *gunyah.*"

Alan blanched.

Lawless reacted to the look on Alan's face. "Oh Gawd, guverner! What is it? What did he say?"

"He said the bad men do not follow us, lad, that they are already at Treehard Hill."

Panic ran through Lawless, filled his whole body until the tips of his fingers prickled. His voice was weak, shocked, almost a whisper. "Oh, no, guverner. How can it be? How can they be here before us?"

"I do not believe they could be, Lawless. It is impossible . . . unless there was a second party of troopers."

"Oh, no!" replied Lawless, shaking his head in despair. "Guv, what'll we do?"

"I'm not sure, laddie, but whatever it is, it must be swift."

Then he looked again to Womballa, asking in a mixture of English and tribal language, how many men were at Treehard, when did they come, and what had happened?

"Bad magic, *ungawilla*," Womballa replied, and the others with him murmured and shuffled their feet and waved their hands in spirals. Then the tribal elder gave the sign for rifle shots, and telling Alan and Lawless not to continue on, but to leave this place now, said, "Clever Fletcher must . . . *yanawa, nar-randa*." Then he held up his fingers to show the sign for more than ten men. "Bad medicine *noondha*, Fletcher *gunyah*. You no go Fletcher *gunyah*!"

Alan shook his head. "But I cannot leave here, Womballa. I must help my *igeelu*."

Then Womballa hesitated. His eyes blinked, and looking down, he gave the tribal sign for sorrow, before answering entirely in English. "Father no more. Clever Fletcher father dead, little man dead, Clever Fletcher woman live."

"Oh Gawd, oh no!" exclaimed Lawless, looking skyward.

Alan closed his eyes. His heart was beating wildly in his chest. For the first time in many years, the situation was beyond him. He did not know what to do. Danny, Danny. Sam. No . . . no . . . Eve. He wanted to rush carelessly on, no matter what. To be there with Daniel and with Sam, to hold Eve in his arms.

Then Womballa's strong voice broke through his thoughts. "Womballa and people see. *Thulga*. You no help dead men. In *yamminga* now. Too late."

Alan opened his eyes to look down at the face of his friend. There was sympathy in the old, black eyes looking up at him, and once more Womballa made the sign for sorrow, and so, too, did Mulgatta and the others.

He dismounted, moving spiritlessly, consumed by shock. "Thank you, my *wamindas*."

Lawless followed the action of his leader, and they both stood facing Womballa and his men.

The tribal elder gestured with his spear to the southwest. "Clever Fletcher woman and *thulga jerribong darwong*."

Alan looked intently at his friend. "What is that you say, Womballa?"

"Clever Fletcher woman go *yarraman, yanni thulga jerri-bong.*"

Lawless's anxious face turned to Alan. "What is it, guverner? What does he say about Mistress Eve?"

"He says she is being taken away on horseback."

Lawless sighed. It was a brokenhearted sigh, and he leaned on Waterloo hopelessly. "Jordan!" he exclaimed. "Blast ye for the evil devil ye be!"

Alan put his arm around him. "Lawless, lad, perhaps there is a chance to rescue Eve and still carry out part of our plan. We must try, for the sake of our Daniel and Sam."

Lawless nodded feebly. He was eaten up with pain and anguish for Dan and Sam, and hatred for Jordan, but he would do whatever the guverner wanted.

Alan faced back to Womballa and asked how far away Eve was and how many men were escorting her. The aborigine turned his spear on end, which was the sign for not far in a straight line, and said, *"Pulwarra thulga jerribong. Cooranga yangennanock ngauwun."*

Alan again put his arm around Lawless, and there was a faint hope in his expression as he translated. "There are two men escorting her, and Womballa says it is not far. He can take us through the bush so that we can get in front of them, lad. What do you think of that?"

Lawless had to force himself to be alert. "Oh Gawd, guv! At least we might be able to save the mistress." Then he faltered. "But we can't. Waterloo and Freedom are spent. They could not do it."

Alan knew Lawless was right; the horses were completely exhausted. With a gesture of defeat, he pointed to the sweating, panting animals.

An inscrutable expression passed across Womballa's face, and he turned to Goodool and said something. Goodool nodded and removed his headband, a knotted strip of kangaroo skin. At the back was a folded piece of hide attached to the band. He untied it and handed it to Womballa. The tribal elder emptied the contents into Alan's palm, signaling that Alan should give it to the horses. There were eight long seeds lying in his hand. He gave four to Freedom and four to Waterloo. The horses seemed to like the taste, for they swallowed them easily.

Womballa shook his spear. "Good, good."

And so it proved to be, for while the animals continued to sweat, they soon ceased to breathe in a labored fashion, and it was not long before they were standing quietly. Womballa nodded with satisfaction as he looked into the horses' eyes. "*Marook*, good," he said, and Mulgatta and the others muttered approvingly.

The party set off almost directly south to cross the valley at right angles, Womballa, Mulgatta, Gannawarra, and Goodool running in front of the riders. Then they turned at an angle southwest and had covered close to four miles when Womballa held up his hand and halted them. He spoke to Mulgatta and Goodool so quietly that Alan caught only a few words. Mulgatta nodded. Then Womballa turned to look up at Alan, and there was a weary look in his face. "Womballa no run more," he said. "Good medicine no help old man." He waved his hand toward a rocky hill in the distance. "Clever Fletcher woman and *thulga jerribong, yalanga. Mulgatta, Goodool*, take Clever Fletcher." Then an unmistakable expression of sadness covered his face. He lifted his long, thin arm, the veins raised in intersecting pattern across it, and took hold of Alan's right hand in his. "Womballa and Clever Fletcher, *yannawah. Womballa yallambee* Clever Fletcher *yanna*. Dreaming come, see Clever Fletcher."

He was saying a last good-bye to Alan.

Alan recognized the look of final parting in his friend's eyes. He knew he would never see this wonderful old face again with the coal black eyes and the white beard, and the deep, intersecting life grooves time-aged in his bronze skin. All his sorrow rose as a constricting pain in his throat. He had to remind himself of this chance to rescue Eve. He let go the aborigine's hand and dismounted. For a second or two they stared at each other, then Alan took hold of Womballa's shoulders and gripped them. "Good-bye, my dear, true *waminda. Yannawah* and thank you . . . for everything." He dropped his hands and gave the tribal sign for many thanks.

Womballa made a sad, broken sound and touched Alan's face as he had done the day Eve was with them, only this time he touched the corners of each of Alan's eyes as well. It was a moment of unadulterated love. Then he stepped back and said decidedly, "Good-bye, Clever Fletcher. We meet in Dreaming."

After a second or two, Alan drew his eyes from his friend's

to Gannawarra, who was remaining with Womballa, and took his hand in farewell.

They left the aborigines standing beneath the tall gums, two gaunt, dark, still figures. Lawless turned in his saddle and waved good-bye to them, but Alan did not look back.

Close to three miles later, Mulgatta called a halt, arm raised as his father had done. They were in sparse bushland on the crest of a long hill. The two young men scaled up a rough, rocky shelf and disappeared while Alan and Lawless scrambled up and followed across the striated stone floor.

When Mulgatta first pointed eagerly through the trees, stamping his feet as he did so, Alan and Lawless strained to find what the young man saw, but they could see nothing.

Mulgatta continued to point, saying, *"Billandry, billandry."*

Half a minute passed, and then, sure enough, "far away," as Mulgatta had been saying, Alan thought he perceived three black dots moving.

Mulgatta nodded. "Fletcher voomaan."

Alan patted the aborigine's shoulder. "Yes, Mulgatta, you are right." Then he looked to Lawless. "It's likely they will come up here almost within yards of this ledge."

When Alan shook hands with Mulgatta and Goodool, he thanked them and told them they were strong and brave, that he would always remember them and Womballa, and all the people of the Welba Welba. The two young men departed, passing swiftly down the grade on their long, thin legs.

In the minutes left to them, Alan and Lawless worked at speed, tethering the two horses well away in the trees and covering their faces with the dark cloths they always carried. It was more important than ever that their faces not be seen.

The trees leading up the hill on the side the troopers approached gave ample room for passage. They were tall, red gums, ancient trees with great trunks one and two yards thick. Alan stationed himself behind one of these at an angle of seven o'clock from the riders, while some fifty yards away, at an angle of four o'clock, Lawless hid. The oncomers did not divert from their line. One policeman rode in front and Eve, and the other came side by side.

Eve battled defeat. At times during the ride, she had cried softly, the tears running silently down her face as she averted it far from the trooper beside her. She kept seeing Danny and little Sam, twisted like corruptions of themselves, in pools of blood. Then at other times, she rallied and tried to believe that all was not lost, that their deaths would not be for nothing. For she knew in her heart Alan was alive; her very soul told her that. She must live in that thought.

What did they intend to do with her? Those she loved were dead, or in custody, or goodness knew where. Strangely, she kept visualizing Alan and John Stuart, side by side, as she often did. Two men lost to her. She lifted her eyes as they came through giant, red gums. Where are you, Alan? What have they done with you?

Suddenly a figure in gray leaped out in front of them and fired his revolver in the air!

The troopers' horses both reared wildly, and their riders could do nothing. It was placid Milford who did not rise on her hind feet, but merely whinnied and shook her head, then recognizing Alan, doggedly trotted forward to deliver Eve to him. By the time the troopers had taken control of their animals, Eve was at Alan's side.

"Alan! Oh, Alan! Thank God!"

As the troopers realized the situation, Dorando turned his horse to gallop back the way he had come, but there stood Lawless with his Terry carbine trained on the man's heart.

"Hold still, fella, unless ye be sick o' this world!"

"Dismount, constables. Now!" Alan shouted, holding Milford's bridle for Eve to do the same. The troopers did so.

Eve clung to Alan. He was here by her side. It was a miracle! She felt his hands gently push her to position himself between her and the troopers.

"You cannot do this. Mrs. Wakeman is our responsibility," observed Trooper Peters, a conscientious law enforcer.

Alan ignored the statement. "I must ask you to remove your boots, and be swift."

With the incentive of Lawless's rifle thrust in their faces, they did so.

"You'll not get away with this. I know you must be Alan Fletcher!" said Dorando boldly.

"Shut up!" shouted Lawless, brandishing his rifle again. There was a look of hate in his amiable eyes, making him more fierce than he had ever been in his life. "All I be wantin' is an excuse to fill ye with lead, after what ye devils have done this day."

There was animosity, too, in Alan, and the chilling tone in his voice was more threatening even than Lawless's anger. "My partner also speaks for me. I should stay quiet if I were you. I shall keep your compass and your horses.''

"But we need our boots," spoke up Peters. "We must make poor progress without them."

"I am counting on that," replied Alan.

"But we will freeze," Dorando insisted, though more tentatively than before. "It is only an hour to dusk. The night . . . . We will be lost."

"Who flamin' cares?" answered Lawless, picking up their boots.

Eve remounted and sat watching as Alan said to Lawless, "Throw them your horse blanket, lad. It will be of some use to them tonight against the wind."

Lawless's expression disagreed with his leader's generosity, but he untied the blanket roll from the back of his saddle and threw it reluctantly to them.

Half a minute later, Alan led them away from the troopers northward across the valley in the cold evening. When they were a few hundred yards distant and hidden from the police, he halted them. Removing his mask, he turned to look at Eve. "We know what happened at Treehard. Womballa waylaid us down in the valley."

She closed her eyes. "Thank God he did. For there was naught for you to do there except be executed like Daniel and Sam."

"Ahh, Mistress Eve," groaned Lawless, his face a complexity of anger, frustration, and sorrow, "what an unhappy day."

Eve looked from one to the other, she was so relieved to see them, and yet the corpses of Danny and Sam kept filling her mind. Her eyes filled with tears. "It was horrible."

Alan nodded. "Jordan deserted us in the middle of the night. I assume he went to Rutherford Blake. We only just evaded a unit of troopers heading to our camp. I did not know . . . did not realize, there was another party who reached Treehard before us."

"Yes, David Elrington led them. Jordan was with them, I saw him. Danny and Sam never had a chance. . . . Oh dear Lord!" Eve finished, dropping her head.

"There, lass," Alan consoled her, though he felt weighed down by his losses. "We will not talk of it now, though I fear I must ask you to relate it all soon." He looked to Lawless. "We will return on the path we were taking to Treehard. That way we can water the horses in the same stream we stopped at earlier, and leave the troopers' horses there."

"Where are we heading, guv?"

"I do not wish to place any man in jeopardy, but I must, and as I am positive the one man we can still trust is Bluey, we shall take the chance of heading to his hut."

"Good idea, guverner; Bluey would not see us in need." Lawless turned in his saddle and looked across to face in the direction of Treehard. He used Alan's name. Eve had never heard him use it before, and it surprised her. "So, Alan, we will never see Treehard Hill again?"

Alan did not speak, he simply shook his head.

"Good-bye, mateys," Lawless said softly. "The world won't be the same without ye." He tipped his hat in salute.

Eve murmured sadly. She kept seeing Daniel dead in her arms, and Sam's twisted, blood-covered body.

"You are right, Lawless," answered Alan, a hard, determined sound in his voice, "and for their memory alone, we must continue with our plan. As they would want us to do. Continue and succeed."

"But the Theresa Town gold is at Treehard, and we've no money other than what we be carryin' in our pockets."

"I know, lad, but we will discover a way."

THIRTY-TWO

Time to Reassess

It was well after dark when Sir Rutherford finally arrived at Treehard Hill.

By the time he had reached the point on the highway where he was to turn east, four troopers were waiting for him. Sergeant Samuel and two others had come down from Treehard and joined the one left there earlier in the day.

All the long journey from Kettle's Creek, Sir Rutherford had seethed with anger. He had spoken sharply to the troopers with him and had grumbled over minor matters. Frustration and short temper had been his companions all the tedious day. Innumerable times, he had gone over the events of the morning. If only he had caught Fletcher, what a coup it would have been. But he had not. Once more he had been so close, and once more the infernal outlaw had evaded him.

Then, at last, a short time after sunset, he had smiled.

As he approached the campfire of the men waiting for him on the highway, they hailed him with the words "We got 'em, Sir Rutherford. Daniel Dwyer and Samuel Cooper. We got 'em." And at this news Sir Rutherford smiled, even though subsequently he had been disappointed to hear they were both dead.

"And what of Fletcher?" he inquired eagerly.

"No, sir," answered Sergeant Samuel. "There has been no sign of him or Drake, although we've had men at vantage points up to three miles and more from the hideout since we arrived."

When he questioned the sergeant, he learned that Mrs. Wakeman had been there, too, and that she had been transferred by police escort to the magistrate at Young as he had commanded. "Good work indeed!" He beamed in the firelight.

While Sir Rutherford's humor had improved, he was baffled by Fletcher's failure to appear. He wondered where the devil the man could be.

The wind accompanied them all the way up the valley to the hideout, and it was with amazement that he rode through the concealed tunnel onto the cliff top beyond. O'Day had been absolutely right; there was no possibility of finding this place unless one knew it was here. Now, he had always known Fletcher was different from other bushrangers, but what he saw at Treehard Hill impressed him far beyond anything he had imagined.

His troopers had lit fires all around the backyard. He could hardly believe what he saw. There was a solid, well-constructed house with a veranda, and there were gardens . . . landscaping even, and a stable and sheds and a water tank. He recognized admiration in his feelings and was for a time disconcerted.

He viewed the bodies of the dead men, although there was not much left of Cooper to see. The body had disintegrated when they had tried to move it, and they had needed to use shovels to lift it. His own motto ran through his head, "Break those who break the law!" It certainly applied to Samuel Cooper. Standing there studying them, he found himself wondering about Dwyer. He looked the age they said, about seventy. The vague half-truths he had heard in the wayside inns came to his mind. How they said, years before during a holdup, Alan Fletcher had taken to a man with his whip when he had insulted Dwyer; that he loved this Irishman like a father, and how Dwyer was said to call him "son." Ah yes, these men had meant a lot to Fletcher; he was sure of that. Fletcher really should turn up any minute.

He asked David Elrington to give him an account of the shootings.

"Ah yes . . . I see, so it was a wooden spoon Dwyer was holding, not a revolver, Mr. Elrington. I fancy some of our men had nervous trigger fingers?"

"I'm afraid so, but of course, it is law to shoot on sight now, Sir Rutherford."

He looked closely at the face of his young assistant. "Ah yes . . . it is," he replied almost to himself as he turned away. Afterward, he gave orders for the bodies to be interred on the cliff top the following morning.

When David Elrington told him about Mrs. Wakeman, he was most interested to hear there had been no sign of a child as they had been told; and he listened to how she had been devastated by the deaths of her two companions. Ah yes, she certainly seemed to be one of them. John Stuart Wakeman's wife and Alan Fletcher's consort! How very demeaning for the great Wakeman name! He hoped his friend would not be disappointed when he met her in Young.

He did not speak with the informer, although he was told the man wished to see him. He would interview him tomorrow. He was sorry he had to interview the scum at all. Nevertheless, O'Day might shed some light on Fletcher and thus could be helpful.

He left grumbling lookouts at various posts outside the entrance to the tunnel, and wandered all over Treehard Hill in the cold night air, with David Elrington carrying a hurricane lamp. He examined everything, even down to the henhouse.

He smiled again as Sergeant Samuel showed him the bags of gold from Theresa Town found in a box in one of the rooms. There were perhaps two thirds of what had been stolen. Somehow it made up for the indignity he had suffered that awful night last October.

When at last he was satisfied with his inspection, he ate at Daniel's kitchen table, and he slept in Alan's bed. He did not sleep well. His rest was troubled by bad dreams, and he felt uneasy when he awoke early in the morning. He breakfasted off the Treehard crockery and drank from Lawless's mug.

There had been no sight of Fletcher in the night, which very much surprised him, for he thought he knew Fletcher well enough to be certain he would come back. Unless somehow he had found out what had taken place, and how could that possibly be?

He determined to complete things here this morning, and begin the long ride back to Bathurst early in the afternoon.

At thirty minutes past the hour of eight, he witnessed the burial of the bushrangers near the cliff edge. There was no clergyman, of course, so he said what little of the burial ceremony he could remember. As his men heaped the last sods of earth on the graves, he mused on the eccentricities of life; that he, of all men, should say prayers over the bodies of Dwyer and Cooper. He caught himself wondering about them again.

He turned and walked to the edge of the escarpment and looked east into the morning sun. He should have felt satisfied with the way things were progressing. He was inside the Fletcher hideout, where he had dreamed of being; he had two more bushrangers' crosses to go on his map. The Wakeman woman was on her way to Young. It was all very promising, and yet he felt discontented. There was a film of frost on the grass at his feet, and the chilly air bit through his velvet jacket. Looking down from where he stood, the view was vast; the morning lay upon the earth like a gauze of lemon over the patchwork patterns of the valley below. What a remarkable place this Treehard Hill was.

He turned back to the two mounds behind him, the graves of Dwyer and Cooper, and for the space of a few seconds, he felt glad that they had such a resting place. Then he coughed, almost embarrassed at the thought, and rubbing his hands together, strode back through the trees.

He spent a long time studying everything once more in daylight, and he wrote up his reports at Daniel's kitchen table.

Now he must interview O'Day.

He had just called Constable Crystal to him, with the intention of sending for the man, when he heard the sound of Sergeant Samuel's voice calling from the yard, "Sir Rutherford, the troopers Dorando and Peters have just returned. They have been lost all night. They were the men with Mrs. Wakeman. Alan Fletcher ambushed them and took her away!"

He leaped from the table, knocking over his chair, hot anger rippling through him. He bounded out the door, across the veranda, and down the steps. "Bring the blasted informer to me now!" he shouted. "And make ready for half the troop to ride."

Alan, Eve, and Lawless had finally arrived at Bluey's, although for the last few miles, they had moved at a plodding pace, for Waterloo had become lame and badly needed new shoes.

The moon was covered with clouds, and a few spots of rain were falling as they came through the dense bush that led to Bluey's hut. The wind blew violently and the horses strained. It was with immense relief that Eve saw the black shape of the dwelling appear ahead, lamplight flickering invitingly through the broken windowpane.

The fatigue showed in Lawless's face as he reined in Waterloo. "Gawd, I hope Bluey's here, guv, for I cannot go much farther this night. We have taken no food since yesterday."

As Alan rode through the broken fence to Bluey's tumbledown veranda, the front door opened, and a rifle poked through.

"Who is it there?" called Bluey's voice. "Who is traveling on such a night?"

Alan's voice sounded in reply. "It is I, Bluey. I have need of your hospitality again."

Bluey's answer drew a sigh of relief from Lawless. "Oh, it's you, governer, is it?" He lowered his rifle as he came through the door. "Come on in, Alan. I'm all alone here."

Eve and Lawless rode forward, and as they dismounted, Alan explained, "I don't want to take advantage of your generosity or place you in any danger, Bluey, my friend, but we are on the run. The troopers are at Treehard. Jordan informed on us."

Bluey shook his craggy head. "Oh hell, the bastard! What has happened?"

Lawless answered, all the pain and fury of the day sounding in his voice. "They killed Daniel and Sam. The mistress here witnessed it. All I be wantin' is my hands round Jordan's throat." He turned away, making a frustrated sound of fury.

Bluey looked to Alan, shock making his face somber beneath his beard. "Oh no, what an awful thing. Quick, my allies, come in out of the rain and tell me."

Lawless faced back to the horses. "I must be bein' a blacksmith first, Bluey. I am hopin' ye have shoes enough for Waterloo; one has come almost entirely loose." He patted Waterloo's mane. "They've carried us farther than ye'd believe possible from three o'clock this morn."

"Certainly, certainly," replied Bluey. "I've enough shoes in the lean-to to reshoe all the nags 'tween here and Bathurst, so if you head in there, you'll find a hurricane lamp at the entrance to work by, and feed in the box."

"I'll join you, lad," Alan said to Lawless as he moved Eve toward the door. "Bluey, this is Mistress Eve. Ah . . . Mrs. Wakeman from Mayfield. Please, take her inside while we attend to the animals."

Bluey's expression of disbelief remained, but he did as he was asked. Alan would explain if it were necessary.

Eve took off her cape, then stood warming herself and looking along the titles of his books that lay in disarray on a shelf above. She was surprised to see among them works she had seen before only in the Mayfield library: Aristotle and Plato, and more recent thinkers, Thomas Carlyle and David Hume and John Locke. She had never heard of the latter two until she had met John Stuart. Momentarily she thought of her husband, and sadness settled over her. She turned her eyes from the Scottish philosopher's autobiography to look at the bushman behind her with new interest.

"Well now," he said thoughtfully as he started cutting the meat into slices, "from mighty Mayfield, eh?"

Eve nodded.

"Life is not simple, eh?" the bushman remarked softly, sympathetically.

"I see by the books you read that you maintain that point of view."

He smiled at her. "Ah, you recognize my soul companions. You know the Descartes axiom? 'I think, therefore I am.' Well, perhaps a solitary man thinks too much, but it is meditations that are my comforts on a cold winter's night such as this."

Eve liked this strange, solitary person. "Have you ever been married, Bluey?"

"No, never. Got a girl, though, good girl, Christina Lyon of Wattamondara."

When at last Alan and Lawless came in, they gave their host a description of the unhappy events that brought them to him.

Eve knew she must tell them what had occurred at Treehard. She took a deep breath to calm herself and began. She told them how Sam had taken his tranter revolver and worn it in his belt. "It was so odd, his doing that." She related the sighting of the porcupine and her conversation with Samuel in the stables. "We talked of America. And I had only been gone from him for a few minutes when I heard rifle shots. I stood stock-still in fright, but a few seconds later there were more. I ran back through the trees to find them both lying dead on the ground. Sam was just a . . . a bloody heap, and Daniel had fallen to the bottom of the steps. I screamed, I think, and ran to Dan and took him in my arms." She could go no further for a few moments, and Alan took her hands in his. "There, lass, there."

Lawless's eyes were wet, and Bluey pulled at his beard, his expression grim.

"After I had been taken into the house, David Elrington came in. He told me I was to be escorted to the magistrate in Young. He acted as if I were a sort of embarrassment to them at Treehard, and he was very anxious to get me to the magistrate. After having lived with you all for over six months . . . no doubt I was to be charged, under the new act."

Alan nodded thoughtfully.

"There was a single trooper who had compassion for me. He was the sergeant we met on the road on Boxing Day; remember him? He was sympathetic, kind, wished me good luck. I believe Rutherford Blake was to arrive at Treehard tonight." Eve turned her eyes to Alan's. "There was one thing Sam said to me. How very strange he would say it to me today."

Alan was looking questioningly at her.

"He said . . . that I was not the only one who . . . loved you."

Alan leaned forward and put his head in his hands. He sat that way as the seconds turned into an entire minute, and no one spoke. The wind was whipping around the little shack, and something was rattling on the roof. Then he ran his hands across his eyes and sat upright. "And tell me of Jordan; did you see him?"

"Yes, he was there among the troopers. He . . . seemed shocked. He was ashen and his face was . . . full of fear."

"Oh, how I would fill him with fear if I could!" Lawless lashed out again, smashing his fist down on the table.

"Calm, lad," advised Alan. "Though I feel the same way, there is little we can do about Jordan at this distance." He shook his head. "From what you say, Eve, perhaps Jordan believed Danny and Sam would be taken prisoner, not shot down in front of him. He may have expected they would swiftly be removed from Treehard, in which case he would not have witnessed what happened afterward, and he would have been able to rationalize it all.''

Bluey grunted angrily. "The bloody, stinking rat."

"I misjudged the caliber of the man; that is certain," Alan said softly.

Bluey shook his head sadly, then pointed to his bed against the wall. "I'll be offering you my cot, Mistress Eve. It's a night's sleep in peace you all need."

The rain continued falling on the tin roof, and for a time Eve lay listening to it, but no sleep came. She could see the shapes of the three men lying on the floor under their blankets, Alan closest to her. There was a painful, empty place in her chest when she thought of Danny and Sam, and hot tears were running from her eyes. Slowly, quietly, she raised herself up and moved the few feet to Alan. She knelt down, and he turned toward her. She could not really see in the darkness, but she sensed that he lifted his arms and opened them. With a long sigh, she bent forward and lay down inside them, head resting on his chest. He covered her with the blanket, and she felt him kiss the curls on the top of her head. Soon she drifted into sleep, curled securely against him, while Alan lay staring into the blackness, his eyes fixed, listening to the night rain on the tin roof.

Close to nine hours later, they wrapped themselves well against the wind and said their farewells. It was a moodily overcast, cold day, but at least the rain had stopped.

When Alan came to say good-bye to Bluey, he put a gold sovereign in his hand. Bluey looked down at it, then handed it back. "It's hard for me to say no to a sovereign, but I reckon you'll be needin' it more than me, Alan."

"Bluey, I want you to have it. It is but small payment for what you've done."

"Don't want it, old ally," the bushman answered sternly. "Just don't get caught. That will be ample payment for me, governor, for I doubt I'll be seeing the fine sight that is your face again."

As they rode away, Eve hoped Bluey would marry his Chrissy and be happy, and she turned at the same moment as Alan to wave a last good-bye to him standing there in the thick undergrowth, near his fallen fence.

Before they reached the highway, Alan halted them. "The whole force of police in the West will be after us soon. I still propose to get us away to America, but now we have no money, it leaves us little choice. We need to do another job, quickly, and one that will pay us well.''

Eve interjected. ''What do you mean by 'pay well,' Alan? The coach with the wages was to pay a lot of money. But—'' her voice dropped ''—now there are only three of us. Surely we don't need as much.''

He fell silent for a few moments. ''What you say is true. We could get by with less . . . probably much less.''

''Well, I know somewhere that we can get three hundred and fifty pounds, and there is no risk involved.''

Lawless's face brightened. ''That'll do. That'll do. But where, Mistress Eve?''

''In Bathurst.''

''Bathurst?''

''Yes, it's my money. You know about it, Alan, the money Father left to me. I wrote the letter to Mr. Lees, the solicitor, in February, and we sent it to Lottie to deliver. The legacy is three hundred and fifty pounds, and it should be there waiting for me.''

Lawless spoke eagerly. ''Gawd, that's wonderful, mistress. Isn't it grand, guv?''

Alan was less enthusiastic. ''Eve, that is your money, yours alone. By all means, you should get it, but it is not for us to buy passage with it.''

Eve frowned. ''Oh, Alan, it is my money, yes, to do with as I will. It is wrong of you to once more place yourself in jeopardy to get funds for passage when I have enough for us all. Lawless, you know I am right.''

''I think the mistress has a favorable argument, guv,'' said Lawless meekly.

Alan did not speak immediately. When he did so, it was as he urged Freedom forward. His words came back at them. ''Perhaps we should head to Bathurst, where you can get your money, lass, after which we will discuss all this again.''

Eve made a small, groaning sound, and shaking her head at Lawless, moved Milford after him. They continued to ride mostly in silence, and Eve watched Alan. She knew he was concentrating on the next moves he should make.

He was thinking it very probable that Rutherford Blake was at Treehard, and once the two troopers who had been escorting Eve found their way back to him, he would start immediately for Bathurst. They did not have much time. Once more in their lives, they were truly on the run. Now, too, the woman he loved was in danger. She was wanted in custody. Escaping to America was paramount.

Nearing Cowra, they avoided the old, rustic bridge and forded the river at a shallow spot to the east, skirting the township. Then between two and three o'clock, they ate a meal near a tiny creek half a mile off the road and not far from Carcoar.

When Lawless was dousing the fire, Eve was washing the billy and the mugs in the creek; she lifted her eyes to see Alan regarding her. He looked concerned, and when she came back to the horses, he came to her. "Eve, I do not want you sleeping out tonight. I have upon me some gold sovereigns, and one of those will be more than enough to get you a good meal and a bed in an hotel. We will ride into Carcoar and put you on the afternoon mail coach to Bathurst. It gets into that settlement around eight o'clock tonight. You can sleep there comfortably, and we can meet with you on the morrow."

She looked at him severely for the second time in a few hours. "Alan, I am not made of glass."

"What is that?"

"I am not made of glass. I shall sleep where you sleep. I do not want to be separated from either of you. I refuse to be put on the mail coach."

Lawless continued quietly to break camp as she went on, "And in any event, I have an idea of my own. One which will have us all under a good roof and will cost us none of the sovereigns in your pocket."

"Oh, and what is that, lass?"

"Lottie . . . Lottie Thatcher. You said she told you she would be living in one of the church's river cottages. I know she will help us. I could get my money, and then we could go on to Sydney, and meanwhile we could stay with her in safety."

Alan weighed her argument before he replied. "I see you are ahead of me. I agree, Mistress Lottie would be willing to help. But you forget, there must still be some troopers in Bathurst, and we place all these good folk in dire peril when they assist us."

"But Lottie would want to help. That is the sort of woman she is."

Lawless, who had listened earnestly to the conversation, broke in. "This Mistress Lottie, she was the instrument of your escape from Bathurst last January, guverner. She has always sounded like a plucky one to me, and reliable."

Alan looked thoughtful. "I appear outnumbered. But it is still a thirty-mile ride, and I fear you overtax yourself, lass."

She shook her head vigorously. "I can make the ride."

It was some hours after dark when the three travelers rode down the deserted, windswept streets of Bathurst and reined in near a clump of young casuarinas that made a tolerable windbreak not far from the river cottages. They looked at one another in the pale light of the bleak winter moon. Eve thought all the emotional strain and physical exertion of the last forty-eight hours echoed in Lawless's voice as he spoke. "Guvérner, how in Heaven's name are we to know which place is Mistress Lottie's? There look to be a number of cottages over there trailin' along the river. We cannot go knockin' upon doors."

Alan replied as he dismounted. "You are right, lad, we cannot knock upon doors. But there are other ways perhaps of divining Mistress Lottie's home. Wait here."

Eve and Lawless climbed down as his dark shape disappeared across the field and melded with the night. All was still except for the wind around them. They looked at each other. They heard dogs barking. A few more minutes passed, and Eve spoke anxiously. "He seems to be taking a long time, Lawless."

"Don't worry, Mistress Eve; of all the men in the world, he knows what he's doing."

Alan had passed up and down by the small houses. There were six, and he examined everything he could see, meticulously, including the gardens and little sheds and the paths leading to the doors. A large dog had barked at the fifth cottage, and its cry was taken up by another at the sixth, but no one came out to observe the disturbance, and before long, they fell into silence.

Alan came back to the very first cottage, and walking quietly to the door, tapped on it. All was still, and he knocked again, a little louder this time. His heart quickened ever so slightly as he heard someone stir inside, and a few moments later, draw back the latch. It clicked and the door moved ajar some inches. A face peered out into the darkness. "Who comes aknocking on a poor woman's door this dark cold night?" asked Lottie, peering out into the blackness.

A mild sound, much like a sigh, issued from Alan's mouth as he answered softly, "Mistress Lottie, it is Alan Fletcher. I have need of your help."

The opening of the door widened, and he fancied that in the

gloom, Lottie's eyes widened with it. "Well, I never," she said. "Come on in, don't be astanding in the cold."

"I have Eve with me, and Lawless, the last of my band. I shall go and get them."

"Oh, do . . . do," the good woman replied.

"We are on horseback; I am concerned about where to put the animals so they won't be seen."

She nodded thoughtfully. "Now, wait a bit, I'll just pop and get my shawl." With that she turned back in to the house, and a few seconds later, emerged covered in a long, woolen wrap.

They crossed the field together.

"Do ye know," she said as they walked, "there was a lot of talk here yesterday morn. Sir Rutherford and all his troopers rode out in the middle of the night Sunday, and only three returned. The gossip all over was that they were after ye and that Sir Rutherford had gone to a place called Tree Yard." Her voice dropped as she added, "Well, I'm going to tell ye now that I was aworried about ye, I was. It's a true relief to see ye here beside me."

"Thank you, Mistress Lottie. I would ask if you know whether any more than the troopers you mention have come back since."

"Not as I know of, and I reckon I would be aknowing, for news travels fast in this place."

"That is a good sign for us."

"And to think two minutes ago I was areading by the fire," she continued, half running at his side, "and now here I am with ye again, Mr. Fletcher. What a wonder is this life."

Eve and Lawless saw the two figures approaching. Eve recognized Lottie and ran forward to meet her. "Lottie, oh, Lottie, how wonderful to see you."

"Eve . . . Miss Eve," Lottie whispered excitedly as she took Eve in her arms, "and how grand it is to be aseeing ye."

As they joined Lawless, Alan's arm went around his shoulder. "This is my partner, Lawless Drake, Mistress Lottie Thatcher."

Lottie beamed at the dark shape that was Lawless, and taking him by the hand he extended, said, "A pleasure to meet ye, sir."

They followed Lottie back across the field to her cottage.

When the animals had been put in Lottie's shed and watered, fed, and covered with blankets, the humans collected around her warm fire, where Alan gave her a brief description of the important events of the last two days. She bustled about as she listened, getting food and drink for them. Alan finished his account with the words "So we are here for Eve to collect her legacy, and then we make haste for Sydney town. We do not want to endanger you, or be here when Rutherford Blake and his troopers return."

Lottie shook her head sadly. "My, that Jordan O'Day deserves to swing, but of course, he shan't now that he's in cohoots with Rutherford Blake." Then she wagged the knife she was using to cut the meat as she added, "And never ye mind about putting me in danger. I'm an old hand at it. Haven't we been through this once before, Mr. Fletcher?"

"Yes," Alan answered quietly, "that we have, Mistress Lottie, but now there is even more jeopardy for a friend such as you."

For reply, she simply smiled at him. Then she asked, "How on earth did ye know this was my cottage?"

"In the end, it was a guess. But I knew you did not like large dogs, so that helped to discount two places. And this was the neatest cottage of all, the garden beds being tidy and the fence whitewashed. It had the stamp of Mistress Lottie upon it."

"Why, thank ye, Mr. Fletcher."

Eve moved to Lottie. "Did you receive the letter I wrote to Mr. Lees?"

"I did indeed. Came here to me on February sixth, and I opened it and took out the sealed missive inside. Delivered it bright and early to him the following morning. Demanded a private interview and got one," she finished proudly.

Alan turned to Eve. "You instructed the solicitor to hold the funds in readiness?"

"Yes. I said I would come at a future time to collect the legacy. That I was not sure when it would be, but for him to do what was legally necessary, and would he hold the money until I came for it. How did he react when you gave him the letter, Lottie?"

"Well now, he read it through in front o' me, looking very formal, and then he says, 'Miss Thatcher, do you know the whereabouts of Mrs. Wakeman?' and I answered I did not. Then he shook his head and looked a mite absorbed and said, 'Do ye know what this letter is about?' I replied once more in the negative, and then he bade me good morning, and in half a minute more, I be back in the street."

Eve patted Lottie's shoulder. "Thank you, dear. It is six months since Father's death. There has been ample time for probate to have been granted, as it was Mr. Lees himself who was to be executor.''

They sat at Lottie's small table and took the refreshment she had prepared.

''What happens now?'' Eve asked.

''Lawless and I shall ride out before dawn,'' Alan answered. ''Our presence endangers Mistress Lottie too much. As for you, Eve, you will be an object of much discussion in Bathurst once folk are aware of you.'' He smiled briefly. ''Now, as you are not on the wanted list, they won't arrest you, and I would be certain the troopers here do not know of the plan to deliver you to the magistrate's hands; that would be something private between Rutherford Blake and his deputy. There is no reason for those here to connect you with us. Nevertheless, we wish to expedite matters, and caution should be exercised.''

''Aye, that be true enough,'' agreed Lawless, ''and witless as some of the traps be, they can make lots of trouble.''

Eve's face clouded; she disliked the thought of any separation from them. ''So you leave first. Where shall I meet up with you again? What will happen if Rutherford Blake comes back in the morning?''

''Lass,'' answered Alan, ''I do not see how he can possibly be back before tomorrow afternoon if he went on to Treehard. But to be sure, I shall take up a position where I am hidden from the highway but have a view of all who ride into Bathurst from the west. If perchance I see him, I will be back to remove you from Bathurst immediately.''

Eve brightened considerably.

''I expect tomorrow morning to pass quietly. Nevertheless, I want you to catch the noontime Cobb and Company coach that goes to Meadow Flat, Lithgow, Bell, and Mount Victoria.'' He leaned toward her. ''Leave the vehicle at Lithgow. It stops at the Gibraltar Hotel. I choose that location because I have just now had an idea that I will explain shortly.''

They were all attentive, their faces alert. ''I do not believe we can expect to be farther than twenty-four hours' ahead of Rutherford Blake, perhaps not even that long. If he has the knowledge of Eve's escape from the troopers, she is in danger of being taken. She must avoid being here when he returns. I have little doubt Jordan has told him of our plan to get away to America. Blake will most certainly follow us.''

Eve nodded. ''But we must be well ahead of him, Alan, for

we were at Bluey's last night, whereas you thought he would be at Treehard Hill.''

Alan considered the point. ''Yes, what you say may be so, lass, but when the troopers who were conveying you to Young appear, then I think he will ride rapidly in this direction, for he will quickly realize we have had the advantage on him.''

''We should have bound the troopers, guv, we really should have,'' said Lawless grimly.

Alan peered into the flames of the fire as he answered. ''No, lad, that would have been wrong. Roped up there in that isolated valley, they might never have been found. It would have amounted to murder, and we do not deal in killing.''

''Aye, I know in my heart ye be right, but the traps deal in it. They murdered Sam and Danny.''

''They do not see it as murder, lad.''

''I know, guverner, but it was, it damn well was.''

Alan stood and moved to the fireplace. He lifted the poker and stoked the fire before he turned back into the room. Eve felt his sadness. He looked to her. ''Eve, do you know where Mr. Lees, the solicitor, lives?''

''If it's where he used to live, it's no more than a quarter of a mile from here, in Rankin Street.''

''Yes,'' said Lottie, ''that's right.''

''Then it is my opinion that you should be there before he goes to his offices in the morning.''

Eve nodded. ''Yes, I understand. To speak with him at home and make certain that everything can be arranged before I catch the noon coach?''

''Right. And if it cannot be, then you must catch the coach anyway. We will decide what to do later.''

Alan regarded Lottie contemplatively for some moments. She returned his gaze with a smile. He seemed to come to a decision and he asked, ''Mistress Lottie, can you ride?''

Lottie looked surprised. ''I can. Used to ride a great deal. Why?''

He motioned for Eve and Lottie to rise. ''Would you both be kind enough to stand up side by side?''

Their interest aroused, the two women did so.

Alan looked to Lawless. ''Am I right to suggest they are the same height, size, and coloring?''

''I believe ye are, guv.''

''Mistress Lottie, I will understand if you do not agree to my suggestion, but I ask if you ride because if you would accompany Lawless tomorrow morning and take a room at the Gibraltar Hotel in Lithgow, when Eve arrives there, you could be of great help.''

Lottie smiled. ''I'll do anything I can. Ye should know that full well.''

''Hear my plan first, Mistress Lottie,'' Alan continued as the two women sat down, ''then we shall see if you agree. Tomorrow, Eve wears a hat and heavy veil when she catches the coach, and when she disembarks at Lithgow, she buys a room at the Gibraltar Hotel. Now, Lawless and you, Mistress Lottie, are already there, having left here at dawn on Waterloo and Milford. You two women, being so similar in build, will then change clothes and hats. Mistress Lottie becomes Eve and decides to quit her room and take the night coach south to Oberon, while the couple that came in on horseback after a few hours' rest continue on their way, up the Blue Mountains.''

Lawless slapped his hand down upon his thigh. ''I see it, guverner, I see it. Blake will follow Mistress Lottie, thinkin' she be Mistress Eve.''

While Eve liked the idea, suddenly she felt apprehensive. ''But there is a telegraph line from Bathurst to Sydney. Sir Rutherford could telegraph ahead and have a trooper waiting for me in Lithgow.''

Alan nodded thoughtfully and then spoke in a reluctant tone ''I do not approve of destruction, and it is something I am not proud to perform, but to protect Eve from Rutherford Blake, I am forced to ask you, Lawless, to choose a point between Bathurst and Lithgow and to bring down the line. The poles are nine inches in diameter at the base and a strong arm and a sharp ax will bring one down in five minutes.''

''Good as done, guv.''

''I shall await Blake here and follow him, for he is certain to continue the chase, and I want to be sure that he follows Lottie in Eve's guise. That is, if you agree to be involved, Mistress Lottie. Understand that there is danger and you will make an enemy of Rutherford Blake.''

Lottie gave him a wide smile. ''I am not worried by such as he. Of course, I agree.''

THIRTY-THREE

On through Bathurst and Lithgow

John Stuart and Joe had ridden south on the bleak, wet western plains and arrived cold and miserable at Kiddley's Inn some hours after dark on Monday night.

Joe looked tired, the lines in his face showing clearly, and John Stuart felt guilty at having brought him on another long ride in such inclement weather. At breakfast he even suggested that Joe bide at Kiddley's until his return. "For I can ride on to Young and bring Eve back. I shall be all right on my own."

Joe shook his head. "No, m'boy, you do not ride alone, not as long as I can sit a horse. I'm coming with you, and besides, it's not raining this morning."

When they dismounted outside Mr. Finimore's wooden house with wide veranda and whitewashed fence, it was close to noon.

Joe rapped on the front door with his solid fist, and a woman opened it.

"Mrs. Finimore?"

"Yes."

Joe gestured to John Stuart. "This is Mr. Wakeman."

The good woman looked amazed. "Mr. Wakeman? Gracious, sir, what brings you here?"

Joe looked surprised. "There is no one here waiting for Mr. Wakeman?"

"Good heavens, no, sir. Should there be?"

John Stuart gave a loud, disappointed sigh, grasping the veranda rail in frustration.

Joe spoke again. "Is your husband in?"

"Yes, sir, he has just come home for luncheon. He is out the back seeing to the cleaning of the dray. Do please come into the parlor; I shall get him for you.''

Mr. Finimore was as astonished as his wife. ''No, sirs. I have seen no police or Mrs. Wakeman, and I have had no message from Sir Rutherford Blake about anything.''

Joe nodded. ''We shall wait.''

And they did . . . all day, and into the early twilight of the winter evening, until a horse and rider in police uniform came up the dirt road at a goodly pace.

John Stuart and Joe met Sergeant Rodney Samuel at the Finimores' gate. He tipped his cap, his good-natured face serious. ''Mr. Wakeman, Mr. Larmer, I come with a message from Sir Rutherford.''

''Yes . . . yes.''

''He says to tell you he is very sorry. He had done exactly as you asked. Mrs. Wakeman was on her way here when it appears that she was stopped by two masked men, and carried off again. He believes it was Alan Fletcher.''

John Stuart said nothing. He could not even bring himself to thank the trooper. He turned away and smashed his fist into the palm of his hand.

Joe looked up to where the sergeant sat astride his horse, and lifting his hand, held the man's dusty boot in friendly fashion. ''We are very grateful. Thank you, Sergeant, for bringing us the news. Where is Sir Rutherford now?''

''He has ridden on to Bathurst. He has information that Fletcher is on his way to Sydney, sir.''

''Thank you.''

''And sir?''

Joe, who was in the act of turning away to John Stuart, looked back. ''Yes?''

Sergeant Samuel cleared his throat. ''Sir Rutherford asked me to give you this.'' He handed Joe a folded piece of paper. Then he saluted and, pulling his horse's head around, rode back the way he had come.

The crumpled paper Joe held had ''John Stuart Wakeman'' written on it. Inside, in the police detective's sprawling hand, was the concise but adequate sentence, ''There is no child.''

''Yes, Mrs. Wakeman, I think I can have a letter of authorization written for you this morning,'' Mr. Lees said, his small eyes growing even smaller with scrutiny behind his tiny spectacles. ''But you realize that because of the nature of the money, it being a legacy, I mean, you will have to collect it at the principal Office of Bequests, at the Bank of New South Wales, in Sydney.''

"But why was the money not kept here in Bathurst?''

"My dear Mrs. Wakeman,'' he answered, removing his spectacles and looking severely at her. "This was a most extraordinary case. You were the beneficiary, the only beneficiary, of Reverend Billings's will. But the only document in my possession pertaining to the matter was a letter. There was no return address. You were not to be found, and only a vague suggestion was made that you would come at some time for your money. Obviously I did not know whether the claim would be made this year, next year, or the one after. A certificate of verification was delivered and probate granted, but you were not in evidence to appropriate the monies. Thus, it was transferred to the Office of Bequests in Sydney.''

"So all I need to do is take your letter there and they will give it to me?''

"I should imagine so.''

"Then you shall be good enough to write it for me, this morning?''

Mr. Lees scratched the top of his hairless head, and his eyes found the stuffed and mounted lyrebird reposing beyond Eve near his study window. "Mrs. Wakeman, where have you been?''

"I beg your pardon?''

"Where have you been?'' he repeated, still concentrating on the lyrebird. Then his eyes came back to her face. "These last six months. Is it true what I have read in the newspapers?''

Eve looked steadily back at him. He was a portly little man of around sixty years. His florid face was stern as he sat surveying her.

"Mr. Lees, I don't know what you have read.''

"Oh, come now, Mrs. Wakeman, today is the fifth of July; you have been missing since Christmas. When the wife of the richest, most prestigious man in New South Wales disappears, there is naturally much speculation.'' He clicked his tongue in remonstrance. "Do you know, only two weeks ago there was an article in the *Sydney Morning Herald* that insinuated your husband should make a statement to the people in regard to your whereabouts?''

Oh dear, poor John Stuart. How awful for him. Eve shivered.

Her eyes met Mr. Lees's. "I did not know. The suggestion seems very insensitive."

Eve could see that Mr. Lees was judging her, as everybody would. How could they be expected to know the intricacies that had brought her to this day? She sighed. "Mr. Lees, I am asking you to do me the great favor of writing my letter of authority this morning, and I will be indebted to you for doing so. Because of that, I will answer you. I have been away with . . . my family."

His eyebrows lifted in surprise as he sat appraising her. "Your family? I thought you were from America and had no family here."

Eve stood up as he said this, and as a gentleman, he was forced to stand also.

"Ah, but I have always had family here, Mr. Lees, even though I did not spend time with them until this year." She held out her hand to him. "I am truly very grateful to you for seeing me in your home, and I shall call at your offices for my letter at eleven o'clock this morning."

"Very well, Mrs. Wakeman. When do you believe you will be in Sydney? I shall send a telegraph message to alert them of your coming. It will serve also to identify you."

Dismay quivered through Eve's frame. She thought of Lawless on his way to bring down the wire. "What do you mean, identify me? Will not the letter be sufficient?"

He clicked his tongue. "It was my intent merely to help you, to give the manager an idea of when you would be arriving, so that he is expecting you, and does not think you happened upon the letter you carry by accident, in the street."

With difficulty, she replied evenly, "I shall be traveling there directly, perhaps Friday."

He smiled perfunctorily, "Well then, I shall organize to send a telegraph message to prepare them, either today or tomorrow."

Eve's thoughts raced. "Oh yes, thank you, Mr. Lees. Would you? That is . . . could you send it first thing this morning? Yes . . . for in fact, I am hoping to catch an express mail coach from Lithgow. It is a recent, a very recent, innovation. It continues overnight. I actually hope to be there perhaps as early as tomorrow. Would you be so very kind as to send the telegraph message this morning?"

Mr. Lees's gaze had entirely forgone the stuffed lyrebird and was directed keenly at her. He coughed. "Are you sure of catching this 'express' mail coach? I'm not familiar with it."

Eve felt so uncomfortably hot, she wanted air, and it was a very cold day. Calmly, Eve, calmly. "I . . . No, the express mail does not run every day. I will not know until I arrive at Lithgow whether I can board it or not." She coughed. "So I would hate to arrive in Sydney and find they did not have the message, when you were so kind and so efficient in sending it. Best to have everything in order, don't you think? You could send it early this morning, couldn't you, sir?"

The legal gentleman put his spectacles back on, replying slowly. "Yes, probably I can arrange what you suggest, Mrs. Wakeman, even though it is all very hasty, and I needs must journey on business to Orange this afternoon."

Eve gave him a wide smile of genuine gratitude. "Oh, thank you, Mr. Lees. Until eleven o'clock this morning then? Good-bye."

He sat shaking his head. He had heard a rumor that her husband had searched hundreds of miles of bush looking for her . . . and here she pops up in his home.

Eve was relieved when she gained the street. Back in the cottage, she made a pot of tea. As she sat alone in Lottie's tiny kitchen, many things ran through her mind. The deaths of Daniel and Sam. She cried for them again. How her life seemed to be filled with losing those she cared for. Her own mother and father, Billy, Clare, Mother and Father Billings, and now Daniel and Sam . . . and even John Stuart, in a way. Oh, please, Lord, keep Alan safe. She loved him so. She saw him in her mind's eye looking at her . . . into her.

It was an interminable morning, but at last fifteen minutes to eleven o'clock arrived, and she was ready to go to the solicitor's office.

When she was ushered in to see Mr. Lees, he was still looking at her disapprovingly, but he had kept his word, and he handed over the envelope to her at six minutes after the appointed hour.

"Thank you so very much, Mr. Lees." And at the risk of sounding unreasonably repetitious, she asked, "Was all in order with the sending of the telegraph message?"

Mr. Lees frowned. "Actually, I'm not sure. I know young Turner, the office boy, was sent to have it transmitted. I assume it went."

Eve sighed. "I see. Thank you very much, Mr. Lees, and good-bye." She walked quickly through his rooms to the street.

There was nothing she could do. The telegraph message had gone, or had not gone, and she must continue in the hopes that it had.

She drove Lottie's horse, Daisy, to Cobb and Company, the coaching company around the corner, to purchase a ticket for Lithgow. With relief, she saw the face behind the counter was one she did not know instead of the usual ticket seller, Mrs. Janklor, the town gossip.

There were forty-five minutes before the coach departed. Back she drove swiftly to Lottie's and unharnessed Daisy. She locked the door and put the key under the mat. Clutching her bag of possessions, she passed out through the gate. She carried her small bag and Lottie's hat and veil, beneath her cloak.

A voice called to her, but she ignored it.

The streets were blessedly quiet. She covered the six hundred yards to All Saints' Church in just under six minutes.

When she entered the empty churchyard, her own eyes roved across the graves. There it was! Over near the parsonage fence beside a native cherry tree, the marble tablet with the cross and the angel carved into the pale stone. She moved through the row of headstones, her eyes brimming with tears. "My dearest ones . . ." she whispered as she read the inscriptions. They had been devoted to bringing peace and goodwill to everyone. How truly she had loved them. For a moment she pictured her real mother and father, and then the clergyman and his wife. She saw them all together as one. She closed her eyes and began a prayer.

"Well, glory be!" a strident voice sounded behind her.

She turned in fright to see Martin Carlyle and his wife standing there, surveying her with amazement. The church warden made a rumbling sound in his throat. "Goodness gracious! Where have ye sprung from? Whole colony's lookin' out for a sign of ye!"

"Yes. I'm only visiting here briefly. I wished to see the last resting place of Father and Mother."

Mrs. Carlyle's meager lips pursed. "My, how thin ye be. Have ye really left yer husband as everyone's been sayin'?" she barked.

"Please excuse me, but I'd like to go into the church now." Eve moved away to the church porch.

"Will ye be here in Bathurst long?" called Martin Carlyle.

Eve turned her head to reply as she continued inside. "I'm catching the noonday coach."

"My, going on the noon coach, is it?" The woman looked to her husband. "And what do you make of that, Mr. Carlyle?"

"Well, I never . . ." answered her husband.

"Always was uppity, a real miss," decreed his wife.

All Saints' was empty. She passed between the pews, breathing in the memories of her happy years with Father and Mother. She stood in front of the altar, and her wedding day pushed itself into her thoughts. She remembered standing by John Stuart, and the air of excitement all around. She knelt down at the altar rail for a few minutes, then rose, and putting out her hand in reverence, touched the altar cloth.

As she passed through the porch, she remembered standing with Father on her last visit and how he had asked her to tell John Stuart about Clare. His words came gently to her mind on the winter wind. *It is for you to tell him, my darling. It is your responsibility.* She sighed and spoke aloud. "I never could tell him, Father darling. Forgive me."

She took Lottie's hat out from under her cloak and put it on, securing it with a hatpin, then tied the edges of the long, black veil firmly under her chin, covering her face. She looked up to see an elderly lady leave a group of children standing on the far side of the street and come toward her. It was Mrs. Wiggers, her old headmistress, out with some of the girls from All Saints' School.

"Eve, dear, is it you under that veil?"

"Why, yes, I . . . have been saying good-bye to Father and Mother."

"We have all been so worried about you; are you staying here long?"

"No, I am catching the noonday coach. I'm sorry, but I cannot stay and talk, Mrs. Wiggers. I . . . would have come to see you had I time to do so."

The woman nodded. "I know you would have. Is there aught I can do to help you, dear?"

Eve sighed. "No, thank you, but it is good to see you all the same."

Mrs. Wiggers stretched out her gloved hand and took one of Eve's in hers. "Then let me wish you luck, my dear. It does me good just to see you."

"Thank you." Eve's voice caught in her throat. "Thank you so much. Good-bye."

She left the charitable lady and hurried across the street around into the main thoroughfare. Seeing Mrs. Wiggers had lifted her spirits. Yes, there were some good, kind people in the world. But her equanimity was short-lived, for there, standing by the open carriage door, waiting to look at tickets, was the formidable Mrs. Janklor. Eve handed her the small, blue card, and the big woman took it. "To Lithgow," she said, but did not hand the ticket back. She attempted to peer through the veil in brash fashion. "Do I know you? For the life of me, can't see through that thing!" The woman's head came closer as she bent forward inquisitively.

In a swift motion, Eve plucked the ticket from Mrs. Janklor's fingers and quickly entered the coach. Her heart was racing, but she told herself to settle and be still. Didn't she have the letter from Mr. Lees in her bag, and wasn't she on her way to meet Lawless and Lottie? But what of Alan? It would be many hours before she knew if he were safe. She leaned back in the corner of the coach and closed her eyes behind her veil. She said a prayer.

There was a sudden lurch and the coach moved forward, rumbling down William Street and out onto the Sydney road, while three quarters of a mile away, a dark figure on a gray stallion cantered from the western road up and over a long slope to the public reserve.

Alan had spent the morning a mile west of Bathurst in a dense clump of white cedar trees and had seen only eight vehicles and riders in the five hours since dawn, none of whom were troopers.

Now, just after noon, he found himself a position as Lottie had instructed, giving him clear view across the dirt track the locals called Lort Street to the beginning of the settlement and Rutherford Blake's office. From here he had a clear line of sight along the Sydney road to the east. In fact, he could just now see the noonday coach disappearing into the distance. It was right on time, and Eve would be in it.

He did not fasten Freedom to a tree; there was no need. The animal would not stray. He took out his water bottle and poured some water into the crown of his hat and held it for the stallion to drink. Then he put the hat in the sun to dry and unwrapped the food Eve and Lottie had prepared. He kept his eyes on the settlement while he ate, sharing it with Freedom.

Eve would be safely with Lawless and Lottie in Lithgow by five o'clock. In Lawless he had confidence. By now, his old friend would have completed his task and be on his way to the Gibraltar Hotel.

He sat in thought, his eyes on the quiet township, as the hours of the cold afternoon passed. His mind returned to Danny and Sam. He tormented himself with the thought that he should have foreseen Jordan's move. Jordan had always been the weak link, the high risk, right from first meeting the boy. How easy it was to see in hindsight. He should never have let him join. There had been Patricia June, of course, who had wanted him along, but finally there was no one else for Alan to blame but himself. And in the end it had killed Samuel and Danny!

His mouth drew down with emotion, and he put his head in his hands. He remembered the apprehension, the shudder he had experienced when saying good-bye to Daniel last Friday, and the repetition of the odd feeling on Monday night, only hours before Jordan bolted. Jordan must have shown some indication of what he was thinking. Why hadn't he, Alan Fletcher, the governor, read the signs?

There was a constricting feeling in his chest as he thought of Daniel shot dead by the troopers. It was the one death he had always hoped to spare him. He had loved Dan well.

For the first time in many years, Alan Fletcher's eyes brimmed over with tears, while Daniel's voice sounded in his mind: *We'll be expecting you back sometime during the night on Monday. I'll have the fire going and a billy on the boil. . . .* And he heard again truculent, faithful Samuel instructing them in a stern tone. Then he spoke aloud. He did not know to whom he spoke, for he was not a believer in a merciful God. How could he be? Yet, he addressed his words to his Maker. "Whatever happens, let the last of my men get away. Don't kill Lawless! Let the lad and my darling Eve get away to America. Please, God."

He had taken his eyes from the settlement as he spoke, and now he looked back. He sat up taut and alert! Men on horses!

Wide, dusty William Street, vacant a minute or so before, showed activity. He could make out the bright sign on Mrs. Ayres's tea shop, and opposite it, Rutherford Blake's office. Into that building disappeared the five or six riders, men in dark clothing, most certainly troopers.

It was now fast approaching four o'clock. In another hour, night would fall. If only he had his telescope! But that had been in the pile of equipment they had been forced to leave behind in the flight from Kettle's Creek.

Five minutes later, a single figure came out of the office and ran up the street out of sight. What was going on? It all pointed to one thing. Rutherford Blake must be back. He could not hope to catch Eve. At this very moment, the Cobb and Company coach would be within an hour of gaining Lithgow, thirty-four miles away. Yet the man was fanatical, and a fanatical man would follow his quarry when others would not.

Another five minutes passed, and more men issued from the building and went in the same direction as the previous man.

After perhaps fifteen minutes, the door opened again, discharging two final forms along the same course as those who had gone before. He fancied he recognized Rutherford Blake as one of them.

What was happening? The horses they had ridden into town were all still tethered to the rail outside.

He looked at the sky and guessed it must be about half past the hour of four. His eyes swung back and forth from the dirt highway on his left to the building in William Street. Daylight would soon begin to fade, although it would not be dark for some thirty minutes yet.

William Street was deserted, and there were no riders on the Sydney road.

The minutes passed. Suddenly he stood up in surprise! A Cobb and Company coach rumbled into his line of vision on the Sydney highway. But there was no coach out of Bathurst at this hour!

Straining to see, he moved through the trees. Two figures sat atop in the driver's seat, and behind rode two more in dark clothing. Troopers? Of course! Rutherford Blake had commandeered a coach! He was continuing the chase.

He mounted Freedom. Down across the slope he rode to join the Sydney highway behind the vehicle.

Alan had concluded correctly. Inside the rumbling vehicle he followed sat Sir Rutherford. Beside him was David Elrington, and opposite, Constable Ward. Up in front were a driver and Trooper Himsworth, and behind rode two more mounted police. Sir Rutherford's severe features were not unhappy this afternoon. Even though he had camped out last night, ridden almost sixty miles since breakfast, and had taken only a hot bath and a change of clothes before continuing, he was not displeased.

He closed his eyes in contemplation. What an exciting week this had been. Since Jordan O'Day had come to his office in the early hours of Monday morning, he had experienced a gamut of emotions: excitement, anger, disappointment, satisfaction, exasperation, melancholy, confusion, and now again, the acute

exhilaration and stimulation of the chase. And now that he knew
from O'Day that Fletcher's ultimate plan was to leave the country, he knew he had no time to waste. Ah yes, he must get him
this time.

He had been devastated to learn on his arrival at his offices
that the telegraph line was broken between Bathurst and Meadow
Flat. He had been hoping to alert the various police stations over
the Blue Mountains of the probable movements of Fletcher. It
was infuriating! These damn telegraph lines were so unreliable,
such a flimsy little wire stretched across such immense areas.
Ah yes, the tyranny of distance! It was his greatest enemy. Only
his tenacious and uncompromising will kept him going.

When he had heard the news that Mrs. Wakeman had been in
Bathurst and had bought a ticket for Lithgow on the noon Cobb
and Company coach, his spirits had risen again. She was only
hours ahead of him, when he had believed her perhaps a day in
advance. But where was Fletcher?

He discovered she had stayed overnight with Lottie Thatcher.
He had called on her himself to investigate, only to find the
woman not at home. His mouth tightened. That Thatcher woman
aggravated him.

And when he was told Eve Wakeman had visited Mr. Lees,
the solicitor, it had intrigued him immensely. He had sent Constable Ward there to investigate, only to find Mr. Lees had gone
this very afternoon to Orange.

But then he had a more comforting thought. Ah yes, perhaps
Fletcher was beginning to make mistakes at last. He had let the
Wakeman woman stay in Bathurst and catch the coach alone.
To do such a thing, the man must have believed he was a few
days ahead of the chase. Briefly he felt sorry for John Stuart.
The woman was obviously in cahoots with Fletcher, no matter
what her poor, deceived husband thought. He leaned back on
the corner cushion, and his face composed itself. Ah yes, he
would sleep for a few hours. He felt confident again. There was
one thing of which he was absolutely certain: When he caught
up to Mrs. Wakeman, he would catch Alan Fletcher. They were
a pair; he was positive of that now. Ah yes, Alan Fletcher was
not far away.

Since before dawn that morning, Lottie and Lawless had been
in each other's company, and yet how speedily the day had gone.
When they had left Bathurst town, they made good time on the
Sydney road. Lawless had chosen a spot to bring the telegraph

down some seventeen miles from Bathurst. It was where the wire ran twenty yards in from the road, and was strung across a deep gully.

He had stood still and looked at Lottie rather speculatively, as if appraising her. Wondering at his expression, she demanded, "Now, why are ye aweighing me like that, Mr. Drake?"

"Er, well, it's somethin' I do not like to ask a lady like yeself, but . . ."

"But what? Go on, say it."

"All right. If ye were to be climbin' up on top, there—" he pointed to a line of rocks running back from the ravine to higher ground "—ye would be able to have good, clear vision either way on the highway and could tell me if I could use my ax . . . er, excuse me . . . *your* ax. But ye don't have to," he added hastily.

"I'm not made o' glass, ye know, Mr. Drake."

Lawless began to chuckle. "If that don't beat all."

Lottie fixed him with a stare. "Whatever do ye mean?"

"Well, it seems that whenever a man says somethin' that a woman is resentin', she says she's not made of glass. It were the very same thing Mistress Eve was sayin' to the guverner on the ride to Bathurst."

Lottie showed the glimmer of a smile. "Now, where is it ye want me to climb?" She was soon scrambling to a position of good vision, and Lawless lifted the ax. In the five minutes Alan had predicted, the twenty-three-foot-high pole was down. Lawless jumped away and ran as it fell, pulling yards of wire free of the next pole beyond the gully.

Lottie waved her arms. "There's a vehicle in the distance now acoming from the Bathurst side."

"Well then, swiftly down, please, and we'll be on our way."

They lunched together in the shade of some gray gums on the banks of the Cox River three miles from Lithgow.

When they arrived at the Gibraltar Hotel, Lottie waited with the horses while Lawless signed the register as "Mr. and Mrs. A. Green."

There was no one in the front entrance hall when Lawless escorted her to their room, and Mr. Moody glanced up only briefly from his papers at the desk as they passed.

Eve stepped down out of the coach. How she hoped that Lottie and Lawless were here, that nothing had gone wrong.

She followed the four men, her fellow passengers, across the poorly tended lawn to the steps of the Gibraltar Hotel. A man with a leather apron across his sturdy frame met them on the veranda. "Welcome, welcome. Moody's the name, and the Gibraltar Hotel has the fame." He smiled. "The taproom is open, right this way." He pointed along to the left. "Anyone need a room?"

His smile widened as Eve replied, "Yes, please." Today was proving successful. He had five rooms to rent, and now three would be occupied, unusual for a weekday. A couple who had ridden in on horseback were in number three; wished to have a room for perhaps only four or five hours to have a sleep before continuing their journey. And number one was given over to a leather salesman.

Eve signed the register as "Mrs. Jones," and Mr. Moody, jovial and well mannered, insisted on carrying her small cloth bag down the hall to number six.

When he left her and went back to the desk, he assumed she must be in mourning, what with the heavy veil and the subdued attitude. As the cordial publican sat entering his guests' names in his day book, he would have been astounded if he could have seen the activity taking place in number six.

Eve had been so delighted to see Lottie and Lawless that she had hugged them both a long time, and now she and Lottie were exchanging clothes. Eve put on Lottie's skirt and blouse in exchange for her dress. The velvet coat and scarf to complete her transformation lay on the bed.

"Now, what time does the night coach for Oberon leave?" Lottie said to Lawless's back. He stood at the window, looking through a small opening in the faded blue curtains.

"In half an hour, at six o'clock. It's some thirty miles, I suppose. I remember it as bein' a windin' road, though I have been upon it but once. There'll be one stop for change of horses, and all bein' well, ye should alight there before midnight."

"You can turn around now, Lawless," said Eve. "We're dressed."

He came back from the window. "Ye both fit into each other's clothes mighty well."

Eve smoothed her skirt. "Thank you. We have changed over the contents of our bags. I think that is everything."

"Yes," agreed Lottie. "Now ye two had best be returning to number three."

Eve came to her and took hold of her hands. "Now, you know

what to do, Lottie, dear. Wear the cape and carry the dark hat and veil, and go out to the desk in fifteen minutes.''

Lottie nodded. ''I will, and I shall say I've decided to catch the night coach to Oberon. I shall try to talk as much like *ye-oo* as I can, Miss Eve.''

Eve smiled. ''You don't need to be too concerned, Lottie. I said very little when I came in.''

Lawless looked to Eve. ''We should ride out as soon as we know Mistress Lottie is safe on the way to Oberon, for we've eighteen miles of windin' road, to cover tonight, Mistress Eve, much of it uphill, in the wind and chill.''

''Yes, Lawless, I realize.'' Then taking Lottie in her arms, she said, ''I am so loath to say good-bye. Dearest Lottie, you have been wonderful. I will write as soon as we are somewhere safe. You will write back, won't you?''

Lottie sniffed and nodded. ''Bless ye, I will. Oh, I truly will, yet my writing is not up to much. Ye shall have to decipher it, I'm afraid.''

They clung to each other a few moments more, then with tears in her eyes, Eve took up the bag she was now to carry and the bonnet to wear, and went hurriedly to the door. She opened it a fraction and peeped out.

Lawless watched her, a frown on his brow. She was leaving far too quickly. He wanted to speak with Mistress Lottie, and he was about to when Eve looked back at him. ''Don't hurry, Lawless; I'll be waiting. Just come over when you are ready.'' And she was gone.

Lawless and Lottie stood face-to-face to say good-bye.

''I . . . er . . . well, Mistress Lottie, I've had a grand day with ye. And thanks for climbin' up on them rocks for me. It were a real help and no mistake.''

'' 'Twere nothing, Mr. Drake.'' The hint of a flush began to rise to her neck.

''I heard Mistress Eve mention she would write to ye. Would it be too bold if I wrote, too? The guverner taught me how, ye know, many a year ago, and I can read as well.''

''Why . . . I would be more than pleased to hear from ye, truly I would.''

''Then . . . I *will* write, Mistress Lottie, and no mistake.''

She put out her hand. He took it and shook it quite ferociously.

He turned from her and took the five or six steps to the door, then he halted. She heard him take a deep breath, and the words he said rushed from him so quickly, she was not sure of their import for a second or two.

"If, and I'm not meanin' to insult a lady such as yerself, please understand, but *if* a man were to be sendin' money, proper and respectable-like from another country, would ye ever consider doin' him the surpassin' honor of takin' a ship to join with him?" He had not turned around. His face was to the door.

She watched his square shoulders.

She said, "Mr. Drake?"

Slowly he turned back to her.

Their eyes met. They stood looking at each other.

Lottie's expression was singularly grave. "I am all alone in this world." She could feel her heart thumping in her chest. "Yes, I would be considering it."

A smile broke across his face and seemed to ripple down to extend through his whole body. When he spoke, his voice was lighter, more buoyant.

"Good luck, Mistress Lottie."

"Good luck, Mr. Drake."

THIRTY-FOUR

Sydney Town

When Sir Rutherford reached Lithgow, the temperature had fallen to near freezing in the moonlit night.

He bade the driver draw up at the Gibraltar, for that was the watering place for the coaches, and it was there he hoped to find news of the Wakeman woman. He extricated himself from the confines of the vehicle onto his aching, stiff legs. He was exhausted, but the thought of finding her here in the township gave a bounce back to his step.

As there was no coach scheduled at this time, no one was

there to receive them. A dim light was thrown in the entrance hall by a wall lantern and the voice of David Elrington vibrated down the passage. "Innkeeper, where are you? Is anyone in attendance here?"

"Go through to the taproom," Sir Rutherford instructed.

A minute later, Mr. and Mrs. Moody came speedily up the passage. The possibility of seven overnight lodgers was a pleasing prospect, and that one of them was Sir Rutherford Blake was a bonus in itself, for his name was well known this side of the Blue Mountains.

Mrs. Moody smiled. Her beautiful nut brown, almond-shaped eyes widened in greeting, as did her generous mouth. "Sir Rutherford, a pleasure, and how is it that we can help you, indeed?"

Her winsome charm was lost on him; he had only one thing in his mind. "First, madam, you can tell me of a woman we believe dismounted the noon coach from Bathurst. I am led to believe she was the only woman in a party of men, although the complement may have changed as the vehicle stopped at Meadow Flat on its way here."

Mrs. Moody looked to her husband. "You took care of them, didn't you, love?"

Her husband nodded.

"Well?" she prompted.

"There was a woman, all right, dearest. Mrs. Jones; took a room for the night, she did."

"Ah yes, yes, that sounds right. She would give such a name," Sir Rutherford decided in an excited voice. "Which room is she in?"

"Well, she ain't in a room, you realize," Mr. Moody replied, nonchalantly.

Sir Rutherford looked irritated. This was all he needed after such a day as he had experienced, a publican playing games. "Explain yourself. Not in a room?"

"She's gone."

"Gone where, love?" Mrs. Moody asked for Sir Rutherford, whose mouth was open, ready to do so.

Mr. Moody smiled benignly at his wife before he turned his face to the impatient police detective. "Just after six o'clock, she comes out here and says she won't be staying after all. Says she wants to catch the night mail to Oberon. Now, as I have a night's rent out of her and she's a grown-up adult, free to make her own decisions, you realize, I told her where to purchase the ticket, and off she goes."

Sir Rutherford's face grew grim. "What the devil is going on?" He examined the faces of the innkeepers. "Describe the woman, if you please."

Mr. Moody's eyes closed in thought. "Well, when she arrived, she was wrapped up against the cold, you realize, wearin' a cape, dark blue, real expensive looking, though a touch worn, and traveling hat and veil, but I could see she were thin. Average height, I think. Oh, when she were leaving, she carried the hat and veil; her hair was fair and curly." Here he looked down at his wife, and said to her, and not to Sir Rutherford, "And comely. I suppose a man would have to say she was comely."

"Really now?" his wife answered, her well-defined eyebrows arching.

"That description fits her, sir," David Elrington said.

Meanwhile, Sir Rutherford had turned away and walked to the door, where he stood, arms folded, looking out into the night.

"Will you be stayin', then?" Mrs. Moody eagerly questioned David Elrington.

His eyes followed his superior's back. "I . . . I'm not sure, madam."

"It is a thirty-mile ride to Oberon, is it not?" Sir Rutherford threw the words over his shoulder.

"Aye, sir, it is," answered Trooper Ward.

"What time does the mail coach leave Oberon in the morning?"

"Well, as tomorrow's Thursday, there are two," replied Mrs. Moody. "One at eleven o'clock goes to Rockley, Blayney, and Bathurst."

"And the other?" urged David Elrington.

"Noontime, and it goes south to Black Springs, doesn't it, love?" She turned to touch her husband's sleeve.

"Indeed, my love."

David Elrington moved to his leader's side in the wan light. His face was drained from fatigue. "We are spent, sir; should we not bide here? We will have plenty of time to reach Oberon before either of the coaches departs from there in the morning."

"My dear Mr. Elrington, have I not taught you better than this? You are tired, I know, and hence I forgive the lapse, but who is to say the woman is catching an onward coach? She may be meeting someone in Oberon and going elsewhere, in separate fashion altogether."

The younger man looked abashed. "Yes, of course, sir, I'm sorry. But even if that's so, she must sleep somewhere in Oberon this night. She's been traveling since noon, and the coach will not arrive in that settlement until late tonight.''

"Probably midnight, you realize," interjected Mr. Moody.

"Probably midnight," repeated David Elrington. "So surely, if we depart here early in the morning—"

"All right, young man, all right. Ah yes, it is true we are drained, consumed by a long day of overtaxing events. We will bide here the night."

David Elrington sighed with relief and turned back to the Moodys, who also sighed with relief. They had thought they were to lose their seven lodgers.

Sir Rutherford stood silhouetted, looking out into the night.

Fourteen feet away, in the deep shadows of the veranda, Alan listened to the conversation. Relief came to his face, too, as he heard they would rest here the night and follow Lottie's false trail in the morning. He, too, was weary, but there was no halting for him yet. He must continue on, up the Blue Mountains, and make Newton's Inn this night.

Sir Rutherford's face was a mixture of emotions as he eyed the black shadows of the night. He stepped aside as the driver moved by him to tend the coach and horses, then he sighed and turned back in to the dimly lit hall of the Gibraltar Hotel. At the same time, Alan left the shadows and rapidly covered the distance back to where Freedom waited.

It was midnight and sleet was falling when Alan and Freedom finally arrived at Newton's Inn. A figure rose from the old leather couch against the wall and came quickly across the covered veranda as Alan reined in.

"Guverner," came the soft tones of Lawless, "thank the Lord ye be here."

"Hallo there, lad, good to see you."

"The inn is asleep, all but the mistress, who waits within."

Alan was now under the protection of the veranda and he shook the rain and sleet from his coat.

"So all went well, then? According to our plan?"

"Aye, that it did."

Alan took hold of Lawless's shoulders. "Good. Good. I knew you'd do it."

"I'll take Freedom around to the stables, guv. It's ye should get inside. The mistress is in number ten, straight up the stairs."

Thursday morning was bitterly cold all over the west country. Deke Edwards shivered as he brought the Mayfield coach around to the front door of the big house, and beside him Leeroy Barton, wrapped in a blanket with just his nose showing, complained about, "Being awake at this God-forsaken hour."

It was half past three o'clock in the morning as John Stuart and Joe crossed the veranda to climb into the coach, followed by a half-awake Timothy. Thelma and Mrs. Smith stood watching, hurricane lanterns in hand.

"Travel safely," Thelma called to her husband as the vehicle creaked forward to gain speed down the carriageway.

Over a hundred road miles away, Sir Rutherford, mindful of his problems, was shaking David Elrington awake.

Even though every limb had ached from fatigue and the police detective had fallen asleep quickly, he had woken after a few hours, and could not go back to sleep. Thus it was, at half past the hour of three, he had the need to be on the road again.

"B-but, sir, I thought you said we should awaken at five o'clock!" the young man complained.

"I have changed my mind. I want to be breakfasted and away in half an hour."

Sir Rutherford's orders were carried out, and it was just after four o'clock that Mr. and Mrs. Moody, puffy-eyed and with candles in hand, wearing dressing gowns over their night attire, saw off a tired and surly crew.

They made slow progress during the three hours of darkness, for it had rained heavily around midnight, and the road was muddy and soft. Twice the wheels caught fast in the mud, and they needed to haul the vehicle out. They were not halfway there when the sun came up. Nevertheless, the dauntless leader pushed onward, and as ten o'clock passed, the coach rumbled up the single street of Oberon.

Sir Rutherford was displeased, and his men were sullen.

"But if she is catching either mail," David Elrington ventured optimistically, "then we shall have her, sir."

His leader nodded. "Ah yes, that's true, but there is something odd in it all. That Eve Wakeman caught a coach to Lithgow had sense to it. Lithgow is on the way to Sydney. But that she detoured south to Oberon is odd. Why? That is what I ask? Why is she traveling south?"

"I wish I knew, sir."

"I attempted to get here earlier in case she was meeting someone and has gone off on horseback, but as misfortune has prevailed, all we can hope is that wherever she spent the night, her landlord was inquisitive. Ah yes, I shall be mighty surprised if she is still here.''

And she was not still there, but he was mighty surprised all the same! For on alighting at Stopford's Inn, he was informed that the lady of his description had caught the half-past-nine-o'clock mail directly westward to Rockley.

"Half past nine o'clock?" Sir Rutherford exploded. "But the blasted thing doesn't go until the hour of eleven!"

"No, that be the summer schedule, sir," answered the informant. "We been on winter schedule over a month now."

"Get us all a hot drink!" Sir Rutherford hurled at Constable Ward. "These damnable icy days and this damnable chase are beginning to tell on me."

"They be bloody well tellin' on us all," mumbled Ward to himself, after he turned away to do his leader's bidding.

Oberon was a minute settlement, but Rockley was what was called a "one-horse town." The road that joined the two places was narrow and potholed, not much more than a track. In bad weather, the coach didn't run at all. But it had left this morning, and Sir Rutherford stood drinking his hot coffee and pondering on the enigma that was Eve Wakeman's movements.

"It doesn't make sense," he said over and over to himself. "That the woman catches a coach heading *back* toward the part of the country she has just escaped from. Farther south to Black Springs, I might have accepted; but returning west to Rockley? No, no sense in it. But I must follow her, for she is my link with him.''

And follow, they did, along the twenty-mile track that led them to Rockley.

Some of the anger and frustration of the last forty-eight hours disappeared when finally they saw the Cobb and Company coach standing by the veranda of the Rockley Hotel.

Sir Rutherford jumped down into the wind, calling over his shoulder, "You men, get yourselves some refreshment; I don't know how long we hold here! Come on, Mr. Elrington . . . Ward!"

Across the uneven dirt street, Sir Rutherford bounded in great strides, to the man watering the horses at the side of the plain wooden establishment.

"Are you the Cobb and Company coachman?"

"No, sir, I ain't. He be in the barroom justifyin' a few pints of ale."

Sir Rutherford mounted the battered steps and proceeded on under the precariously hanging wooden sign that read, THE ROCKLEY HOTEL, into the public barroom. David Elrington and Trooper Ward made up the rear. Sir Rutherford's eyes ran over the few drinkers. "Who is the driver of the coach outside?"

"I be the man," answered a bearded individual moving out from the bar.

"I believe a woman who had sojourned overnight at Stopford's Inn in Oberon, one 'Mrs. Jones,' caught your coach this morning."

"Aye, a lady boarded there for certain, though fact is, I picked up two ladies, not just one, sir, and I be picking up another here, for she has need to be in Blayney this day. So, as of when the coach departs, ye can say I have three ladies in my care."

Sir Rutherford hardly contained his impatience. "For heaven's sake, man, I am only interested in the one from Oberon. Where is she?"

"Yonder in the parlor, sir. I believe she be partakin' of some tea."

In mere seconds, Sir Rutherford had passed out of the barroom and across the hall to the parlor. The parlor door was weak on its hinges, and he thrust it open with such force that one of the joints came entirely away from the wall.

The two women who were taking tea looked up from their cups in alarm.

"Good God!" Sir Rutherford exclaimed as he stopped stock-still, and David Elrington, coming up behind him, cannoned into his back, moving him forward a pace. "What the devil is going on?"

The younger man looked over his leader's shoulder, and a hissing sound of disbelief issued from his lips as he, too, recognized Lottie, sitting teacup in hand.

The other lady, who was a governess on her way to new employment, spoke up. "Who are you? What is the meaning of this blasphemous intrusion?"

"Ah yes . . . forgive me, ma'am. I am Sir Rutherford Blake, and this is my assistant, Mr. Elrington. It is not with you that I have dispute." He trained his gaze on Lottie. "But with you, Miss Thatcher, I do. Be good enough to follow me, please; I have questions for you."

To the infuriation of Sir Rutherford and the extreme interest of the governess, Lottie refused. "Well, that's as may be," she answered, putting down her teacup, "but I have naught to speak with ye about, and as I am a passenger on the mail, which is due to depart any minute, I must ask ye to leave me alone.''

"Damn you, woman!" His voice rose sharply, as the governess glared at him. "I don't know how you achieved it, but I see the pretty trick you have played me. Don't think it isn't all clear to me now, for it is. I *demand* you come with me.''

Lottie did not move. Her knees were shaking, but that was not in evidence. She replied in a voice sounding much more sure than she was. "I shan't. There is no law says I have to speak with ye, if I wish not to.''

Sir Rutherford's mouth drew tight, and his face was beginning to flush with anger. His voice grew threateningly quiet. "Miss Thatcher! I do not have a subpoena in my pocket to make you do as I ask, but believe me, I shall. Ah yes, your little artifice has managed to deceive me and has waylaid me from my purpose for a time. But I will be back for you when I have caught the Wakeman woman and Fletcher, and then you shall pay. Ah yes, pay with a long jail sentence, when I prove your guilt and the part you have played this day.''

"I don't know what ye refer to at all,'' replied Lottie bravely. "It's a fine thing when a body cannot take a coach trip into her *own* country, without the likes of ye turning up to be a harassment.''

Back out into the street, Sir Rutherford strode. Rage made his voice high, rasping. "Get the men from their drinks, Mr. Elrington. We turn back immediately. It's Sydney they were making for all the time, and we the bloody fools to be duped!''

It was two o'clock in the afternoon of Friday when Alan, Eve, and Lawless stepped off the train at Sydney's city station in the inner suburb of Redfern.

They had ridden in the biting winter winds and drifting sleet east over the Blue Mountains and down to the Penrith railhead. There they had joined the train, and with Freedom, Waterloo, and Milford in the horse van, had traveled the thirty-five miles into Sydney town.

Eve smiled to see how Lawless was enthralled with the train. He had never before traveled on one. Having begun his days in St. Giles, that part of London north of the Strand, he had seen them and had often pilfered from gentlemen leaving Charing Cross station, but he had never been aboard one. He leaned out the window as a child would do, bright with excitement. Only once did his face cloud over sorrowfully. It was as he turned from the delights of the passing countryside to Alan. "Gawd, guverner, wouldn't Sam and Daniel have thought this a treat? How I wish they could have been here. Gee, I miss them."

"Yes, Lawless, I, too."

Eve turned away and looked out the window, her eyes filling with tears.

At Redfern station they fought their way through the melee of travelers, station officials, and peddlers, and found the animal van. The horses whinnied in a mixture of recognition and joy at release, as down the ramp from the carriage and across the platform, they were led.

The first requirement was for Eve to find out about her legacy. She and the two men mounted up and set off toward the harbor. The main office of the Bank of New South Wales, which held the Principal Office of Bequests, was on Pitt Street, number 170.

Bright yellow horse-drawn tramcars ran along Pitt Street, and they followed one that led them to the brown stone building carrying the right number.

Eve went in alone. The letter was taken from her, and five minutes later, a clerk escorted her from the front desk to a large, enclosed office at the back.

When Mr. Bull, the bank manager, entered, letter in hand, his eyes ran over her from head to toe. He was extremely interested in his caller. She was a celebrated "missing person." "So you are Mrs. Wakeman."

"Yes," Eve replied, "I am she."

He gestured her to a chair. "We received a telegraph message from your solicitor in Bathurst, one Mr. Lees. We were expecting you yesterday."

Eve sighed with relief as she sat. He pointed to the letter lying on the desk in front of him.

"By this, I see you wish to remove *all* of your money. Now, madam, I must ask you to reflect. Are you sure? Is it not judicious to leave some with us?"

Eve smiled. "Mr. Bull, I do not need to reflect. I want to remove *all* of my money, now, this afternoon."

"Very well, madam, you know best. But it's a great deal of money for one woman to be carrying."

Half an hour later, after signing numerous forms, she was outside again.

"I have it," she said, patting her handbag and smiling jubilantly. "Three hundred and twenty-eight pounds, twenty-two being the cost of the probate, documentation, and fees."

On horseback once more, they crossed to George Street. After eight years, Eve still remembered the buildings and laneways, the shops and streets. On the left was a store with a sign that read, SULLY TOMPKIN'S HABERDASHERY. She felt peculiar reading that.

Down George Street they continued to the general post office, now a brick building with keystoned arches, a portico, and pillars. It was as they passed it that Eve drew back on Milford's reins. "Oh, Alan, look."

There, free-standing on the footpath, set in mortar, was the large wooden planked board covered with *wanted* postered, just as she remembered it. And right in the middle, easily readable from the roadway, was one that said:

WANTED
DEAD OR ALIVE

ALAN FLETCHER

2,000 POUNDS!
FOR BUSHRANGING ACTS
SUN-BROWNED COMPLEXION
LIGHT BROWN HAIR
THOUGHT TO BE CLEAN-SHAVEN
AND
FIVE FEET ELEVEN INCHES TALL
GRAY-BLUE EYES
KNOWN TO WEAR DARK
OR GRAY CLOTHING

Underneath was another poster describing all the members of the band, including Jordan O'Day.

"Makes me sick to be seein' his name with ours!" Lawless said as they rode on.

"I would not like to be Jordan," Eve answered. "Night and day, forever, he will not be able to escape the memory of what he did."

Lawless turned in the saddle toward her. "Do ye really believe he will suffer, Mistress Eve?"

"Yes, I do."

He shook his head. "How I do hope ye be right, but I lived nigh on eight years with the rat, and I doubt it."

An hour later, Alan had found them two inns, one a quiet establishment called the Prince of Wales in Grosvener Street, which was not far from Circular Quay and the central dockyards, and the other, a small but lively place named Paget's Hotel in the Rocks. They did not go as far as Dawes Point Battery, so Eve did not see whether the Ship Inn was still there.

Lawless lodged at the hotel in the Rocks, and Alan and Eve, registered as brother and sister, stayed at the other. Alan hoped that by separating, they would be more difficult to trace.

All their energies now were concentrated on finding a ship to take them immediately from Sydney.

Most of the shipping agents were located in and around Circular Quay and when the shops and workplaces closed their doors at six o'clock, they had been to them all. They looked at one another with disappointment, for there was no ship available to them. Oh, there were plenty going to America, and with berths for sale. But the sailing dates were a week hence or ten days in advance, and they could not wait that long. One of the agents had said, "You'll not find any ships that sail in the next seventy-two hours remaining in our books. They are removed, you see. We need to have time to get the money in and do the paperwork, and in any case, we have more work than we can handle, don't you know? No, you shan't get a passage now under a week's notice."

They stood together in the cold night air, outside the last agent's door.

Eve looked discouraged. "What shall we do now, Alan?"

"Don't be despondent, lass. There is perhaps one chance yet."

"Aye?" said Lawless. "And what would that be?"

"Let us walk by the ships themselves. Perhaps we can find one going where we wish to go, and the master will take us. Three late fares might be desirable. We must try."

As they walked along the many wharfs of Sydney town, Eve's mind was filled with her yesterdays: memories of her and Clare, the teenagers of the Rocks, and of the day she had met Father, and the other day when he had given her the watch, of the sewing business, and the move to Bathurst that had so changed her life. At times she would look sidelong at Alan and wonder what he was thinking.

It was with a confusion of sentiments that Alan strode at her side. All the memories of his past life at sea claimed his thoughts as he passed the vessels tied to the quays. He saw a picture of the *Coral Regis* setting sail and drifting down Southampton Water toward The Solent. He had been a bushranger so long, had lived in wide, empty spaces for so long. He had not been prepared for the gamut of feelings that ships and docks and lapping water brought.

For Lawless there was the same delight he had felt when traveling on the train, for the ships were wonderful; but he was quiet now, aware that this was a serious quest and their lives rested upon it. But when they passed a single iron steamship with a sharply angled bow and a brightly striped funnel with lanterns lighting it from stem to stern, he could not help but remark in admiration, "Hey, guv, if that don't beat all."

For two hours they walked the docks from Circular Quay west toward Darling Harbor. Each and every ship, they investigated. Many were destined for England; others were cargo ships, bound only for China and the East. It was after eight o'clock at night when they came to the tall-masted American clipper ship *Port Dennison*, a ship of the Golden Eagle Line, the American partner to the British Black Ball Line. Long and sleek, measuring over 250 feet, it was the last vessel on the Pyrmont wharf in Darling Harbor.

Alan looked from Eve to Lawless. "Wait here. I shall investigate this one."

The glow of its lanterns threw pale light amidships as they watched him go up the gangplank. Eve shivered.

It was very cold now, but there were a few sailors smoking beneath two lifeboats secured beside the mainmast. Alan approached them.

"Excuse me, mateys, but where is this vessel bound for, and when does she leave?"

"America," they answered in unison. Then one man removed the pipe from his mouth and added, "We leave tomorrow on the evening tide."

"I see you carry a cargo of wool." Alan motioned to the bales piled aft.

"Aye, wool and the odd passenger," replied the same man.

Alan's voice lifted slightly. "Where can I find the master? Or the officer in charge?"

"Why? Comin' with us?" asked another of the sailors, smoking a cheroot.

"Perhaps."

"It's Mr. Holmes you need," spoke up the first man again, tapping his pipe on the hatch beside him. "He's first mate, and he's forward on the upper deck now." He pointed with his pipe toward the raised section on the deck.

"Thank you. What is your destination port?"

"New York, though we sail Auckland, Easter Island, around the Horn to Montevideo, Rio de Janeiro, Trinidad, and Baltimore first."

"And what about Charleston, eh?" spoke up the third man.

"Oh, yes, that's right," replied the pipe smoker, "we were just informed this morning. We call in at Charleston, too."

Alan looked puzzled. "What do you mean Charleston? How is it a Yankee ship calls in at a Confederate port?"

The three men laughed. Then the one who had remained silent spoke. "Where have you been hidin'? Don't you read the newspapers? The war's over, friend."

"I see," Alan replied. "I assume the Union won."

"You assume correctly," answered the man with the cheroot. "We did. Fact is, we didn't know ourselves until we reached here. Lee surrendered to Grant on April ninth, and Johnson to Sherman on the twenty-sixth."

The pipe smoker laughed. "We have one of the owners on board, you see, and he had a tidy little business in Charleston before the war. He wants to investigate matters on his way home."

"I see. Thank you again," answered Alan, turning away to find the first mate. He found Grantley Holmes, a big man with a mustache and long sideburns, in conversation beside the wheel. When Alan explained that they needed three berths to America, the first mate shook his head. "Our shipping agents are the Bright Brothers. You should book passage through them."

"We have been to them," Alan told him, "but they close off the books and take no more fares seventy-two hours before sailing."

"Do they now?" said Mr. Holmes as if it were the first he had heard of such a thing. "How is it you know this?"

"I called on them this afternoon. They say there is more work than they can handle, and it gives them time to get the money and do the paperwork."

"Is that correct?" remarked Mr. Holmes thoughtfully.

Alan smiled at him. "We would like to come with you to New York. We can be ready tomorrow, and we have money to pay. Is there anything you can do?"

Grantley Holmes looked keenly at Alan. "What is your name, sir?"

Alan looked steadily back. "Trent, James Trent."

"How do you do." Mr. Holmes shook his hand.

The first mate had partaken of a pleasant evening meal and four rums, and was in good spirits. He was an honest, sensible man, and fair-minded. He felt slight resistance to the statement that the agents closed their books three days in advance of a sailing date, for sometimes ships left with only half as many passengers as they could take. Obviously the agents were making plenty of money. More work than they could handle, eh? Once more he looked closely at Mr. Trent. The man was quality; you could see that. He came to a decision.

"Mr. Trent, sir, it is irregular, and we do not have many berths for passengers, but I think I can talk to the purser and arrange something. Can you come back in the morning, say eight bells, and ask for me?"

"I can and I thank you."

Eve saw the look on his face as he came down the *Port Dennison*'s gangplank in the lantern light. So, too, did Lawless, and he whistled with delight.

They had a meal in the small dining room at the Prince of Wales, and at thirty minutes past ten o'clock, Lawless was ready to return the short distance to his lodgings.

Alan took Eve's hand. "I shall accompany Lawless; won't be long."

"But I would like to come with you."

Lawless looked toward the window. "It be pretty chilly out there."

That did not daunt Eve, and so all three set off together again. The footpaths and roadways were quiet until they reached the noisy taverns and inns of the Rocks. A few drunken sailors passed them, and the drifters of Sydney still slept on benches and down alleyways as they always had.

At the entrance to a narrow lane not far from the cutting known as the Argyle Cut, Lawless stopped. "I shall say good night here. Paget's is only a few paces along. I shall be at yer hotel in time to go with ye in the mornin', guv."

Alan shook his head. "No, lad, I think it is best if I go back to the *Port Dennison* and pay the fares alone, but do come to the Prince of Wales, for I would like you and Eve to be together while I'm gone."

Eve smiled at Lawless. "It will be an opportunity for us to go out and buy some clothes and items for the voyage."

"Aye, then I shall be with ye at half past seven of the clock, Mistress Eve."

Alan looked from one to the other and added, "Yes, but we must be careful."

They waved Lawless up the steps of the passage, and Alan drew Eve's arm through his as they walked away from the hustle and noise of the Rocks.

They passed silently along the empty street. Suddenly Alan stopped.

Eve looked up at him and saw an enigmatic expression on his face. She sensed something different in him. Her heartbeat quickened. How she loved him! How she truly loved him . . . for always. She did not care what people thought of her or said of her. It magnified her soul simply being with him. And the miracle and glory was that he, too, loved her. How she wished she could be closer to him. She knew he wanted to wait until they were in America, and yet, what was time? Did not they love each other now, this night, and forever?

He moved beside her, and holding her arm, walked her across the street to where a dozen clippers lay berthed around Circular Quay. They were a striking picture, their tall, black masts reaching skyward in the weak night lights. Two large fig trees grew alone close to the dockside, and he stopped in the jet black darkness of their shadows. Most of the lanterns above decks had been put out; only a few below threw dim radiance through the portholes. The hum of the noise from the Rocks in the distance was almost indistinguishable; only the water lapping against the hulls and the side of the quay came to their ears.

"It's wonderful being here alone with you," she said softly, but he did not answer. For a time she thought he seemed entranced by the ships; he was staring straight ahead at them. After perhaps a minute, he made a sound, a painful sound, and turned to her. He lifted his hand and stroked her cheek.

It was the intangible difference she had felt in him across the street. He was not here merely to look at the ships as she had thought. What was happening inside Alan Fletcher? Her heart was racing. She felt almost hot, though it was a cold winter's night. She lifted her hand to his arm and moved around his body to face him. "My darling," she said, putting her hand up to his face. "What is it? I am so happy to be here with you. Tomorrow our new life will begin, and we'll be together always."

He made no reply. He was looking at her strangely.

She put her arms up to him, just as she had the day in the beautiful glade. He did not turn away, but brought his head slowly down, his mouth slowly down, to hers.

Alan . . . Alan . . . She was vividly aware of him, his hands in her hair, on her shoulders, moving over her spine. When he lifted his mouth from hers, there were a few seconds when she was unaware of what was happening, when the world became a dark, glorious blur. Then she felt him moving down her body, sinking slowly to his knees. He was inside her cape now and his face was pressed against her, his arms encircling and holding her.

She was bewildered, excited, overpowered. His face pressed through her clothes . . . his hands pressed through her clothes . . . he murmured softly against her body. Time slowed.

She became aware that he was standing again, and she heard her name.

"Eve," he said, he spoke it in that way he had of elongating the e and the sound was sensual, "let's go back." He moved swiftly along the dockside with her hand held tightly in his own. Her face glowed. Her eyes shone. She felt revitalized. She knew at last he wanted her, this minute, as she wanted him.

When they passed through the door of the Prince of Wales, and by the hotel register where they were entered as sister and brother, and on up the cedar staircase, she was conscious only of him. Strange sensations rippled through her stomach, and in quick succession, up into her chest and around her throat.

Inside the room, Alan turned from her and closed the door.

In the clear patch of light stretching across the floor from the brilliant moon, Eve watched his long, brown fingers leave the brass knob and cut in an arc across the space between them to take her shawl from her shoulders and drop it aside. He moved to the fireplace and stoked the dying embers; the firelight and moonbeams blended, strangely intensified, and became for Eve the white light of Alan Fletcher's love as the material world drifted away and vanished.

She became aware he had returned to her and his lips were resting on her forehead. New spasms of excitement tingled along her limbs. His hands moved down and undid her coat.

She did not question why Alan had changed his mind. She did not know what secret he had seen there at the quayside; all she knew was her own expectation, her heart pounding, sending vibrations through all her senses.

She lifted her eyes at the same moment she lifted her hands to the button at the top of his jacket. As she unfastened his coat, he smiled at her. His eyes glinted in the dancing light. In their infinite depths, she read all that she had longed for: passion, desire, excitement, need, love.

They stepped over the two garments, and he drew her closer. His voice sounded husky in the stillness of the night. "Eve, I want you always to be happy; remember that." In the faint light, his face grew serious. He was looking into her again, seeing the soul of her, and she felt herself opening to him as if layer by layer. She heard him say the things she had longed to hear, love things, wonderful things, reverent, adoring. She shivered as she brought her hand to his face, the rounded tips of her fingers sliding between his lips and feeling the moisture of his mouth. The wetness on her fingers was arousing, erotic. She touched his strong white teeth.

"Yes," she whispered, "yes."

His arms slid around her body, feeling through her clothes the slender planes and gentle undulations of her, his Eve. To her, this action was the promise of encompassing her forever in his life, and in duplicate movement, in a promise of her own, she enfolded him in her arms. For the first time, Alan's eyes closed with yearning as he relished the intensity in her embrace, the one he truly loved. He murmured softly as she whispered another "Yes," unfinished before his mouth came down on hers to close the word inside his lips.

Desire, undisguised now, rushed up through Alan's body as they explored each other's mouths. All the restraint of the past months, Alan threw aside, disregarded, for he knew now was the moment.

Eve heard a voice in her head repeat, "This is it. This is the time you have waited for, dreamed about."

The taste of him and the feel of his body molding itself to hers spread a burning heat through her as if it seeped through her skin into her blood and very bones. Alan's mouth moved down across her neck to rest momentarily at the hollow of her throat. His lips realized the pulsating, the throbbing, within her as they drifted on down the opening in her bodice to rest against the tops of her breasts. She arched backward as his hands pressed up the sides of her ribs to cup her breasts. She felt the heat of his mouth in nerve-tingling sensation through her clothes, closing over her nipples as they hardened in tense expectation. She had dreamed about this so many times. . . .

She was aware he had moved away a step and was looking at her, openly, greedily, and she held out her arms, tempting him back to where she might possess him. He laughed, a soft, caressing sound, and knelt in front of the fire, drawing off his brilliant, gleaming, black boots and then beckoning her. She glided across the space between them to join him in the warmth of the firelight. Tenderly, adoringly, he ran his hands up her arms and unfastened her bodice and chemise. Her garments fell away to expose her round, firm breasts, and she murmured gently as his head came forward, hiding nothing now, mouth open, eyes wanting, to find her waiting nipples. His iron-hard, brown arms easily raised her, placing her astride him as he rolled back on the rug to tease and suckle her breasts above.

She groaned in deep pleasure, and lifting herself up from the waist so his mouth left her breasts, she sat upon him while her nimble fingers swiftly removed his warm shirt and undervest. The blood coursed furiously through Alan's veins as he lay looking up at her naked breasts in the firelight above him. Urgently, he tugged at her skirt and petticoat, and in turn she undid the silver buckle on his black leather belt. She murmured and rolled over to lie beside him as he kissed the gentle curve at the inside of her elbow.

The passion reflected in their eyes was a charged mixture of sweet fever, pleasure, and love. She came up to him in a graceful movement, and her hands eased his gray trousers down over his lean hips to show all of his beautiful body in the flickering fireglow.

Now he rose above her, like Adonis returned to life. She watched him bending forward, removing her pantalets; she lifted her hips smoothly up for him to slide the garment down. He groaned. It was a sound of wonderful indulgence as his tongue touched her belly and found the indentation there. She saw everything about him, heightened in her head, as if she must remember each small detail of him, forever: his sun-lightened hair falling softly forward across his gleaming brow, the perfection of his eyes and face, his flawless chin-line and neck, the wide, earth-colored smoothness of his shoulders and chest, his sleek, sinewy stomach, his muscle-hard legs, his slender, brown fingers, the fair hairs shining on his forearms, and the L-shaped scar in among them on his left arm.

He was removing her gartered stockings, and as the clinging material was pulled over her ankles, he kissed the inside of her calf and looked back down at her, his eyes shining with boundless love, with need and longing. There she lay, a tantalizingly beautiful, nymphlike creature, her voluptuous lips apart, an expression in her eyes that radiated undisguised love, simultaneously earthy and tenderly sweet. She lifted her slender arms, and his eyes fed greedily on her full breasts, erect, demanding, and below them, the flat, soft belly. His gaze came down across her abdomen, and he lifted her right foot to kiss the inside of her ankle and to watch the tangle of curls nestling between her legs. There was a crescendo of desire building within him now. This was his Eve. Finally, after the long months of starving for her, battling his yearning for her, he was allowing himself to exalt in her, to be consumed by the touch and feel of her, his one true love.

Eve gave a small, erotic, loving murmur as their mouths met again, and in the depth and intensity of her arousal, she slid her palms down the back of his neck, savoring the smooth, resilient texture of his skin, delighting in the rigid muscles of his back. He was perfect, he was beautiful, inside and out, and he was hers. How could life have given anyone more? She felt released, free, as if she were floating in the smell and feel of him. Her senses were filled with Alan. She spoke, although she hardly knew she had. "I am a part of you, I am a part of you, my darling, my own."

As his hands drifted down her silken skin, adoring her breasts, kneading her stomach, he answered thickly, "You will always be a part of me."

Giddy spirals of delight were bursting through his limbs as his fingers stroked across her belly to enter between her legs and explore at last the aroused, wet folds of her flesh. His fingers experienced the velvet-soft heat, the wetness, inviting them to probe carefully wider and deeper. How he, too, had dreamed of this, his angel and his devil, here and vulnerable, and his. He smiled as he heard her gasp of surprise, a wonderful, wanton sound.

They fell gently back to the rug as Eve's hands found the stiffened length of him, inflexible and hot. Thrill upon thrill rose and descended to knot in her womb and spread down through her as she moved his fluid skin back and forth.

In unison, they groaned, and through the paroxysms of pleasure, she felt his lips move from her mouth, down across her neck and over her tingling breasts and stomach to lodge in the swell of hair between her legs. His fingers came out of her to part her wetness for his tongue to search and knead. She gasped again; never had she felt like this. She was floating, falling into bursts of light and fire. She murmured, "Yes . . . yes," feeling as if her whole body were expanding and contracting in explosions of delight, and all the while her fingers twined the thick, waving hair at the back of his head.

He lifted his own mouth from her and came up to find her mouth again. Rippling with ecstasy, she clasped him at the small of his back while she tasted him. She wanted to give as he had given, please as he had pleased. She drew her lips from his and descended across his firm body to his waist and down to the male hardness of him. She ran her tongue around the tip, and he moaned, his breath catching in his throat. She squeezed and stroked him, teasing him with her tongue, until she opened her lips to receive him, the wondrous strength of him, to move restlessly in the burning willingness of her mouth. As he moved, his continuous rumbling moan intensified all the rapturous sensations tumbling in confusion through her limbs.

She felt his hands on the sides of her head, lifting her mouth from him. He moved her, lying her shimmering nakedness across the rug, her fair curls near the sensual firelight, and now his breath came in rasping sounds as he reared over her pale, inviting body.

Pushing between her legs at last, he thrust himself inside her, expanding her and filling her. She came up to him, to meet and join, entwining her legs around him, every sensation acute, the moist channel of herself throbbing with the ecstasy of at last receiving him, taking him down into the extent of her. She rode with him, exulting in the slow, sliding, delicious pressure of him inside her, while their bodies molded as one in the glorious, abandoned, decadent firelight. For some moments, Alan stopped to hold himself still within her, his head bowed into the curve of her shoulder, his lips caressing the side of her throat as he murmured thickly, unsteadily, "I love you, always." She heard his words, and all the emptiness, all the losses, all the pain and hurt that had been traveling with her, hidden in her heart, burst like a volcano inside her, then dissipated and disappeared. She was no longer alone. It was an exquisite, vivid moment. She was possessing him, and she was possessed by him; her answer came with a rush of glorious tenderness, "And I love you, my Alan, my own."

All thought and will faded as he began to move again, strong and endlessly enduring. The blood surged through their veins as their breathing shuddered and caught, their shadows delirious, waving shapes in the prodigal night.

There was an awareness of his iron-hard body abrading her breasts and belly and thighs, the pulsating urgency of his plunging into her and drawing back. She tasted the salt dampness of his bronze shoulder against her open mouth. Her fingers skimmed down the sweat on his back, lightly scoring the resilient skin, while the rhythm of his thrusts created a new and intense harmony. He was tending her, merging with her, sweeping her into a blinding light of space and color, immortal.

There were no thoughts now; their world was only continually connected spasms of thrilling, turbulent energy, and the final explosion consumed them, impelling them into bliss, sensation after sensation rumbling into something wider, magical, everlasting, shattering and re-creating, violently, beautifully powerful.

Time passed.

Eve became aware that he was pressing kisses on her forehead. Her lips were resting upon that part of him, at the base of his throat, that she had first noticed the day in the bush when she had fallen from Moonlight. It had thrilled her then, just looking at it, and from that day she had longed to touch and caress it. She kissed it now.

THIRTY-FIVE

The Parting

Saturday the eighth of July was a windy, cold winter's day, and the sun shone only intermittently on the straggling collection of buildings and byways that was Sydney town. And while the environs of the Prince of Wales Hotel comprised rubbish-strewn streets, Eve's eyes saw none of it, for she had been loved by Alan Fletcher, and that had colored her perception of things.

It was the first morning she had not awakened with an ache in her chest for Daniel and Sam, and now as the day advanced, she felt guilty at her happiness. Yet she could not suppress the overwhelming love that lifted from her being and composed her. The night before had brought her all she had dreamed about from the first day she had looked into his eyes at the coach door.

Alan had gone to the ship as arranged at eight o'clock, and half an hour before, Lawless had joined her.

When the shops opened, the two left the hotel to buy the necessary items for the voyage. As they passed through the front door, a small frown lodged between Lawless's eyes. "Ye know, Mistress Eve, this mornin' there be somethin' impressin' me, concernin' ye."

Eve, who was holding his arm, turned to look in his face. "Why, Lawless, what do you mean?"

"It's not as I can say exactly. It be hard for me, as I don't have the guverner's gift with words. Like you are calm or . . . or I don't know; there be a grace about ye this mornin'. Now, not as ye are not graceful all the time," he added, nodding to himself, "but ye are more so today."

She was silent for a few moments then she said, "Dear Lawless, yes, perhaps you are right. You are such a candid and sensitive man."

He smiled as if her words were enough explanation, and she squeezed his arm as they continued down to the shops.

By the time the clock on the general post office had struck eleven times, the two shoppers were returning up the hill of Grosvenor Street, laden with parcels. They had ordered two traveling trunks to be delivered to the Prince of Wales by noon, and into these they would pack their purchases and belongings.

Alan was waiting for them with good news of their embarkation. "It is all arranged. We can board the *Port Dennison* this afternoon. She sails with the evening tide, which is precisely at nightfall. The animals are last to be taken aboard, after cargo, supplies, and passengers. So we shall have to return here for the horses later."

"Aye, guv. Wonder what Waterloo will think of shipboard life."

Eve turned from her purchases. "How long will the voyage take, Alan? When will we be in New York?"

He smiled gently at her, lifting his hand to touch her cheek.

"The clipper is a very fast ship, lass. They tell me it will be less than one hundred days."

Lawless whistled, then he looked thoughtful. "Come to think of it, the old *Mount Stewart Elphinstone* wasn't too bad then, eh, if these here clippers are supposed to be the swiftest things afloat? She did the journey from the Old Dart in a hundred and fifty days, seventeen years ago, and we were blown off course as well."

"You are right, laddie, she was a good ship."

A few minutes before noon, the two wooden trunks were delivered, and while Eve packed them, Alan and Lawless went to hire a dray to convey them to the ship.

It was as they returned up the hill toward York Street that Lawless asked, "Guverner, when ye bought passage, what relationship did ye say as the mistress holds to us?"

"I said she was my wife, Lawless."

Lawless made a sound of approval. "Good, guverner, and that is what she wishes to be and all."

Nothing else was said for a time, then Lawless spoke again. "Do you think as a man would be disloyal to the dead woman he loved dearly if he began to like another . . . a mighty lot?"

"You cannot live with the dead, lad. It is fine and proper to remember them with all the love you bore them, and perhaps the places they had are never quite filled again, but life continues."

Lawless nodded. "I think Patricia Junie would see it that way."

Alan smiled. "Yes, she would; I have no doubt of it. She was one of the best there is, lad, and she would approve of Mistress Lottie."

"Gawd, guverner!" declared Lawless, turning in the seat to face him. "How did you know?"

Alan smiled again and patted him on the back. "Lawless lad, it wasn't hard to guess."

The younger man grinned self-consciously. Then he shook his finger in the air. "And here I am goin' to this America and as far away from Mistress Lottie as a man can get."

"Yes, but at the moment you have no alternative. Perhaps she will join you."

"Aye, guv, that's bein' my very plan. In fact, I shall be writin' a letter to her and post it before we sail."

"That's the spirit."

They drew up outside the Prince of Wales and climbed down.

Alan took the younger man's arm. "Lawless, lad, from now on we must be cautious. It is just possible that if Rutherford Blake followed us, he could be in Sydney this afternoon, though I do not deem it likely. Still we must remain discreet and wary."

"Aye, guv, that's as I shall be."

Lawless turned away to fasten the horse's reins to the hitching rail.

"And, lad . . ."

"Yes, guv?" he turned back.

Alan stood regarding him, a tender look in his eyes. A number of intense expressions ran in quick succession across his face before he answered, "Nothing, lad . . . it's just that you are the best companion a man could ever have dreamed of having. The best, and the most courageous."

They were standing looking at each other amid the noise and clamor. People and vehicles were all around and a street vendor shouted nearby, but the two companions were alone, holding each other's gazes, while the wind blew cold down York Street.

The seconds passed.

Lawless swallowed hard. "If I am that, Alan, my guverner, then it is as *ye* have made me."

Alan continued staring at his friend, a long look that said so very many things. Then he shook his head.

"Ah, Lawless," he answered, looking quickly away, "you pay me too high a compliment."

By two o'clock they were safely aboard the *Port Dennison*.

This first day, men and women were allowed to roam between decks at will, but once at sea, the women would sleep on a different deck from the men. There was to be communal living during the day on the main deck, a major difference from ships that carried passengers exclusively, where they often separated the sexes, keeping the females aft, and allowing the men and women together only on a Sunday.

The "sea stable," the name given to the hold where the animals were kept, was ready to take horses from three o'clock in the afternoon, and shortly before that hour, Lawless came to Alan and Eve on the main deck, against the bulwark.

Eve was fascinated with the scene. All around were the boisterous sounds of preparation for departure. Sailors shouted and officers called orders. Children squealed and ran about the decks, and parents reprimanded. People and baggage were bustled down hatchways and along gangways. This was to be the third major voyage of her life, and she felt exhilarated.

"I'll be away now, guverner, and shall have Waterloo, Freedom, and Milford back on board before the hour's out."

"Yes, lad, but I am coming with you."

"It only needs one man, guverner. I will ride Waterloo and lead the others."

"Yes, but two can keep a weather eye out better than one."

Eve looked from one to the other. "Now, both go, and the sooner you leave, the sooner you'll be back. I shall have everything unpacked when you return."

Alan took Eve's hand in a brief farewell. Lawless said, "Bye for now then, Mistress Eve," as he turned and led the way across the deck toward the port side and the quay. He was two or three yards ahead of Alan, and as he passed the wide mainmast, there was a shout from above, and sailors up in the rigging yelled, "Watch out below!"

"Falling chain!"

"Danger!"

Above the general hustle and din, very few people heard the shout. The heavy length of chain, which had been secured around the topmost yard near the crow's nest, had slipped from the grasp of the two men who were refastening it; it fell amidships, crashing down straight through a sail, bringing ropes with it.

Eve saw it falling and screamed in shock as she realized Lawless was directly beneath. He looked up too late to avoid it. His reflexes were excellent, and he dived to the side, but it was useless, and as Alan shouted, "Lawless!" the chain smashed into his shoulder and dragged him to the deck amid tangles of rope. He lay inertly facedown.

They ran to him. Alan knelt and lifted him in his arms. There was blood running from a cut on his shoulder, and he appeared unconscious.

"Lawless! Lawless, my boy."

A second or two passed, then Lawless opened his eyes, and grimacing with pain, said, "Gawd, guverner, these clipper ships are dangerous!"

Alan and Eve let out long sounds of relief.

The *Port Dennison*'s doctor, one Larry McManus, was called to attend, and the patient was carried belowdecks to a small but well-equipped hospital.

"He's broken his shoulder blade," Dr. McManus informed

Eve and Alan a short time later, "but I have strapped it well, and by the time this voyage is half-over, he shall be as good as new."

Eve remained to sit with Lawless, who was to spend the night in the hospital bunk. Alan left to get the horses alone.

"Let us know as soon as you are aboard again, my love, so we can cease to worry," Eve said to him.

He kissed her fingers. "Of course."

His journey was without incident, and when he arrived back with Freedom, Waterloo, and Milford, the *Port Dennison* was sitting low in the high water, for full tide and departure were less than an hour away. One at a time, he took the horses up the wide gangplank that led to the elliptical stern, the place for the embarkation of animals. The sea stable was in an aft hold. Down there, he met Mr. Brown, the second mate, a capable, softly spoken man, in charge of live cargo. He marked down the three horses on his record book and inquired, "Disembarkation port?"

"New York."

Mr. Brown pointed to Freedom and Waterloo. "Beautiful animals, both of them," he said appreciatively. "Now, you know the feedin' of these fine specimens of horseflesh is up to you."

Alan nodded. "Yes, I understand that. I ordered sufficient seed and grain this morning. I shall be back to bed them down."

"Be here before we sail, then," called the second mate. "I want the sea stable shipshape before we pass Farm Cove."

As he entered the hospital, Eve stood and came to his side. He put his arm around her waist, and she felt a wonderful surge of happiness. She smiled up in welcome, and Lawless attempted to do the same. He spent a brief time with them, and as it neared the hour of embarkation, he stood to leave and take care of the horses.

"In less than half an hour, the ship will sail; I must feed and bed them down."

"Wish I could help, guv," Lawless sighed from where he lay. Then, with his good arm, he gestured toward the door. "Go on, Mistress Eve, accompany the guv. I'll be all right and no mistake."

Eve patted his arm. "No, it is best I stay here. I can see you have a temperature."

Alan touched Lawless affectionately on the arm, and bent down and kissed Eve on the top of her head. She watched him turn away to the door and halt before he stepped through into the companionway. He looked back, his eyes gleaming with love for them both.

"My dear ones," he said, "soon the *Port Dennison* will be sailing, and that means freedom and new lives."

Eve felt a tremor of love run through her. For a few seconds, he stood perfectly motionless, looking at them with his deep blue-gray, matchless eyes, his dark figure framed by the doorway.

The sun was setting as he returned above to the aft deck.

The hatch entrance was close to the bulwark of the stern, and as he neared it, he glanced over the side to the *Saint Louis*, the ship berthed adjacent to the *Port Dennison*, which also sailed with the evening tide.

He stood stock-still, and the blood coursed more swiftly in his veins as he recognized the man who now was striding up the single gangplank of the *Saint Louis*. Rutherford Blake was followed by David Elrington and a trooper, and below at the quayside, two police constables stood on the wharf waiting.

Speedily, mind racing, Alan evaluated the situation. He took a graphite pencil from his inside coat pocket. The only piece of paper upon him was the receipt for payment from the hotel, and on the back of this he wrote hastily.

Along past the mizzenmast, through the bodies milling on the main deck, he ran. He knew exactly where to find the man he sought. Up the companionway to the raised deck and the ship's wheel he went.

I must have time . . . I must.

There, among the activity of getting under way, stood the first mate, Grantley Holmes, arms raised, giving orders. He was surprised to see Alan, for all the passengers had been asked to remain aft and to view the departure from there, out of the way of the sailors.

"I must speak with you, Mr. Holmes."

The first mate felt the urgency in the man beside him. "Please be quick then, sir, as you know we prepare to depart."

"Mr. Holmes, I have no other to trust at this moment but you. I would give you a long and detailed explanation if I had time, but I do not. I am not coming on the voyage."

Mr. Holmes's thick eyebrows rose in confusion.

"I ask you to give this note to . . . my wife. She is below in the hospital with my brother. But please do not give it to her until you are beyond the Sydney Heads and out at sea."

"Mr. Trent, whatever is going on?"

"I wish I could tell you, but I cannot, sir. The two I leave with you are more to me than life itself. Will you do as I ask? Please?"

There are moments in men's lives when they recognize that the decision they make has enormous bearing on the lives of others; Mr. Holmes recognized that he was in that position now. He heard himself answer, "Yes, I will."

"My eternal thanks to you, sir." Alan gave him the note and shook the first mate by the hand, before he left him standing there.

To the port side he ran.

Mr. Brown was standing with four sailors at the ship's side in readiness to draw up the plank. His freckled brow wrinkled in amazement as Alan came past. "Where the devil are you off to?" he demanded, his soft voice rising. "In a few minutes we pull this up."

"Never mind, sail without me. I am not coming . . . definitely not coming." Then he stepped through the opening and went rapidly down the gangway to the wooden planking of the wharf.

Humanity in all its forms shuffled and moved about, shouting farewells and waving. Through the crowded quayside, he strode to the base of the *Saint Louis*'s gangplank. Three yards away stood the police constables.

At the same moment above him on the deck of the *Saint Louis* appeared Rutherford Blake. He turned from the ship's master, saying, "I'm grateful for your cooperation, Captain. Ah yes, and may your voyage find fair winds." Then he gestured to David Elrington to hurry. "Come on, now to this *Port Dennison*; we perhaps have enough time at least to see the manifest of passengers, before she sails." In the gathering dusk, he stepped through the ship's side and began to descend. Below him, a man stepped onto the other end of the plank and began to ascend.

Sir Rutherford looked down at the man.

The man looked up at Sir Rutherford.

For a second it seemed as if the tumult and the excitement around them were gone. They both halted as the impact of recognition took hold on Sir Rutherford. Then Alan turned and leaped to the wharf, running away through the noise and clamor.

"Stop him!" screamed Sir Rutherford, impelling himself forward to stumble in his haste as he pointed at the figure. "It's Alan Fletcher! Stop him!"

The two constables, roused by Sir Rutherford's shout, turned to see Alan disappearing through the throng. Along Pyrmont wharf they ran, calling and shouting for Alan to stop, but he did not. He led them up and away from the wharfs toward the city. By the warehouses he ran, and over an open field to a lane leading uphill. Very few people were here, and although it was quickly darkening, his pursuers could see him clearly making for the street.

"I'll not lose you this time," Sir Rutherford said as he stopped and withdrew his pistol from inside his coat. His eyes narrowed in clinical appraisal of the distance between himself and his quarry.

"Don't! You might hit one of the men, sir!" David Elrington protested beside him.

"I hope not," came the grim answer as he pulled the trigger.

The explosion sounded, and Alan stumbled and fell to his knees.

The constables stopped running, and looked back in fright. But when they realized Sir Rutherford was not intending to fire again, they continued the chase.

Alan rose to maintain his flight, but the wound and fall had cost him dearly, and the constables were soon upon him. He knocked one to the ground and threw off the other before he vaulted a low wall at the lane's end and made for the street. But the injury slowed him down badly, and when the two police reached him the second time, they held him fast.

Sir Rutherford came, pistol in hand, over the unpaved ground toward them. He did not hurry; in fact, just the opposite. He dawdled, seeming to savor the walk up to his captive, as a cat might to its injured prey. He was elated! His pulse was thumping with excitement. Beads of perspiration covered his forehead and his temples. He was smiling with gratification and exhilaration.

Blood ran from the wound in Alan's thigh, down across his knee into the top of his highly polished, black boot.

The expert on the bushrangers strolled up to within two feet of Alan, his eyes locked with his captive's. "Surely you did not expect I would let you escape this time, Alan Fletcher," Sir Rutherford said, coming face-to-face with the man he had wanted more than any other in his life.

"No, I did not," Alan answered, steadily returning his gaze.

While this exchange took place, the gangplank was being stowed aboard the *Port Dennison*, and Mr. Holmes and Captain Cruthers were shouting orders to their men in the rigging.

Mr. Brown saw that the flags were furled, and the *Port Dennison* drifted inexorably away from Pyrmont wharf.

When Eve felt the ship drift away from the dock, she did not go above. She felt she should remain with Lawless while he slept, and for some reason, she did not want to witness the ship's departure. Her thoughts were full of the future, not the past she was leaving behind. What would America hold in store for her and Alan? She presumed they would live together as man and wife. An odd thought came to her. Perhaps John Stuart would divorce her. Some people did such things nowadays. He might agree if she wrote from America and asked him. Surely he would be glad to be rid of her. In any case, it didn't matter; she perceived things differently now, and in the new land, she would be Alan's wife in all that mattered.

Where *was* Alan? She wondered why he had not come down. It must be over half an hour since they had left the wharf.

A sailor had come in and lit the wall lamp earlier and told her that the ship's surgeon would be by shortly. She stood and moved to the porthole. She could hear the wind but could see nothing except the blackness of the night. She shivered, and walking back to the bunk, drew a second blanket up over Lawless.

Where was Alan? Surely he would have bedded the horses down by now?

Suddenly it came to her. Of course! He was once a man of the sea. He will be on deck, watching and enjoying the activity and thinking all the things that sailors think. Satisfied, she sat down again.

The door opened, and she turned sharply in expectation, a smile on her face. It was Dr. McManus with a tray and some broth for Lawless.

"Have you seen . . . Mr. Trent?"

"No, I have not, but I have been in ship's medical stores until I went to the galley to get this for Mr. Miller." He put down the tray and lifted Lawless's good arm to take his pulse.

At the movement, he woke. "Hallo, Doctor." His eyes found Eve. "Where's the guverner?"

"I don't know, dear. Will you be all right while I go above to find him?"

"Yes, you go; of course I will."

She closed the hospital door and moved swiftly along the dimly lit corridor and up a companionway to a second corridor, then to the deck. It was cold, and the wind swept her hair high from her shoulders. Men were moving about and calling to one another in the vague light of the hurricane lanterns. Where was he?

It was close to eight miles by water from Pyrmont wharf to the north and south heads at the entrance to Sydney Harbor. An hour after departing the dockside, the *Port Dennison*, under full sail, headed out across the Tasman Sea.

Eve had been on all the decks, and now there was fear in her eyes as she rushed along, almost falling once or twice as the ship rolled. Perhaps he had returned to the hospital and Lawless. . . . Yes, yes, that would be it.

Back down the companionway she went, and there was Mr. Holmes coming toward her along one of the corridors. He called to her and she halted. His pleasant face was serious, for he held the impression that he was not the bringer of good news. He was an honorable man and had not read the folded note carried in his pocket, though he had been tempted to during the last hour.

"Mrs. Trent, your husband asked me to give you this. He was particular about the time. He made it distinctly plain, you were not to receive it until we were at sea." He was holding the paper out to her.

She went cold with dread. The pulse in her throat throbbed as she took it from him. She could not speak. She made a strange sound that was meant to be "thank you" and turned from him.

In the cold, dark corridor she dragged her eyes down to read Alan's words.

Eve,

Rutherford Blake is upon us.

There is only one hope for you both. I am returning to shore as a decoy, for I must know that you two whom I love above all else are free.

Live in the knowledge that I love you, now and always,

Alan

She stood unmoving in the passage. Then she crumpled sideways into the bulkhead, and for a long time she leaned there. She became aware of Dr. McManus's voice and his bespectacled, kindly face looking at her with concern. "Mrs. Trent, Mrs. Trent, are you all right? Whatever is the matter?"

Like a stranger, she listened to the sound of her voice replying, "It's . . . it's nothing I can discuss with you, Doctor. I'm sorry, forgive me." And she stumbled by to the hospital door.

Lawless was sitting up. He had finished his broth. His mouth broke into a smile as she entered, but his face changed as he registered Eve's look.

"What is it, mistress? By the Lord in Heaven, what is it?"

She came to him and handed him the note. She stood impotently beside the bunk, watching the color drain out of his face as he read. He lifted his eyes from the paper, and they brimmed over with tears.

"Oh, my guverner, my beloved guverner, whatever shall we do without ye?"

They had taken Alan to Liverpool Street police barracks, less than a mile from the docks. There they disinfected and doctored his wound, fed him, and put him in a cold cell with a wall candle, a table and a chair, a wooden bunk, and two blankets.

He heard a clock chime eight times somewhere in the distance. About a minute later, footsteps stopped outside his cell. The lock rattled and the heavy timber door squeaked open on its hinges.

The adviser on the bushrangers entered, carrying a hurricane lantern. He placed it on the table as two police peered tentatively in from the doorway.

"Come in, Wright," Sir Rutherford said to one of them who held a notebook and pencil.

The door closed and Constable Wright stood inside. Sir Rutherford sat on the single chair, and Alan remained where he was, sitting on the bunk.

For perhaps thirty seconds no one spoke; the captor and the captive watched each other across the chilly air of the room, each quite openly examining the other.

A self-satisfied smile sat on Sir Rutherford's mouth as he determined to break the silence. "So, Fletcher, is there anything you wish to say?"

"No."

"Then perhaps you will be good enough to answer my questions?"

"Perhaps."

The captor tapped with his oval fingernail on the table, once again observing his prisoner. "They removed my bullet from your leg, eh?"

"They did."

He gave an indulgent chuckle. ''Ah yes, you'll be able to walk to the gallows after all.''

Alan did not speak.

''How long did you reside at Treehard Hill?''

''Six years.''

''I buried your companions there, you know . . . Dwyer and Cooper.''

Sir Rutherford was sure he detected his prisoner flinch. Yes, yes, there was pain in his eyes.

''I did not know. . . . '' Alan replied slowly.

''And where is the last remaining member of your gang? Lawless Drake.''

Alan made a sound that could have been mistaken for a sigh. ''We were never a *gang*, and it does not conform with my estimation of your intelligence to expect me to answer your question.''

''Then perhaps you will tell me why you were about to board the *Saint Louis* this evening?''

''I will not.''

''Ah, yes, I see. I did not really think you would cooperate, unlike your former associate, Jordan O'Day. Now, he has told me quite a lot about you already.'' Sir Rutherford folded his arms and leaned back in his chair. ''He won't swing, you know. Ah yes, he will turn Queen's evidence at your trial. In fact, he shall probably be allotted a portion of your reward money.''

Alan did not answer; he sat motionlessly, staring steadily at his inquisitor.

''What do you think of that, Alan Fletcher? O'Day collecting money for your head and living the high life?''

''Jordan O'Day is as nothing to me. Discussing his future will be a very one-sided conversation.''

The captor forced a smile. ''Ah yes. You are well controlled, Alan Fletcher. You do not disappoint me. I expected as much. I am learning a great deal about you simply having this conversation, one-sided or not.''

Alan smiled, and for some seconds the two men observed each other in silence, the only noise the scratching of Constable Wright's pencil on his notebook.

Sir Rutherford shivered and moved his eyes from Alan's face. It was damned cold in here. He noted an empty fireplace in one corner, no doubt from previous days when it had been other than a detention room. He motioned with his right hand to the constable's book. "For the record, Alan Fletcher, I must ask you once more why you were boarding the *Saint Louis*."

Alan did not reply.

Sir Rutherford sighed and stood up. "I have kept her in port, you realize. She is being searched this very minute for stowaways."

Then he pointed to the door and looked to his companion. "You may leave, Constable. I will join you outside in a moment."

When the door closed, his eyes returned to his prisoner's face. "This is a very delicate matter. Ah yes. It concerns Mrs. Wakeman. Do you know where she is?" He was watching his prisoner with all the scrutiny available to him, and he thought he noticed a change of expression come into his eyes.

"I do," Alan answered.

Sir Rutherford's brows drew together in a frown. "Where? Where is she?"

Alan hesitated a few seconds. "Out of New South Wales, away from anywhere that you, or those you associate with, can do her harm."

The police detective did not like this information. John Stuart would not like this information. He stood and walked to the cell door. There, he paused. His face was a mixture of emotions, and his angular profile in shadow looked even more hawklike than ever. He was about to leave, but he decided to ask for the information that he had been inquisitive about from the first. He turned his head back to his prisoner, and they locked eyes once again. "Why is it that in all the raids you have made in twelve years, your target has been the government on all occasions except two, and those were upon the most wealthy in the land?"

Alan sat staring at his inquisitor, and for some seconds Sir Rutherford believed he was not going to answer. Then he did. "My differences are only with those who exercise authority."

The expert on the bushrangers nodded; he had thought as much. "I shall see you in the morning, Alan Fletcher. I hope your wound does not trouble you too much."

He dismissed the two constables and stood outside the cell, watching them depart. The satisfaction and sheer rejoicing he had experienced three hours before, when he had caught the bushranger, had waned. The interview had disturbed him, no matter how he pretended to himself it had not. He felt unhappy with the whole turn of events. Fletcher had integrity. It was confusing to compare him with other bushrangers. He was nothing like the informer, O'Day, or any of the other scum who had been caught. Now that he had spent even this short time in the man's company, Sir Rutherford admitted there was a sort of morality in the very essence of the man. He conceded that this was what he had suspected when he was at Treehard Hill; why he had felt uncomfortable there, like an intruder.

Yet Fletcher was a cold-blooded murderer. . . .

Sir Rutherford certainly was disconcerted and uneasy. He hated to feel this way. It was not conducive to being efficient and effective. He looked back at the door of Alan's cell. He shook his head.

Down the corridor and through the iron gate he hurried. Turning left, he entered a small, warm room where three constables sat at desks. A fire burned in the grate. They all looked up at him; one was the smooth-faced Wright, who was now turning his shorthand notes into longhand.

Sir Rutherford was the talk of the barracks. His reputation, already substantial among the rank and file of the force, was now, with the capture of Alan Fletcher, indestructible. They all stood from their desks as a mark of respect.

He coughed. "Ah, yes, gentlemen. I want you to . . . I would like a fire lit in the prisoner's cell. Immediately. There is a fireplace in there." He coughed again. "He is wounded, after all. . . . It is a cold night. Keep it fed. You understand?"

The surprise on the three constables' faces remained after Sir Rutherford had closed the door and was ten yards along the corridor.

He crossed the yard, where a fine rain drizzled, and joined David Elrington, who waited for him in the superintendent's office.

Twenty minutes later, they had ridden to their billets in the police training school, a section of the Redford Barracks, situated a half mile away. Their horses were taken and they said good night to each other in the wide, paved quadrangle. Light rain continued falling.

"What time do you wish to see me in the morning, sir?"

"The usual, Mr. Elrington; we shall meet at seven o'clock for breakfast."

"Very good, sir," his assistant said as he made to depart. Then he added, "Oh, and what a great afternoon's work, sir. Congratulations!"

It seemed to David Elrington that his superior's answer lacked the enthusiasm he had expected. "Ah yes . . . Well, good night, Mr. Elrington."

As Sir Rutherford mounted the stone steps and opened the door that led into the building containing his quarters, a young constable came up to him. He saluted.

"Constable Henry Garner, sir. I have been assigned to you."

Sir Rutherford nodded to the tall, neat young man.

"What would you like to eat, sir? Cook's gone for the night, but there are ham sandwiches in the kitchen."

The preoccupied face frowned. "What's that? Sandwiches? Yes . . . yes, Garner, anything will do."

"And there are two men here, sir, to see you. Came some twenty minutes ago. They are waiting in the duty officer's room, sir."

Before the expert on the bushrangers opened the door to the duty officer's area, he had guessed who they might be: John Stuart and Joe sat by the fire, waiting.

As they stood to meet him, Joe said, "Rutherford, we followed you and arrived just this evening. We stay at the Royal."

"My friends." He frowned. "While I am happy to see you, I have mixed news for you, I fear."

John Stuart took his friend's hand. "Have you found her?"

He shook his head. "No. But I have Alan Fletcher in custody. I think we should go to my rooms, and I shall tell you all I know."

When Sir Rutherford had related the story of his long ride and the capture of Alan, he leaned back and tapped the arm of his chair restlessly. "So you see, I have the bushranger in my hands. And while that makes me happy, I am sorry I cannot give you the wherabouts of Mrs. Wakeman. All he has told me is that she is out of New South Wales."

John Stuart was dispirited and tired. "What does that mean?"

"I don't know. Now, of course, he could be lying to put me off the track. That is always possible. Because I do not see how she could be out of New South Wales. Even now, I have experts searching the *Saint Louis*. If she is on board, we will find her."

John Stuart looked to Joe. As always, his feelings were transparent to the older man, his misgivings and disillusion obvious. Joe's expression of concern and encouragement helped him to ask his ultimate question. "Are we to take it that you believe they were running away to America together? That they were . . . lovers?"

Rutherford Blake lifted his hands, palms upward, to him. "I'm sorry, my friend. From appearances, I can only assume . . ."

"Yes," John Stuart replied. "I understand."

When Joe and John Stuart left, it was with the understanding that if Sir Rutherford learned anything, he would send a message immediately to them, and in any case, they would return here to the Redfern Barracks to meet with the police detective at noon tomorrow.

Sir Rutherford sat listening to the heavily falling rain. His earlier discomforting sentiments about Alan Fletcher had given way to irritation with himself. He must return to seeing things as they were. He had begun to romanticize the man. He was going soft. The man was a killer, a convict, and an outlaw. Of course, he could give the appearance of integrity and honesty. Ah yes, couldn't many criminals?

At half past nine, young Garner knocked gently on the door with the news that the *Saint Louis* had been searched from stem to stern and no stowaways had been found. Sir Rutherford nodded, and after the constable had gone, stood for a long time looking out into the cold, dark, wet night. Poor John Stuart. He felt deeply sorry for the man.

At eleven o'clock he went to bed, and at midnight was still awake. It had ceased to rain, and he lay thinking in the silence. Suddenly his eyes opened widely, and his voice echoed around the room. "Of course! He wanted me to see him. He wanted me to chase him. It was not the *Saint Louis* at all!" He moved in his bed and sat up. He lit the candle on his bedside table.

He understood now.

Alan Fletcher had lured him away from the wharf deliberately, had given himself up to ensure that the others would not be taken. It was the next ship that Drake and the Wakeman woman were on . . . the *Port Dennison*. It had sailed with the evening tide, while he had held in port the one that did not matter. Ah yes, it all made sense. Had not Fletcher said she was "out of New South Wales, away from anywhere that you, or those you associate with, can do her harm"? John Stuart had truly lost his wife this time. And he, Sir Rutherford Blake, had been fooled by Fletcher one more time.

"Blasted bushrangers. The devil take them all!" He sighed, a long, miserable sound. Well, he had Fletcher, didn't he? Fletcher was the coup. The greatest coup of them all! Ah, yes, he had Fletcher.

Sometime later, he dropped off to sleep. He awoke early and

was fully dressed and had written a note to John Stuart before seven o'clock. He thought it only fair to alert his friend of his convictions.

Sunday, July 8

Dear John Stuart,

The American ship Saint Louis *was thoroughly searched, and no stowaways found.*

It is now my opinion that your wife and Lawless Drake were on the clipper ship Port Dennison, *which left Sydney last night on the evening tide, bound for the United States of America. I fear it was a deliberate ploy of Alan Fletcher's to have me believe his companions were on the* Saint Louis.

I am deeply sorry, my friend, and shall be available to you at the Redfern Barracks at noon today as arranged.

Your friend,
Rutherford

Fresh-faced, Constable Garner had just gone off to deliver the note when there was an excited knock on his door. David Elrington entered to his call.

"Sir," he began before his superior could open his mouth, "I have it here, here in my hands, the transcript of the Fletcher trial. Would you believe it? It was handed to me not five minutes since. Remember, we sent for it last year? It arrived aboard the HMS *Gallant* on Thursday. Inspector McClelland has had it sitting here in his office among a batch of letters for postage. He found it last night, and when he met me in the corridor just now, he went and retrieved it."

Sir Rutherford's hand shook as he took the sealed envelope.

An hour later, he still had not eaten breakfast. He sat looking out into the cobbled yard, his back ramrod-stiff, his eyes glassy.

It is sometimes said that worry makes people age overnight. There is no doubt that Sir Rutherford Blake aged in the hour it took him to voraciously read the transcript of the Fletcher trial.

He had changed. Never would he be the same again. For he now knew what only Alan Fletcher knew!

His face was ashen, and he was weighed down with guilt. He spoke to himself in a subdued voice and he said over and over, "He is innocent . . . innocent. . . . Alan Fletcher is innocent."

Having read the report of the trial, it was all apparent to him. It was obvious that Abel Crenshaw perpetrated the crime to get Alan Fletcher's lands. The name of the chief witness had leaped off the pages at him! Benjamin Breely! Benjamin Breely, alias Rufus Short, alias Victor Hawke, alias Clifton Kempe. The man had been a vile murderer, though not, it was clear, when Alan Fletcher was tried. That was later. Sir Rutherford would never forget him. Hadn't his been one of the last convictions he had made before he came out to this country?

Breely, the most immoral of men, who had looked as innocent as he was guilty. He, with the face of an incorruptible man, was of the devil's own vintage. He had used his looks to marry wealthy, older women, and he had killed them for their estates. Four women he had married and murdered between 1853 and '61. He had died on the gibbet, brought to justice only weeks before Sir Rutherford had come out to New South Wales. His evidence in a court of law was not worth a tinker's curse!

Sir Rutherford remembered the name Christoper Scales, too. A thief and burglar in London, caught in '57 for robbery with violence, and sentenced to ten years on the prison hulk *Redoubtable*. This man had been another witness who had sworn he had seen Alan Fletcher commit the murder! It was ghastly! These men had been paid by Abel Crenshaw to convince the jury. Without them, the prosecution had no case, no case at all.

It made Sir Rutherford feel physically ill.

Ah yes, but none had yet been caught for unlawful acts in 1849 when Alan Fletcher was on trial. They were at the beginning of their nefarious careers then. And why was the case not reopened? Because there had been only one man who would have known about their subsequent careers, and he was dead! Finnigan McGuire, who had been Alan's defense lawyer, had drowned off Torquay in 1854. Sir Rutherford had known of him, a clever young barrister set to go far.

He brought his fist down heavily on the window ledge. His whole life had been dedicated to bringing criminals to justice. These last three years had been devoted to catching bushrangers, and none had he wanted more than the one who was a half mile away . . . the innocent one, who had lost his lands and been degraded into convictism. Of course, he had escaped and become a bushranger. Would not Sir Rutherford have done the very same?

Alan Fletcher, who had allowed himself to be caught so that his associates might live. Alan Fletcher, who had never used violence; who had never robbed any but the government and the acutely rich. Of course. All clear now . . . all so sickeningly clear. He turned from the window and strode to the door.

It was unbelievable, but it was true!

He must go to Alan Fletcher. Tell him. Set him free.

David Elrington thought he had never seen his superior so excited. There was a tense, unnatural look about him, and when Sir Rutherford asked for his horse, he said in agitated tones, "Bring him here to me, posthaste. I must go to the Liverpool Street barracks immediately."

They were standing in the quadrangle. At that moment, Henry Garner appeared, and marching formally up to them, he said, "Sir Rutherford, Inspector McClelland sends his respects and requests your company in his office. He asks if you would be good enough to see him forthwith?"

"Damn!" Sir Rutherford said, frowning. Then he decided. "Mr. Elrington, you must go for Alan Fletcher. Go immediately. Bring him straight back to me here. Do not deviate. Do you understand? Hurry! It is most urgent!"

A surprised David Elrington did as he was told.

Sir Rutherford strode across the quadrangle and up the stairs into the building that contained the offices. At the senior officer's door, he knocked and entered.

Inspector Mark McClelland's bearded face looked up from a pile of papers. "There you are, Sir Rutherford. Good morning. I want to talk to you. Now, where do you propose to incarcerate Fletcher until his trial? The Darlinghurst jail?"

Sir Rutherford shivered, but not from the cold of the winter's morning. He dropped into the chair opposite the police officer. "My God, McClelland, you will find this hard to believe, but Fletcher is innocent . . . innocent of the murder charge which made him a convict in the first place." He put the transcript of the trial on the desk as the police officer's mouth opened in amazement.

"Listen, and I will tell you what I have found out this morning."

For a few seconds, Inspector McClelland thought it was a joke, but as the explanation continued, he knew it was very serious.

"And so you see," Sir Rutherford finished, after he had told the story, "the wheel has come full circle, for I, who was his enemy, must now be his champion. We must see the inspector general, the governor, the premier. Set him free. No matter who is against it."

Mark McClelland had been a policeman for thirty years. First in Bristol and the west country of England. He had come out to

New South Wales in 1844, and for twenty-one years he had worked as hard as anyone to gain respect for the colonial police. He hated the way his men were often the target of lampoons, and in particular, how they had been made to look foolish in the eyes of the public these last few years when bushranging had become a social menace. He had been annoyed when the inspector general had seen fit to appoint this famous criminalist from London to advise on the problem. But he was a fair man, an honest policeman, and a good administrator, and had to admit that Sir Rutherford Blake had made a difference. The man had been a veritable bloodhound, tenacious and resolute. He had been instrumental in bringing in many, if not all, of the notorious outlaws of the last two years, and now, finally, he had caught the elusive Alan Fletcher. He was an erudite antagonist of all who broke the law, and hence, more than any man alive, if he said a man was innocent, he was to be believed.

Mark McClelland nodded. "You are right."

Ten minutes later, both men waited impatiently on the small balcony outside the office building. The adviser on the bushrangers was still speaking his agitated thoughts aloud. "I have been a criminalist studying crimes and the law for twenty years. I have been a detective policeman since the phrase was coined ten years ago, and never have I seen an innocent man sentenced, *never*, until now."

Inspector McClelland shook his head. "What is he like?" he asked. A question from time immemorial, when ordinary beings wish an insight into the extraordinary. And Sir Rutherford, in answer, sighed, and then attempted description.

"What does one say about a man like him? Dispassionate? Clever? Heroic? Noble? I suspect he is all these things. Perhaps at another time he would have been an Alexander, a Wolfe, a Nelson. There is one thing I know. He is not afraid of you or me or any man."

The cold wind that had been blowing for the last twenty-four hours picked up some stray papers and moved them across the court in front of them as Sir Rutherford lifted his hand with excitement. "Here, here they come now!"

Over the heads of the dozen police cadets drilling beyond the arched entrance to the yard, they saw the escort riding toward them. Two troopers in front, David Elrington riding alongside Alan Fletcher, ah yes, and it looked like two more police behind.

Followed by the police inspector, the adviser on the bushrangers jumped down the stone steps to the cobbled yard, a look of anticipation upon his grave face.

Alan had been surprised when an armed constable had unlocked the door of his cell and held it open while two more entered, carrying armfuls of wood. He watched as a fire was lit in the grate.

"Orders of Sir Rutherford Blake," the man lighting the fire explained, looking at Alan with awe.

"Thank you," Alan said as they departed.

The heat had certainly made a difference. After it pervaded the cold, dank room, his leg, which had been aching continuously, improved to where it was but a dull discomfort.

It was now two hours since he had been put in the cell, and there had been a flow of visitors. Rutherford Blake, the constables to light his fire, the superintendent, the police duty officer, and only a few minutes ago, the doctor. All had eyed him with ill-concealed interest.

He lay back on the bunk and looked at the flickering firelight.

Rutherford Blake had proved an able adversary. A peculiar individual, arrogant, egotistical, but unquestionably clever, discerning, and determined. Curious that the man had ordered him a fire. Curious, but surprisingly kind.

A wan smile came to Alan's mouth. It was a pity that he could not know Blake better; there was something about him that, in other circumstances, he felt he would have liked.

So he was a prisoner again. . . . After twelve and a half years, they had him once more.

Transcending everything was the fact that his two remaining loved ones were safe. That was what mattered to him; that was all that mattered now. Two lives exchanged for two lives. Danny and Sam were gone, and Eve and Lawless were free. He had given the only thing he finally had to give that would make a difference . . . his own freedom.

He felt confidence in their resilience and courage. He closed his eyes and saw her looking at him from inside the coach, wearing her green traveling dress and a white bow at her throat as she had been the first time he had seen her. And then there she was sitting in the bush, her head bandaged in strips of his shirt, gazing up at him with her darling brown eyes. He looked over to the corner of his cell where the fire burned brightly, warming the small space around him. He pictured her slender nakedness on the hearth rug in the fire-glow of last night; was

it only last night? He imagined the gentle curves of her body
and heard the soft, seductive laughter of their perfect union. He
made a sad sound. "I wish you happiness, my love," he said
aloud.

When he fell asleep, it was to the sound of rain falling against
the windowpane outside the iron bars, and when he awoke, it
was to the dull light of a cold, gray day.

They continued to keep his fire burning.

His breakfast was a small bowl of porridge, a thick slice of
bacon, and a slab of bread.

He thought it must have been sometime between eight and
nine o'clock when the door of his cell was unlocked again, and
this time he saw the face of the same constable who had lit his
fire the night before. Standing behind him were two armed men.
The young man coughed nervously. "Mr. Fletcher, you are requested to come, and bring your coat with you. You are being
transferred."

As Alan followed the constable down the hall, in his office in
a wing across the yard, the superintendent signed the release
form and handed it to David Elrington. Then he turned to watch
through his window as the prisoner was brought from confinement down into the yard, within the precincts of the barracks.
He looked on as David Elrington joined them and they mounted
up, the prisoner swinging his bandaged leg up over the horse
with no show of difficulty. The company moved away down the
lane between the buildings, and was lost to his sight.

It was a short ride of some one thousand yards from the barracks to the police training school on the far side of Hyde Park,
and as they issued into the street, Alan spoke to David Elrington, who rode beside him.

"Where do we go?"

Sir Rutherford's assistant was as fascinated by the captive as
everyone else, and he was glad to speak with him. "To the other
side of the park, College Street Police Training School. Sir Rutherford Blake especially requested me to bring you there immediately. No doubt you are in for a morning's interrogation before
they transfer you to Darlinghurst jail."

"No doubt," Alan answered.

David Elrington would have liked to continue the conversation,
but being aware of his position, he did not feel it appropriate, and
in any case, the prisoner looked away.

In the street, the mounted, armed entourage caused great interest. Alan, handcuffed and escorted by armed police, became

the subject of loud speculation from the idle, the loiterers, the hawkers, and passersby. He was certainly a striking figure for the Sydney streets in his dark clothes and knee-high, black leather boots, with his bandaged leg. Even manacled, he rode easily, expertly, and the horse responded to his authority, lifting its hooves in lively fashion. He ignored the noisy observations shouted at him, for his mind was not in the dusty streets of Sydney town, but far away with those he could see no more. Their faces were a jumble in his mind. Eve . . . his mother . . . Danny . . . Lawless . . . Sam . . . Swiftie . . . Womballa . . . and even Bluey, for an instant.

And so, after all, it had come down to this day. Sunday, the eighth of July, 1865.

Another trial! What defense could he possibly have?

Jordan would be there to give evidence against him, and all the men the Crown could muster would stand in line to convict him. Once more, he would have to listen to the slander and the lies. Once more, they would malign him and show him culpable. Though this time they would not send him as a convict to a place thirteen thousand miles across the sea. This time they would hang him. Snap his neck at the end of a rope.

Was he angry at the injustice? Did he feel rancor? No. There was no rage or resentment. He had acknowledged years ago that those sentiments were useless. What had occurred could not be altered. And, too, there had been joys, many joys, the love he felt for Eve surpassing them all. He felt the skin of her body again, smelt the dreamy, heady scent of her. The ultimate treasure was here in his mind, the memory of lying with her in the firelight. He could take that to eternity with him. His vision clouded momentarily as he stared straight ahead.

Into his mind, out of the well of his yesterdays, came the words that the soldier Parker had said to him so long ago in the convict tent when they were escaping: *You'll hang, Fletcher. They'll hang you for sure in the end.*

No. It was no way for a man to die! The most dishonorable death of all.

He could not join Danny and Sammy that way.

For a few seconds he visualized the *Coral Regis*, and Long Moss House and his mother.

Then he saw Eve again. She was on the deck of the *Port Dennison* with the wind in her curls, and her hands reaching out to him across a rolling, blue sea.

He came out of his reverie to see that they had crossed Hyde

Park and were in the precincts of the training school. They were riding over a grass-covered yard. In front of them was a stone archway, and beyond, police drilling in a quadrangle.

"Enough," he said, aloud.

David Elrington, hearing him speak, turned expectantly in the saddle toward him. The young man's face dropped as Alan's horse lurched. The animal, tired of the walking pace, responded to its rider's insistence. It sprang to the side as Alan brought its head around and urged it away. The horse gathered speed, thudding through the grass.

He was fifty yards from them in the seven seconds it took the four police troopers to rally from the shock, lift their rifles, aim, and fire.

Three bullets smashed into his back; the fourth went wide. The explosions drowned out the scream from Sir Rutherford, who had witnessed the event as he came forward across the court.

Alan fell heavily to the ground.

"No! No! Stop!" screamed Sir Rutherford as he ran, arms waving, through the archway toward the fallen man. "He's innocent! Oh God, what have you done? He's innocent!"

Mark McClelland ran after him, his face full of despair.

David Elrington and the troopers were amazed. They could not believe what they saw and heard. They dismounted and stood in confusion, watching wide-eyed as Sir Rutherford ran to the bushranger and, turning him over, lifted him gently in his arms.

"Oh, God! Forgive me! I am so sorry . . . so sorry," Sir Rutherford said softly now to the upturned face. "Alan Fletcher . . . Alan Fletcher, can you hear me? I know you are innocent."

Alan's eyes opened and focused on the face above him.

"Oh, God, man, I'm sorry. I know you are innocent. Forgive us. Please . . . I'm sorry. . . . Oh, God!"

Alan's eyes registered Sir Rutherford's. His lips parted, and he said something that the police detective could not understand.

"What? Oh God, what is that you say? Please . . ."

But he did not speak again.

To Sir Rutherford it was as if time stopped. He knelt in anguish, his features ashen, gazing only at Alan's face.

Then the life-light went out of the wonderful eyes; they glazed over in death, and he quivered and lay still.

Men were running from the training school, shouting and calling out. There was din and disorder all around. But Rutherford Blake did not hear it. He was conscious of nothing but the dead man in his arms.

Tenderly he lifted the handsome face very close to his own. His lips actually touched the rigid cheek as he murmured, "Please . . . forgive us."

He was oblivious of the astonished stares of his assistant and his troopers; he was oblivious of the blood that seeped into his velvet jacket and stained his expensive breeches. For a very long time, he continued to kneel on the wet ground, holding Alan Fletcher tightly to him.

Eve had not eaten breakfast. She could not. She was too distraught.

It was sometime between eight and nine o'clock that she donned her warm cape and went above to make her way aft. There she stood alone, looking back into the white, frothy wake of the clipper.

She prayed for Alan, though no longer was she sure of the efficacy of prayer. She stood with the wind blowing her curls, staring at the sea and the purple-gray line of the horizon.

The ship streaked through the water, carrying her ever farther from the man she loved more than herself. She pictured him in the cabin doorway as she had last seen him looking down at her . . . the way she was to picture him forevermore.

Suddenly she froze.

It was as if deep inside her, something had left her soul. She felt it stir and break away. She clutched the bulwark. "Oh no . . . no . . . no . . ."

And then she knew, as surely as if she had seen it happen.

Alan was gone.

When she came along the corridor to the hospital door, she stood still. She remembered his words, *My dear ones, soon the* Port Dennison *will be sailing, and that means freedom and new lives.*

Alan, oh, Alan, what is a new life without you? I am soul-dead.

She opened the door and entered. Once more, she found Lawless. He had spent the night in hospital, and now, with his shoulder firmly strapped, was dressed to leave.

She came to him and took his hand. "We are alone, Lawless," she said. "There are only two of us now, just you and me."

THIRTY-SIX

Revelation

It was two o'clock in the afternoon of the day that Alan Fletcher left the earth when John Stuart and Joe made their way across Hyde Park toward the Royal Hotel. The sun had come through the clouds and had turned Sydney town's weather into a crisp winter's day.

They had been with Sir Rutherford at Redfern Barracks. A changed, subdued Sir Rutherford who had told them the disturbing story of Alan Fletcher's innocence and his death. The police detective had recounted how Abel Crenshaw had coveted the Fletcher lands and had arranged for Alan to be falsely charged with murder. He told them of the trial and the sentencing. Afterward, he had looked at them with a haunted, distracted expression. "It's been hard to tell you, John Stuart, for you of all people have been affected by your wife's association with him, but I must be the one to set things right. I shall return to England and will not rest until he is pardoned. It is my duty."

They had not spoken much since leaving Sir Rutherford, and as they came by a small stone wall where an old man and a child, wrapped well against the cold, sat feeding four or five pigeons, John Stuart halted, and Joe turned to him.

"Old man, there has been a lot to contend with this last week. I feel at a loss to know what is what."

Joe nodded sympathetically. "I know, m'boy."

"I have to accept that my wife left me and somehow went to the bushranger, that they planned to go to America together." He stiffened slightly and his moody eyes rested on the child feeding the birds. "That is the part that hurts me more than I can express.

574

"And now we know that he was innocent, forced into his way of life to survive. It is a great deal for any man to take in."

"It is . . . that."

"I don't understand any of it, and the way I feel this minute, I don't know if I ever want to. My wife is on a ship to America. I've truly lost her. There's nothing for me to do but to go home and take care of my responsibilities."

"A wise decision, m'boy."

John Stuart and Joe spent a night in Bathurst on their way back to Mayfield.

They had arrived just before three o'clock in the afternoon, and after washing off the dust of travel had taken a stroll to get some exercise. When they came to the corner of Rocket Street, John Stuart pointed to Mrs. Ayres's Tea Room. "Would you like a cup of tea or coffee, old man?"

"Yes, m'boy, I might at that."

They did not remain in the little establishment long, only for enough time to have coffee and one of Mrs. Ayres's jam rolls, and to become the center of attention. They had departed about ten minutes before Lottie came back to the tea shop after running an errand for Mrs. Ayres. The proprietress's pretty, elfin face was all agog. "Guess who just took tea here, Lottie, love."

"Who?"

"Mr. John Stuart Wakeman, that's who!"

Lottie's expression was thoughtful. "Really now?"

"Terrible shame, isn't it?" her employer said, wrinkling up her fine nose.

"What is?" asked Lottie.

"Why, haven't you read today's *Bathurst Times*?"

Lottie shook her head.

"Well, you should. Tells all about him, poor man, says the truth's only just come out, after many months. Do you know, he's been searching the bush for his wife, and she was seen here in Bathurst only last week! Says he mounted search parties in January, February, May, and June. Examined hundreds of miles of this country, back and forth like a beaver, if the truth is written. Apparently the rumor was true that she left him on Boxing Day last. From what's been printed, he's a broken man, and him so handsome and wonderful and kind to his Mayfield folk. I think it's awfully sad." She sighed dreamily. "I could *never* leave *him*."

Lottie did not answer, but later on her way home, she bought herself a *Bathurst Times*.

It was not by accident that after the tea shop, the two men had gone by a circuitous route to return to the Royal Hotel. Although nothing was said, neither wanted to go near the Bathurst park and the memories it held.

The early-falling winter night was beginning to descend, and as they passed an old wares shop on the corner of Keppel Street opposite the jail, they noticed a man bend inside the window to place a lantern in the display.

Joe nodded through the glass to the man. "That's young George Bonner, the famous local cricketer. He pitched the ball one hundred and nineteen yards from a standing position here, last twenty-fourth of May."

"Looks strong enough," commented John Stuart, moving away. Then he suddenly halted. His eye had been taken by a small wooden inlaid casket with the initials L.B. on the side.

He stood in thought for a few seconds and then entered the door. Joe followed, and George Bonner, well aware of the identity of his customer, grinned in welcome. "Good afternoon, Mr. Wakeman, sir."

John Stuart nodded, and pointed to the item. "Can I look at the case?"

"Most definitely, sir, of course," George Bonner leaned into the window and brought it out. As he did, he lifted the lid, adding, "The top here opens, but this side drawer won't pull out. The latch be broken on the inside, and I'm afraid there be no key. But then, ye could have it mended, assuredly ye could."

"Yes, it be a lovely thing, to my way of thinking," spoke up Mr. Bonner's helper, a tall, bright-eyed girl who was polishing some candlesticks.

John Stuart held it in his hand and looked at it. It was some twelve inches long and perhaps ten wide. There were many such about; people kept letters and papers in them, or sometimes jewels. He had a number of them at Mayfield. He turned it at an angle to peruse the initials L.B. carved in the front side on the drawer that would not open.

Joe stood silently watching him.

"Tell me, Mr. Bonner, where did this come from?"

"Why, er . . ." He inclined his head to the girl. "Where did this come from, Maggie?"

And Maggie, a clever child and part-time student at All Saints' Church School, rising to the occasion, answered, "Well, a lot of this here stuff were sold to us by the new Reverend Cornish, old stuff like, from the rectory. That there box His Worship holds came direct from him.''

"I knew it, I knew it," John Stuart said, half to himself. It was the initials that had attracted him in the first place. He felt sure that this had belonged to Eve's "Father," as she had called him. Leslie Billings. He would buy it. He did not know why; he simply would.

Joe, who now understood that his boy wanted it, immediately paid for it, and they were shown to the door by Maggie, who was smiling winsomely.

Back in their rooms at the hotel, John Stuart held out the box to Joe. "I'd like to open this drawer, old man. Do you have your penknife on you?''

Joe laughed. "Yes, m'boy, I do. I carry it even in a dress suit, which my wife thinks odd.''

It was not as easy as John Stuart had imagined, and after some minutes of trying, they looked at each other in defeat.

"Don't think we can do it tonight, m'boy. Best leave it and give it to a locksmith in the morning.''

"I'm not sure why I wanted to open it, actually. Just a feeling. Thought there might be something in it, but in all probability it is empty.'' He took the penknife from Joe's hand, then one last time inserted it in the lock and twisted it from side to side. He felt something give way, and when he pulled, the drawer moved.

"Well done,'' Joe said. "Perseverance, eh?''

John Stuart nodded, pulling the drawer out farther.

There, lying inside, were a number of folded papers and envelopes. He took an envelope. "Ah, so it *did* belong to the Reverend Billings, as we thought. This is addressed to him.'' Then he leafed quickly through the rest. "They mostly look like personal letters and the odd list of church requirements. Best we just burn them in the gra— What's this?'' He stopped speaking. His eye had caught the handwriting on the top of a sheet of paper, and he could not help but notice the date and the address:

1st February 1863
General Post Office
Postal Letter Box Number 72
King William Street
Adelaide

"It is Eve's handwriting!" he exclaimed, mystified. "I'd know it anywhere."

He looked at Joe, then back down to the letter, and he could not stop himself from reading it.

Dear Reverend Billings,

Thank you for the numerous letters you have so considerately written to me over the years.

It seems that you and my darling sister believe that I am unhappy with my life and would regain peace and respectability living in Bathurst, under your influence. Now, you are both so solicitous, and I must admit your offers at times are tempting, but you see, I am not dissatisfied with my lot and am indeed quite happy.

Oh, I know you must regard it as shameful and unnatural to live as I have done, but I have a new friend here now who is very good to me, and I could not leave him for anything. The trappings of respectability—home and family and husband—have no appeal for me. Oh, I do hope that does not shock you.

I thank you once again for your charitable attention. It does most certainly make me feel special.

I do not need to see Eve, for whilst we are hundreds of miles apart, twin sisters are born to a unique condition, and thus I can feel close to her without seeing her. Indeed it is better this way, I know.

Unfortunately I am not an able correspondent, as you doubtless are aware by now, so do please forgive my lack of discipline. I know you are at pains to take care of my dear sister, and for that I am eternally grateful. Do be so kind as to accept that I am competent to do the same for myself.

                                        I remain
                                        Yours sincerely,
                                        Clare Herman

John Stuart was unable to speak. He did not lift his eyes from the paper. He simply stood there.

"What is it, m'boy? What the devil is wrong?"

The truth had hit him instantaneously. He was overwhelmed by the significance of the words on the paper he held. He sat down, and with a listless movement, handed the letter up to Joe. Then he bent forward, head down in his hands, while Joe read it.

After what seemed a long time, the older man spoke. "A twin sister. It was this Clare who was in Adelaide, this Clare who lived with Lake. Why didn't she tell us?"

"Why, indeed?" came John Stuart's strained voice.

Joe sighed, and he, too, sat. As he did, his hand went out mechanically and ruffled the younger man's hair. The face beneath looked up, full of suffering, and there they remained staring at each other.

Thunder rolled in the distance, and shortly afterward, the sounds of rain began on the windowpane.

"I see all the mistakes I made. In truth, I have seen them since the moment of her departure. I had decided all grown women were like my mother . . . all but Eve. I was once told not to 'weave a dream about Eve,' but I did. I continued to tell her she was good and pure and different from other women. I, who am scornful of the church, did my own canonizing. Of course, she feared to tell me of her twin, for this Clare was living the sort of life I so repeatedly told her I despised. I made it impossible for her."

Joe's face was full of sorrow. He wanted more than anything for this "child" of his to be happy. He shook his head. "Do not be too harsh upon yourself, m'boy. Eve was the only one in possession of the knowledge. How could you possibly understand if she did not tell you?"

"Ah, Joe, you minimize my misdeeds. I was proud . . . ah, the arrogance and self-conceit attached to pride. . . . I was interpreter, censor, and critic."

"Perhaps you judged her wrongly at the time, that is true, but you have tried consistently to find her to make her aware you felt differently. Her successive actions should not be passed over."

John Stuart closed his eyes and made a gesture of confusion in the air with his hands. "Joe, she left Mayfield thinking I loathed her. She believed I thought her mean and vile."

They were very late going to bed that night, for he insisted on reciting the unhappy events of Christmas time.

When finally Joe bade him good night, he took John Stuart's hands in his and counseled him. "Listen to me, m'boy. I don't want you to blame yourself. The circumstances which prevailed at that time were beyond one man's power to alter."

In reply, John Stuart gave a weak, grateful smile. He met the older man's eyes. "What would I do without you, Joe?"

* * *

Robert Robinson-Pike's main office was in Sydney. Four times a year, he journeyed into the West to meet with his most important client, and he kept a small office in Bathurst for one reason only: it was the nearest town on the telegraph line to Mayfield. And it was his most important client who came the following morning at opening time to the Bathurst branch of R. Robinson-Pike to see the man in charge, the solicitor James McIntosh.

John Stuart had lain awake thinking a long, long time before falling asleep the night before, and he had come to a decision.

Mr. McIntosh was a sincere, intelligent young man, and had listened gravely to all that Mr. Wakeman and Mr. Larmer said. Now he made his reply.

"Well, sirs, there is such a thing, in the United States of America, known as the Pinkerton National Detective Agency, run, I think, by an ex-sheriff, as they call their law officers over there. They find people for a fee. Mind you, what with the recent civil war, they may not be operating now. But Mr. Robinson-Pike and Mr. Noah, my superiors, know more about this sort of thing than I do. Would you like me to telegraph them, sirs?"

John Stuart looked to Joe. The older man shook his head. "I don't think this can be explained in a telegraphed message, m'boy."

John Stuart nodded and faced back to the solicitor. "Mr. Larmer is right, and this is most urgent. How would you like to leave on the noon mail coach today? You'll be in Sydney on Saturday, which will allow Mr. Robinson-Pike to have a letter written to these Pinkerton people by Monday, and it can be on the first ship leaving Sydney for America next week."

Joe smiled. "Yes, m'boy, that's the answer."

THIRTY-SEVEN

Daydee

Eve looked around at the sound of Lawless's voice.

"She's comin'! Oh, Eve, Lottie's comin'!"

He came across the few yards of grass from the back door of their stone house, waving a letter high in the air in the warm September sunlight.

Eve put down the purple honeysuckle she had been gathering from the creeper near the yew tree. "How wonderful, Arnold. Let me see."

It was the second letter they had received from Lottie in the thirteen months since they had left the Australian shores. They had written to her immediately upon their arrival here in Boston.

Often it had been almost impossible for them to carry on without the strength of Alan. And there were times when both of them had thought life hardly worth living. But then they would bring out the note written on the back of the receipt from the Prince of Wales Hotel, and the very sight of his handwriting would reinforce their wills.

They had been lucky, for there had been enough money left from Eve's legacy to rent this house, and a piano had been one of the items of furniture. Eve had begun to teach music as soon as she had found pupils, and Lawless had tried a few jobs before finally settling into a position that suited him perfectly: guard on the Boston Railroad Company line between Boston and Providence.

Oh, they had to be practical and could not be extravagant and spend on luxuries; nevertheless, it had not been long before they knew they would soon have enough money for Lottie's passage. And Lawless had made arrangements to pay her fare through the Golden Eagle Line, the very one they had come over upon.

As Eve took the letter from Lawless, she thought back to the first letter they had received from Lottie. She reread that letter every week. Lottie had written it on the twentieth of March, 1866, after receiving their first letter from Boston the day before. It had told them of Alan's death in Sydney, and how Sir Rutherford Blake had held Alan in his arms as he died. It explained that Sir Rutherford had declared him innocent and had resigned from the police force and returned to England to fight for a posthumous pardon for Alan. Eve had cried a long time when she read that.

Then came some paragraphs about John Stuart. Eve had read, with complex emotions, the story of John Stuart's search across hundreds of miles of country for her. She remembered how she had told Alan at Treehard Hill that she was certain John Stuart would not look for her. How wrong she had been! Lottie had enclosed a newspaper cutting with a banner that read, THE STRANGE STORY OF THE MISSING WIFE OF AUSTRALIA'S RICHEST MAN. Her stomach had given an odd little lurch when she had read what was said to be a quote from John Stuart. "Yes, I searched for my wife for many months, that is so. There had been an unfortunate difference between us, which was entirely my fault, and I sought to resolve it." Fancy John Stuart saying that for all the world to read. She had felt deep sorrow at that, sorrow that he had to expose himself that way.

She sighed as she brought her eyes down to Lottie's second letter. Yes, Lottie was coming to Boston. She had received notification that her passage had been paid from America, and she would be on a ship leaving Sydney in August.

Eve turned to Lawless. "Oh, Arnold that means she could be here in early December if we are lucky!"

Lawless smiled in answer, and for some seconds they stood unspeaking in the sunshine.

Eve was so happy for Arnold, as she called him these days. Her "brother" Arnold to the folk of Boston town. He and Lottie would make a fine pair.

"Well, Eve," Lawless said, breaking into her meditations, "with this wonderful news, I'm off to work. Do ye know, with that new horse car they have put on in Mount Vernon Street, I get to work ten minutes earlier. I reckon it's the horses; they're beauties. Do you know they say there's a man experimentin' on a car for the streets that uses electric power . . . so they won't need horses anymore.''

He left in long strides across the lawn, and Eve found herself thinking of the man who was experimenting on an electric street-car. How such a thing would intrigue John Stuart. Yes, she could visualize him now, reading all about it in one of his journals in the summerhouse on a Sunday afternoon. Her heart gave a strange little tremor as she pictured him, and she sighed in remembrance before she turned to gather more honeysuckle. As she did, there was an awakening cry from the bassinet that lay beside her on the grass.

She bent to it. ''Oh, my darling, you are awake.'' And she lifted the baby up into her arms, and kissed him. ''Uncle Arnold has just gone to work, and what do you know? Auntie Lottie is coming from Australia to live with us.''

John Stuart walked out of the new dairy and over to Diomed.

As he did, the words of a song one of the dairymen was singing floated over to him. His brows drew together in a frown. It was a song about Alan Fletcher. It called him brave, and bold, and innocent. Ballads about the bushranger were now sung all over the west country.

The Crown Proclamation of Alan Fletcher's posthumous pardon had appeared in the colonial newspapers only a few weeks ago, but already they had made a hero of him here in the bush. He had overheard Tommy Barnes boast more than once how he had met the man.

Rutherford had been instrumental in having the pardon granted, just as he had said he would. He had resigned his appointment with the Colonial police force and gone back to England and reopened the case.

The report in the *Sydney Morning Herald* had said that the false charge of murder against Alan Fletcher had been brought about by his cousin Abel Crenshaw, who had coveted his lands. Rutherford had obtained a confession from the one remaining living witness from the Fletcher trial. The report stated Crenshaw had died of smallpox six years after the trial, in 1855, and the Fletcher estate had passed to a cousin of Alan Fletcher's mother, a single lady from Falmouth.

It was difficult for John Stuart to think of Alan Fletcher impartially. Of course, the man had been most fearfully ill-treated, and it was only proper and fitting that his name was cleared. Still, it sometimes felt as if it were he who had taken Eve away.

For a moment he pictured Eve as he had first seen her coming through the park in Bathurst. She wore a light floral gown, and the skin of her throat was faintly golden in the setting sun. She walked vigorously and swung in her hand a small bag on pink strings.

He made a sharp, sad sound and brought his mind back to the present.

He mounted Diomed and rode up the hill toward Mayfield House.

He was going back home for luncheon with Daydee, and would work the afternoon there, for today was her birthday, her twenty-first, and there was to be a grand celebration tonight.

Last Sunday she had found him in the summerhouse and asked if on her birthday could she eat luncheon there. He had agreed. And then she had stood up and mock bowed and continued in a comical fashion, "I think I should like to have my birthday luncheon *alone* with the master of Mayfield, please, for during the rest of the day, I shall be surrounded by so many."

"If I am not busy," he had answered.

Fortunately, this morning she had been at Mayfield House when he had come out after breakfast, and she had reminded him, for he had forgotten all about it.

Joe's daughter was to gain her majority in grand style. A huge marquee had been erected on the lawns in the park, and all the Mayfield House staff were invited for refreshments and music and dancing, at four o'clock. Then at eight o'clock, there was a private party to which a number of Daydee's friends from school days had been invited.

In April, Daydee and Thelma had traveled to Sydney, and Daydee had been presented at the grand ball at Government House for the young debutantes of the colony. She had been made quite a fuss over by some of Sydney's eligible bachelors, and she had written a number of letters to John Stuart telling him about it.

One matter that John Stuart and Joe were delighted about was Daydee's change of heart toward Roy Ford. In the last year, she had been openly friendly to him, and Roy had traveled to Sydney to be Daydee's partner at her coming-out ball. In fact, they had planned a surprise for her, and Roy was arriving unbeknownst to Daydee for the party tonight.

John Stuart would not have ridden up from the dairy toward

Mayfield House so unconcernedly had he known the real reason for Daydee's apparently altered attitude toward Roy. Oh yes, Daydee had been nice to Roy, even amicable over the previous months, for one reason only: to make John Stuart jealous. When she had written from Sydney to him with the news of the boys who doted on her, she had prayed he would not like it.

And today was her birthday. She would be twenty-one at last! Now, finally, John Stuart would take her seriously.

She smiled into her mirror as Rosy brushed her hair and tied a large pink bow into it. She was having luncheon with him, just the two of them. And then tonight she would dance with him. Since *that woman* had gone away, life had been wonderful. Yet Daydee had made a mistake in flirting with Roy. That had not worked very well, and she would never do it again. She was a woman at last. She would make John Stuart love her!

She knew all about love now. She had taken the final step in Sydney with Sir Jeffrey Hughes's son, Andrew. He was handsome and played polo. John Stuart played polo. Yet in going all the way with Andrew Hughes, it had not been as marvelous as she had thought it would be. She gave a giggle thinking of him; he had said he loved her, and she had said it, too, but she had been pretending he was John Stuart.

Luncheon was a delight for Daydee. She and the master alone, waited on by Baines and the servants. The hour passed far too quickly.

They left the summerhouse together and were wandering back across the lawn when in the distance, through a gap in the shrubs and trees, they saw an open carriage coming up the drive.

Daydee recognized it as the Fords' vehicle. She started, and her mouth turned down unpleasantly as a sound of anger escaped her lips. "But *they* have not been invited. John Stuart, that is the Fords' carriage. What are they doing here?"

"But, my dear, your father and I thought you would be pleased to have Roy here. Lately you have been so happy in his company."

They were standing in a secluded part of the garden, beside a long white granite colonnade overgrown with climbing rose and jasmine vines. Even in winter, when there were no blooms, the setting was beautiful.

Her skirt brushed the uneven granite stones as she walked a step or two away from him in what seemed to him a petulant movement.

He shook his head and was just about to speak severely when

she turned back to face him. Her dark eyes were wide, and there were wrinkles of unhappiness on her brow. Her mouth quivered nervously as her eyes filled with tears. And then it came rushing from her at last.

"Oh, John Stuart, you don't understand, do you? You never have . . . I only flirted with Roy to . . . to make you *see* me . . . notice me. It's you I want. I love you. I have always loved you. All my life . . ."

She stepped quickly back to him, and as the tears brimmed from her eyes, she threw herself into his arms. "Oh, please . . . please love me as I love you. It's you I want . . . it's you. . . ."

There was a time when John Stuart would have been appalled by this outburst. But he was more moderate in his views these days, and he simply moved her tenderly from him. He looked down into the upturned, tearstained face. "Oh, Daydee, dear Daydee. I had no idea of this. You are a child to me, don't you see? I remember your being born. I am almost old enough to be your father."

She stood clinging with her small hands to his arms, a desperate look in her eyes. "I have loved you all my life; what is age to me?" The tears streamed down her face. She was sobbing helplessly.

He drew her over to a stone seat in the vine-covered colonnade. He sat her down and knelt in front of her, taking her hands in his.

"Now, listen to me carefully, Daydee, and attend what I say." She nodded.

"I cannot change how I feel about you. It is impossible. You are little Daydee to me. Like a baby sister." Then he took a deep breath and spoke his innermost thought. "I love Eve. . . ."

Daydee's pretty face twisted with hate. "But you cannot love her. . . . She is gone. You told me yourself, she was never coming back."

"Daydee, listen, I know what I said, and undoubtedly it is true. But I did not explain things properly, for I *do* love her, and I always will."

Daydee's look was peevish and she dropped her eyes as she said between sobs, "But she has gone forever. Why cannot you love me now?"

He was quiet for a few seconds before he stood up and lifted her to her feet. He stroked her cheek, then handed her his handkerchief. "Come now, Daydee," he said, "wipe your eyes and take my arm. You must face your guests. It is your birthday. In two hours you must be in the marquee, and tonight you will be the belle of the ball.''

She sniffed. ''You treat me like a child.''

''No, I do not,'' he answered, tucking her hand in his arm, ''for I have told you today what is in my heart.''

They walked slowly under the pergola to the open lawn and across through the hedges and trees to the graveled carriageway. Here they could see servants coming and going from the house to the marquee, all activity in every direction.

They halted.

His look was grave and he bent forward toward her as he said, ''Now, give me a smile and promise me that you will enjoy yourself tonight.''

She returned his look and, making a half smile, nodded.

''Good,'' he replied, patting her hand affectionately and then raising it to his lips. Then he stepped off the lawn onto the drive and strode across to the steps. ''And we shall have the first dance together,'' he called back to her.

She watched him mount the steps and cross the veranda and enter the house.

''The devil take you, Eve,'' she said aloud. ''I hate you, I detest you, I loathe you!'' Then she hurried away toward her own home.

''Happy birthday, Miss Daydee!'' shouted Timothy, who had been commandeered to help Mr. Baines, and was crossing the lawn laden with an armful of napkins.

She waved peremptorily and passed on. She was running by the time she reached the gate in the hedge, and hot tears were spilling from her eyelids again.

It wasn't fair. How could he still love *her*? Well, she wouldn't dance with that Roy Ford. He could go to hell!

As she came in the door, her mother was coming out.

''Ah, Daydee, there you are. Did you have a nice luncheon?''

Her daughter looked at her with scorn and brushed hurriedly past her. ''I'm going out for a ride, and don't you dare suggest I take Leith, for I shan't.''

Just over fifteen minutes later, Daydee was in the saddle and riding hard toward Larmer's Crossing.

''He mustn't love her . . . he mustn't love her . . . he mustn't love her . . .'' she chanted as she took Boots from a trot to a canter, along the far bank of the Lachlan to the west. She rode a mile spiritedly, aggressively.

The river path climbed here to high ground. Over the centuries the water had eroded the earth, and at times her way took her thirty and forty feet above the Lachlan.

As she came near a group of men driving a herd of cattle from a river paddock to higher ground, two held up their hands to her, and Tommy Barnes shouted for her to stop. Daydee ignored their signals. She would stop for no one! How dare they call and shout to her! Horrid stockmen. . . .

She was furious with her father for inviting Roy Ford . . . furious with her mother . . . she hated Eve . . . and John Stuart was treating her like a child. She hated everyone . . . hated them all. . . .

She urged Boots to even more speed, and remained oblivious to the warnings shouted by the men, who now waved even more excitedly at her.

"Don't stay on the river path, Miss Daydee; the ground is undermined along the high bend! There have been cave-ins!"

"Stop, Miss Daydee! Stop!"

But on she sped, her mind full of fury, pushing Boots to even more speed. His hooves flung dirt up behind as his mistress careered along the high path above the Lachlan.

Tommy Barnes spurred his horse and rode after her, calling all the while for her to stop. His shouts died as he saw her disappear. He pulled sharply back on his reins, and his horse reared in the air as her scream came back, high-pitched in terror. She and Boots fell, the ground beneath her giving way and crashing with her into the river.

They lifted her as gently as they could and took her back the two miles to Larmer's Crossing, where Joe and Thelma came to meet them. They had been alerted of the accident by Barnes, who had galloped up to tell them. The men transferred her to the first aid cart they used to carry injured men. In this they took her little broken body home. Dr. Douglas could do nothing for her.

She remained unconscious until, three hours later, she opened her eyes briefly. She saw above her the strained faces of her father and her mother and John Stuart, and beyond them, a clergyman's. He was the new minister from Cowra and had been visiting in the married workers' cottages.

He came forward as Daydee's eyes opened. She did not look at him; her gaze was for John Stuart.

Joe spoke. "Daydee, Daydee love, we are all here, and the Reverend Bailey is here to say a prayer for you."

Daydee, whose eyes had been trained on John Stuart until now, shifted her eyes to her father. "Am I dying, Dada?"

"Oh, Daydee . . . Daydee love . . ." was all Joe could find to answer.

"Oh, Lord, watch over Daydee Bronwyn Larmer," she heard the minister say, "and help her to make her peace with You and come in purity, as we all will on the Day of Judgment."

She looked up at the pain-filled faces and she thought of all that had happened. She stared at John Stuart and recalled her secret, the secret she had told no one. How she had found the photographic likeness of Eve and her sister, Clare, and how she had burnt it, so that John Stuart would never know. . . .

Little did she realize he knew the truth now anyway.

She lifted her tiny hand toward him, and he took it tenderly. "You . . . d-do love me . . . don't you . . . John Stuart?"

And with tears brimming in his eyes, he answered, "Oh yes, Daydee, yes, my little one, of course I do."

A smile almost beatific settled on her face.

"Good," she answered as she closed her eyes.

An hour later she died.

A week later, John Stuart came to Thelma and Joe.

It was a cold night and they sat before the fire. Thelma was knitting a shawl, and Joe was attempting to peruse plans for a modern community hall, but his mind kept wandering to his daughter's funeral.

"John Stuart," Thelma said as Rosy brought him in. "What a lovely surprise."

He sat down on the sofa opposite them. "I have something to discuss with you. Both of you." He coughed. "My dears, I do not want to upset you by mentioning Daydee, but her death is somehow the final bewildering event in a series of bewildering events in our lives . . . in my life."

He looked from one to the other. "This is hard for me to say, but I have been thinking. All my life I have been offended by what I called immorality. I hated my mother, because of her adultery. I judged her as my father appeared to judge her. I also judged my wife, and in doing so, lost her."

He brought his hands together, clasping them. "I see things differently these days. Life is constant metamorphosis. Perhaps time runs out and then we find ourselves sorry for the past when it's too late."

Joe met his gaze. He thought he had guessed what was going on in his boy's mind.

"It is thirty-five years since my mother went home to Scotland, is it not?"

The older man nodded. "Yes, I'd say that was right, m'boy."

"How old was she when she went away?"

Joe looked to Thelma. She thought for a second or two. "Why, she was a year or two younger than you, Joe. I'd say she was about twenty-eight, yes, or twenty-nine."

"So she would be in her early sixties now?"

"She would."

John Stuart looked directly at Joe. "I am saying all this because I want to go and see my mother."

Joe nodded. That is what he had thought, and he was taking it dispassionately, for that was his nature. It was Thelma's heart that pounded as she attended his words.

"She came from Fort William, didn't she?"

Joe nodded. "Hard by, near Ben Nevis, wasn't it, Thelma?"

"Y-Yes, love, that's right. . . . The old laird had property there."

John Stuart looked to Thelma. "Is that where she wrote from? The letters she wrote to me?"

"Why, yes, dear, from Dunain Lodge, via Fort William. It's in the Highlands."

"I see. And all we know is that she was alive and living there until I was fifteen." He sighed loudly and rested his chin in his hands.

Thelma made a small, uncomfortable sound in her throat and moved a touch closer to Joe. "No, John Stuart dear, I know a little more than that."

Both men looked at her.

Joe touched her hand. "What is it, Thel? What do you know?"

She swallowed and looked directly at John Stuart. "Well, I wrote to her after Sir Arthur . . . your father died, and she replied."

Joe shook his head in disbelief. "You wrote to her? Heavens, woman, when will you cease to amaze me?"

Thelma looked abashed, but in defense she explained, "I thought she should know, you see. It didn't seem right that Arthur was dead, and she none the wiser. Why, don't you remember? He wore her wedding bracelet on the night he passed on. I believe he wanted her to know."

"It's all right, Thelma dear," John Stuart said. "I'm glad you wrote. But she answered, you say?"

"Yes, and her letter was lovely, although I burned it." Here she looked at Joe. "Out of fear you would find it and carry on."

Joe continued to shake his head.

"She said she held naught against Arthur, that he did what he had to do and that was the way of things, but the rest of the letter, while of course, I can't recall the detail, was all about you, John Stuart, being the new master of Mayfield, about how proud she was of you and all. . . ."

John Stuart, to Thelma's delight, was smiling. "What you did was right. I am so very pleased."

"You are?" the good woman asked, emotion making the words catch in her throat.

"Indeed I am. I only wish you had continued to correspond. . . . At least I would know if I still had a mother."

Thelma was now turning very pink. Her cheeks had become florid and she was tapping her knitting needles together nervously. "Oh . . . you do? Well, then, I can answer that for you right enough."

"What?" exclaimed John Stuart.

Joe was watching the exchange with an expression of astonishment.

His wife continued, "You see, dear, she was desperate to know about you and she *begged* me to write back, so . . ." She turned again to her husband, giving a small, embarrassed cough. "You may have noticed I've been getting a Scottish periodical each six months all these years."

"Yes," her husband replied, "it's household articles and stories. Isn't that one over there?" He pointed to a small stacked pile of reading matter.

"It is, my love." She turned back to John Stuart. "Well now, it is inside one of those she has been sending me letters since your father died. I always post my replies on a Bathurst visit, or when I'm in Cowra. . . . Oh, John Stuart, she loves you so, always has. She calls me her lifeline. To you, she means."

John Stuart was smiling tenderly.

"You do not hold it against me, then, for corresponding?"

"Thelma . . . Thelma . . ." He stood, and coming to her, lifted her to her feet and put his arms around her. For the first time since he was thirteen years old, he actually hugged her to him.

"No. No, I am not angry. I am truly glad."

He knew she was crying. She was pressing him close and holding on to him so tightly. He stood there with her for a long time, looking over her head at Joe, before she moved a step back to look up at him. On her face a jumble of expressions fought for supremacy . . . love, relief, anxiety.

"Ah, Thelma, don't be sad," he said gently. "I am so lucky to have you, and you've had the burden of this for so long. I've been such a damn fool. An arrogant, damn fool. Please forgive me."

"Oh no, no, no," she said, drying her eyes, "You have not. It's I who've often wondered whether I've done right or wrong, but I was so sorry for her, the poor thing. Take no notice of me. It's just such a release after all these years."

She sat down, and Joe spoke at last. "You're a wonder, Thelma Larmer, that you are."

She gave a small smile. "Well, there was no telling you, Joe, for you would have thought me an interfering old biddy."

"And so you have been," he answered. "Though it seems just as well." He leaned over and kissed her cheek, putting his arm protectively around her.

"So my mother is still alive," John Stuart sighed. "Is she well?"

"Ah, now, that's just it and all. It's a constant racking cough she's had in recent years. Her last letter came about a month ago. She was none too well. It was shorter than usual. Although all about you, as always."

"I would like to leave soon . . . as soon as I can."

Joe looked at Thelma, and Thelma smiled. "Then, Joseph Larmer, you had best be arranging to leave as well. No doubt Jack Hennessy and Stephen Brown and Mrs. Smith and I shall manage without you two. Haven't we always?"

It was the day before they were to leave Mayfield to travel to Sydney to board the SS *Donaghadee*, September 2, 1866. John Stuart rode in from the east gate and dismounted. Up the steps to his white cedar front door he leapt and into the hall. There he met Mrs. Smith.

"Good afternoon, sir. The mail coach arrived while ye were out. There be a pile of missives on yer desk in the study."

Ten minutes later he was going through his mail.

When he opened the letter from Robert Robinson-Pike, his hand shook a little. Enclosed was a page from the Pinkerton

National Detective Agency. It was dated April 2, 1866, and it read:

> Dear Mr. Pike,
>
> I am happy to inform you that the woman you asked us to find has been located.
>
> She lives in a rented house at number 32 Russell Street, Beacon Hill, Boston, Massachusetts, in the United States of America. It is a very modest dwelling, but the area is a superior one. She is known as Mrs. Fletcher.
>
> There is a man living with her, her brother, Arnold Drake. She is in the ninth month of a pregnancy.
>
> Thank you for the payment you made available to us through the Bank of North America.
>
> It is always a pleasure to help people in foreign lands, and if we can be of further assistance, please write to us at the same address.
>
> Sincerely,
Allan Pinkerton,
Founder

John Stuart folded the page and put it in his pocket.

He opened no more mail.

He stood and left his study and walked down the corridor.

For the first time in many months, he opened the door to the bedroom he used to share with Eve and walked by the bed to the long casement windows. He opened them and moved across the veranda and down the steps.

It was growing dark and there was a cold wind blowing.

He went to the trunk of the poinciana tree and stood there under the leafless branches, looking up through them to the pitiless sky.

And then he wept.

THIRTY-EIGHT

Honor and Strength

Eve moved up the stairs and inside the door of Saint Martin's Church. In her arms she carried her nine-and-a-half-month-old son, wrapped well against the early January winds. Ahead of her walked Lottie and Arnold.

She followed them to the altar rail, where the Presbyterian minister waited. He had been happy to marry them. Eve had met the cleric during her pregnancy, for this had been the nearest church to Russell Street, and she often came to service. As Arnold had said, "A church is a church to me. Ain't it the one, single God who is supposed to be abidin' in them all?"

Eve moved into the pew near her next-door neighbor, Mrs. Mason, pretty, reliable, and obliging, who many times had taken care of Eve's son.

Briefly the winter sun broke through the clouds, and the stained-glass window behind the altar radiated a glorious light down upon the few gathered in the church. Eve sighed. Her two dear friends were being joined together. She thought of her other friend, Thelma, so far away, and prayed that she was well.

This was the first wedding she had been to since her own, and her memory insisted on leading her through the moments when she had held John Stuart's hand at the altar in All Saints', Bathurst. How happy she had been. How excited she had been. She found herself wondering about John Stuart. She had run away from him thinking he hated her, and apparently that was not so at all.

Her son moved in her arms, and she bent her head to kiss him. Alan Fletcher's son, the living proof of her perfect love. Lottie had brought the news of Alan's posthumous pardon, and

Eve rejoiced to know the world now recognized his innocence. As in everything else, Sir Rutherford Blake had proven tenacious in his desire to see Alan's name cleared. The proclamation had been published in the colonial newspapers just before Lottie had sailed for America. Alan's ultimate victory over meanness, hatred, and injustice. Alan, oh, Alan, you affected all those who ever came in contact with you.

When she lifted her gaze from her child's face, Mr. Willson was saying nice things about Arnold. "A genial man . . . polite . . . charitable . . . a law-abiding citizen." Oh, gracious, Arnold's shoulders lifted. Were they shaking in mirth? Arnold, "law-abiding"? Well, these days, yes, he was. Don't laugh, Arnold! Don't laugh!

"I now pronounce you man and wife."

They celebrated at the restaurant in Babette's Hotel across the Common, while Mrs. Mason minded the baby. It was a cheerful occasion, and sad memories only joined them once, when Lawless made his short speech after the meal.

"Today has been a day of mixed blessings for me. I am pleased and content to be married to Lottie, the woman I love. And it is a fine thing that I could share it with ye, Eve. But I wish God had seen fit to let me share it with Swiftie, Sam, and Danny, as well, and my beloved guverner most of all." His eyes filled with tears, but he took a deep breath, swallowed quickly, and finished. "Alan once said to me, 'Ye cannot live with the dead, lad. It is fine and proper to remember them with all the love ye bore them, and perhaps the places they had are never quite filled again, but life continues.' " He lifted his glass in the air, and looking upward with shining eyes, said, "Alan, we're doin' our best, as ye would have wanted."

That night, Eve sat alone by the fire. Arnold and Lottie were spending their wedding night at Babette's. She attempted to busy herself by knitting a pair of booties, but her eyes kept lifting to the window, where, in the firelight, she could see snow gathering, little by little, against the glass on the ledge outside. After a while, her knitting fell from her fingers and she sat staring at the fluttering, jerking flames of the fire. She thought of the wedding and Arnold's speech. And finally she thought about Alan. She imagined him, faultless visions of him, striding through her mind as he had through her life. She saw him in the fireglow of their one night of love, how sublime it had been. For a long time she sat staring, reliving the feel of his body, his arms around her, the touch of his fingers, the taste of his mouth.

Soft tears left her eyes and ran in little trickles down her face as she saw him laughing with Danny, and riding through the bush on Freedom. She saw him holding Womballa's hand. She saw him jump down from Freedom's back and leap up the steps at Treehard. She saw him slap Bluey on the back. She saw him come down the gangplank of the *Port Dennison*. She saw him standing in the doorway of the ship's hospital looking down at her. She saw him smiling. She saw his incomparable eyes and then she saw him near the Mayfield coach, dressed in gray, his black boots gleaming, his sun-lightened hair long under his dark hat, his sun-browned hand raised in the air, and standing beside him . . . John Stuart, staring at her across the dark flow of time. . . .

That very same night, snow fell heavily in the west of Scotland north of Rannoch Moor when two travelers and their attendant alighted at Fort William railway station, wrapped in many layers to fight the cold. They passed out from the dim, gaslit platform into the blast of the wind from Loch Linne, and looked for a vehicle to take them the few, lonely miles to their destination.

There was a single dog cart parked at the side of the station, and after inquiring at the inn across the street, the driver was found in the barroom.

"We wish to be taken to Dunain Lodge," Joe said to the driver, a long individual whose legs snaked around a barstool. He sipped his stout and looked Joe up and down, and beyond him to John Stuart, standing by the door. "Weel, it be three miles, blowing snow and sleet. Cost ye a shilling a mile, not a penny less."

It was too much, but Joe agreed to pay it.

They took rooms and left Timothy with the luggage at the inn.

The driver was silent for the entire journey, as the force of the wind hardly allowed conversation. Over an hour later, the stone fence beyond which their objective lay appeared in the swirling mists ahead of them.

John Stuart had no way of letting his mother know he was coming. The miracle of the undersea telegraph cable had only been laid from Great Britain as far as the United States of America and Ceylon, and in any case, it was used only for news of world events.

"Dunain Lodge," the driver called back over his shoulder.

When they reached the front of the house, a large building with Gothic figures looming above them, Joe and John Stuart climbed down. Joe turned to the driver. "We would appreciate if you would wait. We may wish to go back with you."

"Aye. But I'll need to be cooming in out of this 'ere gale."

As they mounted the stone steps, the pale light from the windows of the house fell on them. Joe looked at John Stuart; his face was a mixture of anticipation and apprehension. "Now, m'boy," he said softly, "this will be a great night for both of you."

John Stuart's pulse quickened. At last he was to see his mother, the woman who had given him life. All his years of despising her had rolled away; he was different now. He truly wanted to know her, talk to her, hold her. "Yes. Yes, I hope so, Joe."

As Joe pulled the bell, he put his arm around John Stuart. The door swung open, and a lady in her middle years, wearing a black dress and white apron, looked out into the night. "I canna see you," she said. "Please announce yearselves."

Joe replied, "We are here to see Mrs. Wakeman, Caroline, the old laird's daughter. We have come from Australia. This gentleman is her son. May we come in?"

The woman's eyes widened, and she took a step backward. She crossed herself. "Oh, dear Lord Jesus in Heaven above, preserve us!"

"What is that you say?" Joe stepped over the threshold, bringing John Stuart with him, while the dog cart driver quickly followed into the warm hall.

She was staring at John Stuart in shock. "I didna know as her ladyship had a son. Oh, Lordy me."

John Stuart stepped forward. "May I see her?"

The woman was scrutinizing him, barring the way.

"Look, I've come thirteen thousand miles to see my mother. Please."

Her eyes narrowed in the lamplight. "Aye, it's as ye look like her, got her eyes for certain, ye do. And why would ye be here on a night such as this, I ask, if ye be not who ye say ye be?"

Joe spoke firmly. "Yes, we are who we say, my good woman. Where is Mr. Wakeman's mother?"

She pointed a crooked finger in the air above her head. "In her bed. It's ill she is for sure. Her lungs are proper bad."

"I must see her." John Stuart's voice had the edge of desperation to it, the sound that manifests when a person has waited too long.

The woman nodded. "Ah, all right. Follow me." She turned on her downtrodden heel and led them along the passage and up the stairway, repeating now and then to herself as she trotted on, "A son indeed, a son indeed."

They halted before a large oak door, the metal hinges gleam-

ing in the vague lamplight. The servant woman rapped and
called, "M'lady, may I come in? I've someone here to see you."

A small voice answered, "Yes, Mabel."

John Stuart looked expectantly to Joe. The older man smiled
reassuringly.

As the door swung back, they saw a small figure in a large
bed turn to them. "This gentleman says he is your son, m'lady;
from Australia and all," Mabel said.

The lovely, dark, sad eyes of Caroline Wakeman, so like her
son's, lifted, and a look of consternation covered her pallid face.
At the same time she pushed herself upward. "My son?" The
two words somehow ricocheted in the long wall hangings of the
room, embodying all the grief of a mother who has never known
her only child.

John Stuart almost stumbled in his haste to get to her side.
"Mother, it's truly me. I'm here."

Caroline Wakeman looked intently upon John Stuart. There
was a strange silent moment of recognition, and then her arms
lifted to reach out across thirty-six years to take hold of him, a
love-light reviving in her eyes that had died the day she left him,
a little three-year-old, and stepped out of his life and into the
Mayfield coach.

Three weeks went by. During that time John Stuart hardly
ever left his mother's side, except for one day when, in company
with a local guide, he climbed Ben Nevis to look out over her
lands. He could not climb to the top, for the mountain was snow-
covered, making passage impossible. The sun shone briefly that
day, and the temperature rose marginally. For the middle of
winter, it was a charitable day.

He had met his two surviving uncles and his aunts and cousins, and life had taken on a kindlier note for him, so that as the
days passed, his gentle half smile came more easily.

It was a bitterly cold night when the mother and son sat alone
before a wonderful fire. Joe had gone early to bed, complaining
that his feet were frozen and he must have them on a warming
pan.

John Stuart took his mother's hand in his and said, "Mother,
I have something to do in London soon."

She smiled. While Caroline Wakeman was still frail and the
congestion in her lungs was quite apparent, she had improved
in mind and body from the minute her son had appeared. "Then
you should go."

"I shall return."

She looked intently at him, deeply at him. "John Stuart, to have had you with me these last weeks was beyond my wildest hope. My prayers have been answered. You have rejuvenated me. Do not feel bound to stay or return here if you cannot."

"But now that I have found you, I am loath to leave you."

"What is your business in London, my son?" She said "son" with a feeling of utmost joy; it thrilled her to pronounce the word.

John Stuart's mouth turned down. "Oh, Mother, there is so much in me that is unfulfilled." He looked away and his words came very slowly. "I have told you of the estrangement between Eve and myself, and that she is now in the United States of America."

Caroline Wakeman was no fool, and when John Stuart had given his brief explanation of the sad events in his life, she had been filled with guilt. She had guessed that her son's attitudes toward women, and in particular his wife, had been shaped by her own behavior to his father.

She nodded her head sympathetically. She must help him if she could.

He hesitated before he went on, "I did not tell you everything. There is something I feel I must do for Eve, and to do it, I must go to London."

"Then delay no longer. Go, John Stuart, and when you have completed this thing, perhaps you will come briefly to me again and tell me of it."

John Stuart took his mother in his arms. "Oh I will, Mother, I will."

In London they rented a house in Curzon Street, Mayfair.

On the day after their arrival, they took the letter of introduction given to them by Robert Robinson-Pike before they left Australia, and sought out Forrest Rowell Pty. Ltd., a well-known legal firm. Forrest Rowell was the brother of Robert Robinson-Pike's wife, she and her parents having migrated to Australia fifteen years before.

Mr. Rowell himself greeted them. He was a large man with a wide forehead and intelligent blue eyes. He was aware of the Wakeman name and what it meant, and in convivial manner offered them tea. After these formalities, Joe spoke first. "There is a property in Somerset called Long Moss. We have no idea how big it is; all we do know is that it supports some tenant farmers, and we believe a single lady is the owner. She is a relative of the Fletcher family, in whose hands the estate has been for generations. We wish you to purchase it for Mr. Wakeman.''

Mr. Rowell's eyebrows rose. "And what if the lady does not wish to sell?"

John Stuart leaned forward in his chair. "You have my authority to make her an offer that is overly generous."

Mr. Rowell's eyebrows rose even farther. "May I ask why we are buying it?"

John Stuart held his chin in thought for a moment before he answered, "Mr. Rowell, I hope you will understand, but I wish to attain it first, to know it is mine. Then I shall explain."

If Mr. Rowell deemed this eccentric behavior, he concealed it well. He nodded sagely.

"We would like you to make the purchase immediately," Joe added. "Do whatever you have to do to expedite matters."

Three weeks later, on a wet, miserably cold February day, Mr. Rowell knocked on the door in Curzon Street. Timothy let him in. He carried a large envelope which he had wrapped in leather against the rain, and when he had removed his overcoat, Timothy showed him into the parlor, where a fire crackled cozily in the grate.

John Stuart and Joe entered a minute later, and Forrest Rowell came forward with a gratified smile on his large face. "Congratulations, Mr. Wakeman," he said, holding out his hand to shake John Stuart's. "You are now the owner of the estate of Long Moss, eight hundred and forty acres in Somerset. Oh, and with it comes a freehold of several smaller properties in Wales." He took the envelope from under his arm. "It is a very profitable estate, although I must say you did not get it exactly at bargain price. Here are the deeds, sir."

John Stuart and Joe smiled in unison, and Joe motioned their visitor to a chair and ordered coffee.

"Now, Mr. Wakeman," Mr. Rowell asked, "is there anything more for me to do for you?"

John Stuart inclined his head but did not answer. He glanced at Joe, and the older man replied. "Yes, there is. The matter is far from ended. You come highly recommended to us by Robert Robinson-Pike, whom we trust implicitly, and therefore we are prepared to put our trust in you. As Australia lies three to four months by ship away from these shores, it is unlikely we will ever make the long voyage to this country again." He looked to John Stuart. "At least *I* will not. Thus, we need someone here to manage and maintain the properties that Mr. Wakeman has obtained."

Forrest Rowell smiled calmly. "We do similar things for one or two estates now."

At that moment, Timothy brought in the coffee. When he had poured it and departed, John Stuart broke the silence. "The reason I have bought Long Moss is to hold it in trust for someone who is yet a baby. I want the child to inherit Long Moss when it reaches its majority."

"You say 'it,' Mr. Wakeman. Do you not know the sex of the child?"

"That is correct. I do not."

Mr. Rowell looked slightly startled, and adroitly Joe continued the explanation. "The child is in America, in Boston. As you are aware, Long Moss belonged to the Fletcher family, and as you will be handling the estate's affairs, you should be aware that Sir Graham Fletcher's son, Alan Fletcher, who was the heir, was wrongly accused of a crime and sent to Australia for life, as a convict. Hence, it went to the lady from whom we purchased. Now, in purchasing the estate, we have ensured that Long Moss will return to Alan Fletcher's child."

Mr. Rowell looked at John Stuart with a mixed expression of admiration and surprise. "That's a very commendable deed, sir. Most magnanimous. Mr. Fletcher, the convict, must have been very important to you. Was he a relative, sir?"

Joe actually turned in his chair to see the younger man's eyes cloud for a moment. Joe knew he had never stopped loving Eve and had come to London expressly to buy Long Moss, to make sure that Eve and her child would be taken care of through the years. Joe's heart swelled with pride, and he smiled with love and encouragement at the pensive eyes opposite. A flicker of a sad smile lifted the corner of John Stuart's mouth. Then he turned his eyes to the solicitor. "Alan Fletcher's life and mine were—" he hesitated briefly "—intertwined." He hesitated again. "It is the child's mother who is a relative of mine. I want her to be the recipient of the proceeds from the estate until the child comes of age. I desire a copy of the deeds with the information on a trust that I want you to arrange for her and her child. The originals, I wish taken to her in Boston without delay. Do you have a man you trust to do this?"

Mr. Rowell's eyebrows rose again. Mr. Wakeman wanted *everything* done without delay, as far as he could see. Perhaps it was a colonial trait to push forward so brusquely. He had to think. He took a deep breath. "A man to sail to Boston, you ask? One I can trust, a good man. Well, now, I'm not sure, but one does comes to mind. He is twenty-nine, reliable, has just come out of his time, just acquired his letters. Finnigan McGuire is his name."

John Stuart started. Joe also recognized the name, for he, too, had read every word of the Fletcher trial transcripts.

"Do you know him?" Mr. Rowell asked.

John Stuart shook his head. "No, but did his father have the same name? And was he a barrister-at-law?"

"Yes, that is so, a clever young man who unfortunately was drowned when Finnigan was only a child."

John Stuart closed his eyes for a few seconds in thought as he tapped the polished oak of the armchair with his long fingers. "Mr. Rowell, this is one of those coincidences in life that we say do not happen. It is very appropriate that your young Finnigan McGuire is the man to take the deeds of Alan Fletcher's estate to his child, for Finnigan's father defended Alan Fletcher at his trial in 1849."

Mr. Rowell's eyebrows rose again for an extended period of time. "You don't say!"

"There is one more thing," John Stuart added.

By this time, Forrest Rowell thought he was ready for any pecularity whatsoever.

"The mother of the child must never know that I am her benefactor."

Forrest Rowell actually gulped. He had been wrong; he was not ready for this. "But, Mr. Wakeman, I don't understand."

John Stuart sighed. It was a deeply sorrowful sound, and Joe's heart gave a little lurch in sympathy as his boy continued, "I merely want the papers handed over to the child's mother. It would be helpful if young Finnigan McGuire were to have the impression that someone here in England had arranged for the inheritance. I am very serious about this particular, very serious."

Mr. Rowell was looking quite amazed as Joe completed the meeting with the words "We realize it takes sometimes six weeks for a steamship to cross from here to Boston and back, so Mr. Wakeman and I have decided to return to Scotland in the interim. Can you get Finnigan McGuire on a ship to Boston before the end of this week?''

"Who on earth is this?" Eve looked up as she read the name on the card Lottie gave her. "I have never heard of Mr. Finnigan McGuire, solicitor of Forrest Rowell Pty. Ltd., London."

"Me neither. I wonder what he wants."

"I have a piano lesson at half past ten tomorrow," Eve answered. "So he had better be quick with his business, whatever it is."

The following day, Finnigan indeed proved swift, for Eve was so overwhelmed by the nature of his assignment, he soon took leave of her; and when little Rosy Daniels arrived for her piano lesson, she was sent home. After Finnigan had gone, Eve sat for a long time staring at the deeds to Long Moss.

When the visitor had given her the envelope and she had read the accompanying letter, she was speechless. It was like a miracle. She was to receive the proceeds from Alan's estate until her child came of age and inherited. She had looked again and again from the letter to Mr. McGuire's face and back down to the letter again. It took quite some time for her to believe it. Finally she spoke. "I cannot comprehend this. It is like something out of a dream. I am overcome. Who is responsible for this . . . magnanimous deed?"

Finnigan's long brow, so reminiscent of his father's, wrinkled in concern as he replied, "Actually, madam, I never met your benefactor. Mr. Rowell was particular that I did not have the gentleman's name. But he did mention that it was someone in England, a gentleman, important, of the upper classes, I believe. Probably titled, I would say, the respectful way he spoke of him."

Eve's mind was in turmoil. There was only one person she could imagine it was. Yes, it had to be. A man who cared enough about the injustice done to Alan Fletcher. A man who had gone back to England and cleared Alan's name, had a posthumous pardon bestowed. A man of the upper classes, rich and titled, who could afford to do this . . . Sir Rutherford Blake. Oh, how wonderful. How could she ever express her gratitude?

When she had finally calmed her racing mind, she offered Finnigan some tea, which he had the good sense to refuse. He could see the woman needed to be alone.

"I shall not take up any more of your time," he said, rising to his feet.

Eve was trying to talk in a self-possessed manner, but her heart was racing. "Yes, thank you, Mr. McGuire, I would appreciate being left alone." Then her befuddled mind realized she was not being very hospitable. "Oh, you mentioned earlier that you are here only briefly."

"Yes, I leave for Plymouth the day after tomorrow."

"Would you come back to tea tomorrow? I shall be more able to be congenial then, I am sure."

At three o'clock the next day, Eve and Finnigan took tea together. Lottie brought in the refreshments and remained to be introduced before she left them. They spoke of the journey from England and of ships and the sea. When he stood to leave, Eve handed him the letter she had written the night before to Sir Rutherford Blake. "Please give this to your superior, Mr. Rowell. I am sure he will be able to get it to its destination."

Finnigan took it and bowed over her hand. "Certainly, madam."

At the front door, he hesitated. There was something he wished to tell this lady. "Mrs. Fletcher, there is a connection between myself and yourself."

"Really?"

"Yes. Mr. Rowell said that it was very fitting that I be the one to carry the deeds of the Long Moss estate to you, for it was my father who defended your husband at his trial in Southampton in 1849. I was named after my father."

Eve shook her head in wonder. "That is astonishing. The son has in effect completed what his father set out to do. Yes, yes, how appropriate." She stood looking into the honest gray eyes, and then she said something that shocked both herself and Finnigan. "While I loved him beyond words, I was never married to Mr. Fletcher."

Finnigan was a well-bred young man, but he could not help being startled. He had been commissioned to bring the deeds of Long Moss across the Atlantic to Mrs. Fletcher of 32 Russell Street, Beacon Hill, Boston. He knew the story of Alan Fletcher and the wrong done to him. This act undid some of the wrong. But always he had assumed that the mother of the child had been married to the father.

"I see," he said.

Eve held out her hand. "Thank you, manifoldly, for the part you have played in this charitable and noble-minded deed. Thank you and good-bye."

Finnigan took Eve's hand once more and shook it. "All the best to you," he said softly before he turned away.

As Eve closed the door, Lottie spoke behind her. "Why on earth did ye tell him that?"

"I don't know. I am mixed up, Lottie. This is a miracle. That man helped it happen. I will never see him again, and I wanted to be honest with him."

Lottie shook her head. "Sometimes you do the oddest things, Miss Eve." Then she sniffed. "Who would have believed Sir Rutherford would turn up trumps? What a simply marvelous man." She pursed her lips in memory before she added, "And to think there was a time I was athinking him quite the reverse."

During his stay in London, John Stuart had made inquiries about Sir Rutherford. He was working for the London police force at Scotland Yard but spent much of his spare time interviewing prisoners who had pleaded innocent to charges of major crimes, examining their records and studying their files. He had been so affected by Alan Fletcher, he had determined never to let another innocent man suffer.

They were disappointed to find he was holidaying in the south of France with his new wife, a woman named Coralea. He was not expected back in England until April. John Stuart was determined to remain in Great Britain and spend more time with his mother, at least until he knew that the Long Moss deeds were in Eve's hands, so with luck, he would yet see Sir Rutherford. He said so to Joe as they traveled back to London by coach after a day's outing to Windsor.

Joe nodded. "What do you intend to do if young Finnigan accomplishes his task?"

John Stuart did not reply straightaway; he sat with his head turned, looking through the window into the gloom of the overcast night.

"It depends on my mother."

Joe sighed. "I know you, m'boy, and I'm guessing you have an idea to take your mother home to Mayfield."

John Stuart did not speak.

Joe leaned forward in the darkness. "Your mother is not strong enough to make the long voyage to Australia, son."

"Nevertheless, I shall ask her. I am so glad to have found her that I would like her near me always."

This time Joe did not speak at once. He remained silently musing for some minutes. Then he bent forward to touch John Stuart's knee. "M'boy, don't you want to see Eve?"

When John Stuart finally answered, his voice was controlled, but there was that edge of troubled emotion in it that Joe recognized so well.

"I think of it constantly. But if Finnigan has done his job, then I know she will always be well looked after. I am content to have found my mother."

"Content?" Joe sat back and folded his arms. "Yes, finding Caroline was wonderful, and I know it has made you happy, but would you not be even more content if you finished this whole thing properly? If you saw Eve one more time and made your peace with her?"

"What? Go to Boston, do you mean?"

Joe leaned forward again and this time took up his boy's hands in his own. He spoke slowly, reflectively. "Yes, that is what I mean. I have known you all your life, and you cannot hide things from me. I'm certain you want to see her, to make your peace with her, too; you just have not yet admitted it. Now, Eve made choices that I do not agree with; they were mistakes, to my mind. But I know you have never stopped loving her. Didn't I ride beside you through hundreds of miles of bush trying to find her? Look, m'boy, I want what you want, and I believe you want to see her; give this whole sorry business some sort of completion."

"But, old man, if I arrive suddenly, she might suspect that I'm the one who has sent her the deeds, and the last thing I want from her is any damned gratitude."

Joe continued to grip his hands tightly. "M'boy. You know full well that Finnigan was told no lies, but what he was led to believe was that Eve's benefactor was a wealthy Englishman of the upper classes. She will not suspect it is you." He let go John Stuart's hands to ruffle his hair as he often did when they were alone. He had said his piece and he leaned back into his seat.

A few seconds later, John Stuart spoke softly. "I will consider it." Then he called out the window to the driver, who halted the coach near Prince's Gate on the southern side of the park. "I shall walk the remainder of the way, Joe."

"There's a chill wind, m'boy, and it might rain again. Are you sure?"

"Yes, I am," he answered, jumping down from the coach. "Have Tim pour me a brandy to warm me on my return."

The coach squeaked away, and John Stuart walked into the park. There was a ghostly moon illuminating the stark limbs of the leafless trees. He pulled his overcoat more tightly around him as he trudged across the sodden earth of Rotten Row and came to a halt by the Serpentine. In the dreary light of a gas lamp, he stood staring at the floes on the surface of the water.

He turned and took the path leading up by the bandstand to Park Lane. There was an ache in his chest as he strode along in the wind. He would always love her. When he had realized she carried Alan Fletcher's child, it had cut into his soul, but he had lived with that for eight months now, and the pain had dulled. At times he even thought that having a child to love and cherish would be good for her. He had done his best now for her and her child. He lifted his gloved hand to his eyes. He wished by all that was sacred that the child had been his. But life was not like that. Life was "a tale, Told by an idiot, full of sound and fury, Signifying nothing."

Joe thought he should go to Boston and see her face-to-face. Dear Joe, who wanted only what was best for him. John Stuart knew the man was tired and wanted to go home, and yet he was willing to wait with him here while he tarried with his mother and then to travel on to Boston. How lucky he was to have Joe.

As he reached Park Lane and stood waiting for some carriages to pass, he thought of Mayfield. He should go home, home to the imperfect consolation of his beautiful rolling hills and valleys. Tomorrow he would ask his mother to come with him. He truly rejoiced with the reward of knowing her at last. Yes, perhaps he could find some sort of peace back there.

He stepped into the street to hurry across Park Lane between the vehicles. A fine rain was falling as he passed the newspaper seller on the corner of Curzon Street, but he was hardly aware of anything, for in his mind he watched a dream woman coming across the Bathurst park at twilight. When he arrived at the three stone steps that led up to his front door, he took off his glove and put his hand inside his coat and touched the thing he always carried, the olive-branch hairpin she had left behind on her pillow the morning she had gone away.

When he entered the warm, comfortable hall of his house, Joe was waiting with a brandy for him. "I'm glad you're home, m'boy. I see it has begun to rain."

John Stuart managed a meager smile. "Has it? Yes, I suppose it has." He noticed the dampness on his overcoat as Timothy removed it for him. He took the brandy and followed Joe into the parlor.

"Joe?"

"Yes?"

"I want to leave as early as possible for Scotland tomorrow."

The following day they alighted at Fort William railway station for the second time and traveled with the same taciturn individual in the same dog cart to Dunain Lodge. The wind was as bitter as ever.

Caroline Wakeman welcomed them with open arms and a smiling face.

The next morning at breakfast John Stuart asked his mother to return to Australia with him.

Her face crinkled into a sad smile. "My dear, dear boy," she said, taking up his hand, "if I were younger, hardier, I might say yes, but I am not. You have given me new life by coming here to me." She looked briefly across the table to Joe. "All those years when I wrote to dear Thelma, this is more than I ever dreamed of, but no, I must stay and you must go, for your life is on Mayfield. Do not think of me, do not worry for me. I am happier than I thought possible. My life is very comfortable, Mabel takes fine care of me, and your only two uncles are keen to live elsewhere, so Dunain Lodge is mine. I need for nothing, and now God has given me the memory of you to sustain me through the time left to me. My prayers have been answered. I am content."

"It's just so hard, having found you again, to think of losing you."

Now her finger rose and wagged at him. "John Stuart, my dear son, you are not losing me. I shall always be present in your heart." She smiled gently and took up his hand. "But tell me of your London business if you will. I know it was to do with Eve."

So then he explained what he had set in motion, and she listened silently. He finished by saying, "Joe thinks that if all has gone well with Finnigan and she has the deeds, I should go to Boston and make peace with her."

A look of compassion came to her face. "Darling, Joe is right. You should. Go and make your peace with Eve, no matter what the outcome. Even though she does not realize it, she is very greatly loved, and you, my son, are the finest of men. No wonder Joe is so proud of you."

"Does it show?" Joe asked.

Caroline Wakeman laughed, gently. "Oh yes, Joe, it does."

* * *

By the third week of their stay, the weather was slightly more equable, and Joe and John Stuart often took Caroline for exercise. While she managed to get around the small garden near the terrace, she coughed a lot and tired quickly and was never able to go farther.

All too soon the day came when they had to return to London to meet Finnigan. They stood atop the stone steps beneath the watching gargoyles as they had on the night of their first arrival. They would catch the train from Fort William at one in the afternoon.

The air smelled damp, and a wind was rising. Caroline leaned on her cane. Around her neck, next to the Franciscan cross she always wore, sparkled a splendid gold chain and heart-shaped locket, which John Stuart had commissioned in London. It contained his likeness and was inscribed with the words "My darling mother found." Unconsciously she raised her hand to clutch it as Joe stepped over to her and said, "Good-bye, dear Caroline, and thank you for your hospitality."

She hugged him. "Good-bye, old friend. Tell Thelma I shall write as often as I am able, and give her my love."

When John Stuart took her in his arms, his pulse raced. He had found her, and all too soon must give her up again.

"Remember, my darling," she said, "you will never again be without me."

John Stuart kissed her hair. "I shall write often, Mother, and I shall think of you all the time."

As they stepped into the dog cart that would once again take them to the railway station, Caroline Wakeman's controlled voice sounded, "Go to Boston, John Stuart, my dearest, go and settle things."

They had not been back in Curzon Street for five days before Joe came to John Stuart one afternoon, holding a letter.

"Timothy just gave me this, m'boy. It's from Forrest Rowell." He handed a small, dark envelope to John Stuart.

Inside was a short note.

Inns of Court
London
April 26th, 1867

Dear Messrs. Wakeman and Larmer,
   This is to advise you of the safe return this day to London of Mr. Finnigan McGuire. He has carried out your wishes.

*With your permission, I shall wait on you at ten o'clock
tomorrow morning.*

> Sincerely,
> Forrest Rowell

"And another thing," Joe said as John Stuart lifted his eyes
from the note. "Another message has come today to say that
Rutherford is back in London."

The next morning, sharply at ten o'clock, Timothy answered
the doorbell and Forrest Rowell was ushered in. He told them
all had gone well and that Finnigan had delivered the deeds to
Mrs. Fletcher and that she had been quite overcome.

Only Joe noticed John Stuart's almost imperceptible flinch
when Forrest Rowell said, "Mrs. Fletcher."

"And did she ask who sent the deeds?" Joe prompted.

"Yes. He told her exactly what he had been instructed to say.
I am here to tell you, the lady in question must have believed
him, for on his departure the next day, she gave him this." Mr.
Rowell withdrew a letter from inside his coat and handed it to
John Stuart. It was the letter Eve had given Finnigan on his
departure. She had addressed it: "To Sir Rutherford Blake, per
kind favor of Mr. McGuire and his Associates."

"I assume you will know what to do with it, Mr. Wakeman?"

John Stuart put it down on the sofa beside him. "Yes, we shall
be seeing Rutherford. You may leave it with us."

Then Forrest Rowell informed them of Eve's situation. "She
teaches music . . . piano, and she lives with a married couple.
Finnegan saw no sign of the child, but it was obvious that there
was one, for there were baby's toys about."

John Stuart nodded slowly. His face was expressionless, but
his chest hurt, and the ache was filling him. "Anything else?"
he forced himself to say.

"He said she was quite in control the second day, unlike the
day before. And he told me of an odd incident when he was
leaving her."

"Oh?" Joe interjected. "What was that?"

"He was at the door, apparently departing. He said he informed her of what I had told him, which was that his own father
had defended Alan Fletcher at his trial nearly twenty years ago.
Finnigan said he referred to Alan Fletcher as her 'husband,' and
she answered with the words 'While I loved Alan Fletcher, I

was never married to him.' '' Forrest Rowell waited to see what effect his words would have on his two listeners. Joe looked to John Stuart and saw his boy struggle to remain impassive as his nervous fingers rapped in telltale fashion on the edge of the armchair.

"Did you know this?" Mr. Rowell asked.

"We did," Joe replied.

John Stuart stood and walked to the fire. His back was to the room as he spoke. "Mr. Rowell, you will be handling the estate of Long Moss probably for decades to come, and we will remain in communication. It is time I was completely honest with you." He turned around, and a succession of expressions traveled quickly across his strong features. "It is true that the lady who calls herself Mrs. Fletcher was never married to Alan Fletcher. She was . . . is . . . married to me."

"Ah, so that's it," the legal man said with a quite audible sigh.

When Forrest Rowell left the house in Curzon Street, he was acquainted, in essence, with the history of John Stuart and Eve. He would keep Mr. Wakeman's trust—that was his duty, and part of his occupation—but he could not understand the man. "You're a better man than me, John Stuart Wakeman," he said to himself as he turned the corner into Berkeley Square. "If my wife left me to have another man's child, I'd be damned in hell before I'd do what you have done."

The day before they departed for Boston, John Stuart and Joe spent some pleasant hours with Sir Rutherford at his family home in Kent. It was the first day they had felt spring in the air. The sun shone, and the breeze did not have the chill of a week earlier. As the carriage passed up the drive from the main road, Joe pointed to a herd of deer running in Sir Rutherford's park.

The police detective met them at the steps of his ancestral home, and they hugged as old friends do. A minute later, out came Lady Coralea, a fine-looking woman with curly, auburn hair and large hazel eyes. After the introductions, she took them through the beautiful, old house and out into the sunken garden, where a sumptuous luncheon awaited them.

Two hours later, the three men rode along the Medway River and talked of old times. On the return ride, they reined in at the edge of a small forest of oaks atop a long, grassy ridge.

They dismounted and John Stuart walked a few steps to the bole of one of the oaks and tapped upon it with his riding crop before he looked back to Rutherford. "My friend, I have something to tell you."

The detective policeman smiled. "You have told me much already."

"Yes, but this concerns Eve."

He related the events of acquiring Long Moss and how he had constructed the trust for Eve and her son, and of Finnigan's journey to Boston. "So you see, old friend, we believe Eve thinks you are the man who purchased Long Moss. I have a letter here from her, which she asked McGuire to deliver to you. Of course, I have not opened it, but I suspect I know the contents." He took it from his breast pocket and gave it to him.

Sir Rutherford read the letter, then handed it to John Stuart. "Here, my friend. She does indeed believe it is me who has endowed her so very munificently."

John Stuart read.

> 32 Russell St.
> Beacon Hill
> Boston
> 1st April, 1867

Dear Sir Rutherford,

A legal gentleman, by name, Mr. Finnigan McGuire, has been to see me today, and now, in my hands, I hold the deeds to the estate of Long Moss in Somerset, England. I cannot believe what you have done. It is so benevolent, so magnanimous, so wonderful.

For you see, Sir Rutherford, I realize the benefactor must be yourself, although I understand you wish to remain anonymous. Not only did you have Alan Fletcher posthumously pardoned (a most honorable act), but you have returned his inheritance to his son, and in doing so, have generously made provision for me as well. For my son I accept your bountiful offer. It is only right that he should inherit his father's goods and lands. But I am confused by your extraordinary generosity to me. It is not proper for me to take the proceeds from the Fletcher estate. I manage to keep myself, as I have always done, and I have wonderful friends. Therefore, any money I receive in beneficiary, I shall place into a bank to ensure it will be used only to enhance my son's life.

Sir Rutherford, we were never friends, you and I. There was always reserve between us.

*I misjudged you badly. Forgive me. It was more than enough
that you cleared Alan Fletcher's name.*

*Yours Faithfully,
Evelyn May*

"Odd that she signed no surname," Rutherford said when
John Stuart lifted his eyes.

John Stuart handed over the letter for Joe to read as he answered, "Yes, it is odd." He sighed. "So the child is a boy."

Rutherford took hold of John Stuart's shoulder. "My friend,
I am relieved that she thinks it more than enough to have cleared
the bushranger's name, for that was the extent of my doing. You
are an amazing man, John Stuart, to do as you have done." His
eyes narrowed in habitual scrutiny as he added, "I wonder if
she will ever realize how very greatly loved she is."

John Stuart met Rutherford's eyes. He shook his head as if to
say it did not matter. After some seconds, he spoke. "Even
when I duped myself into thinking ill of her, somehow I loved
her through it all." He turned quickly away and moved a few
paces to look down across the Medway to the patchwork quilt
of the fields beyond. The breeze had turned a little cooler, and
clouds now drifted in front of the sun.

Sir Rutherford's high forehead wrinkled. "I can't allow it,
you know," he said.

"What?"

"For her to think it is I who have been so beneficent."

John Stuart turned back to him. "I thought as much, my
friend. But even if you tell her it is not you, I must ask you never
to divulge the truth. Would you be so kind as to wait a few
weeks before you answer her? Do not write back posthaste. I
want to . . . go to her first. I leave for Boston tomorrow. Will
you do me the very great favor of giving me time to see her
before you reply to this letter? I should like to be departed from
Boston when it arrives."

Sir Rutherford took up John Stuart's hand. "You are the best
of men, my good friend. I don't agree with your decision, but
shall do as you request."

THIRTY-NINE
Realization

May 1867

May in Boston is a pleasant time. The wind has lost its chill, the trees are in blossom, the flowers were budding, and the days are lengthening.

A comforting breeze blew across the Boston Common, so that the woman who walked swiftly along the graveled path opened her cape to let it cool her.

She had been to Boylston Street, on the far side of the Common, where she taught piano at a private home one evening a week. She was a little later than usual, but she was not concerned, for Lottie was in Russell Street now to take care of things, and she did not need to rely on Mrs. Mason's good nature so much. It was odd to think that she lived at 32 Russell Street, Boston; in Australia, she had lived at 22 Russell Street, Bathurst. For a few moments she reflected on Bathurst and Father and Mother and how serene her life had been then. She thought of the day she had burst into Father's study and met John Stuart. She shook her head gently at the memory.

The sky was beginning to darken, and she quickened her step as she came to the black row of pine trees that ran along the gravel path.

Suddenly she heard someone call her name, "Eve? Eve . . ."

She halted as if petrified. She knew that voice intimately but it was impossible. Slowly she turned. A tall figure stepped out of the ebony shadows of the pine trees not six feet away.

"John Stuart?"

"Eve."

"I don't understand. How can this be?"

He stood looking at the face he had so longed to see, and his heart thumped wildly. It was like a dream to be with her again. Greedily his eyes took her in. She was the same and yet not the same. Her face was more angular than he remembered, and her brown eyes seemed darker and more enigmatic. Yet her features still held the gentility and beauty and grace he knew so well.

It was an awkward speech he made to her there in the dying day. "Eve, I have come to see you. So much has happened. I am here to make peace with you, if I can. The truth is, I tried to do this before you left Australia. I wanted to from the very moment you left Mayfield . . . left me . . . and even before that. I searched for you." His long fingers made a hopeless gesture in the air. "For many weary months, I searched."

Eve was in shock. It was as if he had risen out of the ground beside her. She took a deep breath and regarded him. Never, could she have believed this would happen, that John Stuart would come to Boston. The rising wind lifted her cape and blew it forward to touch his trousers. She shook her head. It was a strange, complicated, pleasant feeling, looking up at him again. "I don't know what to say."

"You need not say anything. I have simply come here to make amends."

"John Stuart," she said with a sigh, "what happened between us was not your fault alone. Truly it was not. I was not always honest with you. We both made mistakes."

"Yes. I know about Clare."

This surprised her. "I see."

"I was very wrong about all that . . . all that business with Lake. I saw you and my mother as one, and I did not give you a chance. When finally I wanted to right things between us, on Boxing Day morning, I came to you, but you were gone."

A tingle of sorrow rose in her chest. Poor John Stuart. Yes, he had suffered, too, and greatly, she could see. She was looking at him closely, examining him. He looked older but was just as handsome, just as imposing.

He took a deep breath. "I believe that you must know of the posthumous pardon for . . . Mr. Fletcher. Sir Rutherford Blake was instrumental in having it conferred. He was untiring in his efforts to have it granted."

"Yes, I know about it." She looked away up to Beacon Street where a lamplighter moved slowly along. It was peculiar to hear him call Alan "Mr. Fletcher." She brought her eyes back to his. "I now realize Sir Rutherford is a most remarkable man. Lottie told me about the pardon."

"Yes, I heard Lottie Thatcher had gone abroad. I thought she must have come to you."

She was still having difficulty believing he was here. It was weird, overwhelming. Her voice sounded odd and thin to her own ears. "She and her husband live with me. He, too, you will remember. His name is Arnold Drake, but you would know him as Lawless Drake. He is . . . my best friend."

Of course, "her brother," as the Pinkerton men had called him; the last of the Fletcher band.

It was darkening around them now, but neither really noticed, each was so taken with the presence of the other.

"How did you find me?" she asked suddenly.

He moved off the path to let two people pass by before he answered. "There are men who do such things now . . . find people . . . for a fee."

She thought how diligent he had been to know of such people, to actually find her here, but then, he was always thorough in everything. He had always done things well.

"Eve, I know I wronged you. I am truly sorry, but you wronged me, too. I have been wanting to know for so long. That day in Cowra? At first I thought you had been kidnapped by Alan Fletcher. Eve . . . you were not, were you?"

She was looking up into his eyes, his pensive, brown eyes, in the gloom of dusk. "No, John Stuart, I was not."

She noticed the fleeting expression of pain that crossed his face, and she found herself not wanting to hurt him, wanting to explain how it really had been. "John Stuart, please, do not misunderstand. I was unconscious in Cowra when Alan found me . . . took care of me. In fact, he wanted to bring me home to you, but I believed you and I were forever estranged. What happened was not *anyone's* fault . . . it just happened."

She thought he made a bitter sound as he asked, "Did you love him very deeply?"

Unconsciously she half raised her hand between herself and John Stuart. "Yes. Very deeply."

He said nothing.

She sighed, closing her eyes. "John Stuart, I am a mother. I have a son; Alan Fletcher's son."

"Yes, I know," he said.

They stood, eyes locked, until he spoke again. "Perhaps you should be on your way home. It's getting dark."

She nodded. "It does grow late."

"This way?" He pointed up the steps.

"Yes."

They moved off together in silence. Under the lamp on the corner of Joy Street, they halted. The gentle wind was still blowing, but was cooler now. She pulled her cape around her.

"I live there," she said, pointing up the hill.

"Yes." He looked keenly at her, studying her face again; the face of his sleepless nights and dream-filled imaginings. "We have survived, Eve, you and I. I have wondered about you every day. Are you happy?"

For some reason, she shivered. "Ah, John Stuart as happy as it is possible for me to be. I have my son; that makes me happy. Are you happy?"

And now he actually smiled. He was thinking of having found his mother and how that had brought him true joy. He wanted dearly to tell Eve about it, but he could not. She must never know he had been to Great Britain.

His smile remained. "I am happy to have seen you, cleared things between us a little." He looked away, pointing up the hill. "Come. I will see you to your door."

"No, it is not necessary. But thank you."

They stood looking at each other.

"All right," he replied, reluctantly.

"Before you go," she said, "how is Thelma?"

"She is well. She was always your true friend."

She nodded. "And Joe?"

"He is here with me."

Yes, yes, of course he would be. "And Mayfield, how is Mayfield?"

Now he wanted to say, *Not the same without you*, but he did not. He answered, "As beautiful as ever."

She thought of Mayfield then: the glorious rolling hills and valleys; the morning rays breaking through the branches of the trees of the park; the Lachlan wending its way through the orchards and crops. John Stuart must long for it, she knew. He loved it so. "How long . . . do you remain in Boston?"

He shrugged his shoulders. "Not long. I don't know."

Silence fell. It was very quiet under the dim streetlight. No horses or carriages passed by. They both felt it, the unreality of this little slice of time as they stood regarding each other.

Suddenly she put out her hand to him, and he took it. She

was very aware of his touch, the sensation of his palm on hers. "Would you care to come to tea tomorrow?"

He did not answer immediately, but continued looking intently at her until he dropped her hand and nodded. "What time should I come?"

"I teach music in the afternoon. Would five o'clock be all right?"

He nodded. "I'll be there."

Another smile broke across his mouth. She had always liked his smile; she saw in it what she used to believe was the benevolent essence of him. Involuntarily she smiled back before she turned and walked away into the night.

He felt a surge of sadness. He loved her so, but she seemed so in command of herself, with the same strength of character and spirit she had always shown. He stood under the lamp until he could see her no more, then he crossed the street to descend into the darkened Common. He put his hand into his breast pocket and touched the olive-branch hairpin, then he strode on in the night.

When Eve came to the front door of her home, she hesitated on the doorstep. John Stuart was here in Boston. It was hard to believe. Such strange things were happening lately: the appearance of Mr. McGuire with Sir Rutherford's wonderful gift a few months ago, and now John Stuart's arrival all the way from Australia. He had tracked her down, halfway around the globe, to make his peace with her. "How truly amazing he is," she said softly as she opened the door. Inside, Lottie and Lawless appeared from the kitchen.

"Eve," Lottie said, concern in her eyes. "We were just beginning to aworry about ye."

The expression on Eve's face was so extraordinary, they came quickly to her. "What has happened?" Lawless asked.

She did not reply immediately. She took off her cape and put her satchel on the hall stand before she spoke. "I'm not sure I believe it myself yet. Come into the parlor. I've something astonishing to tell you."

John Stuart's appearance evoked so many recollections for Eve that she spent the night recounting the years gone by: her mother and the wasting disease; the death of her father on the voyage from America to New South Wales; her exacting teenage years in Sydney town; Clare's dying of consumption; her marriage and life at Mayfield; the terrible experience with Lake and the rejection of her by John Stuart; her fight for life at Treehard and all the days spent there; the deaths of Father and Mother; the loss of Alan and the struggle to continue on without him; and her lonely pregnancy here in Boston, with dear Arnold. No, life had not been easy, but she was resilient, and she was strong. These were the experiences of her existence, the events that had made her who she was today. She had survived. Hadn't John Stuart said something about survival tonight? *We have survived, Eve . . . you and I.* Well, that was true, but his life had been gentle in comparison with hers. Yet he had changed. She had seen that tonight. He had matured; he was not at all judgmental or censorious.

She felt a sensation of guilt. To think he had come to see her at Mayfield on that fateful Boxing Day to make amends, and she had left just a few short hours before. . . . How odd, how very chancefully odd. If she had remained merely one more day . . .

Before she went to bed, she stood holding the side of her son's cot, looking at him in the flickering lamplight. How like Alan he was. Already he had startlingly beautiful eyes. "You shall inherit what is rightfully yours, my darling," she said softly. "That is the miracle."

She left the cot and walked to the window. She looked out into the blackness and pictured Alan. *My wonderful Alan . . . your lands will return to your son.* She saw his face. How desperately she missed him. Tears rose to her eyes, then her mind played the trick that it often did, and Alan's face changed; it was her wedding day, and the coach was being held up. There, side by side, stood Alan and John Stuart.

When John Stuart came the following day, he remained an hour. It was a unique time for both of them, filled with drifting thoughts and memories, delicate, sensitive, and singular. Lottie served tea and departed quickly. Later, she confided to Eve. "He does look so regal, doesn't he? Always was, but now he's sort of sad-looking; makes him more handsome, to my way of thinking."

Eve had been particular with Lottie. Once she had served tea, she was to take the baby out for a walk. Somehow, she wanted to save John Stuart any discomfiture that seeing her son might bring.

They had spoken of many things and she asked many questions about Thelma and Stephanie, Baines, Dr. Douglas, the Hennessys, the Watsons, and Mrs. Smith. They were all still with John Stuart, all still at Mayfield. She felt very peculiar when he told her of Daydee's death. "It was on her twenty-first birthday. Terrible for Joe and Thel."

She found it hard to think of Daydee gone; all that useless energy the girl had expended in vicious hatred. "Oh, Daydee, why?" she said to herself.

They conversed not as old friends would, but not as strangers would either. When John Stuart looked at his fob watch and said, "I've been here an hour. It's time I left," Eve realized it had not been an awkward hour at all.

"How long did the ship take from Sydney?" she asked as John Stuart stood.

"What's that?"

"Your voyage here. Did you come around the Horn or the Cape Colony?"

She thought he hesitated before he answered, "Around the Cape, yes, and then across the Atlantic. A hundred days or so."

"It's a long voyage, isn't it?"

He nodded and, turning, walked out into the hall. He had answered her question truthfully about his route to America; he had merely omitted to say he went to Great Britain first.

She followed him as he retrieved his hat from the stand and opened the front door. He tipped his hat and walked out.

"John Stuart," she called, and he turned on the top step to face her, "I have no idea how long you are in Boston, but if you are still in town on Saturday . . . perhaps we could dine here, together? You and Joe and me."

"And what of Lottie and her husband?"

Eve looked inquiringly at him. "What of them?"

"They live with you. They are your day-to-day companions. Joe and I will be happy to dine with you *all* on Saturday."

It was a pleasant meal. Lottie had worked untiringly to clean and tidy the small house, and she had managed to haggle with a street vendor and purchase a fresh hen, a real treat in Russell Street. With the help of Mrs. Mason, she had made vegetable soup, roast hen, and a lemon pie.

They had only four chairs, so Lottie sat on a kitchen stool brought into the parlor. John Stuart talked to Arnold about Boston. He was very knowledgeable about the city, for someone who had just arrived. For a long time they discussed electricity and the experiments being done on electric tramcars while an interested Lottie listened. Joe and Eve talked of Thelma and

Mayfield. When he mentioned Daydee, she could see the suffering in his face.

"I'm so sorry, Joe," she said.

He nodded sadly. "Yes, my little girl is gone, but at least I've still got m'boy." He nodded in John Stuart's direction as he added, "And he's the best there is in this world."

Dear Joe, dear, loyal Joe.

It was close to eleven o'clock when they departed. They made their good-nights on the doorstep, and Lottie and Lawless returned to the house, while Joe went ahead a few paces, leaving John Stuart alone with Eve.

As he took her hand in good-night, he said something utterly unexpected. "Once again, I did not see your son."

Surprise registered in Eve's face. "I did not think you would want to see him. Tonight he sleeps next door with our neighbor."

"Eve . . ." There was a disappointed tone in the way he said her name. "Many months ago, in your garden bower under the poinciana tree, I accepted that you and Alan Fletcher had a child." His eyes appeared almost black in the pale light from the entry hall. "You need not hide him from me if we meet again." He retained her hand. "In fact, if you agree, I shall come to see him tomorrow or the next day." He increased the pressure on her palm momentarily before he let it go and followed Joe into the night.

When she closed the door, she stood there a few moments contemplating what John Stuart had said and thinking just how very enjoyable the dinner had been, before she passed into the kitchen to find Lottie and Lawless washing up.

Lawless half turned to her. "Joe's a nice old bloke."

"Yes . . . and?"

"Well, Eve, the fact is, we both liked John Stuart Wakeman, didn't we, Lottie, love?"

"Yes, we did. There's no astanding on ceremony with him and nothing snobbish about him at all."

Eve's eyes had a thoughtful, faraway expression in them as she looked from one to the other. "No, there never was," she answered quietly.

John Stuart did not come the next day. It was the day after, on the Monday evening, that Eve heard the knock on her front door.

Neither Lottie nor Lawless were home, and she was playing

with her son on the living room floor. She answered the door holding him in her arms.

For some seconds, John Stuart stood there regarding them motionlessly. Then he smiled his crooked smile. "I see him at last."

"Won't you come in?"

She was strangely disappointed when he said, "No, I won't stay." The child wriggled in her arms, and she put him down. He took a few steps and sat on the stone entry, his head tilted, watching John Stuart.

John Stuart looked from infant to mother. "I saw his father only once, but the child has his eyes."

Up into Eve's head came the habitual vision of the single time John Stuart had seen Alan: in the bush, on their wedding day, when she had watched them both side by side. She shivered now as she had shivered then. "Yes, he does," she answered.

Her son had crawled to John Stuart's boot and was touching it. He bent and patted the soft, fair curls of the little one's head, which gave Eve an odd feeling.

"What have you named him?" John Stuart asked, squatting down beside him.

"Christopher."

John Stuart looked up quickly, then after a few seconds, he said in an indifferent tone, "I suppose there could be only one *Alan* Fletcher."

"Yes." She said it so softly, he almost thought she had not spoken.

He tried to smile, but he could not.

Her son was now making happy noises and hitting his small hand on the shining boot in front of him. She watched as John Stuart held out a finger and Christopher took hold of it. John Stuart continued to look at her son, and now his voice broke with emotion. "Christopher is a good, strong name. You will grow up a good, strong boy." He ruffled Christopher's hair again in a lingering movement before he stood up and tipped his hat to Eve. With a final look down at the child, he walked away.

John Stuart had been hurt when she had said "yes" to his statement about Alan; she had seen that quite clearly. How hard it must have been for him to see her with her child, the child that could have been his. He was being so accepting, so wonderful, her heart felt quite heavy for him.

She fell quickly to sleep that night and dreamed of riding

across Mayfield on Moonlight, but in the early hours of the
morning, she woke and lay for a long time looking into the
darkness around her. Christopher was sleeping deeply in his
little bed beside her. She did not know at what point she fell
back to sleep, but she awoke to the most brilliant sunshine and
a day of warmth and cheer.

That morning she went to the Common with Lottie and Christopher, for she had no music classes until the afternoon. They
spread a blanket on the grass near a hedge just bursting into
blossom, and Lottie tatted a lace doily while Eve read the newspaper. On and off, they played with Christopher, and Lottie was
giving him his morning bottle of orange juice when Eve stood
up. "If you don't mind, dear, I shall just go for my walk. Christopher should sleep a little soon."

Eve started off at a brisk pace. She took a walk most days, a
habit she had always kept. She was soon across the Common
and found herself over in the Public Garden, where she walked
along until she halted to look through the trees to Arlington
Street. There stood the Regency, the best hotel in Boston. The
facade was very classical-looking, and men in uniform were
darting about. She knew it was where John Stuart was staying,
although she had never been inside.

She had been standing there a couple of minutes when a voice
behind her said, "Eve." She turned around to find John Stuart.

"My goodness, what a surprise. I have been with Lottie and
Christoper; they are over in the Common." She pointed.

He smiled his half smile, taking off his fashionable hat. "How
lovely to see you." He was dressed in brown gabardine and silk;
she, in honey-colored muslin, and while it was only a serviceable
dress, the color picked up her creamy skin and the light sheen of
her fair curls. Standing together, they looked quite exceptional
and people passing by glanced at them a second time.

He motioned to a seat and they sat down.

At first they spoke of the beautiful day and the pleasant spring
Boston was enjoying. He did not tell her he had just left Joe at
the Seaward Line Booking Office, where the older man was
purchasing three passenger tickets for Thursday's noon sailing;
destination Sydney, Australia.

After a time, he crossed his legs, his brilliantly polished boot
catching the sun as he half turned toward her. He was looking
steadily at her and thinking how lovely she was, just as she had
always been; she even made cheap muslin look like rare silk.

"It seems a long time since I was passing through Bathurst and saw you in the park."

"It does," she replied, "and yet, it's not really. It's just that so much has happened."

He nodded. "Indeed it has."

She shook her head. "And to think you followed me home, and I did not know."

Now he turned even farther toward her, his arm up on the back of the seat. He made a mild sound that could have been a laugh. "Yes, what a month that was. I fell in love with you at first sight, and then I had to convince you to marry me."

"Yes, I suppose it was like that."

He turned to the front and lifted his right knee in his hands. "Do you recall our picnic on the day I asked you to marry me?"

She nodded. "I do."

"It was on the riverbank with the reverend and his wife. He was a fine man, and she a fine woman."

"Yes," she replied quietly, "I think of them every day."

He closed his eyes briefly, leaning back a little. "Whenever I go through Bathurst these days, I pass through swiftly, but sometimes I go to the graveyard at All Saints' and place a flower on their grave. I shall continue to do that." He did not tell her the reason was for her.

She was moved to think he did such a thing. "John Stuart, that is so kind of you. After all, you are not a one for churchyards and things."

He looked away. "No." When he turned back to her, his face was cheerful. "Do you remember on that same picnic, I asked you what you wanted more than anything in the world, and you became angry because I was amused by your serious sentiments."

She nodded. "I do."

"Well, I promise I won't laugh now."

She met his eyes. "What do you mean?"

"I'm asking you what you want more than anything in the world, now, today. And I will not laugh."

He smiled his adorable smile, and she thought how Lottie was absolutely right; he was more handsome than ever. She wondered why he would ask such a thing. It was almost impossible for her to answer him. What could she say? Perhaps, if he had asked her a couple of months ago, before Sir Rutherford's benevolence, she would have said the thing she wanted most was for her son to grow up with some security.

Two small children were rolling hoops nearby; one lost control, and the hoop wobbled sideways toward John Stuart. He bent forward and caught it, standing to give it back to the child.

When he sat down, she answered him with the words "John Stuart, it's a difficult question. I am not sure. No doubt I could still answer with the same replies I gave you years ago, but now I think I want peace . . . happiness and peace."

"Yes, Eve," he said with a sigh. "We all want that."

She was looking at his long, slender hands and oval fingernails. His hands had lost some of the heavy brown from the Australian sun but were not as pale as her own, lying in her lap.

She decided to tell him about Sir Rutherford's philanthropy and Christopher's inheritance. She was not sure why she wanted to tell him; it was just something to do with wanting to be truthful and honest with him. She took a deep breath. "John Stuart?"

"Yes?" He turned his eyes to hers.

"I want to tell you something. If you had asked me your question some months ago, I would have answered differently. I would have wished for security for my son. But something has occurred, a sort of miracle, really. In March a man came here from London. He was a solicitor, representing a legal firm. He gave me the deeds to the property of Long Moss in Somerset, England. Long Moss was Alan's ancestral home. Christopher is now the legal heir. You see, Sir Rutherford Blake has purchased the property and is holding it in trust for him until he comes of age. There are funds that will arrive regularly, and my son will never want." She sat looking at him. "I'll be grateful to that man as long as I live. He's done so much. It is just too wonderful."

He faced away from her, so she would not see his eyes. Forcing delight into his tone, he remarked, "Eve, I am so very pleased to hear that. That's marvelous. So you, too, are provided for?"

"Yes, there is money for me, but I shall keep it for Christopher. I can manage to take care of myself."

He thought how indomitable her spirit was, one of the things he had always loved, respected, about her. He loved her so very deeply. He was troubled, though, for he had bought Long Moss as much for her as for the child. He was unsure how to say it, but say it he must. "It is not my business, but if there has been money provided for you, then I think you should use it."

"I see it as my son's," she replied.

He thought of her small rented house and tiny parlor with the threadbare chairs, and forced himself to sound matter-of-fact.

"No doubt Rutherford did also, but perhaps he believed that if the mother was well provided for, then the son would naturally be."

"Yes, perhaps," was her answer.

He did not dare continue with this subject, so he finished with the words "You will know best." His eyes followed two elderly women passing by as he spoke again. "Eve, now I want you to know something."

"Yes?" She turned to him.

"I must tell you this." He looked up at the treetops and then back to her. "When I knew you were actually with Alan Fletcher, that you were not coming back home, I was hurt, jealous, angry, bitter, disillusioned. When I found out you had his child, something in my heart died. But for some long time now, I have realized that Alan Fletcher was no ordinary man, and those sentiments no longer exist in me. And you, my dear, are an extraordinary woman. Now that I have seen you . . . and Christopher . . . I am pleased that I made the journey to Boston, to have been with you again and to know you are with good friends who care." He stood up, and taking up her right hand, bent over it and brought it to his lips.

The whole of her attention was on him. She did not see the gardens or the children playing or the people walking; she saw only his face and lips on her hand. A peculiar thought filled her mind. She was still married to John Stuart; this was her legal husband kissing her hand.

When he straightened up, he said, "Would it be possible to call on you again?"

"Certainly, of course." She wondered when he was leaving, but somehow she did not want to mention it. She did not want to remind him of leaving.

"Are you in tomorrow?"

"No, I teach at private homes until close to five o'clock."

"Then I might come the day after tomorrow, on Thursday afternoon?"

"Anytime Thursday afternoon; I give no lessons then."

For a few moments he stayed staring down at her, his gaze lingering on her. He knew he would not see her Thursday, and he was sorry for the subterfuge, but he did not want to tell her he was leaving that day; he did not want to say good-bye.

His pulse quickened as he acknowledged this would be the last time he looked on her face. He did so hope she would be happy, and he had much to be happy about himself. He had been reunited with his mother and he had Mayfield, beautiful Mayfield . . . waiting for him. He nodded good-bye, and turned from her.

She watched him as he walked through the trees, his long stride moving him swiftly out of sight, and she recognized that she was already looking forward to Thursday when she would see him again. Suddenly she remembered Lottie and Christopher, and she left the seat at a run.

When John Stuart entered their rooms at the Regency, Joe stood from his chair by the window. "M'boy, I was surprised to find you not here."

"Yes, of all things, I ran into Eve." But that was all the information he gave.

Joe took an envelope from his breast pocket. "I have the tickets; we sail noon Thursday, as you desire."

Later, after a meal in the hotel's dining room, Joe said good night to his boy and went early to bed. He lay there thinking, looking at the evening sky, still faintly light through the window. It would be wonderful to be home at Mayfield again. How badly he had missed it and his darling Thel. There had been times while they had been here in Boston that he had actually thought a miracle might happen, that somehow Eve would come home with them, but that was just an old man's dream. He had even fancied that John Stuart might adopt Eve's son, and that they could get a pardon for Lawless Drake. The other night, he had actually dreamed about arriving at Mayfield. Eve and John Stuart, at last, home together. The whole of Mayfield had echoed with the roar of hundreds of delighted cheers. . . . Ah, what a grand dream that had been. He rolled over and closed his eyes.

At the same time, in Russell Street, Eve sat on the tiny back porch, looking at the waning light in the late evening sky. Little Christopher was asleep, and Lottie and Arnold were next door with Mrs. Mason. They had asked her to come with them, but she had preferred to be alone.

The perfume of an early-blooming honeysuckle vine hung in the air, evocatively reminding her of how she used to pick the diverse bush smells on Mayfield. She thought of the miles of gum trees and scrub, of the valleys and hills, and remembered the day she fell from Moonlight. She recalled the wonderful, fearful excitement she had felt when she realized who had found her. She stood up and went to the porch railing. She grasped it tightly seeing that other small veranda at Treehard Hill and thinking of how often she had held the railing there.

She heard the words Alan said to her on the rug in front of the glowing fire on their one consummate night. *Eve, I want you always to be happy; remember that.* And my darling Alan, while I have loved your son, and been strong and faced the world without you, I have not been happy. Forgive me, for I know you want me to be happy. I love you, Alan, as I always will love you, but you have gone from this earth. My darling one, what we had together was too exquisite to last. I understand that now. I have wept for you until I feel I have no more tears. I have mourned your death in some way every single day, and thus I have not let your spirit rest, and have kept you in troubled unsleep. That was selfish and so very wrong of me. At last, I realize I must leave you in tranquillity. The very words you said to Arnold are truth, like all the things you ever said. *You cannot live with the dead. It is fine and proper to remember them with all the love you bore them, and perhaps the places they had are never quite filled again, but life continues.* I am here, I must live with those who are here, and I must let you go. It is time. I must release your soul and let you be happy, too. . . . She put up her hands to the sky, arms extended, palms open. "Good-bye, my darling, Alan Fletcher." Suddenly a rain cloud seemed to come quickly from nowhere. Somber and mysterious, it hung low in the sky, and then drops were falling heavily on the palms of her hands; clean, pristine drops of water from the heavens, from the place beyond human comprehension, and quite surely, she knew he had heard her.

It was the following afternoon, and her young pupil was not well, so that when Eve arrived at his home, a maid informed her there would be no music lesson. Eve went home, walking the mile and a half to Russell Street.

She took Mrs. Mason's side gate and went through her backyard to the gate in the adjoining fence of number 32. She was mounting the few steps to the porch when she heard voices around in the tiny side garden. Peering through the trees and vines, she saw Lottie, and close by, Christopher wandering around investigating.

They were not alone. To her surprise, John Stuart was with them. What was he doing here? It was Wednesday, and he was not coming to see her until tomorrow afternoon.

Something stopped her from going down to join them, and full of curiosity, she leaned forward intently as he spoke with Lottie, who smiled and nodded. Then he walked over to Chris-

topher. Her heart rate accelerated as John Stuart bent down and
picked up her child in his arms. He spoke, and Christopher
clapped his hands with pleasure, and they both laughed. To Eve,
standing there watching, unknown to any of them, it seemed
unreal. For the next seconds, her awareness was heightened, as
if she saw her son and John Stuart close up, their faces side by
side. Her son hugged him and laughed and talked. She stared
enthralled as John Stuart kissed him on his cheek. Then he held
the merry boy out at arm's length, to dangle laughing in the air,
before he put him down. He spoke again to Lottie, knelt back
upon the ground to ruffle Christopher's curls, stood, and walked
away.

Once she was sure he was gone, she rushed down the steps
and around to Lottie.

"My gracious, Eve. Ye be home already? I was not expecting
ye yet."

"What did John Stuart want?"

"Oh, he just came to say he would not be able to avisit with
ye here tomorrow. He had some sort of an arrangement with ye,
but he cannot keep it. Said something important was astopping
him."

"Did he say when he *would* come?"

"No, but no doubt he'll be amaking another time with ye. It
was nice to see him today. He was so lovely to Christopher;
kissed him, he did. Oh, and when he was aspeaking of ye, he
called ye Evvy. Was that his pet name for ye, like it was with
the reverend?"

Eve did not know why, but she felt troubled. "Once or twice
he called me that . . . once or twice."

She did not sleep well that night; she tossed and turned and
kept waking and looking at the blackness. It was close to dawn
when at last she fell into a deep sleep. She woke to Lottie's
voice. "Eve, Eve, you have overslept; young Dorothy Dence
will be here within half an hour."

She went through the music lesson in a distracted fashion,
and during the one that followed, her concentration lapsed continually, until halfway through, she came to a decision and sent
the child home.

Lottie looked up from her sewing in amazement when Eve
came bursting into the parlor. "Lottie, I am going to the Regency. I must see John Stuart. You and Christopher will be all
right, won't you?"

Lottie recovered quickly and nodded, smiling at her charge.

Eve did not know why she was doing this. All she knew was that something was amiss, that she felt very uneasy, and that she must see John Stuart.

She grabbed her bonnet and cape from the hook in the front hall and hurried through the house to the back door and down the steps of the porch. She went through Mrs. Mason's backyard and was soon out in the laneway and hurrying into Irving Street. The fastest way to the Regency Hotel was to weave through a number of back streets and lanes down the hill.

By the time she entered Arlington Street, she was moving very briskly, and as she neared the hotel, a hansom cab pulled away from the front door and went at an easy pace in the opposite direction. She was soon inside, where huge chandeliers hung in the foyer, and grand staircases went up to right and left. There was the hustle and bustle of guests and page boys and porters.

At the rosewood reception desk, a clerk looked over his eyeglasses at her.

"I have come to see Mr. John Stuart Wakeman."

"He's gone, madam."

"Gone? Gone where?"

"Left the hotel, departed, madam."

"But he can't have."

The clerk's colleague, standing beside him, looked up from the guest book. "Yes, he's only just gone, actually; saw him get in a hansom just now."

Eve must have looked so distraught that the clerk with the eyeglasses inquired. "You're not Mrs. Fletcher, by any chance, are you madam?"

"Yes, I am."

"Oh, then he left a letter for you." He turned back to a pile of papers and found what he looked for. "Here it is."

Eve felt sick; her head was aching. "Thank you." No, he could not have gone, not without saying good-bye. She did not want him to go. She walked away from the desk, ripping the letter open in her haste. Now she realized why he had come to Russell Street yesterday. Oh God, he came to say good-bye to Christopher; that is why he kissed him. . . .

She read what he had written through the tears that sprang to her eyes.

Dearest Eve,
　　I cannot face you and say good-bye. You see, my dear, dear

one, I have always loved you, from the moment I saw you in the Bathurst park, and I shall continue to love you, until the last breath departs from my body.

I wish you the "peace and happiness" you said you wanted more than anything in the world when we spoke in the garden Tuesday. If I could have told you what I wanted, I would have said, "You," but that was not to be.

I will treasure the moments we have had together in the short, short time I spent in Boston. To see you and be near you again was more than all the world's treasure to me, and that will sustain me all the days of my life. You have your son, and I now have things to recall that will bring me a certain contentment. Among other memories, I have one beautiful, bittersweet picture in my mind, and I shall keep it as the years pass by. It's you and your son together at the door of your home.

Good-bye, Evvy.
John Stuart

Oh no! It could not be. The words were like stab wounds in her heart. She had loved only four men in her life. Three were gone from this earth; John Stuart was the lone remaining one. He must not leave her. Not now.

She ran out the hotel door, calling frantically to the page boys and porters, "Tell me, please, which way did Mr. Wakeman's cab go? Where was he going? Please help me."

One of the youths spoke up. "That's it, there, lady," He pointed through the trees. "It's just turned the corner of the Public Garden. Driver's got a red hat on."

"But where is he going? Please, do you know where he's going?"

"To Commercial wharf; he sails on the noon tide."

Noon? Oh no! There was no time. She must stop him. But how? There were no hansoms anywhere. No time to wait. What could she do?

Abruptly she started running, her mind distracted. Don't go, John Stuart, please. I cannot lose you, not now, not when I realize you love me so much. I don't want you to go.

She avoided the vehicles in Arlington Street, and seconds later was in the Public Garden, running by children and nannies and people who looked up in amazement to see her speeding by. She ran, her heart pounding, her mind reeling from thought to thought. A red hat, the driver of the hansom wore a red hat. . . .

Now she was crossing Charles Street, darting in and out between horses and carriages and carts and people; now she was in the Common.

John Stuart was heading to Commercial wharf; that meant he would continue on past the deer park and around the Common into Tremont Street. She must stop him, reach him, tell him how she felt. A red hat, where was the red hat? She was impelling herself on, accelerating, dodging people and garden beds and bushes and trees. No, don't leave me, not you, too. John Stuart, wait.

Keep running, Eve, keep running. She felt the ties of her bonnet slacken, then come undone as the tails flew back over her shoulder while she tried to hold it on. She was really racing now, moving faster, faster. She could hold the bonnet no longer and she let it go to feel it dangle briefly behind her before it was gone. She heard someone call out, but she did not stop. Then her cape, too, became loose and began to slip from her shoulders. It was slowing her down when suddenly it caught in some bushes and ripped from her shoulders, but still she did not stop; she was glad it was gone.

She was along the Tremont side of the Common now, her eyes reaching, straining, alert and searching. Cabs going to Commercial wharf took Bromfield Street. Was that a hansom turning up there, ahead?

A number of carts and street vendors plied their trades along here, and a few shouted at the woman racing by, eyes frantic, head bonnetless. Running, running, like a person possessed. Her heart pounded, her pulse raced, her eyes searched the street. On she went, until at last she was at the corner of Bromfield Street, her breath coming in short gasps, and there at the bottom of the road, just turning left, she saw it, a hansom and a scarlet spot up on top. She screamed out, "Stop! Stop!" But it disappeared.

The perspiration was in beads on her temples and her brow; there was a pain in her throat, her chest hurt, and her shoes had come loose. In a swift decision, and to the amazement of a group of elderly women, she threw off her shoes, setting off again, willing herself to continue, to run like she had never run before.

Now, like a fleeing gypsy girl, barefoot, capeless, bonnetless, she sped on. At the bottom of the street, she turned to continue the chase, but her heart sank. The hansom with the crimson spot perched on top was accelerating, gaining speed. It was hopeless.

Her eyes grew wide with dismay. She had lost him. She halted there on the corner, her gaze never leaving the bright speck as it got farther and farther away, more indistinct, taking the only man on earth she wanted away.

Her throat hurt, her head hurt, her feet hurt, her heart hurt. She stood, eyes fixed on the vehicle. Her chest heaved. Then the words came out, from the core of her, from the innermost sanctuary of her psyche: the truth, the clear admission, the fact. "I still truly love you," she said aloud, and as if the acknowledgment gave her the miracle of renewed strength, she began to run again, even though she knew it was useless and the speck of red was getting ever farther away. Smaller, remoter, the little dot of red faded away.

People halted and pointed at her, shouted and laughed, but she did not see them; she saw nothing but the point of scarlet disappearing through her tears. She was gasping now, her breath coming in short, painful bursts, but still she forced herself forward, running, running, her mind obsessively set on continuing onward.

And then a miracle happened.

The dot of crimson was not getting smaller anymore. It remained the same size. It was stationary. Oh Lord, it was stationary!

On, on she flew, toward it as it became more and more distinct. She did not feel the pain in her feet and chest; her whole consciousness was centered on the hansom. Then she heard drums and music, and still the red spot did not move. It grew bigger. Now it became a hat, on a head, on top of the one-horse cab. Then the music became louder and she saw there was some sort of parade, which had held the vehicle up. A band of men were walking and playing in the intersecting street in front of the hansom where it stood waiting in a line of other vehicles and horses.

Oh God, thank you, thank you.

Closer she came, closer, closer . . . the sound of music louder in her ears; past the lined-up carriages and carts and horsemen, she came. She could see the driver distinctly now, sitting jauntily up on top of the small carriage, and there, strapped securely behind him, was the small chest in which John Stuart always carried his personal papers. She was only yards away, so near now that she could read his name on the side, JOHN STUART WAKEMAN, and underneath were two stamps. In big, blue letters, one read, SYDNEY—SOUTHAMPTON, and below it, another in yellow said, SOUTHAMPTON—BOSTON.

Then she understood! Penetrating her mind, the realization burst upon her . . . the impact of the words ramming into her head like a physical blow and bringing her to a standstill two yards from the back of the hansom. It was clear at last. John Stuart had been in England! He had been in England! It was not Sir Rutherford who had bought Long Moss. It was John Stuart. The wonderful, modest, decent, good man, the essential John Stuart, the one she had never stopped loving. He had done it to take care of her and her son.

She stumbled to the side of the cab as the driver gaped down in shock at the barefooted, fierce-eyed lady.

Her heart expanded with joy and gratitude as she lifted her hand, damp from her massive exertion, to take hold of the side of the vehicle as the two men inside saw her and reacted with sudden, startled movement.

"Eve!"

Her eyes shone, her face gleamed, as her arms reached out to John Stuart and she uttered the words, "Please, please, don't leave without us."

She saw the change explode inside him. It was as if a flame of rapture ignited in his eyes. The troubled lines left his forehead and his cheeks, smoothing his face in a flood of love and happiness.

Suddenly he was on the cobbled street with her, lifting her into his arms, holding her as if never to put her down. "My darling Evvy!" She felt his kisses in her hair, on her eyes, her cheeks, her lips, felt his arms entwined around her.

This was peace, this was happiness. She could feel it in the very trembling of his body, a promise of lasting, eternal trust.

She lifted her mouth from his to look through her blissful tears into the face of her husband. There was truth and understanding filling the air around them, no misunderstandings or fears, nothing unrevealed or secret.

From her heart came the words "Take me home to Mayfield."